BEN JONSON

Ben Jonson
from the painting in the National Portrait Gallery
by an unknown artist

BEN JONSON

Edited by C. H. Herford
and Percy Simpson

VOLUME V

Volpone, or *The Fox*
Epicoene, or *The Silent Woman*
The Alchemist
Catiline

OXFORD
At the Clarendon Press

Oxford University Press, Amen House, London E.C.4

GLASGOW NEW YORK TORONTO MELBOURNE WELLINGTON
BOMBAY CALCUTTA MADRAS KARACHI LAHORE DACCA
CAPE TOWN SALISBURY NAIROBI IBADAN ACCRA
KUALA LUMPUR HONG KONG

FIRST EDITION 1937
REPRINTED LITHOGRAPHICALLY IN GREAT BRITAIN
AT THE UNIVERSITY PRESS, OXFORD
FROM CORRECTED SHEETS OF THE FIRST EDITION
1954, 1965

PREFACE

AS this volume goes to press, it is a pleasant duty to acknowledge the help which has lightened the labour of producing it. Mr. T. J. Wise, generous as ever, deposited for our use in the Bodleian his beautiful first Quartos of *Volpone, The Alchemist*, and *Catiline*. The Quarto of *The Alchemist* belonging to Corpus Christi College, Oxford, was also deposited there by the librarian, Dr. J. G. Milne. Mr. H. L. Ford lent his two large-paper copies of the 1616 Folio. The Committee of the Clifton Shakespere Society, through their librarian, Mr. H. W. Crundell, lent their copy of the Quarto of *The Alchemist*. The opportunity thus given for leisurely collation and verification is of the utmost value to an editor. Equally helpful were the rotograph of the Quarto of *Catiline* in the Cambridge University Library, taken by permission of the librarian, Mr. A. F. Scholfield, and the photostat of the Harvard copy of *Epicoene*, taken by permission of the librarian, Mr. A. C. Potter.

For permission to photograph title-pages we have to thank the authorities of the British Museum and the Bodleian, and two Oxford librarians, Sir Charles Oman of All Souls College, and Mr. C. H. Wilkinson of Worcester College.

For the frontispiece of the newly acquired painting of Ben Jonson in the National Portrait Gallery we are indebted to the Trustees. The comments and elucidation of the Director and Keeper, Mr. Henry M. Hake, furnish the substance of an important note which we print on this painting.

For help on textual points we are specially indebted to Dr. W. W. Greg, who gave valuable help with *Volpone* and the problem of the missing Quarto of *Epicoene*. Mr. C. E. Batey, of the Oxford University Press, advised us on some acute difficulties of typography. By the courtesy of Mr. Philip Robinson we obtained from the American collector, Mr. Frank Capra, a photostat of some special pages of his large-paper copy of the 1616 Folio. Mr. C. K. Edmonds supplied some readings in the Quarto text of *Catiline* not found in the copies which we have collated. Mrs. Simpson has again given valuable help in collating and in checking the proofs.

For the readjustment of the readings in the Quarto of *Cynthia's Revels*, printed in the supplementary notes at the end of the volume, we are indebted to the scholarly help of Mr. A. K. McIlwraith.

With each new volume we are conscious more and more of the debt we owe to the printing staff of the Oxford University Press for the way they have handled proofs which make a severe call on their skill and patience.

The Editor acknowledges with much gratitude the grant of a Leverhulme Research Fellowship made by the late Lord Leverhulme's Trustees for the two years 1935 to 1937, to give him leisure to complete his work on the text of Jonson. It has quickened the last stage of preparation of the text as nothing else has done since he undertook the edition. It has also enabled him to prepare the text of the sixth volume, which is virtually ready for the printer.

P. S.

Oriel College, Oxford,
14 January 1937.

CONTENTS

LIST OF ILLUSTRATIONS AND FACSIMILES

VOLUME V

In 1935 the National Portrait Gallery acquired a painting of Ben Jonson, which, by kind permission of the Trustees, is reproduced as a frontispiece to the present volume. It is stated to have been formerly in the collection of the Webb family at Odstock House in Wiltshire, but its earlier history has not been traced. It is fortunate that it has now found a permanent home in the national collection.

The portraits of Jonson which have come down to us all conform to a single type. It is a testimony to the high place which he held in the world of letters that over twenty copies should have been made, if not in his lifetime, at least shortly after his death. A likely date for Jonson to have given a sitting to a painter is not long before the stroke which crippled him in November or December, 1628; by that time, even if his literary powers were failing, his fame was secure. The author of *Volpone* and *The Alchemist*, the 'rare Ben Jonson' acclaimed by a whole-hearted admirer after a performance of *Bartholomew Fair*, the 'arch-poet' who presided over the 'lyric feasts' at the Dog, the Sun, the Three Tuns, and in the Apollo room at the Devil, was one of the best-known figures of contemporary London.

The artist to whom this type of portrait is usually ascribed is Gerard Honthorst. A fine example is the painting in Lord Sackville's collection at Knole, which was reproduced as the frontispiece to our first volume. The attribution to Honthorst appears to have been first made by George Vertue in 1711 when he engraved a bust from a painting in the collection of Lord Somers. The ascription is not without its difficulties. The fine collection of Lord Somers was dispersed after his death, and it is not known what became of the original painting. Further Honthorst was in England only for six months, from June to December, 1628, and he was engaged not only in painting elaborate groups of royal or noble families, such as that of the first Duke of Buckingham and his family in the National Portrait Gallery, but also in the decoration of Whitehall. King Charles worked him hard, and Jonson broke down while he was still in England.

Since only one type of Jonson's features has been handed down to us in a large number of reproductions, there must have been an archetype taken from the life, but whether this was a painting in oils on canvas or a drawing is not likely to be determined now. It has been claimed for the new acquisition of the National Portrait Gallery that it is this original, but in the absence of any real body of similar oil sketches of the period the question remains open. It is true to say with *The Times* critic[1] that the portrait has traces of hesitation and clumsiness in the painting which would not be expected in a copy; the portrait has also an air of 'aliveness' which copies tend to lose. Out of the twenty odd versions known it is the best which has so far come to light and therefore the nearest we possess to a living likeness of Jonson.

The earliest dated likeness of him is the engraved portrait by Robert Vaughan, which was used as frontispiece for the Benson quarto of the *Execration against Vulcan. With divers Epigrams* in 1640, and later in the year as the frontispiece to the first volume of the 1640 Folio. It was issued earlier as a separate print, and cannot be later than 1627. It was reproduced, with a note on its history, in our third volume. Mr. Henry M. Hake, the Director of the National Portrait Gallery, has made an expert examination of the relation of the painting to the engraving. 'In the painting', he writes, 'the head is turned to the right and in the engraving to the left, but the set of the head inside the linen collar is very similar. The engraving shews two loops of the string which fastens the linen collar; the painting shews something like the beginning of one loop. The engraving has a cloak over the left shoulder. In the painting there is something which may be meant for a cloak over the left shoulder. If the engraving is reversed from a drawing, the cloak on that drawing might be expected on the right shoulder. The painting shews the head turned in the opposite direction and the cloak in the same direction as the engraving. The features are very close, especially the shape of the nose.'

The short black curls of the painting and the thin beard look

[1] In the notice of the year's acquisitions, *The Times*, 28 December 1935.

older in the engraving; Jonson's beard had been satirized by Dekker in 1601: 'thou hast such a terrible mouth that the beard's afraid to peep out.'[1] The engraving has the poet's laurel wreath round the head, a decorative feature which rather obscures the treatment of the hair. 'So far as one can see the hair underneath it', Mr. Hake comments, 'the growth corresponds to the growth which is shown in the painting. The engraving shews a black silk doublet buttoning down the front: if the garment in the painting is intended to be a doublet, the buttons, which are also black, have sunk away. But the doublet of the engraving may be only a conventional embellishment.'

[1] *Satiro-mastix*, 1602, quarto, sig. L4 verso.

THE TEXT: INTRODUCTORY NOTES

IN the present volume we reach the end of a definite stage in the text of Jonson's plays. It includes the masterpieces and the play of *Catiline*, which was the last to be printed in the authoritative Folio of 1616. This is the basis of our text. The folio text of *Epicoene, or The Silent Woman* is the earliest we possess; if that play was printed in quarto in 1612, no copy is now known. The other plays were first printed in quarto, *Volpone* in 1606, *The Alchemist* in 1610, and *Catiline* in 1611. Jonson revised these texts for the Folio, but with a more sparing hand than in his earlier plays. There is nothing that can be called re-writing, no insertion of new scenes, but only occasional retouchings of word or phrase. He was at the height of his powers, and even his keen critical mind found little to reject or alter. One after-effect of this was that his proof-reading was less rigorous. Further, the punctuation of the later plays is much freeer than was usual with Jonson, and also less correct.

Seven copies of the Folio of 1616 have been collated for the text of the present edition: two in the British Museum, two in Bodley, and three belonging to the Editor. For the Folio reprint of 1640, two copies belonging to the Editor have been collated, and copies in public libraries have been consulted whenever a reading seemed doubtful. The Quarto texts which have been collated are noticed in detail in the introduction to the separate plays.

The following symbols and abbreviations are used in the critical apparatus:

F1 = the Folio of 1616.
F2 = the Folio of 1640.
Ff = readings common to the Folios of 1616 and 1640.
F3 = the Folio of 1692.

Q = the first Quarto.
Q2 = the second Quarto.
W = Whalley's edition of 1756.
G = Gifford's edition of 1816.
om. = an earlier reading omitted from a later text.
not in Q = a new reading first found in the 1616 Folio.
corr. Q or *corr. F* is a formula used to indicate author's or printer's correction, the earlier reading being indicated by *Q originally* or *F originally*.

Re in the critical apparatus of *Epicoene* = readings in the reset quire Yy of the 1616 Folio (Act I, and Act II up to scene ii, line 64) described on pages 148–9.

In stage directions *add Q* indicates a brief direction such as '*Exit.*' printed at the end of a line; a stage direction centred in the text and taking up a line by itself is indicated by '*After* . . .' and the line number of the end of the preceding speech.

Words inserted in the text by the Editor are enclosed in conical brackets; words wrongly inserted or retained in the original text are enclosed in square brackets to show that they should be deleted.

Gifford's scene-numberings and scene-location are quoted in the critical apparatus, and also his stage directions, except where they are identical with the marginal directions in the Folio.

VOLPONE *or* THE FOX

THE TEXT

THE comedy of *Volpone, or The Fox*, stated on the Folio title-page to have been 'Acted in the yeere 1605', was published by Thomas Thorpe in 1607. The printer is unknown. Thorpe had published *Sejanus* in 1605, the copyright of which had been transferred to him by Edward Blount on 6 August. On 4 September he had entered *Eastward Hoe* along with William Aspley, though only Aspley's name appeared on the title-page. On 21 April 1608 he entered *The Masques of Blackness and of Beauty*, which he published in that year, and followed these with *Hymenaei*, the signatures of which are continuous with those of the two masques. From 1605 to 1608, therefore, he was Jonson's publisher. The date 1607 on the title-page of the *Volpone* Quarto is probably a calendar date, i.e. beginning the year on 1 January.[1] If so, the play was printed early in the year. But Thorpe did not enter it on the Stationers' Register till he transferred it along with *Sejanus* on 3 October 1610 to Walter Burre, the publisher of *The Alchemist*. The entry is as follows:

3° Octobris.

Walter Burre. Entred for his Copyes by assignemente from Thomas Thorpe and with the consente of Th'wardens vnder their handes, 2 bookes thone called, Seianus his fall, thother, Vulpone or the ffoxe. xij^{d}

Arber, *Transcript*, III. 445.

Following the precedent of the *Sejanus* Quarto, Jonson prefaced the play with verse tributes from his friends. Very appropriately Donne, Chapman, Beaumont, and Fletcher[2] were among the eulogists of this great play. There was

[1] See W. W. Greg, 'The Riddle of Jonson's Chronology', in *The Library*, fourth series, vol. vi, pp. 340–7.

[2] So we interpret the initials 'I. F.' here and in the similar copy contributed to the Quarto of *Catiline*. The suggestion that the writer was John Florio (made in *The Times Literary Supplement* of 17 January 1918, and accepted by Miss Yates in her monograph on Florio) is plausible for *Volpone*, but less likely for *Catiline*. Dyce accepted Fletcher's authorship in his edition of Beaumont and Fletcher.

shrewd critical insight in Edmund Bolton's comment that Jonson had rehandled the ancient drama 'Tanquam explorator' and Donne's tribute—

> *Tam nemo veterum est sequutor, vt tu*
> *Illos quòd sequeris nouator audis.*

They saw that he was no blind copyist of the classics.

The collation—two preliminary leaves, four leaves of ¶, A to N in fours, two leaves of O—is in detail: first preliminary leaf blank, preserved in the British Museum copy with the inscription to Florio and in the Cottrell-Dormer copy sold by T. Thorp in 1925; second preliminary leaf, the title with verso blank; ¶ recto, the Dedication; ¶ verso to ¶ 4 recto, the Epistle; ¶ 4 verso, 'E. B.', i.e. Edmund Bolton, '*AD VTRAMQVE ACADEMIAM*'; A recto, 'I. D.', i.e. John Donne, '*Amicissimo, & meritissino* BEN: IONSON'; A verso, '*To my friend Mr.* IONSON. EPIGRAMME' and '*To the Reader. Vpon the worke.*', the latter signed '*T. R.*'; A 2 recto, 'F. B.', i.e. Francis Beaumont, 'To my deare friend, Mr. Beniamin Ionson, vpon his FOXE.'; A 2 verso, 'D. D.', probably Dudley Digges, '*To my good friend. Mr. Ionson.*' and '*I. C.*', '*To the ingenious Poet.*'; A 3 recto, 'G. C.', i.e. George Chapman, 'To his deare Friend, Beniamin Ionson'; A 3 verso, 'E. S.', conjectured by Gifford to be Edward Scory, '*To my worthily-esteemed Mr. Ben: Ionson.*', and 'I. F.', i.e. John Fletcher, '*To the true Mr. in his Art, B. Ionson.*'; A 4 recto, '*THE PERSONS OF* THE COMOEDYE', and 'THE ARGVMENT.'; A 4 verso, 'The PROLOGVE'; B to N and one leaf of O, the text of the play; O 2 blank, preserved in the Cottrell-Dormer copy.

This is the normal collation of the Quarto, giving sheet A as finally adjusted by the compositor. He had made an error in perfecting the inner forme of A, putting signature A 2 at the foot of what should be A 4. The result was that he had printed the inner forme the wrong way round in respect to the outer forme. This blunder is preserved in Mr. T. J. Wise's copy, which gives this absurd arrangement:

A verso, Scory's and Fletcher's poems; A 2, '*THE PERSONS OF* THE COMOEDYE' and 'THE ARGVMENT'; A 3 verso, T. R.'s lines preceded by the unsigned 'EPIGRAMME'; A 4, Beaumont's verses. One other copy, once Mr. W. A. White's, is recorded with this dislocation. Probably the error was discovered at once when the sheet was folded; the signature was then rectified in the course of printing.

This is not the only variation of sheet A. A set of verses signed 'N. F.' was added to the preliminary tributes after the sheet had been set up. It survives in two copies, Mr. Wise's and the British Museum copy with the autograph dedication to Florio. In the Museum copy it is inserted between the original A 3 verso and A 4, before the last leaf containing the 'The Persons of the Comedy', 'The Argument', and 'The Prologue', which thus becomes A 5: this was the proper place for it. But in the Wise copy it is inserted in the middle of the sheet between A 2 verso and the original A 3 with Chapman's verses.

'N. F.' is Nathan Field. The opening lines of his tribute to his 'worthiest Maister' explain that this poem was an afterthought.

> For mee, your *Worke* or you, most worthy Friend,
> (Mongst these vn-æquall'd Men) to dare commend,
> Were damnable presumption; whose weake flame
> Can neither dimme, or light your full grow'n fame:
> How can my common knowledge set you forth,
> When it wants art, and *Art* it selfe wants worth?
> Therefore, how vaine (although by you, made one)
> Am I, to put such saucy boldnesse on
> To send you *Verses*?

The verses were therefore written at Jonson's request. Field had acted in two plays of Jonson before this, *Cynthia's Revels* and *Poetaster*. 'Nid field', Jonson told Drummond, 'was his Schollar & he had read to him the Satyres of Horace & some Epigrames of Martiall.'[1] Verses by Field are prefixed to *The Faithful Shepherdess*, initial-signed in

[1] Drummond Conversations, ll. 164–5: see vol. i, p. 137.

the first edition, which appeared in 1609 or 1610, and to Jonson's *Catiline* in the quarto of 1611. The lines before *Volpone* are thus the earliest verses yet traced to him; their modest tone, not unfitting a young writer who appeared in the company of famous contemporaries, has something of the youthful, almost boyish, note which charms us in his writings. It adds a new and kindly glimpse to what we know of his relations with Jonson, that the great dramatist, amid the homage paid to a brilliant and successful play, sought the tribute of the young actor who revered him. In the equally modest verses to his 'loved friend', John Fletcher, on *The Faithful Shepherdess*, Field had a significant allusion, which has passed unnoticed, to Jonson:

Opinion, that great foole, makes fooles of all,
And (once) I feard her till I met a minde
Whose graue instructions philosophicall,
Toss'd it like dust vpon a March strong winde,
He shall for euer my example be,
And his embraced doctrine grow in me.

Seven copies of the Quarto have been collated for the text of the present edition:

(1) The British Museum copy with press-mark C. 12. e. 17: this was the copy which Jonson gave to John Florio, with an autograph inscription styling him 'his louing Father, & worthy Freind, . . . The ayde of his Muses'.[1] It has the autograph of 'Mary Leigh' at the foot of the title-page and the bookplate of Charles Chauncy, and came from the library of George III (marked A in the following list).

(2) The British Museum copy with press-mark C. 34. d. 2, formerly the Garrick copy (marked B).

(3) The Bodleian copy with press-mark Malone 809 (marked C).

(4) An imperfect copy in Bodley, Malone 225 (4), with the title-page and the last leaf in manuscript (marked D).

(5) The Dyce copy at South Kensington, formerly the Heber copy (marked E).

[1] See the facsimile in volume i opposite page 56.

(6) Mr. T. J. Wise's copy (marked F).

(7) An imperfect copy belonging to the Clifton Shakspere Society, wanting the two first leaves and signature O, the text of which is supplied in an early seventeenth-century hand (marked G).

The following corrections were made by Jonson while the sheets were passing through the press:

Sig. B 2^{r}	I. i. 74	too *B*	to *the rest*
	80	returne *B*	returne, *the rest*
	81	Ten-fold *B*	Ten-fold, *the rest*
Sig. B 4^{r}	I. ii. 122	*Harpyeis* B	*Harpyies* the rest
	124	*Pthisick* B	*Phthisick*, the rest
	125	Ca*tarrhe* B	*Catarrhe* the rest
Sig. C 2^{r}	I. iv. 52	*Scotomy*, he *D*	*Scotomy*; he, *the rest*
Sig. D 2^{v}	II. i. 39	pray *G*	Pray *the rest*
	52	worthy *G*	Worthy *the rest*
	57	knowen *G*	knowne *the rest*
Sig. E 1^{r}	II. ii. 97	' pray *A, B, D, E, F*	' Pray *C, G*
	104	*remedy*. A, B, D, E, F	*remedy:* C, G
	106	Stoppings *A, B, D, E, F*	stoppings *C, G*
Sig. E 3^{r}	247	*seats* A, B, D, E, F	*seat's* C, G
Sig. H 2	III. vii. 162	a racted *A, B, C, E, F, G*	attracted *D*[1]
Sig. H 4^{v}	III. ix. 28	tóld *A, D, E*	I tóld *B, C, F, G*
	29	he Imight *A, D, E*[2]	he might *B, C, F, G*
Sig. M 1^{r}	V. iii. 91	malice *B, C, G*	malice, *A, D, E, F*
Sig. M 2^{v}	V. iv. 68	*creepes* B, C, G	*creepes*, A, D, E, F
Sig. M 3^{r}	80	where's *B, C, G*	Where's *A, D, E, F*
	89	shell, *B, C, G*	shell. *A, D, E, F*

Signature F is misprinted E in A, C, and G, and signature K 3 is not marked.

There are no changes of reading, nothing in fact but press-corrections. Some of them, such as 'Ca*tarrhe*', 'a racted', or the dropped letter of III. ix. 28, 29, might have been made by the compositor, but a correction in punctuation such as 'returne, Ten-fold, vpon them' in I. i. 80–1, and the correction of the mis-spelt '*Harpyeis*' in I. ii. 122, show unmistakably the hand of Jonson.

The printing of the Quarto has one peculiar feature—its

[1] That it is not the accidental dropping out of a letter is shown by the fact that the spacing of the imperfect form admits only of a single *t* while the correction has *tt*.

[2] The 'I' had dropped from the previous line.

use of accents. Where they indicate the pronunciation of Italian words, they undoubtedly come from Jonson, as '*Romagnía*' (I. i. 58), '*Ostería*'(II. vi. 15), '*Soría*' (IV. i. 102); and to these may be added '*Montagnié*' (III. iv. 90). The Folio keeps '*Romagnía*' and '*Soría*', and adds 'procuratía' (II. ii. 36) to the examples found in the Quarto. But the Quarto also has such preposterous pointing as 'alóne' (Epistle, 29); '*Before the bést houndes, thou dost, still, but play*' in Chapman's preliminary verses; 'Gentlewóman' five times;[1] 'wóman-kind' (V. ii. 11); 'Hé' (V. iii. 26, xi. 6); 'Bút' (V. xii. 5). And there are a few others. Why Jonson passed these oddities is a mystery.

The play was next printed by William Stansby in the Folio of 1616 from a carefully corrected copy of the Quarto. Purely textual changes are slight. It is significant that, when Jonson returned to his play after such an interval, he found nothing to recast. He excised, of course, from the dedicatory Epistle the allusion to the preface of his still-unpublished notes on the *Ars Poetica*.[2] But other changes are only verbal—'filth' for 'garbage', in the dedicatory epistle, l. 89; 'goodnesse' for 'vertue' in IV. v. 43; 'catholique' for '*Christian*' (ibid., 130); 'Fitted' for 'Apted' in V. iv. 55. On the other hand, he worked minutely over the punctuation, recasting it systematically, especially in the longer speeches; most of his changes are recorded in the critical apparatus. He inserted a number of stage directions, and he used the interjection, parenthesis bracket, and the dash more freely. In one speech, however, he put in his cold, logical punctuation where the Quarto suggests a hurried delivery for the actor: it is Celia's cry of agony when she flings herself at Volpone's feet and implores him to spare her.[3]

> If you haue eares, that will be pierc'd—or eyes,
> That can be open'd—a heart, may be touch'd—
> Or any part, that yet sounds *man*, about you—

[1] IV. ii. 34, 39; iii. 15; V. 3; V. xii. 3.

[2] ll. 123–4.

[3] III. vii. 240–6, and similarly in the later lines.

If you haue touch of holy *Saints*—or *Heauen*—
Do mee the grace, to let me scape—if not,
Be bountifull, and kill mee—you do knowe,
I am a creature, hether ill betrayed, . . .

Except in the mere point of formal presentment Jonson felt he could not improve on his original text.

A few corrections of the Folio text have been made on the authority of the Quarto: the chief are '*osteria*' in II. vi. 15, 'TASSO?' or DANTE?' in III. iv. 79, and 'I'am past already!' in III. vii. 81. The accent and the metrical apostrophes were omitted by Stansby's compositor, and Jonson overlooked the omission.[1]

The Folio of 1640, printed by Richard Bishop, is a slightly inferior text. It tends to modernize both spelling and punctuation, using the semicolon more frequently. It was set up from an uncorrected copy of the 1616 Folio. The practice of gathering up the uncorrected sheets and binding them impartially with the corrected, is invaluable for tracing the stages of correction when an author read his proofs, but it had its disadvantages if they were bound up for what we may call the office copy and used for a reprint.

The 1640 text has some careless errors. Examples are '*masc'line* enter-ludes' in the Epistle, l. 87, for '*misc'line*', which puzzled the printer, who had not heard of *ludi miscelli*; '*keep up thy station*' in I. ii. 52, for '*take vp*', which seems purely arbitrary; '*dispositions*' for '*depositions*' in II. ii. 139, and 'brought' for 'bought' in III. vii. 195. More serious is the omission of lines: in v. viii. 19, 20, the 1616 text

You shall perceiue, sir, I dare beate you. Approch.
VOLP. No haste, sir, I doe know your valure, well:

is shortened to

You shall perceive, sir, I doe know your valure, well.

Similarly in v. x. 8–12:

(CORV. Will he betray himselfe?) VOLT. Whom, equally,

[1] For the metrical apostrophe see vol. iv, pp. 338–40.

I haue abus'd, out of most couetous endes—
(CORV. The man is mad! CORB. What's that?
CORV. He is possest.)
VOLT. For which; now strooke in conscience, here I prostrate
My selfe, at your offended feete, for pardon.—

the 1640 text left out the second and third of these lines.

One reading of this Folio, however, is an ingenious emendation—'*Yea fright all aches from your bones?*' in Nano's song (II. ii. 203) for '*Yet fright*' in the earlier texts. Whalley printed 'Yea', but Gifford restored the original reading.

The Quarto text was reprinted in 1898 with a frontispiece of Volpone adoring his treasures, five initial letters, and a cover design by Aubrey Beardsley, who had planned twenty-four drawings to illustrate the play; Vincent O'Sullivan prefixed a critical essay on Jonson, and Robert Ross wrote a eulogy of the artist.

The Folio text has also been reprinted. In 1906 Horace Hart privately printed the play as a doctorate thesis of Paris by Henry Blackstone Wilkins; the verse-lining and the punctuation are erratic, though there are no serious errors in the text. W. Bang's scholarly reprint of the Folio in his *Materialien zur Kunde des älteren englischen Dramas*, included *Volpone* in his seventh volume, the second part of which was issued in 1908; it was his last complete play: he stopped short at the beginning of the third act of *Epicoene*. Dr. John D. Rea also reprinted the Folio text in *Yale Studies in English*, volume lix, in 1919, from a copy in the Library of Congress, collated with the Yale copies of the Quarto and the Folio and a Folio copy in the University of Pennsylvania; he noted some variant readings of the Folio. He ignored the 1640 Folio, but collated Gifford, with the result that he credited Gifford with being the author of some of the 1640 readings.

BEN: IONSON

his

VOLPONE

Or

THE FOXE.

—*Simul & iucunda, & idonea dicere vitæ.*

Printed for *Thomas Thorppe.*
1607.

The title-page of the Quarto.

VOLPONE,

OR

THE FOXE.

A Comœdie.

Acted in the yeere 1605. By
the K. MAIESTIES
SERVANTS.

The Author B. I.

HORAT.
Simul & iucunda, & idonea dicere vitæ.

LONDON,
Printed by WILLIAM STANSBY.

M. DC. XVI.

The title-page of the 1616 Folio.

VOLPONE, OR THE FOX.

A Comedy.

First Acted in the yeere 1605. By the
Kings MAIESTIES Servants.
With the allowance of the Master
of REVELLS.

The Author *B. J.*

HORAT.
Simul & jucunda, & idonea dicere vitæ.

LONDON,
Printed by RICHARD BISHOP.

M. DC. XL.

The title-page of the 1640 Folio.

TO

THE MOST

NOBLE AND

MOST EQVALL

SISTERS

THE TWO FAMOVS

VNIVERSITIES

FOR THEIR LOVE

AND

ACCEPTANCE

SHEW'N TO HIS POEME IN THE

PRESENTATION

BEN. IONSON

THE GRATEFVLL ACKNOWLEDGER

DEDICATES

BOTH IT AND HIMSELFE.

DEDICATION. 4 EQVALL] ÆQVALL *Q* 5 SISTERS] SISTERS, *F2* 7 VNIVERSITIES] VNIVERSITIES, *Q* : UNIVERSITIES, *F2* 12 PRESENTATION] PRESENTATION : *Q* : *Presentation, F2* 13 BEN.] BEN : *Q* IONSON] IOHNSON *F2* 16 *IT*] IT, *Q* *HIMSELFE.*] HIMSELFE. | There follows an *Epistle*, if you dare venture on the length. *Q*

N*Euer (most equall* S I S T E R S) *had any man a wit so presently excellent, as that it could raise it selfe; but there must come both matter, occasion, commenders, and fauourers to it: If this be true, and that the fortune of all writers doth daily proue it, it behoues the carefull to prouide, well, toward these accidents; and, hauing acquir'd them, to preserue that part of reputation most tenderly, wherein the benefit of a friend is also defended. Hence is it, that J now render my selfe gratefull, and am studious to iustifie the bounty of your act: to which, though your mere authority were satisfying, yet, it being an age, wherein* Poetrie, *and the Professors of it heare so ill, on all sides, there will a reason bee look'd for in the subiect. Jt is certayne, nor can it with any fore-head be oppos'd, that the too-much licence of* Poetasters, *in this time, hath much deform'd their Mistris; that, euery day, their manifold, and manifest ignorance, doth sticke vnnaturall reproches vpon her: But for their petulancy, it were an act of the greatest iniustice, either to let the learned suffer; or so diuine a skill (which indeed should not bee attempted with vncleane hands) to fall, vnder the least contempt. For, if men will impartially, and not à-squint, looke toward the offices, and function of a Poet, they will easily conclude to themselues, the impossibility of any mans being the good Poet, without first being a good man. He that is said to be able to informe yong-men to all good disciplines, inflame growne-men to all great vertues, keepe old-men in their best and supreme state, or as they decline to child-hood, recouer them to their first strength; that comes forth the interpreter, and arbiter of nature, a teacher of things diuine, no lesse then humane, a master in manners; and can alone (or with a few) effect the businesse of man-kind: this, I take him, is no subiect for pride, and ignorance to exercise their rayling rhetorique vpon. But,*

THE EPISTLE. *The running title is printed in italic in Q, and the text in roman.* 1 *equall*] *æquall* Q 4 *it* :] it. *Q* 11 Poetrie] *Poëtry* Q. So 37 13 *oppos'd,*] oppos'd) *Q, which failed to print* '(nor' *in* 13 14 Poetasters] *Poëtasters* Q 15 *Mistris*] *Mistresse* Q 21, 23 *Poet*] *Poët* Q. So 35 25 *old-men*] *old men* Q 28 *then*] than *F2* (*et passim*) 29 *alone*] alóne *Q* 30 *man-kind : this*] Man-kind. This *Q*

it will here be hastily answer'd, that the writers of these dayes are other things; that, not only their manners, but their natures are inuerted; and nothing remayning with them of the dignitie of Poet, but the abused name, which euery Scribe vsurps: that now, especially in dramatick, *or* (*as they terme it*) *stage-*poetrie, *nothing but ribaldry, profanation, blasphemy, all licence of offence to god, and man, is practis'd. J dare not denie a great part of this* (*and am sorry, J dare not*) *because in some mens abortiue features* (*and would they had neuer boasted the light*) *it is ouer-true: But, that all are embarqu'd in this bold aduenture for hell, is a most vncharitable thought, and, vtter'd, a more malicious slander. For my particular, I can* (*and from a most cleare conscience*) *affirme, that J haue euer trembled to thinke toward the least prophanenesse; haue lothed the vse of such foule, and vn-wash'd baudr'y, as is now made the foode of the* scene. *And, howsoeuer I cannot escape, from some, the imputation of sharpnesse, but that they will say, I haue taken a pride, or lust, to be bitter, and not my yongest infant but hath come into the world with all his teeth; I would aske of these supercilious politiques, what nation, societie, or generall order, or state J haue prouok'd? what publique person? whether I haue not* (*in all these*) *preseru'd their dignitie, as mine owne person, safe? My workes are read, allow'd,* (*I speake of those that are intirely mine*) *looke into them: What broad reproofes haue J vs'd? Where haue I beene particular? Where personall? except to a mimick, cheater, bawd, or buffon, creatures* (*for their insolencies*) *worthy to be tax'd? Yet, to which of these so pointingly, as he might not, either ingenuously haue confest, or wisely dissembled his disease? But it is not rumour can make men guiltie, much lesse entitle me, to other mens crimes. J know, that nothing can bee so innocently writ, or carryed, but may be made obnoxious to construction; mary, whil'st J beare mine innocence about mee, J feare it not. Application, is now, growne a trade with many; and there are,*

38 *god . . . man*] God . . . Man *Q*   47 scene. *And* corr. F1 : scene : And *F1 originally* : *Scene* : And *Q*   49 *lust,*] lust *Q*   54 *workes*] WORKES *Q*   55 *them :*] them, *Q*   56 *vs'd ?*] vsd : *Q*   *beene*] bin *Q*   58 *Yet,*] or *Q*   59 *ingenuously*] ingeniously *Q*

that professe to haue a key for the decyphering of euery thing: but let wise and noble persons take heed how they be too credulous, or giue leaue to these inuading interpreters, to bee ouer-familiar with their fames, who cunningly, and often, vtter their owne virulent malice, vnder other mens simplest meanings. As for those, that will (by faults which charitie hath rak'd vp, or common honestie conceal'd) make themselues a name with the multitude, or (to draw their rude, and beastly claps) care not whose liuing faces they intrench, with their petulant stiles; may they doe it, without a riuall, for me: I choose rather to liue grau'd in obscuritie, then share with them, in so preposterous a fame. Nor can I blame the wishes of those seuere, and wiser patriots, who prouiding the hurts these licentious spirits may doe in a state, desire rather to see fooles, and deuils, and those antique reliques of barbarisme retriu'd, with all other ridiculous, and exploded follies: then behold the wounds of priuate men, of princes, and nations. For, as HORACE *makes* TREBATIVS *speake, among these*

——Sibi quisq; timet, quanquam est intactus, & odit.

And men may iustly impute such rages, if continu'd, to the writer, as his sports. The increase of which lust in liberty, together with the present trade of the stage, in all their misc'line enter-ludes, *what learned or liberall soule doth not already abhor? where nothing but the filth of the time is vtter'd, and that with such impropriety of phrase, such plenty of* solœcismes, *such dearth of sense, so bold* prolepse's, *so rackt* metaphor's, *with brothelry, able to violate the eare of a pagan, and blasphemy, to turne the bloud of a christian to water. J cannot but be serious in a cause of this nature, wherein my fame, and the reputations of diuers honest, and learned are the question; when a Name, so ful of authority, antiquity, and all great marke, is (through their insolence) become the lowest scorne of the age:*

68 *interpreters,*] Interpreters *Q*   74 *intrench,*] intrench *Q*   75 *choose*] chuse *Q*   77 *seuere*] graue *Q*   *wiser*] *wise* F2, F3   79 *deuils*] Diuells *Q*   83 *among*] in *Q*   86 *sports*] *spots* F2, F3   *increase*] encrease *Q*   87 *misc'line*] *masc'line* F2, F3   89 *filth*] garbage *Q*   92 *brothelry,*] brothelry *Q*   95 *diuers*] diuerse *Q*   96 *Name*] NAME *Q*

and those men subiect to the petulancy of euery vernaculous Orator, that were wont to bee the care of Kings, and happiest Monarchs. This it is, that hath not only rap't me to present indignation, but made me studious, heretofore; and, by all my actions, to stand off, from them: which may most appeare in this my latest worke (which you, most learned ARBITRESSES, *haue seene, iudg'd, and to my crowne, approu'd) wherein I haue labour'd, for their instruction, and amendment, to reduce, not onely the ancient formes, but manners of the* scene, *the easinesse, the propriety, the innocence, and last the doctrine, which is the principall end of* poesie, *to informe men, in the best reason of liuing. And though my* catastrophe *may, in the strict rigour of* comick *law, meet with censure, as turning back to my promise; J desire the learned, and charitable critick to haue so much faith in me, to thinke it was done off industrie: For, with what ease J could haue varied it, neerer his scale (but that I feare to boast my owne faculty) J could here insert. But my speciall ayme being to put the snaffle in their mouths, that crie out, we neuer punish vice in our* enterludes, *&c. I tooke the more liberty; though not without some lines of example, drawne euen in the ancients themselues, the goings out of whose* comœdies *are not alwaies ioyfull, but oft-times, the bawdes, the seruants, the riuals, yea, and the masters are mulcted: and fitly, it being the office of a* comick-Poet, *to imitate iustice, and instruct to life, as well as puritie of language, or stirre vp gentle affections. To which, I shall take the occasion else-where to speake. For the present (most reuerenced* SISTERS) *as J haue car'd to be thankefull for your affections past, and here made the vnderstanding acquainted with some ground of your fauours; let me not despaire their continuance, to the maturing of some worthier fruits: wherein, if*

98 *men*] MEN *Q* 100 *is,*] is *Q* 101 *heretofore;*] heretofore, *Q* 102 *off*] of *Q* *them :*] them ; *Q* 103 *worke*] WORKE *Q* 108 poesie,] POESY *Q* 113 *For,*] For *Q* 116 enterludes,] *Enterludes Q* 118 *example,*] example *Q* 120 *masters*] maisters *Q* 121 -Poet,] -POET *Q* 123–4 *I shall take . . . to speake*] vpon my next opportunity toward the examining & digesting of my *notes,* I shall speake more wealthily, and pay the World a debt. *Q* 124 *For the present*] In the meane time *Q, beginning a new paragraph.* 127 *fauours*] fauors *Q*

my MVSES *be true to me, J shall raise the despis'd head of* poetrie *againe, and stripping her out of those rotten and base rags, wherwith the Times haue adulterated her form, restore her to her primitiue habit, feature, and maiesty, and render her worthy to be imbraced, and kist, of all the great and master-* spirits *of our world. As for the vile, and slothfull, who neuer affected an act, worthy of celebration, or are so inward with their owne vicious natures, as they worthily feare her; and thinke it a high point of policie, to keepe her in contempt with their declamatorie, and windy inuectiues: shee shall out of iust rage incite her seruants (who are* genus ir⟨r⟩itabile) *to spout inke in their faces, that shall eate, farder then their marrow, into their fames; and not* CINNAMVS *the barber, with his arte, shall be able to take out the brands, but they shall liue, and bee read, till the wretches dye, as things worst deseruing of themselues in chiefe, and then of all mankind.*

130 poetrie] POETRY *Q* 133 *master*-spirits] Maister *Spirits* Q
145 *mankind.*] *From my house in the Black-Friars this* 11. *of February.* 1607. *add Q*

The Persons of the Play.

VOLPONE, *a Magnifico.*

MOSCA, *his Parasite.*

VOLTORE, *an Aduocate.*

CORBACCIO, *an old Gentleman.*

CORVINO, *a Merchant.*

AVOCATORI, *four Magistrates.*

NOTARIO, *the Register.*

NANO, *a Dwarfe.*

CASTRONE, *an Eunuch.*

GREGE.

POLITIQVE WOVLD-BEE, *a Knight.*

PEREGRINE, *a Gent.-trauailer.*

BONARIO, *a yong Gentleman.*

FINE MADAME WOVLD-BEE, *the Knights wife.*

CELIA, *the Merchants wife.*

COMMANDADORI, *Officers.*

MERCATORI, *three Merchants.*

ANDROGYNO, *a Hermaphrodite.*

SERVITORE, *a Seruant.*

WOMEN.

THE SCENE

VENICE.

The Persons of the Play.] *THE PERSONS OF* | THE COMOEDYE. *Q* 4 CORBACCIO] CORACCIO *F2, F3* 19 SERVITORE, *a Seruant*] *Servitori, Servants two Waiting-women, &c.* G *THE SCENE* VENICE. *not in Q* *After* The Scene *F2 inserts the names of* The principall Comedians *given in F1 at the end of the Play.*

VOLPONE,

OR

THE FOXE.

THE ARGVMENT.

V o l p o n e, *childlesse, rich, faines sicke, despaires,*
O *ffers his state to hopes of seuerall heires,*
L *ies languishing; His Parasite receaues*
P *resents of all, assures, deludes: Then weaues*
O *ther crosse-plots, which ope' themselues, are told.*
N *ew tricks for safety, are sought; they thriue: When, bold,*
E *ach tempts th'other againe, and all are sold.*

PROLOGVE

NOw, luck yet send vs, and a little wit
  Will serue, to make our play hit;
(According to the palates of the season)
  Here is ri'me, not emptie of reason:
This we were bid to credit, from our *Poet,*
  Whose true scope, if you would know it,
In all his *poemes,* stil, hath been this measure,
  To mixe profit, with your pleasure;
And not as some (whose throats their enuy fayling)
  Cry hoarsely, all he writes, is rayling:
And, when his playes come forth, thinke they can flout them,

THE ARGVMENT *roman in Q*   7 *tempts*] tempt's *Q*
PROLOGVE] The PROLOGVE *Q, which prints it in italic, except l.* 8 *and the quotations in ll.* 10, 12   1 yet] God *Q*   2 play] PLAY *Q*   5 *Poet*] Poët *Q*   7 *poemes*] Poëmes *Q*   11 playes] PLAYES *Q*

With saying, he was a yeere about them.
To these there needs no lie, but this his creature,
Which was, two months since, no feature;
And, though he dares giue them fiue liues to mend it,
'Tis knowne, fiue weekes fully pen'd it:
From his owne hand, without a co-adiutor,
Nouice, iourney-man, or tutor.
Yet, thus much I can giue you, as a token
Of his playes worth, no egges are broken;
Nor quaking custards with fierce teeth affrighted,
Wherewith your rout are so delighted;
Nor hales he in a gull, old ends reciting,
To stop gaps in his loose writing;
With such a deale of monstrous, and forc'd action:
As might make *Bet'lem* a faction:
Nor made he'his play, for iests, stolne from each table,
But makes iests, to fit his fable.
And, so presents quick *comœdie*, refined,
As best Criticks haue designed,
The lawes of time, place, persons he obserueth,
From no needfull rule he swerueth.
All gall, and coppresse, from his inke, he drayneth,
Onely, a little salt remayneth;
Wherewith, he'll rub your cheeks, til (red with laughter)
They shall looke fresh, a weeke after.

Act I. *Scene* I.

VOLPONE, MOSCA.

GOod morning to the day; and, next, my gold:
Open the shrine, that I may see my *saint*.
Haile the worlds soule, and mine. More glad then is

Prol. 20 playes . . . no *corr. F1*: Playes . . . No *F1 originally, F2*: PLAYES . . . *No* Q 21 fierce] *feirce* Q 26 *Bet'lem*] Bethlem *Q* 27 play *corr. F1*: Play *F1 originally, F2*: PLAY *Q* 30 designed] designed; *F2* I. i.] ACT. I. SCENE. I. *Q* (*et passim*): *A Room in Volpone's House.* | *Enter Volpone and Mosca.* G After 2 *Mosca withdraws the curtain and discovers piles of gold, plate, jewels, &c.* G

The teeming earth, to see the long'd-for sunne
Peepe through the hornes of the celestiall *ram*,
Am I, to view thy splendor, darkening his :
That, lying here, amongst my other hoords,
Shew'st like a flame, by night ; or like the day
Strooke out of *chaos*, when all darkenesse fled
Vnto the center. O, thou sonne of SOL,
(But brighter then thy father) let me kisse,
With adoration, thee, and euery relique
Of sacred treasure, in this blessed roome.
Well did wise Poets, by thy glorious name,
Title that age, which they would haue the best ;
Thou being the best of things : and far transcending
All stile of ioy, in children, parents, friends,
Or any other waking dreame on earth.
Thy lookes, when they to VENVS did ascribe,
They should haue giu'n her twentie thousand CVPIDS ;
Such are thy beauties, and our loues ! Deare *saint*,
Riches, the dumbe god, that giu'st all men tongues :
That canst doe nought, and yet mak'st men doe all things ;
The price of soules ; euen hell, with thee to boot,
Is made worth heauen ! Thou art vertue, fame,
Honour, and all things else ! Who can get thee,
He shall be noble, valiant, honest, wise——

MOS. And what he will, sir. Riches are in fortune
A greater good, then wisedome is in nature.

VOL. True, my beloued MOSCA. Yet, I glory
More in the cunning purchase of my wealth,
Then in the glad possession ; since I gaine
No common way : I vse no trade, no venter ;
I wound no earth with plow-shares ; fat no beasts
To feede the shambles ; haue no mills for yron,
Oyle, corne, or men, to grinde 'hem into poulder ;

I. i. 4 sunne *corr. F1* : Sunne *F1 originally, F2* : *Sunne* Q 5 celestiall] *Cælestiall* Q *ram* corr. F1 : *Ram* Q, F1 originally, F2 7 That, *corr. F1* : That *Q, F1 originally, F2* 9 Strooke] Struck *F2* 21 loues!] loues. *Q* 22 dumbe] domb *Q* 25 heauen !] heauen. *Q* 26 Honour] Honor *Q* else !] else. *Q* 34 -shares ;.fat *Q, corr. F1* : -shares : I fat *F1 originally, F2, F3* 35 yron] iron *Q* 36 'hem *F3* (*et passim*)

I blow no subtill glasse ; expose no ships
To threatnings of the furrow-faced sea ;
I turne no moneys, in the publike banke ;
Nor vsure priuate—— M o s. No, sir, nor deuoure
Soft prodigalls. You shall ha' some will swallow
A melting heire, as glibly, as your *Dutch*
Will pills of butter, and ne're purge for't ;
Teare forth the fathers of poore families
Out of their beds, and coffin them, aliue,
In some kind, clasping prison, where their bones
May be forth-comming, when the flesh is rotten :
But, your sweet nature doth abhorre these courses ;
You lothe, the widdowes, or the orphans teares
Should wash your pauements ; or their pittious cryes
Ring in your roofes ; and beate the aire, for vengeance.——
V o l. Right, M o s c a, I doe lothe it. M o s. And besides, sir,
You are not like the thresher, that doth stand
With a huge flaile, watching a heape of corne,
And, hungrie, dares not taste the smallest graine,
But feeds on mallowes, and such bitter herbs ;
Nor like the merchant, who hath fill'd his vaults
With *Romagnía*, and rich *Candian* wines,
Yet drinkes the lees of *Lombards* vineger :
You will not lie in straw, whilst moths, and wormes
Feed on your sumptuous hangings, and soft beds.
You know the vse of riches, and dare giue, now,
From that bright heape, to me, your poore obseruer,
Or to your dwarfe, or your *hermaphrodite*,
Your *eunuch*, or what other houshold-trifle
Your pleasure allowes maint'nance.—— V o l. Hold thee, M o s c a,

I. i. 40 priuate—*corr. F1* : priuate. *Q, F1 originally, F2* 43 ne're] nêre *Q* 48 But, *corr. F1* : But *Q, F1 originally, F2* 51 roofes ; *corr. F1* : roofes : *Q, F1 originally, F2* vengeance.— *corr. F1* : vengeance. *Q, F1 originally, F2* 53 the thresher *corr. F1* : a thresher *Q, F1 originally, F2, F3* 57 merchant *Q, corr. F1, F2* : marchant *F1 originally* 58 *Romagnía* Q, corr. F1 : *Romagnia* F1 originally, F2 66 maint'nance.—] maint'nance. *Q* After 66 *Gives him money*. G

Take, of my hand; thou strik'st on truth, in all:
And they are enuious, terme thee parasite.
Call forth my dwarfe, my eunuch, and my foole,
And let 'hem make me sport. What should I doe,
But cocker vp my *genius*, and liue free
To all delights, my fortune calls me to?
I haue no wife, no parent, child, allie,
To giue my substance to; but whom I make,
Must be my heire: and this makes men obserue me.
This drawes new clients, daily, to my house,
Women, and men, of euery sexe, and age,
That bring me presents, send me plate, coyne, iewels,
With hope, that when I die, (which they expect
Each greedy minute) it shall then returne,
Ten-fold, vpon them; whil'st some, couetous
Aboue the rest, seeke to engrosse me, whole,
And counter-worke, the one, vnto the other,
Contend in gifts, as they would seeme, in loue:
All which I suffer, playing with their hopes,
And am content to coyne 'hem into profit,
And looke vpon their kindnesse, and take more,
And looke on that; still bearing them in hand,
Letting the cherry knock against their lips,
And, draw it, by their mouths, and back againe. How now!

Act I. *Scene* II.

NANO, ANDROGYNO, CASTRONE,
VOLPONE, MOSCA.

Now, roome, for fresh gamsters, who doe will you to know,
They doe bring you neither play, nor Vniuersitie *show;*
And therefore doe intreat you, that whatsoeuer they reherse,
May not fare a whit the worse, for the false pase of the verse.

I. i. 67 Take,] Take *Q* 70 sport.] *Exit Mos.* add G 74 to *corr. Q, F1, F2*: too *Q originally* 80, 81 returne, Ten-fold, *corr. Q, F1, F2*: returne Tenfold *Q originally* 82 seeke] see *F3* 88 still] still, *Q* I. ii. *Re-enter Mosca with Nano, Androgyno, and Castrone.* G, continuing the scene

If you wonder at this, you will wonder more, ere we passe,
For know, here is inclos'd the Soule of Pythagoras,
That iuggler diuine, as hereafter shall follow;
Which Soule (fast, and loose, sir) came first from Apollo,
And was breath'd into Æthalides, Mercvrivs *his sonne,*
Where it had the gift to remember all that euer was done.
From thence it fled forth, and made quick transmigration
To goldy-lockt Evphorbvs, *who was kill'd, in good fashion,*
At the siege of old Troy, *by the Cuckold of* Sparta.
Hermotimvs *was next (I find it, in my* charta)
To whom it did passe, where no sooner it was missing,
But with one Pyrrhvs, *of* Delos, *it learn'd to goe a fishing:*
And thence, did it enter the Sophist of Greece.
From Pythagore, *shee went into a beautifull peece,*
Hight Aspasia, *the* meretrix; *and the next tosse of her*
Was, againe, of a whore, shee became a Philosopher,
Crates *the* Cynick: *(as it selfe doth relate it)*
Since, Kings, Knights, and Beggers, Knaues, Lords and Fooles gat it,
Besides, oxe, and asse, cammell, mule, goat, and brock,
In all which it hath spoke, as in the Coblers cock.
But I come not here, to discourse of that matter,
Or his one, two, *or* three, *or his great oath,* by quater,
His musicks, *his* trigon, *his golden thigh,*
Or his telling how elements shift: but I
Would aske, how of late, thou hast suffered translation,
And shifted thy coat, in these dayes of reformation?
And. *Like one of the reformed, a Foole, as you see,*
Counting all old doctrine heresie.
Nan. *But not on thine owne forbid meates hast thou venter'd?*
And. *On fish, when first, a* carthusian *I enter'd.*

I. ii. 6 Pythagoras] Pithagoras *Q*: *so* 59 13 *siege*] *seege* Q 14 charta] Chartâ *Q* 16 Pyrrhvs] Pirrhus *Q* 18 Pythagore] Pithagore *Q*: *so* 38 23 *Besides,*] *Besides* F2 29 *suffered*] *suffer'd* F2 33 *venter'd*] *ventur'd* F3

NAN. *Why, then thy dogmaticall silence hath left thee?*
AND. *Of that an obstreperous Lawyer bereft mee.*
NAN. *O wonderfull change! when Sir Lawyer forsooke thee,*
For PYTHAGORE'S *sake, what body then tooke thee?*
AND. *A good dull moyle.* NAN. *And how! by that meanes,*
Thou wert brought to allow of the eating of beanes?
AND. *Yes.* NAN. *But, from the moyle, into whom did'st thou passe?*
AND. *Into a very strange beast, by some writers cal'd an asse;*
By others, a precise, pure, illuminate brother,
Of those deuoure flesh, and sometimes one another:
And will drop you forth a libell, or a sanctified lie,
Betwixt euery spoonefull of a natiuitie-pie.
NAN. *Now quit thee, for heauen, of that profane nation;*
And gently, report thy next transmigration.
AND. *To the same that I am.* NAN. *A creature of delight?*
And (what is more then a Foole) an hermaphrodite?
Now 'pray thee, sweet Soule, in all thy variation,
Which body would'st thou choose, to take vp thy station?
AND. *Troth, this I am in, euen here would I tarry.*
NAN. *'Cause here, the delight of each sexe thou canst vary?*
AND. *Alas, those pleasures be stale, and forsaken;*
No, 'tis your Foole, wherewith I am so taken,
The onely one creature, that I can call blessed:
For all other formes I haue prou'd most distressed.
NAN. *Spoke true, as thou wert in* PYTHAGORAS *still.*
This learned opinion we celebrate will,
Fellow eunuch (as behooues vs) with all our wit, and art,
To dignifie that, whereof our selues are so great, and speciall a part.
VOL. Now very, very pretty: MOSCA, this
Was thy inuention? MOS. If it please my patron,
Not else. VOL. It doth, good MOSCA. MOS. Then it was, sir.

I. ii. 39 *how!*] *how?* Q 51 *'pray thee*] *'pry thee* F2 52 *take*] *keep* F2, F3 61 behooues] behoves *F2*

SONG.

Fooles, they are the onely nation
Worth mens enuy, or admiration ;
Free from care, or sorrow-taking,
Selues, and others merry-making :
All they speake, or doe, is sterling.
Your Foole, he is your great mans dearling,
And your ladies sport, and pleasure ;
Tongue, and bable are his treasure.
Eene his face begetteth laughter,
And he speakes truth, free from slaughter ;
Hee's the grace of euery feast,
And, sometimes, the chiefest guest :
Hath his trencher, and his stoole,
When wit waites vpon the foole.
O, who would not bee
Hee, hee,.hee ?

One knocks without.

VOL. Who's that ? away, looke MOSCA. MOS. Foole, be gone,
'Tis signior VOLTORE, the Aduocate,
I know him, by his knock. VOL. Fetch me my gowne,
My furres, and night-caps ; say, my couch is changing :
And let him entertayne himselfe, awhile,
Without i' th' gallerie. Now, now, my clients
Beginne their visitation ! vulture, kite,
Rauen, and gor-crow, all my birds of prey,
That thinke me turning carcasse, now they come :
I am not for 'hem yet. How now ? the newes ?
MOS. A piece of plate, sir. VOL. Of what bignesse ? MOS. Huge,

I. ii. After 65 SONG.] *Nano and Castrone sing.* G 69 *Selues*] *Themselues* Q 71 *dearling*] *darling* F2 74 *Eene his*] *His very* Q 79 *waites*] *shall waite* Q 82 *Stage direction not in Q.* After 'away' [*Exeunt Nano and Castrone.*] G After 'gone' [*Exit Androgyno.*] G 85 couch is] couch's *F2, F3* 86 entertayne] intertaine *Q* 87 Without] Within *Q* After 'gallerie.' *Exit Mosca.* G 88 visitation !] visitation ; *Q* 89 and *om. F2, F3*

Massie, and antique, with your name inscrib'd,
And armes ingrauen. Vol. Good! and not a foxe
Stretch'd on the earth, with fine delusiue sleights,
Mocking a gaping crow? ha, Mosca? Mos. Sharpe,
sir.
Vol. Giue me my furres. Why dost thou laugh so,
man?
Mos. I cannot choose, sir, when I apprehend
What thoughts he has (without) now, as he walkes:
That this might be the last gift, he should giue;
That this would fetch you; if you dyed to day,
And gaue him all, what he should be to morrow;
What large returne would come of all his venters;
How he should worship'd be, and reuerenc'd;
Ride, with his furres, and foot-clothes; waited on
By herds of fooles, and clients; haue cleere way
Made for his moyle, as letter'd as himselfe;
Be cald the great, and learned Aduocate:
And then concludes, there's nought impossible.
Vol. Yes, to be learned, Mosca. Mos. O, no: rich
Implies it. Hood an asse, with reuerend purple,
So you can hide his two ambitious eares,
And, he shall passe for a cathedrall Doctor.
Vol. My caps, my caps, good Mosca, fetch him in.
Mos. Stay, sir, your ointment for your eyes. Vol.
That's true;
Dispatch, dispatch: I long to haue possession
Of my new present. Mos. That, and thousands more,
I hope, to see you lord of. Vol. Thankes, kind Mosca.
Mos. And that, when I am lost in blended dust,
And hundred such, as I am, in succession——
Vol. Nay, that were too much, Mosca. Mos. You
shall liue,
Still, to delude these *harpyies*. Vol. Louing Mosca,

I. ii. After 93 *Re-enter Mosca, wtih the gown, &c.* G 97 After 'furres' [*Puts on his sick dress.*] G 99 without] within *Q* 106 herds] heards *Q* 110 Mosca.] *Mosca*; Q 122 *harpyies*] *Harpyies* corr. Q: *Harpyeis* Q originally

'Tis well, my pillow now, and let him enter.
Now, my fain'd cough, my phthisick, and my gout,
My apoplexie, palsie, and catarrhes,
Helpe, with your forced functions, this my posture,
Wherein, this three yeere, I haue milk'd their hopes.
He comes, I heare him (vh, vh, vh, vh) ô.

Act I. *Scene* III.

MOSCA, VOLTORE, VOLPONE.

YOu still are, what you were, sir. Onely you
(Of all the rest) are he, commands his loue :
And you doe wisely, to preserue it, thus,
With early visitation, and kind notes
Of your good meaning to him, which, I know,
Cannot but come most gratefull. Patron, sir.
Here's signior VOLTORE is come—— VOLP. What say you ?
MOS. Sir, signior VOLTORE is come, this morning,
To visit you. VOLP. I thanke him. MOS. And hath brought
A piece of antique plate, bought of S. MARKE,
With which he here presents you. VOLP. He is welcome.
Pray him, to come more often. MOS. Yes. VOLT. What sayes he ?
MOS. He thanks you, and desires you see him often.
VOLP. MOSCA. MOS. My patron ? VOLP. Bring him neere, where is he ?
I long to feele his hand. MOS. The plate is here, sir.
VOLT. How fare you, sir ? VOLP. I thanke you, signior VOLTORE.
Where is the plate ? mine eyes are bad. VOLT. I'm sorry,
To see you still thus weake. MOS. That he is not weaker.

I. ii. After 123 *Exit Mosca.* G 124 phthisick] *Phthisick* corr. Q : *Pthisick* Q originally 125 catarrhes] *Catarrhe* Q originally: *Catarrhe* corr. Q I. iii. *Re-enter Mosca, introducing Voltore with a piece of Plate.* G 7 VOLP.] *Volp.* [*faintly.*] G 17 VOLT.] *Volt.* [*putting it into his hands.*] G 18 weaker.] *Aside.* add G

VOLP. You are too munificent. VOLT. No, sir, would to heauen,
I could as well giue health to you, as that plate.
VOLP. You giue, sir, what you can. I thanke you. Your loue
Hath taste in this, and shall not be vn-answer'd.
I pray you see me often. VOLT. Yes, I shall, sir.
VOLP. Be not far from me. MOS. Doe you obserue that, sir?
VOLP. Harken vnto me, still: It will concerne you.
MOS. You are a happy man, sir, know your good.
VOLP. I cannot now last long—— (MOS. You are his heire, sir.
VOLT. Am I?) VOLP. I feele me going, (vh, vh, vh, vh.)
I am sayling to my port, (vh, vh, vh, vh?)
And I am glad, I am so neere my hauen.
MOS. Alas, kind gentleman, well, we must all goe——
VOLT. But, MOSCA—— MOS. Age wil conquer. VOLT. 'Pray thee heare me.
Am I inscrib'd his heire, for certayne? MOS. Are you?
I doe beseech you, sir, you will vouchsafe
To write me, i' your family. All my hopes,
Depend vpon your worship. I am lost,
Except the rising sunne doe shine on me.
VOLT. It shall both shine, and warme thee, MOSCA. MOS. Sir.
I am a man, that haue not done your loue
All the worst offices: here I weare your keyes,
See all your coffers, and your caskets lockt,
Keepe the poore inuentorie of your iewels,
Your plate, and moneyes, am your steward, sir,
Husband your goods here. VOLT. But am I sole heire?
MOS. Without a partner, sir, confirm'd this morning;

I. iii. 25 still:] still. *Q* 27 long—] long. *Q* (Mos.] Mos. *Q* 28 I?)] I? *Q* 31 goe—] go. *Q* 32 MOSCA—] *Mosca.* Q 'Pray thee] 'Pry thee *F2* 36 worship.] worship; *Q* 38 warme] warn *F3* 40 offices:] offices, *Q* 43 moneyes, am] moneyes; I'm *F2, F3*

The waxe is warme yet, and the inke scarse drie
Vpon the parchment. VOLT. Happy, happy, me!
By what good chance, sweet MOSCA? MOS. Your desert, sir;
I know no second cause. VOLT. Thy modestie
Is loth to know it; well, we shall requite it.
MOS. He euer lik'd your course, sir, that first tooke him.
I, oft, haue heard him say, how he admir'd
Men of your large profession, that could speake
To euery cause, and things mere contraries,
Till they were hoarse againe, yet all be law;
That, with most quick agilitie, could turne,
And re-turne; make knots, and vndoe them;
Giue forked counsell; take prouoking gold
On either hand, and put it vp: these men,
He knew, would thriue, with their humilitie.
And (for his part) he thought, he should be blest
To haue his heire of such a suffering spirit,
So wise, so graue, of so perplex'd a tongue,
And loud withall, that would not wag, nor scarce
Lie still, without a fee; when euery word
Your worship but lets fall, is a *cecchine!*
Another knocks. Who's that? one knocks, I would not haue you seene, sir.
And yet——pretend you came, and went in haste;
I'le fashion an excuse. And, gentle sir,
When you doe come to swim, in golden lard,
Vp to the armes, in honny, that your chin
Is borne vp stiffe, with fatnesse of the floud,
Thinke on your vassall; but remember me:
I ha' not beene your worst of clients. VOLT. MOSCA——
MOS. When will you haue your inuentorie brought, sir?
Or see a coppy of the will? (anon)
I'le bring 'hem to you, sir. Away, be gone,

I. iii. 47 happy,] happy *Q* 50 loth] not *G* 51 sir,] sir; *F2* 57 re-turne; make] re-return; could make *G* 64 would] could *F2* 66 *cecchine!*] *Cecchine.* Q 67 *Stage direction not in Q* 76 (anon)] Anone, *Q*

Put businesse i' your face. VOLP. Excellent, MOSCA!
Come hither, let me kisse thee. MOS. Keepe you still, sir.
Here is CORBACCIO. VOLP. Set the plate away,
The vulture's gone, and the old rauen's come.

Act I. *Scene* IIII.

MOSCA, CORBACCIO, VOLPONE.

BEtake you, to your silence, and your sleepe:
Stand there, and multiply. Now, shall wee see
A wretch, who is (indeed) more impotent,
Then this can faine to be; yet hopes to hop
Ouer his graue. Signior CORBACCIO!
Yo' are very welcome, sir. CORB. How do's your patron?
MOS. Troth, as he did, sir, no amends. CORB. What? mends he?
MOS. No, sir: he is rather worse. CORB. That's well. Where is he?
MOS. Vpon his couch, sir, newly fall'n asleepe.
CORB. Do's he sleepe well? MOS. No winke, sir, all this night,
Nor yesterday, but slumbers. CORB. Good! He should take
Some counsell of physicians: I haue brought him
An *opiate* here, from mine owne Doctor——
MOS. He will not heare of drugs. CORB. Why? I my selfe
Stood by, while 't was made; saw all th'ingredients:
And know, it cannot but most gently worke.
My life for his, 'tis but to make him sleepe.
VOLP. I, his last sleepe, if he would take it. MOS. Sir,
He ha's no faith in physick. CORB. 'Say you? 'say you?
MOS. He ha's no faith in physick: he do's thinke,
Most of your Doctors are the greater danger,

I. iii. 78 After 'face'] *Exit Voltore.* G VOLP.] *Volp.* [*springing up.*] G I. iv. *G continues the scene, with* Enter Corbaccio *at l.* 5 2 After 'multiply' [*Putting the plate to the rest.*] G 7 sir,] sir; *F2* 11 yesterday,] yesterday; *F2* Good!] Good. *Q* should] shall *F3* After 18 *Aside.* G

And worse disease, t'escape. I often haue
Heard him protest, that your physitian
Should neuer be his heire. CORB. Not I his heire?
MOS. Not your physitian, sir. CORB. O, no, no, no,
I doe not meane it. MOS. No, sir, nor their fees
He cannot brooke: he sayes, they flay a man,
Before they kill him. CORB. Right, I doe conceiue you.
MOS. And then, they doe it by experiment;
For which the law not onely doth absolue 'hem,
But giues them great reward: and, he is loth
To hire his death, so. CORB. It is true, they kill,
With as much licence, as a iudge. MOS. Nay, more;
For he but kills, sir, where the law condemnes,
And these can kill him, too. CORB. I, or me:
Or any man. How do's his apoplexe?
Is that strong on him, still? MOS. Most violent.
His speech is broken, and his eyes are set,
His face drawne longer, then 't was wont—— CORB. How? how?
Stronger, then he was wont? MOS. No, sir: his face
Drawne longer, then 't was wont. CORB. O, good. MOS. His mouth
Is euer gaping, and his eye-lids hang. CORB. Good.
MOS. A freezing numnesse stiffens all his ioynts,
And makes the colour of his flesh like lead. CORB. 'Tis good.
MOS. His pulse beats slow, and dull. CORB. Good symptomes, still.
MOS. And, from his brain—— CORB. Ha? how? not from his brain?
MOS. Yes, sir, and from his brain—— (CORB. I conceiue you, good.)
MOS. Flowes a cold sweat, with a continuall rhewme,
Forth the resolued corners of his eyes.
CORB. Is't possible? yet I am better, ha!

I. iv. 27 flay] flea *Q* 28 doe *not in Q* 35 too.] too; *Q*
40 Mos.] CORB. *Q* 47 (CORB. . . . good.)] CORB. . . . good. *Q*

How do's he, with the swimming of his head?
  Mos. O, sir, 'tis past the *scotomy*; he, now,
Hath lost his feeling, and hath left to snort:
You hardly can perceiue him, that he breathes.
  Corb. Excellent, excellent, sure I shall out-last him:
This makes me yong againe, a score of yeeres.
  Mos. I was a comming for you, sir. Corb. Has he made his will?
What has he giu'n me? Mos. No, sir. Corb. Nothing? ha?
  Mos. He has not made his will, sir. Corb. Oh, oh, oh.
What then did Voltore, the Lawyer, here?
  Mos. He smelt a carcasse, sir, when he but heard
My master was about his testament;
(As I did vrge him to it, for your good——)
  Corb. He came vnto him, did he? I thought so.
  Mos. Yes, and presented him this piece of plate.
  Corb. To be his heire? Mos. I doe not know, sir. Corb. True,
I know it too. Mos. By your owne scale, sir. Corb. Well,
I shall preuent him, yet. See, Mosca, looke,
Here, I haue brought a bag of bright *cecchines*,
Will quite weigh downe his plate. Mos. Yea, mary, sir!
This is true physick, this your sacred medicine,
No talke of *opiates*, to this great *elixir*.
  Corb. 'Tis *aurum palpabile*, if not *potabile*.
  Mos. It shall be minister'd to him, in his bowle?
  Corb. I, doe, doe, doe. Mos. Most blessed cordiall!
This will recouer him. Corb. Yes, doe, doe, doe.
  Mos. I thinke, it were not best, sir. Corb. What?
  Mos. To recouer him.

I. iv. 52 past *F3*: past, *Q, Ff* scotomy; he,] *Scotomy*; he, *corr. Q*: *Scotomy*, he *Q originally, F2* 60 What then] But what *Q* 62 master] maister *Q* 63 (As . . . good—) *corr. F1*: As . . . good— *Q, F1 originally, F2* 67 After 'sir'] *Aside.* G 70 Mos.] *Mos.* [*taking the bag.*] G sir! *corr. F1*: sir. *F1 originally, F2*: Sir. *Q* 71 medicine,] medecine; *F2* 74 Mos. *om. F2* 75 cordiall! *corr. F1*: cordiall. *F1 originally, F2*: Cordiall. *Q*

CORB. O, no, no, no; by no meanes. MOS. Why, sir, this
Will worke some strange effect, if he but feele it.
CORB. 'Tis true, therefore forbeare, I'le take my venter:
Giue me 't againe. MOS. At no hand, pardon me;
You shall not doe your selfe that wrong, sir. I
Will so aduise you, you shall haue it all.
CORB. How? MOS. All, sir, 'tis your right, your owne; no man
Can claime a part: 'tis yours, without a riuall,
Decree'd by destinie. CORB. How? how, good MOSCA?
MOS. I'le tell you, sir. This fit he shall recouer——
CORB. I doe conceiue you. MOS. And, on first aduantage
Of his gayn'd sense, will I re-importune him
Vnto the making of his testament:
And shew him this. CORB. Good, good. MOS. 'Tis better yet,
If you will heare, sir. CORB. Yes, with all my heart.
MOS. Now, would I counsell you, make home with speed;
There, frame a will: whereto you shall inscribe
My master your sole heire. CORB. And disinherit
My sonne? MOS. O, sir, the better: for that colour
Shall make it much more taking. CORB. O, but colour?
MOS. This will, sir, you shall send it vnto me.
Now, when I come to inforce (as I will doe)
Your cares, your watchings, and your many prayers,
Your more then many gifts, your this dayes present,
And, last, produce your will; where (without thought,
Or least regard, vnto your proper issue,
A sonne so braue, and highly meriting)
The streame of your diuerted loue hath throwne you
Vpon my master, and made him your heire:

I. iv. 79 effect,] effect *Q* 80 forbeare,] forbeare; *Q* 81 hand,] hand; *F2* 87 recouer— *corr. F1*: recouer; *Q, F1 originally, F2* 94 will: *corr. F1*: will; *F1 originally*: Will; *Q, F2* 95, 106 master] maister *Q*

He cannot be so stupide, or stone dead,
But, out of conscience, and mere gratitude——
CORB. He must pronounce me, his? MOS. 'Tis true.
CORB. This plot
Did I thinke on before. MOS. I doe beleeue it.
CORB. Doe you not beleeue it? MOS. Yes, sir.
CORB. Mine owne proiect.
MOS. Which when he hath done, sir—— CORB. Publish'd me his heire?
MOS. And you so certayne, to suruiue him—— CORB. I.
MOS. Being so lusty a man—— CORB. 'Tis true.
MOS. Yes, sir——
CORB. I thought on that too. See, how he should be
The very organ, to expresse my thoughts!
MOS. You haue not onely done your selfe a good——
CORB. But multiplyed it on my sonne? MOS. 'Tis right, sir.
CORB. Still, my inuention. MOS. 'Lasse sir, heauen knowes,
It hath beene all my studie, all my care,
(I e'ene grow grey withall) how to worke things——
CORB. I doe conceiue, sweet MOSCA. MOS. You are he,
For whom I labour, here. CORB. I, doe, doe, doe:
I'le straight about it. MOS. Rooke goe with you, rauen.
CORB. I know thee honest. MOS. You doe lie, sir——
CORB. And——
MOS. Your knowledge is no better then your eares, sir.
CORB. I doe not doubt, to be a father to thee.
MOS. Nor I, to gull my brother of his blessing.
CORB. I may ha' my youth restor'd to me, why not?
MOS. Your worship is a precious asse—— CORB. What say'st thou?

I. iv. 112 sir—] Sir. *Q* 113 him—] him. *Q* 114 man—] man. *Q* sir—] Sir. *Q* 117 good—] good, *Q* 121 I e'ene] I'eene *Q*, *Ff* 124 After 'it'] *Going.* G 125 sir—] Sir. *Q* *Aside.* add G, who does not mark the asides in ll. 124, 126, 128, 130. 128 I,] I *F2* 130 asse—] asse. *Q*

Mos. I doe desire your worship, to make haste, sir.
Corb. 'Tis done, 'tis done, I goe. Volp. O, I shall burst;
Let out my sides, let out my sides—— Mos. Contayne
Your fluxe of laughter, sir: you know, this hope
Is such a bait, it couers any hooke.
Volp. O, but thy working, and thy placing it!
I cannot hold; good rascall, let me kisse thee:
I neuer knew thee, in so rare a humour.
Mos. Alas, sir, I but doe, as I am taught;
Follow your graue instructions; giue 'hem wordes;
Powre oyle into their eares: and send them hence.
Volp. 'Tis true, 'tis true. What a rare punishment
Is auarice, to it selfe? Mos. I, with our helpe, sir.
Volp. So many cares, so many maladies,
So many feares attending on old age,
Yea, death so often call'd on, as no wish
Can be more frequent with 'hem, their limbs faint,
Their senses dull, their seeing, hearing, going,
All dead before them; yea, their very teeth,
Their instruments of eating, fayling them:
Yet this is reckon'd life! Nay, here was one,
Is now gone home, that wishes to liue longer!
Feeles not his gout, nor palsie, faines himselfe
Yonger, by scores of yeeres, flatters his age,
With confident belying it, hopes he may
With charmes, like Æson, haue his youth restor'd:
And with these thoughts so battens, as if fate
Would be as easily cheated on, as he,
Another knocks. And all turnes aire! Who's that, there, now? a third?
Mos. Close, to your couch againe: I heare his voyce.
It is Corvino, our spruce Merchant. Volp. Dead.
Mos. Another bout, sir, with your eyes. Who's there?

I. iv. 132 After 'goe' [*Exit.*] G Volp.] *Volp.* [*leaping from his couch.*] G 138 humour] humor *Q* 148 going,] going *Q* 159 *Stage direction not in Q* 161 Volp.] *Volp.* [*lies down as before.*] G 162 After 'eyes' [*anointing them.*] G

Act I. *Scene* V.

MOSCA, CORVINO, VOLPONE.

SIgnior CORVINO! come most wisht for! O,
How happy were you, if you knew it, now!
CORV. Why? what? wherein? MOS. The tardie houre is come, sir.
CORV. He is not dead? MOS. Not dead, sir, but as good;
He knowes no man. CORV. How shall I doe, then? MOS. Why, sir?
CORV. I haue brought him, here, a pearle. MOS. Perhaps, he has
So much remembrance left, as to know you, sir;
He still calls on you, nothing but your name
Is in his mouth: Is your pearle orient, sir?
CORV. *Venice* was neuer owner of the like.
VOLP. Signior CORVINO. MOS. Harke. VOLP. Signior CORVINO.
MOS. He calls you, step and giue it him. H'is here, sir,
And he has brought you a rich pearle. CORV. How doe you, sir?
Tell him, it doubles the twelfe *caract*. MOS. Sir,
He cannot vnderstand, his hearing's gone;
And yet it comforts him, to see you—— CORV. Say,
I haue a diamant for him, too. MOS. Best shew 't, sir,
Put it into his hand; 'tis onely there
He apprehends: he has his feeling, yet.
See, how he grasps it! CORV. 'Lasse, good gentleman!
How pittifull the sight is! MOS. Tut, forget, sir.
The weeping of an heire should still be laughter,
Vnder a visor. CORV. Why? am I his heire?
MOS. Sir, I am sworne, I may not shew the will,
Till he be dead: But, here has beene CORBACCIO,

I. v. *Enter Corvino.* G, continuing the scene 8 you,] you; *F2* 11 VOLP.] *Volp.* [*faintly.*] G 12 He] 'He *Q*, *F1*: Hee *F2* 17 diamant] Diamond *F3* Best shew 't] Beshrew 't *F2 originally*

Here has beene VOLTORE, here were others too,
I cannot number 'hem, they were so many,
All gaping here for legacies; but I,
Taking the vantage of his naming you,
(Signior CORVINO, Signior CORVINO) tooke
Paper, and pen, and inke, and there I ask'd him,
Whom he would haue his heire? CORVINO. Who
Should be executor? CORVINO. And,
To any question, he was silent too,
I still interpreted the nods, he made
(Through weakenesse) for consent: and sent home th'others,
Nothing bequeath'd them, but to crie, and curse.

They embrace.

CORV. O, my deare MOSCA. Do's he not perceiue vs?
MOS. No more then a blind harper. He knowes no man,
No face of friend, nor name of any seruant,
Who 't was that fed him last, or gaue him drinke:
Not those, he hath begotten, or brought vp
Can he remember. CORV. Has he children? MOS. Bastards,
Some dozen, or more, that he begot on beggers,
Gipseys, and *Iewes*, and black-*moores*, when he was drunke.
Knew you not that, sir? 'Tis the common fable,
The Dwarfe, the Foole, the Eunuch are all his;
H' is the true father of his family,
In all, saue me: but he has giu'n 'hem nothing.
CORV. That's well, that's well. Art sure he does not heare vs?
MOS. Sure, sir? why, looke you, credit your owne sense.
The poxe approch, and adde to your diseases,
If it would send you hence the sooner, sir.
For, your incontinence, it hath deseru'd it
Throughly, and throughly, and the plague to boot.
(You may come neere, sir) would you would once close
Those filthy eyes of yours, that flow with slime,

I. v. 26 Vo■TORE *F2 originally*; so 84 Vo■P., 89 Vo■PONE 27 number] nomber *Q* 32, 33 CORVINO.] *Coruino*: *Q* 33 executor?] executor, *Q* 38 *Stage direction not in Q* 43 Bastards] Bastads *F2* 46 fable,] fable. *Q, Ff* After 51 *Shouts in Vol.'s ear.* G

Like two frog-pits ; and those same hanging cheeks,
Couer'd with hide, in stead of skin : (nay, helpe, sir)
That looke like frozen dish-clouts, set on end.
CORV. Or, like an old smok'd wall, on which the raine
Ran downe in streakes. MOS. Excellent, sir, speake out ;
You may be lowder yet : a culuering,
Discharged in his eare, would hardly bore it.
CORV. His nose is like a common sewre, still running.
MOS. 'Tis good ! and, what his mouth ? CORV. A very draught.
MOS. O, stop it vp—— CORV. By no meanes. MOS. 'Pray you let me.
Faith, I could stifle him, rarely, with a pillow,
As well, as any woman, that should keepe him.
CORV. Doe as you will, but I'le be gone. MOS. Be so ;
It is your presence makes him last so long.
CORV. I pray you, vse no violence. MOS. No, sir ? why ?
Why should you be thus scrupulous ? 'pray you, sir.
CORV. Nay, at your discretion. MOS. Well , good sir, be gone.
CORV. I will not trouble him now, to take my pearle ?
MOS. Puh, nor your diamant. What a needlesse care
Is this afflicts you ? Is not all, here, yours ?
Am not I here ? whom you haue made ? your creature ?
That owe my being to you ? CORV. Gratefull MOSCA !
Thou art my friend, my fellow, my companion,
My partner, and shalt share in all my fortunes.
MOS. Excepting one. CORV. What's that ? MOS. Your gallant wife, sir.
Now, is he gone : we had no other meanes,
To shoot him hence, but this. VOLP. My diuine MOSCA !
Thou hast to day out-gone thy selfe. Who's there ? *Another knocks.*

I. v. 65 sewre] shewre *F2* : shewer *F3* running.] running ; *Q* 66 good !] good : *Q* 67 meanes.] meanes ; *Q* 68–9 *Originally in F2 the initial capitals dropped to the line below, and the* It *of l.* 71 *disappeared* 78 made ?] made *F3* 79 MOSCA !] *Mosca : Q* After 82 *Exit Corv.* G 83 no] on *F2* 85 *Stage direction not in Q*

I will be troubled with no more. Prepare
Me musicke, dances, banquets, all delights;
The *Turke* is not more sensuall, in his pleasures,
Then will VOLPONE. Let mee see, a pearle?
A diamant? plate? *cecchines?* good mornings purchase;
Why, this is better then rob churches, yet:
Or fat, by eating (once a mon'th) a man.
Who is't? MOS. The beauteous lady WOVLD-BEE, sir,
Wife, to the *English* Knight, Sir POLITIQVE WOVLD-
BEE,
(This is the stile, sir, is directed mee)
Hath sent to know, how you haue slept to night,
And if you would be visited. VOLP. Not, now.
Some three houres, hence—— MOS. I told the Squire, so
much.
VOLP. When I am high with mirth, and wine: then,
then.
'Fore heauen, I wonder at the desperate valure
Of the bold *English*, that they dare let loose
Their wiues, to all encounters! MOS. Sir, this knight
Had not his name for nothing, he is politique,
And knowes, how ere his wife affect strange aires,
Shee hath not yet the face, to be dishonest.
But, had shee signior CORVINO's wiues face——
VOLP. Has shee so rare a face? MOS. O, sir, the
wonder,
The blazing starre of *Italie!* a wench
O' the first yeere! a beautie, ripe, as haruest!
Whose skin is whiter then a swan, all ouer!
Then siluer, snow, or lillies! a soft lip,
Would tempt you to eternitie of kissing!
And flesh, that melteth, in the touch, to bloud!
Bright as your gold! and louely, as your gold!

I. v. 89 After 'VOLPONE' [*Exit Mos.*] G 92 mon'th] moneth *F2* *originally, corrected to* month After 92 *Re-enter Mosca.* G 93 sir, *F2*: sir. *F1*: Sir. *Q* 100 valure] valour *F2* 106 wiues] wifes *F2* 108 *Italie !*] *Italy ;* Q 109 yeere !] yeare, *Q* 114 gold ! and] gold, and *Q*

VOLP. Why had not I knowne this, before? MOS. Alas, sir.
My selfe, but yesterday, discouer'd it.
VOLP. How might I see her? MOS. O, not possible;
Shee's kept as warily, as is your gold:
Neuer do's come abroad, neuer takes ayre,
But at a windore. All her lookes are sweet,
As the first grapes, or cherries: and are watch'd
As neere, as they are. VOLP. I must see her—— MOS. Sir.
There is a guard, of ten spies thick, vpon her;
All his whole houshold: each of which is set
Vpon his fellow, and haue all their charge,
When he goes out, when he comes in, examin'd.
VOLP. I will goe see her, though but at her windore.
MOS. In some disguise, then. VOLP. That is true. I must
Maintayne mine owne shape, still, the same: wee'll thinke.

Act II. *Scene* I.

POLITIQVE WOVLD-BEE, PEREGRINE.

SIr, to a wise man, all the world's his soile.
It is not *Italie*, nor *France*, nor *Europe*,
That must bound me, if my fates call me forth.
Yet, I protest, it is no salt desire
Of seeing countries, shifting a religion,
Nor any dis-affection to the state
Where I was bred (and, vnto which I owe
My dearest plots) hath brought me out; much lesse,
That idle, antique, stale, grey-headed proiect
Of knowing mens minds, and manners, with VLYSSES:
But, a peculiar humour of my wiues,
Laid for this height of *Venice*, to obserue,

I. v. 120, 127 windore] Window *F3* 128 then.] then? *Q* After 129 *Exeunt*. G II. i. ACT II. SCENE I. | *St. Mark's Place; a retired corner before Corvino's House.* | *Enter Sir Politick Would-be, and Peregrine*. G

To quote, to learne the language, and so forth——
I hope you trauell, sir, with licence? PER. Yes.
POL. I dare the safelier conuerse—— How long, sir,
Since you left *England?* PER. Seuen weekes. POL. So lately!
You ha' not beene with my lord Ambassador?
PER. Not yet, sir. POL. 'Pray you, what newes, sir, vents our climate?
I heard, last night, a most strange thing reported
By some of my lords followers, and I long
To heare, how 't will be seconded! PER. What was't, sir?
POL. Mary, sir, of a rauen, that should build
In a ship royall of the Kings. PER. This fellow
Do's he gull me, trow? or is gull'd? your name, sir?
POL. My name is POLITIQVE WOVLD-BEE. PER. O, that speaks him.
A Knight, sir? POL. A poore knight, sir. PER. Your lady
Lies here, in *Venice*, for intelligence
Of tyres, and fashions, and behauiour,
Among the curtizans? the fine lady WOVLD-BEE?
POL. Yes, sir, the spider, and the bee, oft-times,
Suck from one flowre. PER. Good sir POLITIQVE!
I cry you mercie; I haue heard much of you:
'Tis true, sir, of your rauen. POL. On your knowledge?
PER. Yes, and your lyons whelping, in the *Tower*.
POL. Another whelpe! PER. Another, sir. POL. Now, heauen!
What prodigies be these? The fires at *Berwike!*
And the new starre! these things concurring, strange!
And full of omen! Saw you those meteors?
PER. I did, sir. POL. Fearefull! Pray you sir, confirme me,
Were there three porcpisces seene, aboue the bridge,

II. i. 24 After 'gull'd' [*Aside.*] G After 25 *Aside.* G 31 flowre] flower *Q* 33 sir,] sir *F1* 35 whelpe!] whelpe? *Q* 39 Pray *corr. Q, F1, F2*: pray *Q originally* 40 porcpisces] porcpises *F2*

As they giue out? PER. Sixe, and a sturgeon, sir.
POL. I am astonish'd! PER. Nay, sir, be not so;
Ile tell you a greater prodigie, then these——
POL. What should these things portend! PER. The verie day
(Let me be sure) that I put forth from *London*,
There was a whale discouer'd, in the riuer,
As high as *Woolwich*, that had waited there
(Few know how manie mon'ths) for the subuersion
Of the *Stode*-Fleet. POL. Is't possible? Beleeue it,
'Twas either sent from *Spaine*, or the *Arch-dukes!*
SPINOLA's whale, vpon my life, my credit!
Will they not leaue these proiects? Worthie sir,
Some other newes. PER. Faith, STONE, the foole, is dead;
And they doe lacke a tauerne-foole, extremely.
POL. Is MASS' STONE dead! PER. H'is dead, sir, why? I hope
You thought him not immortall? O, this Knight
(Were he well knowne) would be a precious thing
To fit our *English* stage: He that should write
But such a fellow, should be thought to faine
Extremely, if not maliciously. POL. STONE dead!
PER. Dead. Lord! how deeply, sir, you apprehend it?
He was no kinsman to you? POL. That I know of.
Well! that same fellow was an vnknowne foole.
PER. And yet you knew him, it seemes? POL. I did so. Sir,
I knew him one of the most dangerous heads
Liuing within the state, and so I held him.
PER. Indeed, sir? POL. While he liu'd, in action.
He has receiu'd weekely intelligence,
Vpon my knowledge, out of the *low Countries*,

II. i. 41 and] and and *F1* 42 astonish'd!] astonish'd. *Q* 48 mon'ths] moneths *Q* 50 *Arch-dukes!*] *Arch-duke*, Q 51 credit!] credit; *Q* 52 Worthie] Worthy *corr. Q*: worthy *Q originally* 55, 60 dead!] dead? *Q* 57 knowne *corr. Q, F1*: knowen *Q originally* 60 After 'maliciously' [*Aside.*] G 64 knew] know *Q*

(For all parts of the world) in cabages ;
And those dispens'd, againe, to' Ambassadors,
In oranges, musk-melons, apricotes,
Limons, pome-citrons, and such like : sometimes,
In *Colchester*-oysters, and your *Selsey*-cockles.
PET. You make me wonder ! POL. Sir, vpon my knowledge.
Nay, I haue obseru'd him, at your publique ordinarie,
Take his aduertisement, from a traueller
(A conceal'd states-man) in a trencher of meat :
And, instantly, before the meale was done,
Conuey an answere in a tooth-pick. PER. Strange !
How could this be, sir ? POL. Why, the meat was cut
So like his character, and so laid, as he
Must easily reade the cypher. PER. I haue heard,
He could not reade, sir. POL. So, 'twas giuen out,
(In politie) by those, that did imploy him :
But he could read, and had your languages,
And to't, as sound a noddle—— PER. I haue heard, sir,
That your *Bab'ouns* were spies ; and that they were
A kind of subtle nation, neere to *China*.
POL. I, I, your *Mamuluchi*. Faith, they had
Their hand in a *French* plot, or two ; but they
Were so extremely giuen to women, as
They made discouery of all : yet I
Had my aduises here (on wensday last)
From one of their owne coat, they were return'd,
Made their relations (as the fashion is)
And now stand faire, for fresh imployment. PER. 'Hart !
This, sir POLL. will be ignorant of nothing.
It seemes, sir, you know all ? POL. Not all, sir. But,
I haue some generall notions ; I doe loue
To note, and to obserue : though I liue out,

II. i. 71 to' Ambassadors] to *Ambassadors* Q 72 apricotes] apricocks *Q* 78 meat : *corr. F1* : meat ; *F1 originally, F2* : meate ; *Q* 88 *Bab'ouns* corr. F1 : *Babiouns* Q, F1 originally, F2 94 aduise *corr. F1* : *aduises* Q : aduices *F1 originally* 98 This,] This *Q, F2* POLL. *corr. F1* : POLL : *F1 originally* : *Poll:* Q : POL. *F2* After 98 *Aside.* G

Free from the actiue torrent, yet I'ld marke
The currents, and the passages of things,
For mine owne priuate vse ; and know the ebbes,
And flowes of state. PER. Beleeue it, sir, I hold
My selfe, in no small tie, vnto my fortunes,
For casting me thus luckily, vpon you ;
Whose knowledge (if your bountie equall it)
May doe me great assistance, in instruction
For my behauiour, and my bearing, which
Is yet so rude, and raw—— POL. Why ? came you forth
Emptie of rules, for trauaile ? PER. Faith, I had
Some common ones, from out that vulgar *grammar*,
Which he, that cry'd *Italian* to me, taught me.
POL. Why, this it is, that spoiles all our braue blouds ;
Trusting our hopefull gentrie vnto pedants :
Fellowes of out-side, and mere barke. You seeme
To be a gentleman, of ingenuous race——
I not professe it, but my fate hath beene
To be, where I haue beene consulted with,
In this high kind, touching some great mens sonnes,
Persons of bloud, and honour—— PER. Who be these, sir ?

Act II. *Scene* II.

MOSCA, POLITIQVE, PEREGRINE,
VOLPONE, NANO,
GREGE.

VNder that windore, there 't must be. The same.
POL. Fellowes, to mount a banke ! Did your instructer
In the deare tongues, neuer discourse to you
Of the *Italian* mountebankes ? PER. Yes, sir. POL. Why,

II. i. 115 blouds ; *corr. F1* : blouds, *Q, F1 originally, F2* 116 pedants : *corr. F1* : *Pedants*, Q : pedants, *F1 originally, F2* II. ii. *Enter Mosca and Nano disguised, followed by persons with materials for erecting a Stage.* G, continuing the scene 1 same.] same : *Q*

Here shall you see one. PER. They are quack-saluers,
Fellowes, that liue by venting oyles, and drugs?
POL. Was that the character he gaue you of them?
PER. As I remember. POL. Pitie his ignorance.
They are the onely-knowing men of *Europe!*
Great generall schollers, excellent phisicians,
Most admir'd states-men, profest fauourites,
And cabinet-counsellors, to the greatest princes!
The onely languag'd-men, of all the world!
PER. And, I haue heard, they are most lewd impostors;
Made all of termes, and shreds; no lesse belyers
Of great-mens fauours, then their owne vile med'cines;
Which they will vtter, vpon monstrous othes:
Selling that drug, for two pence, ere they part,
Which they haue valu'd at twelue crownes, before.
POL. Sir, calumnies are answer'd best with silence:
Your selfe shall iudge. Who is it mounts, my friends?
MOS. SCOTO of *Mantua*, sir. POL. Is't he? nay, then
I'le proudly promise, sir, you shall behold
Another man, then has beene phant'sied to you.
I wonder, yet, that he should mount his banke
Here, in this nooke, that has beene wont t'appeare
In face of the *piazza!* Here, he comes.
VOLP. Mount, *Zany*. GRE. Follow, follow, follow, follow, follow.
POL. See how the people follow him! h'is a man
May write 10000 crownes, in banke, here. Note,
Marke but his gesture: I doe vse to obserue
The state he keeps, in getting vp! PER. 'Tis worth it, sir.

VOLP. *Most noble gent: and my worthy patrons, it may seeme strange, that I, your* SCOTO MANTVANO, *who*

II. ii. 5 They are *Q, corr. F1, F2*: They' are *F1 originally* 9 *Europe!*] *Europe,* Q 10 Great] Great, *Q* 11 fauourites] *Fauorites* Q 12 princes!] *Princes:* Q 16 fauours] fauors *Q* 20 silence:] silence; *Q* After 27 *Enter Volpone disguised as a mountebank Doctor, and followed by a crowd of people.* G 28 *Zany.*] *Zany,* Q After '*Zany*' [*To Nano.*] G 29 h'is] hee's *Q, F2* After 30 *Volpone mounts the Stage.* G 31 gesture:] gesture; *Q*

was euer wont to fixe my banke in face of the publike piazza, *neere the shelter of the* portico; *to the* procuratìa, *should, now* (*after eight months absence, from this illustrous city of* Venice) *humbly retire my selfe, into an obscure nooke of the* piazza.

POL. Did not I, now, obiect the same? PER. Peace, sir.

VOLP. *Let me tell you : I am not* (*as your* Lombard *prouerb saith*) *cold on my feet ; or content to part with my commodities at a cheaper rate, then I accustomed : looke not for it. Nor, that the calumnious reports of that impudent detractor, and shame to our profession,* (ALESSANDRO BVTTONE, *I meane*) *who gaue out, in publike, I was condemn'd a* 'Sforzato *to the galleys, for poysoning the Cardinall* BEMBO'*s*—*Cooke, hath at all attached, much lesse deiected me. No, no, worthy gent.* (*to tell you true*) *I cannot indure, to see the rabble of these ground* Ciarlitani, *that spread their clokes on the pauement, as if they meant to do feates of actiuitie, and then come in, lamely, with their mouldy tales out of* BOCCACIO, *like stale* TABARINE, *the Fabulist : some of them discoursing their trauells, and of their tedious captiuity in the* Turkes *galleyes, when indeed* (*were the truth knowne*) *they were the Christians galleyes, where very temperately, they eate bread, and drunke water, as a wholesome penance* (*enioyn'd them by their Confessors*) *for base pilferies.*

POL. Note but his bearing, and contempt of these.

VOLP. *These turdy-facy-nasty-paty-lousy-farticall rogues, with one poore groats-worth of vn-prepar'd* antimony, *finely wrapt vp in seuerall* 'scartoccios, *are able, very well, to kill their twentie a weeke, and play ; yet, these meagre staru'd spirits, who haue halfe stopt the organs of their mindes with earthy appilations, want not their fauourers among your shriuel'd, sallad-eating* artizans : *who are ouer-ioy'd, that they may haue their halfe-pe'rth of physick, though it purge 'hem into another world, 't makes no matter.*

II. ii. 36 procuratìa] Procuratia *Q* 38 piazza.] Piazza; *Q* 41 *feet ;*] *feete,* Q 42 *accustomed :*] accustomed ; *Q* 45 *a* 'Sforzato *Q* : *a'* Sforzato *Ff* 46 BEMBO's] Bemboo's *Q* 61 *seuerall* 'scartoccios] *seuerall'*Scartoccios *Q* : *seuerall'* Scartoccios *F1* : *severall* scartoccios *F2* 62 *staru'd*] *steru'd* Q 64 *fauourers*] *fauorers* Q 66 *halfe-pe'rth*] *halfeperth* Q 67 *'t makes*] *makes* Q

POL. Excellent! ha' you heard better language, sir?

VOLP. *Well, let 'hem goe. And gentlemen, honorable gentlemen, know, that for this time, our banke, being thus remou'd from the clamours of the* canaglia, *shall be the* scene *of pleasure, and delight: For, I haue nothing to sell, little, or nothing to sell.*

POL. I told you, sir, his end. PER. You did so, sir.

VOLP. *I protest, I, and my sixe seruants, are not able to make of this precious liquor, so fast, as it is fetch'd away from my lodging, by gentlemen of your city; strangers of the* terra-ferma; *worshipfull merchants; I, and senators too: who, euer since my arriuall, haue detayned me to their vses, by their splendidous liberalities. And worthily. For, what auailes your rich man to haue his* magazines *stuft with* moscadelli, *or of the purest grape, when his physitians prescribe him (on paine of death) to drinke nothing but water, cocted with* anise-seeds? *O, health! health! the blessing of the rich! the riches of the poore! who can buy thee at too deare a rate, since there is no enioying this world, without thee? Be not then so sparing of your purses, honorable gentlemen, as to abridge the naturall course of life——*

PER. You see his end? POL. I, is't not good?

VOLP. *For, when a humide fluxe, or catarrhe, by the mutability of aire, falls from your head, into an arme, or shoulder, or any other part; take you a duckat, or your* cecchine *of gold, and apply to the place affected: see, what good effect it can worke. No, no, 'tis this blessed* vnguento, *this rare extraction, that hath only power to disperse all malignant humours, that proceed, either of hot, cold, moist, or windy causes——*

PER. I would he had put in drie to. POL. 'Pray you, obserue.

VOLP. *To fortifie the most indigest, and crude stomack, I, were it of one, that (through extreme weakenesse) vomited bloud,*

II. ii. 69 *honorable*] *honourable* Q 70 *banke*] *Banque* Q 73 *sell.*] *sell:* Q 74 you, sir,] you, Sir ; *Q* 77 terra-] Tèrra- *Q* 80 *For,*] *For* Q 82 *of* not in Q 84 *rich !*] rich, *Q* 85 *too*] *to* Q 91 *arme,*] *arme* Q 95 *humours*] *humors* Q 97 'Pray *corr. Q, Ff*: 'pray *Q originally*

applying only a warme napkin to the place, after the vnction, and fricace ; for the vertigine, *in the head, putting but a drop into your nostrills, likewise, behind the eares ; a most soueraigne, and approued remedie : the* mal-caduco, *crampes, conuulsions, paralysies, epilepsies,* tremor-cordia, *retyred-nerues, ill vapours of the spleene, stoppings of the liuer, the stone, the strangury,* hernia ventosa, iliaca passio ; *stops a* disenteria, *immediately ; easeth the torsion of the small guts ; and cures* melancolia hypocondriaca, *being taken and applyed, according to my printed receipt. For, this is the physitian, this the medicine ; this counsells, this cures ; this giues the direction, this workes the effect : and* (*in summe*) *both together may bee term'd an abstract of the theorick, and practick in the* Æsculapian *arte. 'Twill cost you eight crownes. And,* ZAN FRITADA, *'pray thee sing a verse,* extempore, *in honour of it.* ***Pointing to his bill and his glasse.***

POL. How doe you like him, sir? PER. Most strangely, I!

POL. Is not his language rare? PER. But *Alchimy,*
I neuer heard the like : or BROVGHTONS bookes.

SONG.

H*Ad old* HIPPOCRATES, *or* GALEN,
(*That to their bookes put med'cines all in*)
But knowne this secret, they had neuer
(*Of which they will be guiltie euer*)
Beene murderers of so much paper,
Or wasted many a hurtlesse taper :
No Indian *drug had ere beene famed,*
Tabacco, sassafras *not named ;*
Ne yet, of guacum *one small stick, sir,*
Nor RAYMVND LVLLIES *great* elixir.
Ne, had been knowne the Danish GONSWART,
Or PARACELSVS, *with his long-sword.*

II. ii. 104 *remedie :* F1 : *remedy :* corr. Q, F2 : *remedy.* Q originally 106 *stoppings* corr. Q, Ff: *Stoppings* Q originally 110 *Stage direction not in Q* 115 *'pray thee*] *pr'y thee* F2 118 *Alchimy,* Q, F2: *Alchimy* F1 Before 121 SONG.] *Nano sings.* G 131 GONSWART,] GONSWART. *Q, Ff*

PER. All this, yet, will not doe, eight crownes is high.

VOLP. *No more. Gentlemen, if I had but time to discourse to you the miraculous effects of this my oile, surnamed* oglio del SCOTO; *with the count-lesse catalogue of those I haue cured of th'aforesaid, and many more diseases; the pattents and priuiledges of all the Princes, and common-wealths of Christendome; or but the depositions of those that appear'd on my part, before the* signiory *of the* Sanitâ, *and most learned colledge of physitians; where I was authorized, vpon notice taken of the admirable vertues of my medicaments, and mine owne excellency, in matter of rare, and vnknowne secrets, not onely to disperse them publiquely in this famous citie, but in all the territories, that happily ioy vnder the gouernement of the most pious and magnificent states of* Italy. *But may some other gallant fellow say, O, there be diuers, that make profession to haue as good, and as experimented receipts, as yours: Indeed, very many haue assay'd, like apes in imitation of that, which is really and essentially in mee, to make of this oyle; bestow'd great cost in furnaces, stilles, alembeks, continuall fires, and preparation of the ingredients, (as indeede there goes to it sixe hundred seuerall simples, besides some quantity of humane fat, for the conglutination, which we buy of the anatomistes) but, when these practitioners come to the last decoction, blow, blow, puff, puff, and all flies in* fumo: *ha, ha, ha. Poore wretches! I rather pittie their folly, and indiscretion, then their losse of time, and money; for those may be recouered by industrie: but to bee a foole borne, is a disease incurable. For my selfe, I alwaies from my youth haue indeuour'd to get the rarest secrets, and booke them; either in exchange, or for money: I spared nor cost, nor labour, where any thing was worthy to bee learned. And gentlemen, honourable gentlemen, I will vndertake (by vertue of chymicall art) out of the honour-*

II. ii. 133 doe,] doe; *F2* 134 *more.*] *more;* Q 136 SCOTO;] Scoto, *Q* 137 *diseases;*] *diseases,* Q 139 *Christendome;*] Christendome, *Q* *depositions*] *dispositions* F2 140 signiory] Signiry *Q* 149 *apes*] *Apes,* Q 150 *really*] *really,* Q 152 (*as*] *as* Q 153 *besides*] *besides,* Ff: *beside* Q 154 *anatomistes*)] Anatomistes; *Q* 158 *recouered*] *recouer'd* Q 159 *borne,*] *borne* Q 162 *money:*] *money;* Q

able hat, that couers your head, to extract the foure elements; that is to say, the fire, ayre, water, and earth, and returne you your felt without burne, or staine. For, whil'st others haue beene at the balloo, *I haue beene at my booke: and am now past the craggie pathes of studie, and come to the flowrie plaines of honour, and reputation.*

POL. I doe assure you, sir, that is his ayme.

VOLP. *But, to our price.* PER. And that withall, sir
POL.

VOLP. *You all know (honourable gentlemen) I neuer valu'd this* ampulla, *or viall, at lesse then eight crownes, but for this time, I am content, to be depriu'd of it for sixe; sixe crownes is the price; and lesse in courtesie, I know you cannot offer me: take it, or leaue it, howsoeuer, both it, and I, am at your seruice. I aske you not, as the value of the thing, for then I should demand of you a thousand crownes, so the Cardinals* MONTALTO, FERNESE, *the great duke of* Tuscany, *my gossip, with diuers other princes haue giuen me; but I despise money: onely to shew my affection to you, honourable gentlemen, and your illustrous state here, I haue neglected the messages of these princes, mine owne offices, fram'd my iourney hither, onely to present you with the fruits of my trauels. Tune your voices once more to the touch of your instruments, and giue the honourable assembly some delightfull recreation.*

PER. What monstrous, and most painefull circumstance
Is here, to get some three, or foure *gazets!*
Some three-pence, i'th' whole, for that 'twill come to.

SONG.

YOu that would last long, list to my song,
Make no more coyle, but buy of this oyle.
Would you be euer faire? and yong?
Stout of teeth? and strong of tongue?

II. ii. 174 *viall*] *violl* Q *crownes,*] *crownes;* F2 177 *me:*] *mee;* Q *I,*] *I* Q 181 *me;*] *me;* Q 182, 187 *honourable*] *honorable* Q 183 *illustrous*] *illustrious* F2 185 *fruits*] *fruicts* Q 186 *more*] *more,* Q 189 *gazets!*] *Gazets?* Q 190 i'th'] i'th *F1* Before 191 SONG.] *Nano sings.* G

Tart of palat? quick of eare?
Sharpe of sight? of nostrill cleare?
Moist of hand? and light of foot?
(Or I will come neerer to't)
Would you liue free from all diseases?
Doe the act, your mistris pleases;
Yet fright all aches from your bones?
Here's a med'cine, for the nones.

VOLP. *Well, I am in a humour (at this time) to make a present of the small quantitie my coffer containes: to the rich, in courtesie, and to the poore, for Gods sake. Wherefore, now marke; I ask'd you sixe crownes; and sixe crownes, at other times, you haue paid me; you shall not giue me sixe crownes, nor fiue, nor foure, nor three, nor two, nor one; nor halfe a duckat; no, nor a* muccinigo: *sixe—pence it will cost you, or sixe hundred pound—expect no lower price, for by the banner of my front, I will not bate a* bagatine, *that I will haue, only, a pledge of your loues, to carry something from amongst you, to shew, I am not contemn'd by you. Therefore, now, tosse your handkerchiefes, chearefully, chearefully; and be aduertised, that the first heroique spirit, that deignes to grace me, with a handkerchiefe, I will giue it a little remembrance of something, beside, shall please it better, then if I had presented it with a double pistolet.*

CELIA at the windo' throwes downe her handkerchiefe.

PER. Will you be that heroique sparke, sir POL? O, see! the windore has preuented you.

VOLP. *Lady, I kisse your bountie: and, for this timely grace, you haue done your poore* SCOTO *of* Mantua, *I will returne you, ouer and aboue my oile, a secret, of that high, and inestimable nature, shall make you for euer enamour'd on that minute, wherein your eye first descended on so meane, (yet not altogether to be despis'd) an obiect. Here is a poulder, conceal'd in this paper, of which, if I should speake to the worth,*

II. ii. 202 *Yet*] *Yea* F2, F3 204 *humour*] *humor* Q 207 *crownes; and*] Crownes, *and* Q 210 *sixe—pence*] *six pence* Q 220 *Stage direction not in Q* *windo'*] *window* F2 226 (*yet*] *yet* Q 227 *despis'd*)] *despis'd* Q

nine thousand volumes were but as one page, that page as a line, that line as a word : so short is this pilgrimage of man (which some call life) to the expressing of it. Would I reflect on the price ? why, the whole world were but as an empire, that empire as a prouince, that prouince as a banke, that banke as a priuate purse, to the purchase of it. I will, onely, tell you ; It is the poulder, that made VENVS *a goddesse (giuen her by* APOLLO) *that kept her perpetually yong, clear'd her wrincles, firm'd her gummes, fill'd her skin, colour'd her haire ; from her, deriu'd to* HELEN, *and at the sack of* Troy *(vnfortunately) lost : till now, in this our age, it was as happily recouer'd, by a studious Antiquarie, out of some ruines of* Asia, *who sent a moyetie of it, to the court of* France *(but much sophisticated) wherewith the ladies there, now, colour their haire. The rest (at this present) remaines with me ; extracted, to a quintessence : so that, where euer it but touches, in youth it perpetually preserues, in age restores the complexion ; seat's your teeth, did they dance like virginall iacks, firme as a wall ; makes them white, as iuory, that were black, as——*

Act II. *Scene* III.

CORVINO, POLITIQVE,
PEREGRINE.

SPight o' the deuill, and my shame ! come downe, here ; *He beates away the monte-banke, &c*
Come downe : no house but mine to make your *scene ?*
Signior FLAMINIO, will you downe, sir ? downe ?
What is my wife your FRANCISCINA ? sir ?
No windores on the whole *piazza*, here,
To make your properties, but mine ? but mine ?
Hart ! ere to morrow, I shall be new christen'd,

II. ii. 230 *word :*] *word ;* Q 231 *it. Would*] *it: would* Q 246 *seat's* corr. Q, Ff : *seats* Q originally II. iii. *Enter Corvino.* G, continuing the scene 1 *Stage direction a correction in F1 : not in Q or in F1 originally or in F2* Spight] Bloud *Q* 5 *piazza* corr. F1 : *Piazza* Q, F1 originally, F2 After 6 *Beats away Volpone, Nano, &c.* G

And cald the PANTALONE *di besogniosi*,
About the towne. PER. What should this meane, sir POL?
POL. Some trick of state, beleeue it. I will home.
PER. It may be some designe, on you. POL. I know not.
I'le stand vpon my guard. PER. It is your best, sir.
POL. This three weekes, all my aduises, all my letters,
They haue beene intercepted. PER. Indeed, sir?
Best haue a care. POL. Nay, so I will. PER. This knight,
I may not lose him, for my mirth, till night.

Act II. *Scene* IIII.

VOLPONE, MOSCA.

O, I am wounded. MOS. Where, sir? VOLP. Not without;
Those blowes were nothing: I could beare them euer.
But angry CVPID, bolting from her eyes,
Hath shot himselfe into me, like a flame;
Where, now, he flings about his burning heat,
As in a fornace, an ambitious fire,
Whose vent is stopt. The fight is all within me.
I cannot liue, except thou helpe me, MOSCA;
My liuer melts, and I, without the hope
Of some soft aire, from her refreshing breath,
Am but a heape of cinders. MOS. 'Lasse, good sir!
Would you had neuer seene her. VOLP. Nay, would thou
Had'st neuer told me of her. MOS. Sir, 'tis true;
I doe confesse, I was vnfortunate,
And you vnhappy: but I'am bound in conscience,
No lesse then duty, to effect my best
To your release of torment, and I will, sir.

II. iii. 8 *di besogniosi* corr. F1: DI BESOGNIOSI *F1 originally, F2*: *di Besogniosi* Q 11 designe,] designe *Q* you.] you: *Q* 12 It is *corr. F1*: 'Tis *Q, F1 originally, F2* 13 letters,] letters *Q* 16 lose] loose *Q* *Exeunt.* add G II. iv. SCENE II. | *A Room in Volpone's House.* | *Enter Volpone and Mosca.* G 3 bolting] boulting *Q* 6 fornace] furnace *Q* an *corr. F1*: some *Q, F1 originally, F2* 11 sir! *corr. F1*: sir, *F1 originally, F2*: Sir, *Q*

VOLP. Deare MOSCA, shall I hope? MOS. Sir, more then deare,
I will not bid you to despaire of ought,
Within a humane compasse. VOLP. O, there spoke
My better Angell. MOSCA, take my keyes,
Gold, plate, and iewells, all's at thy deuotion;
Employ them, how thou wilt; nay, coyne me, too:
So thou, in this, but crowne my longings. MOSCA?
MOS. Vse but your patience. VOLP. So I haue. MOS. I doubt not
To bring successe to your desires. VOLP. Nay, then,
I not repent me of my late disguise.
MOS. If you can horne him, sir, you need not. VOLP. True:
Besides, I neuer meant him for my heire.
Is not the colour o' my beard, and eye-browes,
To make me knowne? MOS. No iot. VOLP. I did it well.
MOS. So well, would I could follow you in mine,
With halfe the happinesse; and, yet, I would
Escape your *epilogue*. VOLP. But, were they gull'd
With a beliefe, that I was SCOTO? MOS. Sir,
SCOTO himselfe could hardly haue distinguish'd!
I haue not time to flatter you, now, wee'll part:
And, as I prosper, so applaud my art.

Act II. *Scene* V.

CORVINO, CELIA, SERVITORE.

DEath of mine honour, with the cities foole?
A iuggling, tooth-drawing, prating mountebanke?
And, at a publike windore? where whil'st he,
With his strain'd action, and his dole of faces,

II. iv. 26 To] But *Q* 30 o' *corr. F1*: of *Q*: of o' *F1 originally, preserved in the Yale copy*: *other copies have a white space before and after the* of, *which was picked out without adjusting the spacing.* 32, 33 and, . . . *epilogue.*] —and . . . epilogue. [*Aside.* G 36 distinguish'd !] distinguish'd; *Q* 37 now, *not in Q* II. v. SCENE III. | *A Room in Corvino's House.* | *Enter Corvino, with his sword in his hand, dragging in Celia.* G

To his drug-lecture drawes your itching eares,
A crue of old, vn-marri'd, noted lechers,
Stood leering vp, like *Satyres:* and you smile,
Most graciously! and fan your fauours forth,
To giue your hot spectators satisfaction!
What, was your mountebanke their call? their whistle?
Or were you'enamour'd on his copper rings?
His saffron iewell, with the toade-stone in't?
Or his imbroidred sute, with the cope-stitch,
Made of a herse-cloth? or his old tilt-feather?
Or his starch'd beard? well! you shall haue him, yes.
He shall come home, and minister vnto you
The fricace, for the moother. Or, let me see,
I thinke, you'had rather mount? would you not mount?
Why, if you'll mount, you may; yes truely, you may:
And so, you may be seene, downe to th' foot.
Get you a citterne, lady *vanitie*,
And be a dealer, with the vertuous man;
Make one: I'le but protest my selfe a cuckold,
And saue your dowrie. I am a *Dutchman*, I!
For, if you thought me an *Italian*,
You would be damn'd, ere you did this, you whore:
Thou'ldst tremble, to imagine, that the murder
Of father, mother, brother, all thy race,
Should follow, as the subiect of my iustice!
CEL. Good sir, haue patience! CORV. What could'st thou propose
Lesse to thy selfe, then, in this heat of wrath,
And stung with my dishonour, I should strike
This steele into thee, with as many stabs,
As thou wert gaz'd vpon with goatish eyes?
CEL. Alasse sir, be appeas'd! I could not thinke
My being at the windore should more, now,

II. v. 7 *Satyres:*] *Satyres;* *Q* 8 graciously!] graciously? *Q* 9 satisfaction!] satisfaction? *Q* 10 What,] What; *Q* 15 well!] well, *Q* 17 moother] *Mother* *Q* 20 to th'] to' th' *F1* 24 I!] I; *Q* 29 iustice!] iustice. *Q* 30 patience!] pacience. *Q* could'st] coul'dst *F1* 33 into *F2*, *F3*: vnto *Q*, *F1* 35 appeas'd!] appeas'd; *Q* I could] Icould *F1*

Moue your impatience, then at other times.
CORV. No? not to seeke, and entertaine a parlee,
With a knowne knaue? before a multitude?
You were an actor, with your handkerchiefe!
Which he, most sweetly, kist in the receipt,
And might (no doubt) returne it, with a letter,
And point the place, where you might meet: your sisters,
Your mothers, or your aunts might serue the turne.
CEL. Why, deare sir, when doe I make these excuses?
Or euer stirre, abroad, but to the church?
And that, so seldome—— CORV. Well, it shall be lesse;
And thy restraint, before, was libertie,
To what I now decree: and therefore, marke me.
First, I will haue this bawdy light dam'd vp;
And, til 't be done, some two, or three yards off,
I'le chalke a line: o're which, if thou but chance
To set thy desp'rate foot; more hell, more horror,
More wilde, remorcelesse rage shall seize on thee,
Then on a coniurer, that, had heedlesse left
His circles safetie, ere his deuill was laid.
Then, here's a locke, which I will hang vpon thee;
And, now I thinke on't, I will keepe thee backe-wards;
Thy lodging shall be backe-wards; thy walkes back-wards;
Thy prospect—all be backe-wards; and no pleasure,
That thou shalt know, but backe-wards: Nay, since you force
My honest nature, know, it is your owne
Being too open, makes me vse you thus.
Since you will not containe your subtle nostrils
In a sweet roome, but, they must snuffe the ayre
Of ranke, and sweatie passengers—— One knockes. *Knocke within.*
Away, and be not seene, paine of thy life;
Not looke toward the windore: if thou dost——
(Nay stay, heare this) let me not prosper, whore,

II. v. 37 times.] times: *Q* 38 parlee,] *parlee;* Q 40 handkerchiefe!] handkercheife; *Q* 51 off] of *Q* 52–3 chance To] (chance To) *Q* 60 prospect—all] prospect-all *Q, Ff* 61 know, *Q*: know *Ff* 63 too] to *Q* 65 but, *Q*: but *Ff* 66 *Stage direction not in Q*

But I will make thee an anatomie,
Dissect thee mine owne selfe, and read a lecture
Vpon thee, to the citie, and in publique.
Away. Who's there? SER. 'Tis signior MOSCA, sir.

Act II. *Scene* VI.

CORVINO, MOSCA.

LEt him come in, his master's dead: There's yet
Some good, to helpe the bad. My MOSCA, welcome,
I ghesse your newes. MOS. I feare you cannot, sir.
CORV. Is't not his death? MOS. Rather the contrarie.
CORV. Not his recouerie? MOS. Yes, sir. CORV. I am curst,
I am bewitch'd, my crosses meet to vex me.
How? how? how? how? MOS. Why, sir, with SCOTO's oyle!
CORBACCIO, and VOLTORE brought of it,
Whil'st I was busie in an inner roome——
CORV. Death! that damn'd mountebanke! but, for the law,
Now, I could kill the raskall: 't cannot be,
His oyle should haue that vertue. Ha' not I
Knowne him a common rogue, come fidling in
To th'*osteria*, with a tumbling whore,
And, when he ha's done all his forc'd trickes, beene glad
Of a poore spoonefull of dead wine, with flyes in't?
It cannot be. All his ingredients
Are a sheepes gall, a rosted bitches marrow,
Some few sod earewigs, pounded caterpillers,
A little capons grease, and fasting spittle:

II. v. 73 After 'Away' *Exit Celia.* | *Enter Servant.* G II. vi. *G continues the scene, marking the Servant's exit at l.* 2 ('Let him come in') *and Mosca's entry at l.* 3 *after* ' help the bad'. 3 ghesse] gesse *Q* 5 sir. *F2*: sir, *F1*: Sir, *Q* 7 oyle!] oyle; *Q* 10 mountebanke!] *Mountebanke*; Q 14 *osteria*] *Osteria* Q: *osteria* F1: *Osteria* F2 16 Of a] Ofa *F1*

I know 'hem, to a dram. Mos. I know not, sir,
But some on't, there, they powr'd into his eares,
Some in his nostrils, and recouer'd him ;
Applying but the fricace. Corv. Pox o' that fricace.
Mos. And since, to seeme the more officious,
And flatt'ring of his health, there, they haue had
(At extreme fees) the colledge of physicians
Consulting on him, how they might restore him ;
Where, one would haue a cataplasme of spices,
Another, a flayd ape clapt to his brest,
A third would ha' it a dogge, a fourth an oyle
With wild cats skinnes : at last, they all resolu'd
That, to preserue him, was no other meanes,
But some yong woman must be streight sought out,
Lustie, and full of iuice, to sleepe by him ;
And, to this seruice (most vnhappily,
And most vnwillingly) am I now imploy'd,
Which, here, I thought to pre-acquaint you with,
For your aduice, since it concernes you most,
Because, I would not doe that thing might crosse
Your ends, on whom I haue my whole dependance, sir :
Yet, if I doe it not, they may delate
My slacknesse to my patron, worke me out
Of his opinion ; and there, all your hopes,
Venters, or whatsoeuer, are all frustrate.
I doe but tell you, sir. Besides, they are all
Now striuing, who shall first present him. Therefore——
I could intreat you, briefly, conclude some-what :
Preuent 'hem if you can. Corv. Death to my hopes !
This is my villanous fortune ! Best to hire
Some common curtezan ? Mos. I, I thought on that, sir.
But they are all so subtle, full of art,
And age againe doting, and flexible,
So as——I cannot tell——we may perchance
Light on a queane, may cheat vs all. Corv. 'Tis true.
Mos. No, no : it must be one, that ha's no trickes, sir,

II. vi. 22 there, *Q* (*comma faint*) : there *Ff* 30 flayd] flead *Q*
53 againe] againe, *Q*

Some simple thing, a creature, made vnto it;
Some wench you may command. Ha' you no kinswoman?
Gods so—— Thinke, thinke, thinke, thinke, thinke, thinke, thinke, sir.
One o' the Doctors offer'd, there, his daughter.
CORV. How! MOS. Yes, signior LVPO, the physician,
CORV. His daughter? MOS. And a virgin, sir. Why? Alasse
He knowes the state of 's bodie, what it is;
That nought can warme his bloud, sir, but a feuer;
Nor any incantation rayse his spirit:
A long forgetfulnesse hath seiz'd that part.
Besides, sir, who shall know it? some one, or two——
CORV. I pray thee giue me leaue. If any man
But I had had this lucke—— The thing, in't selfe,
I know, is nothing—— Wherefore should not I
As well command my bloud, and my affections,
As this dull Doctor? In the point of honour,
The cases are all one, of wife, and daughter.
MOS. I heare him comming. CORV. Shee shall doo't: 'Tis done.
Slight, if this Doctor, who is not engag'd,
Vnlesse 't be for his counsell (which is nothing)
Offer his daughter, what should I, that am
So deeply in? I will preuent him: wretch!
Couetous wretch! MOSCA, I haue determin'd.
MOS. How, sir? CORV. We'll make all sure. The party, you wot of,
Shall be mine owne wife, MOSCA. MOS. Sir. The thing,
(But that I would not seeme to counsell you)
I should haue motion'd to you, at the first:
And, make your count, you haue cut all their throtes.
Why! 'tis directly taking a possession!

II. vi. 67 two—] two. *Q*   68 pray thee] pr'y thee *F2*   leaue.] leaue : *Q* : leave. [*walks aside.*] G   69 thing, *Q* (*comma faint*) : thing *Ff*   74 After 'comming'] *Aside.* G   75 who] that *Q*   78 him: *corr. F1* : him, *Q*, *F1 originally*

And, in his next fit, we may let him goe.
'Tis but to pull the pillow, from his head,
And he is thratled: 't had beene done, before,
But for your scrupulous doubts. CORV. I, a plague on't,
My conscience fooles my wit. Well, I'le be briefe,
And so be thou, lest they should be before vs;
Goe home, prepare him, tell him, with what zeale,
And willingnesse, I doe it: sweare it was,
On the first hearing (as thou maist doe, truely)
Mine owne free motion. MOS. Sir, I warrant you,
I'le so possesse him with it, that the rest
Of his staru'd clients shall be banisht, all;
And onely you receiu'd. But come not, sir,
Vntill I send, for I haue some-thing else
To ripen, for your good (you must not know't)
CORV. But doe not you forget to send, now. MOS. Feare not.

Act II. *Scene* VII.

CORVINO, CELIA.

WHere are you, wife? my CELIA? wife? what, blubbering?
Come, drie those teares. I thinke, thou thought'st me in earnest?
Ha? by this light, I talk'd so but to trie thee.
Me thinkes, the lightnesse of the occasion
Should ha' confirm'd thee. Come, I am not iealous.
CEL. No? CORV. Faith, I am not, I, nor neuer was:
It is a poore, vnprofitable humour.
Doe not I know, if women haue a will,
They'll doe 'gainst all the watches, o' the world?
And that the fiercest spies, are tam'd with gold?

II. vi. 91 And] And, *Q* vs; *corr. F1*: vs: *Q, F1 originally* 93 it': *corr. F1*: it; *Q, F1 originally, F2* 97 staru'd] steru'd *Q* 99 some-thing] something, *Q* 101 *Exit.* add G II. vii. After 'wife?' *Re-enter Celia.* G, continuing the scene 5 iealous.] iealous: *Q* 6 not, I *corr. F1, F2*: not I *Q, F1 originally* 7 humour] humor *Q*

Tut, I am confident in thee, thou shalt see't :
And see, I'le giue thee cause too, to beleeue it.
Come, kisse me. Goe, and make thee ready straight,
In all thy best attire, thy choicest iewells,
Put 'hem all on, and, with 'hem, thy best lookes :
We are inuited to a solemne feast,
At old VOLPONE'S, where it shall appeare
How far I am free, from iealousie, or feare.

Act III. *Scene* I.

MOSCA.

I Feare, I shall begin to grow in loue
With my deare selfe, and my most prosp'rous parts,
They doe so spring, and burgeon ; I can feele
A whimsey i' my bloud : (I know not how)
Successe hath made me wanton. I could skip
Out of my skin, now, like a subtill snake,
I am so limber. O ! Your Parasite
Is a most precious thing, dropt from aboue,
Not bred 'mong'st clods, and clot-poules, here on earth.
I muse, the mysterie was not made a science,
It is so liberally profest ! almost
All the wise world is little else, in nature,
But Parasites, or Sub-parasites. And, yet,
I meane not those, that haue your bare towne-arte,
To know, who's fit to feede 'hem ; haue no house,
No family, no care, and therefore mould
Tales for mens eares, to bait that sense ; or get
Kitchin-inuention, and some stale receipts
To please the belly, and the groine ; nor those,
With their court-dog-tricks, that can fawne, and fleere,
Make their reuennue out of legs, and faces,
Eccho my-Lord, and lick away a moath :
But your fine, elegant rascall, that can rise,

II. vii. 18 I am] I'am *F2* 18 *Exeunt.* add G III. i. ACT III. SCENE I. | *A Street.* | *Enter Mosca.* G 11 almost] Almost, *Q* 21 reuennue] reuenue *Q* : revenue *F2*

And stoope (almost together) like an arrow;
Shoot through the aire, as nimbly as a starre;
Turne short, as doth a swallow; and be here,
And there, and here, and yonder, all at once;
Present to any humour, all occasion;
And change a visor, swifter, then a thought!
This is the creature, had the art borne with him;
Toiles not to learne it, but doth practise it
Out of most excellent nature: and such sparkes,
Are the true Parasites, others but their *Zani's*.

Act III. *Scene* II.

MOSCA, BONARIO.

WHo's this? BONARIO? old CORBACCIO's sonne?
The person I was bound to seeke. Faire sir,
You are happ'ly met. BON. That cannot be, by thee.
MOS. Why, sir? BON. Nay, 'pray thee know thy way, & leaue me:
I would be loth to inter-change discourse,
With such a mate, as thou art. MOS. Courteous sir,
Scorne not my pouertie. BON. Not I, by heauen:
But thou shalt giue me leaue to hate thy basenesse.
MOS. Basenesse? BON. I, answere me, is not thy sloth
Sufficient argument? thy flatterie?
Thy meanes of feeding? MOS. Heauen, be good to me.
These imputations are too common, sir,
And eas'ly stuck on vertue, when shee's poore;
You are vnequall to me, and how ere
Your sentence may be righteous, yet you are not,
That ere you know me, thus, proceed in censure:

III. i. 29 thought!] thought. *Q* III. ii. *Enter Bonario.* G, continuing the scene 4 Nay, *F2*: Nay *Q*, *F1* 'pray thee] pr'y thee *F2* 7 heauen :] heauen, *Q*

S^t^. MARKE beare witnesse 'gainst you, 'tis inhumane.
BON. What? do's he weepe? the signe is soft, and good!
I doe repent me, that I was so harsh.
MOS. 'Tis true, that, sway'd by strong necessitie,
I am enforc'd to eate my carefull bread
With too much obsequie; 'tis true, beside,
That I am faine to spin mine owne poore rayment,
Out of my mere obseruance, being not borne
To a free fortune: but that I haue done
Base offices, in rending friends asunder,
Diuiding families, betraying counsells,
Whispering false lyes, or mining men with praises,
Train'd their credulitie with periuries,
Corrupted chastitie, or am in loue
With mine owne tender ease, but would not rather
Proue the most rugged, and laborious course,
That might redeeme my present estimation;
Let me here perish, in all hope of goodnesse.
BON. This cannot be a personated passion!
I was to blame, so to mistake thy nature;
'Pray thee forgiue me: and speake out thy bus'nesse.
MOS. Sir, it concernes you; and though I may seeme,
At first, to make a maine offence, in manners,
And in my gratitude, vnto my master,
Yet, for the pure loue, which I beare all right,
And hatred of the wrong, I must reueale it.
This verie houre, your father is in purpose
To disinherit you—— BON. How! MOS. And thrust you forth,
As a mere stranger to his bloud; 'tis true, sir:
The worke no way ingageth me, but, as
I claime an interest in the generall state
Of goodnesse, and true vertue, which I heare

III. ii. 17 *Weeps.* add G 18 good !] good; *Q* 19 *Aside.* add G 20 that, sway'd] that sway'd, *Q* 22 too] to *Q* 24 borne] borne, *Q* 26 rending] rendring *F3* 33 redeeme] redeeme, *Q* 35 passion !] passion. *Q* *Aside.* add G 36 to] too *Q, F2*

T'abound in you : and, for which mere respect,
Without a second ayme, sir, I haue done it.
  BON. This tale hath lost thee much of the late trust,
Thou hadst with me ; it is impossible :
I know not how to lend it any thought,
My father should be so vnnaturall.
  MOS. It is a confidence, that well becomes
Your pietie ; and form'd (no doubt) it is,
From your owne simple innocence : which makes
Your wrong more monstrous, and abhor'd. But, sir,
I now, will tell you more. This verie minute,
It is, or will be doing : And, if you
Shall be but pleas'd to goe with me, I'le bring you,
(I dare not say where you shall see, but) where
Your eare shall be a witnesse of the deed ;
Heare your selfe written bastard : and profest
The common issue of the earth. BON. I'm maz'd !
  MOS. Sir, if I doe it not, draw your iust sword,
And score your vengeance, on my front, and face ;
Marke me your villaine : You haue too much wrong,
And I doe suffer for you, sir. My heart
Weepes bloud, in anguish—— BON. Lead. I follow thee.

Act III. *Scene* III.

VOLPONE, NANO, ANDROGYNO, CASTRONE.

MOSCA stayes long, me thinkes. Bring forth your sports
And helpe, to make the wretched time more sweet.
  NAN. *Dwarfe, Foole, and Eunuch, well met here we be.*
  A question it were now, whether of vs three,

III. ii. 65 maz'd !] maz'd. *Q* 70 *Exeunt.* add G III. iii. SCENE II. | *A Room in Volpone's House.* | *Enter Volpone.* G After 2 *Enter Nano, Androgyno, and Castrone.* G

Being, all, the knowne delicates of a rich man,
In pleasing him, claime the precedencie can?
CAS. *I claime for my selfe.* AND. *And, so doth the foole.*
NAN. *'Tis foolish indeed: let me set you both to schoole.*
First, for your dwarfe, hee's little, and wittie,
And euery thing, as it is little, is prittie;
Else, why doe men say to a creature of my shape,
So soone as they see him, it's a pritty little ape?
And, why a pritty ape? but for pleasing imitation
Of greater mens action, in a ridiculous fashion.
Beside, this feat body of mine doth not craue
Halfe the meat, drinke, and cloth, one of your bulkes will haue.
Admit, your fooles face be the mother of laughter,
Yet, for his braine, it must alwaies come after:
And, though that doe feed him, it's a pittifull case,
His body is beholding to such a bad face.
One knocks.
VOLP. Who's there? my couch, away, looke, NANO, see:
Giue me my cappes, first—— go, enquire. Now, CVPID
Send it be MOSCA, and with faire returne.
NAN. It is the beauteous madam—— VOLP. WOVLD-BE—is it?
NAN. The same. VOLP. Now, torment on me; squire her in:
For she will enter, or dwell here for euer.
Nay, quickely, that my fit were past. I feare
A second hell too, that my loathing this
Will quite expell my appetite to the other:
Would shee were taking, now, her tedious leaue.
Lord, how it threates me, what I am to suffer!

III. iii. 5 *Being, all,* Q: *Being all* Ff *delicates*] *delicates,* Q 11 *of . . . shape,*] (*of . . . shape*) Q 14 *action*] *actions* F2: *Actions* F3 21 *Exe. And. and Cas.* add G 22 After 'enquire' [*Exit Nano.*] G 23 be] by *F2, F3* 24, 25 NAN.] *Nan.* [*within.*] G WOVLD-BE—] *Would-bee?* Q 27 After 'quickely' [*Retires to his couch.*] G

Act III. *Scene* IIII.

LADY, VOLPONE, NANO,
WOMEN. 2.

I Thanke you, good sir. 'Pray you signifie
Vnto your patron, I am here. This band
Shewes not my neck inough (I trouble you, sir,
Let me request you, bid one of my women
Come hither to me) in good faith, I, am drest
Most fauourably, to day, it is no matter,
'Tis well inough. Looke, see, these petulant things!
How they haue done this! VOLP. I do feele the feuer
Entring, in at mine eares; ô, for a charme,
To fright it hence. LAD. Come neerer: is this curle
In his right place? or this? why is this higher
Then all the rest? you ha' not wash'd your eies, yet?
Or do they not stand euen i' your head?
Where's your fellow? call her. NAN. Now, St. MARKE
Deliuer vs: anon, shee'll beate her women,
Because her nose is red. LAD. I pray you, view
This tire, forsooth: are all things apt, or no?
WOM. One haire a little, here, sticks out, forsooth.
LAD. Do's 't so forsooth? and where was your deare sight
When it did so, forsooth? what now? bird-ey'd?
And you, too? 'pray you both approch, and mend it.
Now (by that light) I muse, yo' are not asham'd!
I, that haue preach'd these things, so oft, vnto you,
Read you the principles, argu'd all the grounds,
Disputed euery fitnesse, euery grace,
Call'd you to counsell of so frequent dressings——
(NAN. More carefully, then of your fame, or honour)

III. iv. *Re-enter Nano with Lady Politick Would-be.* G, continuing the scene 5 hither] hether *Q* 6 fauourably] fauorably *Q, F2* to day,] to day; *F2* 7 After 'inough.' *Enter 1. Waiting-woman.* G things!] things, *Q* 10 After 'hence.' [*Aside.*] G 14 After 'her.' *Exit 1. Woman.* G 16 After 'red.' *Re-enter 1. and 2. Woman.* G 17 forsooth:] forsooth; *Q* 22 asham'd!] asham'd, *Q* 27 honour] honor *Q* *Aside.* add G

LAD. Made you acquainted, what an ample dowrie
The knowledge of these things would be vnto you,
Able, alone, to get you noble husbands
At your returne: and you, thus, to neglect it?
Besides, you seeing what a curious nation
Th'*Italians* are, what will they say of me?
The *English* lady cannot dresse her selfe;
Here's a fine imputation, to our countrie!
Well, goe your wayes, and stay, i' the next roome.
This *fucus* was too course too, it's no matter.
Good-sir, you'll giue 'hem entertaynement?
VOLP. The storme comes toward me. LAD. How do's my VOLP?
VOLP. Troubled with noise, I cannot sleepe; I dreamt
That a strange *furie* entred, now, my house,
And, with the dreadfull tempest of her breath,
Did cleaue my roofe asunder. LAD. Beleeue me, and I
Had the most fearefull dreame, could I remember 't——
VOLP. Out on my fate; I ha' giu'n her the occasion
How to torment me: shee will tell me hers.
LAD. Me thought, the golden mediocritie
Polite, and delicate—— VOLP. O, if you doe loue me,
No more; I sweat, and suffer, at the mention
Of any dreame: feele, how I tremble yet.
LAD. Alas, good soule! the passion of the heart.
Seed-pearle were good now, boild with syrrope of apples,
Tincture of gold, and corrall, citron-pills,
Your elicampane roote, mirobalanes——
VOLP. Ay me, I haue tane a grasse-hopper by the wing.
LAD. Burnt silke, and amber, you haue muscadell
Good i' the house—— VOLP. You will not drinke, and part?
LAD. No, feare not that. I doubt, we shall not get
Some *english* saffron (halfe a dram would serue)
Your sixteene cloues, a little muske, dri'd mints,

III. iv. 35 countrie!] Country: *Q* After 38 *Exeunt Nano and Waiting-women.* G 46 *Aside.* add G So 55, 62, 64, 82, 85, 87, 113, 115 55 tane] tâne *Q*

Buglosse, and barley-meale—— VOLP. Shee's in againe,
Before I fayn'd diseases, now I haue one.
LAD. And these appli'd, with a right scarlet-cloth——
VOLP. Another floud of wordes! a very torrent!
LAD. Shall I, sir, make you a poultise? VOLP. No, no, no;
I' am very well: you need prescribe no more.
LAD. I haue, a little, studied physick; but, now,
I'am all for musique: saue, i' the fore-noones,
An houre, or two, for painting. I would haue
A lady, indeed, t'haue all, letters, and artes,
Be able to discourse, to write, to paint,
But principall (as PLATO holds) your musique
(And, so do's wise PYTHAGORAS, I take it)
Is your true rapture; when there is concent
In face, in voyce, and clothes: and is, indeed,
Our sexes chiefest ornament. VOLP. The Poet,
As old in time, as PLATO, and as knowing,
Say's that your highest female grace is silence.
LAD. Which o' your Poets? PETRARCH? or TASSO?' or DANTE?
GVERRINI? ARIOSTO? ARETINE?
CIECO *di Hadria?* I haue read them all.
VOLP. Is euerything a cause, to my destruction?
LAD. I thinke, I ha' two or three of 'hem, about me.
VOLP. The sunne, the sea will sooner, both, stand still,
Then her eternall tongue! nothing can scape it.
LAD. Here's PASTOR FIDO—— VOLP. Professe obstinate silence,
That's, now, my safest. LAD. All our *English* writers,
I meane such, as are happy in th'*Italian*,
Will deigne to steale out of this author, mainely;
Almost as much, as from MONTAGNIE:
He has so moderne, and facile a veine,

III. iv. 61 againe,] againe; *F2* 73 PYTHAGORAS] *Pithagoras* Q 78 your] our *F2, F3* 79 TASSO?' or] *Tasso?'* or *Q*: TASSO? or *Ff* 85 eternall tongue!] æternall tongue; *Q* 90 MONTAGNIE:] *Montagnié;* Q

Fitting the time, and catching the court-eare.
Your PETRARCH is more passionate, yet he,
In dayes of sonetting, trusted 'hem, with much:
DANTE is hard, and few can vnderstand him.
But, for a desperate wit, there's ARETINE!
Onely, his pictures are a little obscene——
You marke me not? VOLP. Alas, my mind's perturb'd.
LAD. Why, in such cases, we must cure our selues,
Make vse of our philosophie—— VOLP. O'y me.
LAD. And, as we find our passions doe rebell,
Encounter 'hem with reason; or diuert 'hem,
By giuing scope vnto some other humour
Of lesser danger: as, in politique bodies,
There's nothing, more, doth ouer-whelme the iudgement,
And clouds the vnderstanding, then too much
Settling, and fixing, and (as't were) subsiding
Vpon one obiect. For the incorporating
Of these same outward things, into that part,
Which we call mentall, leaues some certaine *fæces*,
That stop the organs, and, as PLATO sayes,
Assassinates our knowledge. VOLP. Now, the spirit
Of patience helpe me. LAD. Come, in faith, I must
Visit you more, a dayes; and make you well:
Laugh, and be lusty. VOLP. My good angell saue me.
LAD. There was but one sole man, in all the world,
With whom I ere could sympathize; and he
Would lie you often, three, foure houres together,
To heare me speake: and be (sometime) so rap't,
As he would answere me, quite from the purpose,
Like you, and you are like him, iust. I'le discourse
(And't be but only, sir, to bring you a-sleepe)
How we did spend our time, and loues, together,
For some sixe yeeres. VOLP. Oh, oh, oh, oh, oh, oh.
LAD. For we were *coætanei*, and brought vp——
VOLP. Some power, some fate, some fortune rescue me.

III. iv. 94 trusted] trusting *F2* 96 ARETINE!] *Aretine;* Q 100 O'y] O'ay *Q* 105 more,] more. *Q* 115 angell] angels *F2*: Angels *F3*

Act III. *Scene* V.

MOSCA, LADY, VOLPONE.

GOd saue you, Madam. LAD. Good sir. VOLP. MOSCA? welcom,
Welcome to my redemption. MOS. Why, sir? VOLP. Oh,
Rid me of this my torture, quickly, there;
My Madam, with the euerlasting voyce:
The bells, in time of pestilence, ne're made
Like noise, or were in that perpetuall motion;
The cock-pit comes not neere it. All my house,
But now, steam'd like a bath, with her thicke breath.
A lawyer could not haue beene heard; nor scarse
Another woman, such a hayle of wordes
Shee has let fall. For hells sake, rid her hence.
MOS. Has shee presented? VOLP. O, I doe not care,
I'le take her absence, vpon any price,
With any losse. MOS. Madam—— LAD. I ha' brought your patron
A toy, a cap here, of mine owne worke—— MOS. 'Tis well,
I had forgot to tell you, I saw your Knight,
Where you'ld little thinke it—— LAD. Where? MOS. Mary,
Where yet, if you make haste, you may apprehend him,
Rowing vpon the water in a *gondole*,
With the most cunning curtizan, of *Venice*.
LAD. Is't true? MOS. Pursue 'hem, and beleeue your eyes:
Leaue me, to make your gift. I knew, 't would take.
For lightly, they that vse themselues most licence,
Are still most iealous. VOLP. MOSCA, hearty thankes,
For thy quicke fiction, and deliuery of mee.
Now, to my hopes, what saist thou? LAD. But, doe you heare, sir?——

III. v. *Enter Mosca.* G, continuing the scene 5 ne're] nêre *Q* 18 you may] youmay *F1* 22 After 'gift.' [*Exit Lady P. hastily.*] G 26 After 'thou?' *Re-enter Lady P. Would-be.* G 26 But, *Q*: But *Ff*

VOLP. Againe; I feare a *paroxisme*. LAD. Which way
Row'd they together? MOS. Toward the *rialto*.
LAD. I pray you lend me your dwarfe. MOS. I pray you, take him.
Your hopes, sir, are like happie blossomes, faire,
And promise timely fruit, if you will stay
But the maturing; keepe you, at your couch,
CORBACCIO will arriue straight, with the will:
When he is gone, ile tell you more. VOLP. My blood,
My spirits are return'd; I am aliue:
And like your wanton gam'ster, at *primero*,
Whose thought had whisper'd to him, not goe lesse,
Methinkes I lie, and draw—for an encounter.

Act III. *Scene* VI.

MOSCA, BONARIO.

SIr, here conceald, you may heare all. But 'pray you
Haue patience, sir; the same's your father, knocks: *One knockes.*
I am compeld, to leaue you. BON. Do so. Yet,
Cannot my thought imagine this a truth.

Act III. *Scene* VII.

MOSCA, CORVINO, CELIA, BONARIO, VOLPONE.

DEath on me! you are come too soone, what meant you?
Did not I say, I would send? CORV. Yes, but I feard
You might forget it, and then they preuent vs.

III. v. After 29 *Exit Lady P.* G 31 fruit] fruict *Q* 34 After 'more.' [*Exit.*] G After 38 *The scene closes upon Volpone.* G III. vi.] SCENE II. | *The Passage leading to Volpone's Chamber.* | *Enter Mosca and Bonario.* G 1 After 'conceald,' [*shews him a closet.*] G 2 *Stage direction not in Q* 3 After 'you.' [*Exit.*] G After 4 *Goes into the closet.* G III. vii.] SCENE III. | *Another Part of the Same.* | *Enter Mosca and Corvino, Celia following.* G MOSCA] Mosco *Q* 1 too] to *Q*

MOS. Preuent? did ere man haste so, for his hornes?
A courtier would not ply it so, for a place.
Well, now there's no helping it, stay here;
Ile presently returne. CORV. Where are you, CELIA?
You know not wherefore I haue brought you hither?
CEL. Not well, except you told me. CORV. Now, I will:
Harke hither. MOS. Sir, your father hath sent word, *To Bonario.*
It will be halfe an houre, ere he come;
And therefore, if you please to walke, the while,
Into that gallery——at the vpper end,
There are some bookes, to entertaine the time:
And ile take care, no man shall come vnto you, sir.
BON. Yes, I will stay there, I doe doubt this fellow.
MOS. There, he is farre enough; he can heare nothing:
And, for his father, I can keepe him off.
CORV. Nay, now, there is no starting backe; and therefore,
Resolue vpon it: I haue so decree'd.
It must be done. Nor, would I moue 't afore,
Because I would auoide all shifts and tricks,
That might denie me. CEL. Sir, let me beseech you,
Affect not these strange trials; if you doubt
My chastitie, why locke me vp, for euer:
Make me the heyre of darkenesse. Let me liue,
Where I may please your feares, if not your trust.
CORV. Beleeue it, I haue no such humor, I.
All that I speake, I meane; yet I am not mad:
Not horne-mad, see you? Go too, shew your selfe
Obedient, and a wife. CEL. O heauen! CORV. I say it,
Do so. CEL. Was this the traine? CORV. I' haue told you reasons;

III. vii. After 5 *Aside.* G 7 After 'returne.' [*Exit.*] G 10 hither] hether *Q*: hither. [*Exeunt.* G Mos. Sir,] SCENE IV. | *A Closet opening into a Gallery. Enter Mosca and Bonario.* G *To Bonario* not in Q After 16 *Aside, and Exit.* G 17 Mos.] *Mos.* [*Looking after him.*] G After 18 *Exit.* G 19 CORV.] SCENE V. | *Volpone's Chamber.—Volpone on his couch. Mosca sitting by him.* | *Enter Corvino forcing in Celia.* G 21 moue 't] moue 't, *Q* 22 shifts] shifts, *Q*

What the physitians haue set downe ; how much,
It may concerne me ; what my engagements are ;
My meanes ; and the necessitie of those meanes,
For my recouery : wherefore, if you bee
Loyall, and mine, be wonne, respect my venture.
CEL. Before your honour ? CORV. Honour ? tut, a breath ;
There's no such thing, in nature : a meere terme
Inuented to awe fooles. What is my gold
The worse, for touching ? clothes, for being look'd on ?
Why, this 's no more. An old, decrepit wretch,
That ha's no sense, no sinew ; takes his meate
With others fingers ; onely knowes to gape,
When you doe scald his gummes ; a voice ; a shadow ;
And, what can this man hurt you ? CEL. Lord ! what spirit
Is this hath entred him ? CORV. And for your fame,
That's such a Iigge ; as if I would goe tell it,
Crie it, on the *piazza !* who shall know it ?
But hee, that cannot speake it ; and this fellow,
Whose lippes are i' my pocket : saue your selfe,
If you'll proclaime't, you may. I know no other,
Should come to know it. CEL. Are heauen, and saints then nothing ?
Will they be blinde, or stupide ? CORV. How ? CEL. Good Sir,
Be iealous still, æmulate them ; and thinke
What hate they burne with, toward euery sinne.
CORV. I grant you : if I thought it were a sinne,
I would not vrge you. Should I offer this
To some yong *Frenchman*, or hot *Tuscane* bloud,
That had read ARETINE, conn'd all his printes,
Knew euery quirke within lusts laborinth,
And were profest critique, in lechery ;
And I would looke vpon him, and applaud him,

III. vii. 47 After 'him?' [*Aside.*] G 52 If . . . may.] (If . . . may,) G 57 grant you :] graunt you ; Q

This were a sinne: but here, 'tis contrary,
A pious worke, mere charity, for physick,
And honest politie, to assure mine owne.
CEL. O heauen! canst thou suffer such a change?
VOLP. Thou art mine honor, MOSCA, and my pride,
My ioy, my tickling, my delight! goe, bring 'hem.
MOS. Please you draw neere, sir. CORV. Come on, what——
You will not be rebellious? by that light——
MOS. Sir, signior CORVINO, here, is come to see you.
VOLP. Oh. MOS. And hearing of the consultation had,
So lately, for your health, is come to offer,
Or rather, sir, to prostitute—— CORV. Thankes, sweet MOSCA.
MOS. Freely, vn-ask'd, or vn-intreated—— CORV. Well.
MOS. (As the true, feruent instance of his loue)
His owne most faire and proper wife; the beauty,
Onely of price, in *Venice*—— CORV. 'Tis well vrg'd.
MOS. To be your comfortresse, and to preserue you.
VOLP. Alasse, I'am past already! 'pray you, thanke him,
For his good care, and promptnesse, but for that,
'Tis a vaine labour, eene to fight, 'gainst heauen;
Applying fire to a stone: (vh, vh, vh, vh.)
Making a dead leafe grow againe. I take
His wishes gently, though; and, you may tell him,
What I' haue done for him: mary, my state is hopelesse!
Will him, to pray for me; and t'vse his fortune,
With reuerence, when he comes to't. MOS. Do you heare, sir?
Go to him, with your wife. CORV. Heart of my father!
Wilt thou persist thus? come, I pray thee, come.

III. vii. 67 heauen!] heauen, *Q* 69 delight!] delight: *Q* 70 Mos.] *Mos.* [*advancing.*] G 72 you] you, *Q* 76 *om. F3* vn-ask'd] vna-sk'd *Q* 78 faire] faire, *Q* 81 I'am *Q*: I am *Ff* thanke him] thanke 'him *Q, Ff* 82 promptnesse, but] promptnesse. But, *Q*: promptnesse; but *F2* 87 hopelesse!] hopelesse. *Q* 89 to't] to it *Q*

Thou seest 'tis nothing: CELIA. By this hand,
I shall grow violent. Come, do't, I say.
CEL. Sir, kill me, rather: I will take downe poyson,
Eate burning coales, doe any thing—— CORV. Be damn'd.
(Heart) I will drag thee hence, home, by the haire;
Cry thee a strumpet, through the streets; rip vp
Thy mouth, vnto thine eares; and slit thy nose,
Like a raw rotchet—— Do not tempt me, come.
Yeld, I am loth—— (Death) I will buy some slaue,
Whom I will kill, and binde thee to him, aliue;
And at my windore, hang you forth: deuising
Some monstrous crime, which I, in capitall letters,
Will eate into thy flesh, with *aqua-fortis*,
And burning cor'siues, on this stubborne brest.
Now, by the bloud, thou hast incens'd, ile do't.
CEL. Sir, what you please, you may, I am your martyr.
CORV. Be not thus obstinate, I ha' not deseru'd it:
Thinke, who it is, intreats you. 'Pray thee, sweet;
(Good'faith) thou shalt haue iewells, gownes, attires,
What thou wilt thinke, and aske. Do, but, go kisse him.
Or touch him, but. For my sake. At my sute.
This once. No? not? I shall remember this.
Will you disgrace me, thus? do'you thirst my'vndoing?
MOS. Nay, gentle lady, be aduis'd. CORV. No, no.
She has watch'd her time. God's precious, this is skiruy;
'Tis very skiruie: and you are—— MOS. Nay, good sir.
CORV. An errant locust, by heauen, a locust. Whore,
Crocodile, that hast thy teares prepar'd,
Expecting, how thou'lt bid 'hem flow. MOS. Nay, 'pray you, sir,
Shee will consider. CEL. Would my life would serue
To satisfie. CORV. (S'death) if shee would but speake to him,

III. vii. 92 nothing:] *Q*: nothing. *F1*: nothing, *F2* 102 And] And, *Q* 103 capitall] CAPITAL *Q* 109 'Pray thee] 'Pr'y thee *F2* 111 thou wilt] thou' wilt *Q* aske.] aske— *Q* 116 precious,] precious— *Q* 117 good] good, *Q*, *F1* 119 thy] thy thy *F1* 120 'pray *F2*: 'Pray *Q*, *F1* 122 satisfie.] satisfie— *Q*

And saue my reputation, 'twere somewhat;
But, spightfully to affect my vtter ruine.
MOS. I, now you' haue put your fortune, in her hands.
Why i' faith, it is her modesty, I must quit her;
If you were absent, shee would be more comming;
I know it: and dare vndertake for her.
What woman can, before her husband? 'pray you,
Let vs depart, and leaue her, here. CORV. Sweet CELIA,
Thou mayst redeeme all, yet; I'le say no more:
If not, esteeme your selfe as lost. Nay, stay there.
CEL. O god, and his good angels! whether, whether
Is shame fled humane brests? that with such ease,
Men dare put off your honours, and their owne?
Is that, which euer was a cause of life,
Now plac'd beneath the basest circumstance?
And modestie an exile made, for money?
VOLP. I, in CORVINO, and such earth-fed mindes, *He leapes off from his couch.*
That neuer tasted the true heau'n of loue.
Assure thee, CELIA, he that would sell thee,
Onely for hope of gaine, and that vncertaine,
He would haue sold his part of paradise
For ready money, had he met a cope-man.
Why art thou maz'd, to see me thus reuiu'd?
Rather applaud thy beauties miracle;
'Tis thy great worke: that hath, not now alone,
But sundry times, rays'd me, in seuerall shapes,
And, but this morning, like a mountebanke,
To see thee at thy windore. I, before
I would haue left my practice, for thy loue,
In varying figures, I would haue contended
With the blue PROTEVS, or the horned *Floud.*
Now, art thou welcome. CEL. Sir! VOLP. Nay, flie me not.

III. vii. 124 ruine.] ruine: *Q* 132 lost.] lost,— *Q* After 132 *Shuts the door, and exit with Mosca.* G 133–4 whether Is *Q*: whether. Is *Ff* that] that, *Q* 135 off] of *Q* honours] honors *Q* 139 *St. dir. not in Q* 146 Rather] Rather, *Q* 148 rays'd *F2*: 'rays'd *Q, F1* 153 blue] blew *Q* 154 not.] not; *Q*

Nor, let thy false imagination
That I was bedrid, make thee thinke, I am so:
Thou shalt not find it. I am, now, as fresh,
As hot, as high, and in as iouiall plight,
As when (in that so celebrated *scene*,
At recitation of our *comœdie*,
For entertainement of the great VALOYS)
I acted yong ANTINOVS; and attracted
The eyes, and eares of all the ladies, present,
T'admire each gracefull gesture, note, and footing.

SONG.

Come, my CELIA, *let vs proue,*
While we can, the sports of loue;
Time will not be ours, for euer,
He, at length, our good will seuer;
Spend not then his gifts, in vaine.
Sunnes, that set, may rise againe:
But if, once, we lose this light,
'Tis with vs perpetuall night.
Why should wee deferre our ioyes?
Fame, and rumor are but toies.
Cannot we delude the eyes
Of a few poore houshold-spies?
Or his easier eares beguile,
Thus remooued, by our wile?
'Tis no sinne, loues fruits to steale;
But the sweet thefts to reueale:
To be taken, to be seene,
These haue crimes accounted beene.

CEL. Some *serene* blast me, or dire lightning strike
This my offending face. VOLP. Why droopes my CELIA?
Thou hast in place of a base husband, found

III. vii. 161 entertainement] entertayment *Q* 162 ANTINOVS] *Antinoüs* Q attracted *corr. Q, Ff*: a racted *Q originally* 170 *gifts*] *guiftes* Q 172 *lose*] *loose* Q 180 *fruits*] *fruicts* Q

A worthy louer: vse thy fortune well,
With secrecie, and pleasure. See, behold,
What thou art queene of; not in expectation,
As I feed others: but possess'd, and crown'd.
See, here, a rope of pearle; and each, more orient
Then that the braue *Ægyptian* queene carrous'd:
Dissolue, and drinke 'hem. See, a carbuncle,
May put out both the eyes of our S^t^. MARKE;
A diamant, would haue bought LOLLIA PAVLINA,
When she came in, like star-light, hid with iewels,
That were the spoiles of prouinces; take these,
And weare, and loose 'hem: yet remaines an eare-ring
To purchase them againe, and this whole state.
A gem, but worth a priuate patrimony,
Is nothing: we will eate such at a meale.
The heads of parrats, tongues of nightingales,
The braines of peacoks, and of estriches
Shall be our food: and, could we get the phœnix,
(Though nature lost her kind) shee were our dish.
CEL. Good sir, these things might moue a minde affected
With such delights; but I, whose innocence
Is all I can thinke wealthy, or worth th'enioying,
And which once lost, I haue nought to loose beyond it,
Cannot be taken with these sensuall baites:
If you haue conscience—— VOLP. 'Tis the beggers vertue,
If thou hast wisdome, heare me, CELIA.
Thy bathes shall be the iuyce of iuly-flowres,
Spirit of roses, and of violets,
The milke of vnicornes, and panthers breath
Gather'd in bagges, and mixt with *cretan* wines.
Our drinke shall be prepared gold, and amber;
Which we will take, vntill my roofe whirle round
With the *vertigo*: and my dwarfe shall dance,

III. vii. 195 bought] brought *F2* LOLLIA] *Laullia* F3 196 -light, *Q* (*comma faint*): -light *Ff* 198, 209 loose] lose *F2* 198 yet] Yet, *Q* 202 parrats] parrots *Q* 209 And] And, *Q*

My eunuch sing, my foole make vp the antique.
Whil'st, we, in changed shapes, act OVIDS tales,
Thou, like EVROPA now, and I like IOVE,
Then I like MARS, and thou like ERYCINE,
So, of the rest, till we haue quite run through
And weary'd all the fables of the gods.
Then will I haue thee in more moderne formes,
Attired like some sprightly dame of *France*,
Braue *Tuscan* lady, or proud *Spanish* beauty;
Sometimes, vnto the *Persian Sophies* wife;
Or the grand-*Signiors* mistresse; and, for change,
To one of our most art-full courtizans,
Or some quick *Negro*, or cold *Russian;*
And I will meet thee, in as many shapes:
Where we may, so, trans-fuse our wandring soules,
Out at our lippes, and score vp summes of pleasures,

That the curious shall not know,
How to tell them, as they flow;
And the enuious, when they find
What their number is, be pind.

CEL. If you haue eares that will be pierc'd; or eyes,
That can be open'd; a heart, may be touch'd;
Or any part, that yet sounds man, about you:
If you haue touch of holy saints, or heauen,
Do me the grace, to let me scape. If not,
Be bountifull, and kill me. You doe know,
I am a creature, hither ill betrayd,
By one, whose shame I would forget it were.
If you will daigne me neither of these graces,
Yet feed your wrath, sir, rather then your lust;
(It is a vice, comes neerer manlinesse)
And punish that vnhappy crime of nature,

III. vii. 226 thee] thee, *Q* 240 pierc'd;] pierc'd— *Q* 241 open'd;] open'd— *Q* touch'd;] touch'd— *Q* 242 you:] you— *Q* 243 saints,] *Saints*— Q heauen,] *Heauen*— Q 244 scape. If] scape—if *Q* 245 me. You] mee—you *Q* 246 hither] hether *Q* 247 were.] were— *Q*: were, *F1*: were; *F2* 249 lust;] lust— *Q* 250 manlinesse)] manlinesse-) *Q*

Which you miscal my beauty : flay my face,
Or poison it, with oyntments, for seducing
Your bloud to this rebellion. Rub these hands,
With what may cause an eating leprosie,
E'ene to my bones, and marrow : any thing,
That may disfauour me, saue in my honour.
And I will kneele to you, pray for you, pay downe
A thousand hourely vowes, sir, for your health,
Report, and thinke you vertuous—— VOLP. Thinke me cold,
Frosen, and impotent, and so report me ?
That I had NESTOR'S *hernia*, thou wouldst thinke.
I doe degenerate, and abuse my nation,
To play with oportunity, thus long :
I should haue done the act, and then haue parlee'd.
Yeeld, or Ile force thee. CEL. O ! iust God. VOLP. In vaine——
BON. Forbeare, foule rauisher, libidinous swine, *He leapes out from where Mosca had plac'd him.*
Free the forc'd lady, or thou dy'st, impostor.
But that I am loth to snatch thy punishment
Out of the hand of iustice, thou shouldst, yet,
Be made the timely sacrifice of vengeance,
Before this altar, and this drosse, thy idoll.
Lady, let's quit the place, it is the den
Of villany ; feare nought, you haue a guard :
And he, ere long, shall meet his iust reward.
VOLP. Fall on me, roofe, and bury me in ruine,
Become my graue, that wert my shelter. O !
I am vn-masqu'd, vn-spirited, vn-done,
Betray'd to beggery, to infamy——

III. vii. 252 beauty : flay] beauty—Flea *Q* 254 rebellion.] rebellion— *Q* 256 marrow :] marrow— *Q* 257 honour.] honour— *Q* 258 pray] 'pray *Q* 259 health,] health— *Q* 266 After 'thee' *Seizes her.* G O !] O, *Q* (*so* 277) *Stage direction not in Q* After 275 *Exeunt Bon. and Cel.* G

Act III. *Scene* VIII.

MOSCA, VOLPONE.

WHere shall I runne, most wretched shame of men,
To beate out my vn-luckie braines? VOLP. Here, here.
What! dost thou bleed? MOS. O, that his wel-driu'n sword
Had beene so courteous to haue cleft me downe,
Vnto the nauill; ere I liu'd to see
My life, my hopes, my spirits, my patron, all
Thus desperately engaged, by my error.
VOLP. Woe, on thy fortune. MOS. And my follies, sir.
VOLP. Th'hast made me miserable. MOS. And my selfe, sir.
Who would haue thought, he would haue harken'd, so?
VOLP. What shall we do? MOS. I know not, if my heart
Could expiate the mischance, I'ld pluck it out.
Will you be pleas'd to hang me? or cut my throate?
And i'le requite you, sir. Let's die like *Romanes*,
They knock without. Since wee haue liu'd, like *Grecians*. VOLP. Harke, who's there?
I heare some footing, officers, the *Saffi*,
Come to apprehend vs! I doe feele the brand
Hissing already, at my fore-head: now,
Mine eares are boring. MOS. To your couch, sir, you
Make that place good, how euer. Guilty men
Suspect, what they deserue still. Signior CORBACCIO!

III. viii. *Enter Mosca, wounded and bleeding*. G, continuing the scene. G 3 What!] What? *Q* 4 courteous] curteous, *Q*: couetous *F2* 5 ere] êre *Q* 9 Th'hast] Thou hast *Q* 11 not,] not; *F2* 12 I'ld] Il'd *Q*, *F1* 15 *St. dir. not in Q* 20 After 'euer.' [*Volpone lies down as before.*] G

Act III. *Scene* IX.

CORBACCIO, MOSCA, VOLTORE, VOLPONE.

WHy! how now? MOSCA! MOS. O, vndone, amaz'd, sir.
Your sonne (I know not, by what accident)
Acquainted with your purpose to my patron,
Touching your will, and making him your heire;
Entred our house with violence, his sword drawne,
Sought for you, call'd you wretch, vnnaturall,
Vow'd he would kill you. CORB. Me? MOS. Yes, and my patron.
CORB. This act, shall disinherit him indeed:
Here is the will. MOS. 'Tis well, sir. CORB. Right and well.
Be you as carefull now, for me. MOS. My life, sir,
Is not more tender'd, I am onely yours.
CORB. How do's he? will he die shortly, think'st thou? MOS. I feare,
He'll out-last *May*. CORB. To day? MOS. No, last-out *May*, sir.
CORB. Couldst thou not gi' him a dram? MOS. O, by no meanes, sir.
CORB. Nay, I'le not bid you. VOLT. This is a knaue, I see.
MOS. How, signior VOLTORE! did he heare me? VOLT. Parasite.
MOS. Who's that? O, sir, most timely welcome—— VOLT. Scarse,
To the discouery of your tricks, I feare.
You are his, onely? and mine, also? are you not?
MOS. Who? I, sir! VOLT. You, sir. What deuice is this

III. ix. *Enter Corbaccio.* G, continuing the scene 3 purpose] purpose, *Q* 10 After 'me.' [*Enter Voltore behind.*] G 12 feare,] feare. *Q, F1* 14 Mos.] Mos, *Q* 15 VOLT.] *Volt.* [*coming forward*]. G This is] This's *Q* 16. Mos.] *Mos.* [*seeing Volt.*] G After 'me?' [*Aside.*] G 20 I, sir!] I, Sir? *Q*

About a will? Mos. A plot for you, sir. Volt. Come,
Put not your foist's vpon me, I shall sent 'hem.
Mos. Did you not heare it? Volt. Yes, I heare, Corbaccio
Hath made your patron, there, his heire. Mos. 'Tis true,
By my deuice, drawne to it by my plot,
With hope—— Volt. Your patron should reciprocate?
And, you haue promis'd? Mos. For your good, I did, sir.
Nay more, I told his sonne, brought, hid him here,
Where he might heare his father passe the deed;
Being perswaded to it, by this thought, sir,
That the vnnaturalnesse, first, of the act,
And then, his fathers oft disclaiming in him,
(Which I did meane t'helpe on) would sure enrage him
To doe some violence vpon his parent.
On which the law should take sufficient hold,
And you be stated in a double hope:
Truth be my comfort, and my conscience,
My onely ayme was, to dig you a fortune
Out of these two, old rotten sepulchers——
(Volt. I cry thee mercy, Mosca.) Mos. Worth your patience,
And your great merit, sir. And, see the change!
Volt. Why? what successe? Mos. Most haplesse! you must helpe, sir.
Whilst we expected th' old rauen, in comes
Corvino's wife, sent hither, by her husband——
Volt. What, with a present? Mos. No, sir, on visitation:
(I'le tell you how, anone) and, staying long,
The youth, he growes impatient, rushes forth,
Seizeth the lady, wound's me, makes her sweare
(Or he would murder her, that was his vow)

III. ix. 28 I told *Ff*: I tóld *corr. Q*: tóld *Q originally* 29 he might *corr. Q, Ff*: he Imight *Q originally, the* 'I' *having dropped from the line above* 33 (Which . . . on)] Which . . . on *Q* 34 parent.] parent, *Q* 40 (Volt. I . . . Mosca.)] Volt. I . . . *Mosca. Q* 44 hither] hether *Q*

T'affirme my patron to haue done her rape :
Which how vnlike it is, you see ! and, hence,
With that pretext, hee's gone, t'accuse his father ;
Defame my patron ; defeate you—— VOLT. Where's her husband ?
Let him be sent for, streight. MOS. Sir, I'le goe fetch him.
VOLT. Bring him, to the *Scrutineo*. MOS. Sir, I will.
VOLT. This must be stopt. MOS. O, you do nobly, sir.
Alasse, 'twas labor'd all, sir, for your good ;
Nor, was there want of counsel, in the plot :
But fortune can, at any time, orethrow
The proiects of a hundred learned *clearkes*, sir.
CORB. What's that ? VOLT. Wilt please you sir, to goe along ?
MOS. Patron, go in, and pray for our successe.
VOLP. Neede makes deuotion : heauen your labor blesse.

Act IIII. *Scene* I.

POLITIQVE, PEREGRINE.

I Told you, sir, it was a plot : you see
What obseruation is. You mention'd mee,
For some instructions : I will tell you, sir,
(Since we are met, here, in this height of *Venice*)
Some few particulars, I haue set downe,
Onely for this *meridian ;* fit to be knowne
Of your crude traueller, and they are these.
I will not touch, sir, at your phrase, or clothes,
For they are old. PER. Sir, I haue better. POL. Pardon,
I meant, as they are *theames*. PER. O, sir, proceed :

III. ix. 50 to] would *Q* 61 CORB.] *Corb.* [*listening.*] G *Exit Corbaccio followed by Voltore.* add G 63 VOLP.] *Volp.* [*rising from his couch.*] G *Exeunt.* add G IV. i. ACT IV. SCENE I. | *A Street.* | *Enter sir Politick Would-be and Peregrine.* G 4 here, *Q*: here, *F1* 5 particulars] perticulars *Q* 6 *meridian ;*] *meridian,* Q 7 traueller] Trauailer *Q* 9 Pardon, *F2* : Pardon *Q*, *F1*

I'le slander you no more of wit, good sir.
POL. First, for your garbe, it must be graue, and serious;
Very reseru'd, and lock't; not tell a secret,
On any termes, not to your father; scarse
A fable, but with caution; make sure choise
Both of your company, and discourse; beware,
You neuer speake a truth—— PER. How! POL. Not to strangers,
For those be they you must conuerse with, most;
Others I would not know, sir, but, at distance,
So as I still might be a sauer, in 'hem:
You shall haue tricks, else, past vpon you, hourely.
And then, for your religion, professe none;
But wonder, at the diuersitie of all;
And, for your part, protest, were there no other
But simply the lawes o' th' land, you could content you:
NIC: MACHIAVEL, and monsieur BODINE, both,
Were of this minde. Then, must you learne the vse,
And handling of your siluer forke, at meales;
The mettall of your glasse: (these are maine matters,
With your *Italian*) and to know the houre,
When you must eat your melons, and your figges.
PER. Is that a point of state, too? POL. Here it is.
For your *Venetian*, if he see a man
Preposterous, in the least, he has him straight;
He has: he strippes him. I'le acquaint you, sir,
I now haue liu'd here ('tis some fourteene monthes)
Within the first weeke, of my landing here,
All tooke me for a citizen of *Venice*:
I knew the formes, so well—— PER. And nothing else.
POL. I had read CONTARENE, tooke me a house,
Dealt with my *Iewes*, to furnish it with moueables——
Well, if I could but finde one man, one man,

IV. i. 12 serious;] serious, *Q* 15 with] with with *Q* 17 speake] spake *F1* How!] How? *Q* 18 they] they, *Q* 25 lawes] *Lawes*, *Q* 29 glasse: (these] glasse— These *Q* 30 *Italian*)] *Italian*, *Q* houre] hower *Q* 39 *Aside.* add G 42 man, one] man-one *Q*

To mine owne heart, whom I durst trust, I would——
PER. What? what, sir? POL. Make him rich; make him a fortune:
He should not thinke, againe. I would command it.
PER. As how? POL. With certaine proiects, that I haue:
Which, I may not discouer. PER. If I had
But one to wager with, I would lay odds, now,
He tels me, instantly. POL. One is, (and that
I care not greatly, who knowes) to serue the state
Of *Venice*, with red herrings, for three yeeres,
And at a certaine rate, from *Roterdam*,
Where I haue correspondence. There's a letter,
Sent me from one o' th' States, and to that purpose;
He cannot write his name, but that's his marke.
PER. He is a chaundler? POL. No, a cheesemonger.
There are some other too, with whom I treate,
About the same negotiation;
And, I will vndertake it: For, 'tis thus,
I'le do't with ease, I'haue cast it all. Your hoigh
Carries but three men in her, and a boy;
And she shall make me three returnes, a yeare:
So, if there come but one of three, I saue,
If two, I can defalke. But, this is now,
If my mayne proiect faile. PER. Then, you haue others?
POL. I should be loath to draw the subtill ayre
Of such a place, without my thousand aymes.
Ile not dissemble, sir, where ere I come,
I loue to be consideratiue; and, 'tis true,
I haue, at my free houres, thought vpon
Some certaine goods, vnto the state of *Venice*,
Which I doe call my cautions: and, sir, which
I meane (in hope of pension) to propound
To the great councell, then vnto the forty,
So to the ten. My meanes are made already——

IV. i. 43 trust,] trust— *Q* 49 After 'instantly' [*Aside.*] G 57 other] others *F2* too] two *Q* 59 And,] And— *Q*

PER. By whom? POL. Sir, one, that though his place b⟨e⟩'obscure,
Yet, he can sway, and they will heare him. H'is
A *commandadore*. PER. What, a common sergeant?
POL. Sir, such, as they are, put it in their mouthes,
What they should say, sometimes: as well as greater.
I thinke I haue my notes, to shew you—— PER. Good, sir,
POL. But, you shall sweare vnto me, on your gentry,
Not to anticipate—— PER. I, sir? POL. Nor reueale
A circumstance—— My paper is not with mee.
PER. O, but, you can remember, sir. POL. My first is,
Concerning tinder-boxes. You must know,
No family is, here, without it's boxe.
Now sir, it being so portable a thing,
Put case, that you, or I were ill affected
Vnto the state; sir, with it in our pockets,
Might not I goe into the *arsenale?*
Or you? come out againe? and none the wiser?
PER. Except your selfe, sir. POL. Goe too, then. I, therefore,
Aduertise to the state, how fit it were,
That none, but such as were knowne patriots,
Sound louers of their countrey, should be sufferd
T'enioy them in their houses: and, euen those,
Seal'd, at some office, and, at such a bignesse,
As might not lurke in pockets. PER. Admirable!
POL. My next is, how t'enquire, and be resolu'd,
By present demonstration, whether a ship,
Newly arriued from *Soria*, or from
Any suspected part of all the *leuant*,
Be guilty of the plague: And, where they vse,
To lie out fortie, fifty daies, sometimes,
About the *Lazaretto*, for their triall;
Ile saue that charge, and losse vnto the merchant,

IV. i. 77 H'is] Hee's *F2* 81 After 'you' [*Searching his pockets.*] G 87 boxe.] boxe; *Q* 90 state;] State: *Q* it] it, *Q* 93 PER.] POL. *Q*

And, in an houre, cleare the doubt. PER. Indeede, sir?
POL. Or—— I will loose my labour. PER. 'My faith, that's much.
POL. Nay, sir, conceiue me. 'Twill cost me, in onions,
Some thirtie *liu'res*—— PER. Which is one pound sterling.
POL. Beside my water-workes: for this I doe, sir.
First, I bring in your ship, 'twixt two brickwalles;
(But those the state shall venter) on the one
I straine me a faire tarre-paulin; and, in that,
I stick my onions, cut in halfes: the other
Is full of loope-holes, out at which, I thrust
The noses of my bellowes; and, those bellowes
I keepe, with water-workes, in perpetuall motion,
(Which is the easi'st matter of a hundred)
Now, sir, your onion, which doth naturally
Attract th'infection, and your bellowes, blowing
The ayre vpon him, will shew (instantly)
By his chang'd colour, if there be contagion,
Or else, remaine as faire, as at the first.
Now 'tis knowne, 'tis nothing. PER. You are right, sir.
POL. I would, I had my note. PER. 'Faith, so would I:
But, you ha' done well, for once, sir. POL. Were I false,
Or would be made so, I could shew you reasons,
How I could sell this state, now, to the *Turke;*
Spight of their galleis, or their—— PER. Pray you, sir POLL.
POL. I haue 'hem not, about me. PER. That I fear'd.
They'are there, sir? POL. No, this is my *diary*,
Wherein I note my actions of the day.
PER. 'Pray you, let's see, sir. What is here? *notandum*,
A rat had gnawne my spurre-lethers; notwithstanding,
I put on new, and did goe forth: but, first,
I threw three beanes ouer the threshold. *Item*,.
I went, and bought two tooth-pickes, whereof one
I burst, immediatly, in a discourse

IV. i. 116 in] iu *Q* 131 After 'their' [*Examining his papers.*] G Pray] 'Pray *F2* 135 *Reads.* add G 137 put] pnt *Q*

With a *dutch* merchant, 'bout *ragion del stato.*
From him I went, and payd a *moccinigo,*
For peecing my silke stockings ; by the way,
I cheapen'd sprats : and at St. MARKES, I vrin'd.
'Faith, these are politique notes ! POL. Sir, I do slippe
No action of my life, thus, but I quote it.
PER. Beleeue me it is wise ! POL. Nay, sir, read forth.

Act IIII. *Scene* II.

LADY, NANO, WOMEN, POLITIQVE, PEREGRINE.

WHere should this loose knight be, trow ? sure, h'is hous'd.
NAN. Why, then he's fast. LAD. I, he plaies both, with me :
I pray you, stay. This heate will doe more harme
To my complexion, then his heart is worth.
(I do not care to hinder, but to take him)
How it comes of ! WOM. My master's, yonder. LAD. Where ?
WOM. With a yong gentleman. LAD. That same's the party !
In mans apparell. 'Pray you, sir, iog my knight :
I will be tender to his reputation,
How euer he demerit. POL. My lady ! PER. Where ?
POL. 'Tis shee indeed, sir, you shall know her. She is,
Were she not mine, a lady of that merit,
For fashion, and behauiour ; and, for beauty
I durst compare—— PER. It seemes, you are not iealous,
That dare commend her. POL. Nay, and for discourse——
PER. Being your wife, she cannot misse that. POL. Madame,
Here is a gentleman, 'pray you, vse him, fairely,

IV. ii. *Enter, at a distance, Lady Politick Would-be, Nano, and two Waiting-women.* G, continuing the scene   1 h'is] he's *F2*   6 of] off *F2*: off! [*Rubbing her cheeks.* G   master's] maister's *Q*   7 party!] party, *Q*   10 POL.] *Pol.* [*seeing her.*] G   16 POL.] *Sir P.* [*introducing Per.*] G

He seemes a youth, but he is—— L A D. None? P O L. Yes, one
Has put his face, as soone, into the world——
L A D. You meane, as earely? but to day? P O L. How's this!
L A D. Why in this habit, sir, you apprehend me.
Well, master W O V L D-B E E, this doth not become you;
I had thought, the odour, sir, of your good name,
Had beene more precious to you; that you would not
Haue done this dire massacre, on your honour;
One of your grauity, and ranke, besides!
But, knights, I see, care little for the oath
They make to ladies: chiefely, their owne ladies.
P O L. Now, by my spurres (the symbole of my knight-hood)
(P E R. Lord! how his braine is humbled, for an oath)
P O L. I reach you not. L A D. Right, sir, your politie
May beare it through, thus. Sir, a word with you.
I would be loth, to contest publikely,
With any gentlewoman; or to seeme
Froward, or violent (as the courtier sayes)
It comes too neere rusticity, in a lady,
Which I would shun, by all meanes: and, how-euer
I may deserue from master W O V L D-B E E, yet,
T'haue one faire gentlewoman, thus, be made
Th'vnkind instrument, to wrong another,
And one she knowes not, I, and to perseuer;
In my poore iudgement, is not warranted
From being a *solœcisme* in our sexe,
If not in manners. P E R. How is this! P O L. Sweet madame,
Come neerer to your ayme. L A D. Mary, and will, sir.
Since you prouoke me, with your impudence,
And laughter of your light land-*siren*, here,
Your S P O R V S, your *hermaphrodite*—— P E R. What's here?

IV. ii. 20 this!] this? *Q* 26 besides!] besides: *Q* 30 *Aside.* add G 32 *To Per.* add G 33 contest] contest, *Q* 34, 39 gentle-woman] Gentlewóman *Q* 36 too] to *Q* 41 not,] not; *Q* perseuer;] perseuer: *Q* 45 and will] and I will *F2* 47 light *om. F2, F3*

Poetique fury, and historique stormes !
POL. The gentleman, beleeue it, is of worth,
And of our nation. LAD. I, your *white-Friers* nation ?
Come, I blush for you, master WOVLD-BEE, I ;
And am asham'd, you should ha' no more forehead,
Then, thus, to be the patron, or St. GEORGE
To a lewd harlot, a base fricatrice,
A female deuill, in a male out-side. POL. Nay,
And you be such a one ! I must bid adieu
To your delights. The case appeares too liquide.
LAD. I, you may carry 't cleare, with your state-face !
But, for your carniuale concupiscence,
Who here is fled for liberty of conscience,
From furious persecution of the Marshall,
Her will I disc'ple. PER. This is fine, i'faith !
And do you vse this, often ? is this part
Of your wits exercise, 'gainst you haue occasion ?
Madam—— LAD. Go to, sir. PER. Do you heare me, lady ?
Why, if your knight haue set you to begge shirts,
Or to inuite me home, you might haue done it
A neerer way, by farre. LAD. This cannot work you,
Out of my snare. PER. Why ? am I in it, then ?
Indeede, your husband told me, you were faire,
And so you are ; onely your nose enclines
(That side, that's next the sunne) to the queene-apple.
LAD. This cannot be endur'd, by any patience.

Act IIII. *Scene* III.

MOSCA, LADY, PEREGRINE.

WHat's the matter, madame ? LAD. If the *Senate*
Right not my quest, in this ; I will protest 'hem,
To all the world, no *aristocracie*.

IV. ii. 57 And . . . one !] An' . . . one, *W* bid] bid, *Q* 58 *Exit.* add G 61 fled] fled, *Q* 69 farre.] farre : *Q* 73 -apple.] -*apple* : Q
IV. iii. *Enter Mosca.* G, continuing the scene

MOS. What is the iniurie, lady? LAD. Why, the callet,
You told me of, here I haue tane disguis'd.
MOS. Who? this? what meanes your ladiship? the creature
I mention'd to you, is apprehended, now,
Before the *Senate*, you shall see her—— LAD. Where?
MOS. I'le bring you to her. This yong gentleman
I saw him land, this morning, at the port.
LAD. Is't possible! how has my iudgement wander'd!
Sir, I must, blushing, say to you, I haue err'd:
And plead your pardon. PER. What! more changes, yet?
LAD. I hope, yo' ha' not the malice to remember
A gentlewomans passion. If you stay,
In *Venice*, here, please you to vse me, sir——
MOS. Will you go, madame? LAD. 'Pray you, sir, vse mee. In faith,
The more you see me, the more I shall conceiue,
You haue forgot our quarrell. PER. This is rare!
Sir POLITIQVE WOVLD-BEE? no, sir POLITIQVE bawd!
To bring me, thus, acquainted with his wife!
Well, wise sir POL: since you haue practis'd, thus,
Vpon my freshman-ship, I'le trie your salt-head,
What proofe it is against a counter-plot.

Act IIII. *Scene* IIII.

VOLTORE, CORBACCIO, CORVINO, MOSCA.

WEll, now you know the carriage of the businesse,
Your constancy is all, that is requir'd
Vnto the safety of it. MOS. Is the lie

IV. iii. 5 tane] tâne *Q* 11 wander'd!] wander'd? *Q* 14 yo'] you *Q* 15 gentlewomans] Gentlewómans *Q* 18 see] vse *Q* 19 After 'quarrell.' *Exeunt Lady Would-be, Mosca, Nano, and Waiting-women.* G 20 bawd!] Baud. *Q* 24 *Exit.* add G IV. iv. SCENE II. | *The Scrutineo, or Senate House.* | *Enter Voltore, Corbaccio, Corvino, and Mosca.* G

Safely conuai'd amongst vs? is that sure?
Knowes euery man his burden? CORV. Yes. MOS. Then, shrink not.
CORV. But, knowes the Aduocate the truth? MOS. O, sir,
By no meanes. I deuis'd a formall tale,
That salu'd your reputation. But, be valiant, sir.
CORV. I feare no one, but him; that, this his pleading
Should make him stand for a co-heire—— MOS. Co-halter.
Hang him: we will but vse his tongue, his noise,
As we doe croakers, here. CORV. I, what shall he do?
MOS. When we ha' done, you meane? CORV. Yes. MOS. Why, we'll thinke,
Sell him for *mummia*, hee's halfe dust already.
To Voltore. Do not you smile, to see this *buffalo*,
How he doth sport it with his head?—— I should
To Corbaccio. If all were well, and past. Sir, onely you
Are he, that shall enioy the crop of all,
And these not know for whom they toile. CORB. I, peace.
To Coruino, then to Voltore againe. MOS. But you shall eate it. Much! Worshipfull sir,
MERCVRY sit vpon your thundring tongue,
Or the *French* HERCVLES, and make your language
As conquering as his club, to beate along,
(As with a tempest) flat, our aduersaries:
But, much more, yours, sir. VOLT. Here they come, ha' done.
MOS. I haue another witnesse, if you neede, sir,
I can produce. VOLT. Who is it? MOS. Sir, I haue her.

IV. iv. 15, 17, 20 *Stage directions not in Q* 16 doth] do's *Q* I should] I'should *Q, F1* 17 After 'past.' [*Aside.*] G 20 Much!] Much. *Q*: Much! [*Aside.*] G

Act IIII. *Scene* V.

AVOCATORI, 4. BONARIO, CELIA, VOLTORE, CORBACCIO, CORVINO, MOSCA, NOTARIO, COMMANDADORI.

THe like of this the *Senate* neuer heard of.
AVOC. 2. 'Twil come most strange to them, when we report it.
AVOC. 4. The gentlewoman has beene euer held
Of vn-reproued name. AVOC. 3. So, the yong man.
AVOC. 4. The more vnnaturall part that of his father.
AVOC. 2. More of the husband. AVOC. 1. I not know to giue
His act a name, it is so monstrous!
AVOC. 4. But the impostor, he is a thing created
T'exceed example! AVOC. ⟨1.⟩ And all after times!
AVOC. 2. I neuer heard a true voluptuary
Describ'd, but him. AVOC. 3. Appeare yet those were cited?
NOTA. All, but the old magnifico, VOLPONE.
AVOC. 1. Why is not hee here? MOS. Please your father-hoods,
Here is his Aduocate. Himselfe's, so weake,
So feeble—— AVOC. 4. What are you? BON. His parasite,
His knaue, his pandar: I beseech the court,
He may be forc'd to come, that your graue eyes
May beare strong witnesse of his strange impostures.
VOLT. Vpon my faith, and credit, with your vertues,
He is not able to endure the ayre.
AVO. 2. Bring him, how euer. AVO. 3. We will see him. AVO. 4. Fetch him.

IV. V. *Enter Avocatori and take their seats, Bonario, Celia, Notario, Commandadori, Saffi, and other Officers of justice.* G VOLTORE,] VOLTORE, *F1* NOTARIO] NotArio *F1* 3 gentlewoman] Gentle-wóman *Q* 4 So, . . . man] So has the youth *Q* 6 More] More, *Q* 9 Avoc. 1. *F2* 11 Describ'd] Discrib'd *Q* 16 pandar:] Pandar—*Q*

VOLT. Your father-hoods fit pleasures be obey'd,
But sure, the sight will rather mooue your pitties,
Then indignation; may it please the court,
In the meane time, he may be heard in me:
I know this place most voide of preiudice,
And therefore craue it, since we haue no reason
To feare our truth should hurt our cause. AVOC. 3.
Speake free.
VOLT. Then know, most honor'd fathers, I must now
Discouer, to your strangely'abused eares,
The most prodigious, and most frontlesse piece
Of solid impudence, and trecherie,
That euer vicious nature yet brought foorth
To shame the state of *Venice.* This lewd woman
(That wants no artificiall lookes, or teares,
To helpe the visor, she has now put on)
Hath long beene knowne a close adulteresse,
To that lasciuious youth there; not suspected,
I say, but knowne; and taken, in the act;
With him; and by this man, the easie husband,
Pardon'd: whose timelesse bounty makes him, now,
Stand here, the most vnhappie, innocent person,
That euer mans owne goodnesse made accus'd.
For these, not knowing how to owe a gift
Of that deare grace, but with their shame; being plac'd
So'aboue all powers of their gratitude,
Began to hate the benefit: and, in place
Of thankes, deuise t'extirpe the memorie
Of such an act. Wherein, I pray your father-hoods,
To obserue the malice, yea, the rage of creatures
Discouer'd in their euils; and what heart
Such take, euen, from their crimes. But that, anone,
Will more appeare. This gentleman, the father,

IV. v. 22 obey'd,] obey'd; *F2* *Exeunt Officers.* add G 33 foorth] forth *Q* 38 there;] there, *Q* 39 act;] act, *Q* 41 timelesse] timely *F3* 43 goodnesse] vertue *Q* 48 Of] Af *F1* *originally, as recorded by W. Bang* 49 act. Wherein] act: wherein *Q* 50 To obserue] T'observe *F2*

Hearing of this foule fact, with many others,
Which dayly strooke at his too-tender eares,
And, grieu'd in nothing more, then that he could not
Preserue him selfe a parent (his sonnes ills
Growing to that strange floud) at last decreed
To dis-inherit him. Avoc. 1. These be strange turnes!
Avoc. 2. The yong mans fame was euer faire, and honest.
Volt. So much more full of danger is his vice,
That can beguile so, vnder shade of vertue.
But as I said (my honour'd sires) his father
Hauing this setled purpose, (by what meanes
To him betray'd, we know not) and this day
Appointed for the deed; that parricide,
(I cannot stile him better) by confederacy
Preparing this his paramour to be there,
Entred Volpone's house (who was the man
Your father-hoods must vnderstand, design'd
For the inheritance) there, sought his father:
But, with what purpose sought he him, my lords?
(I tremble to pronounce it, that a sonne
Vnto a father, and to such a father
Should haue so foule, felonious intent)
It was, to murder him. When, being preuented
By his more happy absence, what then did he?
Not check his wicked thoughts; no, now new deeds:
(Mischiefe doth euer end, where it begins)
An act of horror, fathers! he drag'd forth
The aged gentleman, that had there lien, bed-red,
Three yeeres, and more, out off his innocent couch,
Naked, vpon the floore, there left him; wounded
His seruant in the face; and, with this strumpet,
The stale to his forg'd practise, who was glad
To be so actiue, (I shall here desire

IV. v. 55 Which] That *Q* strooke] struck *F2* 66 deed;] deed, *Q* 68 paramour] Paramour, *Q* 72 lords] *Sires* Q 79 euer] never *W. conj.* 81 bed-red] bed-rid *Q*, *F2* 84 strumpet,] Strumpet, *F3*: strumpet *Q*, *Ff* 85 forg'd] for'gd *Q*

Your father-hoods to note but my collections,
As most remarkable) thought, at once, to stop
His fathers ends; discredit his free choice,
In the old gentleman; redeeme themselues,
By laying infamy vpon this man,
To whom, with blushing, they should owe their liues.
AVOC. 1. What proofes haue you of this? BON. Most honour'd fathers,
I humbly craue, there be no credit giuen
To this mans mercenary tongue. AVOC. 2. Forbeare.
BON. His soule moues in his fee. AVOC. 3. O, sir.
BON. This fellow,
For six *sols* more, would pleade against his maker.
AVOC. 1. You do forget your selfe. VOLT. Nay, nay, graue fathers,
Let him haue scope: can any man imagine
That he will spare'his accuser, that would not
Haue spar'd his parent? AVO. 1. Well, produce your proofes.
CEL. I would I could forget, I were a creature.
VOLT. Signior CORBACCIO. AVO. 4. What is he?
VOLT. The father.
AVO. 2. Has he had an oth? NOT. Yes. CORB. What must I do now?
NOT. Your testimony's crau'd. CORB. Speake to the knaue?
I'le ha' my mouth, first, stopt with earth; my heart
Abhors his knowledge: I disclaime in him.
AVO. 1. But, for what cause? CORB. The meere portent of nature.
He is an vtter stranger, to my loines.
BON. Haue they made you to this! CORB. I will not heare thee,
Monster of men, swine, goate, wolfe, parricide,
Speake not, thou viper. BON. Sir, I will sit downe,

IV. V. 91 infamy] infamy, *Q* 97 *sols*] *souz* F2 99 scope:] scope; *Q* 103 After 'CORBACCIO.' [*Corbaccio comes forward.*] G 110 this!] this? *Q*

And rather wish my innocence should suffer,
Then I resist the authority of a father.
VOLT. Signior CORVINO. AVO. 2. This is strange!
AVO. 1. Who's this?
NOT. The husband. AVO. 4. Is he sworn? NOT. He is. AVO. 3. Speak then.
CORV. This woman (please your father-hoods) is a whore,
Of most hot exercise, more then a partrich,
Vpon record—— AVO. 1. No more. CORV. Neighes, like a iennet.
NOT. Preserue the honour of the court. CORV. I shall,
And modestie of your most reuerend eares.
And, yet, I hope that I may say, these eyes
Haue seene her glew'd vnto that peece of cedar;
That fine well-timber'd gallant: and that, here,
The letters may be read, thorough the horne,
That make the story perfect. MOS. Excellent! sir.
CORV. There is no shame in this, now, is there? MOS. None.
CORV. Or if I said, I hop'd that she were onward
To her damnation, if there be a hell
Greater then whore, and woman; a good catholique
May make the doubt. AVO. 3. His griefe hath made him frantique.
AVO. 1. Remoue him, hence. AVO. 2. Looke to the woman. CORV. Rare! *She swownes.*
Prettily fain'd! againe! AVO. 4. Stand from about her.
AVO. 1. Giue her the ayre. AVO. 3. What can you say? MOS. My wound
(May't please your wisdomes) speakes for me, receiu'd
In ayde of my good patron, when he mist
His sought-for father, when that well-taught dame

IV. v. 115 After 'CORVINO.' [*Corvino comes forward.*] G 119 iennet] gennet *Q* 126 Excellent !] Excellent, *Q* 127 shame] harme *Q* After 'there?' [*Aside to Mosca.*] G 130 catholique] *Christian* Q 132 *Stage direction not in Q* 137 sought-for] sought for *Q*

Had her cue giuen her, to cry out a rape.
BON. O, most lay'd impudence! Fathers—— AVO. 3. Sir, be silent,
You had your hearing free, so must they theirs.
AVO. 2. I do begin to doubt th'imposture here.
AVO. 4. This woman, has too many moodes. VOLT. Graue fathers,
She is a creature, of a most profest,
And prostituted lewdnesse. CORV. Most impetuous!
Vnsatisfied, graue fathers! VOLT. May her fainings
Not take your wisdomes: but, this day, she baited
A stranger, a graue knight, with her loose eyes,
And more lasciuious kisses. This man saw 'hem
Together, on the water, in a *gondola*.
MOS. Here is the lady her selfe, that saw 'hem too,
Without; who, then, had in the open streets
Pursu'd them, but for sauing her knights honour.
AVO. 1. Produce that lady. AVO. 2. Let her come. AVO. 4. These things,
They strike, with wonder! AVO. 3. I am turn'd a stone!

Act IIII. *Scene* VI.

MOSCA, LADY, AVOCATORI, &C.

BEe resolute, madame. LAD. I, this same is shee.
Out, thou *chameleon* harlot; now, thine eies
Vie teares with the *hyæna*: dar'st thou looke
Vpon my wronged face? I cry your pardons.
I feare, I haue (forgettingly) transgrest
Against the dignitie of the court—— AVO. 2. No, madame.
LAD. And beene exorbitant—— AVO. 4. You haue not, lady.

IV. v. 138 cue] *Qu:* Q 139 Fathers—] *Fathers.* Q 140 free,] free; *F2* 141 imposture] imposture, *Q* 145 VOLT.] VOLT, *Q* 152 Pursu'd] Pursew'd *Q* 153 After 'come.' *Exit Mosca.* G
IV. vi. *Re-enter Mosca with Lady Would-be.* G, continuing the scene. 1 *Pointing to Celia.* add G

AVO. 4. These proofes are strong. LAD. Surely, I had no purpose :
To scandalize your honours, or my sexes.
AVO. 3. We do beleeue it. LAD. Surely, you may beleeue it.
AVO. 2. Madame, we do. LAD. Indeede, you may; my breeding
Is not so course—— AVO. 4. We know it. LAD. To offend
With pertinacy—— AVO. 3. Lady. LAD. Such a presence :
No, surely. AVO. 1. We well thinke it. LAD. You may thinke it.
AVO. 1. Let her o'recome. What witnesses haue you,
To make good your report ? BON. Our consciences.
CEL. And heauen, that neuer failes the innocent.
AVO. 4. These are no testimonies. BON. Not in your courts,
Where multitude, and clamour ouercomes.
AVO. 1. Nay, then you do waxe insolent. VOLT. Here, here,
The testimonie comes, that will conuince, *Volpone is brought in, as impotent.*
And put to vtter dumbnesse their bold tongues.
See here, graue fathers, here's the rauisher,
The rider on mens wiues, the great impostor,
The grand voluptuary ! do you not think,
These limbes should affect *venery ?* or these eyes
Couet a concubine ? 'pray you, marke these hands.
Are they not fit to stroake a ladies brests ?
Perhaps, he doth dissemble ? BON. So he do's.
VOLT. Would you ha' him tortur'd ? BON. I would haue him prou'd.
VOLT. Best try him, then, with goades, or burning irons;

IV. vi. 8 Avo. 4. *Q, Ff* : *query* Avo. 1 : *F3 substitutes* Avo. 2. *in l.* 7 purpose :] purpose, *Q* : purpose *F2* 13 presence :] presence ; *Q* 16 consciences.] consciences : *Q* 18 Not] Not, *Q* 21 *Stage direction not in Q* 22 dumbnesse] dumbnesse, *Q* 25 voluptuary !] Voluptuary : *Q* 29 dissemble ?] dissemble. *Q* 31 irons] Irons *Q, Ff*

Put him to the strappado: I haue heard,
The racke hath cur'd the gout, faith, giue it him,
And helpe him of a maladie, be courteous.
I'le vndertake, before these honour'd fathers,
He shall haue, yet, as many left diseases,
As she has knowne adulterers, or thou strumpets.
O, my most equall hearers, if these deedes,
Acts, of this bold, and most exorbitant straine,
May passe with sufferance, what one citizen,
But owes the forfeit of his life, yea fame,
To him that dares traduce him? which of you
Are safe, my honour'd fathers? I would aske
(With leaue of your graue father-hoods) if their plot
Haue any face, or colour like to truth?
Or if, vnto the dullest nostrill, here,
It smell not rancke, and most abhorred slander?
I craue your care of this good gentleman,
Whose life is much indanger'd, by their fable;
And, as for them, I will conclude with this,
That vicious persons when they are hot, and flesh'd
In impious acts, their constancy abounds:
Damn'd deeds are done with greatest confidence.
  Avoc. 1. Take 'hem to custody, and seuer them.
  Avoc. 2. 'Tis pittie, two such prodigies should liue.
  Avoc. 1. Let the old gentleman be return'd, with care:
I'am sorry, our credulitie wrong'd him.
  Avo. 4. These are two creatures! Avo. 3. I haue an earthquake in me!
  Avo. 2. Their shame (euen in their cradles) fled their faces.
  Avo. 4. You'haue done a worthy seruice to the state, sir,
In their discouerie. Avo. 1. You shall heare, ere night,
What punishment the court decrees vpon 'hem.

IV. vi. 33 gout,] *goute*; Q 34 courteous.] courteous: *Q* 35 honour'd] honor'd *Q* 40 sufferance,] suffrance; *Q* 43 honour'd] honord *Q* 51 they are] they'are *F2* 56 care :] care; *Q* *Exeunt Officers with Volpone.* add G 61 After 'discouerie.' [*To Volt.*] G After 62 *Exeunt Avocat. Not. and Officers with Bonario and Celia.* G

VOLT. We thanke your fatherhoods. How like you it? MOS. Rare.
I'ld ha' your tongue, sir, tipt with gold, for this;
I'ld ha' you be the heire to the whole citie;
The earth I'ld haue want men, ere you want liuing:
They'are bound to erect your statue, in St. MARKES.
Signior CORVINO, I would haue you goe,
And shew your selfe, that you haue conquer'd. CORV. Yes.
MOS. It was much better, that you should professe
Your selfe a cuckold, thus, then that the other
Should haue beene prou'd. CORV. Nay, I consider'd that:
Now, it is her fault. MOS. Then, it had beene yours.
CORV. True, I doe doubt this Aduocate, still. MOS. I'faith,
You need not, I dare ease you of that care.
CORV. I trust thee, MOSCA. MOS. As your owne soule, sir. CORB. MOSCA.
MOS. Now for your businesse, sir. CORB. How? ha' you busines?
MOS. Yes, yours, sir. CORB. O, none else? MOS. None else, not I.
CORB. Be carefull then. MOS. Rest you, with both your eyes, sir.
CORB. Dispatch it. MOS. Instantly. CORB. And looke, that all,
What-euer, be put in, iewels, plate, moneyes,
Household-stuffe, bedding, cortines. MOS. Cortine-rings, sir,
Onely, the Aduocates fee must be deducted.
CORB. I'le pay him, now: you'll be too prodigall.
MOS. Sir, I must tender it. CORB. Two *cecchines* is well?

IV. vi. 67 to erect] t'erect *Q* 73 fault.] fault: *Q* 76 After 'MOSCA.' [*Exit.*] G your] your, *Q* 79 carefull] carefull, *Q* 80 it.] it, *Q* 82 cortines . . . Cortine-] curtines . . . Curtine- *Q*

Mos. No, six, sir. Corb. 'Tis too much. Mos. He talk'd a great while,
You must consider that, sir. Corb. Well, there's three——
Mos. I'le giue it him. Corb. Doe so, and there's for thee.
Mos. Bountifull bones! What horride strange offence
Did he commit 'gainst nature, in his youth,
Worthy this age? you see, sir, how I worke
Vnto your ends; take you no notice. Volt. No,
I'le leaue you. Mos. All, is yours; the deuill, and all:
Good Aduocate. Madame, I'le bring you home.
Lad. No, I'le goe see your patron. Mos. That you shall not:
I'le tell you, why. My purpose is, to vrge
My patron to reforme his will; and, for
The zeale you' haue shew'n to day, whereas before
You were but third, or fourth, you shall be now
Put in the first: which would appeare as beg'd,
If you were present. Therefore—— Lad. You shall sway me.

Act v. *Scene* i.

Volpone.

WEll, I am here; and all this brunt is past:
I ne're was in dislike with my disguise,
Till this fled moment; here, 'twas good, in priuate,
But, in your publike, *Caue*, whil'st I breathe.
'Fore god, my left legge 'gan to haue the crampe;
And I apprehended, straight, some power had strooke me
With a dead palsey: well, I must be merry,

IV. vi. 86 while,] while; *F2* 88 *Exit.* add *Q* 91 After 'age?' [*Aside.*] G 93 After 'you.' *Exit.* G all:] all, *Q* 99 or *Q*, *F2*: or, *F1* 101 were] be *Q* *Exeunt.* add G V. i. ACT V. SCENE I. | *A Room in Volpone's House.* | *Enter Volpone.* G 2 ne're] nêre *Q* 3 priuate,] private; *F2* 4 breathe] breath *Q* 5 god] God *Q* 6 apprehended] apprênded *Q* strooke] struck *F2*

And shake it off. A many of these feares
Would put me into some villanous disease,
Should they come thick vpon me: I'le preuent 'hem.
Giue me a boule of lustie wine, to fright
This humor from my heart; (hum, hum, hum) *He drinkes.*
'Tis almost gone, already: I shall conquer.
Any deuice, now, of rare, ingenious knauery,
That would possesse me with a violent laughter,
Would make me vp, againe! So, so, so, so. *Drinkes againe.*
This heate is life; 'tis bloud, by this time: MOSCA!

Act V. *Scene* II.

MOSCA, VOLPONE, NANO,
CASTRONE.

HOw now, sir? do's the day looke cleare againe?
Are we recouer'd? and wrought out of error,
Into our way? to see our path, before vs?
Is our trade free, once more? VOLP. Exquisite MOSCA!
MOS. Was it not carry'd learnedly? VOLP. And stoutly.
Good wits are greatest in extremities.
MOS. It were a folly, beyond thought, to trust
Any grand act vnto a cowardly spirit:
You are not taken with it, enough, me thinkes?
VOLP. O, more, then if I had enioy'd the wench:
The pleasure of all woman-kind's not like it.
MOS. Why, now you speake, sir. We must, here, be fixt;
Here, we must rest; this is our master-peece:
We cannot thinke, to goe beyond this. VOLP. True,
Thou'hast playd thy prise, my precious MOSCA. MOS. Nay, sir,
To gull the court—— VOLP. And, quite diuert the torrent,

v. i. 12, 16 *Stage directions not in Q* 12 *drinkes*] *doinkes* F2
v. ii. *Enter Mosca.* G, continuing the scene 11 woman-] wóman- *Q*
12 here,] here *Q, Ff* 13 master-] maister- *Q*

Vpon the innocent. Mos. Yes, and to make
So rare a musique out of discordes—— Volp. Right.
That, yet, to me's the strangest! how th'hast borne it!
That these (being so diuided 'mongst themselues)
Should not sent some-what, ór in me, or thee,
Or doubt their owne side. Mos. True, they will not see't.
Too much light blinds 'hem, I thinke. Each of 'hem
Is so possest, and stuft with his owne hopes,
That any thing, vnto the contrary,
Neuer so true, or neuer so apparent,
Neuer so palpable, they will resist it——
Volp. Like a temptation of the diuell. Mos. Right, sir.
Merchants may talke of trade, and your great signiors
Of land, that yeelds well; but if *Italy*
Haue any glebe, more fruitfull, then these fellowes,
I am deceiu'd. Did not your Aduocate rare?
Volp. O (my most honor'd fathers, my graue fathers,
Vnder correction of your father-hoods,
What face of truth, is here? If these strange deeds
May passe, most honour'd fathers——) I had much a doe
To forbeare laughing. Mos. 'T seem'd to mee, you sweat, sir.
Volp. In troth, I did a little. Mos. But confesse, sir,
Were you not daunted? Volp. In good faith, I was
A little in a mist; but not deiected:
Neuer, but still my selfe. Mos. I thinke it, sir.
Now (so truth helpe me) I must needes say this, sir,
And, out of conscience, for your aduocate:
He' has taken paines, in faith, sir, and deseru'd,
(In my poore iudgement, I speake it, vnder fauour,
Not to contrary you, sir) very richly——

v. ii. 18 musique] *Musique,* Q 22 True, they] True. They *Q* see't.] see't; *Q* 23 thinke. Each] thinke: each *Q* 28 diuell] Deuill *Q* 31 fruitfull] fruictfull *Q* 33–6 (my . . . fathers—)] *my* . . . Fathers— Q, *which prints the mock-quotations in italic* 35 truth, is] truth is, *Q, Ff* 38 did] did, *Q originally, but the comma, faintly printed, disappeared* 41 sir.] sir *F1* 42 sir,] Sir, *Q*: sir. *Ff* 43 conscience,] conscience; *Q* 45–6 (In . . . sir)] In . . . Sir, *Q*

Well—to be cosen'd. VOLP. 'Troth, and I thinke so too,
By that I heard him, in the latter end.
MOS. O, but before, sir; had you heard him, first,
Draw it to certaine heads, then aggrauate,
Then vse his vehement figures—— I look'd still,
When he would shift a shirt; and, doing this
Out of pure loue, no hope of gaine—— VOLP. 'Tis right.
I cannot answer him, MOSCA, as I would,
Not yet; but for thy sake, at thy intreaty,
I will beginne, eu'n now, to vexe 'hem all:
This very instant. MOS. Good, sir. VOLP. Call the dwarfe,
And eunuch, forth. MOS. CASTRONE, NANO. NAN. Here.
VOLP. Shal we haue a jig, now? MOS. What you please, sir. VOLP. Go,
Streight, giue out, about the streetes, you two,
That I am dead; doe it with constancy,
Sadly, doe you heare? impute it to the griefe
Of this late slander. MOS. What doe you meane, sir?
VOLP. O,
I shall haue, instantly, my vulture, crow,
Rauen, come flying hither (on the newes)
To peck for carrion, my shee-wolfe, and all,
Greedy, and full of expectation——
MOS. And then to haue it rauish'd from their mouthes?
VOLP. 'Tis true, I will ha' thee put on a gowne,
And take vpon thee, as thou wert mine heire;
Shew 'hem a will: open that chest, and reach
Forth one of those, that has the blankes. I'le straight
Put in thy name. MOS. It will be rare, sir. VOLP. I,
When they e'ene gape, and finde themselues deluded——
MOS. Yes. VOLP. And thou vse them skiruily. Dispatch,

v. ii. 48 latter] later *Q* 56 eu'n] euen *Q* 58 After 'NANO.' *Enter Castrone and Nano.* G 62 Sadly,] Sadly; *F2* 63 After 'slander.' [*Exeunt Cast. and Nano.*] G 71 will:] Will; *Q* 73 After 'sir.' [*Gives him a paper.*] G I,] I *Q* 74 e'ene] ev'n *F2* deluded—] deluded, *Q* 75 And] And, *Q*

Get on thy gowne. Mos. But, what, sir, if they aske
After the body? Volp. Say, it was corrupted.
Mos. I'le say, it stunke, sir; and was faine t'haue it
Coffin'd vp instantly, and sent away.
Volp. Any thing, what thou wilt. Hold, here's my will.
Get thee a cap, a count-booke, pen and inke,
Papers afore thee; sit, as thou wert taking
An inuentory of parcels: I'le get vp,
Behind the cortine, on a stoole, and harken;
Sometime, peepe ouer; see, how they doe looke;
With what degrees, their bloud doth leaue their faces!
O, 'twill afford me a rare meale of laughter.
Mos. Your Aduocate will turne stark dull, vpon it.
Volp. It will take off his oratories edge.
Mos. But your *Clarissimo*, old round-backe, he
Will crumpe you, like a hog-louse, with the touch.
Volp. And what Corvino? Mos. O, sir, looke for him,
To morrow morning, with a rope, and a dagger,
To visite all the streetes; he must runne mad.
My Lady too, that came into the court,
To beare false witnesse, for your worship—— Volp. Yes,
And kist mee 'fore the fathers; when my face
Flow'd all with oyles. Mos. And sweate, sir. Why, your gold
Is such another med'cine, it dries vp
All those offensiue sauors! It transformes
The most deformed, and restores 'hem louely,
Cestus. As 't were the strange poeticall girdle. Iove
Could not inuent, t'himselfe, a shroud more subtile,
To passe Acrisivs guardes. It is the thing
Makes all the world her grace, her youth, her beauty.

v. ii. 76 Mos.] *Mos.* [*putting on a gown.*] G 77 corrupted.] corrupted, *Q* 84 cortine] curtine *Q* 86 faces!] faces; *Q* 88 Mos.] *Mos.* [*putting on a cap, and setting out the table, &c.*] G 97 kist] kisse *F2* 98 sweate,] sweate— *Q* 102 *Marginal note not in Q*

VOLP. I thinke, she loues me. MOS. Who? the lady, sir?
Shee's iealous of you. VOLP. Do'st thou say so? MOS. Harke,
There's some already. VOLP. Looke. MOS. It is the vulture:
He has the quickest sent. VOLP. I'le to my place,
Thou, to thy posture. MOS. I am set. VOLP. But, MOSCA,
Play the artificer now, torture 'hem, rarely.

Act V. *Scene* III.

VOLTORE, MOSCA, CORBACCIO, CORVINO, LADY, VOLPONE.

HOw now, my MOSCA? MOS. Turkie carpets, nine——
VOLT. Taking an inuentory? that is well.
MOS. Two sutes of bedding, tissew—— VOLT. Where's the will?
Let me read that, the while. CORB. So, set me downe:
And get you home. VOLT. Is he come, now, to trouble vs?
MOS. Of cloth of gold, two more—— CORB. Is it done, MOSCA?
MOS. Of seuerall vellets, eight—— VOLT. I like his care.
CORB. Dost thou not heare? CORV. Ha? is the houre come, MOSCA?
VOLP. I, now, they muster. CORV. What do's the aduocate here? *Volpone peepes from behinde a trauerse.*

v. ii. 107 After 'so?' [*Knocking within.*] G 108 some] some, *Q* 110 After 'posture.' [*Goes behind the curtain.*] G v. iii.] *Enter Voltore.* G, continuing the scene 1–78 *Q italicizes quotations from the inventory* 1 Mos.] *Mos.* [*writing.*] G 4 After 'while.' *Enter Servants with Corbaccio in a chair.* G 5 And] And, *Q* After 'home.' [*Exeunt Servants.*] G 7 vellets] velvets *F2* 8 After 'heare?' [*Enter Corvino.*] G the houre] th'houre *Q* 9 aduocate] Aduocate, *Q* St. dir. not in *Q*

Or this CORBACCIO? CORB. What do these here?
LAD. MOSCA?
Is his thred spunne? MOS. Eight chests of linnen——
VOLP. O,
My fine dame WOVLD-BEE, too! CORV. MOSCA, the will,
That I may shew it these, and rid 'hem hence.
MOS. Six chests of diaper, foure of damaske—— There.
CORB. Is that the will? MOS. Down-beds, and boulsters—— VOLP. Rare!
Be busie still. Now, they begin to flutter:
They neuer thinke of me. Looke, see, see, see!
How their swift eies runne ouer the long deed,
Vnto the name, and to the legacies,
What is bequeath'd them, there—— MOS. Ten sutes of hangings——
VOLP. I, i'their garters, MOSCA. Now, their hopes
Are at the gaspe. VOLT. MOSCA the heire! CORB. What's that?
VOLP. My aduocate is dumbe, looke to my merchant,
Hee has heard of some strange storme, a ship is lost,
He faints: my lady will swoune. Old glazen-eyes,
He hath not reach'd his dispaire, yet. CORB. All these
Are out of hope, I'am sure the man. CORV. But, MOSCA——
MOS. Two cabenets—— CORV. Is this in earnest? MOS. One
Of ebony.—— CORV. Or, do you but delude me?
MOS. The other, mother of pearle—I am very busie.
Good faith, it is a fortune throwne vpon me——
Item, one salt of agat——not my seeking.
LAD. Do you heare, sir? MOS. A perfum'd boxe—— 'pray you forebeare,

v. iii. 10 After 'here?' [*Enter Lady Pol. Would-be.*] G After 14 *Gives them the Will carelessly, over his shoulder.* G 22 heire!] heire? *Q* 24 lost,] lost: *Q* 25 faints: my] faintes. My *Q* 26 He] Hé *Q* 27 After 'man.' [*Takes the Will.*] G 28 cabenets] *Cabinets* Q

You see I am troubled——made of an *onyx*—— LAD. How!

MOS. To morrow, or next day, I shall be at leasure,
To talke with you all. CORV. Is this my large hopes issue?

LAD. Sir, I must haue a fayrer answer. MOS. Madame!
Mary, and shall: 'pray you, fairely quit my house.
Nay, raise no tempest with your lookes; but, harke you:
Remember, what your ladiship offred me,
To put you in, an heire; goe to, thinke on't.
And what you said, eene your best madames did
For maintenance, and, why not you? inough.
Goe home, and vse the poore sir POL, your knight, well;
For feare I tell some riddles: go, be melancholique.

VOLP. O, my fine diuell! CORV. MOSCA, 'pray you a word.

MOS. Lord! will not you take your dispatch hence, yet?
Me thinkes (of all) you should haue beene th'example.
Why should you stay, here? with what thought? what promise?
Heare you, doe not you know, I know you an asse?
And, that you would, most faine, haue beene a wittoll,
If fortune would haue let you? that you are
A declar'd cuckold, on good termes? this pearle,
You'll say, was yours? right: this diamant?
I'le not deny't, but thanke you. Much here, else?
It may be so. Why, thinke that these good works
May helpe to hide your bad: I'le not betray you,
Although you be but extraordinary,
And haue it onely in title, it sufficeth.
Go home, be melancholique too, or mad.

v. iii. 37 Madame!] Madame? *Q* 40 offred] offerd *Q* 45 riddles:] riddles; *Q* melancholique] melancholy *F3*: *so* 60 *Exit Lady Would-be.* add G 46 diuell] Deuill *Q* 50 you, doe] you; do *Q* 51 would,] would; *Q* 57 your *Q, F2*: you *F1* 60 home,] home; *Q* melancholique too,] melancholique, too: *Q* *Exit Corvino.* add G

VOLP. Rare, MOSCA! how his villany becomes him!
VOLT. Certaine, he doth delude all these, for me.
CORB. MOSCA, the heire? VOLP. O, his foure eyes haue found it!
CORB. I'am cosen'd, cheated, by a parasite-slaue;
Harlot, t⟨h⟩'hast gul'd me. MOS. Yes, sir. Stop your mouth,
Or I shall draw the onely tooth, is left.
Are not you he, that filthy couetous wretch,
With the three legges, that here, in hope of prey,
Haue, any time this three yeere, snuft about,
With your most grou'ling nose; and would haue hir'd
Me to the pois'ning of my patron? sir?
Are not you he, that haue, to day, in court,
Profess'd the dis-inheriting of your sonne?
Periur'd your selfe? Go home, and die, and stinke;
If you but croake a sillable, all comes out:
Away and call your porters, go, go, stinke.
VOLP. Excellent varlet! VOLT. Now, my faithfull MOSCA,
I finde thy constancie. MOS. Sir? VOLT. Sincere. MOS. A table
Of porphiry——I mar'le, you'll be thus troublesome.
VOLT. Nay, leaue off now, they are gone. MOS. Why? who are you?
What? who did send for you? O 'cry you mercy,
Reuerend sir! good faith, I am greeu'd for you,
That any chance of mine should thus defeate
Your (I must needs say) most deseruing trauels:
But, I protest, sir, it was cast vpon me,
And I could, almost, wish to be without it,
But, that the will o' th' dead, must be obseru'd.
Mary, my ioy is, that you need it not,
You haue a gift, sir, (thanke your education)
Will neuer let you want, while there are men,

v. iii. 61 Rare,] Rare *Q* him!] him. *Q* 63 MOSCA,] *Mosca Q* it!] it. *Q* 76 After 'porters,' [*Exit Corbaccio.*] G 78 Mos.] *Mos.* [*writing.*] G 82 sir!] Sir: *Q* 84 trauels] trauailes *Q* 87 dead,] dead *Q*

And malice, to breed causes. Would I had
But halfe the like, for all my fortune, sir.
If I haue any suites (as I doe hope,
Things being so easie, and direct, I shall not)
I wil make bold with your obstreperous aide,
(Conceiue me) for your fee, sir. In meane time,
You, that haue so much law, I know ha' the conscience,
Not to be couetous of what is mine.
Good sir, I thanke you for my plate: 'twill helpe
To set vp a yong man. Good faith, you looke
As you were costiue; best go home, and purge, sir.
VOLP. Bid him, eat lettuce well: my wittie *mischiefe*,
Let me embrace thee. O, that I could now
Transforme thee to a VENVS—— MOSCA, goe,
Streight, take my habit of *Clarissimo;*
And walke the streets; be seene, torment 'hem more:
We must pursew, as well as plot. Who would
Haue lost this feast? MOS. I doubt it will loose them.
VOLP. O, my recouery shall recouer all.
That I could now but thinke on some disguise,
To meet 'hem in: and aske 'hem questions.
How I would vexe 'hem still, at euery turne?
MOS. Sir, I can fit you. VOLP. Canst thou? MOS. Yes, I know
One o' the *Commandadori*, sir, so like you,
Him will I streight make drunke, and bring you his habit.
VOLP. A rare disguise, and answering thy braine!
O, I will be a sharpe disease vnto 'hem.
MOS. Sir, you must looke for curses—— VOLP. Till they burst;
The *Foxe* fares euer best, when he is curst.

v. iii. 91 malice, *corr. Q, Ff*: malice *Q originally* 99 you] you, *Q* 101 *Exit Voltore.* add G 102 VOLP.] *Volp.* [*comes from behind the curtain.*] G 105 *Clarissimo;*] *Clarissimo,* Q 107 pursew] pursue *F2* 108 doubt] doubt, *Q* loose] lose *F2* 109 all.] all, *Q* 114 *Commandadori* Q: *Commandatori* Ff 119 *Exeunt.* add G

Act V. *Scene* IIII.

PEREGRINE, MERCATORI. 3. WOMAN, POLITIQVE.

AM I enough disguis'd? MER. I. I warrant you.
PER. All my ambition is to fright him, onely.
MER. 2. If you could ship him away, 'twere excellent.
MER. 3. To *Zant*, or to *Alepo?* PER. Yes, and ha' his
Aduentures put i' th' *booke of voyages*,
And his guld story registred, for truth?
Well, gentlemen, when I am in, a while,
And that you thinke vs warme in our discourse,
Know your approaches. MER. I. Trust it to our care.
PER. Saue you, faire lady. Is sir POLL. within?
WOM. I do not know, sir. PER. 'Pray you, say vnto him,
Here is a merchant, vpon earnest businesse,
Desires to speake with him. WOM. I will see, sir. PER. 'Pray you.
I see, the family is all female, here.
WOM. He sai's, sir, he has waighty affaires of state,
That now require him whole, some other time
You may possesse him. PER. 'Pray you, say againe,
If those require him whole, these will exact him,
Whereof I bring him tidings. What might be
His graue affaire of state, now? how, to make
Bolognian sauseges, here, in *Venice*, sparing
One o' th' ingredients. WOM. Sir, he sai's, he knowes
By your word, tidings, that you are no states-man,
And therefore, wills you stay. PER. Sweet, 'pray you returne him,

v. iv.] SCENE II. | *A Hall in sir Politick's House.* | *Enter Peregrine disguised, and three Merchants.* G 3 excellent.] excellent, *Q* 4 ha' his] haue's *Q* 7 while,] while; *Q* 9 it] it, *Q* *Exeunt Merchants.* add G After 9 *Enter Waiting-woman.* G 13 After 'sir.' [*Exit.*] G After 14 *Re-enter Waiting-woman.* G 16, 18 whole,] whole; *Q* 17 you, *Q*: you *F1* 19 After 'tidings.' [*Exit Woman.*] G 22 After 'ingredients.' [*Re-enter Waiting-woman.*] G

I haue not read so many proclamations,
And studied them, for words, as he has done,
But—— Here he deignes to come. POL. Sir, I must craue
Your courteous pardon. There hath chanc'd (to day)
Vnkinde disaster, 'twixt my lady, and mee:
And I was penning my apologie
To giue her satifaction, as you came, now.
PER. Sir, I am grieu'd, I bring you worse disaster;
The gentleman, you met at th' port, to day,
That told you, he was newly arriu'd—— POL. I, was
A fugitiue punke? PER. No, sir, a spie, set on you:
And, he has made relation to the Senate,
That you profest to him, to haue a plot,
To sell the state of *Venice*, to the *Turke*.
POL. O me! PER. For which, warrants are sign'd by this time,
To apprehend you, and to search your study,
For papers—— POL. Alasse, sir. I haue none, but notes,
Drawne out of play-bookes—— PER. All the better, sir.
POL. And some essayes. What shall I doe? PER. Sir, best
Conuay your selfe into a sugar-chest,
Or, if you could lie round, a fraile were rare:
And I could send you, aboard. POL. Sir, I but talk'd so,
For discourse sake, merely. PER. Harke, they are there. *They knocke without.*
POL. I am a wretch, a wretch. PER. What, will you doe, sir?
Ha' you ne're a curren-but to leape into?
They'll put you to the racke, you must be sudden.
POL. Sir, I haue an ingine—— (MER. 3. Sir POLITIQVE WOVLD-BE?

v. iv. 27 But— Here] But, here *Q* After 'come.' *Exit Woman.* | *Enter Sir Politick.* G Sir,] Sir! *Q* 28 pardon.] pardon; *Q* 29 'twixt] 'twixt *Q* 35 fugitiue punke] fugitiue-*Punke* Q you:] you, *Q* 39 O me!] O' mee. *Q* 44 selfe] selfe, *Q* (*comma faint*) 45 could] would *F2* 47 *Stage direction not in Q* 49 Ha' *F2*: Ha *Q, F1* 50 sudden] sodaine *Q* 51–2 (MER. . . . he?)] MER. . . . hee? *Q*

MER. 2. Where is he?) POL. That I haue thought vpon, before time.
PER. What is it? POL. (I shall ne're indure the torture.)
Mary, it is, sir, of a tortoyse-shell,
Fitted, for these extremities: 'pray you sir, helpe me.
Here, I' haue a place, sir, to put backe my leggs,
(Please you to lay it on, sir) with this cap,
And my blacke gloues, I'le lye, sir, like a tortoyse,
Till they are gone. PER. And, call you this an ingine?
POL. Mine owne deuice—— good sir, bid my wiues women
They rush in. To burne my papers. MER. I. Where's he hid? MER. 3. We must,
And will, sure, find him. MER. 2. Which is his study? MER. I. What
Are you, sir? PER. I' am a merchant, that came heere
To looke vpon this tortoyse. MER. 3. How? MER. I. St. MARKE!
What beast is this? PER. It is a fish. MER. 2. Come out, here.
PER. Nay, you may strike him, sir, and tread vpon him:
Hee'll beare a cart. MER. I. What, to runne ouer him? PER. Yes.
MER. 3. Let's iump, vpon him. MER. 2. Can he not go? PER. He creeps, sir.
MER. I. Let's see him creepe. PER. No, good sir, you will hurt him.
MER. 2. (Heart) I'le see him creepe; or pricke his guts.
MER. 3. Come out, here. PER. 'Pray you sir, (creepe a little) MER. I. Foorth.

v. iv. 53 (I . . . torture.)] I . . . torture. *Q* ne're] nêre *Q* 55 Fitted] Apted *Q* 57 (Please . . . sir)] Please . . . Sir, *Q* After 'sir' [*Lies down while Per. places the shell upon him.*] G 59 gone.] gone, *Q* 60 wiues] wifes *Q* 61 After 'papers.' [*Exit Per.*] G *Stage direction not in Q* 62 After 'study?' [*Re-enter Peregrine.*] G 67 Yes.] Yes. (sir *F2, taking the last word of l. 68, printed above the end of the line in F1* 68 him.] him; *Q* He creeps, sir.] *He creepes, Sir.* corr. Q (*creepes* Q originally), italicizing as if it were a stage direction 71 After 'little' [*Aside to sir Pol.*] G Foorth] Forth *Q*

MER. 2. Yet furder. PER. Good sir, (creep) MER. 2. We'll see his legs.

MER. 3. Gods'so, he has garters! MER. 1. I, and gloues! MER. 2. Is this
Your fearefull tortoyse? PER. Now, sir POLL. we are euen;
For your next proiect, I shall be prepar'd:
I am sorry, for the funerall of your notes, sir.

They pull of the shell and discouer him.

MER. 1. 'Twere a rare motion, to be seene in *Fleet-street!*

MER. 2. I, i'the terme. MER. 1. Or *Smithfield*, in the faire.

MER. 3. Me thinkes, tis but a melancholique sight!

PER. Farewell, most politique tortoyse. POL. Where's my lady?
Knowes shee of this? WOM. I know not, sir. POL. Enquire.
O, I shall be the fable of all feasts;
The freight of the *gazetti;* ship-boyes tale;
And, which is worst, euen talke for ordinaries.

WOM. My lady's come most melancholique, home,
And say's, sir, she will straight to sea, for physick.

POL. And I, to shunne, this place, and clime for euer;
Creeping, with house, on backe: and thinke it well,
To shrinke my poore head, in my politique shell.

Act V. *Scene* V.

VOLPONE, MOSCA.

The first, in the habit of a Commandadore: the other, of a Clarissimo.

AM I then like him? MOS. O; sir, you are he:
No man can seuer you. VOLP. Good. MOS. But, what am I?

VOLP. 'Fore heau'n, a braue *Clarissimo*, thou becom'st it!

v. iv. 72 furder] farther *F2* 73 *Stage direction not in Q* 74 PER.] *Per.* [*discovering himself.*] G 79, 85 melancholique] melancholy *F3* 80 After 'tortoyse.' *Exeunt Per. and Merchants.* | *Re-enter Waiting-Woman.* G 80 Where's *corr. Q, Ff*: where's *Q originally* 89 shell. *corr. Q*: shell, *Q originally* *Exeunt.* add G v. v. Misnumbered Act IV in *Q, Ff, F3* *Marginal note not in Q* SCENE III | *A Room in Volpone's House.* | *Enter Mosca in the habit of a clarissimo, and Volpone in that of a commandadore.* G

Pitty, thou wert not borne one. Mos. If I hold
My made one, 'twill be well. Volp. I'le goe, and see
What newes, first, at the court. Mos. Doe so. My
Foxe
Is out on his hole, and, ere he shall re-enter,
I'le make him languish, in his borrow'd case,
Except he come to composition, with me:
Androgino, Castrone, Nano. All. Here.
Mos. Goe recreate your selues, abroad; goe, sport:
So, now I haue the keies, and am possest.
Since he will, needes, be dead, afore his time,
I'le burie him, or gaine by him. I'am his heire:
And so will keepe me, till he share at least.
To cosen him of all, were but a cheat
Well plac'd; no man would construe it a sinne:
Let his sport pay for't, this is call'd the Foxe-trap.

Act V. *Scene* VI.

Corbaccio, Corvino, Volpone.

THey say, the court is set. Corv. We must maintaine
Our first tale good, for both our reputations.
Corb. Why? mine's no tale: my sonne would, there, haue kild me.
Corv. That's true, I had forgot: mine is, I am sure.
But, for your will, sir. Corb. I, I'le come vpon him,
For that, hereafter, now his Patron's dead.
Volp. Signior Corvino! and Corbaccio! sir,
Much ioy vnto you. Corv. Of what? Volp. The sodaine good,
Dropt downe vpon you—— Corb. Where? Volp. (And, none knowes how)

v. v. 5 After 'well.' [*Aside.*] G 6 After 'court.' [*Exit.*] G 10 After 'Nano.' [*Enter Androgyno, Castrone, and Nano.*] G 11 Goe] Go, *Q* *Exeunt.* add G 14 him.] him; *Q* 18 *Exit.* add G v. vi.] SCENE IV. | *A Street.* | *Enter Corbaccio and Corvino.* G 4 forgot:] forgot; *Q* After 'sure.' *Aside.* G 6 hereafter,] hereafter; *Q* After 6 *Enter Volpone.* G

From old VOLPONE, sir. CORB. Out, errant knaue.
VOLP. Let not your too much wealth, sir, make you furious.
CORB. Away, thou varlet. VOLP. Why sir? CORB. Do'st thou mocke me?
VOLP. You mocke the world, sir, did you not change wills?
CORB. Out, harlot. VOLP. O! belike you are the man,
Signior CORVINO? 'faith, you carry it well;
You grow not mad withall: I loue your spirit.
You are not ouer-leauen'd, with your fortune.
You should ha' some would swell, now, like a wine-fat,
With such an *Autumne*—— Did he gi' you all, sir?
CORV. Auoid, you rascall. VOLP. Troth, your wife has shew'ne
Her selfe a very woman: but, you are well,
You neede not care, you haue a good estate,
To beare it out, sir, better by this chance.
Except CORBACCIO haue a share? CORB. Hence, varlet.
VOLP. You will not be a'knowne, sir: why, 'tis wise.
Thus doe all gam'sters, at all games, dissemble.
No man will seeme to winne. Here, comes my vulture,
Heauing his beake vp i' the ayre, and snuffing.

Act V. *Scene* VII.

VOLTORE, VOLPONE.

OVt-stript thus, by a parasite? a slaue?
Would run on errands? and make legs, for crummes?
Well, what I'le do—— VOLP. The court staies for your worship.

v. vi. 18 now, *Q*, *F2*: now *F1* 23 sir,] Sir: *Q* 25 why, *Q*: why *Ff* 26 dissemble.] dissemble; *Q* 27 winne. Here] winne: here *Q*: win. [*Exeunt Corvino and Corbaccio.*]—Here *G* v. vii.] *Enter Voltore.* G, continuing the scene 3 your *Q*, *F2*: you *F1*

I eêne reioyce, sir, at your worships happinesse,
And that it fell into so learned hands,
That vnderstand the fingering.—— VOLT. What doe you meane?
VOLP. I meane to be a sutor to your worship,
For the small tenement, out of reparations;
That, at the end of your long row of houses,
By the *piscaria*: it was, in VOLPONE's time,
Your predecessor, ere he grew diseas'd,
A handsome, pretty, custom'd, bawdy-house,
As any was in *Venice* (none disprais'd)
But fell with him; his body, and that house
Decay'd, together. VOLT. Come, sir, leaue your prating.
VOLP. Why, if your worship giue me but your hand,
That I may ha' the refusall; I haue done.
'Tis a meere toy, to you, sir; candle rents:
As your learn'd worship knowes—— VOLT. What doe I know?
VOLP. Mary no end of your wealth, sir, god decrease it.
VOLT. Mistaking knaue! what, mock'st thou my misfortune?
VOLP. His blessing on your heart, sir, would 'twere more.
(Now, to my first, againe; at the next corner.)

Act V. *Scene* VIII.

CORBACCIO, CORVINO, (MOSCA, *passant*) VOLPONE.

SEe, in our habite! see the impudent varlet!
CORV. That I could shoote mine eies at him, like gun-stones.
VOLP. But, is this true, sir, of the parasite?

v. vii. 6 fingering.—] fingering. *Q* 7 VOLP.] VOLP, *Q* 11 ere] êre *Q* 20 god] God *Q* 21 *Exit.* add G 23 (Now . . . corner.)] Now . . . corner. *Q* *Exit.* add G v. viii.] SCENE V. | *Another part of the Street.* | *Enter Corbaccio and Corvino;—Mosca passes over the Stage, before them.* G After 2 *Enter Volpone.* G

CORB. Againe, t'afflict vs? monster! VOLP. In good faith, sir,
I'am hartily greeu'd, a beard of your graue length
Should be so ouer-reach'd. I neuer brook'd
That parasites haire, me thought his nose should cosen:
There still was somewhat, in his looke, did promise
The bane of a *Clarissimo*. CORB. Knaue—— VOLP. Me thinkes,
Yet you, that are so traded i' the world,
A witty merchant, the fine bird, CORVINO,
That haue such morall *emblemes* on your name,
Should not haue sung your shame; and dropt your cheese:
To let the FOXE laugh at your emptinesse.
CORV. Sirrah, you thinke, the priuiledge of the place,
And your red saucy cap, that seemes (to me)
Nayl'd to your iolt-head, with those two *cecchines*,
Can warrant your abuses; come you, hither:
You shall perceiue, sir, I dare beate you. Approch.
VOLP. No haste, sir, I doe know your valure, well:
Since you durst publish what you are, sir. CORV. Tarry,
I'ld speake, with you. VOLP. Sir, sir, another time——
CORV. Nay, now. VOLP. O god, sir! I were a wise man,
Would stand the fury of a distracted cuckold.
CORB. What! come againe? VOLP. Vpon 'hem, MOSCA; saue me. *Mosca walkes by 'hem.*
CORB. The ayre's infected, where he breathes. CORV. Lets flye him.
VOLP. Excellent *Basiliske!* turne vpon the *vulture*.

v. viii. 7 cosen:] cosen, *Q* 12 morall] mortall *F2* 13 your shame *Q, F2*: you shame *F1* 19, 20 I dare beate . . . haste, sir *om. F2* 23 god] God *Q* After 24 *As he is running off, re-enter Mosca.* G 25 *Stage direction not in Q* me.] me, *F1* 26 *Exeunt Corv. and Corb.* add G

Act V. *Scene* IX.

VOLTORE, MOSCA, VOLPONE.

WEll, flesh-flie, it is sommer with you, now;
Your winter will come on. MOS. Good Aduocate,
'Pray thee, not raile, nor threaten out of place, thus;
Thou 'lt make a *solœcisme* (as madame sayes.)
Get you a biggen, more: your braine breakes loose.
VOLT. Well, sir. VOLP. Would you ha' me beate the insolent slaue?
Throw dirt, vpon his first good cloathes? VOLT. This same
Is, doubtlesse, some familiar! VOLP. Sir, the court
In troth, stayes for you. I am mad, a mule,
That neuer read IVSTINIAN, should get vp,
And ride an Aduocate. Had you no quirke,
To auoide gullage, sir, by such a creature?
I hope you doe but iest; he has not done 't:
This's but confederacy, to blind the rest.
You are the heire? VOLT. A strange, officious,
Trouble-some knaue! thou dost torment me. VOLP. I know——
It cannot be, sir, that you should be cosen'd;
'Tis not within the wit of man, to doe it:
You are so wise, so prudent, and, 'tis fit,
That wealth, and wisdome still, should goe together.

V. ix.] *Enter Voltore.* G, continuing the scene 1 sommer] summer *F2* 3 'Pray thee] Pr'y thee *F2* 5 *Exit.* add G 6 ha'] haue *Q* 7 VOLT.] VOLT, *F1* 13 hope] hope, *Q* 19 prudent, and] prudent—And *Q* 20 together.] together— *Q* *Exeunt.* add G

Act V. *Scene* X.

AVOCATORI, 4. NOTARIO, COMMANDADORI, BONARIO, CELIA, CORBACCIO, CORVINO, VOLTORE, VOLPONE.

ARe all the parties, here? NOT. All, but the Aduocate.
AVO. 2. And, here he comes. AVO. ⟨I.⟩ Then bring 'hem foorth to sentence.
VOLT. O, my most honour'd fathers, let your mercy
Once winne vpon your iustice, to forgiue——
I am distracted—— (VOLP. What will he doe, now?)
VOLT. O,
I know not which t'addresse my selfe to, first,
Whether your father-hoods, or these innocents——
(CORV. Will he betray himselfe?) VOLT. Whom, equally,
I haue abus'd, out of most couetous endes——
(CORV. The man is mad! CORB. What's that?
CORV. He is possest.)
VOLT. For which; now strooke in conscience, here I prostrate
My selfe, at your offended feet, for pardon.
AVO. I. 2. Arise. CEL. O heau'n, how iust thou art!
VOLP. I'am caught
I' mine owne noose—— CORV. Be constant, sir, nought now
Can helpe, but impudence. AVO. I. Speake forward.
COM. Silence.
VOLT. It is not passion in me, reuerend fathers,

V. X.] SCENE VI. | *The Scrutineo or Senate House.* | *Enter Avocatori, Notario, Bonario, Celia, Corbaccio, Corvino, Commandadori, Saffi, &c.* G COMMANDADORI *Q*: COMMANDADORE *Ff* 2 After 'comes.' [*Enter Voltore and Volpone.*] G AVO. I. *F3* foorth] forth *Q* 5 (VOLP. . . . now?)] VOLP. . . . now? *Q* After 'now?' [*Aside.*] G VOLT.] VOLP. *Q, Ff* 6 t'addresse] to addresse *Q* 8 (CORV. . . . himself?)] CORV. . . . himselfe, *Q* After 'himselfe?' [*Aside.*] G 9, 10 I haue . . . possest *om. F2*: *F3 supplied the gap in the sense by inserting* I have abus'd, by my false Accusation: 10 (CORV. . . . possest.)] CORV. . . . possest. *Q* 11 strooke] struck *F2* 14 After 'noose' [*Aside.*] G CORV.] *Corv.* [*to Corbaccio.*] G

But onely conscience, conscience, my good sires,
That makes me, now, tell truth. That parasite,
That knaue hath been the instrument of all.
AVO. ⟨2.⟩ Where is that knaue? fetch him. VOLP. I goe. CORV. Graue fathers,
This man's distracted; he confest it, now:
For, hoping to be old VOLPONE's heire,
Who now is dead—— AVOC. 3. How? AVO. 2. Is VOLPONE dead?
CORV. Dead since, graue fathers—— BON. O, sure vengeance! AVO. 1. Stay,
Then, he was no deceiuer? VOLT. O no, none:
The parasite, graue fathers. CORV. He do's speake,
Out of meere enuie, 'cause the seruant's made
The thing, he gap't for; please your father-hoods,
This is the truth: though, I'le not iustifie
The other, but he may be some-deale faulty.
VOLT. I, to your hopes, as well as mine, CORVINO:
But I'le vse modesty. Pleaseth your wisdomes
To viewe these certaine notes, and but conferre them;
As I hope fauour, they shall speake cleare truth.
CORV. The deuill ha's entred him! BON. Or bides in you.
AVO. 4. We haue done ill, by a publike officer,
To send for him, if he be heire. AVO. 2. For whom?
AVO. 4. Him, that they call the parasite. AVO. 3. 'Tis true;
He is a man, of great estate, now left.
AVO. 4. Goe you, and learne his name; and say, the court
Intreates his presence, here; but, to the clearing
Of some few doubts. AVO. 2. This same's a labyrinth!

V. x. 17 conscience, my *Q*: conscience my *Ff* 19 all.] all— *Q* 20 Avo. 2.] 1 *Avoc.* G After 'goe.' *Exit.* G 21 distracted;] distracted, *Q* 24 Stay,] Stay,— *Q* 26 fathers.] *Fathers*— *Q* 30 some-deale] somewhere *Q* 32 Pleaseth] 'Pleaseth *Q* 35 him!] him. *Q* 37 heire.] heire; *Q* 41 presence,] presence *Q* 42 After 'doubts.' [*Exit Notary.*] G

AVO. 1. Stand you vnto your first report? CORV. My state,
My life, my fame—— BON. (Where is't?) CORV. Are at the stake.
AVO. 1. Is yours so too? CORB. The Aduocate's a knaue:
And has a forked tongue—— AVO. 2. (Speake to the point.)
CORB. So is the parasite, too. AVO. 1. This is confusion.
VOLT. I doe beseech your father-hoods, read but those;
CORV. And credit nothing, the false spirit hath writ:
It cannot be, but he is possest, graue fathers.

Act v. *Scene* xi.

VOLPONE, NANO, ANDROGINO, CASTRONE.

TO make a snare, for mine owne necke! and run
My head into it, wilfully! with laughter!
When I had newly scap't, was free, and cleare!
Out of mere wantonnesse! ô, the dull deuill
Was in this braine of mine, when I deuis'd it;
And MOSCA gaue it second: he must now
Helpe to seare vp this veyne, or we bleed dead.
How now! who let you loose? whither goe you, now?
What? to buy ginger-bread? or to drowne kitlings?
NAN. Sir, master MOSCA call'd vs out of doores,
And bid vs all goe play, and tooke the keies. AND. Yes.
VOLP. Did master MOSCA take the keyes? why, so!
I am farder, in. These are my fine conceipts!
I must be merry, with a mischiefe to me!

v. x. 44 (Where is't?)] Where is't? *Q* 46 (Speake . . . point.)] Speake . . . point. *Q* 48 *Giving them papers.* add G 50 but he is possest, graue fathers] (my *Sires*) but he is possest. *Q* *The scene closes.* add G v. xi.] SCENE VII. | *A Street.* | *Enter Volpone.* G 6 he] Hé *Q* After 7 *Enter Nano, Androgyno, and Castrone.* G 8 whither] whether *Q*, *F2* 10, 12 master] Maister *Q*

What a vile wretch was I, that could not beare
My fortune soberly? I must ha' my crotchets!
And my *conundrums!* well, goe you, and seeke him:
His meaning may be truer, then my feare.
Bid him, he streight come to me, to the court;
Thither will I, and, if 't be possible,
Vn-screw my aduocate, vpon new hopes:
When I prouok'd him, then I lost my selfe.

Act V. *Scene* XII.

AVOCATORI, &C.

THese things can nere be reconcil'd. He, here,
Professeth, that the gentleman was wrong'd;
And that the gentlewoman was brought thither,
Forc'd by her husband: and there left. VOLT. Most true.
CEL. How ready is heau'n to those, that pray! AVO. I. But, that
VOLPONE would haue rauish'd her, he holds
Vtterly false; knowing his impotence.
CORV. Graue fathers, he is possest; againe, I say,
Possest: nay, if there be possession,
And obsession, he has both. AVO. 3. Here comes our officer.
VOLP. The parasite will streight be here, graue fathers.
AVO. 4. You might inuent some other name, sir varlet.
AVO. 3. Did not the notarie meet him? VOLP. Not that I know.
AVO. 4. His comming will cleare all. AVO. 2. Yet it is mistie.

v. xi. 16 fortune] fortune, *Q* 20 Thither] Thether *Q* 22 *Exeunt.* add G v. xii. *Misnumbered* Scene 10. *in Q* SCENE VIII. | *The Scrutineo, or Senate House.* | *Avocatori, Bonario, Celia, Corbaccio, Corvino, Commandadori, Saffi, &c. as before.* G, who omits Voltore. 1 nere] nêre *Q* *Shewing the papers.* add G 3 gentlewoman] Gentlewóman *Q* thither] thether *Q* 5 pray!] pray. *Q* But] Bút *Q* After 10 *Enter Volpone.* G 11 be *F2*: be, *Q, F1* 13 Not] Not, *Q*

VOLT. May't please your father hoods—— VOLP. Sir, the parasite *Volpone whispers the Aduocate.*
Will'd me to tell you, that his master liues;
That you are still the man; your hopes the same;
And this was, onely a iest—— VOLT. How? VOLP. Sir, to trie
If you were firme, and how you stood affected.
VOLT. Art' sure he liues? VOLP. Doe I liue, sir?
VOLT. O me!
I was to violent. VOLP. Sir, you may redeeme it,
They said, you were possest; fall downe, and seeme so:
I'le helpe to make it good. God blesse the man! *Voltore falls.*
(Stop your wind hard, and swell) see, see, see, see!
He vomits crooked pinnes! his eyes are set,
Like a dead hares, hung in a poulters shop!
His mouth's running away! doe you see, signior?
Now, 'tis in his belly. (CORV. I, the deuill!)
VOLP. Now, in his throate. (CORV. I, I perceiue it plaine.)
VOLP. 'Twill out, 'twill out; stand cleere. See, where it flies!
In shape of a blew toad, with a battes wings!
Doe not you see it, sir? CORB. What? I thinke I doe.
CORV. 'T is too manifest. VOLP. Looke! he comes t'himselfe!
VOLT. Where am I? VOLP. Take good heart, the worst is past, sir.
You are dis-possest. AVO. 1. What accident is this?
AVO. 2. Sodaine, and full of wonder! AVO. 3. If he were
Possest, as it appeares, all this is nothing.
CORV. He has beene, often, subiect to these fits,
AVO. 1. Shew him that writing, do you know it, sir?

v. xii. 15 *Stage direction not in Q* 16 master] Maister *Q* 19 were *Q, F2*: were, *F1* 21 to] too *Q* 23 *Stage direction not in Q* 24 (Stop . . . swell)] Stop . . . swell: *Q* 28 belly.] belly! *Q* (CORV. . . . deuill!)] CORV. . . . Deuill! *Q* 29 (CORV. . . . plaine.)] CORV. . . . plaine. *Q* 30 'twill] t'will *F1* 31 a battes] batts *F2* 35 AVO.] ATO. *F1* 36 AVO. 2. *Q*: AVO. *F1* AVO. 3.] ATO. 3 *F1* were] were. *F1* 38 subiect] subbiect *F1*

VOLP. Deny it, sir, forsweare it, know it not.
VOLT. Yes, I doe know it well, it is my hand:
But all, that it containes, is false. BON. O practise!
AVO. 2. What maze is this! AVO. 1. Is he not guilty, then,
Whom you, there, name the parasite? VOLT. Graue fathers,
No more then, his good patron, old VOLPONE.
AVO. 4. Why, he is dead? VOLT. O no, my honor'd fathers.
He liues—— AVO. 1. How! liues? VOLT. Liues. AVO. 2. This is subtler, yet!
AVO. 3. You said, he was dead? VOLT. Neuer. AVO. 3. You said so? CORV. I heard so.
AVO. 4. Here comes the gentleman, make him way. AVO. 3. A stoole.
AVOC. 4. A proper man! and were VOLPONE dead,
A fit match for my daughter. AVOC. 3. Giue him way.
VOLP. MOSCA, I was a'most lost, the Aduocate
Had betray'd all; but, now, it is recouer'd:
Al's o' the hinge againe——say, I am liuing.
MOS. What busie knaue is this! most reuerend fathers,
I sooner, had attended your graue pleasures,
But that my order, for the funerall
Of my deare patron did require me—— VOLP. (MOSCA!)
MOS. Whom I intend to bury, like a gentleman.
VOLP. I, quicke, and cosen me of all. AVO. 2. Still stranger!
More intricate! AVO. 1. And come about againe!
AVO. 4. It is a match, my daughter is bestow'd.
MOS. (Wil you gi' me halfe? VOLP. First, I'le be hang'd. MOS. I know,

v. xii. 40 VOLP.] *Volp.* [*whispers Volt.*] G 42 BON. O *F2*: BON. 3. O *Q, F1*: *the* '3' *perhaps a corruption of an ill-written* ô 49 gentleman, *F2*: gentleman *F1*: Gentleman, *Q* After 'way.' [*Enter Mosca.*] G 51 After 'daughter.' [*Aside.*] G 52 a'most] almost *Q* 54 hinge] henge *Q* *Aside to Mos.* add G 58 *Aside.* add G 59 gentleman.] Gentleman— *Q* 60 After 'all.' [*Aside.*] G 61 about] about, *Q* 62 *Aside.* add G 63 After 'halfe?' [*Aside to Volp.*] G

Your voice is good, cry not so lowd) AVO. I. Demand
The Aduocate. Sir, did not you affirme,
VOLPONE was aliue? VOLP. Yes, and he is;
This gent'man told me so, (thou shalt haue halfe.)
MOS. Whose drunkard is this same? speake some, that know him:
I neuer saw his face. (I cannot now
Affoord it you so cheape. VOLP. No?) AVO. I. What say you?
VOLT. The officer told mee. VOLP. I did, graue fathers,
And will maintaine, he liues, with mine owne life.
And, that this creature told me. (I was borne,
With all good starres my enemies.) MOS. Most graue fathers,
If such an insolence, as this, must passe
Vpon me, I am silent: 'twas not this,
For which you sent, I hope. AVO. 2. Take him away.
(VOLP. MOSCA.) AVO. 3. Let him be whipt. (VOLP. Wilt thou betray me?
Cosen me?) A⟨v⟩OC. 3. And taught to beare himselfe
Toward a person of his ranke. AVO. 4. Away.
MOS. I humbly thank your father-hoods. VOLP. Soft, soft: whipt?
And loose all that I haue? if I confesse,
It cannot be much more. AVO. 4. Sir, are you married?
VOLP. They'll be ally'd, anon; I must be resolute:
The FOXE shall, here, vncase. (MOS. Patron.) VOLP. Nay, now, *He puts off his disguise.*
My ruines shall not come alone; your match
I'le hinder sure: my substance shall not glew you,
Nor screw you, into a family. (MOS. Why, patron!)

v. xii. 64 lowd] low'd *Q*: lowd' *F1* 67 *Aside to Mos.* add G 70 After 'cheape.' [*Aside to Volp.*] G 70 Avo.] Avo *F1* 73 After 'creature' [*points to Mosca.*] G 74 After 'enemies' [*Aside.*] G 79 Avoc.] Aoc. *F1* taught] taught, *Q*: be taught *T. Keightley conj.* 80 *The Officers seize Volpone.* add G 82 loose] lose *F2* 83 After 'more.' [*Aside.*] G 84 *Stage direction not in Q*

VOLP. I am VOLPONE, and this is my knaue;
This, his owne knaue; this, auarices foole;
This, a *Chimæra* of wittall, foole, and knaue;
And, reuerend fathers, since we all can hope
Nought, but a sentence, let's not now despaire it.
You heare me briefe. CORV. May it please your fatherhoods—— COM. Silence.
AVOC. 1. The knot is now vndone, by miracle!
AVOC. 2. Nothing can be more cleare. AVO. 3. Or can more proue
These innocent. AVOC. 1. Giue 'hem their liberty.
BON. Heauen could not, long, let such grosse crimes be hid.
AVOC. 2. If this be held the high way to get riches,
May I be poore. AVOC. 3. This 's not the gaine, but torment.
AVOC. 1. These possesse wealth, as sicke men possesse feuers,
Which, trulyer, may be said to possesse them.
AVOC. 2. Disroabe that parasite. CORV. MOS. Most honor'd fathers.
AVOC. 1. Can you plead ought to stay the course of iustice?
If you can, speake. CORV. VOLT. We beg fauor, CEL. And mercy.
AVOC. 1. You hurt your innocence, suing for the guilty.
Stand forth; and, first, the parasite. You appeare
T'haue beene the chiefest minister, if not plotter,
In all these lewd impostures; and now, lastly,
Haue, with your impudence, abus'd the court,
And habit of a gentleman of *Venice*,
Being a fellow of no birth, or bloud:
For which, our sentence is, first thou be whipt;
Then liue perpetuall prisoner in our gallies.

v. xii. 89 *Pointing to Mosca.* add G 90 this,] This, [*to Volt.*] G this,] this, [*to Corb.*] G 91 This,] This, [*to Corv.*] G 93 despaire] dispaire *Q* 94 Silence] silence *F1* 96 Or] Or, *Q* 99 way] way, *Q* 102 trulyer, *Q*: trulyer *F1* 103 fathers.] *Fathers*— Q

VOLP. I thanke you, for him. MOS. Bane to thy wooluish nature.
AVOC. I. Deliuer him to the *Saffi*. Thou, VOLPONE,
By bloud, and ranke a gentleman, canst not fall
Vnder like censure; but our iudgement on thee
Is, that thy substance all be straight confiscate
To the hospitall, of the *Incurabili*:
And, since the most was gotten by imposture,
By faining lame, gout, palsey, and such diseases,
Thou art to lie in prison, crampt with irons,
Till thou bee'st sicke, and lame indeed. Remoue him.
VOLP. This is call'd mortifying of a FOXE.
AVOC. I. Thou VOLTORE, to take away the scandale
Thou hast giu'n all worthy men, of thy profession,
Art banish'd from their fellowship, and our state.
CORBACCIO, bring him neere. We here possesse
Thy sonne, of all thy state; and confine thee
To the monasterie of *San' Spirito*:
Where, since thou knew'st not how to liue well here,
Thou shalt be learn'd to die well. CORB. Ha! what said he?
COM. You shall know anone, sir. AVOC. ⟨I.⟩ Thou CORVINO, shalt
Be straight imbarqu'd from thine owne house, and row'd
Round about *Venice*, through the *grand canale*,
Wearing a cap, with faire, long asses eares,
In stead of hornes: and, so to mount (a paper
Pin'd on thy brest) to the *berlino*—— CORV. Yes,
And, haue mine eies beat out with stinking fish,
Bruis'd fruit, and rotten egges——'Tis well. I'am glad,
I shall not see my shame, yet. AVOC. I. And to expiate
Thy wrongs done to thy wife, thou art to send her
Home, to her father, with her dowrie trebled:

v. xii. 115 VOLP. *G*: VOLT. *Q*, *Ff* (*a retort to l.* 81) wooluish] woluish *Q* 116 After '*Saffi.*' *Mosca is carried out.* G 119 be straight] be, straight, *Q* 120 To the . . . of the] To th' . . . of th' *W* After 124 *He is taken from the Bar.* G 130 thy state] thy 'estate *Q* 134 AVO. I. *F2*: AVO. *F1*: AVOC. *Q* 139 *berlino*] *Berlina* W

And these are all your iudgements. (A L L. Honour'd fathers.)
A V O C. I. Which may not be reuok'd. Now, you begin,
When crimes are done, and past, and to be punish'd,
To thinke what your crimes are : away with them.
Let all, that see these vices thus rewarded,
Take heart, and loue to study 'hem. Mischiefes feed
Like beasts, till they be fat, and then they bleed.

V O L P O N E.

THe seasoning of a play is the applause.
Now, though the F O X be punish'd by the lawes,
He, yet, doth hope there is no suffring due,
For any fact, which he hath done 'gainst you ;
If there be, censure him : here he, doubtfull, stands.
If not, fare iouially, and clap your hands.

THE END

V. xii. 145 iudgements.] Iudgements— *Q* 146 begin,] begin *Q* 148 are :] are ; *Q* 151 *Exeunt.* add G EPILOGUE. *Volpone comes forward.* G 1 applause.] applause, *Q* 5 censure] sensure *F1* 6 *Exit.* add G

This Comoedie was first
acted, in the yeere
1605.

By the Kings Maiesties
SERVANTS.

The principall Comœdians were,

RIC. BVRBADGE.	IOH. HEMINGS.
HEN. CONDEL.	IOH. LOWIN.
WILL. SLY.	ALEX. COOKE.

With the allowance of the Master of REVELLS.

This page was added in F1. In F2 the statements about the date, the Company, and the Master of the Revels were omitted, and the list of 'The principall Comœdians' *was transferred to the back of the half-title, where it followed* 'The Persons of the Play' *and* 'The Scene'.

EPICOENE *or* THE SILENT WOMAN

THE TEXT

The printing and publishing of *Epicoene, or The Silent Woman* have some perplexing points. The play was entered on the Stationers' Register for John Browne and John Busby junior on 20 September 1610.

20mo Septembris

John Browne John Busby junior	Entred for their Copye vnder thandes of Sir George Bucke and master Waterson for master warden Leake, A booke called, Epicoene or the silent woman by Ben: Johnson. vj^d

Arber, *Transcript*, III. 444.

Browne transferred his rights to Walter Burre on 28 September 1612.

.28. Septembris

Walter Burre /	Entred for his copie by assignment from John Browne and consent of the Wardens in full Court holden this Day /. A booke called the Commodye of the silent Woman vj^d

Ibid. 498.

The next entry is irregular, and it is cancelled.[1] On 17 February 1623 Mistress Browne, whose husband died on 10 October 1622, assigned the copyright of eleven books to John Marriott, the ninth being 'Epicœne or the silent woman', which is crossed out, with a side-note 'vide 28° Septembris 1612'. She evidently did not know that her husband had assigned the copyright to Burre.

The next entry is also irregular.[2] Mistress Burre, whose husband died in 1622, assigned to John Spencer on 3 July 1630 her rights in *Cynthia's Revels*, *The Alchemist*, and *Epicoene*, and in six other books. For these nine books she should have paid four shillings and sixpence; she actually paid four shillings. It looks as if the registering clerk found out that she had no rights in *Epicoene*, and did not charge her the fee for it, but omitted to delete the entry.

1 Arber, *Transcript*, IV. 92.   2 Ibid. 238.

During Walter Burre's lifetime Stansby had published *Epicoene* in folio in 1616 and reissued it in quarto in 1620. He must have had some understanding with Burre, though there is no record of it at either of these dates. He could not have ignored Burre's interest in seven plays which he printed in the Folio—*Every Man in his Humour*, *Cynthia's Revels*, *Sejanus*, *Volpone*, *The Silent Woman*, *The Alchemist*, and *Catiline*. But it is not till 4 July 1635 that a belated entry in the Register finally establishes his rights:

Master Stansby — Entred for his Copies by vertue of a noate under the hand of Walter Burre and master Mathew Lowndes warden bearing date the 10th of June 1621 as therby appeareth these Copies following (*vizt*.) by order of a Court iii^s^ vj^d^

Arber, *Transcript*, IV. 342.

The copies are those of the seven plays. Apparently, after Stansby had published them, he judged it desirable to safeguard his rights by a formal agreement with Burre, which was submitted to the then Warden of the Stationers' Company but, for some unexplained reason, was not entered on the Register.

When was the play first published? This is a far more serious question which has been fully investigated in an important article by Dr. W. W. Greg, 'Was there a 1612 Quarto of *Epicene*?' contributed to *The Library* in December 1934 (vol. xv, pp. 306–15). Gifford stated in 1816: 'The *Silent Woman* was printed in quarto with this motto:

Ut sis tu similis Cœli, Byrrhique latronum,
Non ego sim Capri, neque Sulci. Cur metuas me?

and went through several editions. I have one dated 1620. The *Companion to the Playhouse* mentions another, printed in 1609 (as does Whalley, in the margin of his copy),[1] which I have not been able to discover; the earliest which has

[1] Gifford had access to a copy of Whalley's edition of 1756 which Whalley had annotated, no doubt with a view to a second edition.

fallen in my way, bearing the date 1612. All these are exclusive of the folio, 1616.'

For this alleged quarto of 1609, D. E. Baker's *Companion to the Play-House*, 1764, says ' EPICÆNE, or *the silent Woman.* Com. by *Ben Jonson*, 4to. 1609 '. But the date ' 1609 ' is copied from the date of performance on the title-page of the play in the Folio. Publication of an authorized text a year before it was entered in the Stationers' Register would be an extraordinary and a pointless proceeding on the part of such a man as Burre. Whalley's note is merely a copy from Baker. On the evidence we have the Quarto of 1609 may be dismissed as impossible.

It is otherwise with the missing Quarto of 1612. Gifford says he had seen it, though he never mentions it again and, contrary to his usual practice with the Quartos, he made no use of it. He does not, for example, record any disagreement with the later texts. We should expect the Quarto, if it existed, to have been published by Burre. An edition by Browne and Busby is, of course, possible; but Burre was evidently anxious to secure Jonson's plays, and the transfer of *Epicoene* to him in 1612 suggests that he contemplated an edition. In that year he published *The Alchemist*, which he had registered in 1610. Was there any reason for his holding up *The Silent Woman*?

There are clear signs that the play caused trouble. Jonson virtually says so in the dedication to Sir Francis Stuart and in the second prologue ' *occasion'd by some persons impertinent exception* ' and not intended for delivery on the stage. ' Thinke nothing true ', he says in the prologue; the play is pure fiction.

For he knowes, *Poet* neuer credit gain'd
  By writing truths, but things (like truths) well fain'd.
If any, yet, will (with particular slight
  Of application) wrest what he doth write;
And that he meant or him, or her, will say:
  They make a libell, which he made a play.

And in the dedication he makes a statement which will

reconcile us to the loss of an earlier Quarto if it had been published: 'There is not a line, or syllable in it chang'd from the simplicity of the first Copy.' If Jonson had been forced to suppress anything in that copy, it was characteristic of him to retrieve it in a later text.[1] 'And, when you shall consider,' he tells Stuart, 'through the certaine hatred of some, how much a mans innocency may bee indanger'd by an vn-certaine accusation; you will, I doubt not, so beginne to hate the iniquitie of such natures, as I shall loue the contumely done me, whose end was so honorable, as to be wip'd off by your sentence.'

The passage which is likely to have brought Jonson into trouble was at the beginning of the fifth act, where La-Foole describes Daw as having a box of writing-materials

> to draw maps of euery place, and person, where he comes.
>
> CLE. How, maps of persons!
>
> LA-F. Yes, sir, of NOMENTACK, when he was here, and of the Prince of MOLDAVIA, and of his mistris, mistris EPICOENE.
>
> CLE. Away! he has not found out her latitude, I hope.

The words 'his mistris' unquestionably mean Daw's mistress, but in the context and, when spoken on the stage, they could be, and apparently were, interpreted to mean the Prince of Moldavia's mistress.

This sham prince was Stephano Janiculo, sometimes called Bogdan, for 'Bugdania' was another name for Moldavia.[2] He visited England in 1601 and enlisted the support of Elizabeth. He went to the English embassy at Constantinople, was lured from it and imprisoned by the Turks; he escaped disguised as a woman in 1606. He came to England in 1607 and left in November; King James was

[1] For instance, the Apologetical Dialogue to *Poetaster* was retrieved in the 1616 Folio (vol. iv, pp. 317 foll.).

[2] A full account of Stephano is given in Sir William Foster's edition of *The Travels of John Sanderson in the Levant 1584–1602*, pp. xxxv–vii, published by the Hakluyt Society, 1931. There is a contemporary notice of his adventures in *Newes from Poland* (1621, sigs. A 4 verso–B 4 verso), one of the countries to which he fled for refuge.

fool enough to give him a grant of £300, and next year to warrant the Levant Company to spend £3,000 in securing his 'restitution'.[1] Wotton's letters from Venice to Lord Salisbury throw further light on him. On 22 February 1608 Wotton writes that Stephano has arrived in Venice and proposes to quarter himself on Wotton. Wotton found Stephano and his portmanteaux one day at the embassy and asked for his credentials from the King. 'Whereupon he asked me very wonderingly whether I had no direction touching him from your Lordship, nor from my lady Arabella'—Arabella Stuart—'with a few other wild questions.'[2] Wotton politely packed him off, but he announced in Venice that, when he got his princedom, he was going to marry Lady Arabella. He was a safe distance from England before he ventured on this interesting announcement. But it caused a flutter in Venice because he was already married to a Venetian lady. On 7 November 1608 Wotton further reports to Salisbury that 'Stephano Bogdan' has written from Constantinople to the Archbishop of Philadelphia at Venice to divorce him from his Venetian wife. 'The matter is come to the hearing of her friends, who make no small noise of it, and the rather for a certain report, scattered here by the said intendant at his last passage this way (when he came from England), of some motions that had passed between him and the Lady Arabella of marriage, to succeed when he should be settled in his princedom.'[3] The lady's friends believed this, and pointed to James's treatment of him as corroborating the allegation.

The true facts about any proposals for Lady Arabella's marriage were well known in England and are on record. As a cousin of King James she was politically important. She was kept in confinement in December 1609 for promising her hand to an unnamed suitor—probably a rich

[1] See the *Calendar of Domestic State Papers* under the dates 26 October 1607, and 25 September 1608.
[2] See Logan Pearsall Smith, *The Life and Letters of Sir Henry Wotton*, vol. i, p. 414.
[3] Ibid., p. 438.

man, for she pleaded her poverty, and James pardoned her and gave her a pension.[1] On 2 February 1610 she became engaged to Sir William Seymour, and they appeared before the Privy Council and promised not to marry without the King's consent. She was granted a monopoly. But in July the pair married secretly and were imprisoned. In June 1611 she played an epicene part by escaping in boy's clothes from the Bishop of York who had charge of her, got to Blackwall and went on board a French vessel below Lee with several attendants ; she was retaken at sea near Calais and lodged in the Tower.[2] She stayed there till her death in 1615.

Now within a week of her engagement to Seymour the Venetian ambassador on 8 February 1610 made a report which bears on *Epicoene* : 'Lady Arabella is seldom seen outside her rooms and lives in greater dejection than ever. She complains that in a certain comedy the play-wright introduced an allusion to her person and the part played by the Prince of Moldavia. The play was suppressed. Her Excellency is very ill-pleased and shows a determination in this coming Parliament'—which opened on 9 February—'to secure the punishment of certain persons, we don't know who.'[3] *Epicoene* was produced at the end of 1609 or the beginning of 1610: Wotton's report of November 1608 would set the scandal about Stephano afloat in England at once, but the statement of the Venetian ambassador slightly favours the latter date. Mr. Logan Pearsall Smith was the first to suggest that the suppressed play was *Epicoene* ;[4] the suggestion has since been made independently by Sir E. K. Chambers.[5] The authorities would deal promptly with any insult, real or imagined, to a royal personage. Her

[1] *Domestic State Papers* under date 30 December 1609.
[2] See the report of Sir William Waad, lieutenant of the Tower, to Lord Salisbury in the *Domestic State Papers*, 5 June 1611, and Lady Dorothy Cope's letter to Carleton, 24 June.
[3] *Calendar of Venetian State Papers*, xi, no. 794, p. 427. The passage about the play is in cipher.
[4] Op. cit. i, p. 414 n.
[5] *Elizabethan Stage*, iii. 370.

escapade in boy's clothes would lend colour to any rumour that she was referred to in the play.

One other passage in *Epicoene* betrays signs of nervousness. When Truewit disguises Cutberd as a doctor and Otter as a parson—' as able . . . and compleat . . . as may be wish'd '—Jonson adds this very undramatic proviso: 'And, I hope, without wronging the dignitie of either profession, since they are but persons put on, and for mirths sake, to torment him.'[1] The words may have been in the ' first Copy ' which Jonson professed to reprint exactly, for he had got into trouble for satirizing lawyers in *Poetaster*.[2] But they read curiously like an afterthought inserted as a reply to critics.

Jonson should have had no difficulty in explaining the Moldavia allusion to the authorities when once they looked into it. But the further point arises—if they stopped the performance, would it be safe to print the passage in 1612 when Lady Arabella was in the Tower and the scandal fairly recent? By 1616 the affair was forgotten, and Jonson was just the man to let the world know what he had written, in order to show how wilfully he had been maligned.

To sum up this confusing and unsatisfactory evidence, we may say (1) it is clear that Burre at any rate intended to print the play in 1612; (2) Gifford says he had seen a quarto printed that year; (3) no one has seen it since. A quarto of 1612 would probably omit the passage supposed to reflect on Lady Arabella: that would account for Jonson's emphatic statement that the 1616 text was ' the first Copy ' without the change of a line or syllable. A further clue to publication, or at least the intention to publish, in 1612 has been pointed out by Sir E. K. Chambers.[3] The commendatory verses prefixed to the Folio of 1616 include a copy by Francis Beaumont ' Vpon the Silent Woman ', as well as his two poems in praise of *Volpone* and *Catiline* reprinted from the Quartos of those plays. Beaumont dis-

[1] Act IV, scene vii, 47–9. [2] See vol. iv, p. 193.
[3] *Elizabethan State*, vol. iii, pp. 369–70.

cusses personal satire in the drama[1]—its effectiveness or otherwise in competent and incompetent hands—and Sir Edmund Chambers suggests that the lines were written for the Quarto of 1612. The suggestion must certainly be accepted, but it does not prove that Jonson did not keep the verses in his desk and use them for the first time in the Folio. The problem is insoluble unless a copy of the missing Quarto turns up.

The authoritative text is in any case that of the 1616 Folio. Jonson read the proofs, but not with his usual care. The misprints are mostly trivial, such as turned letters or wrong punctuation, but there are forty-seven of them.[2] The worst are 'a sauer i' the man' for 'saver in the main' (III. iii. 34); 'all women are not to be taken alwaies' for 'all ways' (IV. i. 90); and the misspellings '*numbre*' for '*nombre*' (IV. v. 329) and '*Paralisis*' (V. iii. 178).

In three large-paper copies of the 1616 Folio—the Grenville copy in the British Museum, the Fleming Crooks copy, now in the possession of Mr. H. L. Ford, and Sir C. Firth's copy, now in the possession of the editor—sheet Y y (Act I and Act II up to scene ii, line 64) has been reset. The line-arrangements of several pages differ from those of the ordinary issue; there are eighteen variant readings, all of which are wrong; the spelling is freely altered, the punctuation varies, and sometimes roman type is substituted for italic in the printing of proper names. In all, there are nearly two hundred and eighty changes. They have some textual importance because the Folio of 1640 was set up from a copy containing this ill-printed sheet.

The explanation is probably this. Large-paper copies of a work at the present day are usually printed after the ordinary issue on small paper has been worked off: there

[1] Satire at large, such as the character of Morose, not incidental allusions. Dryden was told that Jonson had known such a man (*Essays*, ed. Ker, vol. i, p. 84).

[2] Recorded in the critical apparatus, at II. ii. 37; iii. 28, 56, 80, 113, 125, 134, 137, 139; iv. 17, 18, 51, 53, 54, 101; v. 1, 9, 23, 41, 45, 63, 81; vi. 21; III. iii. 19, 34, 87; v. 11, 28, 40, 45; vii. 32; IV. i. 90; v. 200, 213, 232, 260, 300, 305, 322, 329, 343; V. i. 11; iii. 4, 52, 178; iv. 186.

is no clear proof that this was so in the seventeenth century, but probably it is the traditional practice. The dislocation in sheet Y y must have occurred when the edition was being printed off and after Jonson had passed the proofs. It was probably due to an accident in the printing-house—for instance, to a workman dropping the formes. It was reset without consulting Jonson. What he would have said if he had discovered a copy in this state can be but faintly imagined.

It would be useless to cumber the critical apparatus of *Epicoene* with this array of printer's variants. Thus there are thirty-eight interchanges of ' be ' and ' bee ', ' he ' and ' hee ', ' she ' and ' shee ', ' we ' and ' wee ', the printer taking the spelling which best suited his spacing of the line. A selection has been made giving (1) the deviations from the authorized text, (2) anything reproduced in the 1640 Folio which, but for this evidence, would be regarded as a change or a correction. But in the critical survey of the text which will precede the commentary a full record with a facsimile will be given because of the light it throws on the working methods of a seventeenth-century printer.

Stansby reprinted the play in quarto in 1620. The title-page is in two states. The first copies the Folio : ' Epicoene, or The silent Woman. A Comœdie. Acted in the yeare 1609. By the Children of her Majesties Revels. The Author B. I.' This was replaced by a cancel : ' The Silent Woman. A Comœdie. Acted by the Children of the Revels. The Author B. Ionson.' Had this been done earlier, we might have conjectured that *Epicoene* had disappeared because of its possible association with Lady Arabella, but no reason can be assigned for the change in 1620. ' Epicoene ' is the only clue Jonson gave to the real sex of the character, but would any one but himself grasp its significance ?

The collation, two leaves of A, B to O in fours, is in detail : A 1 recto, title-page ; verso, blank ; A 2 recto, the dedication ; verso, the persons and the scene ; B to O 4 recto, the text of the play ; O 4 verso, blank. The running title is '*The silent Woman*'. Five copies have been collated for the text of the present edition:

(1, 2) Two copies in the British Museum with press-marks 1346.a.9 and 644.b.51, the former T. Jolley's copy with the cancel title-page, the latter defective with sheet A missing.

(3) The Bodleian copy, formerly Malone's, with the original title-page: the press-mark is Malone 229 (3).

(4) The copy in the Harvard University Library, formerly W. A. White's, with the original title-page, from a photostat kindly supplied by the Librarian.

(5) The copy in the Dyce Library, with sheet A missing.

The Quarto is a grossly careless reprint of the 1616 Folio, with only two real departures from that text—'adiudg'd' for 'iudg'd' in III. ii. 57, and 'perpetuall about motion' for 'perpetuall motion' in V. iii. 63. These are not misprints like '*continue you it*' in V. ii. 62 or 'once againe' for 'once' in V. iii. 8, but they obviously have no authority. A stupid misprint of the Folio, 'you you'll' in II. iii. 139, is reproduced, and a speech which is obviously Truewit's is assigned to Clerimont (IV. iv. 186–9). Dropped or misplaced letters, which would strike the eye at once if Stansby or his corrector had glanced at the proofs—'pay' for 'pray', 'grat' for 'great', 'tls' for ''tis', 'id' for 'in'—disfigure the book. No variant readings have been detected in the copies examined.

The Folio of 1640 is a reprint by Richard Bishop of the 1616 Folio. Owing to the unfortunate accident that the copy which Bishop acquired from Stansby contained sheet Y y after it had been reset, the 1640 text reproduced its errors and alterations at the beginning of the play. The most important are the omission of the marginal note to the second prologue, explaining that it was '*Occasion'd by some persons impertinent exception*', and therefore, it may be assumed, never spoken on the stage; the substitution of 'going' for 'marching' in I. i. 178; the omission of 'one CVT-BERD' in I. ii. 33; the assigning of La-Foole's speech ' No, sir . . . Your seruant ' in I. iv. 72–5 to Clerimont ; and the odd change of ' puritane preachings ' to ' Puritane Parlees ' in II. ii. 34–5. It also introduced new blunders. In the list of the ' Persons of the Play ' it duplicated the name of Mavis : she is ' MAD. MAVIS ' in the list of the Collegiates, and also ' M[rs]. MAVIS, *The La.* HAUGHTIES *woman.*' instead of ' M[rs]. TRVSTY '. The chief textual errors are—'speake' for 'spend' (I. i. 36) ; 'particle' for 'article' (ib. 30) ; ' master ' for ' mistris ' (iv. 81) ; ' pitch ' for ' pith ' (III. ii. 44) ; ' ARTEMIDORTS ' for ' ARTEMIDORVS ' (ib. 62) ; ' difference ' for ' diffidence ' (IV. i. 68) ; ' search ' for ' scratch ' (v. 24) ; ' barke ' for ' brake ' (vi. 28) ; and ' *divertendendo* ' for ' *diuertendo* ' (v. iii. 72). The few corrections it makes are obvious, such as ' *They* ' for ' *Thy* ' (I. i. 102) ; ' DAW.' for ' DAV.' (II. iii. 125) ; and '*nombre*' for ' *numbre* ' (IV. v. 329). It changes the punctuation rather freely, especially in the substitution of the more logical semicolon for the comma ; and it modernizes the spelling.

The text of the 1616 Folio has been twice reprinted. Dr. Aurelia Henry edited it for the Yale Studies in English, no. xxxi, in 1906 : she took her text from the copy in the Library of Yale University and collated it with the two copies in the British Museum. Professor C. M. Gayley edited the play in his *Representative English Comedies*, 1913, vol. ii, pp. 113–43 ; he used one of the Bodleian copies. He modernizes the capitals and italics, and prints ' j ' and ' v ' according to current usage. The extremely accurate reprint of the Folio edited by Professor W. Bang at Louvain in the seventh volume of his *Materialien zur Kunde des älteren englischen Dramas* unfortunately stops short at the end of sheet Z z, which ends at Act III, scene i, line 20 of *Epicoene*.

EPICOENE,

OR

The silent VVoman.

A Comœdie.

Acted in the yeere 1609. By
the Children of her Maiesties
REVELLS.

The Author B. I.

HORAT.

Vt sis tu similis Cæli, Byrrhiq; latronum,
Non ego sim Capri, neq; Sulci. Cur metuas me?

LONDON,
Printed by WILLIAM STANSBY.

M. DC. XVI.

The title-page of the 1616 Folio.

EPICOENE,
OR
The silent VVoman.

A Comœdie.

Acted in the yeare 1609.
By the Children of her Majesties
REVELS.

The Author B. I.

HORAT.
Vt sis tu similis Cœli, Byrrhiq; latronum,
Non ego sim Capri, neq; Sulci. Cur metuas me?

LONDON,
Printed by *William Stansby*, and are to be sold by
Iohn Browne at his shop in Saint *Dunstanes*
Church-yard in Fleetstreet.
1620.

The title-page of the 1620 Quarto, first issue.

The

Silent Woman.

A Comœdie.

Acted by the Children of the
REVELS.

The Author B. IONSON.

HORAT.
Vt sis tu similis Cœli, Byrrhiq; latronum,
Non ego sim Capri, neq; Sulci. Cur metuas me?

LONDON,
Printed by *William Stansby*, and are to be sold by
Iohn Browne at his shop in Saint *Dunstanes*
Church-yard in Fleetstreet.
1620.

The title-page of the 1620 Quarto, second issue.

EPICOENE,

OR

The Silent Woman.

A Comedy.

First Acted in the yeere 1609. By the
Children of her MAIESTIES
REVELLS.

With the allowance of the Master
of REVELLS.

The Author *B. J.*

HORAT.

Vt sis tu similis Cæli, Byrrhiq; latronum.
Non ego sim Capri, neq; Sulci. Cur metuas me?

LONDON,
Printed by RICHARD BISHOP.

M. DC. XL.

The title-page of the 1640 Folio.

TO THE TRVLY NOBLE, BY ALL TITLES.

Sir Francis Stuart:

SIR,

MY hope is not so nourish'd by example, as it will conclude, this dumbe peece should please you, by cause it hath pleas'd others before: but by trust, that when you haue read it, you will find it worthy to haue dis-pleas'd none. This makes, that I now number you, not onely in the Names of fauour, but the Names of iustice, to what I write; and doe, presently, call you to the exercise of that noblest, and manlyest vertue: as coueting rather to be freed in my fame, by the authority of a Iudge, then the credit of an Vndertaker. Read therefore, I pray you, and censure. There is not a line, or syllable in it changed from the simplicity of the first Copy. And, when you shall consider, through the certaine hatred of some, how much a mans innocency may bee indanger'd by an vn-certaine accusation; you will, J doubt not, so beginne to hate the iniquitie of such natures, as I shall loue the contumely done me, whose end was so honorable, as to be wip'd off by your sentence.

Your vnprofitable, but true louer,

BEN. IONSON.

DEDICATION. Heading TITLES.] TITLES, *F2* 3 *by cause*] because *F3* 10 *then*] than *F2* (*et passim*) 18 *honorable*] *honourable* F2

The Persons of the Play.

MOROSE. *A Gent. that loues no noise.*
DAVP. EVGENIE. *A Knight his nephew.*
CLERIMONT. *A Gent. his friend.*
TRVE-WIT. *Another friend.*
EPICOENE. *A yong Gent. suppos'd the silent Woman.*
IOH. DAW. *A Knight, her seruant.*
AMOROVS LA FOOLE. *A Knight also.*
THOM: OTTER. *A land, and sea-Captaine.*
CVTBERD. *A Barber.*
MVTE. *One of* MOROSE *his seruants.*

MAD. HAVGHTY. MAD. CENTAVRE. M^{rs}. MAVIS.	*Ladies Collegiates.*

M^{rs}. TRVSTY.	*The La.* HAVGHTIES *woman.*	
M^{rs}. OTTER.	*The Captaines wife.*	*Pretenders.*

PARSON.
PAGES.
SERVANTS.

THE SCENE

LONDON.

THE PERSONS OF THE PLAY. 1, 3 *Gent.*] *Gentleman* Q 1 *no*] *not* F2 11, 12 MAD.] Lady *G* 12 *Collegiates*] *Collegiate* F2, F3 13 M^{rs}.] MAD. *F2* 14 M^{rs}. TRVSTY] M^{rs}. MAVIS *F2, F3* *After* The Scene *F2 inserts the names of* The principall Comœdians *given in F1 at the end of the Play.*

EPICOENE,
OR
The silent Woman.

PROLOGVE.

TRuth sayes, of old, the art of making plaies
Was to content the people ; & their praise
Was to the *Poet* money, wine, and bayes.
But in this age, a sect of writers are,
That, onely, for particular likings care,
And will taste nothing that is populare.
With such we mingle neither braines, nor brests ;
Our wishes, like to those (make publique feasts)
Are not to please the cookes tastes, but the guests.
Yet, if those cunning palates hether come,
They shall find guests entreaty, and good roome ;
And though all relish not, sure, there will be some,
That, when they leaue their seates, shall make 'hem say,
Who wrote that piece, could so haue wrote a play :
But that, he knew, this was the better way.
For, to present all custard, or all tart,
And haue no other meats, to beare a part,
Or to want bread, and salt, were but course art.
The *Poet* prayes you then, with better thought
To sit ; and, when his cates are all in brought,
Though there be none far fet, there will deare-bought
Be fit for ladies : some for lords, knights, squires,
Some for your waiting wench, and citie-wires,
Some for your men, and daughters of *white-Friars*.
Nor is it, onely, while you keepe your seate

Heading EPICOENE,] EPICOENE *Re, F2* PROLOGUE 8 (make . . . feasts)] make . . . feasts, *Re, F2* 9 tastes,] taste *F2* 10 hether] hither *F2* 13 'hem] *'em* F3 (et passim) 21 far fet] far-fet *F2*

Here, that his feast will last; but you shall eate
A weeke at ord'naries, on his broken meat:
If his *Muse* be true,
Who commends her to you.

Another.

Occasion'd by some persons impertinent exception.

THe ends of all, who for the *Scene* doe write,
Are, or should be, to profit, and delight.
And still 't hath beene the praise of all best times,
So persons were not touch'd, to taxe the crimes.
Then, in this play, which we present to night,
And make the object of your eare, and sight,
On forfeit of your selues, thinke nothing true:
Lest so you make the maker to iudge you.
For he knowes, *Poet* neuer credit gain'd
By writing truths, but things (like truths) well fain'd.
If any, yet, will (with particular slight
Of application) wrest what he doth write;
And that he meant or him, or her, will say:
They make a libell, which he made a play.

Act I. *Scene* I.

CLERIMONT, BOY, TRVE-WIT.

He comes out making himselfe ready.

HA' you got the song yet perfect I ga' you, boy? BOY. Yes, sir.
CLE. Let me heare it.
BOY. You shall, sir, but i'faith let no body else.
CLE. Why, I pray?

PROLOGUE 27 ord'naries] ordinaries *Re*: Ordinaries *F2* 2nd PROLOGUE *Marginal note not in Re, F2* 8 you.] you, *Re*: you; *F2* I. i. ACT I. SCENE I. | *A Room in Clerimont's House.* | *Enter Clerimont making himself ready, followed by his Page.* G 4 sir,] sir; *F2* 5 pray] pay *Q*

B o y. It will get you the dangerous name of a *Poet* in towne, sir, besides me a perfect deale of ill will at the mansion you wot of, whose ladie is the argument of it: where now I am the welcom'st thing vnder a man that comes there.

C l e. I thinke, and aboue a man too, if the truth were rack'd out of you.

B o y. No faith, I'll confesse before, sir. The gentlewomen play with me, and throw me o' the bed; and carry me in to my lady; and shee kisses me with her oil'd face; and puts a perruke o' my head; and askes me an' I will weare her gowne; and I say, no: and then she hits me a blow o' the eare, and calls me innocent, and lets me goe.

C l e. No maruell, if the dore bee kept shut against your master, when the entrance is so easie to you—well sir, you shall goe there no more, lest I bee faine to seeke your voyce in my ladies rushes, a fortnight hence. Sing, sir. *Boy sings.*

T r v. Why, here's the man that can melt away his time, and neuer feeles it! what, betweene his mistris abroad, and his engle at home, high fare, soft lodging, fine clothes, and his fiddle; hee thinkes the houres ha' no wings, or the day no post-horse. Well, sir gallant, were you strooke with the plague this minute, or condemn'd to any capitall punishment to morrow, you would beginne then to thinke, and value euery article o' your time, esteeme it at the true rate, and giue all for't.

C l e. Why, what should a man doe?

T r v. Why, nothing: or that, which when 'tis done, is as idle. Harken after the next horse-race, or hunting-match; lay wagers, praise *Puppy*, or *Pepper-corne*, *White-foote*, *Franklin*; sweare vpon *White-maynes* partie; spend aloud, that my lords may heare you; visite my ladies at night, and bee able to giue 'hem the character of euery *Horses o' the time.*

I. i. 7 sir,] sir; *F2* 8 it:] it, *Re, F2* 15 oil'd] oyld *Re, F2* 17 gowne;] gowne? *F2* 22 St. dir. *Boy sings.*] *Page sings.* | *Still to be neat, still to be drest*— | *Enter Truewit.* G 27 strooke] struck *F2* 30 article] particle *F2* 35 *Marginal note not in Re, F2* 36 sweare] swere *Q* spend] speak *F2, F3*

bowler, or better o' the greene. These be the things, wherein your fashionable men exercise themselues, and I for companie.

CLE. Nay, if I haue thy authoritie, I'le not leaue yet. Come, the other are considerations, when wee come to haue gray heads, and weake hammes, moist eyes, and shrunke members. Wee'll thinke on 'hem then; then wee'll pray, and fast.

TRV. I, and destine onely that time of age to goodnesse, which our want of abilitie will not let vs employ in euill?

CLE. Why, then 'tis time enough.

TRV. Yes: as if a man should sleepe all the terme, and thinke to effect his businesse the last day. O, CLERIMONT, this time, because it is an incorporeall thing, and not subiect to sense, we mocke our selues the fineliest out of it, with vanitie, and miserie indeede: not seeking an end of wretchednesse, but onely changing the matter still.

CLE. Nay, thou'lt not leaue now——

TRV. See but our common disease! with what iustice can wee complaine, that great men will not looke vpon vs, nor be at leisure to giue our affaires such dispatch, as wee expect, when wee will neuer doe it to our selues: nor heare, nor regard our selues.

CLE. Foh, thou hast read PLVTARCHS moralls, now, or some such tedious fellow; and it showes so vilely with thee: 'Fore god, 'twill spoile thy wit vtterly. Talke me of pinnes, and feathers, and ladies, and rushes, and such things: and leaue this *Stoicitie* alone, till thou mak'st sermons.

TRV. Well, sir. If it will not take, I haue learn'd to loose as little of my kindnesse, as I can. I'le doe good to no man against his will, certainely. When were you at the colledge?

CLE. What colledge?

TRV. As if you knew not!

CLE. No faith, I came but from court, yesterday.

TRV. Why, is it not arriu'd there yet, the newes? A

I. i. 39 better] bettor *F2* 48 our] ou *Q* 50 Yes:] Yes, *Re, F2* 56 CLE.] *Clo.* Q 60 nor heare] not heare *Re, F2* 72 but] bt *Q*

new foundation, sir, here i' the towne, of ladies, that call themselues the Collegiates, an order betweene courtiers, and country-madames, that liue from their husbands; and giue entertainement to all the *Wits*, and *Braueries* o' the time, as they call 'hem: crie downe, or vp, what they like, or dislike in a braine, or a fashion, with most masculine, or rather *hermaphroditicall* authoritie: and, euery day, gaine to their colledge some new probationer.

CLE. Who is the President?

TRV. The graue, and youthfull matron, the lady HAVGHTY.

CLE. A poxe of her autumnall face, her peec'd beautie: there's no man can bee admitted till shee be ready, now adaies, till shee has painted, and perfum'd, and wash'd, and scour'd, but the boy here; and him shee wipes her oil'd lips vpon, like a sponge. I haue made a song, I pray thee heare it, o' the subiect.

SONG.

Still to be neat, still to be drest,
As, you were going to a feast;
Still to be pou'dred, still perfum'd:
Lady, it is to be presum'd,
Though arts hid causes are not found,
All is not sweet, all is not sound.

Giue me a looke, giue me a face,
That makes simplicitie a grace;
Robes loosely flowing, haire as free:
Such sweet neglect more taketh me,
Then all th'adulteries of art.
They strike mine eyes, but not my heart.

TRV. And I am, clearely, o' the other side: I loue a good dressing, before any beautie o' the world. O, a woman is, then, like a delicate garden; nor, is there one kind of it: she may varie, euery houre; take often counsell

I. i. 88 scour'd] sour'd *Re* 89 pray thee] pr'y thee *F2* 92 *As,*] *As* F2 102 *They* Re, F2: *Thy* F1 not] not, *Re*

of her glasse, and choose the best. If shee haue good eares, shew 'hem ; good haire, lay it out ; good legs, weare short cloathes ; a good hand, discouer it often ; practise any art, to mend breath, clense teeth, repaire eye-browes, paint, and professe it.

CLE. How? publiquely?

TRV. The doing of it, not the manner : that must bee priuate. Many things, that seeme foule, i' the doing, doe please, done. A lady should, indeed, studie her face, when wee thinke shee sleepes : nor, when the dores are shut, should men bee inquiring, all is sacred within, then. Is it for vs to see their perrukes put on, their false teeth, their complexion, their eye-browes, their nailes? you see guilders will not worke, but inclos'd. They must not discouer, how little serues, with the helpe of art, to adorne a great deale. How long did the canuas hang afore *Ald-gate?* were the people suffer'd to see the cities *Loue*, and *Charitie*, while they were rude stone, before they were painted, and burnish'd? No. No more should seruants approch their mistresses, but when they are compleat, and finish'd.

CLE. Well said, my TRVE-WIT.

TRV. And a wise ladie will keepe a guard alwaies vpon the place, that shee may doe things securely. I once followed a rude fellow into a chamber, where the poore madame, for haste, and troubled, snatch'd at her perruke, to couer her baldnesse : and put it on, the wrong way.

CLE. O prodigie!

TRV. And the vn-conscionable knaue held her in complement an houre, with that reuerst face, when I still look'd when shee should talke from the t'other side.

CLE. Why, thou should'st ha' releeu'd her.

TRV. No faith, I let her alone, as wee'l let this argument, if you please, and passe to another. When saw you DAVPHINE EVGENIE?

CLE. Not these three daies. Shall we goe to him this morning? he is very melancholique, I heare.

I. i. 107 choose] chuse *Re, F2* 117 inquiring,] inquiring ; *Re, F2* 121 serues] serue *Q*

TRV. Sicke o' the vncle? is hee? I met that stiffe peece of formalitie, his vncle, yesterday, with a huge turbant of night-caps on his head, buckled ouer his eares.

CLE. O, that's his custome when he walkes abroad. Hee can endure no noise, man.

TRV. So I haue heard. But is the disease so ridiculous in him, as it is made? they say, hee has beene vpon diuers treaties with the Fish-wiues, and Orenge-women; and articles propounded betweene them: mary, the Chimney-sweepers will not be drawne in.

CLE. No, nor the Broome-men: they stand out stiffely. He cannot endure a Costard-monger, he swounes if he heare one.

TRV. Me thinkes, a Smith should be ominous.

CLE. Or any Hammer-man. A Brasier is not suffer'd to dwel in the parish, nor an Armorer. He would haue hang'd a Pewterers 'prentice once vpon a shroue-tuesdaies riot, for being o' that trade, when the rest were quit.

TRV. A Trumpet should fright him terribly, or the Hau'-boyes?

CLE. Out of his senses. The Waights of the citie haue a pension of him, not to come neere that ward. This youth practis'd on him, one night, like the Bell-man; and neuer left till hee had brought him downe to the doore, with a long-sword: and there left him flourishing with the aire.

BOY. Why, sir! hee hath chosen a street to lie in, so narrow at both ends, that it will receiue no coaches, nor carts, nor any of these common noises: and therefore, we that loue him, deuise to bring him in such as we may, now and then, for his exercise, to breath him. Hee would grow resty else in his ease. His vertue would rust without action. I entreated a Beare-ward, one day, to come downe with the dogs of some foure parishes that way, and I thanke him, he did; & cryed his games vnder master MOROSE's windore: till he was sent crying away, with his head made a most

I. i. 151 mary,] mary *Re*: marry *F2* (*so usually*) 158 vpon *Q*: vp on *F1*: on *Re, F2* 159 quit] quiet *F3* 170 in *om. Re, F2* 172 ease. His] ease: his *Re, F2*

bleeding spectacle to the multitude. And, another time, a Fencer, marching to his prize, had his drum most tragically run through, for taking that street in his way, at my request.

TRV. A good wag. How do's he for the bells?

CLE. O, i' the Queenes time, he was wont to goe out of towne euery satterday at ten a clock, or on holy-day-eues. But now, by reason of the sicknesse, the perpetuitie of ringing has made him deuise a roome, with double walls, and treble seelings; the windores close shut, and calk'd: and there he liues by candle-light. He turn'd away a man, last weeke, for hauing a paire of new shooes that creak'd. And this fellow waits on him, now, in tennis-court socks, or slippers sol'd with wooll: and they talke each to other, in a trunke. See, who comes here.

Act I. *Scene* II.

DAVPHINE, TRVE-WIT, CLERIMONT.

HOw now! what aile you sirs? dumbe?

TRV. Strooke into stone, almost, I am here, with tales o' thine vncle! There was neuer such a prodigie heard of.

DAVP. I would you would once loose this subiect, my masters, for my sake. They are such as you are, that haue brought mee into that predicament, I am, with him.

TRV. How is that?

DAVP. Mary, that he will dis-inherit me, no more. Hee thinks, I, and my companie are authors of all the ridiculous acts, and moniments are told of him.

TRV. S'lid, I would be the author of more, to vexe him, that purpose deserues it: it giues thee law of plaguing him. I'll tell thee what I would doe. I would make a false almanack; get it printed: and then ha' him drawne out on a coronation day to the *tower*-wharfe, and kill him with the

I. i. 178 marching] going *Re, F2, F3* 179 through] thorow *Q* 189 sol'd] soal'd *F2* I. ii. *Enter Sir Dauphine Eugenie.* G, continuing the scene 2 Strooke] Stroke *Re*: Struck *F2* 4 loose] lose *F2* 9 authors] Authours *Q*: authours *F2* 10 moniments] mon'ments *Re, F2* 11 author] Authour *Q*

noise of the ordinance. Dis-inherit thee! hee cannot, man. Art not thou next of bloud, and his sisters sonne?

DAVP. I, but he will thrust me out of it, he vowes, and marry.

TRV. How! that's a more portent. Can he endure no noise, and will venter on a wife?

CLE. Yes: why, thou art a stranger, it seemes, to his best trick, yet. He has imploid a fellow this halfe yeere, all ouer *England*, to harken him out a dumbe woman; bee shee of any forme, or any qualitie, so shee bee able to beare children: her silence is dowrie enough, he saies.

TRV. But, I trust to god, he has found none.

CLE. No, but hee has heard of one that's lodg'd i' the next street to him, who is exceedingly soft-spoken; thrifty of her speech; that spends but sixe words a day. And her hee's about now, and shall haue her.

TRV. Is't possible! who is his agent i' the businesse?

CLE. Mary, a Barber, one CVT-BERD: an honest fellow, one that tells DAVPHINE all here.

TRV. Why, you oppresse mee with wonder! A woman, and a barber, and loue no noise!

CLE. Yes faith. The fellow trims him silently, and has not the knacke with his sheeres, or his fingers: and that continence in a barber hee thinkes so eminent a vertue, as it has made him chiefe of his counsell.

TRV. Is the barber to be seene? or the wench?

CLE. Yes, that they are.

TRV. I pray thee, DAVPHINE, let's goe thether.

DAVP. I haue some businesse now: I cannot i' faith.

TRV. You shall haue no businesse shall make you neglect this, sir, wee'll make her talke, beleeue it; or if shee will not, wee can giue out, at least so much as shall interrupt the treatie: wee will breake it. Thou art bound in conscience, when hee suspects thee without cause, to torment him.

I. ii. 16 ordinance] Ordnance *F2* 22 Yes: why,] Yes, why *Re, F2* 27 god] God *Q* 33 Barber,] Barber; *Re, F2* one CVT-BERD: *om. Re, F2, F3* 39 continence] continency *F2, F3* eminent] emient *Q* 43 pray thee] pr'y thee *F2* (*so* 56) thether] thither *F2* (*so* 69) 46 sir,] sir; *F2*

DAVP. Not I, by any meanes. I'll giue no suffrage to't. He shall neuer ha' that plea against me, that I oppos'd the least phant'sie of his. Let it lie vpon my starres to be guiltie, I'll be innocent.

TRV. Yes, and be poore, and beg ; doe, innocent : when some groome of his has got him an heire, or this barber, if hee himselfe cannot. Innocent ! I pray thee, NED, where lyes shee ? let him be innocent, still.

CLE. Why, right ouer against the barbers ; in the house, where sir IOHN DAW lyes.

TRV. You doe not meane to confound me !

CLE. Why ?

TRV. Do's he, that would marry her, know so much ?

CLE. I cannot tell.

TRV. 'Twere inough of imputation to her, with him.

CLE. Why ?

TRV. The onely talking sir i' th' towne ! IACK DAW ! And he teach her not to speake—God b'w'you. I haue some businesse too.

CLE. Will you not goe thether then ?

TRV. Not with the danger to meet DAW, for mine eares.

CLE. Why ? I thought you two had beene vpon very good termes.

TRV. Yes, of keeping distance.

CLE. They say he is a very good scholler.

TRV. I, and hee sayes it first. A poxe on him, a fellow that pretends onely to learning, buyes titles, and nothing else of bookes in him.

CLE. The world reports him to be very learned.

TRV. I am sorry, the world should so conspire to belie him.

CLE. Good faith, I haue heard very good things come from him.

TRV. You may. There's none so desperately ignorant to denie that: would they were his owne. God b'w'you gentlemen.

CLE. This is very abrupt !

I. ii. 60 doe *om. F2* 67 speake—] speake, *Re, F2* 83 *Exit hastily.* add G

Act I. *Scene* III.

DAVPHINE, CLERIMONT, BOY.

COme, you are a strange open man, to tell euery thing, thus.

CLE. Why, beleeue it DAVPHINE, TRVE-WIT'S a very honest fellow.

DAVP. I thinke no other: but this franke nature of his is not for secrets.

CLE. Nay, then, you are mistaken DAVPHINE: I know where he has beene well trusted, and discharg'd the trust very truely, and heartily.

DAVP. I contend not, NED, but, with the fewer a businesse is carried, it is euer the safer. Now we are alone, if you'll goe thether, I am for you.

CLE. When were you there?

DAVP. Last night: and such a *decameron* of sport fallen out! BOCCACE neuer thought of the like. DAW do's nothing but court her; and the wrong way. Hee would lie with her, and praises her modestie; desires that shee would talke, and bee free, and commends her silence in verses: which hee reades, and sweares, are the best that euer man made. Then railes at his fortunes, stamps, and mutines, why he is not made a counsellor, and call'd to affaires of state.

CLE. I pray thee let's goe. I would faine partake this. Some water, Boy.

DAVP. Wee are inuited to dinner together, he and I, by one that came thether to him, sir LA-FOOLE.

CLE. O, that's a precious mannikin!

DAVP. Doe you know him?

CLE. I, and he will know you too, if ere he saw you but once, though you should meet him at church in the midst of praiers. Hee is one of the *Braueries*, though he be none o' the *Wits*. He will salute a Iudge vpon the bench, and a Bishop in the pulpit, a Lawyer when hee is pleading at

I. iii. *G continues the scene* 11 thether] thither *F2* (*so* 24 14 out !] out, *Re, F2* 21 pray thee] pr'y thee *F2* (*so* 50) 22 *Exit Page.* add G 25 mannikin !] mannikin. *Re, F2*

the barre, and a Lady when shee is dauncing in a masque, and put her out. He do's giue playes, and suppers, and inuites his guests to 'hem, aloud, out of his windore, as they ride by in coaches. He has a lodging in the *Strand* for the purpose. Or to watch when ladies are gone to the *China* houses, or the *Exchange*, that hee may meet 'hem by chance, and giue 'hem presents, some two or three hundred pounds-worth of toyes, to be laught at. He is neuer without a spare banquet, or sweet-meats in his chamber, for their women to alight at, and come vp to, for a bait.

DAVP. Excellent! He was a fine youth last night, but now he is much finer! what is his christen-name? I ha' forgot.

CLE. Sir AMOROVS LA-FOOLE.

BOY. The gentleman is here below, that ownes that name.

CLE. Hart, hee's come, to inuite me to dinner, I hold my life.

DAVP. Like enough: pray thee, let's ha' him vp.

CLE. Boy, marshall him.

BOY. With a truncheon, sir?

CLE. Away, I beseech you. I'le make him tell vs his pedegree, now; and what meat he has to dinner; and, who are his guests; and, the whole course of his fortunes: with a breath.

Act I. *Scene* IIII.

LA-FOOLE, CLERIMONT, DAVPHINE.

S'Aue, deare sir DAVPHINE, honor'd master CLERIMONT.

CLE. Sir AMOROVS! you haue very much honested my lodging, with your presence.

I. iii. 36 purpose. Or] purpose: or *Re, F2* 38 presents] persents *Re* 40 for *om. Re, F2, F3* After 44 *Re-enter Page.* G 45 Sir] Sis *Re* 46 below *om. Re, F2, F3* ownes] owes *Re, F2* 53 After 'you.' *Exit Page.* G I. iv. *Enter sir Amorous La-Foole.* G, continuing the scene 1 honor'd] honour'd *F2*

LA-F. Good faith, it is a fine lodging! almost, as delicate a lodging, as mine.

CLE. Not so, sir.

LA-F. Excuse me, sir, if it were i' the *Strand*, I assure you. I am come, master CLERIMONT, to entreat you wait vpon two or three ladies, to dinner, to day.

CLE. How, sir! wait vpon 'hem? did you euer see me carry dishes?

LA-F. No, sir, dispence with me; I meant, to beare 'hem companie.

CLE. O, that I will, sir. The doubtfulnesse o' your phrase, beleeue it, sir, would breed you a quarrell, once an houre, with the terrible boyes, if you should but keepe 'hem fellowship a day.

LA-F. It should be extremely against my will, sir, if I contested with any man.

CLE. I beleeue it, sir; where hold you your feast?

LA-F. At TOM OTTERS, sir.

DAVP. TOM OTTER? what's he?

LA-F. Captaine OTTER, sir; he is a kind of gamster: but he has had command, both by sea, and by land.

DAVP. O, then he is *animal amphibium?*

LA-F. I, sir: his wife was the rich *China*-woman, that the courtiers visited so often, that gaue the rare entertainment. She commands all at home.

CLE. Then, she is Captaine OTTER?

LA-F. You say very well, sir; she is my kins-woman, a LA-FOOLE by the mother side, and will inuite, any great ladies, for my sake.

DAVP. Not of the LA-FOOLES of *Essex?*

LA-F. No, sir, the LA-FOOLES of *London*.

CLE. Now, h'is in.

LA-F. They all come out of our house, the LA-FOOLES o' the north, the LA-FOOLES of the west, the LA-FOOLES of the east, and south—we are as ancient a

I. iv. 17 but *om. Re, F2, F3* 24 gamster :] gamster, *Re*: gamester, *F2* 28 often,] often; *Re, F2* 38 of the west] o' the west *Q*

family, as any is in *Europe*—but I my selfe am descended lineally of the *french* LA-FOOLES—and, wee doe beare for our coate *Yellow*, or *Or*, checker'd *Azure*, and *Gules*, and some three or foure colours more, which is a very noted coate, and has, some-times, beene solemnely worne by diuers nobilitie of our house—but let that goe, antiquitie is not respected now—I had a brace of fat Does sent me, gentlemen, & halfe a dosen of phesants, a dosen or two of godwits, and some other fowle, which I would haue eaten, while they are good, and in good company—there will be a great lady, or two, my lady HAVGHTY, my lady CENTAVRE, mistris DOL MAVIS—and they come a' purpose, to see the silent gentlewoman, mistris EPICOENE, that honest sir IOHN DAW has promis'd to bring thether—and then, mistris TRVSTY, my ladies woman, will be there too, and this honorable Knight, sir DAVPHINE, with your selfe, master CLERIMONT—and wee'll bee very merry, and haue fidlers, and daunce—I haue beene a mad wag, in my time, and haue spent some crownes since I was a page in court, to my lord LOFTY, and after, my ladies gentleman-vsher, who got mee knighted in *Ireland*, since it pleas'd my elder brother to die—I had as faire a gold ierkin on that day, as any was worne in the *Iland*-voyage, or at *Caliz*, none disprais'd, and I came ouer in it hither, show'd my selfe to my friends, in court, and after went downe to my tenants, in the countrey, and suruai'd my lands, let new leases, tooke their money, spent it in the eye o' the land here, vpon ladies—and now I can take vp at my pleasure.

DAVP. Can you take vp ladies, sir?

CLE. O, let him breath, he has not recouer'd.

DAVP. Would I were your halfe, in that commoditie—

LA-F. No, sir, excuse mee: I meant money, which can take vp any thing. I haue another guest, or two, to inuite,

I. iv. 42 for *om. Re, F2, F3* 50 great] grat *Q* 55 honorable] honourable *Q, F2* 63 *Caliz*] *Cadiz* F3 71 commoditie— commodity. *Re, F2* 72 LA-F.] CLE. *Re, F2, F3*

and say as much to, gentlemen. I'll take my leaue abruptly, in hope you will not faile—Your seruant.

Davp. Wee will not faile you, sir precious La-foole; but shee shall, that your ladies come to see: if I haue credit, afore sir Daw.

Cle. Did you euer heare such a wind-fucker, as this?

Davp. Or, such a rooke, as the other! that will betray his mistris, to be seene. Come, 'tis time, we preuented it.

Cle. Goe.

Act II. *Scene* I.

Morose, Mvte.

CAnnot I, yet, find out a more compendious method, then by this trunke, to saue my seruants the labour of speech, and mine eares, the discord of sounds? Let mee see: all discourses, but mine owne, afflict mee, they seeme harsh, impertinent, and irksome. Is it not possible, that thou should'st answere me, by signes, and, I apprehend thee, fellow? speake not, though I question you. You haue taken the ring, off from the street dore, as I bad you? answere me not, by speech, but by silence; vnlesse, it be otherwise (——) very good. And, you haue fastened on a thicke quilt, or flock-bed, on the out-side of the dore; that if they knocke with their daggers, or with bricke-bats, they can make no noise? but with your leg, your answere, vnlesse it be otherwise (——) very good. This is not, onely, fit modestie in a seruant, but good state, and discretion in a master. And you haue been with Cvtberd, the barber, to haue him come to me? (——) good. And, he will come presently? answere me not but with your leg, vnlesse it be otherwise: if it be otherwise, shake your head, or shrug (——) so. Your *Italian*, and *Spaniard*, are wise in

At the breaches, still the fellow makes legs: or signes.

I. iv. 75 *Exit.* add G 79 -fucker] -sucker *F3* 81 mistris] master *F2*: Master *F3* 82 *Exeunt.* add G II. i. Act II. Scene I. | *A Room in Morose's House.* | *Enter Morose with a tube in his hand, followed by Mute.* G 1 Cannot] Can not *Re, F2* 9 vnlesse,] unlesse *F2* 13 your answere] you answer *F2, F3* 20 shrug (—) so] shrug. (—) So *Re, F2*

these! and it is a frugall, and comely grauitie. How long will it bee, ere CVTBERD come? stay, if an houre, hold vp your whole hand; if halfe an houre, two fingers; if a quarter, one; (——) good: halfe a quarter? 'tis well. And haue you giuen him a key, to come in without knocking? (——) good. And, is the lock oild, and the hinges, to day? (——) good. And the quilting of the staires no where worne out, and bare? (——) very good. I see, by much doctrine, and impulsion, it may be effected: stand by. The *Turke*, in this diuine discipline, is admirable, exceeding all the potentates of the earth; still waited on by mutes; and all his commands so executed; yea, euen in the warre (as I haue heard) and in his marches, most of his charges, and directions, giuen by signes, and with silence: an exquisite art! and I am heartily asham'd, and angrie often-times, that the Princes of *Christendome*, should suffer a *Barbarian*, to transcend 'hem in so high a point of felicitie. I will practise it, hereafter. How now? oh! oh! what villaine? what prodigie of mankind is that? looke. Oh! cut his throat, cut his throat: what murderer, hell-hound, deuill can this be?

One windes a horne without. Againe.

MVT. It is a post from the court——

MOR. Out rogue, and must thou blow thy horne, too?

MVT. Alas, it is a post from the court, sir, that sayes, hee must speake with you, paine of death——

MOR. Paine of thy life, be silent.

Act II. *Scene* II.

TRVE-WIT, MOROSE, CVTBERD.

BY your leaue, sir (I am a stranger here) is your name, master MOROSE? is your name, master MOROSE? fishes! *Pythagoreans* all! this is strange! What say you, sir, nothing? Has HARPOCRATES beene here, with

II. i. 24 After 'one' *holds up a finger bent.* G 39 After 'looke.' *Exit Mute.* G 40 deuill] divell *F2* After 41 *Re-enter Mute.* G 45 with *om. Re, F2, F3* II. ii. *Enter Truewit with a post-horn, and a halter in his hand.* G, continuing the scene 1 sir (I . . . here)] sir, I . . . here: *Re, F2* 3 all!] all? *Re, F2* strange!] strange. *Re, F2*

his club, among you? well sir, I will beleeue you to bee the man, at this time: I will venter vpon you, sir. Your friends at court commend 'hem to you, sir——

(MOR. O men! ô manners! was there euer such an impudence?)

TRV. And are extremely sollicitous for you, sir.

MOR. Whose knaue are you!

TRV. Mine owne knaue, and your compere, sir.

MOR. Fetch me my sword——

TRV. You shall taste the one halfe of my dagger, if you do (groome) and you, the other, if you stirre, sir: be patient, I charge you, in the kings name, and heare mee without insurrection. They say, you are to marry? to marry! doe you marke, sir?

MOR. How then, rude companion!

TRV. Mary, your friends doe wonder, sir, the *Thames* being so neere, wherein you may drowne so handsomely; or *London*-bridge, at a low fall, with a fine leape, to hurry you downe the streame; or, such a delicate steeple, i' the towne, as *Bow*, to vault from; or, a brauer height, as *Pauls;* or, if you affected to doe it neerer home, and a shorter way, an excellent garret windore, into the street; or, a beame, in the said garret, with this halter; which they haue sent, and desire, that you would sooner commit your graue head to this knot, then to the wed-lock nooze; or, take a little sublimate, and goe out of the world, like a rat; or a flie (as one said) with a straw i' your arse: any way, rather, then to follow this goblin *matrimony.* Alas, sir, doe you euer thinke to find a chaste wife, in these times? now? when there are so many masques, plaies, puritane preachings, mad-folkes, and other strange sights to be seene daily, priuate and publique? if you had liu'd in king ETHELRED'S time, sir, or EDWARD the Confessors,

He shewes him a halter.

II. ii. 6 venter] venture *F3* 14 taste] taste, *Re, F2* 21 drowne] drowne, *Re, F2* 25 *Pauls;* Re, F2: *Pauls,* F1, Q 26 windore] window *Re, F2* 27 halter;] halter, *Re, F2* 31 or] or, *Re, F2* 35 preachings] parlee's *Re*: Parlees *F2, F3* seene] seene, *F2* 37 ETHELRED'S *Re, F2*: ETHELDRED'S *F1*: *Etheldred's* Q

you might, perhaps, haue found in some cold countrey-hamlet, then, a dull frostie wench, would haue been contented with one man: now, they will as soone be pleas'd with one leg, or one eye. I'll tell you, sir, the monstrous hazards you shall runne with a wife.

MOR. Good sir! haue I euer cosen'd any friends of yours of their land? bought their possessions? taken forfeit of their morgage? begg'd a reuersion from 'hem? bastarded their issue? what haue I done, that may deserue this?

TRV. Nothing, sir, that I know, but your itch of marriage.

MOR. Why? if I had made an assassinate vpon your father; vitiated your mother; rauished your sisters——

TRV. I would kill you, sir, I would kill you, if you had.

MOR. Why? you doe more in this, sir: It were a vengeance centuple, for all facinorous acts, that could be nam'd, to doe that you doe——

TRV. Alas, sir, I am but a messenger: I but tell you, what you must heare. It seemes, your friends are carefull after your soules health, sir, and would haue you know the danger (but you may doe your pleasure, for all them, I perswade not, sir) If, after you are married, your wife doe run away with a vaulter, or the *Frenchman* that walkes vpon ropes, or him that daunces the iig, or a fencer for his skill at his weapon, why it is not their fault; they haue discharged their consciences: when you know what may happen. Nay, suffer valiantly, sir, for I must tell you, all the perills that you are obnoxious too. If shee be faire, yong, and vegetous, no sweet meats euer drew more flies; all the yellow doublets, and great roses i' the towne will bee there. If foule, and crooked, shee'll bee with them, and buy those doublets and roses, sir. If rich, and that you marry her dowry, not her; shee'll raigne in your house, as imperious

II. ii. 39 frostie] frostrie *Q* 43 cosen'd] cosen'd, *Re, F2* 44 yours] yours, *Re, F2* 45 morgage] Mortgage *F3* 51 mother;] mother: *Re, F2* 53 It] it *Re, F2* 59 them,] them; *F2* 60 If] if *Re, F2* 62 fencer] fencer, *Re, F2* 66 yong, and] and young, *Q*

as a widow. If noble, all her kindred will be your tyrannes. If fruitfull, as proud as *May*, and humorous as *April;* she must haue her doctors, her midwiues, her nurses, her longings euery houre: though it be for the dearest morsell of man. If learned, there was neuer such a parrat; all your patrimony will be too little for the guests, that must be inuited, to heare her speake *Latine* and *Greeke:* and you must lie with her in those languages too, if you will please her. If precise, you must feast all the silenc'd brethren, once in three daies; salute the sisters; entertaine the whole family, or wood of 'hem; and heare long-winded exercises, singings, and catechisings, which you are not giuen to, and yet must giue for: to please the zealous matron your wife, who, for the holy cause, will cosen you, ouer and aboue. You beginne to sweat, sir? but this is not halfe, i' faith: you may do your pleasure notwithstanding, as I said before, I come not to perswade you. Vpon my faith, master seruingman, if you doe stirre, I will beat you. *The Mute is stealing away.*

MOR. O, what is my sinne! what is my sinne?

TRV. Then, if you loue your wife, or rather, dote on her, sir: ô, how shee'll torture you! and take pleasure i' your torments! you shall lye with her but when she lists; she will not hurt her beauty, her complexion; or it must be for that iewell, or that pearle, when she do's; euery halfe houres pleasure must be bought anew: and with the same paine, and charge, you woo'd her at first. Then, you must keepe what seruants shee please; what company shee will; that friend must not visit you without her licence; and him shee loues most shee will seeme to hate eagerliest, to decline your ielousie; or, faigne to bee ielous of you first; and for that cause goe liue with her she-friend, or cosen at the colledge, that can instruct her in all the mysteries, of writing letters, corrupting seruants, taming spies; where shee must haue that rich goune for such a great day; a new one for the next; a richer for the third; bee seru'd in siluer; haue the chamber fill'd with a succession of groomes, foot-men,

II. ii. 80 brethren] bethren *F2*   100 most] most, *F2*

vshers, and other messengers ; besides embroyderers, iewellers, tyre-women, sempsters, fether-men, perfumers ; while shee feeles not how the land drops away ; nor the acres melt ; nor forsees the change, when the mercer has your woods for her veluets ; neuer weighes what her pride costs, sir : so shee may kisse a page, or a smoth chinne, that has the despaire of a beard ; bee a states-woman, know all the newes, what was done at *Salisbury*, what at the *Bath*, what at court, what in progresse ; or, so shee may censure *poets*, and authors, and stiles, and compare 'hem, DANIEL with SPENSER, IONSON with the tother youth, and so foorth ; or, be thought cunning in controuersies, or the very knots of diuinitie ; and haue, often in her mouth, the state of the question : and then skip to the *Mathematiques*, and demonstration and answere, in religion to one ; in state, to another, in baud'ry to a third.

MOR. O, ô !

TRV. All this is very true, sir. And then her going in disguise to that coniurer, and this cunning woman : where the first question is, how soone you shall die ? next, if her present seruant loue her ? next that, if she shall haue a new seruant ? and how many ? which of her family would make the best baud, male, or female ? what precedence shee shall haue by her next match ? and sets downe the answers, and beleeues 'hem aboue the scriptures. Nay, perhaps she'll study the art.

MOR. Gentle sir, ha' you done ? ha' you had your pleasure o' me ? I'll thinke of these things.

TRV. Yes sir : and then comes reeking home of vapor and sweat, with going afoot, and lies in, a moneth, of a new face, all oyle, and birdlime ; and rises in asses milke, and is clens'd with a new *fucus* : god b'w'you, sir. One thing more (which I had almost forgot.) This too, with whom you are to marry, may haue made a conuayance of her

II. ii. 111 forsees] foresees *Q, F2* 118 IONSON] *Iohnson* Q : JOHNSON *F2* 136 vapor] vapour *F2* 138 rises] rinses *F. Cunningham conj.* 139 god] God *Q*

virginity aforehand, as your wise widdowes doe of their states, before they marry, in trust to some friend, sir: who can tell? or if she haue not done it yet, she may doe, vpon the wedding day, or the night before, and antidate you cuckold. The like has beene heard of, in nature. 'Tis no deuis'd impossible thing, sir. God b'w'you: I'll be bold to leaue this rope with you, sir, for a remembrance. Farewell MVTE.

MOR. Come, ha' me to my chamber: but first shut the dore. O, shut the dore, shut the dore: Is he come againe? *The horne againe.*

CVT. 'Tis I, sir, your barber.

MOR. O, CVTBERD, CVTBERD, CVTBERD! here has bin a cut-throate with me: helpe me in to my bed, and giue me physicke with thy counsell.

Act II. *Scene* III.

DAW, CLERIMONT, DAVPHINE, EPICOENE.

NAy, and she will, let her refuse, at her owne charges: 'tis nothing to me, gentlemen. But she will not bee inuited to the like feasts, or guests, euery day.

CLE. O, by no meanes, shee may not refuse—to stay at home, if you loue your reputation: 'Slight, you are inuited thither o' purpose to bee seene, and laught at by the lady of the colledge, and her shadowes. This trumpeter hath proclaim'd you. *They dis-swade her, priuately.*

DAVP. You shall not goe; let him be laught at in your steade, for not bringing you: and put him to his extemporall faculty of fooling, and talking loud to satisfie the company.

CLE. He will suspect vs, talke aloud. 'Pray, mistris EPICOENE, let's see your verses; we haue sir IOHN

II. ii. 144 or if] orif *F1* 146 beene] bin *Q* 149 *Exit.* add G After 151 *Enter Cutbeard.* G 154 bin] beene *F2* II. iii. SCENE II. | *A Room in sir John Daw's House.* | *Enter Daw, Clerimont, Dauphine, and Epicœne.* G 1 and] an' *F2* 8 proclaim'd] proclym'd *Q* 13 'Pray, *Q*: 'Pray' *F1*: 'Pray *F2* 14 verses;] verses, *F2*

DAW's leaue: doe not conceale your seruants merit, and your owne glories.

EPI. They'll proue my seruants glories, if you haue his leaue so soone.

DAVP. His vaine glories, lady!

DAW. Shew 'hem, shew 'hem, mistris, I dare owne 'hem.

EPI. Iudge you, what glories?

DAW. Nay, I'll read 'hem my selfe, too: an author must recite his owne workes. It is a *madrigall* of modestie.

Modest, and faire, for faire and good are neere
Neighbours, how ere.—

DAVP. Very good.

CLE. I, is't not?

DAW. *No noble vertue euer was alone,*
But two in one.

DAVP. Excellent!

CLE. That againe, I pray' sir IOHN.

DAVP. It has some thing in 't like rare wit, and sense.

CLE. Peace.

DAW. *No noble vertue euer was alone,*
But two in one.
Then, when I praise sweet modestie, I praise
Bright beauties raies:
And hauing prais'd both beauty'and modestee,
I haue prais'd thee.

DAVP. Admirable!

CLE. How it chimes, and cries tinke i' the close, diuinely!

DAVP. I, 'tis SENECA.

CLE. No, I thinke 'tis PLVTARCH.

DAW. The *dor* on PLVTARCH, and SENECA, I hate it: they are mine owne imaginations, by that light. I wonder those fellowes haue such credit with gentlemen!

CLE. They are very graue authors.

II. iii. 20 DAW *corr. F1*: Daw *F1 originally* 24 his | owne workes *corr. F1*: his own | workes *F1 originally* workes] Worke *Q* *madrigall* corr. F1, F2: madrigall *F1 originally*: *Madrigall* Q 28 is't] Is't *Ff, Q* 32 pray'] pray *F2* 39 *beauty'and*] *beauty and* F2

DAW. Graue asses! meere *Essaists!* a few loose sentences, and that's all. A man would talke so, his whole age, I doe vtter as good things euery houre, if they were collected, and obseru'd, as either of 'hem.

DAVP. Indeede! sir IOHN?

CLE. Hee must needs, liuing among the *Wits*, and *Braueries* too.

DAVP. I, and being president of 'hem, as he is.

DAW. There's ARISTOTLE, a mere common-place fellow; PLATO, a discourser; THVCIDIDES, and LIVIE, tedious and drie; TACITVS, an entire knot: sometimes worth the vntying, very seldome.

CLE. What doe you think of the *Poets*, sir IOHN?

DAW. Not worthy to be nam'd for authors. HOMER, an old tedious prolixe asse, talkes of curriers, and chines of beefe. VIRGIL, of dunging of land, and bees. HORACE, of I know not what.

CLE. I thinke so.

DAW. And so PINDARVS, LYCOPHRON, ANACREON, CATVLLVS, SENECA the tragœdian, LVCAN, PROPERTIVS, TIBVLLVS, MARTIAL, IVVENAL, AVSONIVS, STATIVS, POLITIAN, VALERIVS FLACCVS, and the rest——

CLE. What a sacke full of their names he has got!

DAVP. And how he poures 'hem out! POLITIAN, with VALERIVS FLACCVS!

CLE. Was not the character right, of him?

DAVP. As could be made, i' faith.

DAW. And PERSIVS, a crabbed cockescombe, not to be endur'd.

DAVP. Why? whom do you account for authors, sir IOHN DAW?

DAW. *Syntagma Iuris ciuilis*, *Corpus Iuris ciuilis*, *Corpus Iuris canonici*, the King of *Spaines* bible.

DAVP. Is the King of *Spaines* bible an author?

II. iii. 51 age,] age; *F2* 57 There's *corr. F1, Q, F2*: There is *F1 originally* common-place fellow *F2*: common place-fellow *F1, Q* 81 *Corpus Iuris canonici*] *Corpns Iuris canonici* F1

CLE. Yes, and *Syntagma*.

DAVP. What was that *Syntagma*, sir?

DAW. A ciuill law⟨i⟩er, a *Spaniard*.

DAVP. Sure, *Corpus* was a *Dutch*-man.

CLE. I, both the *Corpusses*, I knew 'hem: they were very corpulent authors.

DAW. And, then there's VATABLVS, POMPONATIVS, SYMANCHA, the other are not to be receiu'd, within the thought of a scholler.

DAVP. Fore god, you haue a simple learn'd seruant, lady, in titles.

CLE. I wonder that hee is not called to the helme, and made a councellor!

DAVP. He is one extraordinary.

CLE. Nay, but in ordinarie! to say truth, the state wants such.

DAVP. Why, that will follow.

CLE. I muse, a mistris can be so silent to the dotes of such a seruant.

DAW. 'Tis her vertue, sir. I haue written somewhat of her silence too.

DAVP. In verse, sir IOHN?

CLE. What else?

DAVP. Why? how can you iustifie your owne being of a *Poet*, that so slight all the old *Poets*?

DAW. Why? euery man, that writes in verse, is not a *Poet*; you haue of the *Wits*, that write verses, and yet are no *Poets*: they are *Poets* that liue by it, the poore fellowes that liue by it.

DAVP. Why? would not you liue by your verses, sir IOHN?

CLE. No, 'twere pittie he should. A knight liue by his verses? he did not make 'hem to that ende, I hope.

DAVP. And yet the noble SIDNEY liues by his, and the noble family not asham'd.

II. iii. 86 law⟨i⟩er] Lawier *Q* 91 SYMANCHA,] SYMANCHA; *F2* 93 god] God *Q* 114 IOHN?] IOHN. *F1*

CLE. I, he profest himselfe; but sir IOHN DAW has more caution: hee'll not hinder his owne rising i' the state so much! doe you thinke hee will? Your verses, good sir IOHN, and no *poems.*

DAW. *Silence in woman, is like speech in man,*
Deny't who can.

DAV. Not I, beleeue it: your reason, sir.

DAW. *Nor, is't a tale,*
That female vice should be a vertue male,
Or masculine vice, a female vertue be:
You shall it see
Prou'd with increase,
I know to speake, and shee to hold her peace.

Do you conceiue me, gentlemen?

DAV. No faith, how meane you with increase, sir IOHN?

DAW. Why, with increase is, when I court her for the comon cause of mankind; and she says nothing, but *consentire videtur:* and in time is *grauida.*

DAV. Then, this is a ballad of procreation?

CLE. A *madrigall* of procreation, you mistake.

EPI. 'Pray giue me my verses againe, seruant.

DAW. If you'll aske 'hem aloud, you shal.

CLE. See, here 's TRVE-WIT againe!

Act II. *Scene* IIII.

CLERIMONT, TRVE-WIT, DAVPHINE, CVT-BERD, DAW, EPICOENE.

WHere hast thou beene, in the name of madnesse! thus accoutred with thy horne?

TRV. Where the sound of it might haue pierc'd your senses, with gladnes, had you beene in eare-reach of it.

II. iii. 122 and] are *F2, F3* 126 DAW. *F2*: DAV. *F1*: *Daup.* Q *is't* F2: *i'st* F1, Q 130 *increase,*] *increase ;* F2 133 faith,] faith; *F2* 135 nothing] nothiug *F1* 138 procreation] proceation *F1* 140 you'll] you you'll *F1, Q*: you'le *F2* *Walks aside with the papers.* add G After 140 *Enter Truewit with his horn.* G 141 TRVE-WIT] *Tru-wit* Q (which adopts this spelling from this point) II. iv. *G continues the scene*

DAVPHINE, fall downe and worship me: I haue forbid the banes, lad. I haue been with thy vertuous vncle, and haue broke the match.

DAVP. You ha' not, I hope.

TRV. Yes faith; and thou shouldst hope otherwise, I should repent me: this horne got me entrance, kisse it. I had no other way to get in, but by faining to be a post; but when I got in once, I prou'd none, but rather the contrary, turn'd him into a post, or a stone, or what is stiffer, with thundring into him the incommodities of a wife, and the miseries of marriage. If euer GORGON were seene in the shape of a woman, hee hath seene her in my description. I haue put him off o' that sent, for euer. Why doe you not applaud, and adore me, sirs? why stand you mute? Are you stupid? you are not worthy o' the benefit.

DAVP. Did not I tell you? mischiefe!——

CLE. I would you had plac'd this benefit somewhere else.

TRV. Why so?

CLE. Slight, you haue done the most inconsiderate, rash, weake thing, that euer man did to his friend.

DAVP. Friend! if the most malicious enemy I haue, had studied to inflict an iniury vpon me, it could not bee a greater.

TRV. Wherein? for gods-sake! Gent: come to your selues againe.

DAVP. But I presag'd thus much afore, to you.

CLE. Would my lips had beene soldred, when I spak on 't. Slight, what mou'd you to be thus impertinent?

TRV. My masters, doe not put on this strange face to pay my courtesie: off with this visor. Haue good turnes done you, and thanke 'hem this way?

DAVP. Fore heau'n, you haue vndone me. That, which I haue plotted for, and beene maturing now these foure moneths, you haue blasted in a minute: now I am lost,

II. iv. 9 and] an' *F2* 10 entrance,] entrance; *F2* 17 haue] hane *F1* sent] scent *F3* 17 Why] Wby *F1* 32 spak] spake *Q, F2*

I may speake. This gentlewoman was lodg'd here by me o' purpose, and, to be put vpon my vncle, hath profest this obstinate silence for my sake, being my entire friend; and one, that for the requitall of such a fortune, as to marry him, would haue made mee very ample conditions: where now, all my hopes are vtterly miscarried by this vnlucky accident.

CLE. Thus 'tis, when a man will be ignorantly officious; doe seruices, and not know his why: I wonder what curteous itch possess'd you! you neuer did absurder part i' your life, nor a greater trespasse to friendship, to humanity.

DAVP. Faith, you may forgiue it, best: 'twas your cause principally.

CLE. I know it, would it had not.

DAVP. How now CVTBERD? what newes?

CVT. The best, the happiest that euer was, sir. There has beene a mad gentleman with your vncle, this morning (I thinke this be the gentleman) that has almost talk'd him out of his wits, with threatning him from marriage——

DAVP. On, I pray thee.

CVT. And your vnkle, sir, hee thinkes 'twas done by your procurement; therefore he will see the party, you wot of, presently: and if he like her, he sayes, and that she be so inclining to dombe, as I haue told him, he sweares hee will marry her, to day, instantly, and not deferre it a minute longer.

DAVP. Excellent! beyond our expectation!

TRV. Beyond your expectation? by this light, I knewe it would bee thus.

DAVP. Nay, sweet TRVE-WIT, forgiue me.

TRV. No, I was ignorantly officious, impertinent: this was the absurd, weake part.

CLE. Wilt thou ascribe that to merit, now, was meere fortune?

II. iv. 50 to humanity] or humanity *F2, F3* 51 DAVP.] DAVP *F1* it,] it *F2* 53 CLE.] DLE. *F1* After 53 *Enter Cutbeard.* G 54 DAVP.] CAVP. *F1* 56 After 'morning' *seeing Truewit.* G 59 pray thee] pr'y thee *F2* 63 dombe] dumbe *F2* 67 your] our *F2, F3*

TRV. Fortune? mere prouidence. Fortune had not a finger in 't. I saw it must necessarily in nature fall out so: my *genius* is neuer false to me in these things. Shew me, how it could be otherwise.

DAVP. Nay, gentlemen, contend not, 'tis well now.

TRV. Alasse, I let him goe on with inconsiderate, and rash, and what he pleas'd.

CLE. Away thou strange iustifier of thy selfe, to bee wiser then thou wert, by the euent.

TRV. Euent! By this light, thou shalt neuer perswade me, but I fore-saw it, aswell as the starres themselues.

DAVP. Nay, gentlemen, 'tis well now: doe you two entertaine sir IOHN DAW, with discourse, while I send her away with instructions.

TRV. I'll be acquainted with her, first, by your fauour.

CLE. Master TRVE-WIT, lady, a friend of ours.

TRV. I am sorry, I haue not knowne you sooner, lady, to celebrate this rare vertue of your silence.

CLE. Faith, an' you had come sooner, you should ha' seene, and heard her well celebrated in sir IOHN DAW'S *madrigalls.*

TRV. IACK DAW, god saue you, when saw you LA-FOOLE?

DAW. Not since last night, master TRVE-WIT.

TRV. That's miracle! I thought you two had beene inseparable.

DAW. Hee's gone to inuite his guests.

TRV. Gods so! 'tis true! what a false memory haue I towards that man! I am one: I met him e'ne now, vpon that he calls his delicate fine blacke horse, rid into a foame, with poasting from place to place, and person to person, to giue 'hem the *cue*——

CLE. Lest they should forget?

TRV. Yes: there was neuer poore captaine tooke more

II. iv. 78 'tis] tis *F1, Q* After 91 *Exeunt Daup. Epi. and Cutbeard.* G 95 TRV.] *True.* [*advances to Daw.*] G 98 miracle] a miracle *F2, F3* 101 'tis *F2*: tis *F1*: tls *Q* 102 e'ne] ev'n *F2*

paines at a muster to show men, then he, at this meale, to shew friends.

DAW. It is his quarter-feast, sir.

CLE. What! doe you say so, sir Iohn?

TRV. Nay, IACK DAW will not be out, at the best friends hee has, to the talent of his wit: where's his mistris, to heare and applaud him? is she gone!

DAW. Is mistris EPICOENE gone?

CLE. Gone afore, with sir DAVPHINE, I warrant, to the place.

TRV. Gone afore! that were a manifest iniurie; a disgrace and a halfe: to refuse him at such a festiuall time, as this, being a *Brauery*, and a *Wit* too.

CLE. Tut, hee'll swallow it like creame: hee's better read in *iure ciuili*, then to esteeme any thing a disgrace is offer'd him from a mistris.

DAW. Nay, let her eene goe; she shall sit alone, and bee dumbe in her chamber, a weeke together, for IOHN DAW, I warrant her: do's she refuse me?

CLE. No, sir, doe not take it so to heart: shee do's not refuse you, but a little neglect you. Good faith, TRVEWIT, you were too blame to put it into his head, that shee do's refuse him.

TRV. She do's refuse him, sir, palpably: how euer you mince it. An' I were as hee, I would sweare to speake ne're a word to her, to day, for't.

DAW. By this light, no more I will not.

TRV. Nor to any body else, sir.

DAW. Nay, I will not say so, gentlemen.

CLE. It had beene an excellent happy condition for the company, if you could haue drawne him to it.

DAW. I'll be very melancholique, i' faith.

CLE. As a dog, if I were as you, sir IOHN.

TRV. Or a snaile, or a hog-louse: I would roule my selfe vp for this day, introth, they should not vnwinde me.

II. iv. 131 She . . . him, sir,] Sir, she . . . him, *F2* 139, 148 melancholique] melancholick *F2*

DAW. By this pick-tooth, so I will.

CLE. 'Tis well done: he beginnes already to be angry with his teeth.

DAW. Will you goe, gentlemen?

CLE. Nay, you must walke alone, if you bee right melancholique, sir IOHN.

TRV. Yes sir, wee'll dog you, wee'll follow you a farre off.

CLE. Was there euer such a two yards of knighthood, measur'd out by *Time*, to be sold to laughter?

TRV. A meere talking mole! hang him: no mushrome was euer so fresh. A fellow so vtterly nothing, as he knowes not what he would be.

CLE. Let's follow him: but first, let's goe to DAVPHINE, hee's houering about the house, to heare what newes.

TRV. Content.

Act II. *Scene* V.

MOROSE, EPICOENE, CVTBERD, MVTE.

WElcome CVTBERD; draw neere with you⟨r⟩ faire chardge: and, in her eare, softly intreat her to vnmasque (——) So. Is the dore shut? (——) inough. Now, CVTBERD, with the same discipline I vse to my family, I will question you. As I conceiue, CVTBERD, this gentlewoman is shee, you haue prouided, and brought, in hope shee will fit me in the place and person of a wife? Answer me not, but with your leg, vnlesse it be otherwise: (——) very well done CVTBERD. I conceiue, besides, CVTBERD, you haue beene pre-acquainted with her birth, education, and quallities, or else you would not preferre her to my acceptance, in the waighty consequence of

II. iv. 150 *Exit Daw.* add G   153 hang him *om. Q*   II. v. SCENE III. | *A Room in Morose's House.* | *Enter Morose and Mute, followed by Cutbeard with Epicœne.* G   1 your] you *F1*   3 dore] dore' *F2* (*perhaps for* 'dore,')   9 conceiue] concciue *F1*   11 quallities] qualities *Q, F2*

marriage. (——) this I conceiue, C V T B E R D. Answer me not but with your leg, vnlesse it bee otherwise. (——) Very well done C V T B E R D. Giue aside now a little, and leaue me to examine her condition, and aptitude to my affection. *He goes about her, and viewes her.* Shee is exceeding faire, and of a speciall good fauour; a sweet composition, or harmony of limmes: her temper of beauty has the true height of my blood. The knaue hath exceedingly wel fitted me without: I will now trie her within. Come neere, faire gentlewoman: let not my behauiour seeme rude, though vnto you, being rare, it may happely appeare strange. (——) *She curtsies.* Nay, lady, you may speake, though C V T B E R D, and my man, might not: for, of all sounds, onely, the sweet voice of a faire lady has the iust length of mine eares. I beseech you, say lady, out of the first fire of meeting eyes, (they say) loue is stricken: doe you feele any such motion, sodenly shot into you, from any part you see in me? ha, lady? (——) *Curt'sie.* Alasse, lady, these answers by silent curt'sies, from you, are too courtlesse, and simple. I haue euer had my breeding in court: and shee that shall bee my wife, must bee accomplished with courtly, and audacious ornaments. Can you speake lady?

E P I. Iudge you, forsooth. *She speakes softly.*

M O R. What say you, lady? speake out, I beseech you.

E P I. Iudge you, forsooth.

M O R. O' my iudgement, a diuine softnes! but can you naturally, lady, as I enioyne these by doctrine & industry, referre your self to the search of my iudgement, and (not taking pleasure in your tongue, which is a womans chiefest pleasure) thinke it plausible, to answer me by silent gestures, so long as my speeches iumpe right, with what you conceiue? (——) *Curt'sie.* Excellent! diuine! if it were possible she should hold out thus! Peace C V T B E R D, thou art made for euer, as thou hast made mee, if this felicitie haue lasting:

II. v. 23 happely] happily *Q* (—)] (—(*F1* 24 speake,] speak; *F2* 26 eares] eare *Q* 28 sodenly] suddenly *F2* 41 tongue] tougue *F1* 45 CVTBERD] CVTBRD *F1*

but I will trie her further. Deare lady, I am courtly, I tell you, and I must haue mine eares banqueted with pleasant, and wittie conferences, pretty girds, scoffes, and daliance in her, that I meane to choose for my bedpheere. The ladies in court, thinke it a most desperate impaire to their quickenesse of wit, and good carriage, if they cannot giue occasion for a man to court 'hem; and, when an amorous discourse is set on foot, minister as good matter to continue it, as himselfe: and doe you alone so much differ from all them, that, what they (with so much circumstance) affect, and toile for, to seeme learn'd, to seeme iudicious, to seeme sharpe, and conceited, you can bury in your selfe, with silence? and rather trust your graces to the faire conscience of vertue, then to the worlds, or your owne proclamation?

EPI. I should be sorry else.

MOR. What say you, ladie? good ladie, speake out.

EPI. I should be sorrie, else.

MOR. That sorrow doth fill me with gladnesse! O MOROSE! thou art happie aboue mankinde! pray that thou maiest containe thy selfe. I will onely put her to it once more, and it shall be with the vtmost touch, and test of their sexe. But heare me, faire lady, I doe also loue to see her, whom I shall choose for my heicfar, to be the first and principall in all fashions; præcede all the dames at court, by a fortnight; haue her counsell of taylors, linneners, lace-women, embroyderers, and sit with 'hem sometimes twise a day, vpon *French* intelligences; and then come foorth, varied like Nature, or oftner then she, and better, by the helpe of Art, her æmulous seruant. This doe I affect. And how will you be able, lady, with this frugalitie of speech, to giue the manifold (but necessarie) instructions, for that bodies, these sleeues, those skirts, this cut, that stitch, this embroyderie, that lace, this wire, those knots, that ruffe, those roses, this girdle, that fanne, the tother skarfe, these gloues? ha! what say you, ladie?

II. v. 58 conceited] concieted *F2* 63 else.] else *F1* 69 heicfar] heifar *F2* 74 foorth] forth *F2* 78 skirts] Sirkts *Q* 81 ladie?] ladie. *F1*

EPI. I'll leaue it to you, sir.

MOR. How lady? pray you, rise a note.

EPI. I leaue it to wisdome, and you sir.

MOR. Admirable creature! I will trouble you no more: I will not sinne against so sweet a simplicity. Let me now be bold to print, on those diuine lips, the seale of being mine. CVTBERD, I giue thee the lease of thy house free: thanke me not, but with thy leg (——) I know what thou woul⟨d⟩st say, shee's poore, and her friends deceased; shee has brought a wealthy dowrie in her silence, CVTBERD: and in respect of her pouerty, CVTBERD, I shall haue her more louing, and obedient, CVTBERD. Goe thy waies, and get me a minister presently, with a soft, low voice to marry vs, and pray him he will not be impertinent, but briefe as he can; away: softly, CVTBERD. Sirrah, conduct your mistris into the dining roome, your now-mistris. O my felicity! how I shall bee reueng'd on mine insolent kinsman, and his plots, to fright me from marrying! This night I wil get an heire, and thrust him out of my bloud like a stranger; he would be knighted, forsooth, and thought by that meanes to raigne ouer me, his title must doe it: no kinsman, I will now make you bring mee the tenth lords, and the sixteenth ladies letter, kinsman; and it shall doe you no good kinsman. Your knighthood it selfe shall come on it's knees, and it shall be reiected; it shall bee sued for it's fees to execution, and not bee redeem'd; it shall cheat at the tweluepeny ordinary, it knighthood, for it's diet all the terme time, and tell tales for it in the vacation, to the hostesse: or it knighthood shall doe worse; take sanctuary in *Coleharbor*, and fast. It shall fright all it friends, with borrowing letters; and when one of the foure-score hath brought it knighthood ten shillings, it knighthood shall go to the Cranes, or the Beare at the *Bridge*-foot, and be drunk in feare: it shal not haue money

II. v. 87 print, *corr. F1, Q, F2*: print *F1 originally* 94 soft, low *corr. F1, Q, F2*: soft-low *F1 originally* 96 After 'CVTBERD.' *Exit Cut.* G 97 now-mistris *corr. F1, Q, F2*: now—mistris *F1 originally* 98 After 'mistris.' *Exit Mute followed by Epi.* G 105 good] good, *F2*

to discharge one tauerne reckoning, to inuite the old creditors, to forbeare it knighthood; or the new, that should be, to trust it knighthood. It shall be the tenth name in the bond, to take vp the commoditie of pipkins, and stone jugs; and the part thereof shall not furnish it knighthood forth, for the attempting of a bakers widdow, a browne bakers widdow. It shall giue it knighthoods name, for a *stallion*, to all gamesome citizens wiues, and bee refus'd; when the master of a dancing schoole, or (*How* do you call him) the worst reueller in the towne is taken: it shall want clothes, and by reason of that, wit, to foole to lawyers. It shall not haue hope to repaire it selfe by *Constantinople*, *Ireland*, or *Virginia;* but the best, and last fortune to it knighthood shall be, to make DOL TEARE-SHEET, or KATE COMMON, a lady: and so, it knighthood may eate.

Act II. *Scene* VI.

TRVE-WIT, DAVPHINE, CLERIMONT, CVTBERD.

ARe you sure he is not gone by?

DAVP. No, I staid in the shop euer since.

CLE. But, he may take the other end of the lane.

DAVP. No, I told him I would be here at this end: I appointed him hether.

TRV. What a barbarian it is to stay then!

DAVP. Yonder he comes.

CLE. And his charge left behinde him, which is a very good signe, DAVPHINE.

DAVP. How now CVTBERD, succeedes it, or no?

CVT. Past imagination, sir, *omnia secunda;* you could

II. v. 120 jugs] Iugs *Q* knighthood] knighthod *F2* 131 *Exit.* add G II. vi. SCENE IV. | *A Lane, near Morose's House.* | *Enter Truewit, Dauphine, and Clerimont.* G 5 hether] hither *F2* (*so* 32) After 9 *Enter Cutbeard.* G

not haue pray'd, to haue had it so wel: *Saltat senex*, as it is i' the prouerbe, he do's triumph in his felicity; admires the party! he has giuen me the lease of my house too! and, I am now going for a silent minister to marry 'hem, and away.

TRV. Slight, get one o' the silenc'd ministers, a zealous brother would torment him purely.

CVT. *Cum priuilegio*, sir.

DAVP. O, by no meanes, let's doe nothing to hinder it now; when 'tis done and finished, I am for you: for any deuise of vexation.

CVT. And that shall be, within this halfe houre, vpon my dexterity, gentlemen. Contriue what you can, in the meane time, *bonis auibus*.

CLE. How the slaue doth *latine* it!

TRV. It would be made a iest to posterity, sirs, this daies mirth, if yee will.

CLE. Beshrew his heart that will not, I pronounce.

DAVP. And, for my part. What is't?

TRV. To translate all LA-FOOLES company, and his feast hether, to day, to celebrate this bride-ale.

DAVP. I mary, but how will't be done?

TRV. I'll vndertake the directing of all the ladie-guests thether, and then the meat must follow.

CLE. For gods sake, let's effect it: it will be an excellent *comœdy* of affliction, so many seuerall noyses.

DAVP. But are they not at the other place already, thinke you?

TRV. I'll warrant you for the colledge-honors: one o' their faces has not the priming color laid on yet, nor the other her smocke sleek'd.

CLE. O, but they'll rise earlier then ordinary, to a feast.

TRV. Best goe see, and assure our selues.

CLE. Who knowes the house?

II. vi. 17 ministers,] ministers; *F2* 21 now,; *F2*: now *F1*, *Q* 25 *Exit.* add G 33 mary] marry *F2* 36 gods] Gods *Q* (*so* 51, 68) 40 -honors] -honours *Q* 41 color] colour *Q*, *F2*

TRV. I'll lead you, were you neuer there yet?

DAVP. Not I.

CLE. Nor I.

TRV. Where ha' you liu'd then? not know TOM OTTER!

CLE. No: for gods sake, what is he?

TRV. An excellent animal, equall with your DAW, or LA-FOOLE, if not transcendent; and do's *latine* it as much as your barber: hee is his wifes Subiect, he calls her Princesse, and at such times as these, followes her vp and downe the house like a page, with his hat off, partly for heate, partly for reuerence. At this instant, hee is marshalling of his bull, beare, and horse.

DAVP. What be those, in the name of *Sphinx?*

TRV. Why sir? hee has beene a great man at the beare-garden in his time: and from that subtle sport, has tane the witty denomination of his chiefe carousing cups. One he calls his bull, another his beare, another his horse. And then hee has his lesser glasses, that hee calls his deere, and his ape; and seuerall degrees of 'hem too: and neuer is well, nor thinkes any intertainement perfect, till these be brought out, and set o' the cupbord.

CLE. For gods loue! we should misse this, if we should not goe.

TRV. Nay, he has a thousand things as good, that will speake him all day. He will raile on his wife, with certaine common places, behind her backe; and to her face——

DAVP. No more of him. Let's goe see him, I petition you.

II. vi. 66 intertainement] entertaynment *Q*: entertainment *F2* 74 *Exeunt,* add G

Act III. *Scene* I.

OTTER, M^rs^. OTTER, TRVE-WIT, CLERIMONT, DAVPHINE.

NAy, good Princesse, heare me *pauca verba.*

Mrs. OT. By that light, I'll ha' you chain'd vp, with your bul-dogs, and beare-dogges, if you be not ciuill the sooner. I'll send you to kennell, i'faith. You were best baite me with your bull, beare, and horse? Neuer a time, that the courtiers, or collegiates come to the house, but you make it a *shrouetuesday!* I would haue you get your *whitsontide*-veluet-cap, and your staffe i' your hand, to intertaine 'hem: yes introth, doe.

OTT. Not so, Princesse, neither, but vnder correction, sweete Princesse, gi' me leaue—these things I am knowne to the courtiers by. It is reported to them for my humor, and they receiue it so, and doe expect it. TOM OTTERS bull, beare, and horse is knowne all ouer *England,* in *rerum natura.*

Mrs. OT. Fore me, I wil *na-ture* 'hem ouer to *Paris-garden,* and *na-ture* you thether too, if you pronounce 'hem againe. Is a beare a fit beast, or a bull, to mixe in society with great ladies? thinke i' your discretion, in any good politie.

OTT. The horse then, good Princesse.

Mrs. OT. Well, I am contented for the horse: they loue to bee well hors'd, I know. I loue it my selfe.

OTT. And it is a delicate fine horse this. *Poetarum Pegasus.* Vnder correction, Princesse, IVPITER did turne himselfe into a— *Taurus,* or Bull, vnder correction, good Princesse.

Mrs. OT. By my integritie, I'll send you ouer to the

III. i. ACT III. SCENE I. | *A Room in Otter's House.* | *Enter captain Otter with his cups, and mistress Otter* G 8 intertaine] entertaine *Q, F2* 9 introth] in troth *F2* 12 humor] humour *Q, F2* 17 'hem] them *Q* 24 this.] this *F2*: *om. Q* After 27 *Enter Truewit, Clerimont, and Dauphine, behind.* G

banke-side, I'll commit you to the Master of the garden, if I heare but a syllable more. Must my house, or my roofe, be polluted with the sent of beares, and buls, when it is perfum'd for great ladies? Is this according to the instrument, when I married you? That I would bee Princesse, and raigne in mine owne house: and you would be my subiect, and obay me? What did you bring me, should make you thus peremptory? Do I allow you your halfe-crowne a day, to spend, where you will, among your gamsters, to vexe and torment me, at such times as these? Who giues you your maintenance, I pray you? who allowes you your horse-meat, and mans-meat? your three sutes of apparell a yeere? your foure paire of stockings, one silke, three worsted? your cleane linnen, your bands, and cuffes when I can get you to weare 'hem? 'Tis mar'l you ha' 'hem on now. Who graces you with courtiers, or great personages, to speake to you out of their coaches, and come home to your house? Were you euer so much as look'd vpon by a lord, or a lady, before I married you: but on the Easter, or Whitson-holy-daies? and then out at the banquetting-house windore, when NED WHITING, or GEORGE STONE, were at the stake?

(TRV. For gods sake, let's goe staue her off him.)

M^rs^. OT. Answere me to that. And did not I take you vp from thence, in an old greasie buffe-doublet, with points; and greene vellet sleeues, out at the elbowes? you forget this.

(TRV. Shee'll worry him, if we helpe not in time.)

M^rs^. OT. O, here are some o' the gallants! Goe to, behaue your selfe distinctly, and with good moralitie; Or, I protest, I'll take away your exhibition.

III. i. 31 sent] scent *Q, F3* 43 ha' 'hem] ha'hem *Q, Ff* 51 gods] Gods *Q* 54 vellet] velvet *F2* elbowes] eldowes *F2* 56 *They come forward.* add G

Act III. *Scene* II.

TRVE-WIT, Mrs. OTTER, CAP. OTTER, CLERIMONT, DAVPHINE, CVTBERD.

BY your leaue, faire mistris OTTER, I'll be bold to enter these gentlemen in your acquaintance.

Mrs. OT. It shall not be obnoxious, or difficill, sir.

TRV. How do's my noble Captaine? Is the bull, beare, and horse, in *rerum natura* still?

OTT. Sir, *Sic visum superis.*

Mrs. OT. I would you would but intimate 'hem, doe. Goe your waies in, and get tosts, and butter, made for the wood-cocks. That's a fit prouince for you.

CLE. Alas, what a tyrannie, is this poore fellow married too.

TRV. O, but the sport will be anon, when we get him loose.

DAV. Dares he euer speake?

TRV. No Anabaptist euer rail'd with the like licence: but marke her language in the meane time, I beseech you.

Mrs. OT. Gentlemen, you are very aptly come. My cosin, sir AMOROVS, will be here briefly.

TRV. In good time lady. Was not sir IOHN DAW here, to aske for him, and the companie?

Mrs. OT. I cannot assure you, Mr. TRVE-WIT. Here was a very melancholy knight in a ruffe, that demanded my subiect for some body, a gentleman, I thinke.

CLE. I, that was he, lady.

Mrs. OT. But he departed straight, I can resolue you.

DAV. What an excellent choice phrase, this lady expresses in!

TRV. O, sir! shee is the onely authenticall courtier, that is not naturally bred one, in the citie.

III. ii. *Act* III.] *Act.* III F1 originally, miscorrected to '*Act.* III.' *G continues the scene.* After 9 *Drives him off.* G 16 meane time] meane-time *Q* 17 Mrs. OT.] M. OT. *F2, so at ll.* 21, 25, 30, 34, 36, 54, 57, 66 21 Mr.] M. *F2*

M^rs^. O T. You haue taken that report vpon trust, gentlemen.

T R V. No, I assure you, the court gouernes it so, lady, in your behalfe.

Mrs. O T. I am the seruant of the court, and courtiers, sir.

T R V. They are rather your idolaters.

Mrs. O T. Not so, sir.

D A V. How now, C V T B E R D? Any crosse?

C V T. O, no, sir: *Omnia bene.* 'Twas neuer better o' the hinges, all's sure. I haue so pleas'd him with a curate, that hee's gone too't almost with the delight he hopes for soone.

D A V. What is he, for a vicar?

C V T. One that has catch'd a cold, sir, and can scarse bee heard sixe inches off; as if he spoke out of a bull-rush, that were not pickt, or his throat were full of pith: a fine quick fellow, and an excellent barber of prayers. I came to tell you, sir, that you might *omnem mouere lapidem* (as they say) be readie with your vexation.

D A V. Gramercy, honest C V T B E R D, be there abouts with thy key to let vs in.

C V T. I will not faile you, sir: *Ad manum.*

T R V. Well, I'll goe watch my coaches.

C L E. Doe; and wee'll send D A W to you, if you meet him not.

Mrs. O T. Is master T R V E - W I T gone?

D A V. Yes, lady, there is some vnfortunate businesse fallen out.

Mrs. O T. So I iudg'd by the phisiognomy of the fellow, that came in; and I had a dreame last night too of the new pageant, and my lady Maioresse, which is alwaies very ominous to me. I told it my lady H A V G H T Y t'other day; when her honour came hether to see some *China* stuffes: and shee expounded it, out of A R T E M I D O R V S,

III. ii. 32 gouernes] go uernes *F1 originally* After 36 *Enter Cutbeard.* G 38 sir:] Sir, *F2* 44 pith] pitch *F2, F3* 48 there abouts] there-abouts *Q* 50 *Exit.* add G 55 vnfortunate] vnfortnnate *F1* 57 iudg'd] adiudg'd *Q* 61 hether] hither *F2* 62 ARTEMIDORVS] ARTEMIDORTS *F2*

and I haue found it since very true. It has done me many affronts.

CLE. Your dreame, lady?

Mrs. OT. Yes, sir, any thing I doe but dreame o' the city. It staynd me a damasque table-cloth, cost me eighteen pound at one time; and burnt me a blacke satten gowne, as I stood by the fire, at my ladie CENTAVRES chamber in the colledge, another time. A third time, at the Lords masque, it dropt all my wire, and my ruffe with waxe-candle, that I could not goe vp to the banquet. A fourth time, as I was taking coach to goe to *Ware*, to meet a friend, it dash'd me a new sute all ouer (a crimson sattin doublet, and blacke veluet skirts) with a brewers horse, that I was faine to goe in and shift mee, and kept my chamber a leash of daies for the anguish of it.

DAVP. These were dire mischances, lady.

CLE. I would not dwell in the citie, and 'twere so fatall to mee.

Mrs. OT. Yes sir, but I doe take aduise of my doctor, to dreame of it as little, as I can.

DAVP. You doe well, mistris OTTER.

Mrs. OT. Will it please you to enter the house farther, gentlemen?

DAVP. And your fauour, lady: but we stay to speake with a knight, sir IOHN DAW, who is here come. We shall follow you, lady.

Mrs. OT. At your owne time, sir. It is my cosen sir AMOROVS his feast.——

DAVP. I know it lady.

Mrs. OT. And mine together. But it is for his honour; and therefore I take no name of it, more then of the place.

DAVP. You are a bounteous kinswoman.

Mrs. OT. Your seruant, sir.

III. ii. 79 and] an' *F2* After 83 *Enter sir John Daw, and is taken aside by Clerimont.* G 95 *Exit.* add G

Act III. *Scene* III.

CLERIMONT, DAW, LA-FOOLE, DAVPHINE, OTTER.

WHy doe not you know it, sir IOHN DAW?

DAW. No, I am a rooke if I doe.

CLE. I'll tell you then, shee's married by this time! And whereas you were put i' the head, that shee was gone with sir DAVPHINE, I assure you, sir DAVPHINE has beene the noblest, honestest friend to you, that euer gentleman of your quality could boast off. He has discouer'd the whole plot, and made your mistris so acknowledging, and indeed, so ashamed of her iniurie to you, that she desires you to forgiue her, and but grace her wedding with your presence to day—She is to be married to a very good fortune, she saies, his vnkle, old MOROSE: and she will'd me in priuate to tell you, that she shall be able to doe you more fauours, and with more securitie now, then before.

DAW. Did she say so, i' faith?

CLE. Why, what doe you thinke of mee, sir IOHN! aske sir DAVPHINE.

DAW. Nay, I beleeue you. Good sir DAVPHINE, did shee desire mee to forgiue her?

DAVP. I assure you, sir IOHN, she did.

DAW. Nay then, I doe with all my heart, and I'll be *iouiall*.

CLE. Yes, for looke you sir, this was the iniury to you. LA-FOOLE intended this feast to honour her bridale day, and made you the propertie to inuite the colledge ladies, and promise to bring her: and then at the time, shee should haue appear'd (as his friend) to haue giuen you

III. iii. CLERIMONT,] *Cler.* [*coming forward with Daw.*] G, who continues the scene. 1 not *om. F2* 4 i' the] i'th' *F2* 19 DAW. *W*: DAVP. *F1*: *Daup.* Q: DAU. *F2*: *Dau.* F3 21 IOHN,] IHON. *F1* 28 should] would *F2*

the *dor.* Whereas now, sir DAVPHINE has brought her to a feeling of it, with this kinde of satisfaction, that you shall bring all the ladies to the place where shee is, and be verie *iouiall;* and there, she will haue a dinner, which shall be in your name: and so dis-appoint LA-FOOLE, to make you good againe, and (as it were) a sauer i' the ma<i>n.

DAW. As I am a knight, I honour her, and forgiue her hartily.

CLE. About it then presently, TRVE-WIT is gone before to confront the coaches, and to acquaint you with so much, if hee meet you. Ioyne with him, and 'tis well. See, here comes your *Antagonist,* but take you no notice, but be verie *iouiall.*

LA-F. Are the ladies come, sir IOHN DAW, and your mistris? sir DAVPHINE! you are exceeding welcome, and honest master CLERIMONT. Where's my cossen? did you see no collegiats, gentlemen?

DAVP. Collegiats! Doe you not heare, sir AMOROVS, how you are abus'd?

LA-F. How sir!

CLE. Will you speake so kindly to sir IOHN DAW, that has done you such an affront?

LA-F. Wherein, gentlemen? let me be a sutor to you to know, I beseech you!

CLE. Why sir, his mistris is married to day, to sir DAVPHINES vncle, your cosens neighbour, and hee has diuerted all the ladies, and all your company thether, to frustrate your prouision, and sticke a disgrace vpon you. He was here, now, to haue intic'd vs away from you too: but we told him his owne, I thinke.

LA-F. Has sir IOHN DAW wrong'd me so in-humanely?

DAV. He has done it, sir AMOROVS, most maliciously, and trecherously: but if you'll be rul'd by vs, you shall quit him i'faith.

III. iii. 34 main *W. conj.* 37 presently,] presently. *F2* 39 After 'well' *Enter sir Amorous La-Foole.* G 43 After 'mistris?' *Exit Daw.* G 55 thether] thither *F2* 56 prouision] provision *F1* 60 DAV.] *Daw.* Q

LA-F. Good gentlemen! I'll make one, beleeue it. How I pray?

DAV. Mary sir, get me your phesants, and your godwits, and your best meat, and dish it in siluer dishes of your cosens presently, and say nothing, but clap mee a cleane towell about you, like a sewer; and bare-headed, march afore it with a good confidence ('tis but ouer the way, hard by) and we'll second you, where you shal set it o' the boord, and bid 'hem welcome to't, which shall show 'tis yours, and disgrace his preparation vtterly: and, for your cosen, whereas shee should bee troubled here at home with care of making and giuing welcome, shee shall transferre all that labour thether, and bee a principall guest her selfe, sit rank'd with the colledge-Honors, and bee honor'd, and haue her health drunke as often, as bare, and as lowd as the best of 'hem.

LA-F. I'll goe tell her presently. It shall be done, that's resolu'd.

CLE. I thought he would not heare it out, but 'twould take him.

DAVP. Well, there be guests, & meat now; how shal we do for musique?

CLE. The smell of the venison, going through the street, will inuite one noyse of fidlers, or other.

DAVP. I would it would call the trumpeters thether.

CLE. Faith, there is hope, they haue intelligence of all feasts. There's good correspondence betwixt them, and the *London*-cookes. 'Tis twenty to one but we haue 'hem.

DAVP. 'Twill be a most solemne day for my vncle, and an excellent fit of mirth for vs.

CLE. I, if we can hold vp the æmulation betwixt FOOLE, and DAW, and neuer bring them to expostulate.

DAVP. Tut, flatter 'hem both (as TRVE-WIT sayes) and you may take their vnderstandings in a purse-net. They'll beleeue themselues to be iust such men as we make

III. iii. 70 it *om.* *Q* 80 *Exit.* add G 83 now;] now, *F2*
87 DAVP] DAVP: *F1* 90 we] he *F2*, *F3*

'hem, neither more nor lesse. They haue nothing, not the vse of their senses, but by tradition.

CLE. See! Sir AMOROVS has his towell on already. Haue you perswaded your cossen? *He enters like a sewer.*

LA-F. Yes, 'tis verie fæsible: shee'll do any thing she sayes, rather then the LA-FOOLES shall be disgrac'd.

DAVP. She is a noble kinswoman. It will be such a pest'ling deuice, sir AMOROVS! It will pound all your enemies practises to poulder, and blow him vp with his owne mine, his owne traine.

LA-F. Nay, wee'll giue fire, I warrant you.

CLE. But you must carry it priuatly, without any noyse, and take no notice by any meanes——

OTT. Gentlemen, my Princesse sayes, you shall haue all her siluer dishes, *festinate:* and she's gone to alter her tyre a little, and go with you——

CLE. And your selfe too, captaine OTTER.

DAVP. By any meanes, sir.

OTT. Yes, sir, I doe meane it: but I would entreate my cosen sir AMOROVS, and you gentlemen, to be sutors to my Princesse, that I may carry my bull, and my beare, as well as my horse.

CLE. That you shall doe, captaine OTTER.

LA-F. My cosen will neuer consent, gentlemen.

DAVP. She must consent, sir AMOROVS, to reason.

LA-F. Why, she sayes they are no *decorum* among ladies.

OTT. But they are *decora*, and that's better, sir.

CLE. I, shee must heare argument. Did not PASIPHAE, who was a queene, loue a bull? and was not CALISTO, the mother of ARCAS, turn'd into a beare, and made a starre, mistris VRSVLA, i' the heauens?

OTT. O God! that I could ha' said as much! I will haue these stories painted i' the beare-garden, *ex Ouidij metamorphosi.*

III. iii. 98 more] more, *F2* 102 fæsible] feasible *F3* After 110 *Re-enter captain Otter.* G

DAVP. Where is your Princesse, Captaine? pray' be our leader.

OTT. That I shall, sir.

CLE. Make haste, good sir AMOROVS.

Act III. *Scene* IIII.

MOROSE, EPICOENE, PARSON, CVTBERD.

SIr, there's an angel for your selfe, and a brace of angels for your cold. Muse not at this mannage of my bounty. It is fit wee should thanke fortune, double to nature, for any benefit she conferres vpon vs; besides, it is your imperfection, but my solace.

The parson speakes, as hauing a cold.

PAR. I thanke your worship, so is it mine, now.

MOR. What sayes he, CVTBERD?

CVT. He saies, *Præsto*, sir, whensoeuer your worship needes him, hee can be ready with the like. He got this cold with sitting vp late, and singing catches with cloth-workers.

MOR. No more. I thanke him.

PAR. Good keepe your worship, and giue you much ioy with your faire spouse. (Vmh, vmh.)

He coughes.

MOR. O, ô, stay CVTBERD! let him giue me fiue shillings of my money backe. As it is bounty to reward benefits, so is it equity to mulct iniuries. I will haue it. What sayes he?

CVT. He cannot change it, sir.

MOR. It must be chang'd.

CVT. Cough againe.

MOR. What sayes he?

CVT. He will cough out the rest, sir.

Againe.

PAR. (Vmh, vmh, vmh.)

III. iii. 136 *Exeunt.* add G III. iv. SCENE II. | *A Room in Morose's House.* | *Enter Morose, Epicœne, Parson, and Cutbeard.* G EPICOENE] *Epicœne* Q 6 worship,] worship; *F2* 21 *Aside to Parson.* add G

Mor. Away, away with him, stop his mouth, away, I forgiue it.——

Epi. Fye, master Morose, that you will vse this violence to a man of the church.

Mor. How!

Epi. It do's not become your grauity, or breeding, (as you pretend in court) to haue offered this outrage on a waterman, or any more boystrous creature, much lesse on a man of his ciuill coat.

Mor. You can speake then!

Epi. Yes, sir.

Mor. Speake out I meane.

Epi. I sir. Why, did you thinke you had married a statue? or a motion, onely? one of the *French* puppets, with the eyes turn'd with a wire? or some innocent out of the hospitall, that would stand with her hands thus, and a playse mouth, and looke vpon you.

Mor. O immodestie! a manifest woman! what Cvtberd?

Epi. Nay, neuer quarrell with Cvtberd, sir, it is too late now. I confesse, it doth bate somewhat of the modestie I had, when I writ simply maide: but I hope, I shall make it a stocke still competent, to the estate, and dignity of your wife.

Mor. Shee can talke!

Epi. Yes indeed, sir.

Mor. What, sirrah. None of my knaues, there? where is this impostor, Cvtberd?

Epi. Speake to him, fellow, speake to him. I'll haue none of this coacted, vnnaturall dumbnesse in my house, in a family where I gouerne.

Mor. She is my Regent already! I haue married a Penthesilea, a Semiramis, sold my liberty to a distaffe!

III. iv. After 26 *Exit Cut. thrusting out the Par.* G 36 Speake *corr. F1, Q, F2*: Speake, *F1 originally* After 50 *Enter Mute.* G 52 *Mute makes signs.* add G 55 *Exit Mute.* add G

Act III. *Scene* V.

TRVE-WIT, MOROSE, EPICOENE.

WHere's master MOROSE?

MOR. Is he come againe! lord haue mercy vpon me.

TRV. I wish you all ioy, mistris EPICOENE, with your graue and honourable match.

EPI. I returne you the thankes, master TRVE-WIT, so friendly a wish deserues.

MOR. She has acquaintance, too!

TRV. God saue you, sir, and giue you all contentment in your faire choise, here. Before I was the bird of night to you, the owle, but now I am the messenger of peace, a doue, and bring you the glad wishes of many friends, to the celebration of this good houre.

MOR. What houre, sir?

TRV. Your marriage houre sir. I commend your resolution, that (notwithstanding all the dangers I laid afore you, in the voice of a night-crow) would yet goe on, and bee your selfe. It shewes you are a man constant to your own ends, and vpright to your purposes, that would not be put off with left-handed cries.

MOR. How should you arriue at the knowledge of so much!

TRV. Why, did you euer hope, sir, committing the secrecie of it to a barber, that lesse then the whole towne should know it? you might as wel ha' told it the conduit, or the bake-house, or the infant'ry that follow the court, and with more securitie. Could your grauitie forget so olde and noted a remnant, as, *lippis & tonsoribus notum?* Well sir, forgiue it your selfe now, the fault, and be communicable with your friends. Here will bee three or foure fashionable

III. v. *Enter Truewit.* G, continuing the scene. 2 lord] Lord *Q, F2* 11 owle,] owle; *F2*: owle *F1*: Owle *Q* 28 *notum?* F2: *notum.* F1, Q

ladies, from the colledge, to visit you presently, and their traine of minions, and followers.

MOR. Barre my dores! barre my dores! where are all my eaters? my mouthes now? barre vp my dores, you varlets.

EPI. He is a varlet, that stirres to such an office. Let 'hem stand open. I would see him that dares mooue his eyes toward it. Shal I haue a *barricado* made against my friends, to be barr'd of any pleasure they can bring in to me with honorable visitation?

MOR. O *Amazonian* impudence!

TRV. Nay faith, in this, sir, she speakes but reason: and me thinkes is more continent then you. Would you goe to bed so presently, sir, afore noone? a man of your head, and haire, should owe more to that reuerend ceremony, and not mount the marriage-bed, like a towne-bul, or a mountaine-goate; but stay the due season; and ascend it then with religion, and feare. Those delights are to be steep'd in the humor, and silence of the night; and giue the day to other open pleasures, and jollities of feast, of musique, of reuells, of discourse: wee'll haue all, sir, that may make your *Hymen* high, and happy.

MOR. O, my torment, my torment!

TRV. Nay, if you indure the first halfe houre, sir, so tediously, and with this irksomnesse; what comfort, or hope, can this faire gentlewoman make to her selfe hereafter, in the consideration of so many yeeres as are to come——

MOR. Of my affliction. Good sir, depart, and let her doe it alone.

TRV. I haue done, sir.

MOR. That cursed barber!

TRV. (Yes faith, a cursed wretch indeed, sir.)

III. v. 34 After 'now?' *Enter Servants.* G 37 mooue] move *F2* 40 visitation? *F2*: visitation. *F1*, *Q* *Exeunt Ser.* add G 45 reuerend] reueuerend *F1* 49 humor] humour *F2* 50 jollities] iollities *Q* feast] feasting *F2*, *F3* 56 gentlewoman] Geutlewoman *Q*

M o r. I haue married his citterne, that's common to all men. Some plague, aboue the plague——

T r v. (All *Egypts* ten plagues)

M o r. Reuenge me on him.

T r v. 'Tis very well, sir. If you laid on a curse or two, more, I'll assure you hee'll beare 'hem. As, that he may get the poxe with seeking to cure it, sir? Or, that while he is curling another mans haire, his owne may drop off? Or, for burning some male-baudes lock, he may haue his braine beat out with the curling-iron?

M o r. No, let the wretch liue wretched. May he get the itch, and his shop so lousie, as no man dare come at him, nor he come at no man.

T r v. (I, and if he would swallow all his balles for pills, let not them purge him)

M o r. Let his warming pan be euer cold.

T r v. (A perpetuall frost vnderneath it, sir)

M o r. Let him neuer hope to see fire againe.

T r v. (But in hell, sir)

M o r. His chaires be alwaies empty, his scissors rust, and his combes mould in their cases.

T r v. Very dreadfull that! (And may hee loose the inuention, sir, of caruing lanternes in paper)

M o r. Let there be no baud carted that yeare, to employ a bason of his: but let him be glad to eate his sponge, for bread.

T r v. And drinke *lotium* to it, and much good doe him.

M o r. Or, for want of bread——

T r v. Eat eare-waxe, sir. I'll helpe you. Or, draw his owne teeth, and adde them to the lute-string.

M o r. No, beate the old ones to poulder, and make bread of them.

T r v. (Yes, make meale o' the millstones.)

M o r. May all the botches, and burnes, that he has cur'd on others, breake out vpon him.

III. v. 66 *Egypts*] *Ægypts* F2 85 loose] lose *F2* 94 poulder] powder *F2*

TRV. And he now forget the cure of 'hem in himselfe, sir: or, if he do remember it, let him ha' scrap'd all his linnen into lint for 't, and haue not a rag left him, to set vp with.

MOR. Let him neuer set vp againe, but haue the gout in his hands for euer. Now, no more, sir.

TRV. O that last was too high set! you might goe lesse with him i' faith, and bee reueng'd enough: as, that he be neuer able to new-paint his pole——

MOR. Good sir, no more. I forgot my selfe.

TRV. Or, want credit to take vp with a combe-maker——

MOR. No more, sir.

TRV. Or, hauing broken his glasse in a former despaire, fall now into a much greater, of euer getting another——

MOR. I beseech you, no more.

TRV. Or, that he neuer be trusted with trimming of any but chimney-sweepers——

MOR. Sir——

TRV. Or, may he cut a colliers throat with his rasor, by *chance-medlee*, and yet hang for't.

MOR. I will forgiue him, rather then heare any more. I beseech you, sir.

Act III. *Scene* VI.

DAW, MOROSE, TRVE-WIT, HAVGHTY, CENTAVRE, MAVIS, TRVSTY.

THis way, madame.

MOR. O, the sea breakes in vpon me! another floud! an inundation! I shall be orewhelm'd with noise. It beates already at my shores. I feele an earthquake in my selfe, for't.

DAW. 'Giue you ioy, mistresse.

MOR. Has shee seruants too!

DAW. I haue brought some ladies here to see, and know

III. vi. *Enter Daw, introducing lady Haughty, Centaure, Mavis, and Trusty.* G, continuing the scene

She kisses them seuerally as he presents them. you. My ladie HAVGHTY, this my lady CENTAVRE, mistresse DOL MAVIS, mistresse TRVSTIE my ladie HAVGHTIES woman. Where's your husband? let's see him: can he endure no noise? let me come to him.

MOR. What *nomenclator* is this!

TRV. Sir IOHN DAW, sir, your wifes seruant, this.

MOR. A DAW, and her seruant! O, 'tis decreed, 'tis decreed of mee, and shee haue such seruants.

TRV. Nay sir, you must kisse the ladies, you must not goe away, now; they come toward you, to seeke you out.

HAV. I' faith, master MOROSE, would you steale a marriage thus, in the midst of so many friends, and not acquaint vs? Well, I'll kisse you, notwithstanding the iustice of my quarrell: you shall giue me leaue, mistresse, to vse a becomming familiarity with your husband.

EPI. Your ladiship do's me an honour in it, to let me know hee is so worthy your fauour: as, you haue done both him and me grace, to visit so vnprepar'd a paire to entertaine you.

MOR. Complement! Complement!

EPI. But I must lay the burden of that, vpon my seruant, here.

HAV. It shall not need, mistresse MOROSE, wee will all beare, rather then one shall be opprest.

MOR. I know it: and you will teach her the faculty, if shee bee to learne it.

HAV. Is this the silent woman?

CEN. Nay, shee has found her tongue since shee was married, master TRVE-WIT sayes.

HAV. O, master TRVE-WIT! 'saue you. What kinde of creature is your bride here? she speakes, me thinkes!

TRV. Yes madame, beleeue it, she is a gentlewoman of very absolute behauiour, and of a good race.

HAV. And IACK DAW told vs, she could not speake.

TRV. So it was carried in plot, madam, to put her vpon this old fellow, by sir DAVPHINE, his nephew, and one

III. vi. 14 wifes] Wives *F3* 16 and] an' *F2* (*so* 51) *Going.* add G 30 MOROSE,] MOROSE; *F2* 33 *Walks aside while the rest talk apart.* add G

or two more of vs: but shee is a woman of an excellent assurance, and an extraordinarie happie wit, and tongue. You shall see her make rare sport with DAW, ere night.

HAV. And he brought vs to laugh at her!

TRV. That falls out often, madame, that he that thinkes himselfe the master-wit, is the master-foole. I assure your lady-ship, yee cannot laugh at her.

HAV. No, wee'll haue her to the colledge: and shee haue wit, she shall bee one of vs! shall shee not CENTAVRE? wee'll make her a collegiate.

CEN. Yes faith, madame, and MAVIS, and shee will set vp a side.

TRV. Beleeue it madame, and mistris MAVIS, shee will sustaine her part.

MAV. I'll tell you that, when I haue talk'd with her, and try'd her.

HAV. Vse her very ciuilly, MAVIS.

MAV. So I will, madame.

MOR. Blessed minute, that they would whisper thus euer.

TRV. In the meane time, madame, would but your lady-ship helpe to vexe him a little: you know his disease, talke to him about the wedding ceremonies, or call for your gloues, or——

HAV. Let me alone. CENTAVRE, helpe me. Mr. bride-groome, where are you?

MOR. O, it was too miraculously good to last!

HAV. Wee see no ensignes of a wedding, here; no character of a brideale: where be our skarfes, and our gloues? I pray you, giue 'hem vs. Let's know your brides colours, and yours, at least.

CEN. Alas, madame, he has prouided none.

MOR. Had I knowne your ladiships painter, I would.

HAV. He has giuen it you, CENTAVRE, yfaith. But, doe you heare, M. MOROSE, a iest will not absolue you in this manner. You that haue suck'd the milke of the court,

III. vi. 51 wee'll] weell *F1* 61 *Whispers her.* G 62 minute,] minute! *F2* euer.] ever! *F2* *Aside.* add G (*so* 69)

and from thence haue beene brought vp to the very strong meates, and wine, of it; beene a courtier from the biggen, to the night-cap: (as we may say) and you, to offend in such a high point of ceremonie, as this! and let your nuptialls want all markes of solemnitie! How much plate haue you lost to day (if you had but regarded your profit) what guifts, what friends, through your meere rusticitie?

MOR. Madame——

HAV. Pardon mee, sir, I must insinuate your errours to you. No gloues? no garters? no skarfes? no *epithalamium?* no masque?

DAW. Yes, madame, I'll make an *epithalamium*, I promis'd my mistris, I haue begunne it already: will your ladiship heare it?

HAV. I, good IACK DAW.

MOR. Will it please your ladiship command a chamber, and be priuate with your friend? you shall haue your choice of roomes, to retire to after: my whole house is yours. I know, it hath beene your ladiships errand, into the city, at other times, how euer now you haue beene vnhappily diuerted vpon mee: but I shall be loth to breake any honorable custome of your ladiships. And therefore, good madame——

EPI. Come, you are a rude bride-groome, to entertayne ladies of honour in this fashion.

CEN. He is a rude groome, indeed.

TRV. By that light, you deserue to be grafted, and haue your hornes reach from one side of the Iland, to the other. Doe not mistake me, sir, I but speake this, to giue the ladies some heart againe, not for any malice to you.

MOR. Is this your *Brauo*, ladies?

TRV. As god helpe me, if you vtter such another word, I'll take mistris bride in, and beginne to you, in a very sad cup, doe you see? Goe too, know your friends, and such, as loue you.

III. vi. 85 guifts] gifts *Q, F2* 88 you.] you, *F2* 90 promis'd] promise *F3* 97 ladiships] Ladishis *Q* 100 honorable] honourable *F2* 110 god] God *Q, F2* 112 cup,] cup; *F2*

Act III. *Scene* VII.

CLERIMONT, MOROSE, TRVE-WIT, DAVPHINE, LA-FOOLE, OTTER, Mrs. OTTER, &c.

BY your leaue, ladies. Doe you want any musique? I haue brought you varietie of noyses. Play, sirs, all of you.

MOR. O, a plot, a plot, a plot, a plot vpon me! This day, I shall be their anvile to worke on, they will grate me asunder. 'Tis worse then the noyse of a saw. *Musique of all sorts.*

CLE. No, they are haire, rosin, and guts. I can giue you the receipt.

TRV. Peace, boyes.

CLE. Play, I say.

TRV. Peace, rascalls. You see who's your friend now, sir? Take courage, put on a martyrs resolution. Mocke downe all their attemptings, with patience. 'Tis but a day, and I would suffer heroically. Should an asse exceed me in fortitude? No. You betray your infirmitie with your hanging dull eares, and make them insult: beare vp brauely, and constantly. Looke you here, sir, what honour is done you vnexpected, by your nephew; a wedding dinner come, and a Knight sewer before it, for the more reputation: and fine Mrs. OTTER, your neighbour, in the rump, or tayle of it. *La-Foole passes ouer sewing the meate.*

MOR. Is that *Gorgon*, that *Medusa* come? Hide me, hide me.

TRV. I warrant you, sir, shee will not transforme you. Looke vpon her with a good courage. Pray you entertayne her, and conduct your guests in. No? Mistris bride, will you entreat in the ladies? your bride-groome is so shame-fac'd, here——

EPI. Will it please your ladiship, madame?

III. vii. *Enter Clerimont, followed by a number of musicians.* G, continuing the scene 2 *Aside to the musicians, who strike up all together.* add G 3 St. dir. *all* om. F3 (perhaps from a defective copy of F2) 16 *La-Foole passes over the stage as a server, followed by servants carrying dishes, and mistress Otter.* G 25 guests] Guess *F3*

HAV. With the benefit of your companie, mistris.

EPI. Seruant, pray you performe your duties.

DAW. And glad to be commanded, mistris.

CEN. How like you her wit, MAVIS?

MAV. Very prettily, absolutely well.

Mrs. OT. 'Tis my place.

MAV. You shall pardon me, mistris OTTER.

Mrs. OT. Why I am a collegiate.

MAV. But not in ordinary.

Mrs. OT. But I am.

MAV. Wee'll dispute that within.

CLE. Would this had lasted a little longer.

TRV. And that they had sent for the Heralds. Captayne OTTER, what newes?

OTT. I haue brought my bull, beare, and horse, in priuate, and yonder are the trumpetters without, and the drum, gentlemen.

The Drum and Trumpets sound.

MOR. O, ô, ô.

OTT. And we will haue a rouse in each of 'hem, anon, for bold *Britons*, yfaith.

MOR. O, ô, ô.

ALL. Follow, follow, follow.

Act IIII. *Scene* I.

TRVE-WIT, CLERIMONT, DAVPHINE.

WAs there euer poore bride-groome so tormented? or man indeed?

CLE. I haue not read of the like, in the *chronicles* of the land.

TRV. Sure, hee cannot but goe to a place of rest, after all this purgatorie.

III. vii. 32 MAVIS? *F2*: MAVIS. *F1*: *Mauis.* Q 39 *Exeunt Ladies.* add G 41 After 'Heralds.' *Enter captain Otter.* G Captayne OTTER *corr. F1*: Captaine OTTER *F1 originally* 48 *They sound again.* add G 49 *Exit hastily.* add G 50 *Exeunt.* add G
IV. i. ACT IV. SCENE I. | *A Room in Morose's House.* | *Enter Truewit and Clerimont.* G

CLE. He may presume it, I thinke.

TRV. The spitting, the coughing, the laughter, the neesing, the farting, dauncing, noise of the musique, and her masculine, and lowd commanding, and vrging the whole family, makes him thinke he has married a *furie*.

CLE. And shee carries it vp brauely.

TRV. I, shee takes any occasion to speake: that's the height on't.

CLE. And how soberly DAVPHINE labours to satisfie him, that it was none of his plot!

TRV. And has almost brought him to the faith, i' the article. Here he comes. Where is he now? what's become of him, DAVPHINE?

DAV. O, hold me vp a little, I shall goe away i' the iest else. Hee has got on his whole nest of night-caps, and lock'd himselfe vp, i' the top o' the house, as high, as euer he can climbe from the noise. I peep'd in at a crany, and saw him sitting ouer a crosse-beame o' the roofe, like him o' the sadlers horse in *Fleetstreet*, vp-right: and he will sleepe there.

CLE. But where are your collegiates?

DAV. With-drawne with the bride in priuate.

TRV. O, they are instructing her i' the colledge-Grammar. If shee haue grace with them, shee knowes all their secrets instantly.

CLE. Me thinks, the lady HAVGHTY lookes well to day, for all my dispraise of her i' the morning. I thinke, I shall come about to thee againe, TRVE-WIT.

TRV. Beleeue it, I told you right. Women ought to repaire the losses, time and yeeres haue made i' their features, with dressings. And an intelligent woman, if shee know by her selfe the least defect, will bee most curious, to hide it: and it becomes her. If shee be short, let her sit much, lest when shee stands, shee be thought to sit. If shee haue an ill foot, let her weare her gowne the longer, and her shoo the thinner. If a fat hand, and scald nailes, let her carue

IV. i. 18 After 'comes.' *Enter Sir Dauphine.* G

the lesse, and act in gloues. If a sowre breath, let her neuer discourse fasting: and alwaies talke at her distance. If shee haue black and rugged teeth, let her offer the lesse at laughter, especially if shee laugh wide, and open.

CLE. O, you shall haue some women, when they laugh, you would thinke they bray'd, it is so rude, and——

TRV. I, and others, that will stalke i' their gait like an *Estrich*, and take huge strides. I cannot endure such a sight. I loue measure i' the feet, and number i' the voice: they are gentlenesses, that oft-times draw no lesse then the face.

DAV. How cam'st thou to studie these creatures so exactly? I would thou would'st make me a proficient.

TRV. Yes, but you must leaue to liue i' your chamber then a month together vpon AMADIS *de Gaule*, or *Don* QVIXOTE, as you are wont; and come abroad where the matter is frequent, to court, to tiltings, publique showes, and feasts, to playes, and church sometimes: thither they come to shew their new tyres too, to see, and to be seene. In these places a man shall find whom to loue, whom to play with, whom to touch once, whom to hold euer. The varietie arrests his iudgement. A wench to please a man comes not downe dropping from the seeling, as he lyes on his backe droning a tobacco pipe. He must goe where shee is.

DAV. Yes, and be neuer the neere.

TRV. Out heretique. That diffidence makes thee worthy it should bee so.

CLE. He sayes true to you, DAVPHINE.

DAV. Why?

TRV. A man should not doubt to ouer-come any woman. Thinke he can vanquish 'hem, and he shall: for though they denie, their desire is to be tempted. PENELOPE her selfe cannot hold out long. *Ostend*, you saw, was taken at last. You must perseuer, and hold to your purpose. They would sollicite vs, but that they are afraid. How-

IV. i. 52 that] thaa *Q* oft-times] oftentimes *F3* 64 seeling] Ceiling *F3* 68 diffidence] difference *F2, F3* 76 perseuer] persevere *F3*

soeuer, they wish in their hearts we should sollicite them. Praise 'hem, flatter 'hem, you shal neuer want eloquence, or trust: euen the chastest delight to feele themselues that way rub'd. With praises you must mixe kisses too. If they take them, they'll take more. Though they striue, they would bee ouer-come.

CLE. O, but a man must beware of force.

TRV. It is to them an acceptable violence, and has oft-times the place of the greatest courtesie. Shee that might haue beene forc'd, and you let her goe free without touching, though shee then seeme to thanke you, will euer hate you after: and glad i' the face, is assuredly sad at the heart.

CLE. But all women are not to be taken al waies.

TRV. 'Tis true. No more then all birds, or all fishes. If you appeare learned to an ignorant wench, or iocund to a sad, or witty to a foolish, why shee presently begins to mistrust her selfe. You must approch them i' their owne height, their owne line: for the contrary makes many that feare to commit themselues to noble and worthy fellowes, run into the imbraces of a rascall. If shee loue wit, giue verses, though you borrow 'hem of a friend, or buy 'hem, to haue good. If valour, talke of your sword, and be frequent in the mention of quarrels, though you be staunch in fighting. If actiuitie, be seene o' your *barbary* often, or leaping ouer stooles, for the credit of your back. If shee loue good clothes or dressing, haue your learned counsell about you euery morning, your *french* taylor, barber, linnener, &c. Let your poulder, your glasse, and your combe, be your dearest acquaintance. Take more care for the ornament of your head, then the safetie: and wish the common-wealth rather troubled, then a haire about you. That will take her. Then if shee be couetous and crauing, doe you promise any thing, and performe sparingly: so shall you keepe her in appetite still. Seeme as you would giue, but be like a barren field that yeelds little, or vnlucky dice, to foolish,

IV. i. 88 shee then] then shee *F2*, *F3* 90 al waies] alwaies *F1*, *Q*: alwayes *F2*: all ways *W*

and hoping gamesters. Let your gifts be slight, and daintie, rather then pretious. Let cunning be aboue cost. Giue cherries at time of yeere, or apricots; and say they were sent you out o' the countrey, though you bought 'hem in *Cheap-side.* Admire her tyres; like her in all fashions; compare her in euery habit to some deitie; inuent excellent dreames to flatter her, and riddles; or, if shee bee a great one, performe alwaies the second parts to her: like what shee likes, praise whom she praises, and faile not to make the houshold and seruants yours, yea the whole family, and salute 'hem by their names: ('tis but light cost if you can purchase 'hem so) and make her physitian your pensioner, and her chiefe woman. Nor will it bee out of your gaine to make loue to her too, so shee follow, not vsher, her ladies pleasure. All blabbing is taken away, when shee comes to be a part of the crime.

DAV. On what courtly lap hast thou late slept, to come forth so sudden and absolute a courtling?

TRV. Good faith, I should rather question you, that are so harkning after these mysteries. I begin to suspect your diligence, DAVPHINE. Speake, art thou in loue in earnest?

DAV. Yes by my troth am I: 'twere ill dissembling before thee.

TRV. With which of 'hem, I pray thee?

DAV. With all the collegiates.

CLE. Out on thee. Wee'll keepe you at home, beleeue it, i' the stable, and you be such a stallion.

TRV. No. I like him well. Men should loue wisely, and all women: some one for the face, and let her please the eye; another for the skin, and let her please the touch; a third for the voice, and let her please the eare; and where the obiects mixe, let the senses so too. Thou wouldst thinke it strange, if I should make 'hem all in loue with thee afore night!

DAV. I would say thou had'st the best *philtre* i' the

IV. i. 137 pray thee] pr'y thee *F2* 140 and] an' *F2*

world, and couldst doe more then madame MEDEA, or Doctor FOREMAN.

TRV. If I doe not, let me play the mounte-bank for my meate while I liue, and the bawd for my drinke.

DAV. So be it, I say.

Act IIII. *Scene* II.

OTTER, CLERIMONT, DAW, DAVPHINE, MOROSE, TRVE-WIT, LA-FOOLE, Mrs. OTTER.

O Lord, gentlemen, how my knights and I haue mist you here!

CLE. Why, Captaine, what seruice? what seruice?

OTT. To see me bring vp my bull, beare, and horse to fight.

DAW. Yes faith, the Captaine saies we shall be his dogs to baite 'hem.

DAV. A good imployment.

TRV. Come on, let's see a course then.

LA-F. I am afraid my cousin will be offended if shee come.

OTT. Be afraid of nothing. Gentlemen, I haue plac'd the drum and the trumpets, and one to giue 'hem the signe when you are ready. Here's my bull for my selfe, and my beare for sir IOHN DAW, and my horse for sir AMOROVS. Pray set your foot to mine, and yours to his, and——

LA-F. Pray god my cousin come not.

OTT. Saint GEORGE, and saint ANDREW, feare no cousins. Come, sound, sound. *Et rauco strepuerunt cornua cantu.*

TRV. Well said, Captaine, yfaith: well fought at the bull.

CLE. Well held at the beare.

TRV. Low, low, Captayne.

IV. ii. *Enter Otter, with his three cups, Daw, and La-Foole.* G, continuing the scene 17 god] God *Q* 20 *They drink.* add G

DAV. O, the horse has kickt off his dog alreadie.

LA-F. I cannot drinke it, as I am a Knight.

TRV. Gods so, off with his spurres, some-body.

LA-F. It goes againe my conscience. My cousin will bee angrie with it.

DAW. I ha' done mine.

TRV. You fought high and faire, sir IOHN.

CLE. At the head.

DAV. Like an excellent beare-dog.

CLE. You take no notice of the businesse, I hope.

DAW. Not a word, sir, you see we are *iouiall.*

OTT. Sir AMOROVS, you must not æquiuocate. It must bee pull'd downe, for all my cousin.

CLE. Sfoot, if you take not your drinke, they'll thinke you are discontented with some thing: you'll betray all, if you take the least notice.

LA-F. Not I, I'll both drinke, and talke then.

OTT. You must pull the horse on his knees, sir AMOROVS: feare no cousins. *Iacta est alea.*

TRV. O, now hee's in his vaine, and bold. The least hint giuen him of his wife now, will make him raile desperately.

CLE. Speake to him of her.

TRV. Doe you, and I'll fetch her to the hearing of it.

DAV. Captaine hee-OTTER, your shee-OTTER is comming, your wife.

OTT. Wife! Buz. *Titiuilitium.* There's no such thing in nature. I confesse, gentlemen, I haue a cook, a laundresse, a house-drudge, that serues my necessary turnes, and goes vnder that title: But hee's an asse that will be so *vxorious*, to tie his affections to one circle. Come, the name dulls appetite. Here, replenish againe: another bout. Wiues are nasty sluttish *animalls.*

DAV. O, Captaine.

OTT. As euer the earth bare, *tribus verbis.* Where's master TRVE-WIT?

DAW. Hee's slipt aside, sir.

IV. ii. 25 O,] O' *Q* 28 againe] against *F2* 47 *Exit.* add G

CLE. But you must drinke, and be *iouiall.*

DAW. Yes, giue it me.

LA-F. And me, too.

DAW. Let's be *iouiall.*

LA-F. As *iouiall* as you will.

OTT. Agreed. Now you shall ha' the beare, cousin, and sir IOHN DAW the horse, and I'll ha' the bull still. Sound *Tritons* o' the *Thames. Nunc est bibendum, nunc pede libero*——

MOR. Villaines, murderers, sonnes of the earth, and traitors, what doe you there?

Morose speakes from aboue: the trumpets sounding.

CLE. O, now the trumpets haue wak'd him, we shall haue his companie.

OTT. A wife is a sciruy *clogdogdo;* an vnlucky thing, a very foresaid beare-whelpe, without any good fashion or breeding: *mala bestia.*

DAV. Why did you marry one then, Captaine?

His wife is brought out to heare him.

OTT. A poxe——I married with sixe thousand pound, I. I was in loue with that. I ha' not kist my *furie*, these fortie weekes.

CLE. The more to blame you, Captaine.

TRV. Nay, mistris OTTER, heare him a little first.

OTT. Shee has a breath worse then my grand-mothers, *profecto.*

Mrs. OT. O treacherous lyar. Kisse mee, sweet master TRVE-WIT, and proue him a slaundering knaue.

TRV. I'll rather beleeue you, lady.

OTT. And she has a perruke, that's like a pound of hempe, made vp in shoo-thrids.

Mrs. OT. O viper, mandrake!

OTT. A most vile face! and yet shee spends me fortie pound a yeere in *mercury*, and hogs-bones. All her teeth were made i' the Blacke-*Friers:* both her eye-browes i' the *Strand*, and her haire in *Siluer-street.* Euery part o' the towne ownes a peece of her.

IV. ii. After 76 *Re-enter Truewit behind, with mistress Otter.* G 94 *Siluer-*] *Siuer-* Q

Mrs. Ot. I cannot hold.

Ott. She takes her selfe asunder still when she goes to bed, into some twentie boxes; and about next day noone is put together againe, like a great *Germane* clocke: and so comes forth and rings a tedious larum to the whole house, and then is quiet againe for an houre, but for her quarters. Ha' you done me right, gentlemen?

Shee falls vpon him and beates him.

Mrs. Ot. No, sir, I'll do you right with my quarters, with my quarters.

Ott. O, hold, good Princesse.

Trv. Sound, sound.

Cle. A battell, a battell.

Mrs. Ot. You notorious stinkardly beareward, do's my breath smell?

Ott. Vnder correction, deare Princesse: looke to my beare, and my horse, gentlemen.

Mrs. Ot. Doe I want teeth, and eye-browes, thou bull-dog?

Trv. Sound, sound still.

Ott. No, I protest, vnder correction——

Mrs. Ot. I, now you are vnder correction, you protest: but you did not protest before correction, sir. Thou Ivdas, to offer to betray thy Princesse! I'll make thee an example——

Morose descends with a long sword.

Mor. I will haue no such examples in my house, lady Otter.

Mrs. Ot. Ah——

Mor. Mrs. Mary Ambree, your examples are dangerous. Rogues, Hellhounds, *Stentors*, out of my dores, you sonnes of noise and tumult, begot on an ill *May*-day, or when the Gally-foist is a-floate to *Westminster!* A trumpetter could not be conceiu'd, but then!

Dav. What ailes you, sir?

Mor. They haue rent my roofe, walls, and all my windores asunder, with their brazen throates.

iv. ii. 96 Mrs. Ot.] *Mrs. Ott.* [*comes forward.*] G 103 St. dir. *beates*] *beates vpon* Q 122 *Mrs. Otter, Daw, and La-Foole run off.* add G 126 After '*Westminster!*' *Drives out the musicians.* G

TRV. Best follow him, DAVPHINE.

DAV. So I will.

CLE. Where's DAW, and LA-FOOLE?

OTT. They are both run away, sir. Good gentlemen, helpe to pacifie my Princesse, and speake to the great ladies for me. Now must I goe lie with the beares this fortnight, and keepe out o' the way, till my peace be made, for this scandale shee has taken. Did you not see my bull-head, gentlemen?

CLE. Is 't not on, Captayne?

TRV. No: but he may make a new one, by that, is on.

OTT. O, here 'tis. And you come ouer, gentlemen, and aske for TOM OTTER, wee'll goe downe to *Ratcliffe*, and haue a course yfaith: for all these disasters. There's *bona spes* left.

TRV. Away, Captaine, get off while you are well.

CLE. I am glad we are rid of him.

TRV. You had neuer beene, vnlesse wee had put his wife vpon him. His humour is as tedious at last, as it was ridiculous at first.

Act IIII. *Scene* III.

HAVGHTY, Mrs. OTTER, MAVIS, DAW, LA-FOOLE, CENTAVRE, EPICOENE, TRVEWIT, CLERIMONT.

WE wondred why you shreek'd so, Mrs. OTTER.

Mrs. OT. O god, madame, he came downe with a huge long naked weapon in both his hands, and look'd so dreadfully! Sure, hee's beside himselfe.

MAV. Why what made you there, mistris OTTER?

Mrs. OT. Alas, mistris MAVIS, I was chastising my subiect, and thought nothing of him.

DAW. Faith, mistris, you must doe so too. Learne to

IV. ii. 130, 132 *Exit.* add G 142 And] An' *F2* 146 *Exit Otter.* add G 150 *Exeunt.* add G IV. iii. SCENE II. | *A long open Gallery in the same.* | *Enter lady Haughty, mistress Otter, Mavis, Daw, La-Foole, Centaure, and Epicœne.* G 2 god] God *Q*

chastise. Mistris Otter corrects her husband so, hee dares not speake, but vnder correction.

La-f. And with his hat off to her: 'twould doe you good to see.

Hav. In sadnesse 'tis good, and mature counsell: practise it, Morose. I'll call you Morose still now, as I call Centavre, and Mavis: we foure will be all one.

Cen. And you'll come to the colledge, and liue with vs?

Hav. Make him giue milke, and hony.

Mav. Looke how you manage him at first, you shall haue him euer after.

Cen. Let him allow you your coach, and foure horses, your woman, your chamber-maid, your page, your gentleman-vsher, your *french* cooke, and foure groomes.

Hav. And goe with vs, to *Bed'lem*, to the *China* houses, and to the *Exchange*.

Cen. It will open the gate to your fame.

Hav. Here's Centavre has immortaliz'd her selfe, with taming of her wilde male.

Mav. I, shee has done the miracle of the kingdome.

Epi. But ladies, doe you count it lawfull to haue such pluralitie of seruants, and doe 'hem all graces?

Hav. Why not? why should women denie their fauours to men? Are they the poorer, or the worse?

Daw. Is the *Thames* the lesse for the *dyers* water, mistris?

La-f. Or a torch, for lighting many torches?

Trv. Well said, La-Foole; what a new one he has got!

Cen. They are emptie losses, women feare, in this kind.

Hav. Besides, ladies should be mindfull of the approach of age, and let no time want his due vse. The best of our daies passe first.

Mav. We are riuers, that cannot be call'd backe, madame: shee that now excludes her louers, may liue to lie a forsaken beldame, in a frozen bed.

CEN. 'Tis true, MAVIS; and who will wait on vs to coach then? or write, or tell vs the newes then? Make *anagrammes* of our names, and inuite vs to the cock-pit, and kisse our hands all the play-time, and draw their weapons for our honors?

HAV. Not one.

DAW. Nay, my mistris is not altogether vn-intelligent of these things; here be in presence haue tasted of her fauours.

CLE. What a neighing hobby-horse is this!

EPI. But not with intent to boast 'hem againe, seruant. And haue you those excellent receits, madame, to keepe your selues from bearing of children?

HAV. O yes, MOROSE. How should we maintayne our youth and beautie, else? Many births of a woman make her old, as many crops make the earth barren.

Act IIII. *Scene* IIII.

MOROSE, DAVPHINE, TRVE-WIT, EPICOENE, CLERIMONT, DAW, HAVGHTY, LA-FOOLE, CENTAVRE, MAVIS, M^rs^. OTTER, TRVSTY.

O My cursed angell, that instructed me to this fate!

DAV. Why, sir?

MOR. That I should bee seduc'd by so foolish a deuill, as a barber will make!

DAV. I would I had beene worthy, sir, to haue partaken your counsell, you should neuer haue trusted it to such a minister.

MOR. Would I could redeeme it with the losse of an eye (nephew) a hand, or any other member.

DAV. Mary, god forbid, sir, that you should geld your selfe, to anger your wife.

IV. iv. *Enter Morose and Dauphine.* G, continuing the scene 10 god] God *Q*

MOR. So it would rid me of her! and, that I did supererogatorie penance, in a bellfry, at *Westminster*-hall, i' the cock-pit, at the fall of a stagge; the tower-wharfe (what place is there else?) *London*-bridge, *Paris*-garden, *Belinsgate*, when the noises are at their height and lowdest. Nay, I would sit out a play, that were nothing but fights at sea, drum, trumpet, and target!

DAV. I hope there shall be no such need, sir. Take patience, good vncle. This is but a day, and 'tis well worne too now.

MOR. O, 'twill bee so for euer, nephew, I foresee it, for euer. Strife and tumult are the dowrie that comes with a wife.

TRV. I told you so, sir, and you would not beleeue me.

MOR. Alas, doe not rub those wounds, master TRVEWIT, to bloud againe: 'twas my negligence. Adde not affliction to affliction. I haue perceiu'd the effect of it, too late, in madame OTTER.

EPI. How doe you, sir?

MOR. Did you euer heare a more vnnecessary question? as if she did not see! Why, I doe as you see, Empresse, Empresse.

EPI. You are not well, sir! you looke very ill! something has distempered you.

MOR. O horrible, monstrous impertinencies! would not one of these haue seru'd? doe you thinke, sir? would not one of these haue seru'd?

TRV. Yes, sir, but these are but notes of female kindnesse, sir: certaine tokens that shee has a voice, sir.

MOR. O, is't so? come, and 't be no otherwise——what say you?

EPI. How doe you feele your selfe, sir?

MOR. Againe, that!

TRV. Nay, looke you, sir: you would be friends with your wife vpon vn-conscionable termes, her silence——

IV. iv. 14 -wharfe] -warf *F2* 22 so *om. Q* After 29 *Enter Clerimont and Truewit.* G 41 and 't] and *F3*

EPI. They say you are run mad, sir.

MOR. Not for loue, I assure you, of you; doe you see?

EPI. O lord, gentlemen! Lay hold on him for gods sake: what shal I doe? who's his physitian (can you tel) that knowes the state of his body best, that I might send for him? Good sir, speake. I'll send for one of my doctors else.

MOR. What, to poyson me, that I might die intestate, and leaue you possest of all?

EPI. Lord, how idly he talkes, and how his eyes sparkle! He lookes greene about the temples! Doe you see what blue spots he has?

CLE. I, it's melancholy.

EPI. Gentlemen, for heauens sake counsell me. Ladies! Seruant, you haue read PLINY, and PARACELSVS: Ne're a word now to comfort a poore gentlewoman? Ay me! what fortune had I to marry a distracted man?

DAW. I'll tell you, mistris——

TRV. How rarely shee holds it vp!

MOR. What meane you, gentlemen?

EPI. What will you tell me, seruant?

DAW. The disease in *Greeke* is called *Μανία*, in *Latine*, *Insania*, *Furor*, *vel Ecstasis melancholica*, that is, *Egressio*, when a man *ex melancholico*, *euadit fanaticus*.

MOR. Shall I haue a lecture read vpon me aliue?

DAW. But he may be but *Phreneticus*, yet, mistris? and *Phrenetis* is only *delirium*, or so——

EPI. I, that is for the disease, seruant: but what is this to the cure? we are sure inough of the disease.

MOR. Let me goe.

TRV. Why, wee'll intreat her to hold her peace, sir.

MOR. O, no. Labour not to stop her. Shee is like a conduit-pipe, that will gush out with more force, when shee opens againe.

IV. iv. 49 lord] Lord *Q*, *F2* gods] Gods *Q* 52 doctors] Doctours *Q* 65 *Aside to Cler.* add G 68 *Μανία Q, F2*: *Μανὶα F1* 73 so——] so. *F2*

HAV. I'll tell you, MOROSE, you must talke diuinitie to him altogether, or morall philosophie.

LA-F. I, and there's an excellent booke of morall philosophie, madame, of RAYNARD the foxe, and all the beasts, call'd, DONES philosophie.

CEN. There is, indeed, sir AMOROVS LA-FOOLE.

MOR. O miserie!

LA-F. I haue read it, my lady CENTAVRE, all ouer to my cousin, here.

Mrs. OT. I, and 'tis a very good booke as any is, of the Modernes.

DAW. Tut, hee must haue SENECA read to him, and PLVTARCH, and the Ancients; the Modernes are not for this disease.

CLE. Why, you discommended them too, to day, sir IOHN.

DAW. I, in some cases: but in these they are best, and ARISTOTLES *Ethicks.*

MAV. Say you so, sir IOHN? I thinke you are deceiu'd: you tooke it vpon trust.

HAV. Where's TRVSTY, my woman? I'll end this difference. I pr'ythee, OTTER, call her. Her father and mother were both mad, when they put her to me.

MOR. I thinke so. Nay, gentlemen, I am tame. This is but an exercise, I know, a marriage ceremonie, which I must endure.

HAV. And one of 'hem (I know not which) was cur'd with the *Sick-mans salue;* and the other with GREENES *groates-worth of wit.*

TRV. A very cheape cure, madame.

HAV. I, it's very fæsible.

Mrs. OT. My lady call'd for you, mistris TRVSTY: you must decide a controuersie.

HAV. O TRVSTY, which was it you said, your father, or your mother, that was cur'd with the *Sicke-mans salue?*

IV. iv. 82 him] her *Q*   107 'hem] them *F2, F3*   After 110 *Enter Trusty.* G   111 fæsible] feasible *F3*   114 TRVSTY] TTUSTY *F2*

TRVS. My mother, madame, with the *salue.*

TRV. Then it was the *Sicke-womans salue.*

TRVS. And my father with the *Groates-worth of wit.* But there was other meanes vs'd: we had a Preacher that would preach folke asleepe still; and so they were prescrib'd to goe to church, by an old woman that was their physitian, thrise a weeke——

EPI. To sleepe?

TRVS. Yes forsooth: and euery night they read themselues asleepe on those bookes.

EPI. Good faith, it stands with great reason. I would I knew where to procure those bookes.

MOR. Oh.

LA-F. I can helpe you with one of 'hem, mistris MOROSE, the *groats-worth of wit.*

EPI. But I shall disfurnish you, sir AMOROVS: can you spare it?

LA-F. O, yes, for a weeke, or so; I'll reade it my selfe to him.

EPI. No, I must doe that, sir: that must be my office.

MOR. Oh, oh!

EPI. Sure, he would doe well inough, if he could sleepe.

MOR. No, I should doe well inough, if you could sleepe. Haue I no friend that will make her drunke? or giue her a little *ladanum?* or *opium?*

TRV. Why, sir, shee talkes ten times worse in her sleepe.

MOR. How!

CLE. Doe you not know that, sir? neuer ceases all night.

TRV. And snores like a *porcpisce.*

MOR. O, redeeme me, fate, redeeme me, fate. For how many causes may a man be diuorc'd, nephew?

DAV. I know not truely, sir.

TRV. Some Diuine must resolue you in that, sir, or canon-Lawyer.

MOR. I will not rest, I will not thinke of any other hope or comfort, till I know.

IV. iv. 151 *Exit with Dauphine.* add G

CLE. Alas, poore man.

TRV. You'll make him mad indeed, ladies, if you pursue this.

HAV. No, wee'll let him breathe, now, a quarter of an houre, or so.

CLE. By my faith, a large truce.

HAV. Is that his keeper, that is gone with him?

DAW. It is his nephew, madame.

LA-F. Sir DAVPHINE EVGENIE.

CEN. He lookes like a very pittifull knight——

DAW. As can be. This marriage, has put him out of all.

LA-F. He has not a penny in his purse, madame——

DAW. He is readie to crie all this day.

LA-F. A very sharke, he set me i'the nicke t'other night at *primero*.

TRV. How these swabbers talke!

CLE. I, OTTERS wine has swell'd their humours aboue a spring-tide.

HAV. Good MOROSE, let's goe in againe. I like your couches exceeding well: we'll goe lie, and talke there.

EPI. I wait on you, madame.

TRV. 'Slight, I wil haue 'hem as silent as Signes, & their posts too, e're I ha' done. Doe you heare, lady-bride? I pray thee now, as thou art a noble wench, continue this discourse of DAVPHINE within: but praise him exceedingly. Magnifie him with all the height of affection thou canst. (I haue some purpose in't) and but beate off these two rookes, IACK DAW, and his fellow, with any discontentment hither, and I'll honour thee for euer.

EPI. I was about it, here. It angred mee to the soule, to heare 'hem beginne to talke so malepert.

TRV. Pray thee performe it, and thou win'st mee an idolater to thee, euerlasting.

EPI. Will you goe in, and heare me doe it?

IV. iv. 160 DAVPHINE] *Dauphine,* Q 165 i'the] i'th' *F2* 171 *Exeunt Hau. Cen. Mav. Tru. La-Foole, and Daw.* add G 173 'Slight] 'Sligh *F2* 174 posts] post *F2, F3* 180 honour] honor *F2*

TRV. No, I'll stay here. Driue 'hem out of your companie, 'tis all I aske: which cannot bee any way better done, then by extolling DAVPHINE, whom they haue so slighted.

EPI. I warrant you: you shall expect one of 'hem presently.

CLE. What a cast of kastrils are these, to hawke after ladies, thus?

TRV. I, and strike at such an eagle as DAVPHINE.

CLE. He will be mad, when we tell him. Here he comes.

Act IIII. *Scene* V.

CLERIMONT, TRVE-WIT, DAVPHINE, DAW, LA-FOOLE.

O Sir, you are welcome.

TRV. Where's thine vncle?

DAV. Run out o' dores in's night-caps, to talke with a *Casuist* about his diuorce. It workes admirably.

TRV. Thou would'st ha' said so, and thou had'st beene here! The ladies haue laught at thee, most *comically*, since thou wentst, DAVPHINE.

CLE. And askt, if thou wert thine vncles keeper?

TRV. And the brace of Babouns answer'd, yes; and said thou wert a pittifull poore fellow, and did'st liue vpon posts: and had'st nothing but three sutes of apparell, and some few beneuolences that lords ga' thee to foole to 'hem, and swagger.

DAV. Let me not liue, I'll beate 'hem. I'll binde 'hem both to grand Madames bed-postes, and haue 'hem bayted with monkeyes.

TRV. Thou shalt not need, they shall be beaten to thy hand, DAVPHINE. I haue an execution to serue vpon 'hem, I warrant thee shall serue: trust my plot.

IV. iv. 186 TRV.] *Cle.* Q 191 *Exit.* add G IV. v. *Re-enter Dauphine.* G, continuing the scene 12 lords] the lords *F2, F3*

DAV. I, you haue many plots! So you had one, to make all the wenches in loue with me.

TRV. Why, if I doe not yet afore night, as neere as 'tis; and that they doe not euery one inuite thee, and be ready to scratch for thee: take the morgage of my wit.

CLE. 'Fore god, I'll be his witnesse; thou shalt haue it, DAVPHINE: thou shalt be his foole for euer, if thou doest not.

TRV. Agreed. Perhaps 'twill bee the better estate. Doe you obserue this gallerie? or rather lobby, indeed? Here are a couple of studies, at each end one: here will I act such a *tragi-comœdy* betweene the *Guelphes*, and the *Ghibellines*, DAW and LA-FOOLE—which of 'hem comes out first, will I seize on: (you two shall be the *chorus* behind the arras, and whip out betweene the *acts*, and speake.) If I doe not make 'hem keepe the peace, for this remnant of the day, if not of the yeere, I haue faild once——I heare DAW comming: Hide, and doe not laugh, for gods sake.

DAW. Which is the way into the garden, trow?

TRV. O, IACK DAW! I am glad I haue met with you. In good faith, I must haue this matter goe no furder betweene you. I must ha' it taken vp.

DAW. What matter, sir? Betweene whom?

TRV. Come, you disguise it—Sir AMOROVS and you. If you loue me, IACK, you shall make vse of your philosophy now, for this once, and deliuer me your sword. This is not the wedding the CENTAVRES were at, though there be a shee-one here. The bride has entreated me I will see no bloud shed at her bridall, you saw her whisper me ere-while.

DAW. As I hope to finish TACITVS, I intend no murder.

TRV. Doe you not wait for sir AMOROVS?

DAW. Not I, by my knight-hood.

IV. v. 24 scratch] search *F2, F3* 25 god] God *Q* (*so* 97, 221, 292, 338) shalt] shalr *F2* 37 gods *F1*: God *Q*: Gods *F2* After 37 *Re-enter Daw.* G 40 furder] further *F2* 43 it—] it- *F1*: it, *F2* 48 bridall,] Bridall; *F2*

TRV. And your schollership too?

DAW. And my schollership too.

TRV. Goe to, then I returne you your sword, and aske you mercy; but put it not vp, for you will be assaulted. I vnderstood that you had apprehended it, and walkt here to braue him: and that you had held your life contemptible, in regard of your honor.

DAW. No, no, no such thing I assure you. He and I parted now, as good friends as could be.

TRV. Trust not you to that visor. I saw him since dinner with another face: I haue knowne many men in my time vex'd with losses, with deaths, and with abuses, but so offended a wight as sir AMOROVS, did I neuer see, or read of. For taking away his guests, sir, to day, that's the cause: and hee declares it behind your backe, with such threatnings and contempts—— He said to DAVPHINE, you were the errandst asse——

DAW. I, he may say his pleasure.

TRV. And sweares, you are so protested a coward, that hee knowes you will neuer doe him any manly or single right, and therefore hee will take his course.

DAW. I'll giue him any satisfaction, sir——but fighting.

TRV. I, sir, but who knowes what satisfaction hee'll take? bloud he thirsts for, and bloud he will haue: and where-abouts on you he will haue it, who knowes, but himselfe?

DAW. I pray you, master TRVE-WIT, be you a mediator.

TRV. Well, sir, conceale your selfe then in this studie, till I returne. Nay, you must bee content to bee lock'd in: for, for mine owne reputation I would not haue you seene to receiue a publique disgrace, while I haue the matter in managing. Gods so, here hee comes: keepe your breath close, that hee doe not heare you sigh. In good faith, sir AMOROVS, hee is not this way, I pray you bee mercifull, doe not murder him; hee is a christian as good as you: *He puts him vp.*

IV. v. 60 honor] honour *F2* 88 way,] way; *F2*

you are arm'd as if you sought a reuenge on all his race. Good DAVPHINE, get him away from this place. I neuer knew a mans choller so high, but hee would speake to his friends, hee would heare reason. IACK DAW. IACK DAW! a-sleepe?

DAW. Is he gone, master TRVE-WIT?

TRV. I, did you heare him?

DAW. O god, yes.

TRV. What a quick eare feare has?

DAW. And is he so arm'd, as you say?

TRV. Arm'd? did you euer see a fellow, set out to take possession?

DAW. I, sir.

TRV. That may giue you some light, to conceiue of him: but 'tis nothing to the principall. Some false brother i' the house has furnish'd him strangely. Or, if it were out o' the house, it was TOM OTTER.

DAW. Indeed, hee's a Captayne, and his wife is his kinswoman.

TRV. Hee has got some-bodies old two-hand-sword, to mow you off at the knees. And that sword hath spawn'd such a dagger!——but then he is so hung with pikes, halberds, peitronells, calliuers, and muskets, that he lookes like a Iustice of peace's hall: a man of two thousand a yeere, is not sess'd at so many weapons, as he has on. There was neuer fencer challeng'd at so many seuerall foiles. You would think hee meant to murder all Saint PVLCHRES parish. If hee could but victuall himselfe for halfe a yeere, in his breeches, hee is sufficiently arm'd to ouer-runne a countrie.

DAW. Good lord, what meanes he, sir! I pray you, master TRVE-WIT, be you a mediator.

TRV. Well, I'll trie if he will be appeas'd with a leg or an arme, if not, you must die once.

IV. v. 94 IACK DAW] JACK *F2*: *Jack* F3 95 DAW.] *Daw.* [*within.*] G 96 I,] I; *F2* 97 god] God *Q*, *F2* 99 DAW.] *Daw.* [*Comes out of the closet.*] G And] But *F2* 112 peitronells] *Query*, petrionells 120 lord] Lord *Q* 123 arme,] arme; *F2*

DAW. I would be loth to loose my right arme, for writing *madrigalls.*

TRV. Why, if he will be satisfied with a thumb, or a little finger, all's one to me. You must thinke, I'll doe my best.

DAW. Good sir, doe.

He puts him vp againe, and then came forth.

CLE. What hast thou done?

TRV. He will let me doe nothing, man, he do's all afore me, he offers his left arme.

CLE. His left wing, for a IACK DAW.

DAV. Take it, by all meanes.

TRV. How! Maime a man for euer, for a iest? what a conscience hast thou?

DAV. 'Tis no losse to him: he has no employment for his armes, but to eate spoone-meat. Beside, as good maime his body as his reputation.

TRV. He is a scholler, and a *Wit*, and yet he do's not thinke so. But he looses no reputation with vs, for we all resolu'd him an asse before. To your places againe.

CLE. I pray thee, let me be in at the other a little.

TRV. Looke, you'll spoile all: these be euer your tricks.

CLE. No, but I could hit of some things that thou wilt misse, and thou wilt say are good ones.

TRV. I warrant you. I pray forbeare, I'll leaue it off, else.

DAV. Come away, CLERIMONT.

TRV. Sir AMOROVS!

LA-F. Master TRVE-WIT.

TRV. Whether were you going?

LA-F. Downe into the court, to make water.

TRV. By no meanes, sir, you shall rather tempt your breeches.

LA-F. Why, sir?

IV. v. 124 loose] lose *F2* After 129 *Clerimont and Dauphine come forward.* G 134 DAV.] *Daw.* Q 137 losse] lesse *F2* 138 good] goods *Q* 141 looses] loses *F2* After 150 *Daup. and Cler. withdraw as before.* | *Enter La-Foole.* G 155 sir,] sir; *F2*

TRV. Enter here, if you loue your life.

LA-F. Why! why!

TRV. Question till your throat bee cut, doe: dally till the enraged soule find you.

LA-F. Who's that?

TRV. DAW it is: will you in?

LA-F. I, I, I'll in: what's the matter?

TRV. Nay, if hee had beene coole inough to tell vs that, there had beene some hope to attone you, but he seemes so implacably enrag'd.

LA-F. 'Slight, let him rage. I'll hide my selfe.

TRV. Doe, good sir. But what haue you done to him within, that should prouoke him thus? you haue broke some iest vpon him, afore the ladies——

LA-F. Not I, ⟨I⟩ neuer in my life, broke iest vpon any man. The bride was praising sir DAVPHINE, and he went away in snuffe, and I followed him, vnlesse he took offence at me, in his drinke ere while, that I would not pledge all the horse full.

TRV. By my faith, and that may bee, you remember well: but hee walkes the round vp and downe, through euery roome o' the house, with a towell in his hand, crying, where's LA-FOOLE? who saw LA-FOOLE? and when DAVPHINE, and I, demanded the cause, wee can force no answere from him, but (ô reuenge, how sweet art thou! I will strangle him in this towell) which leads vs to coniecture, that the maine cause of his furie is for bringing your meate to day, with a towell about you, to his discredit.

LA-F. Like inough. Why, and he be angrie for that, I'll stay here, till his anger be blowne ouer.

TRV. A good becomming resolution, sir. If you can put it on o' the sudden.

LA-F. Yes, I can put it on. Or, I'll away into the country presently.

TRV. How will you get out o' the house, sir? Hee knowes

IV. v. 158 *Opening the door of the other study.* add G 174 him,] him; *F2* 177 bee,] be; *F2* 182 but] but, *F2*

you are i' the house, and hee'll watch you this se'n-night but hee'll haue you. Hee'll out-wait a sargeant for you.

La-F. Why, then I'll stay here.

Trv. You must thinke, how to victuall your selfe in time, then.

La-F. Why, sweet master Trve-wit, will you entreat my cousin Otter, to send me a cold venison pasty, a bottle or two of wine, and a chamber pot?

Trv. A stoole were better, sir, of sir A-iax his inuention.

La-F. I, that will be better indeed: and a pallat to lie on.

Trv. O, I would not aduise you to sleepe by any meanes.

La-F. Would you not, sir? why, then I will not.

Trv. Yet, there's another feare——

La-F. Is there, sir? What is't?

Trv. No, he cannot breake open this dore with his foot, sure.

La-F. I'll set my backe against it, sir. I haue a good backe.

Trv. But, then, if he should batter.

La-F. Batter! if he dare, I'll haue an action of batt'ry, against him.

Trv. Cast you the worst. He has sent for poulder alreadie, and what he will doe with it, no man knowes: perhaps blow vp the corner o' the house, where he suspects you are. Here he comes, in quickly. I protest, sir Iohn Daw, he is not this way: what will you doe? before god, you shall hang no *petarde* here. I'll die rather. Will you not take my word? I neuer knew one but would be satisfied. Sir Amorovs, there's no standing out. He has made a *petarde* of an old brasse pot, to force your dore. Thinke vpon some satisfaction, or termes, to offer him.

He faines, as if one were present, to fright the other, who is run in to hide himselfe.

IV. v. 200 pot?] pot. *Ff*: Pot. *Q* 214 then,] then *Ff, Q* 220 comes,] comes; *F2* 222 *petarde*] *petar de* (or perhaps *petar'de*) Q 224 After 'Amorovs,' [*speaks through the key-hole,*] G

L A - F. Sir, I'll giue him any satisfaction. I dare giue any termes.

T R V. You'll leaue it to me, then?

L A - F. I, sir. I'll stand to any conditions.

He calls forth Clerimont, and Dauphine.

T R V. How now, what thinke you, sirs? wer't not a difficult thing to determine, which of these two fear'd most?

C L E. Yes, but this feares the brauest: the other a whiniling dastard, I A C K D A W! but L A - F O O L E, a braue heroique coward! and is afraid in a great looke, and a stout accent. I like him rarely.

T R V. Had it not beene pitty, these two should ha' beene conceal'd?

C L E. Shall I make a motion?

T R V. Briefly. For I must strike while 'tis hot.

C L E. Shall I goe fetch the ladies to the *catastrophe?*

T R V. Vmh? I, by my troth.

D A V. By no mortall meanes. Let them continue in the state of ignorance, and erre still: thinke 'hem wits, and fine fellowes, as they haue done. 'Twere sinne to reforme them.

T R V. Well, I will haue 'hem fetch'd, now I thinke on't, for a priuate purpose of mine: doe, C L E R I M O N T, fetch 'hem, and discourse to 'hem all that's past, and bring 'hem into the gallery here.

D A V. This is thy extreme vanitie, now: thou think'st thou wert vndone, if euery iest thou mak'st were not publish'd.

T R V. Thou shalt see, how vniust thou art, presently. C L E R I M O N T, say it was D A V P H I N E's plot. Trust me not, if the whole drift be not for thy good. There's a carpet i' the next roome, put it on, with this scarfe ouer thy face, and a cushion o' thy head, and bee ready when I call A M O R O V S. Away——I O H N D A W.

IV. V. 227 LA-F.] *La-F. [within,]* G 231 St. dir. *He . . . Dauphine*] *beckoning forward Cler. and Dauph.* G 232 most?] most. *Ff, Q* 234 whiniling] whimling *F. Cunningham conj.* 249 to 'hem] to hem *F1* 255 After 'plot.' *Exit Clerimont.* G 259 After 'Away' *Exit Daup.* G After 'DAW.' *Goes to Daw's closet, and brings him out.* add G

DAW. What good newes, sir?

TRV. Faith, I haue followed, and argued with him hard for you. I told him, you were a knight, and a scholler; and that you knew fortitude did consist *magis patiendo quam faciendo, magis ferendo quam feriendo.*

DAW. It doth so indeed, sir.

TRV. And that you would suffer, I told him: so, at first he demanded, by my troth, in my conceipt, too much.

DAW. What was it, sir?

TRV. Your vpper lip, and sixe o' your fore-teeth.

DAW. 'Twas vnreasonable.

TRV. Nay, I told him plainely, you could not spare 'hem all. So after long argument (*pro & con,* as you know) I brought him downe to your two butter-teeth, and them he would haue.

DAW. O, did you so? why, he shall haue 'hem.

TRV. But he shall not, sir, by your leaue. The conclusion is this, sir, because you shall be very good friends hereafter, and this neuer to bee remembred, or vp-braided; besides, that he may not boast, he has done any such thing to you in his owne person: hee is to come here in disguise, giue you fiue kicks in priuate, sir, take your sword from you, and lock you vp in that studie, during pleasure. Which will be but a little while, wee'll get it releas'd presently.

DAW. Fiue kicks? he shall haue sixe, sir, to be friends.

TRV. Beleeue mee, you shall not ouer-shoot your selfe, to send him that word by me.

DAW. Deliuer it, sir. He shall haue it with all my heart, to be friends.

TRV. Friends? Nay, and he should not be so, and heartily too, vpon these termes, he shall haue me to enemie while I liue. Come, sir, beare it brauely.

DAW. O god, sir, 'tis nothing.

TRV. True. What's sixe kicks to a man, that reads SENECA?

IV. v. 260 sir?] sir. *F1* 268 sir? *F2*: sir. *F1*: Sir. *Q* 289 and] an' *F2* 292 god] God *Q*

DAW. I haue had a hundred, sir.

TRV. Sir AMOROVS. No speaking one to another, or rehearsing old matters.

Dauphine comes forth, and kicks him.

DAW. One, two, three, foure, fiue. I protest, sir AMOROVS, you shall haue sixe.

TRV. Nay, I told you ⟨you⟩ should not talke. Come, giue him six, & he will needs. Your sword. Now returne to your safe custody: you shall presently meet afore the ladies, and be the dearest friends one to another——Giue me the scarfe, now, thou shalt beat the other bare-fac'd. Stand by——sir AMOROVS.

LA-F. What's here? A sword.

TRV. I cannot helpe it, without I should take the quarrell vpon my selfe: here he has sent you his sword——

LA-F. I'll receiue none on't.

TRV. And he wills you to fasten it against a wall, and breake your head in some few seuerall places against the hilts.

LA-F. I will not: tell him roundly. I cannot endure to shed my owne bloud.

TRV. Will you not?

LA-F. No. I'll beat it against a faire flat wall, if that will satisfie him: If not, he shall beat it himselfe, for AMOROVS.

TRV. Why, this is strange starting off, when a man vnder-takes for you! I offered him another condition: Will you stand to that?

LA-F. I, what is't?

TRV. That you will be beaten, in priuate.

LA-F. Yes. I am content, at the blunt.

TRV. Then you must submit your selfe to bee hoodwink'd in this skarfe, and bee led to him, where hee will take your sword from you, and make you beare a blow,

IV. v. 300 you *F3* 305 by——] by, *Ff, Q* (*cf. l.* 259): by: *W* After 'by' [*Dauphine retires, and Truewit goes to the other closet, and releases La-Foole.*] G 311 places] place *F2* 322 is't? *F2*: is't. *F1, Q* After 324 *Enter, above, Haughty, Centaure, Mavis, mistress Otter, Epicœne, and Trusty.* G

ouer the mouth, *gules*, and tweakes by the nose, *sans nombre*.

LA-F. I am content. But why must I be blinded?

TRV. That's for your good, sir: because, if hee should grow insolent vpon this, and publish it hereafter to your disgrace (which I hope he will not doe) you might sweare safely and protest, hee neuer beat you, to your knowledge.

LA-F. O, I conceiue.

TRV. I doe not doubt, but you'll be perfect good friends vpon 't, and not dare to vtter an ill thought one of another, in future.

LA-F. Not I, as god helpe me, of him.

TRV. Nor he of you, sir. If he should——Come, sir. All hid, sir IOHN.

LA-F. Oh, sir IOHN, sir IOHN. Oh, ô-ô-ô-ô-ô-Oh——

Dauphine enters to tweake him.

TRV. Good sir IOHN, leaue tweaking, you'll blow his nose off. 'Tis sir IOHN's pleasure, you should retire into the studie. Why, now you are friends. All bitternesse betweene you, I hope, is buried; you shall come forth by and by, DAMON & PYTHIAS vpon 't: and embrace with all the ranknesse of friendship that can be. I trust, wee shall haue 'hem tamer i' their language hereafter. DAVPHINE, I worship thee. Gods will, the ladies haue surpris'd vs!

Act IIII. *Scene* VI.

HAVGHTY, CENTAVRE, MAVIS, Mrs. OTTER, EPICOENE, TRVSTY, DAVPHINE, TRVE-WIT, &c.

Hauing discouerd part of the past scene, *aboue*

CENTAVRE, how our iudgements were impos'd on by these adulterate knights!

CEN. Nay, madame, MAVIS was more deceiu'd then we, 'twas her commendation vtter'd 'hem in the colledge.

IV. v. 329 *nombre* F2: *numbre* F1, Q 339 god] God *Q* 340 After 'should' [*binds his eyes.*] G After 'sir.' [*leads him forward.*] G 343 Good *Q*: Good, *Ff* IV. vi. *Enter Haughty, Centaure, Mavis, mistress Otter, Epicœne, and Trusty behind.* G, continuing the scene. Marginal note—scene] *Scene* F2

MAV. I commended but their wits, madame, and their braueries. I neuer look'd toward their valours.

HAV. Sir DAVPHINE is valiant, and a wit too, it seemes?

MAV. And a brauerie too.

HAV. Was this his proiect?

M^rs^. OT. So master CLERIMONT intimates, madame.

HAV. Good MOROSE, when you come to the colledge, will you bring him with you? He seemes a very perfect gentleman.

EPI. He is so, madame, beleeue it.

CEN. But when will you come, MOROSE?

EPI. Three or foure dayes hence, madame, when I haue got mee a coach, and horses.

HAV. No, to morrow, good MOROSE, CENTAVRE shall send you her coach.

MAV. Yes faith, doe, and bring sir DAVPHINE with you.

HAV. Shee has promis'd that, MAVIS.

MAV. He is a very worthy gentleman, in his exteriors, madame.

HAV. I, he showes he is iudiciall in his clothes.

CEN. And yet not so superlatiuely neat as some, madame, that haue their faces set in a brake!

HAV. I, and haue euery haire in forme!

MAV. That weare purer linnen then our selues, and professe more neatnesse, then the *french hermaphrodite!*

EPI. I ladies, they, what they tell one of vs, haue told a thousand, and are the only theeues of our fame: that thinke to take vs with that perfume, or with that lace, and laugh at vs vn-conscionably when they haue done.

HAV. But, sir DAVPHINES carelesnesse becomes him.

CEN. I could loue a man, for such a nose!

MAV. Or such a leg!

CEN. He has an exceeding good eye, madame!

IV. vi. 28 brake] barke *F2*

MAV. And a very good lock!

CEN. Good MOROSE, bring him to my chamber first.

Mrs. OT. Please your honors, to meet at my house, madame?

TRV. See, how they eye thee, man! they are taken, I warrant thee.

HAV. You haue vnbrac'd our brace of knights, here, master TRVE-WIT.

TRV. Not I, madame, it was sir DAVPHINES ingine: who, if he haue disfurnish'd your ladiship of any guard, or seruice by it, is able to make the place good againe, in himselfe.

HAV. There's no suspition of that, sir.

CEN. God so, MAVIS, HAVGHTY is kissing.

MAV. Let vs goe too, and take part.

HAV. But I am glad of the fortune (beside the discouerie of two such emptie caskets) to gaine the knowledge of so rich a mine of vertue, as sir DAVPHINE.

CEN. We would be al glad to stile him of our friendship, and see him at the colledge.

MAV. He cannot mixe with a sweeter societie, I'll prophesie, and I hope he himselfe will thinke so.

DAV. I should be rude to imagine otherwise, lady.

TRV. Did not I tell thee, DAVPHINE? Why, all their actions are gouerned by crude opinion, without reason or cause; they know not why they doe any thing: but as they are inform'd, beleeue, iudge, praise, condemne, loue, hate, and in æmulation one of another, doe all these things alike. Onely, they haue a naturall inclination swayes 'hem generally to the worst, when they are left to themselues. But, pursue it, now thou hast 'hem.

HAV. Shall we goe in againe, MOROSE?

EPI. Yes, madame.

CEN. Wee'll entreat sir DAVPHINES companie.

IV. vi. 43 honors] Honours *Q* 46 *Haughty comes forward.* add G 49 ingine] inginer *Q* 53 There's] There is *F2* 55 *They come forward.* add G

TRV. Stay, good madame, the inter-view of the two friends, PYLADES and ORESTES: I'll fetch 'hem out to you straight.

HAV. Will you, master TRVE-WIT?

DAV. I, but noble ladies, doe not confesse in your countenance, or outward bearing to 'hem any discouerie of their follies, that wee may see, how they will beare vp againe, with what assurance, and erection.

HAV. We will not, sir DAVPHINE.

CEN. MAV. Vpon our honors, sir DAVPHINE.

TRV. Sir AMOROVS, sir AMOROVS. The ladies are here.

LA-F. Are they?

TRV. Yes, but slip out by and by, as their backs are turn'd, and meet sir IOHN here, as by chance, when I call you. IACK DAW.

DAW. What say you, sir?

TRV. Whip out behind me suddenly: and no anger i' your lookes to your aduersarie. Now, now.

LA-F. Noble sir IOHN DAW! where ha' you beene?

DAW. To seeke you, sir AMOROVS.

LA-F. Me! I honor you.

DAW. I preuent you, sir.

CLE. They haue forgot their rapiers!

TRV. O, they meet in peace, man.

DAV. Where's your sword, sir IOHN?

CLE. And yours, sir AMOROVS?

DAW. Mine! my boy had it forth, to mend the handle, eene now.

LA-F. And my gold handle was broke, too, and my boy had it forth.

DAV. Indeed, sir? How their excuses meet!

CLE. What a consent there is, i' the handles?

IV. vi. 85 TRV.] *True.* [*goes to the first closet.*] G 87 LA-F.] *La-F.* [*within.*] G 90 After 'you.' [*Goes to the other.*] G 91 DAW.] *Daw.* [*within.*] G 93 *La-Foole and Daw slip out of their respective closets, and salute each other.* G 96 honor] honour *Q, F2*

TRV. Nay, there is so i' the points too, I warrant you.

Mrs. T. O me! madame, he comes againe, the mad man, away.

Act IIII. *Scene* VII.

MOROSE, TRVE-WIT, CLERIMONT, DAVPHINE.

He had found the two swords drawne within.

WHat make these naked weapons here, gentlemen?

TRV. O, sir! here hath like to been murder since you went! A couple of knights fallen out about the brides fauours: wee were faine to take away their weapons, your house had beene beg'd by this time else——

MOR. For what?

CLE. For man-slaughter, sir, as being accessary.

MOR. And, for her fauours?

TRV. I, sir, heretofore, not present. CLERIMONT, carry 'hem their swords, now. They haue done all the hurt they will doe.

DAV. Ha' you spoke with a lawyer, sir?

MOR. O, no! there is such a noyse i' the court, that they haue frighted mee home, with more violence then I went! such speaking, and counter-speaking, with their seuerall voyces of *citations*, *appellations*, *allegations*, *certificates*, *attachments*, *intergatories*, *references*, *conuictions*, and *afflictions* indeed, among the Doctors and Proctors! that the noise here is silence too 't! a kind of calme mid-night!

TRV. Why, sir, if you would be resolu'd indeed, I can bring you hether a very sufficient Lawyer, and a learned Diuine, that shall inquire into euery least scruple for you.

MOR. Can you, master TRVE-WIT?

TRV. Yes, and are very sober graue persons, that will dispatch it in a chamber, with a whisper, or two.

IV. vi. After 108 *Enter Morose, with the two swords, drawn, in his hands.* G   109 man,] man! *F2*   110 *Ladies, Daw, and La-Foole run off.* add G   IV. vii. *G continues the scene*   2 murder] muder *Q*   10 *Exit Cler. with the two swords.* add G   17 *intergatories*] *Interrogatories* F2, F3   19 calme *om. Q*   21 hether hither *Q, F2* (*so* 37)   24 TRV. *om. Q*

MOR. Good sir, shall I hope this benefit from you, and trust my selfe into your hands?

TRV. Alas, sir! your nephew, and I, haue beene asham'd, and oft-times mad since you went, to thinke how you are abus'd. Goe in, good sir, and lock your selfe vp till we call you, wee'll tell you more anon, sir.

MOR. Doe your pleasure with me, gentlemen; I beleeue in you: and that deserues no delusion——

TRV. You shall find none, sir: but heapt, heapt plentie of vexation.

DAV. What wilt thou doe now, WIT?

TRV. Recouer me hether OTTER, and the Barber, if you can, by any meanes, presently.

DAV. Why? to what purpose?

TRV. O, I'll make the deepest Diuine, and grauest Lawyer, out o' them two, for him——

DAV. Thou canst not man, these are waking dreames.

TRV. Doe not feare me. Clap but a ciuill gowne with a welt, o' the one; and a canonical cloake with sleeues, o' the other: and giue 'hem a few termes i' their mouthes, if there come not forth as able a Doctor, and compleat a Parson, for this turne, as may be wish'd, trust not my election. And, I hope, without wronging the dignitie of either profession, since they are but persons put on, and for mirths sake, to torment him. The Barber smatters *latin*, I remember.

DAV. Yes, and OTTER too.

TRV. Well then, if I make 'hem not wrangle out this case, to his no comfort, let me be thought a IACK DAW, or LA-FOOLE, or any thing worse. Goe you to your ladies, but first send for them.

DAV. I will.

IV. vi. 33 *Exit.* add G

Act V. *Scene* I.

LA-FOOLE, CLERIMONT, DAW, MAVIS.

WHere had you our swords, master CLERIMONT?

CLE. Why, DAVPHINE tooke 'hem from the mad-man.

LA-F. And he tooke 'hem from our boyes, I warrant you?

CLE. Very like, sir.

LA-F. Thanke you, good master CLERIMONT. Sir IOHN DAW, and I are both beholden to you.

CLE. Would I knew how to make you so, gentlemen.

DAW. Sir AMOROVS, and I are your seruants, sir.

MAV. Gentlemen, haue any of you a pen-and-inke? I would faine write out a riddle in *Italian*, for sir DAVPHINE, to translate.

CLE. Not I, in troth, lady, I am no scriuener.

DAW. I can furnish you, I thinke, lady.

CLE. He has it in the haft of a knife, I beleeue!

LA-F. No, he has his boxe of instruments.

CLE. Like a surgean!

LA-F. For the *mathematiques:* his squire, his compasses, his brasse pens, and black-lead, to draw maps of euery place, and person, where he comes.

CLE. How, maps of persons!

LA-F. Yes, sir, of NOMENTACK, when he was here, and of the Prince of *Moldauia*, and of his mistris, mistris EPICŒNE.

CLE. Away! he has not found out her latitude, I hope.

LA-F. You are a pleasant gentleman, sir.

CLE. Faith, now we are in priuate, let's wanton it a little, and talke waggishly. Sir IOHN, I am telling sir

v. i. ACT V. SCENE I. | *A Room in Morose's House.* | *Enter La-Foole, Clerimont, and Daw.* G   10 I] I, *F2*   After 10 *Enter Mavis.* G   11 -inke ?] -inke. *Ff*: -Inke. *Q*   15 *Exeunt Daw and Mavis.* add G   19 squire] Square *F3*   After 25 *Re-enter Daw.* G

AMOROVS here, that you two gouerne the ladies, where e're you come, you carry the feminine gender afore you.

DAW. They shall rather carry vs afore them, if they will, sir.

CLE. Nay, I beleeue that they doe, withall—But, that you are the prime-men in their affections, and direct all their actions——

DAW. Not I: sir AMOROVS is.

LA-F. I protest, sir IOHN is.

DAW. As I hope to rise i' the state, sir AMOROVS, you ha' the person.

LA-F. Sir IOHN, you ha' the person, and the discourse too.

DAW. Not I, sir. I haue no discourse—and then you haue actiuitie beside.

LA-F. I protest, sir IOHN, you come as high from *Tripoly*, as I doe euery whit: and lift as many ioyn'd stooles, and leape ouer 'hem, if you would vse it——

CLE. Well, agree on't together knights; for betweene you, you diuide the kingdome, or common-wealth of ladies affections: I see it, and can perceiue a little how they obserue you, and feare you, indeed. You could tell strange stories, my masters, if you would, I know.

DAW. Faith, we haue seene somewhat, sir.

LA-F. That we haue—vellet petti-coates, & wrought smocks, or so.

DAW. I, and——

CLE. Nay, out with it, sir IOHN: doe not enuie your friend the pleasure of hearing, when you haue had the delight of tasting.

DAW. Why——a——doe you speake, sir AMOROVS.

LA-F. No, doe you, sir IOHN DAW.

DAW. I' faith, you shall.

LA-F. I' faith, you shall.

DAW. Why, we haue beene——

LA-F. In the great bed at *Ware* together in our time. On, sir IOHN.

v. i. 53 vellet] velvet *F2*

DAW. Nay, doe you, sir AMOROVS.

CLE. And these ladies with you, Knights?

LA-F. No, excuse vs, sir.

DAW. We must not wound reputation.

LA-F. No matter—they were these, or others. Our bath cost vs fifteene pound, when we came home.

CLE. Doe you heare, sir IOHN, you shall tell me but one thing truely, as you loue me.

DAW. If I can, I will, sir.

CLE. You lay in the same house with the bride, here?

DAW. Yes, and conuerst with her hourely, sir.

CLE. And what humour is shee of? is shee comming, and open, free?

DAW. O, exceeding open, sir. I was her seruant, and sir AMOROVS was to be.

CLE. Come, you haue both had fauours from her? I know, and haue heard so much.

DAW. O, no, sir.

LA-F. You shall excuse vs, sir: we must not wound reputation.

CLE. Tut, shee is married, now; and you cannot hurt her with any report, and therefore speake plainely: how many times, yfaith? which of you lead first? Ha?

LA-F. Sir IOHN had her mayden-head, indeed.

DAW. O, it pleases him to say so, sir, but sir AMOROVS knowes what's what, as well.

CLE. Do'st thou yfaith, AMOROVS?

LA-F. In a manner, sir.

CLE. Why, I commend you lads. Little knowes *Don* Bride-groome of this. Nor shall he, for me.

DAW. Hang him, mad oxe.

CLE. Speake softly: here comes his nephew, with the lady HAVGHTY. Hee'll get the ladies from you, sirs, if you looke not to him in time.

LA-F. Why, if he doe, wee'll fetch 'hem home againe, I warrant you.

v. i. 88 lead] led *F2*   101 *Exit with Daw. Cler. walks aside.* G

Act V. *Scene* II.

HAVGHTY, DAVPHINE, CENTAVRE, MAVIS, CLERIMONT.

I Assure you, sir DAVPHINE, it is the price and estimation of your vertue onely, that hath embarqu'd me to this aduenture, and I could not but make out to tell you so; nor can I repent me of the act, since it is alwayes an argument of some vertue in our selues, that we loue and affect it so in others.

DAV. Your ladiship sets too high a price, on my weakenesse.

HAV. Sir, I can distinguish gemmes from peebles——

DAV. (Are you so skilfull in stones?)

HAV. And, howsoeuer I may suffer in such a iudgement as yours, by admitting equality of ranke, or societie, with CENTAVRE, or MAVIS——

DAV. You doe not, madame, I perceiue they are your mere foiles.

HAV. Then are you a friend to truth, sir. It makes mee loue you the more. It is not the outward, but the inward man that I affect. They are not apprehensiue of an eminent perfection, but loue flat, and dully.

CEN. Where are you, my lady HAVGHTY?

HAV. I come presently, CENTAVRE. My chamber, sir, my Page shall show you; and TRVSTY, my woman, shall be euer awake for you: you need not feare to communicate any thing with her, for shee is a FIDELIA. I pray you weare this iewell for my sake, sir DAVPHINE. Where's MAVIS, CENTAVRE?

CEN. Within, madame, a writing. I'll follow you presently. I'll but speake a word with sir DAVPHINE.

DAVP. With me, madame?

v. ii. *Enter Dauphine and Haughty.* G, continuing the scene 4 so *om. Q* 9 peebles] pebles *F2* 20 CEN.] *Cen.* [*within.*] G 25 After 'DAVPHINE.' *Enter Centaure.* G 28 After 'presently.' [*Exit Haughty.*] G

CEN. Good sir DAVPHINE, doe not trust HAVGHTY, nor make any credit to her, what euer you doe besides. Sir DAVPHINE, I giue you this caution, shee is a perfect courtier, and loues no body, but for her vses : and for her vses, shee loues all. Besides, her physitians giue her out to be none o' the clearest, whether she pay 'hem or no, heau'n knowes : and she's aboue fiftie too, and pargets ! See her in a fore-noone. Here comes MAVIS, a worse face then shee ! you would not like this, by candle-light. If you'll come to my chamber one o' these mornings early, or late in an euening, I'll tell you more. Where's HAVGHTY, MAVIS?

MAV. Within, CENTAVRE.

CEN. What ha' you, there ?

MAV. An *Italian* riddle for sir DAVPHINE, (you shall not see it yfaith, CENTAVRE.) Good sir DAVPHINE, solue it for mee. I'll call for it anon.

CLE. How now, DAVPHINE? how do'st thou quit thy selfe of these females ?

DAVP. 'Slight, they haunt me like *fayries*, and giue me iewells here, I cannot be rid of 'hem.

CLE. O, you must not tell, though.

DAVP. Masse, I forgot that : I was neuer so assaulted. One loues for vertue, and bribes me with this. Another loues me with caution, and so would possesse me. A third brings me a riddle here, and all are iealous : and raile each at other.

CLE. A riddle ? pray' le' me see't ? *Sir* DAVPHINE, *I chose this way of intimation for priuacie. The ladies here, I know, haue both hope, and purpose, to make a collegiate and seruant of you. If I might be so honor'd, as to appeare at any end of so noble a worke, I would enter into a fame of taking physique to morrow, and continue it foure or fiue dayes, or longer, for your visitation.* MAVIS. By my faith, a

He reades the paper.

V. ii. 38 After 'candle-light.' *Re-enter Mavis.* G 45 After 'CENTAVRE.' [*Exit Cen.*] G 46 *Exit.* add G 47 CLE.] *Cler.* [*coming forward.*] G 60 *honor'd*] *honour'd* Q, F2 62 *continue*] *continue you* Q

subtle one! Call you this a riddle? What's their plaine dealing, trow?

DAVP. We lack TRVE-WIT, to tell vs that.

CLE. We lack him for somewhat else too: his Knights *reformados* are wound vp as high, and insolent, as euer they were.

DAVP. You iest.

CLE. No drunkards, either with wine or vanitie, euer confess'd such stories of themselues. I would not giue a flies leg, in ballance against all the womens reputations here, if they could bee but thought to speake truth: and for the bride, they haue made their *affidauit* against her directly——

DAVP. What, that they haue lyen with her?

CLE. Yes, and tell times, and circumstances, with the cause why, and the place where. I had almost brought 'hem to affirme that they had done it, to day.

DAVP. Not both of 'hem.

CLE. Yes faith: with a sooth or two more I had effected it. They would ha' set it downe vnder their hands.

DAVP. Why, they will be our sport, I see, still! whether we will, or no.

Act V. *Scene* III.

TRVE-WIT, MOROSE, OTTER, CVTBERD, CLERIMONT, DAVPHINE.

O, Are you here? Come DAVPHINE. Goe, call your vncle presently. I haue fitted my Diuine, & my Canonist, died their beards and all: the knaues doe not know themselues, they are so exalted, and alter'd. Preferment changes any man. Thou shalt keepe one dore, and I another, and then CLERIMONT in the midst, that he may haue no meanes of escape from their cauilling, when they grow hot once. And then the women (as I haue giuen

v. ii. 76 lyen] lain *F3* v. iii. *Enter Truewit.* G, continuing the scene 4 themselues,] themselves, *F2*: themselues *F1*, *Q* 8 once] once againe *Q*

the bride her instructions) to breake in vpon him, i' the *l'enuoy*. O, 'twill be full and twanging! Away, fetch him. Come, master Doctor, and master Parson, looke to your parts now, and discharge 'hem brauely: you are well set forth, performe it as well. If you chance to be out, doe not confesse it with standing still, or humming, or gaping one at another: but goe on, and talke alowd, and eagerly, vse vehement action, and onely remember your termes, and you are safe. Let the matter goe where it will: you haue many will doe so. But at first, bee very solemne, and graue like your garments, though you loose your selues after, and skip out like a brace of iugglers on a table. Here hee comes! set your faces, and looke superciliously, while I present you.

MOR. Are these the two learned men?

TRV. Yes, sir, please you salute 'hem?

MOR. Salute 'hem? I had rather doe any thing, then weare out time so vnfruitfully, sir. I wonder, how these common formes, as *god saue you*, and *you are well-come*, are come to be a habit in our liues! or, *I am glad to see you!* when I cannot see, what the profit can bee of these wordes, so long as it is no whit better with him, whose affaires are sad, & grieuous, that he heares this salutation.

TRV. 'Tis true, sir, wee'll goe to the matter then. Gentlemen, master Doctor, and master Parson, I haue acquainted you sufficiently with the busines, for which you are come hether. And you are not now to enforme your selues in the state of the question, I know. This is the gentleman, who expects your resolution, and therefore, when you please, beginne.

OTT. Please you, master Doctor.

CVT. Please you, good master Parson.

OTT. I would heare the Canon-law speake first.

CVT. It must giue place to positiue Diuinitie, sir.

v. iii. 10 After 'him.' *Exit Dauphine.* | *Enter Otter disguised as a divine, and Cutbeard as a canon lawyer.* G 19 loose] lose *F2* After 22 *Re-enter Dauphine with Morose.* G 27 god] God Q, F2 35 hether] hither *Q, F2*

MOR. Nay, good gentlemen, doe not throw me into circumstances. Let your comforts arriue quickly at me, those that are. Be swift in affoording me my peace, if so I shall hope any. I loue not your disputations, or your court-tumults. And that it be not strange to you, I will tell you. My father, in my education, was wont to aduise mee, that I should alwayes collect, and contayne my mind, not suffring it to flow loosely; that I should looke to what things were necessary to the carriage of my life, and what not: embracing the one, and eschewing the other. In short, that I should endeare my selfe to rest, and auoid turmoile: which now is growne to be another nature to me. So that I come not to your publike pleadings, or your places of noise; not that I neglect those things, that make for the dignitie of the common-wealth: but for the meere auoiding of clamors, & impertinencies of Orators, that know not how to be silent. And for the cause of noise, am I now a sutor to you. You doe not know in what a miserie I haue beene exercis'd this day, what a torrent of euill! My very house turnes round with the tumult! I dwell in a wind-mill! The perpetuall motion is here, and not at *Eltham*.

TRV. Well, good master Doctor, will you breake the ice? master Parson will wade after.

CVT. Sir, though vnworthy, and the weaker, I will presume.

OTT. 'Tis no presumption, *domine* Doctor.

MOR. Yet againe!

CVT. Your question is, for how many causes a man may haue *diuortium legitimum*, a lawfull diuorce. First, you must vnderstand the nature of the word diuorce, *à diuertendo*——

MOR. No excursions vpon words, good Doctor, to the question briefly.

CVT. I answere then, the Canon-law affords diuorce

v. iii. 45 affoording] affording *F2* 52 one,] *F2*: one *Q*, *F1* 58 clamors] clamours *Q*, *F2* impertinences *corr.* *F1*, *Q*: impertinencies *F2*: pertinences *F1 originally* 59 be *corr.* *F1*, *F2*: bee *F1 originally*, *Q* 60 sutor] suitor *F2* 63 motion] about motion *Q* 72 *diuertendo*] *divertendendo* F2, F3

but in few cases, and the principall is in the common case, the adulterous case. But there are *duodecim impedimenta*, twelue impediments (as we call 'hem) all which doe not *dirimere contractum*, but *irritum reddere matrimonium*, as wee say in the Canon-law, *not take away the bond, but cause a nullitie therein.*

MOR. I vnderstood you, before: good sir, auoid your impertinencie of translation.

OTT. He cannot open this too much, sir, by your fauour.

MOR. Yet more!

TRV. O, you must giue the learned men leaue, sir. To your impediments, master Doctor.

CVT. The first is *impedimentum erroris.*

OTT. Of which there are seuerall *species.*

CVT. I, as *error personæ.*

OTT. If you contract your selfe to one person, thinking her another.

CVT. Then, *error fortunæ.*

OTT. If shee be a beggar, and you thought her rich.

CVT. Then, *error qualitatis.*

OTT. If shee proue stubborne, or head-strong, that you thought obedient.

MOR. How? is that, sir, a lawfull impediment? One at once, I pray you gentlemen.

OTT. I, *ante copulam*, but not *post copulam*, sir.

CVT. Mr. Parson saies right. *Nec post nuptiarum benedictionem.* It doth indeed but *irrita reddere sponsalia*, annull the contract: after marriage it is of no obstancy.

TRV. Alas, sir, what a hope are we fall'n from, by this time!

CVT. The next is *conditio:* if you thought her free borne, and shee proue a bond-woman, there is impediment of estate and condition.

OTT. I, but Mr. Doctor, those seruitudes are *sublatæ*, now, among vs christians.

CVT. By your fauour, master Parson——

OTT. You shall giue me leaue, master Doctor.

MOR. Nay, gentlemen, quarrell not in that question ; it concernes not my case : passe to the third.

CVT. Well then, the third is *votum.* If either partie haue made a vow of chastitie. But that practice, as master Parson said of the other, is taken away among vs, thanks be to discipline. The fourth is *cognatio :* if the persons be of kinne, within the degrees.

OTT. I : doe you know, what the degrees are, sir ?

MOR. No, nor I care not, sir : they offer me no comfort in the question, I am sure.

CVT. But, there is a branch of this impediment may, which is *cognatio spiritualis.* If you were her god-father, sir, then the marriage is incestuous.

OTT. That *comment* is absurd, and superstitious, master Doctor. I cannot endure it. Are we not all brothers and sisters, and as much a kinne in that, as god-fathers, and god-daughters ?

MOR. O me ! to end the controuersie, I neuer was a god-father, I neuer was a god-father in my life, sir. Passe to the next.

CVT. The fift is *crimen adulterij :* the knowne case. The sixt, *cultus disparitas,* difference of religion : haue you euer examin'd her what religion shee is of ?

MOR. No, I would rather shee were of none, then bee put to the trouble of it !

OTT. You may haue it done for you, sir.

MOR. By no meanes, good sir, on, to the rest : shall you euer come to an end, thinke you ?

TRV. Yes, hee has done halfe, sir. (On, to the rest) be patient, and expect, sir.

CVT. The seuenth is, *vis :* if it were vpon compulsion, or force.

MOR. O no, it was too voluntarie, mine : too voluntarie.

CVT. The eight is, *ordo :* if euer shee haue taken holy orders.

OTT. That's superstitious, too.

v. iii. 131 in] id *Q* 133 fift] fifth *F2* 134 sixt] sixth *F2*
139 sir,] sir ; *F2* 146 eight] eighth *Q, F2*

MOR. No matter, master Parson: would shee would go into a nunnerie yet.

CVT. The ninth is, *ligamen:* if you were bound, sir, to any other before.

MOR. I thrust my selfe too soone into these fetters.

CVT. The tenth is, *publica honestas:* which is *inchoata quædam affinitas.*

OTT. I, or *affinitas orta ex sponsalibus:* and is but *leue impedimentum.*

MOR. I feele no aire of comfort blowing to me, in all this.

CVT. The eleuenth is, *affinitas ex fornicatione.*

OTT. Which is no lesse *vera affinitas,* then the other, master Doctor.

CVT. True, *quæ oritur ex legitimo matrimonio.*

OTT. You say right, venerable Doctor. And, *nascitur ex eo, quod per coniugium duæ personæ efficiuntur vna caro*——

MOR. Hey-day, now they beginne.

CVT. I conceiue you, master Parson. *Ita per fornicationem æque est verus pater, qui sic generat*——

OTT. *Et vere filius qui sic generatur*——

MOR. What's all this to me?

CLE. Now it growes warme.

CVT. The twelfth, and last is, *si forte coire nequibis.*

OTT. I, that is *impedimentum grauissimum.* It doth vtterly annull, and annihilate, that. If you haue *manifestam frigiditatem,* you are well, sir.

TRV. Why, there is comfort come at length, sir. Confesse your self but a man vnable, and shee will sue to be diuorc'd first.

OTT. I, or if there be *morbus perpetuus, & insanabilis,* as *Paralysis, Elephantiasis,* or so——

DAV. O, but *frigiditas* is the fairer way, gentlemen.

OTT. You say troth, sir, and as it is in the *canon,* master Doctor.

CVT. I conceiue you, sir.

v. iii. 149 nunnerie] nunnery, *F2*   164 MOR.] *True.* G   178 *Paralysis*] *Paralisis* F1

Cle. Before he speakes.

Ott. That *a boy, or child, vnder yeeres, is not fit for marriage, because he cannot reddere debitum.* So your *omnipotentes*——

Trv. Your *impotentes*, you whorson Lobster.

Ott. Your *impotentes*, I should say, are *minime apti ad contrahenda matrimonium.*

Trv. *Matrimonium?* Wee shall haue most vn-matrimoniall *latin*, with you: *matrimonia*, and be hang'd.

Dav. You put 'hem out, man.

Cvt. But then there will arise a doubt, master Parson, in our case, *post matrimonium:* that *frigiditate prœditus*, (doe you conceiue me, sir?)

Ott. Very well, sir.

Cvt. Who cannot *vti vxore pro vxore*, may *habere eam pro sorore.*

Ott. Absurd, absurd, absurd, and merely *apostaticall.*

Cvt. You shall pardon me, master Parson, I can proue it.

Ott. You can proue a Will, master Doctor, you can proue nothing else. Do's not the verse of your owne *canon* say, *Hæc socianda vetant conubia, facta retractant*——

Cvt. I grant you, but how doe they *retractare*, master Parson?

Mor. (O, this was it, I fear'd.)

Ott. *In æternum*, sir.

Cvt. That's false in diuinitie, by your fauour.

Ott. 'Tis false in humanitie, to say so. Is hee not *prorsus invtilis ad thorum?* Can he *præstare fidem datam?* I would faine know.

Cvt. Yes: how if he doe *conualere?*

Ott. He cannot *conualere*, it is impossible.

Trv. Nay, good sir, attend the learned men, they'll thinke you neglect 'hem else.

Cvt. Or, if he doe *simulare* himselfe *frigidum, odio vxoris*, or so?

v. iii. 187 *Aside to Otter.* add G 203 say, *Q*: say. *Ff* *conubia*] *connubia* Q, F2 207 *In*] In *Q, Ff* 213 cannot *corr. F1, Q, F2*: can not *F1 originally*

OTT. I say, he is *adulter manifestus*, then.

DAVP. (They dispute it very learnedly, yfaith.)

OTT. And *prostitutor vxoris*, and this is positiue.

MOR. Good sir, let me escape.

TRV. You will not doe me that wrong, sir?

OTT. And therefore, if he bee *manifeste frigidus*, sir——

CVT. I, if he be *manifeste frigidus*, I grant you——

OTT. Why, that was my conclusion.

CVT. And mine too.

TRV. Nay, heare the conclusion, sir.

OTT. Then, *frigiditatis causa*——

CVT. Yes, *causa frigiditatis*——

MOR. O, mine eares!

OTT. Shee may haue *libellum diuortij*, against you.

CVT. I, *diuortij libellum* shee will sure haue.

MOR. Good *eccho's*, forbeare.

OTT. If you confesse it.

CVT. Which I would doe, sir——

MOR. I will doe any thing——

OTT. And cleere my selfe in *foro conscientiæ*——

CVT. Because you want indeed——

MOR. Yet more?

OTT. *Exercendi potestate.*

Act v. *Scene* IIII.

EPICOENE, MOROSE, HAVGHTY, CENTAVRE, MAVIS, M^rs^. OTTER, DAW, TRVE-WIT, DAVPHINE, CLERIMONT, LA-FOOLE, OTTER, CVTBERD.

I Will not endure it any longer. Ladies, I beseech you helpe me. This is such a wrong, as neuer was offer'd to poore bride before. Vpon her marriage day, to haue her husband conspire against her, and a couple of mercinarie

v. iii. 234 it.] it—— *F2* v. iv. *Epicœne rushes in, followed by Haughty, Centaure, Mavis, Mistress Otter, Daw, and La-Foole.* G, continuing the scene

companions, to be brought in for formes sake, to perswade a separation! If you had bloud, or vertue in you, gentlemen, you would not suffer such eare-wigs about a husband, or scorpions, to creep between man and wife——

Mor. O, the varietie and changes of my torment!

Hav. Let 'hem be cudgell'd out of dores, by our groomes.

Cen. I'll lend you my foot-man.

Mav. Wee'll haue our men blanket 'hem i' the hall.

Mrs. Ot. As there was one, at our house, madame, for peeping in at the dore.

Daw. Content, yfaith.

Trv. Stay, ladies, and gentlemen, you'll heare, before you proceed?

Mav. I'lld ha' the bride-groome blanketted, too.

Cen. Beginne with him first.

Hav. Yes, by my troth.

Mor. O, mankind generation!

Davp. Ladies, for my sake forbeare.

Hav. Yes, for sir Davphines sake.

Cen. He shall command vs.

La-f. He is as fine a gentleman of his inches, madame, as any is about the towne, and weares as good colours when he list.

Trv. Be brief, sir, and confesse your infirmitie, shee'll be a-fire to be quit of you, if shee but heare that nam'd once, you shall not entreat her to stay. Shee'll flie you, like one that had the marks vpon him.

Mor. Ladies, I must craue all your pardons——

Trv. Silence, ladies.

Mor. For a wrong I haue done to your whole sexe, in marrying this faire, and vertuous gentlewoman——

Cle. Heare him, good ladies.

Mor. Being guiltie of an infirmitie, which before I confer'd with these learned men, I thought I might haue conceal'd——

v. iv. 28 list] lists *F2*

TRV. But now being better inform'd in his conscience by them, hee is to declare it, & giue satisfaction, by asking your publique forgiuenesse.

MOR. I am no man, ladies.

ALL. How!

MOR. Vtterly vn-abled in nature, by reason of *frigidity*, to performe the duties, or any the least office of a husband.

MAV. Now, out vpon him, prodigious creature!

CEN. Bride-groome vncarnate.

HAV. And would you offer it, to a young gentlewoman?

Mrs. OT. A lady of her longings?

EPI. Tut, a deuice, a deuice, this, it smells rankly, ladies. A mere comment of his owne.

TRV. Why, if you suspect that, ladies, you may haue him search'd.

DAW. As the custome is, by a iurie of physitians.

LA-F. Yes faith, 'twill be braue.

MOR. O me, must I vnder-goe that!

Mrs. OT. No, let women search him, madame: we can doe it our selues.

MOR. Out on me, worse!

EPI. No, ladies, you shall not need, I'll take him with all his faults.

MOR. Worst of all!

CLE. Why, then 'tis no diuorce, Doctor, if shee consent not?

CVT. No, if the man be *frigidus*, it is *de parte vxoris*, that wee grant *libellum diuortij*, in the law.

OTT. I, it is the same in *theologie*.

MOR. Worse, worse then worst!

TRV. Nay, sir, bee not vtterly dis-heartned, wee haue yet a small relique of hope left, as neere as our comfort is blowne out. CLERIMONT, produce your brace of Knights. What was that, master Parson, you told me *in errore qualitatis*, e'ne now? DAVPHINE, whisper the bride, that shee carry it as if shee were guiltie, and asham'd.

v. iv. 65 why,] why; *F2*, *F3*   72 relique] relike *Q*

OTT. Mary sir, *in errore qualitatis* (which master Doctor did forbeare to vrge) if shee bee found *corrupta*, that is, vitiated or broken vp, that was *pro virgine desponsa*, espous'd for a maid——

MOR. What then, sir?

OTT. It doth *dirimere contractum*, and *irritum reddere* too.

TRV. If this be true, we are happy againe, sir, once more. Here are an honorable brace of Knights, that shall affirme so much.

DAW. Pardon vs, good master CLERIMONT.

LA-F. You shall excuse vs, master CLERIMONT.

CLE. Nay, you must make it good now, Knights, there is no remedie, I'll eate no words for you, nor no men: you know you spoke it to me?

DAW. Is this gentleman-like, sir?

TRV. IACKDAW, hee's worse then sir AMOROVS: fiercer a great deale. Sir AMOROVS, beware, there be ten DAWES in this CLERIMONT.

LA-F. I'll confesse it, sir.

DAW. Will you, sir AMOROVS? will you wound reputation?

LA-F. I am resolu'd.

TRV. So should you be too, IACKDAW: what should keepe you off? shee is but a woman, and in disgrace. Hee'll be glad on't.

DAW. Will he? I thought he would ha' beene angrie.

CLE. You will dispatch, Knights, it must be done, yfaith.

TRV. Why, an' it must it shall, sir, they say. They'll ne're goe backe. Doe not tempt his patience.

DAW. It is true indeed, sir.

LA-F. Yes, I assure you, sir.

MOR. What is true gentlemen? what doe you assure me?

v. iv. 85 honorable] honourable *Q, F2* 90 remedie,] remedie; *F2* 92 -like] -like-like *Q* 100 DAW: what] DAW. What *F2* 106 must] must, *F2*

DAW. That we haue knowne your bride, sir——

LA-F. In good fashion. Shee was our mistris, or so——

CLE. Nay, you must be plaine, Knights, as you were to me.

OTT. I, the question is, if you haue *carnaliter*, or no.

LA-F. *Carnaliter?* what else, sir?

OTT. It is inough: a plaine *nullitie*.

EPI. I am vn-done, I am vn-done!

MOR. O, let me worship and adore you, gentlemen!

EPI. I am vn-done!

MOR. Yes, to my hand, I thanke these Knights: master Parson, let me thanke you otherwise.

CEN. And, ha' they confess'd?

MAV. Now out vpon 'hem, informers!

TRV. You see, what creatures you may bestow your fauours on, madames.

HAV. I would except against 'hem as beaten Knights, wench, and not good witnesses in law.

Mrs. OT. Poore gentlewoman, how shee takes it!

HAV. Be comforted, MOROSE, I loue you the better for't.

CEN. So doe I, I protest.

CVT. But gentlemen, you haue not knowne her, since *matrimonium?*

DAW. Not to day, master Doctor.

LA-F. No, sir, not to day.

CVT. Why, then I say, for any act before, the *matrimonium* is good and perfect: vnlesse, the worshipfull Bride-groome did precisely, before witnesse demand, if shee were *virgo ante nuptias*.

EPI. No, that he did not, I assure you, master Doctor.

CVT. If he cannot proue that, it is *ratum coniugium*, notwithstanding the premises. And they doe no way *impedire*. And this is my sentence, this I pronounce.

OTT. I am of master Doctors resolution too, sir: if you made not that demand, *ante nuptias*.

V. iv. 121 *Weeps.* add G 123 *Gives him money.* add G

MOR. O my heart! wilt thou breake? wilt thou breake? this is worst of all worst worsts! that hell could haue deuis'd! Marry a whore! and so much noise!

DAVP. Come, I see now plaine confederacie in this Doctor, and this Parson, to abuse a gentleman. You studie his affliction. I pray' bee gone companions. And gentlemen, I begin to suspect you for hauing parts with 'hem. Sir, will it please you heare me?

MOR. O, doe not talke to me, take not from mee the pleasure of dying in silence, nephew.

DAVP. Sir, I must speake to you. I haue beene long your poore despis'd kins-man, and many a hard thought has strength'ned you against me: but now it shall appeare if either I loue you or your peace, and preferre them to all the world beside. I will not bee long or grieuous to you, sir. If I free you of this vnhappy match absolutely, and instantly after all this trouble, and almost in your despaire, now——

MOR. (It cannot be.)

DAVP. Sir, that you bee neuer troubled with a murmure of it more, what shall I hope for, or deserue of you?

MOR. O, what thou wilt, nephew! thou shalt deserue mee, and haue mee.

DAVP. Shall I haue your fauour perfect to me, and loue hereafter?

MOR. That, and any thing beside. Make thine owne conditions. My whole estate is thine. Manage it, I will become thy Ward.

DAVP. Nay, sir, I will not be so vn-reasonable.

EPI. Will sir DAVPHINE be mine enemie too?

DAVP. You know, I haue beene long a suter to you, vncle, that out of your estate, which is fifteen hundred a yeere, you would allow me but fiue hundred during life, and assure the rest vpon me after: to which I haue often, by my selfe and friends tendred you a writing to signe, which

v. iv. 153 gone] gone, *F2* 177 DAVPHINE *corr. F1*: DAVPHINE, *F1 originally* 178 long a] a long *Q*

you would neuer consent, or incline too. If you please but to effect it now——

MOR. Thou shalt haue it, nephew. I will doe it, and more.

DAVP. If I quit you not presently, and for-euer of this cumber, you shall haue power instantly, afore all these, to reuoke your act, and I will become, whose slaue you will giue me to, for-euer.

MOR. Where is the writing? I will seale to it, that, or to a blanke, and write thine owne conditions.

EPI. O me, most vnfortunate wretched gentlewoman!

HAV. Will sir DAVPHINE doe this?

EPI. Good sir, haue some compassion on me.

MOR. O, my nephew knowes you belike: away *crocodile.*

CEN. He do's it not sure, without good ground.

DAVP. Here, sir.

MOR. Come, nephew: giue me the pen. I will subscribe to any thing, and seale to what thou wilt, for my deliuerance. Thou art my restorer. Here, I deliuer it thee as my deed. If there bee a word in it lacking, or writ with false orthographie, I protest before——I will not take the aduantage.

DAVP. Then here is your release, sir; you haue married a boy: a gentlemans son, that I haue brought vp this halfe yeere, at my great charges, and for this composition, which I haue now made with you. What say you, master Doctor? this is *iustum impedimentum*, I hope, *error personæ?*

He takes of Epicœnes perruke.

OTT. Yes sir, *in primo gradu.*

CVT. *In primo gradu.*

DAVP. I thanke you, good Doctor CVTBERD, and Parson OTTER. You are beholden to 'hem, sir, that haue taken this paines for you: and my friend, master TRVEWIT, who enabled 'hem for the businesse. Now you may goe in and rest, be as priuate as you will, sir. I'll not

He pulls of their beardes, and disguise.

v. iv. 183 too] to *F2* 186 presently, *F2*: presently? *F1, Q* 195 nephew *corr. F1, F2*: Nephew *Q*: nephew, *F1 originally* 197 *Gives him the parchments.* add G 202 before——] before [heaven] G: *the missing word is* 'God' 203 *Returns the writings.* G 215 After 'sir.' [*Exit Morose.*] G

trouble you, till you trouble me with your funerall, which I care not how soone it come. CVTBERD, I'll make your lease good. Thanke mee not, but with your leg, CVTBERD. And TOM OTTER, your Princesse shall be reconcil'd to you. How now, gentlemen! doe you looke at me?

CLE. A boy.

DAVP. Yes, mistris EPICOENE.

TRV. Well, DAVPHINE, you haue lurch'd your friends of the better halfe of the garland, by concealing this part of the plot! but much good doe it thee, thou deseru'st it, lad. And CLERIMONT, for thy vnexpected bringing in these two to confession, weare my part of it freely. Nay, sir DAW, and sir LA-FOOLE, you see the gentlewoman that has done you the fauours! we are all thankefull to you, and so should the woman-kind here, specially for lying on her, though not with her! You meant so, I am sure? But, that we haue stuck it vpon you to day, in your own imagin'd persons, and so lately; this *Amazon*, the champion of the sexe, should beate you now thriftily, for the common slanders, which ladies receiue from such cuckowes, as you are. You are they, that when no merit or fortune can make you hope to enioy their bodies, will yet lie with their reputations, and make their fame suffer. Away you common moths of these, and all ladies honors. Goe, trauaile to make legs and faces, and come home with some new matter to be laught at: you deserue to liue in an aire as corrupted, as that wherewith you feed rumor. Madames, you are mute, vpon this new *metamorphosis!* but here stands shee, that has vindicated your fames. Take heed of such *insectæ* hereafter. And let it not trouble you that you haue discouer'd any mysteries to this yong gentleman. He is (a'most) of yeeres, & will make a good visitant within this twelue-month. In the meane time, wee'll all

v. iv. 228 in *om. F2, F3* 237 or] of *F2, F3* 240 trauaile] travel *F3* 243 After 'rumor.' [*Exeunt Daw and La-Foole.*] G 246 you] you, *F2*

vndertake for his secrecie, that can speake so well of his silence. Spectators, if you like this *comœdie*, rise cheerefully, and now MOROSE is gone in, clap your hands. It may be, that noyse will cure him, at least please him.

THE END.

v. iv. 251 After 'silence.' [*Coming forward.*] G 253 *Exeunt.* add G

This Comoedie was first
acted, in the yeere
1609.

By the Children of her Maiesties
REVELLS.

The principall Comœdians were,

NAT. FIELD.	WILL. BARKSTED.
GIL. CARIE.	WILL. PEN.
HVG. ATTAWEL.	RIC. ALLIN.
IOH. SMITH.	IOH. BLANEY.

With the allowance of the Master of REVELLS.

This page was added in F1. In F2 the statements about the date, the company, and the Master of the Revels were omitted, and the list of ' The principall Comœdians ' *was transferred to the back of the half-title where it followed* ' The persons of the Play ' *and* ' The Scene '.

THE ALCHEMIST

THE TEXT

The Alchemist was entered on the Stationers' Register by Walter Burre on 3 October 1610. He published it in quarto in 1612. The entry is as follows:

3° Octobris

Walter Burre. Entred for his copy vnder thandes of Sir George Bucke and Th'wardens a Comœdy called, The Alchymist made by Ben: Johnson vj[d]

Arber, *Transcript*, III. 445.

The printer was Thomas Snodham, who did his work badly. John Stepneth was a partner with Burre in the publication; both of them published at the sign of The Crane in Paul's Churchyard. In 1612 Stepneth also entered Jonson's *Epigrams* on the Register.[1]

The collation of the Quarto, A to M, is in detail: A 1 recto, title-page, with the verso blank; A 2, dedication to Lady Mary Wroth; A 3 recto, 'To the Reader', continued on the verso, which also has verses by George Lucy; A 4 recto, 'The Persons of the Comœdie', and 'The Argument'; A 4 verso, 'The Prologue'; B to M, the text of the play. The running title is '*The ALCHEMIST*'. The number of lines on the page varies from thirty-six to thirty-seven, the later pages being fuller to enable the printer to end on sheet M. Owing to the extra line D 3, I 3, and K 3 are not signatured. The catchword on C 3 recto (I. iii. 76–7) is '*Cinoper*;', the text on the verso is '*Cinoper*.' On K 2 (IV. v. 25–32), where the conclusion of Dol's ravings and the dialogue of Mammon and Face are printed in parallel columns, to show that they are all speaking together, the text is in small type spread across the page; of all the copies examined only Mr. Wise's copy is uncropped at this point.

Six copies have been collated for the text of the present edition:

(1) The British Museum copy (marked A in the following list);

[1] On 15 May (Arber, iii. 485).

(2) The Malone copy in Bodley, in which three leaves, A 2 to A 4, are missing (B);

(3) The two Dyce copies at South Kensington, of which one is perfect (C 1), and the other (C 2) lacks E 2 and E 3 and has M 3 supplied in manuscript;

(4) The copy in the Library of Corpus Christi College, Oxford, given to the College with seven other plays by Bryan Twyne in 1644 (D);

(5) Mr. T. J. Wise's copy (E).

The following corrections have been found in the six copies:

A 2ᵛ	Dedication, l. 9	thatremembers *A, E*	that remembers *C 1 & 2, D*
A 3ʳ	To the Reader,		
	l. 6	*Age*, A, E	*Age*) C 1 & 2, D
	l. 7	*Igges, and Daunces*, A, E	*Daunces, and Antickes*, C 1 & 2, D
	l. 15	*Multitude* A, E	*Many* C 1 & 2, D
B 1ʳ	I. i. 18	Will *A*	Will *B, C 1 & 2, D, E*
B 1ᵛ	52	-hahch *C 1 & 2*	-hatch *A, B, D, E*
B 2	68	Sublim'd . . . exalted . . . fix'd *C 1 & 2*	*Sublim'd . . . exalted . . . fix'd* A, B, D, E
	69	third region, the high state of grace *C 1 & 2*	*third region*, the *high state of grace* A, B, D, E
	70	spirit . . . quintessence *C 1 & 2*	*spirit . . . quintessence* A, B, D, E
	71	Philosophers worke *C 1 & 2*	*Philosophers worke* A, B, D, E
	77	great Art *C 1 & 2*	*great Art* A, B, D, E
	79	proiection *C 1 & 2*	*proiection* A, B, D, E
	83	*Equi clibanum* C 1 & 2	*Equi Clibanum* A, B, D, E
B 3ᵛ	I. ii. 1, 2	. . . I thinke, . . . In truth, (Doctor } *C 1 & 2*	(Doctor. . . . I think, . . . In truth, } *A, B, D, E*
B 4ʳ	15	you *C 1 & 2*	you. *A, B, D, E*
	27	*Turque* C 1 & 2	*Turke* A, B, D, E
	28	Doe *C 1 & 2*	Doe, *A, B, D, E*
	39	Sr, *C 1 & 2*	Sir *A, B, D, E*
C 4ᵛ	II. i. 4	*Ophyr* C 1	*Ophir* A, B, C 2, D, E
	7	word. *C 1*	word, *A, B, C 2, D, E*
	9	die *C 1*	Die *A, B, C 2, D, E*
	10	card *C 1*	Card *A, B, C 2, D, E*

D 1^{v}	76	water, *A*	water ? *B, C 1 & 2, D, E*
	88	wood *A*	wood, *B, C 1 & 2, D, E*
	92	*Pythagora's* A	*Pythagora's* B, C 1 & 2, D, E
D 2^{r}	II. ii. 32	be, *A*	be *B, C 1 & 2, D, E*
D 4^{r}	II. iii. 52	Sir *A*	Sir, *B, C 1 & 2, D, E*
E 2^{r}	184	*Elizir* B	*Elixir* A, C 1, D, E
E 3^{r}	266	'Hart *A, C 1*	'Hart, *B, D, E*
E 4^{v}	II. iv. 11	sanguine *C 1*	*sanguine* A, *Sanguine* B, C 2, D, E
	II. v. 9	*dulcefie*, A, C 1	*dulcefie ?* B, C 2, D, E
F 2^{v}	II. vi. 28	impart *E*	impart— *A, B, C 1 & 2, D*
	32	yet, *E*	yet ; *A, B, C 1 & 2, D*
	35	deale. *E*	deale, *A, B, C 1 & 2, D*
	37	here *E*	here, *A, B, C 1 & 2, D*
F 3^{r}	63	Quarrells *E*	Quarrells, *A, B, C 1 & 2, D*
	70	And *E*	And, *A, B, C 1 & 2, D*
	74	Say *A, C 2, E*	Stay *B, C 1, D*
	85	he . . . fayles *E*	he, . . . fayles, *A, B, C 1 & 2, D*
F 3^{v}	III. i. 29	so. *A, C 2, E*	so ; *B, C 1, D*
F4^{v}	III. ii. 36	Friend, *E*	Friend. *A, B, C 1 & 2, D*
H 3^{v}	IV. i. 49	Want *A*	want *B, C 1 & 2, D, E*
H 4^{r}	70	court, *A, B, C 1*	court *C 2, D, E*
	71	Art . . . words *A*	Art, . . . words, *B, C 1 & 2, D, E*
L 3^{r}	V. ii. 41	MEI. 1. *A*	NEI. 1. *B, C 1 & 2, D, E*
	42	deceiu'd *A*	deceiu'd, *B, C 1 & 2, D, E*
		keyes, *A*	keyes : *B, C 1 & 2, D, E*
L 3^{v}	V. iii. 23	Officers ! *A*	Officers, *B, C 1 & 2, D, E*
M 2^{v}	V. v. 7	Braine ? *A, C 2*	Braine. *B, C 1, D, E*
M 3^{r}	46	buthe *A*	but he *B, C 1, D, E*
M 3^{v}	72	they, are *E*	they 'are *A, B, C 1, D*

Lines in which a stop, faint in some copies and missing in others, has dropped out in the printing are not recorded as variants.

In the minor points of spelling and punctuation the Quarto is lax. So also is the Folio. Jonson's metrical apostrophe, as usual, gave the printers trouble. We have restored it on the authority of the Quarto in 'who'are' (II. ii. 67), 'They'are' (III. ii. 122), 'to'you' (IV. iii. 89). The Quarto sometimes inserts the stop wrongly and the Folio reproduces it ;[1] the Folio prints such an absurdity

[1] I. ii. 5, iii. 7, 43 ; II. ii. 95, 105, iii. 43 ; IV. vii. 64.

as ' 'nd ' in I. iii. 85. But there are clear signs in the Folio text of Jonson's care for punctuation. When Mammon is told that his stuff will shortly be changed to gold and silver, he replies, ' Silver, I care not for ' :[1] the comma was added in the Folio. And better still, when Surly is cross-questioning Mammon about the sham lord, Dol's supposed brother whom Mammon professes to know, although, when hard-pressed, he cannot recall his name, Surly asks ' What call you her, brother ? ' The modern punctuation would be ' her—brother ',[2] and the actor could point the innuendo with a mocking emphasis. The comma is retained in the 1640 Folio, and two previous editors of the play note it as a misprint of the Folios.[2]

Generally the punctuation of both texts is careless, and we have had to make many small corrections to bring it up to Jonson's standard in the earlier plays.[3]

The Quarto preserves more of Jonson's classicized spelling of Latin derivatives, such as ' æquall ' (I. i. 145), ' præcise ' (ibid. 164), ' præuaricate ' (II. iii. 19), and ' ædified ' (III. i. 45), though its practice is not uniform.[4] But it gives three misspellings which are impossible for Jonson—' *Metaposcopie* ' (I. iii. 44), ' *solæcisme* ' (IV. i. 101), and *fæces* (IV. v. 31). The Folio copies these and adds ' labaratory ' (IV. i. 171), which the Quarto spells correctly. A similar error is ' *sapor stipstick* ' in both texts in II. v. 10 ; the 1640 Folio corrected to ' *styptick* '. Other errors of the Quarto reproduced in 1616 are—' No ' for ' Now ' (II. iii. 18), ' I haue trick ' for ' a trick ' (III. ii. 142), ' had ' for ' he had ' (V. v. 32), the omission of Face's name before his speeches in III. iii. 62 and IV. iv. 3, and the attribution of Dapper's speech to Face in V. iv. 60.

Textual changes in the Folio are slight. Most of them

[1] IV. i. 4. [2] II. iii. 272.

[3] See the critical apparatus at the Prologue, l. 18 ; I. i. 11, 25, 112, ii. 5, 26, 45, iii. 7, 43, 85, iv. 1, 9 ; II. i. 12, ii. 62, 67, 105, iii. 36, 43, 215, 269, 282, v. 18, 55, 60, 79, 86, vi. 34, 41, 58 ; III. i. 29, ii. 46, 102, 122, iii. 42, 66, 72 ; IV. i. 11, 53, 63, ii. 28, iii. 64, 88, 89, v. 74, vii. 28–9, 47, 64, 65 ; V. i. 28, iii. 33, iv. 44, v. 63, 94, 105.

[4] Compare the examples noted in *Sejanus*, vol. iv, pp. 337–8.

are a toning down of phrases with a mildly Scriptural ring. 'Gods will!' is altered to 'Death on me!' in I. i. 148, and the attenuated 'Gad' to 'IOVE' in I. ii. 135; the language of the Puritans is retouched in several passages. 'They are the exercises of the spirit' disappears from Tribulation's speech at the beginning of the third act, and his 'Seed of Vipers, Sonnes of *Belial*' becomes 'seed of sulphure, sonnes of fire' (V. iii. 44). Similarly with Ananias: his 'vessels Of shame, and of dishonour' is changed to 'vessells Of pride, lust, and the cart' (V. v. 23–4), and even Nimrod, who was secular enough to be let alone, becomes 'Idol' (ibid., 99). These faint echoes of the Bible might, in Jonson's day, be censured as profane. Fortunately Ananias was permitted to testify at the close:

I am strong,
And will stand vp, well girt, against an host
That threaten GAD in exile.

No loss of filthy lucre could daunt the fortitude or dam the piety of this 'silenced saint'. And fortunately Jonson did not sacrifice Subtle's righteous indignation against 'the varlet that cossend the *Apostles*' (II. v. 72–3), though this was sufficiently explicit to be dangerous.

The oddest change is in Face's account of Dapper, the lawyer's clerk. In the Quarto he

Will take his oth, o' the *Greeke Testament*,
If need be, in his pocket. (I. ii. 56–7.)

Dapper might quite well carry a pocket Testament about with him to administer the oath to clients. But the Folio substitutes 'the *greeke* XENOPHON'. Some topical allusion may have given point to the joke, but it reads lamely now, even with Face's further assurance that Dapper 'can court His mistris, out of OVID'. Dapper shows no signs of acquaintance with the *Ars Amatoria*, and he certainly did not get the suggestion for wearing a leaden heart when his mistress forsook him[1] out of the *Remedia Amoris*.

[1] III. v. 45.

Other changes are to emphasize Mammon's refusal to employ for bawds any but fathers and mothers by inserting

They will doe it best.
Best of all others.[1]—

and to transpose two lines in Act II, scene iii, lines 221–4, which read in the Quarto:

FAC.[2] Stay man, what is she? FAC. A Lords Sister, Sir.
MAM. How! Pray thee stay? FAC. She's mad Sir, & sent hether——
(He'll be mad too. MAM. I warrant thee.) Why sent hether?
FAC. Sir, to be cur'd.

The Folio arrangement is—

MAM. How! 'Pray thee stay? FAC. She's mad, sir, and sent hether——
MAM. Stay, man, what is shee? FAC. A lords sister, sir,
(Hee'll be mad too. MAM. I warrant thee.) Why sent hether?
FAC. Sir, to be cur'd.

We have followed Gifford in accepting the order of the Quarto; it is, as he says, much more natural. He thought the change an oversight; it was probably caused by the *ὁμοιοτέλευτον* of 'sent hether' in two succeeding lines of the original text and by correcting 'FAC.' to 'MAM.'

The Folio of 1640 reprints the 1616 text, with hardly any alteration. Two lines

Faith, I haue a confidence in his good nature (I. ii. 115)
Were at the last thred, you see; and downe had gone (III. ii. 2)

are smoother metrically by the omission of 'a' in the first line and 'the' in the second. This Folio makes a few obvious corrections, but otherwise its tendency is to modernize the spelling and punctuation.

A facsimile of the Quarto text was published in the Noel Douglas Replicas in 1927 from the British Museum copy.

[1] II. ii. 58–9. [2] A blunder for MAM.

The Folio text has also been reprinted. Dr. C. M. Hathaway edited it for the Yale Studies in English in 1903, no. XVII. He printed from Professor W. L. Phelps's copy, which he collated with the Hoe copy of the Quarto. In 1904 Professor Felix E. Schelling edited it for Heath's *Belles Lettres* series, in a very accurate text; in 1913 Dr. G. A. Smithson edited it in the second volume of Professor Gayley's *Representative English Comedies*. The last two modernize capitals and italic type, use the modern 'j' and 'v', and insert modern stage directions.

THE ALCHEMIST.

VVritten
by
BEN. IONSON.

——*Neque, me vt miretur turba, laboro:*
Contentus paucis lectoribus.

LONDON,
Printed by *Thomas Snodham*, for *Walter Burre*,
and are to be sold by *Iohn Stepneth*, at the
West-end of Paules.
1612.

The title-page of the 1612 Quarto

THE
ALCHEMIST.

A Comœdie.

Acted in the yeere 1610. By the
Kings MAIESTIES
Seruants.

The Author B. I.

LVCRET.

——*petere inde coronam,*
Vnde priùs nulli velarint tempora Musæ.

LONDON,
Printed by WILLIAM STANSBY

M. DC. XVI.

The title-page of the 1616 Folio.

THE ALCHEMIST.

A Comedy.

Acted in the yeere 1610. By the Kings MAIESTIES SERVANTS.

With the allowance of the Master of REVELLS.

The Author *B. J.*

LUCRET.

——*petere inde coronam,*
Unde prius nulli velarint tempora Musæ.

LONDON,
Printed by RICHARD BISHOP.

M. DC. XL.

The title-page of the 1640 Folio.

TO THE LADY, MOST DESERVING HER NAME, AND BLOVD:

Mary,

La. Wroth.

Madame,

In the age of sacrifices, the truth of religion was not in the greatnesse, & fat of the offrings, but in the deuotion, and zeale of the sacrificers: Else, what could a handfull of gummes haue done in the sight of a hecatombe? *or, how might I appeare at this altar, except with those affections, that no lesse loue the light and witnesse, then they haue the conscience of your vertue? Jf what I offer beare an acceptable odour, & hold the first strength, it is your value of it, which remembers, where, when, and to whom it was kindled. Otherwise, as the times are, there comes rarely forth that thing, so full of authoritie, or example, but by assiduitie and custome, growes lesse, and looses. This, yet, safe in your iudgement (which is a* Sidneys) *is forbidden to speake more; lest*

Dedication *in roman in Q* Heading Deserving . . . Blovd :] most æquall with vertue, *and her Blood :* The Grace, and Glory of women. *Q* 5–8 *or, how . . . vertue ?*] Or how, yet, might a gratefull minde be furnish'd against the iniquitie of *Fortune ;* except, when she fail'd it, it had power to impart it selfe ? A way found out, to ouercome euen those, whom *Fortune* hath enabled to returne most, since they, yet leaue themselues more. In this assurance am I planted ; and stand with those affections at this Altar, as shall no more auoide the light and witnesse, then they doe the conscience of your vertue. *Q* 9 *value of it, which*] valew, that *Q* 10 *which*] that remembers *corr. Q* : thatremembers *Q originally* 11 *as the times are*] in these times *Q* 12 *authoritie,*] *authority* F2 13 *assiduitie*] daylinesse *Q* 14 *looses*] *loses* F2 *This, yet*] But this *Q* 15 *lest*] least *Q*

it talke, or looke like one of the ambitious Faces of the time: who, the more they paint, are the lesse themselues.

Your La:

true honorer,

BEN. IONSON.

To the Reader.

If thou beest more, thou art an Vnderstander, and then I trust thee. If thou art one that tak'st vp, and but a Pretender, beware at what hands thou receiu'st thy commoditie; for thou wert neuer more fair in the way to be cos'ned (then in this Age) in Poetry, *especially in Playes: wherein, now, the Concupiscence of Daunces, and Antickes so raigneth, as to runne away from Nature, and be afraid of her, is the onely point of art that tickles the* Spectators. *But how out of purpose, and place, doe I name Art? when the Professors are growne so obstinate contemners of it, and presumers on their owne Naturalls, as they are deriders of all diligence that way, and, by simple mocking at the termes, when they vnderstand not the things, thinke to get of wittily with their Ignorance. Nay, they are esteem'd the more learned, and sufficient for this, by the Many, through their excellent vice of iudgement. For they commend Writers, as they doe Fencers, or Wrastlers; who if they come in robustuously, and put for it with a great deale of violence, are receiu'd for the brauer fellowes: when many times their owne rudenesse is the cause of their disgrace, and a little touch of their Aduersary giues all that boisterous force the foyle. I deny not, but that these men, who alwaies seeke to doe more then inough, may some time happen on some thing that is good, and great; but very seldome: And when it comes it doth not recompence the rest of their ill. It sticks out perhaps, and is more eminent, because all is sordide, and vile about it: as lights are more discern'd in a thick darknesse, then a faint shadow. I speake not this, out of a hope to doe good on any man, against his will; for I know, if it were put to the question of theirs, and mine, the worse would finde more suffrages: because the most favour common errors. But I giue thee this warning, that there is a great difference between those, that (to gain the opinion of Copie) vtter all they can, how euer vnfitly; and those that vse election, and a meane. For it is onely the disease of the vnskilfull, to thinke rude things greater then polish'd: or scatter'd more numerous then compos'd.*

To the Reader *om. Ff*   5 *Age*) corr. Q: *Age,* Q originally
6 *Daunces, and Antickes* corr. Q: *Iigges, and Daunces* Q originally
15 *Many* corr. Q: *Multitude* Q originally

The Persons of the Play.

SVBTLE, *The Alchemist.*

FACE, *The house-keeper.*

DOL. COMMON, *Their Colleague.*

DAPPER, *A Clarke.*

DRVGGER, *A Tabacco-man.*

LOVE-WIT, *Master of the house.*

EPICVRE MAMMON, *A Knight.*

SVRLEY, *A Gamster.*

TRIBVLATION, *A Pastor of Amsterdã.*

ANANIAS, *A Deacon there.*

KASTRILL, *The angry Boy.*

DA. PLIANT, *His sister: A widdow.*

NEIGHBOVRS.

OFFICERS.

MVTES.

THE SCENE

LONDON.

The Persons of the Play. Play] Comœdie *Q* SURLEY] Pertinax Surly *G* DOL.] DOL: *Q* TRIBVLATION] Tribulation wholesome *G* *Amsterdã*] *Amstredam* Q DA.] DA: *Q* *THE SCENE* LONDON. *not in Q* *After* The Scene *F2 inserts the Actor-list given in F1 at the end of the Play*

The Alchemist.

THE ARGVMENT.

T *he sicknesse hot, a master quit, for feare,*
H *is house in towne : and left one seruant there.*
E *ase him corrupted, and gaue meanes to know*
A *cheater, and his punque ; who, now brought low,*
L *eauing their narrow practise, were become*
C *os'ners at large : and, onely wanting some*
H *ouse to set vp, with him they here contract,*
E *ach for a share, and all begin to act.*
M *uch company they draw, and much abuse,*
I *n casting figures, telling fortunes, newes,*
S *elling of flyes, flat bawdry, with the* stone :
T *ill it, and they, and all in* fume *are gone.*

THE ARGVMENT. *Q prints in roman* 4 *who,*] who *Q* 9 *abuse,*] abuse *Q*

PROLOGVE.

FORTVNE, that fauours fooles, these two short houres
  We wish away; both for your sakes, and ours,
Iudging Spectators: and desire in place,
  To th'Author iustice, to our selues but grace.
Our *Scene* is *London*, 'cause we would make knowne,
  No countries mirth is better then our owne.
No clime breeds better matter, for your whore,
  Bawd, squire, impostor, many persons more,
Whose manners, now call'd humors, feed the stage:
  And which haue still beene subiect, for the rage
Or spleene of *comick*-writers. Though this pen
  Did neuer aime to grieue, but better men;
How e'er the age, he liues in, doth endure
  The vices that shee breeds, aboue their cure.
But, when the wholsome remedies are sweet,
  And, in their working, gaine, and profit meet,
He hopes to find no spirit so much diseas'd,
  But will, with such faire correctiues, be pleas'd.
For here, he doth not feare, who can apply.
  If there be any, that will sit so nigh
Vnto the streame, to looke what it doth run,
  They shall find things, they'ld thinke, or wish, were done;
They are so naturall follies, but so showne,
  As euen the doers may see, and yet not owne.

PROLOGVE] THE PROLOGVE. *Q, which prints in italic* 5 knowne] *knowne.* Q 6 then] than *F2* 10 for] *to* Q 11 *comick*-writers] Comick *writers* Q 18 correctiues,] *Correctiues,* Q: correctiues *F1*: correctives *F2* 23 follies, but] *follies*: But *Q*

Act I. *Scene* I.

FACE, SVBTLE, DOL Common.

BEleeu't, I will. SVB. Thy worst. I fart at thee.
DOL. Ha' you your wits? Why gentlemen! for loue——
FAC. Sirrah, I'll strip you—— SVB. What to doe? lick figs
Out at my—— FAC. Rogue, rogue, out of all your sleights.
DOL. Nay, looke yee! Soueraigne, Generall, are you mad-men?
SVB. O, let the wild sheepe loose. Ile gumme your silkes
With good strong water, an' you come. DOL. Will you haue
The neighbours heare you? Will you betray all?
Harke, I heare some body. FAC. Sirrah—— SVB. I shall marre
All that the taylor has made, if you approch.
FAC. You most notorious whelpe, you insolent slaue,
Dare you doe this? SVB. Yes faith, yes faith. FAC. Why! who
Am I, my mungrill? Who am I? SVB. I'll tell you,,
Since you know not your selfe—— FAC. Speake lower, rogue.
SVB. Yes. You were once (time's not long past) the good,
Honest, plaine, liuery-three-pound-thrum; that kept
Your masters worships house, here, in the *friers*,
For the vacations—— FAC. Will you be so lowd?

I. i. ACT. I. SCENE. I. | FACE. SVBTLE. DOL Common. *Q* (*which so punctuates the headings of act and scene throughout*): ACT I. SCENE I. | *A Room in Lovewit's House.* | *Enter Face, in a captain's uniform, with his sword drawn, and Subtle with a vial, quarrelling, and followed by Dol Common.* G: *so Schelling, omitting* 'with his sword drawn' (*see* l. 115) 7 an' you] an'you *Q, F1* 9 Sirrah——] S[r]ah. *Q* 11 slaue, *Q*: slaue. *Ff* 14 selfe——] selfe. *Q* 18 vacations——] vacations. *Q* Will] Wi̇ll *Q originally*

SVB. Since, by my meanes, translated suburb-Captayne.
FAC. By your meanes, Doctor dog? SVB. Within mans memorie,
All this, I speake of. FAC. Why, I pray you, haue I
Beene countenanc'd by you? or you, by me?
Doe but collect, sir, where I met you first.
SVB. I doe not heare well. FAC. Not of this, I thinke it.
But I shall put you in mind, sir, at *pie-corner*,
Taking your meale of steeme in, from cookes stalls,
Where, like the father of hunger, you did walke
Piteously costiue, with your pinch'd-horne-nose,
And your complexion, of the *romane* wash,
Stuck full of black, and melancholique wormes,
Like poulder-cornes, shot, at th'*artillerie-yard*.
SVB. I wish, you could aduance your voice, a little.
FAC. When you went pinn'd vp, in the seuerall rags,
Yo'had rak'd, and pick'd from dung-hills, before day,
Your feet in mouldie slippers, for your kibes,
A felt of rugg, and a thin thredden cloake,
That scarce would couer your no-buttocks—— SVB. So, sir!
FAC. When all your *alchemy*, and your *algebra*,
Your *minералls*, *vegetalls*, and *animalls*,
Your coniuring, cosning, and your dosen of trades,
Could not relieue your corps, with so much linnen
Would make you tinder, but to see a fire;
I ga' you count'nance, credit for your coales,
Your stills, your glasses, your *materialls*,
Built you a fornace, drew you customers,
Aduanc'd all your black arts; lent you, beside,
A house to practise in—— SVB. Your masters house?
FAC. Where you haue studied the more thriuing skill
Of bawdrie, since. SVB. Yes, in your masters house.

I. i. 25 -*corner*,] -*Corner*, Q: *corner*. F1 37 -buttocks——] -buttockes. Q So, sir!] So S[r]. Q 40 trades,] Trades Q 47 in——] in. Q

You, and the rats, here, kept possession.
Make it not strange. I know, yo'were one, could keepe
The buttry-hatch still lock'd, and saue the chippings,
Sell the dole-beere to *aqua-vitæ*-men,
The which, together with your *christ-masse* vailes,
At *post and paire*, your letting out of counters,
Made you a pretty stock, some twentie markes,
And gaue you credit, to conuerse with cob-webs,
Here, since your mistris death hath broke vp house.
FAC. You might talke softlier, raskall. SVB. No, you *scarabe*,
I'll thunder you, in peeces. I will teach you
How to beware, to tempt a *furie*'againe
That carries tempest in his hand, and voice.
FAC. The place has made you valiant. SVB. No, your clothes.
Thou vermine, haue I tane thee, out of dung,
So poore, so wretched, when no liuing thing
Would keepe thee companie, but a spider, or worse?
Rais'd thee from broomes, and dust, and watring pots?
Sublim'd thee, and *exalted* thee, and *fix'd* thee
I' the *third region*, call'd our *state of grace?*
Wrought thee to *spirit*, to *quintessence*, with paines
Would twise haue won me the *philosophers worke?*
Put thee in words, and fashion? made thee fit
For more then ordinarie fellowships?
Giu'n thee thy othes, thy quarrelling dimensions?
Thy rules, to cheat at horse-race, cock-pit, cardes,
Dice, or what euer gallant tincture, else?
Made thee a second, in mine owne great art?
And haue I this for thanke? Doe you rebell?

I. i. 51 yo'were] you were *Q*   52 -hatch] -hahch *Q originally*   55 *and*] and *Q*, *Ff*   66 would] would not *F2*   68 *Sublim'd* . . . *exalted* . . . *fix'd*] Sublim'd . . . exalted . . . fix'd *Q originally*   69 *third region*] third region *Q originally*   our *state of grace*] the *high state of grace* corr. Q: call'd the high state of grace *Q originally*   70 *spirit* . . . *quintessence*] spirit . . . quintessence *Q originally*   71 *philosophers worke*] *Philosophers worke* corr. Q: Philosophers worke *Q originally*   77 great art] great Art *Q originally*: *great Art* corr. Q   78 thanke] thanks *F2*

Doe you flie out, i' the *proiection?*
Would you be gone, now? DOL. Gentlemen, what meane you?
Will you marre all? SVB. Slaue, thou hadst had no name——
DOL. Will you vn-doe your selues, with ciuill warre?
SVB. Neuer beene knowne, past *equi clibanum,*
The heat of horse-dung, vnder ground, in cellars,
Or an ale-house, darker then deafe IOHN'S: beene lost
To all mankind, but laundresses, and tapsters,
Had not I beene. DOL. Do'you know who heares you, Soueraigne?
FAC. Sirrah—— DOL. Nay, Generall, I thought you were ciuill——
FAC. I shall turne desperate, if you grow thus lowd.
SVB. And hang thy selfe, I care not. FAC. Hang thee, colliar,
And all thy pots, and pans, in picture I will,
Since thou hast mou'd me.—— DOL. (O, this'll ore-throw all.)
FAC. Write thee vp bawd, in *Paules;* haue all thy tricks
Of cosning with a hollow cole, dust, scrapings,
Searching for things lost, with a siue, and sheeres,
Erecting *figures,* in your rowes of *houses,*
And taking in of shaddowes, with a glasse,
Told in red letters: And a face, cut for thee,
Worse then GAMALIEL RATSEY'S. DOL. Are you sound?
Ha' you your senses, masters? FAC. I will haue
A booke, but barely reckoning thy impostures,
Shall proue a true *philosophers stone,* to printers.
SVB. Away, you trencher-raskall. FAC. Out you dog-leach,
The vomit of all prisons—— DOL. Will you be

I. i. 79 *proiection*] proiection *Q originally* 81 name——] Name, *Q* 82 vn-doe] vndoe *Q* 83 *clibanum* Q originally, Ff: *Clibanum* corr. Q 85 then] than *F2* 88 ciuill——] ciuill. *Q* 92 me.——] me. *Q* (O, . . . all.)] ô, . . . all. *Q* 99 RATSEY'S.] *Ratsey*'s, Q

Your owne destructions, gentlemen? Fac. Still spew'd out
For lying too heauy o' the basket. Svb. Cheater.
Fac. Bawd. Svb. Cow-herd. Fac. Coniurer. Svb. Cut-purse. Fac. Witch. Dol. O me!
We are ruin'd! lost! Ha' you no more regard
To your reputations? Where's your iudgement? S'light,
Haue yet, some care of me, o' your *republique*——
Fac. Away this brach. I'll bring thee, rogue, within
The *statute* of *sorcerie*, *tricesimo tertio*,
Of Harry the eight: I, and (perhaps) thy necke
Within a nooze, for laundring gold, and barbing it.
Dol. You'll bring your head within a cocks-combe, will you?
Shee catcheth out Face his sword: and breakes Subtles glasse.
And you, sir, with your *menstrue*, gather it vp.
S'death, you abominable paire of stinkards,
Leaue off your barking, and grow one againe,
Or, by the light that shines, I'll cut your throats.
I'll not be made a prey vnto the *marshall*,
For ne're a snarling dog-bolt o' you both.
Ha' you together cossen'd all this while,
And all the world, and shall it now be said
Yo'haue made most courteous shift, to cosen your selues?
You will accuse him? You will bring him in
Within the *statute?* Who shall take your word?
A whore-sonne, vpstart, *apocryphall* captayne,
Whom not a puritane, in black-*friers*, will trust
So much, as for a feather! And you, too,
Will giue the cause, forsooth? You will insult,
And claime a primacie, in the diuisions?
You must be chiefe? as if you, onely, had
The poulder to proiect with? and the worke

I. i. 105 Fac. *om. F2, F3* 106–7 Cheater. | Fac. Bawd. Svb. *Q, F1*: Cheater. Fac. Bawd. | Svb. *F2* 107 me!] me. *Q* 108 ruin'd! lost!] ruin'd lost. *Q* 110 *republique*——] *Republique.* Q 112 *tertio,*] *tertio* Q, F2: *tertio.* F1 113 eight] Eighth *F3* 114 it *not in Q* 115 *Stage dir. not in Q* *Face his*] Face's F3 117 abominable] abhominable *Q* 126 word?] word, *Q* 129 feather!] fether? *Q*

Were not begun out of equalitie?
The venter *tripartite?* All things in common?
Without prioritie? S'death, you perpetuall curres,
Fall to your couples againe, and cossen kindly,
And heartily, and louingly, as you should,
And loose not the beginning of a *terme*,
Or, by this hand, I shall grow factious too,
And, take my part, and quit you. FAC. 'Tis his fault,
He euer murmures, and obiects his paines,
And sayes, the weight of all lyes vpon him.
SVB. Why, so it do's. DOL. How does it? Doe not we
Sustaine our parts? SVB. Yes, but they are not equall.
DOL. Why, if your part exceed to day, I hope
Ours may, to morrow, match it. SVB. I, they may.
DOL. May, murmuring mastiffe? I, and doe. Death on me!
Helpe me to thrattell him. SVB. DOROTHEE, mistris DOROTHEE,
'Ods precious, I'll doe any thing. What doe you meane?
DOL. Because o' your *fermentation*, and *cibation?*
SVB. Not I, by heauen—— DOL. Your *Sol*, and *Luna*—— helpe me.
SVB. Would I were hang'd then. I'll conforme my selfe.
DOL. Will you, sir, doe so then, and quickly: sweare.
SVB. What should I sweare? DOL. To leaue your faction, sir.
And labour, kindly, in the commune worke.
SVB. Let me not breath, if I meant ought, beside.
I onely vs'd those speeches, as a spurre
To him. DOL. I hope we need no spurres, sir. Doe we?
FAC. 'Slid, proue to day, who shall sharke best. SVB. Agreed.

I. i. 134 equalitie] æqualitie *Q* 137 couples] couples, *Q* 139 loose] lose *F2* 144 DOL.] DAL. *Q* 145 equall] æquall *Q* 148 mastiffe?] mastiffe, *F2* Death on me] Gods will *Q* 149 thrattell] throttle *F2* After 'him.' *Seizes Sub. by the throat.* G 150 'Ods] O'ds *Q*, *F1* 152 heauen——] heauen. *Q* *Luna*——] *Luna:* Q After 'me.' *to Face.* G 154 sir,] sir? *F2* 155 To] 'To *F2*

DOL. Yes, and worke close, and friendly. SVB. 'Slight, the knot
Shall grow the stronger, for this breach, with me.
DOL. Why so, my good baboünes! Shall we goe make
A sort of sober, sciruy, precise neighbours,
(That scarse haue smil'd twise, sin' the king came in)
A feast of laughter, at our follies? raskalls,
Would runne themselues from breath, to see me ride,
Or you t'haue but a hole, to thrust your heads in,
For which you should pay eare-rent? No, agree.
And may *Don Prouost* ride a feasting, long,
In his old veluet ierken, and stayn'd scarfes,
(My noble Soueraigne, and worthy Generall)
Ere we contribute a new crewell garter
To his most worsted worship. SVB. Royall DOL!
Spoken like CLARIDIANA, and thy selfe!
FAC. For which, at supper, thou shalt sit in triumph,
And not be stil'd DOL Common, but DOL Proper,
DOL Singular: the longest cut, at night,
Shall draw thee for his DOL Particular.
SVB. Who's that? one rings. To the windo', DOL. Pray heau'n,
The master doe not trouble vs, this quarter.
FAC. O, feare not him. While there dyes one, a weeke,
O'the plague, hee's safe, from thinking toward *London*.
Beside, hee's busie at his hop-yards, now:
I had a letter from him. If he doe,
Hee'll send such word, for ayring o' the house
As you shall haue sufficient time, to quit it:
Though we breake vp a fortnight, 'tis no matter.
SVB. Who is it, DOL? DOL. A fine yong quodling. FAC. O,
My Lawyers clarke, I lighted on, last night,

I. i. 161 'Slight,] Slight *Q* 162 for] fot *F2* *They shake hands.* add G 164 precise] præcise *Q* 169 eare-rent?] Eare-rent: *Q* 170 a feasting] afeasting *F2* 175 selfe!] selfe. *Q* 180 windo'] wido' *F2* *Exit Dol.* add G 183 thinking] thinking, *Q* 184 now:] now, *Q* 187 it:] it. *Q* After 188 *Re-enter Dol.* G

In *Hol'bourne*, at the dagger. He would haue
(I told you of him) a *familiar*,
To rifle with, at horses, and winne cups.
DOL. O, let him in. SVB. Stay. Who shall doo't?
FAC. Get you
Your robes on. I will meet him, as going out.
DOL. And what shall I doe? FAC. Not be seene, away.
Seeme you very reseru'd. SVB. Inough. FAC. God b'w'you, sir.
I pray you, let him know that I was here.
His name is DAPPER. I would gladly haue staid, but——

Act I. *Scene* II.

DAPPER, FACE, SVBTLE.

CAptaine, I am here. FAC. Who's that? He's come, I think, Doctor.
Good faith, sir, I was going away. DAP. In truth,
I'am very sorry, Captaine. FAC. But I thought
Sure, I should meet you. DAP. I, I'am very glad.
I had a sciruy *writ*, or two, to make,
And I had lent my watch last night, to one
That dines, to day, at the shrieffs: and so was rob'd
Of my passe-time. Is this the cunning-man?
FAC. This is his worship. DAP. Is he a Doctor?
FAC. Yes.
DAP. And ha' you broke with him, Captain? FAC. I.
DAP. And how?
FAC. Faith, he do's make the matter, sir, so daintie,
I know not what to say—— DAP. Not so, good Captaine.

I. i. 196 *Exit Dol.* add G 197 After 'Inough.' *Exit.* G b'] be *Q*
I. ii. *G continues the scene* 1 Captaine] *Dap.* [*within.*] Captain *G*
After 1 *Enter Dapper.* G Doctor.] (Doctor. *Originally ranged with l.* 2 *in Q, afterwards placed above the line* (*see p.* 276) 3 I'am] I am *Q*
4 DAP. *om. F2* I, I'am] I am *Q* 5 I had] I'had *Q, Ff* 7 shrieffs] Sheriffes *F2* 8 After 'passe-time.' *Re-enter Subtle in his velvet cap and gown.* G 12 say——] say. *Q*

FAC. Would I were fairely rid on't, beleeue me.
  DAP. Nay, now you grieue me, sir. Why should you wish so?
I dare assure you. I'll not be vngratefull.
  FAC. I cannot thinke you will, sir. But the law
Is such a thing—— And then, he sayes, *Reade's* matter
Falling so lately—— DAP. *Reade?* He was an asse,
And dealt, sir, with a foole. FAC. It was a clarke, sir.
  DAP. A clarke? FAC. Nay, heare me, sir, you know the law
Better, I thinke—— DAP. I should, sir, and the danger.
You know I shew'd the *statute* to you? FAC. You did so.
  DAP. And will I tell, then? By this hand, of flesh,
Would it might neuer wright good *court*-hand, more,
If I discouer. What doe you thinke of me,
That I am a *Chiause?* FAC. What's that? DAP. The *Turke*, was here——
As one would say, doe you thinke I am a *Turke?*
  FAC. I'll tell the Doctor so. DAP. Doe, good sweet Captaine.
  FAC. Come, noble Doctor, 'pray thee, let's preuaile,
This is the gentleman, and he is no *Chiause.*
  SVB. Captaine, I haue return'd you all my answere.
I would doe much, sir, for your loue—— But this
I neither may, nor can. FAC. Tut, doe not say so.
You deale, now, with a noble fellow, Doctor,
One that will thanke you, richly, and h'is no *Chiause:*
Let that, sir, moue you. SVB. Pray you, forbeare—— FAC. He has
Foure angels, here—— SVB. You doe me wrong, good sir.
  FAC. Doctor, wherein? To tempt you, with these spirits?
  SVB. To tempt my art, and loue, sir, to my perill.

I. ii. 13 on't] of it *G* 15 you. *corr. Q, Ff*: you *Q originally*: you, *F3* 18 lately——] lately. *Q* 21 thinke——] thinke *Q* 24 wright] write *F2* 26 *Turke*, was] *Turke* was, *Q, Ff* 27 *Turke*] *Turque* Q originally 28 Doe,] Doe *Q originally* 37 here——] here. *Q* 39 sir] Sr, *Q originally*: Sir *corr. Q*

'Fore heau'n, I scarse can thinke you are my friend,
That so would draw me to apparant danger.
FAC. I draw you? A horse draw you, and a halter,
You, and your flies together—— DAP. Nay, good Captayne.
FAC. That know no difference of men. SVB. Good wordes, sir.
FAC. Good deeds, sir Doctor dogs-meate. 'Slight I bring you
No cheating CLIM-*o'the*-CLOVGHS, or CLARIBELS,
That looke as bigge as *fiue*-and-*fiftie*, and *flush*,
And spit out secrets, like hot custard—— DAP. Captayne.
FAC. Nor any melancholike vnder-scribe,
Shall tell the *Vicar*: but, a speciall gentle,
That is the heire to fortie markes, a yeere,
Consorts with the small poets of the time,
Is the sole hope of his old grand-mother,
That knowes the law, and writes you sixe faire hands,
Is a fine clarke, and has his cyphring perfect,
Will take his oath, o' the *greeke* XENOPHON,
If need be, in his pocket: and can court
His mistris, out of OVID. DAP. Nay, deare Captayne.
FAC. Did you not tell me, so? DAP. Yes, but I'ld ha' you
Vse master Doctor, with some more respect.
FAC. Hang him proud stagge, with his broad veluet head.
But, for your sake, I'ld choake, ere I would change
An article of breath, with such a puck-fist——
Come let's be gone. SVB. Pray you, le' me speake with you.
DAP. His worship calls you, Captayne. FAC. I am sorry,

I. ii. 43 together——] together. *Q*   45 sir] S^r^. *Q*: sir, *Ff*   dogs-meate] Dogges-mouth *Q*   48 custard——] Custard. *Q*   50 gentle] Genteel *F3*   56 XENOPHON] *Testament* Q   62 choake,] choake *Q*   63 -fist——] fist. *Q*   64 After 'gone.' *Going.* G

I e're imbarqu'd my selfe, in such a businesse.
DAP. Nay, good sir. He did call you. FAC. Will he take, then?
SVB. First, heare me—— FAC. Not a syllable, 'lesse you take.
SVB. Pray ye', sir—— FAC. Vpon no termes, but an *assumpsit.*
SVB. Your humor must be law. FAC. Why now, sir, talke. *He takes the money.*
Now, I dare heare you with mine honour. Speake.
So may this gentleman too. SVB. Why, sir—— FAC. No whispring.
SVB. 'Fore heau'n, you doe not apprehend the losse
You doe your selfe, in this. FAC. Wherein? For what?
SVB. Mary, to be so' importunate for one,
That, when he has it, will vn-doe you all:
Hee'll winne vp all the money i' the towne.
FAC. How! SVB. Yes. And blow vp gamster, after gamster,
As they doe crackers, in a *puppit*-play.
If I doe giue him a *familiar*,
Giue you him all you play for; neuer set him:
For he will haue it. FAC. Y'are mistaken, Doctor.
Why, he do's aske one but for cups, and horses,
A rifling *flye:* none o' your great *familiars.*
DAP. Yes, Captayne, I would haue it, for all games.
SVB. I told you so. FAC. 'Slight, that's a new businesse!
I vnderstood you, a tame bird, to flie
Twise in a *terme*, or so; on friday-nights,
When you had left the office: for a nagge,
Of fortie, or fiftie shillings. DAP. I, 'tis true, sir,
But I doe thinke, now, I shall leaue the law,
And therefore—— FAC. Why, this changes quite the case!

I. ii. 69 sir——] Sr. *Q* 70 humor] humour *F2* *Stage-dir. not in Q* 72 After 'sir' *Offering to whisper Face.* G whispring.] whispring, *Q* 82 Y'are] You are *F2* 86 FAC.] *Face.* [*Taking Dap. aside.*] G 92 therefore——] therefore. *Q*

Do' you thinke, that I dare moue him? DAP. If you please, sir,

All's one to him, I see. FAC. What! for that money?
I cannot with my conscience. Nor should you
Make the request, me thinkes. DAP. No, sir, I meane
To adde consideration. FAC. Why, then, sir,
I'll trie. Say, that it were for all games, Doctor?

SVB. I say, then, not a mouth shall eate for him
At any ordinarie, but o' the score,
That is a gaming mouth, conceiue me. FAC. Indeed!

SVB. Hee'll draw you all the treasure of the realme,
If it be set him. FAC. Speake you this from art?

SVB. I, sir, and reason too: the ground of art.
H'is o' the onely best complexion,
The queene of *Fairy* loues. FAC. What! is he! SVB. Peace.
Hee'll ouer-heare you. Sir, should shee but see him——

FAC. What? SVB. Do not you tell him. FAC. Will he win at cards too?

SVB. The spirits of dead HOLLAND, liuing ISAAC,
You'ld sweare, were in him: such a vigorous luck
As cannot be resisted. 'Slight hee'll put
Sixe o' your gallants, to a cloke, indeed.

FAC. A strange successe, that some man shall be borne too!

SVB. He heares you, man—— DAP. Sir, Ile not be ingratefull.

FAC. Faith, I haue a confidence in his good nature:
You heare, he sayes, he will not be ingratefull.

SVB. Why, as you please, my venture followes yours.

FAC. Troth, doe it, Doctor. Thinke him trustie, and make him.
He may make vs both happy in an houre:
Win some fiue thousand pound, and send vs two on't.

DAP. Beleeue it, and I will, sir. FAC. And you shall, sir.

I. ii. 98 After 'trie.' *Goes to Subtle.* G 114 man——] man. *Q* 115 a *om. F2* 119 houre] hower *Q* 120 on't] o'it *F2* 121 *Takes him aside.* add G

You haue heard all? DAP. No, what was't? nothing, I sir.
FAC. Nothing? DAP. A little, sir. FAC. Well, a rare starre
Raign'd, at your birth. DAP. At mine, sir? no. FAC. The Doctor
Sweares that you are—— SVB. Nay, Captaine, yo'll tell all, now.
FAC. Allyed to the queene of *Faerie*. DAP. Who? that I am?
Beleeue it, no such matter—— FAC. Yes, and that
Yo'were borne with a caule o' your head. DAP. Who saies so? FAC. Come.
You know it well inough, though you dissemble it.
DAP. I-fac, I doe not. You are mistaken. FAC. How!
Sweare by your fac? and in a thing so knowne
Vnto the Doctor? How shall we, sir, trust you
I'the other matter? Can we euer thinke,
When you haue wonne fiue, or sixe thousand pound,
You'll send vs shares in't, by this rate? DAP. By IOVE, sir,
I'll winne ten thousand pound, and send you halfe.
I-fac's no oath. SVB. No, no, he did but iest.
FAC. Goe too. Goe, thanke the Doctor. He's your friend
To take it so. DAP. I thanke his worship. FAC. So?
Another angell. DAP. Must I? FAC. Must you? Slight,
What else is thankes? will you be triuiall? Doctor,
When must he come, for his *familiar?*
DAP. Shall I not ha' it with me? SVB. O, good sir!
There must a world of ceremonies passe,
You must be bath'd, and fumigated, first;
Besides, the Queene of *Faerie* do's not rise,
Till it be noone. FAC. Not, if she daunc'd, to night.

Face takes him aside.

I. ii. 122 *Stage direction not in Q* 127 matter——] matter. *Q* 130 I-fac] I fac *Q* 135 IOVE] Gad *Q* 137 I-fac's] I fac is *Q* 138 He's] He is *Q* friend] friend. *Q* 141 *Dapper gives him the money.* add G 143 sir!] Sir, *Q*

Svb. And she must blesse it. Fac. Did you neuer see
Her royall *Grace*, yet? Dap. Whom? Fac. Your aunt
of *Faerie?*
Svb. Not, since she kist him, in the cradle, Captayne,
I can resolue you that. Fac. Well, see her *Grace*,
What ere it cost you, for a thing that I know!
It will be somewhat hard to compasse: but,
How euer, see her. You are made, beleeue it,
If you can see her. Her *Grace* is a lone woman,
And very rich, and if she take a phant'sye,
She will doe strange things. See her, at any hand.
'Slid, she may hap to leaue you all she has!
It is the Doctors feare. Dap. How will't be done, then?
Fac. Let me alone, take you no thought. Doe you
But say to me, Captayne, I'll see her *Grace*.
One knocks without.
Dap. Captain, I'll see her *Grace*. Fac. Inough. Svb.
Who's there?
Anone. (Conduct him forth, by the backe way)
Sir, against one a clock, prepare your selfe.
Till when you must be fasting; onely, take
Three drops of vinegar, in, at your nose;
Two at your mouth; and one, at either eare;
Then, bath your fingers endes; and wash your eyes;
To sharpen your fiue senses; and, cry *hum*,
Thrise; and then *buz*, as often; and then, come.
Fac. Can you remember this? Dap. I warrant you.
Fac. Well, then, away. 'Tis, but your bestowing
Some twenty nobles, 'mong her *Graces* seruants;
And, put on a cleane shirt: You doe not know
What grace her *Grace* may doe you in cleane linnen.

I. ii. 149 Fac. *om. F2, F3* 152 know!] know. *Q* 158 has!] has: *Q* 160 alone,] alone *Q* 161 me,] me' *F2* 162 *Stage-dir. not in Q* 163 *Aside to Face.* add G 164 a clock] aclock *F2* 168 bath] bathe *F2* 170 *Exit.* add G

Act I. *Scene* III.

SVBTLE, DRVGGER, FACE.

COme in (Good wiues, I pray you forbeare me, now.
Troth I can doe you no good, till after-noone)
What is your name, say you, ABEL DRVGGER?
DRV. Yes, sir.
SVB. A seller of *tabacco?* DRV. Yes, sir. SVB. 'Vmh.
Free of the *Grocers?* DRV. I, and't please you. SVB. Well——
Your businesse, ABEL? DRV. This, and't please your worship,
I am a yong beginner, and am building
Of a new shop, and't like your worship; iust,
At corner of a street: (Here's the plot on't.)
And I would know, by art, sir, of your worship,
Which way I should make my dore, by *necromancie.*
And, where my shelues. And, which should be for boxes.
And, which for pots. I would be glad to thriue, sir.
And, I was wish'd to your worship, by a gentleman,
One Captaine FACE, that say's you know mens *planets,*
And their good *angels,* and their bad. SVB. I doe,
If I doe see 'hem—— FAC. What! my honest ABEL?
Thou art well met, here! DRV. Troth, sir, I was speaking,
Iust, as your worship came here, of your worship.
I pray you, speake for me to master Doctor.
FAC. He shall doe any thing. Doctor, doe you heare?
This is my friend, ABEL, an honest fellow,
He lets me haue good *tabacco,* and he do's not
Sophisticate it, with sack-lees, or oyle,
Nor washes it in muscadell, and graines,

I. iii. *Exeunt Face and Dapper.* G, continuing the scene 1 Come] *Sub.* [*within.*] Come *G* in (Good] in. Good *Q* 2 after-noone)] afternoone. *Q* After 2 *Re-enters, followed by Drugger.* G 4 *tabacco*] *Tobacco* Q (*so* 23) 5, 6, 8 and't] an't *F2* 5 Well——] Well. *Q* 7 I am] I'am *Q, Ff* 11 *necromancie*] *Necromantie* Q 12 boxes.] Boxes, *Q* 17 see 'hem——] see'hem. *Q* After ' 'hem' *Re-enter Face.* G 18 here!] here. *Q*

Nor buries it, in grauell, vnder ground,
Wrap'd vp in greasie leather, or piss'd clouts :
But keeps it in fine lilly-pots, that open'd,
Smell like conserue of roses, or *french* beanes.
He has his maple block, his siluer tongs,
Winchester pipes, and fire of iuniper.
A neate, spruce-honest-fellow, and no gold-smith.
  Svb. H'is a fortunate fellow, that I am sure on——
  Fac. Alreadie, sir, ha' you found it ? Lo' thee Abel !
  Svb. And, in right way to'ward riches—— Fac. Sir.
    Svb. This summer,
He will be of the clothing of his companie :
And, next spring, call'd to the scarlet. Spend what he can.
  Fac. What, and so little beard ? Svb. Sir, you must
    thinke,
He may haue a receipt, to make haire come.
But hee'll be wise, preserue his youth, and fine for't :
His fortune lookes for him, another way.
  Fac. 'Slid, Doctor, how canst thou know this so soone ?
I am amus'd, at that ! Svb. By a rule, Captaine,
In *metoposcopie*, which I doe worke by,
A certaine starre i'the fore-head, which you see not.
Your chest-nut, or your oliue-colour'd face
Do's neuer faile : and your long eare doth promise.
I knew't, by certaine spots too, in his teeth,
And on the naile of his *mercurial* finger.
  Fac. Which finger's that ? Svb. His little finger.
    Looke.
Yo'were borne vpon a wensday ? Drv. Yes, indeed, sir.
  Svb. The thumbe, in *chiromantie*, we giue Venvs ;
The fore-finger to Iove ; the midst, to Satvrne ;
The ring to Sol ; the least, to Mercvrie :
Who was the lord, sir, of his *horoscope*,

I. iii. 32 gold-smith] Goldmith *Q*   33 on——] on. *Q*   35 summer,] Summer. *Q*   36 companie :] company. *Q*   43 I am] I'am *Q, F1*   44 *metoposcopie*] *Metaposcopie* Q : *metaposcopie* Ff : metoposcopy *G*   53 -finger] -finger, *Q, F2*   54 ring] ring, *F2*   Sol ;] *Sol,* Q

His *house of life* being *Libra*, which fore-shew'd,
He should be a merchant, and should trade with ballance.
FAC. Why, this is strange! Is't not, honest NAB?
SVB. There is a ship now, comming from *Ormus*,
That shall yeeld him, such a commoditie
Of drugs—— This is the west, and this the south?
DRV. Yes, sir. SVB. And those are your two sides?
DRV. I, sir.
SVB. Make me your dore, then, south; your broad side, west:
And, on the east-side of your shop, aloft,
Write *Mathlai*, *Tarmiel*, and *Baraborat;*
Vpon the north-part, *Rael*, *Velel*, *Thiel.*
They are the names of those *Mercurial* spirits,
That doe fright flyes from boxes. DRV. Yes, sir. SVB. And
Beneath your threshold, bury me a load-stone
To draw in gallants, that weare spurres: The rest,
They'll seeme to follow. FAC. That's a secret, NAB!
SVB. And, on your stall, a puppet, with a vice,
And a court-*fucus*, to call city-dames.
You shall deale much, with *mineralls*. DRV. Sir, I haue,
At home, alreadie—— SVB. I, I know, you'haue *arsnike*,
Vitriol, *sal-tartre*, *argaile*, *alkaly*,
Cinoper: I know all. This fellow, Captaine,
Will come, in time, to be a great distiller,
And giue a say (I will not say directly,
But very faire) at the *philosophers stone.*
FAC. Why, how now, ABEL! Is this true? DRV. Good Captaine,
What must I giue? FAC. Nay, Ile not counsell thee.
Thou hearst, what wealth (he sayes, spend what thou canst)
Th'art like to come too. DRV. I would gi' him a crowne.

I. iii. 56 *Libra*, which] *Libra*. Which *Q* 57 merchant] Marchant *Q* 59 *Ormus*] *Ormu's* Q 61 drugs——] Drugs. *Q* *Pointing to the plan.* add G 67 *Mercurial*] *Mercurian* Q 68 sir.] Sir, *Q* 77 Cinoper:] *Cinoper.* Q: but catchword of C 3 recto, l. 76, *Cinoper;* 82 After 'giue?' *Aside to Face.* G 83 wealth (he . . . canst)] wealth, he . . . canst, *Q*

FAC. A crowne! '⟨a⟩nd toward such a fortune? Hart,
Thou shalt rather gi' him thy shop. No gold about thee?
DRV. Yes, I haue a *portague*, I ha' kept this halfe yeere.
FAC. Out on thee, NAB; S'light, there was such an offer——
'Shalt keepe 't no longer, I'll gi' it him for thee?
Doctor, NAB prayes your worship, to drinke this: and sweares
He will appeare more gratefull, as your skill
Do's raise him in the world. DRV. I would intreat
Another fauour of his worship. FAC. What is't, NAB?
DRV. But, to looke ouer, sir, my *almanack*,
And crosse out my ill-dayes, that I may neither
Bargaine, nor trust vpon them. FAC. That he shall, NAB.
Leaue it, it shall be done, 'gainst after-noone.
SVB. And a direction for his shelues. FAC. Now, NAB?
Art thou well pleas'd, NAB? DRV. Thanke, sir, both your worships. FAC. Away.
Why, now, you smoky persecuter of nature!
Now, doe you see, that some-thing's to be done,
Beside your beech-coale, and your cor'siue waters,
Your crosse-lets, crucibles, and cucurbites?
You must haue stuffe, brought home to you, to worke on?
And, yet, you thinke, I am at no expence,
In searching out these veines, then following 'hem,
Then trying 'hem out. 'Fore god, my intelligence
Costs me more money, then my share oft comes too,
In these rare workes. SVB. You'are pleasant, sir. How now?

I. iii. 85 'and] And *Q*: 'nd *F1* (cf. IV. vii. 52): and *F2*   88 NAB;] *Nab*, Q: NAB. *F2*   90 this :] this, *Q*   93 fauour] fauor *Q*   99 Thanke] 'Thank *F2*   *Exit Drugger.* add G   100 nature !] *Nature*, Q   106 'hem] 'em *F3* (*et passim*)   107 god] God *Q*   108 Costs] Cost *F2*   then] than *F2*

Act I. *Scene* IIII.

FACE, DOL, SVBTLE.

WHat say's my daintie DOLKIN? DOL. Yonder fish-wife
Will not away. And there's your giantesse,
The bawd of *Lambeth*. SVB. Hart, I cannot speake with 'hem.
DOL. Not, afore night, I haue told 'hem, in a voice,
Thorough the trunke, like one of your *familiars*.
But I haue spied sir EPICVRE MAMMON—— SVB. Where?
DOL. Comming along, at far end of the lane,
Slow of his feet, but earnest of his tongue,
To one, that's with him. SVB. FACE, goe you, and shift.
DOL, you must presently make readie, too——
DOL. Why, what's the matter? SVB. O, I did looke for him
With the sunnes rising: 'Maruaile, he could sleepe!
This is the day, I am to perfect for him
The *magisterium*, our *great worke*, the *stone*;
And yeeld it, made, into his hands: of which,
He has, this month, talk'd, as he were possess'd.
And, now, hee's dealing peeces on't, away.
Me thinkes, I see him, entring ordinaries,
Dispensing for the poxe; and plaguy-houses,
Reaching his dose; walking *more-fields* for lepers;
And offring citizens-wiues pomander-bracelets,
As his preseruatiue, made of the *elixir*;
Searching the spittle, to make old bawdes yong;
And the high-waies, for beggars, to make rich:
I see no end of his labours. He will make

I. iv. *Act* . . . SVBTLE.] *Re-enter Dol.* G, continuing the scene 1 say's] say's, *Q, F1*: sayes *F2* 6 MAMMON——] *Mammon.* Q 9 shift. *F2*: shift, *Q, F1* *Exit Face.* add G 12 rising: 'Maruaile] rising. 'Meruaile *Q*: rising: 'Marvel *F3* sleepe!] sleepe. *Q* 16 possess'd.] possess'd on't, *Q* 24 rich:] rich, *Q*

Nature asham'd, of her long sleepe : when art,
Who's but a step-dame, shall doe more, then shee,
In her best loue to man-kind, euer could.
If his dreame last, hee'll turne the age, to gold.

Act II. *Scene* I.

MAMMON, SVRLY.

COme on, sir. Now, you set your foot on shore
In *nouo orbe ;* Here's the rich *Peru :*
And there within, sir, are the golden mines,
Great SALOMON'S *Ophir!* He was sayling to't,
Three yeeres, but we haue reach'd it in ten months.
This is the day, wherein, to all my friends,
I will pronounce the happy word, *be rich.*
This day, you shall be *spectatissimi.*
You shall no more deale with the hollow die,
Or the fraile card. No more be at charge of keeping
The liuery-punke, for the yong heire, that must
Seale, at all houres, in his shirt. No more,
If he denie, ha' him beaten to't, as he is
That brings him the commoditie. No more
Shall thirst of satten, or the couetous hunger
Of veluet entrailes, for a rude-spun cloke,
To be displaid at *Madame* AVGVSTA's, make
The sonnes of *sword,* and *hazzard* fall before
The golden calfe, and on their knees, whole nights,
Commit idolatrie with wine, and trumpets :
Or goe a feasting, after drum and ensigne.
No more of this. You shall start vp yong *Vice-royes,*
And haue your punques, and punquettees, my SVRLY.

I. iv. 26 sleepe :] sleepe, *Q* 27 then] than *F2* After 29 *Exeunt.* G II. i. ACT II. SCENE I. | *An outer Room in Lovewit's House.* | *Enter Sir Epicure Mammon and Surly.* G 1 foot] foote, *Q* 4 SALOMON'S] *Solomon's* F3 (so 82) *Ophir!* Ff: *Ophyr.* Q originally: *Ophir.* corr. Q to't,] to't *Q* 7 word,] word. *Q originally* 9 die *Q originally, Ff*: Die *corr. Q* 10 card *Q originally, Ff*: Card *corr. Q* 11 the] my *Q* 12 more, *F2* : more *Q, F1* 20 trumpets :] Trumpets *Q*

And vnto thee, I speake it first, *be rich.*
Where is my SVBTLE, there? Within hough? {*Within*} Sir.
Hee'll come to you, by and by. MAM. That's his fire-drake,
His lungs, his *Zephyrus*, he that puffes his coales,
Till he firke nature vp, in her owne center.
You are not faithfull, sir. This night, I'll change
All, that is mettall, in my house, to gold.
And, early in the morning, will I send
To all the plumbers, and the pewterers,
And buy their tin, and lead vp: and to *Lothbury*,
For all the copper. SVR. What, and turne that too?
MAM. Yes, and I'll purchase *Deuonshire*, and *Cornwaile*,
And make them perfect *Indies!* You admire now?
SVR. No faith. MAM. But when you see th'effects of the great med'cine!
Of which one part proiected on a hundred
Of *Mercurie*, or *Venus*, or the *Moone*,
Shall turne it, to as many of the *Sunne*;
Nay, to a thousand, so *ad infinitum*:
You will beleeue me. SVR. Yes, when I see't, I will.
But, if my eyes doe cossen me so (and I
Giuing 'hem no occasion) sure, I'll haue
A whore, shall pisse 'hem out, next day. MAM. Ha! Why?
Doe you thinke, I fable with you? I assure you,
He that has once the *flower of the sunne*,
The perfect *ruby*, which we call *elixir*,
Not onely can doe that, but by it's vertue,
Can confer honour, loue, respect, long life,
Giue safety, valure: yea, and victorie,
To whom he will. In eight, and twentie dayes,
I'll make an old man, of fourescore, a childe.

II. i. 25 {*Within*}] *Face.* [*within.*] G 30 my *Q*: thy *Ff* 35 *Cornwaile*] *Cornwall* F3 36 *Indies!*] *Indies.* Q 44 Giuing 'hem] Giuing'hem *Q* 45 pisse 'hem out,] pisse'hem out *Q* 50 honour] honor *F2* 51 valure] valor *F2*: Valour *F3*

SVR. No doubt, hee's that alreadie. MAM. Nay, I meane,
Restore his yeeres, renew him, like an eagle,
To the fifth age; make him get sonnes, and daughters,
Yong giants; as our *Philosophers* haue done
(The antient *Patriarkes* afore the floud)
But taking, once a weeke, on a kniues point,
The quantitie of a graine of mustard, of it:
Become stout MARSES, and beget yong CVPIDS.
SVR. The decay'd *Vestall's* of *Pickt-hatch* would thanke you,
That keepe the fire a-liue, there. MAM. 'Tis the secret
Of nature, naturiz'd 'gainst all infections,
Cures all diseases, comming of all causes,
A month's griefe, in a day; a yeeres, in twelue:
And, of what age soeuer, in a month.
Past all the doses, of your drugging Doctors.
I'll vndertake, withall, to fright the plague
Out o' the kingdome, in three months. SVR. And I'll
Be bound, the players shall sing your praises, then,
Without their poets. MAM. Sir, I'll doo't. Meane time,
I'll giue away so much, vnto my man,
Shall serue th'whole citie, with preseruatiue,
Weekely, each house his dose, and at the rate——
SVR. As he that built the water-worke, do's with water?
MAM. You are incredulous. SVR. Faith, I haue a humor,
I would not willingly be gull'd. Your *stone*
Cannot transmute me. MAM. PERTINAX, 〈my〉 SVRLY,
Will you beleeue antiquitie? recordes?
I'll show you a booke, where MOSES, and his sister,
And SALOMON haue written, of the art;
I, and a treatise penn'd by ADAM. SVR. How!

II. i. 54 doubt,] doubt *Q* 61 MARSES] *Marsses* Q 65 Cures] Cure *F2* 75 Weekely,] Weekely; *F2* 76 water?] water, *Q originally* 77 humor] humour *F2* 79 my *G conj.* (*cf.* II. ii. 5)

MAM. O' the *Philosophers stone*, and in high-*Dutch*.
SVR. Did ADAM write, sir, in high-*Dutch?* MAM. He did:
Which proues it was the primitiue tongue. SVR. What paper?
MAM. On cedar board. SVR. O that, indeed (they say)
Will last 'gainst wormes. MAM. 'Tis like your *Irish* wood,
'Gainst cob-webs. I haue a peece of IASONS fleece, too,
Which was no other, then a booke of *alchemie*,
Writ in large sheepe-skin, a good fat ram-vellam.
Such was PYTHAGORA's thigh, PANDORA's tub;
And, all that fable of MEDEAS charmes,
The manner of our worke: The Bulls, our fornace,
Still breathing fire; our *argent-viue*, the Dragon:
The Dragons teeth, *mercury* sublimate,
That keepes the whitenesse, hardnesse, and the biting;
And they are gather'd, into IASON's helme,
(Th'*alembeke*) and then sow'd in MARS his field,
And, thence, sublim'd so often, till they are fix'd.
Both this, th'*Hesperian* garden, CADMVS storie,
IOVE's shower, the boone of MIDAS, ARGVS eyes,
BOCCACE his *Demogorgon*, thousands more,
All abstract riddles of our *stone*. How now?

Act II. *Scene* II.

MAMMON, FACE, SVRLY.

DOe wee succeed? Is our day come? and hold's it?
FAC. The euening will set red, vpon you, sir;
You haue colour for it, crimson: the red *ferment*
Has done his office. Three houres hence, prepare you
To see proiection. MAM. PERTINAX, my SVRLY,
Againe, I say to thee, aloud: *be rich*.

II. i. 84–5 high-*Dutch*] *high Dutch Q* 88 wood,] wood *Q originally* 90 then] than *F2* 92 PYTHAGORA'S] *Pythagora's Q originally* 94 fornace] Furnace *F3* (*so usually*) II. ii. *Enter Face, as a servant.* G, continuing the scene 3 crimson :] crimson, *Q* 4 houres] howers *Q*

This day, thou shalt haue ingots: and, to morrow,
Giue lords th'affront. Is it, my ZEPHYRVS, right?
Blushes the *bolts-head?* FAC. Like a wench with child, sir,
That were, but now, discouer'd to her master.
MAM. Excellent wittie *Lungs!* My onely care is,
Where to get stuffe, inough now, to proiect on,
This towne will not halfe serue me. FAC. No, sir? Buy
The couering of o' churches. MAM. That's true. FAC.
Yes.
Let 'hem stand bare, as doe their auditorie.
Or cap 'hem, new, with shingles. MAM. No, good thatch:
Thatch will lie light vpo' the rafters, *Lungs.*
Lungs, I will manumit thee, from the fornace;
I will restore thee thy complexion, *Puffe,*
Lost in the embers; and repaire this braine,
Hurt wi' the fume o'the mettalls. FAC. I haue blowne, sir,
Hard, for your worship; throwne by many a coale,
When 'twas not beech; weigh'd those I put in, iust,
To keepe your heat, still euen; These bleard-eyes
Haue wak'd, to reade your seuerall colours, sir,
Of the *pale citron,* the *greene lyon,* the *crow,*
The *peacocks taile,* the *plumed swan.* MAM. And, lastly,
Thou hast descryed the *flower,* the *sanguis agni?*
FAC. Yes, sir. MAM. Where's master? FAC. At's
praiers, sir, he,
Good man, hee's doing his deuotions,
For the successe. MAM. *Lungs,* I will set a period,
To all thy labours: Thou shalt be the master
Of my *seraglia.* FAC. Good, sir. MAM. But doe you
heare?
I'll geld you, *Lungs.* FAC. Yes, sir. MAM. For I doe
meane
To haue a list of wiues, and concubines,

II. ii. 12 stuffe, inough *Q, F1*: stuffe enough *F2*: *query,* stuffe inough, on,] on *Q* 13 Buy] Take *Q* 14 of] off *F3* 15 auditorie.] Auditorie, *Q* 16 thatch:] Thatch. *Q* 21 wi' the] with the *Q* 24 bleard-eyes] bleard eyes *Q* 29 At's] At his *G* 32 be] be, *Q originally* 33 *seraglia*] *Seraglio* F3 34 you,] you' *Q*

Equall with SALOMON; who had the *stone*
Alike, with me: and I will make me, a back
With the *elixir*, that shall be as tough
As HERCVLES, to encounter fiftie a night.
Th'art sure, thou saw'st it *bloud?* FAC. Both *bloud*, and *spirit*, sir.
MAM. I will haue all my beds, blowne vp; not stuft:
Downe is too hard. And then, mine oual roome,
Fill'd with such pictures, as TIBERIVS tooke
From ELEPHANTIS: and dull ARETINE
But coldly imitated. Then, my glasses,
Cut in more subtill angles, to disperse,
And multiply the figures, as I walke
Naked betweene my *succubæ*. My mists
I'le haue of perfume, vapor'd 'bout the roome,
To loose our selues in; and my baths, like pits
To fall into: from whence, we will come forth,
And rowle vs drie in gossamour, and roses.
(Is it arriu'd at *ruby?*)—— Where I spie
A wealthy citizen, or rich lawyer,
Haue a sublim'd pure wife, vnto that fellow
I'll send a thousand pound, to be my cuckold.
FAC. And I shall carry it? MAM. No. I'll ha' no bawds,
But fathers, and mothers. They will doe it best.
Best of all others. And, my flatterers
Shall be the pure, and grauest of Diuines,
That I can get for money. My mere fooles,
Eloquent burgesses, and then my poets,
The same that writ so subtly of the *fart*,
Whom I will entertaine, still, for that subiect.
The few, that would giue out themselues, to be
Court, and towne-stallions, and, each where, belye
Ladies, who' are knowne most innocent, for them;

II. ii. 36 Equall] Æquall *Q* SALOMON] *Solomon* F3 40 and *F2*: & Q: *and* F1 53 (Is . . . *ruby?*)——] Is . . . *Ruby?* Q 54 rich] a rich *G* 58–9 They . . . others. *Not in Q* 59 And,] And *Q* 60 pure] best *Q* 62 poets,] poets *F1*: Poets *Q*, *F2* 66 each, where] each-where *F2* 67 who' are *Q*: who are *Ff*

Those will I begge, to make me *eunuchs* of:
And they shall fan me with ten estrich tailes
A piece, made in a plume, to gather wind.
We will be braue, *Puffe*, now we ha' the *med'cine.*
My meat, shall all come in, in *Indian* shells,
Dishes of agate, set in gold, and studded,
With emeralds, saphyres, hiacynths, and rubies.
The tongues of carpes, dormise, and camels heeles,
Boil'd i' the spirit of SOL, and dissolu'd pearle,
(APICIVS diet, 'gainst the *epilepsie*)
And I will eate these broaths, with spoones of amber,
Headed with diamant, and carbuncle.
My foot-boy shall eate phesants, caluerd salmons,
Knots, godwits, lamprey's: I my selfe will haue
The beards of barbels, seru'd, in stead of sallades;
Oild mushromes; and the swelling vnctuous paps
Of a fat pregnant sow, newly cut off,
Drest with an exquisite, and poynant sauce;
For which, Ile say vnto my cooke, there's gold,
Goe forth, and be a knight. FAC. Sir, I'll goe looke
A little, how it heightens. MAM. Doe. My shirts
I'll haue of taffata-sarsnet, soft, and light
As cob-webs; and for all my other rayment
It shall be such, as might prouoke the *Persian;*
Were he to teach the world riot, a new.
My gloues of fishes, and birds-skins, perfum'd
With gummes of *paradise*, and easterne aire——
SVR. And do you thinke to haue the *stone*, with this?
MAM. No, I doe thinke, t'haue all this, with the *stone.*
SVR. Why, I haue heard, he must be *homo frugi*,
A pious, holy, and religious man,
One free from mortall sinne, a very virgin.
MAM. That makes it, sir, he is so. But I buy it.
My venter brings it me. He, honest wretch,

II. ii. 69 me] me, *Q* 88 After 'heightens.' *Exit.* G 91 *Persian;*] *Persian:* Q 92 a new] anew *F2* 95 do you] do'you *Q, Ff* 101 venter] venture *F3*

A notable, superstitious, good soule,
Has worne his knees bare, and his slippers bald,
With prayer, and fasting for it: and, sir, let him
Do it alone, for me, still. Here he comes,
Not a prophane word, afore him: 'Tis poyson.

Act II. *Scene* III.

MAMMON, SVBTLE, SVRLY, FACE.

GOod morrow, father. SVB. Gentle sonne, good morrow,
And, to your friend, there. What is he, is with you?
MAM. An heretique, that I did bring along,
In hope, sir, to conuert him. SVB. Sonne, I doubt
Yo'are couetous, that thus you meet your time
I' the iust point: preuent your day, at morning.
This argues something, worthy of a feare
Of importune, and carnall appetite.
Take heed, you doe not cause the blessing leaue you,
With your vngouern'd hast. I should be sorry,
To see my labours, now, e'ene at perfection,
Got by long watching, and large patience,
Not prosper, where my loue, and zeale hath plac'd 'hem.
Which (heauen I call to witnesse, with your selfe,
To whom, I haue pour'd my thoughts) in all my ends,
Haue look'd no way, but vnto publique good,
To pious vses, and deere charitie,
No⟨w⟩ growne a prodigie with men. Wherein
If you, my sonne, should now preuaricate,
And, to your owne particular lusts, employ
So great, and catholique a blisse: be sure,
A curse will follow, yea, and ouertake
Your subtle, and most secret wayes. MAM. I know, sir,

II. ii. 105 Do it] Do'it *Q, Ff* II. iii. *Enter Subtle.* G, continuing the scene 17 charitie,] Charitie *Q* 18 Now *F2*: No *Q, F1* 19 preuaricate] præuaricate *Q* 21 blisse:] blisse; *Q* 23 wayes] way *F3*

You shall not need to feare me. I but come,
To ha' you confute this gentleman. SVR. Who is,
Indeed, sir, somewhat caustiue of beliefe
Toward your *stone:* would not be gull'd. SVB. Well, sonne,
All that I can conuince him in, is this,
The worke is done: Bright SOL is in his *robe.*
We haue a *med'cine* of the *triple Soule,*
The *glorified spirit.* Thankes be to heauen,
And make vs worthy of it. **Ulen spiegel.**
FAC. Anone, sir. SVB. Looke well to the register,
And let your heat, still, lessen by degrees,
To the *Aludels.* FAC. Yes, sir. SVB. Did you looke
O'the *Bolts-head* yet? FAC. Which, on *D.* sir? SVB. I.
What's the complexion? FAC. Whitish. SVB. Infuse vinegar,
To draw his *volatile substance,* and his *tincture:*
And let the water in *Glasse E.* be *feltred,*
And put into the *Gripes egge.* Lute him well;
And leaue him clos'd in *balneo.* FAC. I will, sir.
SVR. What a braue language here is? next to canting?
SVB. I haue another worke; you neuer saw, sonne,
That, three dayes since, past the *Philosophers wheele,*
In the lent heat of *Athanor;* and's become
Sulphur o' nature. MAM. But 'tis for me? SVB. What need you?
You haue inough, in that is, perfect. MAM. O, but——
SVB. Why, this is couetise! MAM. No, I assure you,
I shall employ it all, in pious vses,
Founding of colledges, and *grammar* schooles,
Marrying yong virgins, building hospitalls,
And now, and then, a church. SVB. How now? FAC. Sir, please you,

II. iii. 25 SVR.] SVB. *Q* 27 *stone:* would] Stone. Would *Q* SVB.] SVB- *Q* 32 **Ulen spiegel**] *Vlen spiegle* Q 33 FAC.] *Face.* [*within.*] G (so at 35, 36, 37, 41) 36 Which,] Which *Q, Ff* 43 I haue] I'haue *Q, Ff* 47 is,] is *F2* 52 then,] then *Q* After 'church.' *Re-enter Face.* G now?] now. *Q* Sir,] Sir *Q originally*

Shall I not change the *feltre?* SVB. Mary, yes.
And bring me the complexion of *Glasse B.*
MAM. Ha' you another? SVB. Yes, sonne, were I assur'd
Your pietie were firme, we would not want
The meanes to glorifie it. But I hope the best:
I meane to tinct *C.* in *sand-heat*, to morrow,
And giue him *imbibition.* MAM. Of white oile?
SVB. No, sir, of red. *F.* is come ouer the *helme* too,
I thanke my Maker, in S. MARIES *bath*,
And shewes *lac Virginis.* Blessed be heauen.
I sent you of his *fæces* there, *calcin'd.*
Out of that *calx*, I' ha' wonne the *salt of* MERCVRY.
MAM. By powring on your *rectified water?*
SVB. Yes, and *reuerberating* in *Athanor.*
How now? What colour saies it? FAC. The ground black, sir.
MAM. That's your *crowes-head?* SVR. Your cocks-comb's, is it not?
SVB. No, 'tis not perfect, would it were the *crow.*
That worke wants some-thing. (SVR. O, I look'd for this.
The hay is a pitching.) SVB. Are you sure, you loos'd 'hem
I' their owne *menstrue?* FAC. Yes, sir, and then married 'hem,
And put 'hem in a *Bolts-head*, nipp'd to *digestion*,
According as you bad me; when I set
The *liquor* of MARS to *circulation*,
In the same heat. SVB. The processe, then, was right.
FAC. Yes, by the token, sir, the *Retort* brake,
And what was sau'd, was put into the *Pellicane*,
And sign'd with HERMES *seale.* SVB. I thinke 'twas so.
We should haue a new *amalgama.* (SVR. O, this ferret
Is ranke as any pole-cat.) SVB. But I care not.

II. iii. After 54 *Exit Face.* G 61 Maker] maker *F2* After 66 *Re-enter Face.* G 68 *-head*] *head.* Q is it *G*: is't *Q, Ff* 70, 71 (SVR. O . . . pitching.)] SVR. O . . . pitching. *Q* 71 hay is a] hay is *W*: hay 's *G* 80, 81 (SVR. O, . . . -cat.)] SVR. O, . . . -cat. *Q*

Let him e'ene die ; we haue enough beside,
In *embrion*. *H*. ha's his *white shirt* on ? F A C. Yes, sir,
Hee's ripe for *inceration* : He stands warme,
85 In his *ash-fire*. I would not, you should let
Any die now, if I might counsell, sir,
For lucks sake to the rest. It is not good.
    M A M. He saies right. (S V R. I, are you bolted?)
F A C. Nay, I know't, sir,
I'haue seene th'ill fortune. What is some three ounces
90 Of fresh *materialls*? M A M. Is't no more? F A C. No more, sir,
Of gold, t'*amalgame*, with some sixe of *Mercurie*.
    M A M. Away, here's money. What will serue? F A C. Aske him, sir.
    M A M. How much? S V B. Giue him nine pound : you may gi' him ten.
    S V R. Yes, twentie, and be cossend, doe. M A M. There 'tis.
95   S V B. This needs not. But that you will haue it, so,
To see conclusions of all. For two
Of our inferiour workes, are at *fixation*.
A third is in *ascension*. Goe your waies.
Ha' you set the oile of *Luna* in *kemia* ?
100 F A C. Yes, sir. S V B. And the *philosophers* vinegar ?
    F A C. I.
    S V R. We shall haue a sallad. M A M. When doe you make *proiection* ?
    S V B. Sonne, be not hastie, I *exalt* our *med'cine*,
By hanging him in *balneo vaporoso* ;
And giuing him solution ; then *congeale* him ;
105 And then *dissolue* him ; then againe *congeale* him;
For looke, how oft I iterate the worke,
So many times, I adde vnto his vertue.
As, if at first, one ounce conuert a hundred,
After his second loose, hee'll turne a thousand ;

II. iii. 82 enough] enough, *Q*   83 *H*.] *H* F1   88 (SVR. . . . bolted?)] SVR. . . . bolted? *Q, Ff*   92 serue?] serue. *Q*   93 pound :] pound, *Q*   100 *Exit*. add G

His third solution, ten; his fourth, a hundred.
After his fifth, a thousand thousand ounces
Of any imperfect mettall, into pure
Siluer, or gold, in all examinations,
As good, as any of the naturall mine.
Get you your stuffe here, against after-noone,
Your brasse, your pewter, and your andirons.
  MAM. Not those of iron? SVB. Yes. You may bring them, too.
Wee'll change all mettall's. SVR. I beleeue you, in that.
  MAM. Then I may send my spits? SVB. Yes, and your racks.
  SVR. And dripping-pans, and pot-hangers, and hookes?
Shall he not? SVB. If he please. SVR. To be an asse.
  SVB. How, sir! MAM. This gent'man, you must beare withall.
I told you, he had no faith. SVR. And little hope, sir,
But, much lesse charitie, should I gull my selfe.
  SVB. Why, what haue you obseru'd, sir, in our art,
Seemes so impossible? SVR. But your whole worke, no more.
That you should hatch gold in a fornace, sir,
As they doe egges, in *Egypt!* SVB. Sir, doe you
Beleeue that egges are hatch'd so? SVR. If I should?
  SVB. Why, I thinke that the greater miracle.
No egge, but differs from a chicken, more,
Then mettalls in themselues. SVR. That cannot be.
The egg's ordain'd by nature, to that end:
And is a chicken in *potentia*.
  SVB. The same we say of lead, and other mettalls,
Which would be gold, if they had time. MAM. And that
Our art doth furder. SVB. I, for 'twere absurd
To thinke that nature, in the earth, bred gold
Perfect, i'the instant. Something went before.
There must be remote matter. SVR. I, what is that?

II. iii. 120 SVR.] SVB. *F3*   127 That] That, *Q*   128 *Egypt!*] *Egypt.* Q   132 Then] Than *F2*   137 furder] further *F2*   139 Perfect,] Perfect *Q*

SVB. Mary, we say—— MAM. I, now it heats: stand
Father.
Pound him to dust—— SVB. It is, of the one part,
A humide exhalation, which we call
Materia liquida, or the *vnctuous water*;
On th'other part, a certaine crasse, and viscous
Portion of earth; both which, concorporate,
Doe make the elementarie matter of gold:
Which is not, yet, *propria materia*,
But commune to all mettalls, and all stones.
For, where it is forsaken of that moysture,
And hath more drynesse, it becomes a stone;
Where it retaines more of the humid fatnesse,
It turnes to *sulphur*, or to *quick-siluer*:
Who are the parents of all other mettalls.
Nor can this remote matter, sodainly,
Progresse so from extreme, vnto extreme,
As to grow gold, and leape ore all the meanes.
Nature doth, first, beget th'imperfect; then
Proceedes shee to the perfect. Of that ayrie,
And oily water, *mercury* is engendred;
Sulphure o'the fat, and earthy part: the one
(Which is the last) supplying the place of male,
The other of the female, in all mettalls.
Some doe beleeue *hermaphrodeitie*,
That both doe act, and suffer. But, these two
Make the rest ductile, malleable, extensiue.
And, euen in gold, they are; for we doe find
Seedes of them, by our fire, and gold in them:
And can produce the *species* of each mettall
More perfect thence, then nature doth in earth.
Beside, who doth not see, in daily practice,
Art can beget bees, hornets, beetles, waspes,
Out of the carcasses, and dung of creatures;
Yea, scorpions, of an herbe, being ritely plac'd:

II. iii. 141 say——] say. *Q* heats:] heates, *Q* 142 dust——] Dust. *Q* 170, 176 then] than *F2* 174 ritely] rightly *F3* plac'd:] plac'd. *Q*

And these are liuing creatures, far more perfect,
And excellent, then mettalls. MAM. Well said, father!
Nay, if he take you in hand, sir, with an argument,
Hee'll bray you in a morter. SVR. 'Pray you, sir, stay.
Rather, then I'll be brai'd, sir, I'll beleeue,
That *Alchemie* is a pretty kind of game,
Somewhat like tricks o'the cards, to cheat a man,
With charming. SVB. Sir? SVR. What else are all your termes,
Whereon no one o' your writers grees with other?
Of your *elixir*, your *lac virginis*,
Your *stone*, your *med'cine*, and your *chrysosperme*,
Your *sal*, your *sulphur*, and your *mercurie*,
Your *oyle of height*, your *tree of life*, your *bloud*,
Your *marchesite*, your *tutie*, your *magnesia*,
Your *toade*, your *crow*, your *dragon*, and your *panthar*,
Your *sunne*, your *moone*, your *firmament*, your *adrop*,
Your *lato*, *azoch*, *zernich*, *chibrit*, *heautarit*,
And then, your *red man*, and your *white woman*,
With all your broths, your *menstrues*, and *materialls*,
Of pisse, and egge-shells, womens termes, mans bloud,
Haire o' the head, burnt clouts, chalke, merds, and clay,
Poulder of bones, scalings of iron, glasse,
And worlds of other strange *ingredients*,
Would burst a man to name? SVB. And all these, nam'd
Intending but one thing: which art our writers
Vs'd to obscure their art. MAM. Sir, so I told him,
Because the simple idiot should not learne it,
And make it vulgar. SVB. Was not all the knowledge
Of the *Egyptians* writ in mystick *symboles?*
Speake not the *Scriptures*, oft, in *parables?*
Are not the choisest *fables* of the *Poets*,
That were the fountaines, and first springs of wisedome,

II. iii. 176 mettalls] Mettall *Q* 178 'Pray] Pray *Q* 183 grees] 'grees *F2* 184 *elixir* Ff: *Elizir* Q originally: *Elixir* corr. Q 192 then,] then *Q* 193 broths] Broathes *Q* 195 o' the] o'th *F2* 196 Poulder] *Powder* F3 203 *Egyptians*] *Ægyptians* Q, F3 204 *Scriptures*, oft,] *Scriptures* oft *Q*

Wrapt in perplexed *allegories?* MAM. I vrg'd that,
And clear'd to him, that SISIPHVS was damn'd
To roule the ceaslesse stone, onely, because
Dol is seene. He would haue made ours common. Who is this?
SVB. God's precious—— What doe you meane? Goe in, good lady,
Let me intreat you. Where's this varlet? FAC. Sir?
SVB. You very knaue! doe you vse me, thus? FAC. Wherein, sir?
SVB. Goe in, and see, you traitor. Goe. MAM. Who is it, sir?
SVB. Nothing, sir. Nothing. MAM. What's the matter? good sir!
I haue not seene you thus distemp'red. Who is't?
SVB. All arts haue still had, sir, their aduersaries,
Face returnes. But ours the most ignorant. What now?
FAC. 'Twas not my fault, sir, shee would speake with you.
SVB. Would she, sir? Follow me. MAM. Stay, *Lungs*. FAC. I dare not, sir.
MAM. Stay man, what is shee? FAC. A lords sister, sir.
MAM. How! 'Pray thee stay? FAC. She's mad, sir, and sent hether ——
(Hee'll be mad too. MAM. I warrant thee.) Why sent hether?
FAC. Sir, to be cur'd. SVB. Why, raskall! FAC. Loe you. Here, sir.
He goes out. MAM. 'Fore-god, a BRADAMANTE, a braue piece.
SVR. Hart, this is a bawdy-house! I'll be burnt else.
MAM. O, by this light, no. Doe not wrong him. H'is

II. iii. 210 made *om. F2* 211 SVB. *om. F2* 212 After 'you.' *Dol retires.* G After 'varlet' *Re-enter Face.* G 213 knaue! doe] knaue. Doe *Q* 214 After 'Goe.' *Exit Face.* G Who] who *Q* 215 What's] What is *Q* good] Good *Q*: good, *Ff* 217 sir,] sir; *F2* 218, 224, 234 *Stage directions not in Q* 220 After 'me.' *Exit.* G MAM.] *Mam.* [*stopping him.*] G 221–2 *So in Q, G; transposed in Ff* 220 Stay] stay *Q* 222 'Pray] Pray *Q* hether] hither *F2* 224 SVB.] *Sur.* F3: *Sub.* [*within.*] G 225 -god] -God *Q* piece.] piece! *Q* 226 -house!] House. *Q*

Too scrupulous, that way. It is his vice.
No, h'is a rare physitian, doe him right.
An excellent *Paracelsian!* and has done
Strange cures with *minerall physicke.* He deales all
With *spirits,* he. He will not heare a word
Of GALEN, or his tedious *recipe's.*
How now, *Lungs!* FAC. Softly, sir, speake softly. I meant *Face againe.*
To ha' told your worship all. This must not heare.
MAM. No, he will not be gull'd; let him alone.
FAC. Y'are very right, sir, shee is a most rare schollar;
And is gone mad, with studying BRAVGHTONS workes.
If you but name a word, touching the *Hebrew,*
Shee falls into her fit, and will discourse
So learnedly of *genealogies,*
As you would runne mad, too, to heare her, sir.
MAM. How might one doe t'haue conference with her,
Lungs?
FAC. O, diuers haue runne mad vpon the conference.
I doe not know, sir: I am sent in hast,
To fetch a violl. SVR. Be not gull'd, sir MAMMON.
MAM. Wherein? 'Pray yee, be patient. SVR. Yes, as
you are.
And trust confederate knaues, and bawdes, and whores.
MAM. You are too foule, beleeue it. Come, here, Ulen.
One word. FAC. I dare not, in good faith. MAM. Stay,
knaue.
FAC. H'is extreme angrie, that you saw her, sir.
MAM. Drinke that. What is shee, when shee's out of
her fit?
FAC. O, the most affablest creature, sir! so merry!
So pleasant! shee'll mount you vp, like *quick-siluer,*
Ouer the helme; and *circulate,* like *oyle,*
A very *vegetall:* discourse of *state,*

II. iii. 228 way.] way: *Q* 235 heare.] heare, *Q* 237 right, sir] right. Sir *Q* schollar;] schollar: *Q* 238 BRAVGHTONS] *Broughtons* Q 242 her, sir.] her; Sir, *Q* 246 violl] viale *Q* 249 Ulen] *Zephyrus* Q: U en *in some copies of F2* 250 After 'faith.' *Going.* G 252 After 'that.' *Gives him money.* G 255 *oyle,*] *oyle;* Q

Of *mathematiques*, *bawdry*, any thing——
MAM. Is shee no way accessible? no meanes,
No trick, to giue a man a tast of her—— wit——
Or so?—— **Ulen.** FAC. I'll come to you againe, sir.
MAM. SVRLY, I did not thinke, one o' your breeding
Would traduce personages of worth. SVR. Sir EPICVRE,
Your friend to vse: yet, still, loth to be gull'd.
I doe not like your *philosophicall* bawdes.
Their *stone* is lecherie inough, to pay for,
Without this bait. MAM. 'Hart, you abuse your selfe.
I know the lady, and her friends, and meanes,
The originall of this disaster. Her brother
Ha's told me all. SVR. And yet, you ne're saw her
Till now? MAM. O, yes, but I forgot. I haue (beleeue it)
One o'the trecherou'st memories, I doe thinke,
Of all mankind. SVR. What call you her, brother?
MAM. My lord——
He wi'not haue his name knowne, now I thinke on't.
SVR. A very trecherous memorie! MAM. O' my faith——
SVR. Tut, if you ha' it not about you, passe it,
Till we meet next. MAM. Nay, by this hand, 'tis true.
Hee's one I honour, and my noble friend,
And I respect his house. SVR. Hart! can it be,
That a graue sir, a rich, that has no need,
A wise sir, too, at other times, should thus
With his owne oathes, and arguments, make hard meanes
To gull himselfe? And this be your *elixir*,
Your *lapis mineralis*, and your *lunarie*,
Giue me your honest trick, yet, at *primero*,
Or *gleeke*; and take your *lutum sapientis*,
Your *menstruum simplex*: I'll haue gold, before you,

II. iii. 259–60 her—— wit—— | Or so?——] her—— | Wit? or so? *Q* 260 **Ulen** *not in Q*: *Sub.* [*within.*] Ulen! *G* *Exit.* add G 263 vse: yet] vse. Yet *Q* 266 'Hart,] 'Hart *Q originally* 269 Ha's] H'as *Q, Ff* 271 trecherou'st *corr. F1*: treacherou'st *Q, F1 originally* 272 SVR.] SVB. *Q, Ff* her,] her *Q* 274 O'] O *Q* 282 And *F3*: And, *Q, Ff*

And, with lesse danger of the *quick-siluer ;*
Or the hot *sulphur.* FAC. Here's one from Captaine
FACE, sir, *To Surly.*
Desires you meet him i'the *Temple*-church,
Some halfe houre hence, and vpon earnest businesse.
Sir, if you please to quit vs, now ; and come, *He whispers Mammon.*
Againe, within two houres : you shall haue
My master busie examining o' the workes ;
And I will steale you in, vnto the partie,
That you may see her conuerse. Sir, shall I say,
You'll meet the Captaines worship ? SVR. Sir, I will.
But, by attorney, and to a second purpose.
Now, I am sure, it is a bawdy-house ;
I'll sweare it, were the *Marshall* here, to thanke me :
The naming this Commander, doth confirme it.
Don FACE ! Why, h'is the most autentique dealer
I' these commodities ! The *Superintendent*
To all the queinter traffiquers, in towne.
He is their *Visiter*, and do's appoint
Who lyes with whom ; and at what houre ; what price ;
Which gowne ; and in what smock ; what fall ; what tyre.
Him, will I proue, by a third person, to find
The subtilties of this darke *labyrinth :*
Which, if I doe discouer, deare sir MAMMON,
You'll giue your poore friend leaue, though no *Philosopher*,
To laugh : for you that are, 'tis thought, shall weepe.
FAC. Sir. He do's pray, you'll not forget. SVR. I will
not, sir.
Sir EPICVRE, I shall leaue you ? MAM. I follow you,
streight.
FAC. But doe so, good sir, to auoid suspicion.
This gent'man has a par'lous head. MAM. But wilt thou,
Ulen,

II. iii. 287 *-siluer ;*] *-silver,* F2 288, 291 *Stage directions not in Q*
288 After '*sulphur.*' *Re-enter Face.* G 292 houres] howers *Q* (*so* 305)
296 *Walks aside.* add G 301 autentique] authentique *F2* 302
Superintendent] *Superintendent.* F2 303 queinter] quainter *F3*
313 you ?] you. *Q* : you. [*Exit.* G 315 **Ulen** *not in Q*

Be constant to thy promise? FAC. As my life, sir.

MAM. And wilt thou insinuate what I am? and praise me?
And say I am a noble fellow? FAC. O, what else, sir?
And, that you'll make her royall, with the *stone*,
An Empresse; and your selfe king of *Bantam*.

MAM. Wilt thou doe this? FAC. Will I, sir? MAM. *Lungs*, my *Lungs!*
I loue thee. FAC. Send your stuffe, sir, that my master
May busie himselfe, about proiection.

MAM. Th'hast witch'd me, rogue: Take, goe. FAC. Your iack, & all, sir.

MAM. Thou art a villaine—— I will send my iack;
And the weights too. Slaue, I could bite thine eare.
Away, thou dost not care for me. FAC. Not I, sir?

MAM. Come, I was borne to make thee, my good weasell;
Set thee on a bench: and, ha' thee twirle a chaine
With the best lords vermine, of 'hem all. FAC. Away, sir.

MAM. A *Count*, nay, a *Count-palatine*—— FAC. Good sir, goe.

MAM. Shall not aduance thee, better: no, nor faster.

Act II. *Scene* IIII.

SVBTLE, FACE, DOL.

HAs he bit? Has he bit? FAC. And swallow'd too, my SVBTLE.
I ha' giu'n him line, and now he playes, I faith.

SVB. And shall we twitch him? FAC. Thorough both the gills.
A wench is a rare bait, with which a man
No sooner's taken, but he straight firkes mad.

SVB. DOL, my lord WHATS'HVM's sister, you must now

II. iii. 324 After 'goe.' *Gives him money.* G 332 better:] better; *Q* After 332 *Exit.* G II. iv. *Act . . .* DOL.] *Re-enter Subtle and Dol.* G, continuing the scene 6 WHATS'HVM'S] WHA'TS'HVMS *Ff*: *Whachums* Q.

Beare your selfe ſtatelich. DOL. O, let me alone.
I'll not forget my race, I warrant you.
I'll keepe my distance, laugh, and talke aloud;
Haue all the tricks of a proud sciruy ladie,
And be as rude'as her woman. FAC. Well said, *Sanguine.*
SVB. But will he send his andirons? FAC. His iack too;
And's iron shooing-horne: I ha' spoke to him. Well,
I must not loose my wary gamster, yonder.
SVB. O *Monsieur Caution,* that will not be gull'd?
FAC. I, if I can strike a fine hooke into him, now,
The *Temple*-church, there I haue cast mine angle.
Well, pray for me. I'll about it. SVB. What, more gudgeons!
One knocks.
DOL, scout, scout; stay FACE, you must goe to the dore:
'Pray god, it be my *Anabaptist.* Who is't, DOL?
DOL. I know him not. He lookes like a gold-end-man.
SVB. Gods so! 'tis he, he said he would send. What call you him?
The *sanctified Elder,* that should deale
For MAMMONS iack, and andirons! Let him in.
Stay, helpe me of, first, with my gowne. Away
Ma-dame, to your with-drawing chamber. Now,
In a new tune, new gesture, but old language.
This fellow is sent, from one negotiates with me
About the *stone,* too; for the *holy Brethren*
Of *Amsterdam,* the *exil'd Saints:* that hope
To raise their *discipline,* by it. I must vse him
In some strange fashion, now, to make him admire me.

II. iv. 7 ſtatelich] statelich *Q* 10 ladie,] Lady: *Q* 11 rude'as] rude as *F2* *Sanguine* corr. Q, Ff: *sanguine* Q originally 13 spoke] spoken *F2* 14 loose] lose *F2* 18 *Stage-direction not in Q* 19 After 'scout;' *Dol goes to the window.* G 20 god] God *Q* 24 MAMMONS] *Mammons,* Q 25 After 'gown.' *Exit Face with the gown.* G 26 Ma-dame] Madame *F2* After 'chamber.' *Exit Dol.* G 30 *Amsterdam*] *Amstredam* Q

Act II. *Scene* V.

SVBTLE, FACE, ANANIAS.

WHere is my drudge? FAC. Sir. SVB. Take away the *recipient*,
And rectifie your *menstrue*, from the *phlegma*.
Then powre it, o' the *Sol*, in the *cucurbite*,
And let 'hem macerate, together. FAC. Yes, sir.
And saue the ground? SVB. No. *Terra damnata*
Must not haue entrance, in the *worke*. Who are you?
ANA. A *faithfull Brother*, if it please you. SVB. What's that?
A *Lullianist?* a *Ripley?* *Filius artis?*
Can you *sublime*, and *dulcefie?* *calcine?*
Know you the *sapor pontick?* *sapor stiptick?*
Or, what is *homogene*, or *heterogene?*
ANA. I vnderstand no *heathen* language, truely.
SVB. *Heathen*, you KNIPPER-DOLING? Is *Ars sacra*,
Or *Chrysopœia*, or *Spagirica*,
Or the *pamphysick*, or *panarchick* knowledge,
A *heathen* language? ANA. *Heathen Greeke*, I take it.
SVB. How? *heathen Greeke?* ANA. All's *heathen*, but the *Hebrew*.
SVB. Sirah, my varlet, stand you forth, and speake to him,
Like a *Philosopher*: Answere, i'the language.
Name the vexations, and the martyrizations
Of mettalls, in the worke. FAC. Sir, *Putrefaction*,
Solution, *Ablution*, *Sublimation*,
Cohobation, *Calcination*, *Ceration*, and
Fixation. SVB. This is *heathen Greeke*, to you, now?
And when comes *Viuification?* FAC. After *Mortification*.

II. v. *Act* . . . ANANIAS.] *Enter Ananias.* G, continuing the scene
1 After 'Sir.' *Re-enter Face.* G   3 o'] 'o *Q*   9 *dulcefie ?*] *dulcefie,* Q originally   10 *stiptick*] *stipstick* Q, F1 : *styptick* F2   18 Sirah] S'rah *Q*   him, *F2* : him *Q, F1*

Svb. What's *Cohobation?* Fac. 'Tis the powring on
Your *Aqua Regis*, and then drawing him off,
To the *trine circle* of the *seuen spheares.*
Svb. What's the proper passion of mettalls? Fac. *Malleation.*
Svb. What's your *vltimum supplicium auri?* Fac. *Antimonium.*
Svb. This's *heathen Greeke*, to you? And, what's your *Mercury?*
Fac. A very fugitiue, he will be gone, sir.
Svb. How know you him? Fac. By his *viscositie*,
His *oleositie*, and his *suscitabilitie.*
Svb. How doe you *sublime* him? Fac. With the *calce* of egge-shels,
White marble, *talck.* Svb. Your *magisterium*, now?
What's that? Fac. Shifting, sir, your elements,
Drie into cold, cold into moist, moist in-
to hot, hot into drie. Svb. This's *heathen Greeke* to you, still?
Your *lapis philosophicus?* Fac. 'Tis a *stone*, and not
A *stone;* a *spirit*, a *soule*, and a *body:*
Which, if you doe *dissolue*, it is *dissolu'd*,
If you *coagulate*, it is *coagulated*,
If you make it to *flye*, it *flyeth.* Svb. Inough.
This's *heathen Greeke*, to you? What are you, sir?
Ana. Please you, a seruant of the *exil'd Brethren*,
That deale with widdowes, and with orphanes goods;
And make a iust account, vnto the *Saints:*
A *Deacon.* Svb. O, you are sent from master Wholsome,
Your teacher? Ana. From Tribvlation Wholsome,
Our very zealous *Pastor.* Svb. Good. I haue

II. v. 28 of] off *F2* 29 *Malleation.*] *Malleation,* F1 originally 36 marble, *talck*] marblec, *halke* F2: Marble, *Chalk* F3 40, 41 a *stone,* and not | A] a stone, | And not a *G* 41 *stone;*] *Stone,* Q 44 *Exit Face.* add G 45 sir?] Sir. *Q*

Some orphanes goods to come here. ANA. Of what kind, sir?

SVB. Pewter, and brasse, andirons, and kitchin ware,
Mettalls, that we must vse our med'cine on:
Wherein the *Brethren* may haue a penn'orth,
For readie money. ANA. Were the orphanes parents
Sincere professors? SVB. Why doe you aske? ANA. Because
We then are to deale iustly, and giue (in truth)
Their vtmost valew. SVB. 'Slid, you'ld cossen, else,
And if their parents were not of the *faithfull?*
I will not trust you, now I thinke on't,
Till I ha' talk'd with your *Pastor*. Ha' you brought money
To buy more coales? ANA. No, surely. SVB. No? How so?

ANA. The *Brethren* bid me say vnto you, sir.
Surely, they will not venter any more,
Till they may see *proiection*. SVB. How! ANA. Yo'haue had,
For the *instruments*, as bricks, and lome, and glasses,
Alreadie thirtie pound; and, for *materialls*,
They say, some ninetie more: And, they haue heard, since,
That one, at *Heidelberg*, made it, of an egge,
And a small paper of pin-dust. SVB. What's your name?

ANA. My name is ANANIAS. SVB. Out, the varlet
That cossend the *Apostles!* Hence, away,
Flee *Mischiefe;* had your *holy Consistorie*
No name to send me, of another sound;
Then wicked ANANIAS? Send your *Elders*,
Hither, to make atonement for you, quickly.
And gi' me satisfaction; or out-goes
The fire: and downe th'*alembekes*, and the fornace,
Piger Henricus, or what not. Thou wretch,
Both *Sericon*, and *Bufo*, shall be lost,

II. v. 55 penn'orth, *F2*: penn'orth. *Q*, *F1* 60 And] And, *Q*, *Ff* 65 venter] venture *F3* 70 *Heidelberg*] *Hiedelberg* Q 75 sound;] sound, *F2* 76 Then] Than *F2* 79 fornace,] fornace. *Ff*: Fornace. *Q*

Tell 'hem. All hope of rooting out the *Bishops*,
Or th'*Antichristian Hierarchie* shall perish,
If they stay threescore minutes. The *Aqueitie*,
Terreitie, and *Sulphureitie*
Shall runne together againe, and all be annull'd,
Thou wicked A N A N I A S. This will fetch 'hem,
And make 'hem hast towards their gulling more.
A man must deale like a rough nurse, and fright
Those, that are froward, to an appetite.

Act II. *Scene* VI.

F A C E, S V B T L E, D R V G G E R.

H'Is busie with his spirits, but wee'll vpon him.
S V B. How now! What mates? What *Baiards* ha' wee here?
F A C. I told you, he would be furious. Sir, here's N A B,
Has brought yo' another piece of gold, to looke on:
(We must appease him. Giue it me) and prayes you,
You would deuise (what is it N A B?) D R V. A signe, sir.
F A C. I, a good lucky one, a thriuing signe, Doctor.
S V B. I was deuising now. F A C. ('Slight, doe not say so,
He will repent he ga' you any more.)
What say you to his *constellation*, Doctor?
The *Ballance?* S V B. No, that way is stale, and common.
A townes-man, borne in *Taurus*, giues the bull;
Or the bulls-head: In *Aries*, the ram.
A poore deuice. No, I will haue his name
Form'd in some mystick character; whose *radij*,
Striking the senses of the passers by,
Shall, by a vertuall influence, breed affections,
That may result vpon the partie ownes it:

II. v. 86 annull'd,] annull'd *Q*, *F1* 87 After 'ANANIAS.' *Exit Ananias.* II. vi. *Re-enter Face in his uniform, followed by Drugger.* G, continuing the scene 8, 9 ('Slight . . . more.)] 'Slight . . . more. *Q* 14 No,] No. *Q*

As thus—— FAC. NAB! SVB. He first shall haue a bell, that's ABEL;
And, by it, standing one, whose name is DEE,
In a rugg gowne; there's *D.* and *Rug*, that's DRVG:
And, right anenst him, a Dog snarling *Er;*
There's DRVGGER, ABEL DRVGGER. That's his signe.
And here's now *mysterie*, and *hieroglyphick!*
FAC. ABEL, thou art made. DRV. Sir, I doe thanke his worship.
FAC. Sixe o' thy legs more, will not doe it, NAB.
He has brought you a pipe of *tabacco*, Doctor. DRV. Yes, sir:
I haue another thing, I would impart——
FAC. Out with it, NAB. DRV. Sir, there is lodg'd, hard by me,
A rich yong widdow—— FAC. Good! a *bona roba?*
DRV. But nineteene, at the most. FAC. Very good, ABEL.
DRV. Mary, sh'is not in fashion, yet; shee weares
A hood: but 't stands a cop. FAC. No matter, ABEL.
DRV. And, I doe, now and then, giue her a *fucus*——
FAC. What! dost thou deale, NAB? SVB. I did tell you, Captaine.
DRV. And physick too sometime, sir: for which shee trusts me
With all her mind. Shee's come vp here, of purpose
To learne the fashion. FAC. Good (his match too!) on, NAB.
DRV. And shee do's strangely long to know her fortune.
FAC. Gods lid, NAB, send her to the Doctor, hether.
DRV. Yes, I haue spoke to her of his worship, alreadie:
But shee's afraid, it will be blowne abroad,
And hurt her marriage. FAC. Hurt it? 'Tis the way

II. vi. 25 FAC. *om. Q* 27 *tabacco*] *Tobacco* Q (so 77) 28 impart——] impart *Q originally* 30 widdow——] Widdow. *Q* 32 yet;] yet, *Q originally* 34 then,] then *Q, Ff* *fucus*——] *fucus*, Q 35 deale,] deale. *Q originally* 36 sir:] Sir, *Q* 37 here,] here *Q originally* 38 Good (his . . . too!)] Good, His . . . too! *Q* 40 NAB,] *Nab!* Q send] Send *Q, Ff* hether] hither *F2* 42 abroad, *F2*: abroad *Q, F1*

To heale it, if 'twere hurt ; to make it more
Follow'd, and sought : N A B, thou shalt tell her this.
Shee'll be more knowne, more talk'd of, and your widdowes
Are ne'er of any price till they be famous ;
Their honour is their multitude of sutors :
Send her, it may be thy good fortune. What ?
Thou dost not know. D R V. No, sir, shee'll neuer marry
Vnder a knight. Her brother has made a vow.
F A C. What, and dost thou despaire, my little N A B,
Knowing, what the Doctor has set downe for thee,
And, seeing so many, o'the citie, dub'd ?
One glasse o' thy water, with a *Madame*, I know,
Will haue it done, N A B. What's her brother ? a knight ?
D R V. No, sir, a gentleman, newly warme in'his land, sir,
Scarse cold in'his one and twentie ; that do's gouerne
His sister, here : and is a man himselfe
Of some three thousand a yeere, and is come vp
To learne to quarrell, and to liue by his wits,
And will goe downe againe, and dye i'the countrey.
F A C. How ! to quarrell ? D R V. Yes, sir, to carry quarrells,
As gallants doe, and manage 'hem, by line.
F A C. 'Slid, N A B ! The Doctor is the onely man
In *Christendome* for him. He has made a table,
With *Mathematicall* demonstrations,
Touching the Art of quarrells. He will giue him
An instrument to quarrell by. Goe, bring 'hem, both :
Him, and his sister. And, for thee, with her
The Doctor happ'ly may perswade. Goe to.
'Shalt giue his worship, a new damaske suite
Vpon the premisses. S V B. O, good Captaine. F A C. He shall,
He is the honestest fellow, Doctor. Stay not,

II. vi. 45 Follow'd,] Follow'd *Q* 48 sutors :] Sutors. *Q* 57 newly] newly, *Q* 58 in'his] in his *Q, Ff* 63 quarrells, *Ff*: Quarrells *Q originally* : Quarrells, *corr. Q* 65 NAB !] *Nab.* Q 70 And,] And *Q originally* 72 'Shalt] 'Shat *F3* 74 Stay *corr. Q, Ff* : Say *Q originally*

No offers, bring the damaske, and the parties.
DRV. I'll trie my power, sir. FAC. And thy will too, NAB.
SVB. 'Tis good *tabacco* this! What is't an ounce?
FAC. He'll send you a pound, Doctor. SVB. O, no.
FAC. He will do't.
It is the goddest soule. ABEL, about it.
(Thou shalt know more anone. Away, be gone.)
A miserable rogue, and liues with cheese,
And has the wormes. That was the cause indeed
Why he came now. He dealt with me, in priuate,
To get a med'cine for 'hem. SVB. And shall, sir. This workes.
FAC. A wife, a wife, for one on'vs, my deare SVBTLE:
Wee'll eene draw lots, and he, that failes, shall haue
The more in goods, the other has in taile.
SVB. Rather the lesse. For shee may be so light
Shee may want graines. FAC. I, or be such a burden,
A man would scarse endure her, for the whole.
SVB. Faith, best let's see her first, and then determine.
FAC. Content. But DOL must ha' no breath on't.
SVB. Mum.
Away, you to your SVRLY yonder, catch him.
FAC. 'Pray god, I ha' not stai'd too long. SVB. I feare it.

Act III. *Scene* I.

TRIBVLATION, ANANIAS.

THese chastisements are common to the *Saints*,
And such rebukes we of the *Separation*
Must beare, with willing shoulders, as the trialls
Sent forth, to tempt our frailties. ANA. In pure zeale,

II. vi. 80 *Exit Abel.* add G 86 he, . . . failes,] he . . . fayles *Q originally* 94 god,] God *Q* *Exeunt.* add G III. i. ACT III. SCENE I. | *The Lane before Lovewit's House.* | *Enter Tribulation Wholesome, and Ananias.* G 2–4 we of the . . . Sent forth,] th'*Elect* must beare, with patience; | They are the exercises of the Spirit, | And sent *Q*

I doe not like the man: He is a *heathen.*
And speakes the language of *Canaan*, truely.
TRI. I thinke him a prophane person, indeed. ANA. He beares
The visible marke of the *Beast*, in his fore-head.
And for his *Stone*, it is a worke of darknesse,
And, with *Philosophie*, blinds the eyes of man.
TRI. Good *Brother*, we must bend vnto all meanes,
That may giue furtherance, to the *holy cause.*
ANA. Which his cannot: The *sanctified cause*
Should haue a *sanctified course.* TRI. Not alwaies necessary.
The children of perdition are, oft-times,
Made instruments euen of the greatest workes.
Beside, we should giue somewhat to mans nature,
The place he liues in, still about the fire,
And fume of mettalls, that intoxicate
The braine of man, and make him prone to passion.
Where haue you greater *Atheists*, then your Cookes?
Or more prophane, or cholerick then your Glasse-men?
More *Antichristian*, then your Bell-founders?
What makes the Deuill so deuillish, I would aske you,
Sathan, our common enemie, but his being
Perpetually about the fire, and boyling
Brimstone, and *arsnike?* We must giue, I say,
Vnto the motiues, and the stirrers vp
Of humours in the bloud. It may be so,
When as the *worke* is done, the *stone* is made,
This heate of his may turne into a zeale,
And stand vp for the *beauteous discipline*,
Against the menstruous cloth, and ragg of *Rome.*
We must await his calling, and the comming
Of the good spirit. You did fault, t'vpbraid him
With the *Brethrens* blessing of *Heidelberg*, waighing

III. i. 5 man:] man, *F2* 14 necessary.] necessary: *F2* 15 are, *Q*: are *F1* 21–3 then] than *F2* 23 *Antichristian,*] *Antichristian* Q 24 Deuill] *Diuell* Q 29 humours] humors *Q, F2* so,] so. *Q originally, Ff*: so; *corr. Q* 33 menstruous] mestruous *F2*

What need we haue, to hasten on the worke,
For the restoring of the *silenc'd Saints*,
Which ne'er will be, but by the *Philosophers stone*.
And, so a learned *Elder*, one of *Scotland*,
Assur'd me; *Aurum potabile* being
The onely med'cine, for the ciuill *Magistrate*,
T'incline him to a feeling of the cause:
And must be daily vs'd, in the disease.
ANA. I haue not edified more, truely, by man;
Not, since the *beautifull light*, first, shone on me:
And I am sad, my zeale hath so offended.
TRI. Let vs call on him, then. ANA. The motion's good,
And of the spirit; I will knock first: Peace be within.

Act III. *Scene* II.

SVBTLE, TRIBVLATION, ANANIAS.

O, Are you come? 'Twas time. Your threescore minutes
Were at the last thred, you see; and downe had gone
Furnus acediæ, Turris circulatorius:
Lembeke, Bolts-head, Retort, and *Pellicane*
Had all beene cinders. Wicked ANANIAS!
Art thou return'd? Nay then, it goes downe, yet.
TRI. Sir, be appeased, he is come to humble
Himselfe in spirit, and to aske your patience,
If too much zeale hath carried him, aside,
From the due path. SVB. Why, this doth qualifie!
TRI. The *Brethren* had no purpose, verely,
To giue you the least grieuance: but are ready
To lend their willing hands, to any proiect

III. i. 45 edified] ædified *Q* 47 sad,] sad *Q* 49 After 'first:' *Knocks.* G After 49 *The door is opened, and they enter.* G III. ii. SCENE II. | *A Room in Lovewit's House.* | *Enter Subtle, followed by Tribulation and Ananias.* G 2 the *om.* *F2* 3 *circulatorius:*] *circulatorius,* Q 10 qualifie !] qualefie. *Q*

The spirit, and you direct. SVB. This qualifies more !
TRI. And, for the orphanes goods, let them be valew'd,
Or what is needfull, else, to the holy worke,
It shall be numbred : here, by me, the *Saints*
Throw downe their purse before you. SVB. This qualifies, most !
Why, thus it should be, now you vnderstand.
Haue I discours'd so vnto you, of our *Stone ?*
And, of the good that it shall bring your cause ?
Shew'd you, (beside the mayne of hiring forces
Abroad, drawing the *Hollanders*, your friends,
From th'*Indies*, to serue you, with all their fleete)
That euen the med'cinall vse shall make you a faction,
And party in the realme ? As, put the case,
That some great man in state, he haue the gout,
Why, you but send three droppes of your *Elixir*,
You helpe him straight : there you haue made a friend.
Another has the palsey, or the dropsie,
He takes of your incombustible stuffe,
Hee's yong againe : there you haue made a friend.
A Lady, that is past the feate of body,
Though not of minde, and hath her face decay'd
Beyond all cure of paintings, you restore
With the oyle of *Talck ;* there you haue made a friend :
And all her friends. A lord, that is a *Leper*,
A knight, that has the bone-ache, or a squire
That hath both these, you make 'hem smooth, and sound,
With a bare *fricace* of your med'cine : still,
You increase your friends. TRI. I, 'tis very pregnant.
SVB. And, then, the turning of this Lawyers pewter
To plate, at *Christ-masse*—— ANA. *Christ-tide*, I pray you.
SVB. Yet, ANANIAS ? ANA. I haue done. SVB. Or changing

III. ii. 14 more !] more. *Q* 18 qualifies,] qualifies *F2* most!] most. *Q* 35 paintings,] painting ; *Q* 36 *Talck ;*] *Talck :* Q: *Talek ; Ff* friend :] Friend. *corr. Q :* Friend, *Q originally* 38 -ache,] -ache ; *F2* 41 pregnant] prægnant *Q*

His parcell guilt, to massie gold. You cannot
But raise you friends. Withall, to be of power
To pay an armie, in the field, to buy
The king of *France*, out of his realmes ; or *Spaine*,
Out of his *Indies :* What can you not doe,
Against lords spirituall, or temporall,
That shall oppone you ? TRI. Verily, 'tis true.
We may be temporall lords, our selues, I take it.
SVB. You may be any thing, and leaue off to make
Long-winded exercises : or suck vp,
Your ha, and hum, in a tune. I not denie,
But such as are not graced, in a state,
May, for their ends, be aduerse in religion,
And get a tune, to call the flock together :
For (to say sooth) a tune do's much, with women,
And other phlegmatick people, it is your bell.
ANA. Bells are prophane : a tune may be religious.
SVB. No warning with you ? Then, farewell my patience.
'Slight, it shall downe : I will not be thus tortur'd.
TRI. I pray you, sir. SVB. All shall perish. I haue spoke it.
TRI. Let me find grace, sir, in your eyes ; the man
He stands corrected : neither did his zeale
(But as your selfe) allow a tune, some-where.
Which, now, being to'ard the stone, we shall not need.
SVB. No, nor your holy vizard, to winne widdowes
To giue you legacies ; or make zealous wiues
To rob their husbands, for the *common cause :*
Nor take the start of bonds, broke but one day,
And say, *they were forfeited, by prouidence.*
Nor shall you need, ore-night to eate huge meales,
To celebrate your next daies fast the better :
The whilst the *Brethren*, and the *Sisters*, humbled,
Abate the stiffenesse of the flesh. Nor cast

III. ii. 46 you] your *F2* Withall *F2* : With all *Q*, *F1* 47 field,] field ; *Q* 49 *Indies* :] *Indies.* F2 72 bonds] Bandes *Q* 77 flesh.] flesh ; *Q*

Before your hungrie hearers, scrupulous bones,
As whether a *Christian* may hawke, or hunt;
Or whether, *Matrons, of the holy assembly,*
May lay their haire out, or weare doublets:
Or haue that idoll *Starch*, about their linnen.
ANA. It is, indeed, an idoll. TRI. Mind him not, sir.
I doe command thee, spirit (of zeale, but trouble)
To peace within him. Pray you, sir, goe on.
SVB. Nor shall you need to libell 'gainst the *Prelates*,
And shorten so your eares, against the hearing
Of the next wire-drawne grace. Nor, of necessitie,
Raile against playes, to please the *Alderman*,
Whose daily custard you deuoure. Nor lie
With zealous rage, till you are hoarse. Not one
Of these so singular arts. Nor call your selues,
By names of TRIBVLATION, PERSECVTION,
RESTRAINT, LONG-PATIENCE, and such like, affected
By the whole family, or wood of you,
Onely for glorie, and to catch the eare
Of the *Disciple*. TRI. Truely, sir, they are
Wayes, that the *godly Brethren* haue inuented,
For propagation of the *glorious cause*,
As very notable meanes, and whereby, also,
Themselues grow soone, and profitably famous.
SVB. O, but the *stone*, all's idle to it! nothing!
The art of *Angels*, Natures miracle,
The *diuine secret*, that doth flye in clouds,
From *east* to *west*: and whose tradition
Is not from men, but spirits. ANA. I hate *Traditions*:
I do not trust them—— TRI. Peace. ANA. They are *Popish*, all.
I will not peace. I will not—— TRI. ANANIAS.
ANA. Please the prophane, to grieue the godly: I may not.

III. ii. 80 whether,] whether *F2* 81 doublets:] doublets, *Q* 94 like,] like *F2* 99 *glorious*] *holy* Q 102 to it] to'it *Q, F1*: to't *F2* 100 meanes,] meanes; *Q* 106 *Traditions:*] *Traditions.* Q 107 them——] 'hem. *Q* 109 godly:] godly. *Q*

S V B. Well, A N A N I A S, thou shalt ouer-come.
T R I. It is an ignorant zeale, that haunts him, sir.
But truely, else, a very faithful *Brother*,
A botcher: and a man, by reuelation,
That hath a competent knowledge of the truth.
S V B. Has he a competent summe, there, i' the bagg,
To buy the goods, within? I am made guardian,
And must, for charitie, and conscience sake,
Now, see the most be made, for my poore orphane:
Though I desire the *Brethren*, too, good gayners.
There, they are, within. When you haue view'd, & bought 'hem,
And tane the inuentorie of what they are,
They'are readie for *proiection;* there's no more
To doe: cast on the *med'cine*, so much siluer
As there is tinne there, so much gold as brasse,
I'll gi' it you in, by waight. T R I. But how long time,
Sir, must the *Saints* expect, yet? S V B. Let me see,
How's the moone, now? Eight, nine, ten dayes hence
He will be *siluer potate;* then, three dayes,
Before he *citronise:* some fifteene dayes,
The *Magisterium* will be perfected.
A N A. About the second day, of the third weeke,
In the ninth month? S V B. Yes, my good A N A N I A S.
T R I. What will the orphanes goods arise to, thinke you?
S V B. Some hundred markes; as much as fill'd three carres,
Vnladed now: you'll make sixe millions of 'hem.
But I must ha' more coales laid in. T R I. How! S V B. Another load,
And then we ha' finish'd. We must now encrease
Our fire to *ignis ardens*, we are past
Fimus equinus, Balnei, Cineris,
And all those lenter heats. If the holy purse

III. ii. 112 truely] truley *F2* *Brother,*] *Brother;* Q 122 They'are *Q*: They are *Ff* 123 *med'cine,* so] *med'cine*: So *Q* 132 Yes,] Yes *F2* 135 you'll] you shall *Q* 137 ha'] have *F3*

Should, with this draught, fall low, and that the *Saints*
Doe need a present summe, I haue ⟨a⟩ trick
To melt the pewter, you shall buy now, instantly,
And, with a tincture, make you as good *Dutch* dollers,
As any are in *Holland*. TRI. Can you so?
SVB. I, and shall bide the third examination.
ANA. It will be ioyfull tidings to the *Brethren*.
SVB. But you must carry it, secret. TRI. I, but stay,
This act of coyning, is it lawfull? ANA. Lawfull?
We know no Magistrate. Or, if we did,
This's forraine coyne. SVB. It is no coyning, sir.
It is but casting. TRI. Ha? you distinguish well.
Casting of money may be lawfull. ANA. 'Tis, sir.
TRI. Truely, I take it so. SVB. There is no scruple,
Sir, to be made of it; beleeue ANANIAS:
This case of conscience he is studied in.
TRI. I'll make a question of it, to the *Brethren*.
ANA. The *Brethren* shall approue it lawfull, doubt not.
Where shall't be done? SVB. For that wee'll talke, anone. *Knock without.*
There's some to speake with me. Goe in, I pray you,
And view the parcells. That's the inuentorie.
I'll come to you straight. Who is it? FACE! Appeare.

Act III. *Scene* III.

SVBTLE, FACE, DOL.

HOw now? Good prise? FAC. Good poxe! Yond' caustiue cheater
Neuer came on. SVB. How then? FAC. I ha' walk'd the round,
Till now, and no such thing. SVB. And ha' you quit him?
FAC. Quit him? and hell would quit him too, he were happy.

III. ii. 142 a *F2*: *not in Q, F1*   159 shall't] shall it *F2*   160 *Stage direction not in Q*   162 After 'straight.' *Exeunt Trib. and Ana.* G   FACE !] *Face !* Q   III. iii. *Enter Face in his uniform.* G, continuing the scene   1 caustiue] costiue *Q*   4 and] an' *F2*

'Slight would you haue me stalke like a mill-iade,
All day, for one, that will not yeeld vs graines?
I know him of old. Svb. O, but to ha' gull'd him,
Had beene a maistry. Fac. Let him goe, black Boy,
And turne thee, that some fresh newes may possesse thee.
A noble *Count*, a *Don* of *Spaine* (my deare
Delicious compeere, and my partie-bawd)
Who is come hether, priuate, for his conscience,
And brought munition with him, sixe great slopps,
Bigger then three *Dutch* hoighs, beside round trunkes,
Furnish'd with pistolets, and pieces of eight,
Will straight be here, my rogue, to haue thy bath
(That is the colour,) and to make his battry
Vpon our Dol, our Castle, our *cinque*-Port,
Our *Douer* pire, our what thou wilt. Where is shee?
Shee must prepare perfumes, delicate linnen,
The bath in chiefe, a banquet, and her wit,
For shee must milke his *Epididimis*.
Where is the *Doxie?* Svb. I'll send her to thee:
And but dispatch my brace of little Iohn Leydens,
And come againe my selfe. Fac. Are they within then?
Svb. Numbring the summe. Fac. How much? Svb. A hundred marks, Boy.
Fac. Why, this's a lucky day! Ten pounds of Mammon!
Three o' my clarke! A portague o' my grocer!
This o' the *Brethren!* beside reuersions,
And states, to come i' the widdow, and my *Count!*
My share, to day, will not be bought for fortie—— Dol. What?
Fac. Pounds, daintie Dorothee, art thou so neere?
Dol. Yes, say lord *Generall*, how fares our campe?

III. iii. 12 hether, priuate,] hither, private *F2* 13 slopps] Sloops *F3* 14 then] than *F2* 17 (That . . . colour,)] That . . . colour, *Q* 22 milke] feele *Q* 26 *Exit.* add G 27 Mammon!] *Mammon?* Q 28 clarke! . . . grocer!] Clearke. . . . Grocer. *Q* 29 *Brethren!*] *Brethren*, Q 30 states,] states *F2* *Count!*] *Count*. Q 31 After 'fortie' *Enter Dol*. G

FAC. As, with the few, that had entrench'd themselues
Safe, by their discipline, against a world, DOL:
And laugh'd, within those trenches, and grew fat
With thinking on the booties, DOL, brought in
Daily, by their small parties. This deare houre,
A doughtie *Don* is taken, with my DOL;
And thou maist make his ransome, what thou wilt,
My *Dousabell:* He shall be brought here, fetter'd
With thy faire lookes, before he sees thee; and throwne
In a downe-bed, as darke as any dungeon;
Where thou shalt keepe him waking, with thy drum;
Thy drum, my DOL; thy drum; till he be tame
As the poore black-birds were i' the great frost,
Or bees are with a bason: and so hiue him
I'the swan-skin couerlid, and cambrick sheets,
Till he worke honey, and waxe, my little *Gods-guift.*
DOL. What is he, Generall? FAC. An *Adalantado,*
A *Grande,* girle. Was not my DAPPER here, yet?
DOL. No. FAC. Nor my DRVGGER? DOL. Neither. FAC. A poxe on 'hem,
They are so long a furnishing! Such stinkards
Would not be seene, vpon these festiuall dayes.
How now! ha' you done? SVB. Done. They are gone. The summe
Is here in banque, my FACE. I would, we knew
Another chapman, now, would buy 'hem out-right.
FAC. 'Slid, NAB shall doo't, against he ha' the widdow,
To furnish houshold. SVB. Excellent, well thought on,
Pray god, he come. FAC. I pray, he keepe away
Till our new businesse be o're-past. SVB. But, FACE,
How cam'st thou, by this secret *Don?* ⟨FAC.⟩ A spirit
Brought me th'intelligence, in a paper, here,
As I was coniuring, yonder, in my circle
For SVRLY: I ha' my flies abroad. Your bath

III. iii. 35 Safe,] Safe *F2* 38 houre] hower *Q* (*so* 76) 42 sees] see's *Q, Ff* thee;] thee, *Q* 49 *-guift*] *-gift* F2 50 he,] he *F2* 53 furnishing!] furnishing. *Q* After 54 *Re-enter Subtle.* G 59 Excellent,] Excellent *Q* 60 god] God *Q* 62 secret] secret, *F2* FAC. *F2*: *om. Q, F1*

Is famous, SVBTLE, by my meanes. Sweet DOL,
You must goe tune your virginall, no loosing
O' the least time. And, doe you heare? good action.
Firke, like a flounder; kisse, like a scallop, close:
And tickle him with thy mother-tongue. His great
VERDVGO-ship has not a iot of language:
So much the easier to be cossin'd, my DOLLY.
He will come here, in a hir'd coach, obscure,
And our owne coach-man, whom I haue sent, as guide,
No creature else. Who's that? SVB. It i' not he? *One knocks.*
FAC. O no, not yet this houre. SVB. Who is't? DOL.
DAPPER,
Your Clarke. FAC. Gods will, then, *Queene of Faerie*,
On with your tyre; and, Doctor, with your robes.
Lett's dispatch him, for gods sake. SVB. 'Twill be long.
FAC. I warrant you, take but the *cues* I giue you,
It shall be briefe inough. 'Slight, here are more!
ABEL, and I thinke, the angrie boy, the heire,
That faine would quarrell. SVB. And the widdow?
FAC. No,
Not that I see. Away. O sir, you are welcome.

Act III. *Scene* IIII.

FACE, DAPPER, DRVGGER, KASTRIL.

THe Doctor is within, a mouing for you;
(I haue had the most adoe to winne him to it)
He sweares, you'll be the dearling o' the dice:
He neuer heard her *Highnesse* dote, till now (he sayes.)

III. iii. 66 famous,] famous *Q*, *Ff* 67 loosing] losing *F2* 69 close:] close; *Q* 72 cossin'd,] cozen'd; *F2* DOLLY.] DOLLY *Ff* 75 After 'that?' *Exit Dol.* G: *Dol peeps through the window.* Schelling i'not he?] is not he! *F2* *Stage direction not in Q* 76 After 'houre.' *Re-enter Dol.* G 77 then,] then *F2* 78 After 'tyre;' *Exit Dol.* G 79 Lett's] Lett's vs *Q* gods] Gods *Q* 80 you,] you. *Q* *cues*] QQs. *Q* 81 After 'inough.' *Goes to the window.* G more!] more. *Q* 84 After 'Away.' *Exit Sub.* G III. iv. *Act* ... KASTRIL.] *Enter Dapper.* G, continuing the scene 2 (I ... it)] I ... it; *Q* 4 (he sayes.) *not in Q, G*

Your aunt has giu'n you the most gracious words,
That can be thought on. DAP. Shall I see her *Grace?*
FAC. See her, and kisse her, too. What? honest NAB!
Ha'st brought the damaske? NAB. No, sir, here's *tabacco.*
FAC. 'Tis well done, NAB: Thou'lt bring the damaske too?
DRV. Yes, here's the gentleman, Captaine, master KASTRIL,
I haue brought to see the Doctor. FAC. Where's the widdow?
DRV. Sir, as he likes, his sister (he sayes) shall come.
FAC. O, is it so? 'good time. Is your name KASTRIL, sir?
KAS. I, and the best o'the KASTRILS, I'lld be sorry else,
By fifteene hundred, a yeere. Where is this Doctor?
My mad *tabacco*-Boy, here, tells me of one,
That can doe things. Has he any skill? FAC. Wherein, sir?
KAS. To carry a businesse, manage a quarrell, fairely,
Vpon fit termes. FAC. It seemes sir, yo'are but yong
About the towne, that can make that a question!
KAS. Sir, not so yong, but I haue heard some speech
Of the angrie Boyes, and seene 'hem take *tabacco;*
And in his shop: and I can take it too.
And I would faine be one of 'hem, and goe downe
And practise i'the countrey. FAC. Sir, for the *Duello,*
The Doctor, I assure you, shall informe you,
To the least shaddow of a haire: and shew you,
An instrument he has, of his owne making,
Where-with, no sooner shall you make report
Of any quarrell, but he will take the height on't,
Most instantly; and tell in what degree,
Of saf'ty it lies in, or mortalitie.

III. iv. 7 After 'too.' *Enter Abel, followed by Kastril.* G 8 *tabacco*] *Tobacco* Q (so 16, 22, 127) NAB. *for* DRV. *Q, Ff* 9 done, NAB:] done. *Q* 13 'good] Good *Q* 15 a yeere] ayeare *F2* 29 Where-with] Wherewith *Q, F2* 32 saf'ty] safetie *F2*

And, how it may be borne, whether in a *right line*,
Or a *halfe-circle;* or may, else, be cast
35 Into an *angle blunt*, if not *acute:*
All this he will demonstrate. And then, rules,
To giue, and take the lie, by. K A S. How? to take it?
    F A C. Yes, in *oblique*, hee'll shew you; or in *circle:*
But neuer in *diameter*. The whole towne
40 Studie his *theoremes*, and dispute them, ordinarily,
At the eating *Academies*. K A S. But, do's he teach
Liuing, by the wits, too? F A C. Any thing, what euer.
You cannot thinke that subtiltie, but he reades it.
He made me a Captaine. I was a starke pimpe,
45 Iust o' your standing, 'fore I met with him:
It i' not two months since. I'll tell you his method.
First, he will enter you, at some ordinarie.
    K A S. No, I'll not come there. You shall pardon me.
    F A C. For why, sir?
    K A S. There's gaming there, and tricks. F A C. Why, would you be
50 A gallant, and not game? K A S. I, 'twill spend a man.
    F A C. Spend you? It will repaire you, when you are spent.
How doe they liue by their wits, there, that haue vented
Sixe times your fortunes? K A S. What, three thousand a yeere!
    F A C. I, fortie thousand. K A S. Are there such? F A C. I, sir.
55 And gallants, yet. Here's a yong gentleman,
Is borne to nothing, fortie markes a yeere,
Which I count nothing. H'is to be initiated,
And haue a *flye* o'the Doctor. He will winne you
By vnresistable lucke, within this fortnight,
60 Inough to buy a *baronie*. They will set him
Vpmost, at the Groome-porters, all the *Christmasse!*

    III. iv. 44 Captaine.] Captaine; *Q*   54 I,] I' *F2*   55 yong] young *F2*   57 H'is] He is *F2*   60 *baronie*] Baronry Q   61 *Christmasse !*] *Christmasse.* Q

And, for the whole yeere through, at euerie place,
Where there is play, present him with the chaire;
The best attendance, the best drinke, sometimes
Two glasses of *canarie*, and pay nothing;
The purest linnen, and the sharpest knife,
The partrich next his trencher: and, somewhere,
The daintie bed, in priuate, with the daintie.
You shall ha' your ordinaries bid for him,
As play-houses for a poet; and the master
Pray him, aloud, to name what dish he affects,
Which must be butterd shrimps: and those that drinke
To no mouth else, will drinke to his, as being
The goodly, *president* mouth of all the boord.
KAS. Doe you not gull one? FAC. 'Od's my life! Do you thinke it?
You shall haue a cast commander, (can but get
In credit with a glouer, or a spurrier,
For some two paire, of eithers ware, afore-hand)
Will, by most swift posts, dealing with him,
Arriue at competent meanes, to keepe himselfe,
His punke, and naked boy, in excellent fashion.
And be admir'd for't. KAS. Will the Doctor teach this?
FAC. He will doe more, sir, when your land is gone,
(As men of spirit hate to keepe earth long)
In a vacation, when small monie is stirring,
And ordinaries suspended till the tearme,
Hee'll shew a perspectiue, where on one side
You shall behold the faces, and the persons
Of all sufficient yong heires, in towne,
Whose bonds are currant for commoditie;
On th'other side, the marchants formes, and others,
That, without help of any second broker,
(Who would expect a share) will trust such parcels:

III. iv. 63 chaire;] Chayre, *Q* 74 goodly, *president* mouth] goodly *President*- Mouth *Q* 75 'Od's] God's *Q* 76–8 (can . . . -hand)] can . . . -hand, *Q* 79 with] but with *G* 84 long)] long(*F1 originally* 91 marchants] Merchants *Q*: merchants *F2* 92 That] (That *F1* without] without, *F1 originally*

In the third square, the verie street, and signe
Where the commoditie dwels, and do's but wait
To be deliuer'd, be it pepper, sope,
Hops, or tabacco, oat-meale, woad, or cheeses.
All which you may so handle, to enioy,
To your owne vse, and neuer stand oblig'd.
KAS. I'faith! Is he such a fellow? FAC. Why, NAB here knowes him.
And then for making matches, for rich widdowes,
Yong gentlewomen, heyres, the fortunat'st man!
Hee's sent too, farre, and neere, all ouer *England*,
To haue his counsell, and to know their fortunes.
KAS. Gods will, my suster shall see him. FAC. I'll tell you, sir,
What he did tell me of NAB. It's a strange thing!
(By the way you must eate no cheese, NAB, it breeds melancholy:
And that same melancholy breeds wormes) but passe it,
He told me, honest NAB, here, was ne'er at tauerne,
But once in's life. DRV. Truth, and no more I was not.
FAC. And, then he was so sick—— DRV. Could he tell you that, too?
FAC. How should I know it? DRV. In troth we had beene a shooting,
And had a piece of fat ram-mutton, to supper,
That lay so heauy o' my stomack—— FAC. And he has no head
To beare any wine; for, what with the noise o'the fiddlers,
And care of his shop, for he dares keepe no seruants——
DRV. My head did so ake—— FAC. As he was faine to be brought home,
The Doctor told me. And then, a good old woman——
DRV. (Yes, faith, she dwells in *Sea-coale*-lane) did cure me,
With sodden ale, and pellitorie o'the wall:

III. iv. 97 tabacco] *Tobacco* *Q* 103 too,] too *Q* 106 thing!] thing, *Q* 120 wall:] Wall; *Q*

Cost me but two pence. I had another sicknesse,
Was worse then that. FAC. I, that was with the griefe
Thou took'st for being sess'd at eighteene pence,
For the water-worke. DRV. In truth, and it was like
T'haue cost me almost my life. FAC. Thy haire went off?
DRV. Yes, sir, 'twas done for spight. FAC. Nay, so sayes the Doctor.
KAS. Pray thee, *tabacco*-Boy, goe fetch my suster,
I'll see this learned Boy, before I goe:
And so shall shee. FAC. Sir, he is busie now:
But, if you haue a sister to fetch hether,
Perhaps, your owne paines may command her sooner;
And he, by that time, will be free. KAS. I goe.
FAC. DRVGGER, shee's thine: the damaske. (SVBTLE, and I
Must wrastle for her.) Come on, master DAPPER.
You see, how I turne clients, here, away,
To giue your cause dispatch. Ha' you perform'd
The ceremonies were inioyn'd you? DAP. Yes, o'the vinegar,
And the cleane shirt. FAC. 'Tis well: that shirt may doe you
More worship then you thinke. Your aunt's a fire,
But that shee will not shew it, t'haue a sight on you.
Ha' you prouided for her *Graces* seruants?
DAP. Yes, here are sixe-score EDWARD shillings. FAC. Good.
DAP. And an old HARRY's soueraigne. FAC. Very good.
DAP. And three IAMES shillings, and an ELIZABETH groat,
Iust twentie nobles. FAC. O, you are too iust.
I would you had had the other noble in MARIES.
DAP. I haue some PHILIP, and MARIES. FAC. I, those same
Are best of all. Where are they? Harke, the Doctor.

III. iv. 122 then] than *F2* (*so* 139) 123 sess'd] seast *Q* 132 goe.] goe, Sir. *Q* *Exit*. add G 133 After 'damaske.' *Exit Abel*. G 133–4 (SVBTLE, . . . her.)] *Subtle*, . . . her. *Q* 139 fire,] fire *Q*, *F1*

Act III. *Scene* V.

SVBTLE, FACE, DAPPER, DOL.

Subtle disguisd like a Priest of Faery.

IS yet her *Graces* cossen come? FAC. He is come.
SVB. And is he fasting? FAC. Yes. SVB. And hath cry'd *hum?*
FAC. Thrise, you must answer. DAP. Thrise. SVB. And as oft *buz?*
FAC. If you haue, say. DAP. I haue. SVB. Then, to her cuz,
Hoping, that he hath vinegard his senses,
As he was bid, the *Faery Queene* dispenses,
By me, this robe, the petticote of FORTVNE;
Which that he straight put on, shee doth importune.
And though to FORTVNE neere be her petticote,
Yet, neerer is her smock, the Queene doth note:
And, therefore, euen of that a piece shee hath sent,
Which, being a child, to wrap him in, was rent;
And prayes him, for a scarfe, he now will weare it
(With as much loue, as then her *Grace* did teare it)
About his eyes, to shew, he is fortunate.
They blind him with a rag.
And, trusting vnto her to make his state,
Hee'll throw away all worldly pelfe, about him;
Which that he will performe, shee doth not doubt him.
FAC. Shee need not doubt him, sir. Alas, he has nothing,
But what he will part withall, as willingly,
Vpon her *Graces* word (throw away your purse)
As shee would aske it: (hand-kerchiefes, and all)
Shee cannot bid that thing, but hee'll obay.
(If you haue a ring, about you, cast it off,
Or a siluer seale, at your wrist, her *Grace* will send
Her *Faeries* here to search you, therefore deale
He throwes away, as they bid him

III. v. *Enter Subtle, disguised like a priest of Fairy, with a stripe of cloth.* G, continuing the scene *The stage directions at lines* 1, 15, 25, 31, *and* 58 *are not in Q* 1 Is yet] *Sub.* [*In a feigned voice.*] Is yet G 22 aske it:] aske it, *Q* 24, 28 (If . . . vn-done.)] If . . . vndone. *Q*

Directly with her *Highnesse*. If they find
That you conceale a mite, you are vn-done.)
DAP. Truely, there's all. FAC. All what? DAP. My money, truly.
FAC. Keepe nothing, that is transitorie, about you.
(Bid DOL play musique.) Looke, the *Elues* are come
To pinch you, if you tell not truth. Aduise you.

Dol enters with a citterne: they pinch him.

DAP. O, I haue a paper with a spur-ryall in't. FAC. *Ti, ti,*
They knew't, they say. SVB. *Ti, ti, ti, ti*, he has more yet.
FAC. *Ti, ti-ti-ti.* I'the tother pocket? SVB. *Titi, titi, titi, titi.*
They must pinch him, or he will neuer confesse, they say.
DAP. O, ô. FAC. Nay, 'pray you hold. He is her *Graces* nephew.
Ti, ti, ti? What care you? Good faith, you shall care.
Deale plainely, sir, and shame the *Faeries*. Shew
You are an innocent. DAP. By this good light, I ha' nothing.
SVB. *Ti ti, ti ti to ta.* He do's equiuocate, shee sayes:
Ti, ti do ti, ti ti do, ti da. And sweares by the light, when he is blinded.
DAP. By this good darke, I ha' nothing but a halfe-crowne
Of gold, about my wrist, that my loue gaue me;
And a leaden heart I wore, sin' shee forsooke me.
FAC. I thought, 'twas something. And, would you incurre
Your aunts displeasure for these trifles? Come,
I had rather you had throwne away twentie halfe-crownes.
You may weare your leaden heart still. How now?
SVB. What newes, DOL? DOL. Yonder's your knight, sir MAMMON.

III. v. 31 (Bid . . . musique.)] Bid . . . musique. *Q* 34 *Aside to Face.* add Schelling 35 After 'pocket?' *Aside to Subtle.* G *Titi . . . titi*] *Titi, titi, titi, titi, titi.* F2 41 equiuocate] æquiuocate *Q* 48 *Takes it off.* add G 49 After 'still.' *Enter Dol hastily.* G 50 What] what *F2*

FAC. Gods lid, we neuer thought of him, till now.
Where is he? DOL. Here, hard by. H'is at the doore.
SVB. And, you are not readie, now? DOL, get his suit.
He must not be sent back. FAC. O, by no meanes.
What shall we doe with this same Puffin, here,
Now hee's o'the spit? SVB. Why, lay him back a while,
With some deuice. *Ti, ti ti, ti ti ti.* Would her *Grace* speake with me?

He speakes through the key-hole, the other knocking.

I come. Helpe, DOL. FAC. Who's there? Sir EPICVRE;
My master's i'the way. Please you to walke
Three or foure turnes, but till his back be turn'd,
And I am for you. Quickly, DOL. SVB. Her *Grace*
Commends her kindly to you, master DAPPER.
DAP. I long to see her *Grace*. SVB. Shee, now, is set
At dinner, in her bed; and shee has sent you,
From her owne priuate trencher, a dead mouse,
And a piece of ginger-bread, to be merry withall,
And stay your stomack, lest you faint with fasting:
Yet, if you could hold out, till shee saw you (shee sayes)
It would be better for you. FAC. Sir, he shall
Hold out, and 'twere this two houres, for her *Highnesse;*
I can assure you that. We will not loose
All we ha' done—— SVB. He must nor see, nor speake
To any body, till then. FAC. For that, wee'll put, sir,
A stay in's mouth. SVB. Of what? FAC. Of ginger-bread.
Make you it fit. He that hath pleas'd her *Grace*,
Thus farre, shall not now crinckle, for a little.
Gape sir, and let him fit you. SVB. Where shall we now
Bestow him? DOL. I' the priuie. SVB. Come along, sir,
I now must shew you *Fortunes* priuy lodgings.

III. v. 53 *Exit Dol.* add G 55 Puffin] Puffing *F2* 57 After 'deuice.' *Re-enter Dol with Face's clothes.* G 64 shee *om. F2* 70 houres] howers *Q* 71 loose] lose *F2* 72 done——] done. *Q* 74 in 's] in'is *Q, Ff. Jonson may have written* in'his. 77 After 'you.' *They thrust a gag of gingerbread in his mouth.* G

FAC. Are they perfum'd? and his bath readie? SVB. All.
Onely the Fumigation's somewhat strong.
FAC. Sir EPICVRE, I am yours, sir, by and by.

Act IIII. *Scene* I.

FACE, MAMMON, DOL.

O, Sir, yo'are come i'the onely, finest time——
MAM. Where's master? FAC. Now preparing for proiection, sir.
Your stuffe will b⟨e⟩'all chang'd shortly. MAM. Into gold?
FAC. To gold, and siluer, sir. MAM. Siluer, I care not for.
FAC. Yes, sir, a little to giue beggars. MAM. Where's the lady?
FAC. At hand, here. I ha' told her such braue things, o' you,
Touching your bountie and your noble spirit—— MAM. Hast thou?
FAC. As shee is almost in her fit to see you.
But, good sir, no *diuinitie* i' your conference,
For feare of putting her in rage—— MAM. I warrant thee.
FAC. Sixe men will not hold her downe. And then,
If the old man should heare, or see you—— MAM. Feare not.
FAC. The very house, sir, would runne mad. You know it
How scrupulous he is, and violent,
'Gainst the least act of sinne. *Physick*, or *Mathematiques*,
Poetrie, *State*, or *Bawdry* (as I told you)
Shee will endure, and neuer startle: But
No word of controuersie. MAM. I am school'd, good **Ulen**.

III. v. 82 FAC.] *Face.* [*speaking through the key-hole.*] G After 82 *Exeunt with Dapper.* G IV. i. MAMMON] MAMMOM *F2* ACT IV. SCENE I. | *A Room in Lovewit's House.* | *Enter Face and Mammon.* G 4 Siluer,] Siluer *Q* 6 o'] on *Q* 11 men] men, sir, *G* And then,] And, then *Q, Ff* 12 you——] you. *Q* 18 **Ulen**] *Lungs* Q.

FAC. And you must praise her house, remember that,
And her nobilitie. MAM. Let me, alone:
No *Herald*, no nor *Antiquarie*, *Lungs*,
Shall doe it better. Goe. FAC. Why, this is yet
A kind of moderne happinesse, to haue
DOL Common for a great lady. MAM. Now, EPICVRE,
Heighten thy selfe, talke to her, all in gold;
Raine her as many showers, as IOVE did drops
Vnto his DANAE: Shew the *God* a miser,
Compar'd with MAMMON. What? the *stone* will do't.
Shee shall feele gold, tast gold, heare gold, sleepe gold:
Nay, we will *concumbere* gold. I will be puissant,
And mightie in my talke to her! Here shee comes.
FAC. To him, DOL, suckle him. This is the noble knight,
I told your ladiship—— MAM. Madame, with your pardon,
I kisse your vesture. DOL. Sir, I were vn-ciuill
If I would suffer that, my lip to you, sir.
MAM. I hope, my lord your brother be in health, lady?
DOL. My lord, my brother is, though I no ladie, sir.
FAC. (Well said my *Guiny*-bird.) MAM. Right noble madame——
FAC. (O, we shall haue most fierce idolatrie!)
MAM. 'Tis your prerogatiue. DOL. Rather your courtesie.
MAM. Were there nought else t'inlarge your vertues, to me,
These answeres speake your breeding, and your bloud.
DOL. Bloud we boast none, sir, a poore Baron's daughter.
MAM. Poore! and gat you? Prophane not. Had your father

IV. i. 24 After 'lady.' *Aside, and exit.* G 27 DANAE:] *Danae,*: Q 28 Compar'd] Compa'rd *Q* 31 her!] her. *Q* After 'her!' *Re-enter Face with Dol richly dressed.* G 33 ladiship——] Ladiship. *Q* 35 that,] that; *corr. F2* 36 hope,] hope *F2* 38 (Well . . . -bird.)] Well . . . -bird. *Q* 39 (O, . . . idolatrie!)] O, . . . Idolatry! *Q* 44 Poore!] Poore, *Q* not. Had] not, had *Q*

Slept all the happy remnant of his life
After the act, lyen but there still, and panted,
H'had done inough, to make himselfe, his issue,
And his posteritie noble. DOL. Sir, although
We may be said to want the guilt, and trappings,
The dresse of honor; yet we striue to keepe
The seedes, and the materialls. MAM. I doe see
The old ingredient, vertue, was not lost,
Nor the drug, money, vs'd to make your compound.
There is a strange nobilitie, i' your eye,
This lip, that chin! Me thinks you doe resemble
One o' the *Austriack* princes. FAC. Very like,
Her father was an *Irish* costar-monger.
MAM. The house of *Valois*, iust, had such a nose.
And such a fore-head, yet, the *Medici*
Of *Florence* boast. DOL. Troth, and I haue beene lik'ned
To all these Princes. FAC. I'll be sworne, I heard it.
MAM. I know not how! it is not any one,
But e'en the very choise of all their features.
FAC. I'll in, and laugh. MAM. A certaine touch, or aire,
That sparkles a diuinitie, beyond
An earthly beautie! DOL. O, you play the courtier.
MAM. Good lady, gi' me leaue—— DOL. In faith, I may not,
To mock me, sir. MAM. To burne i' this sweet flame:
The *Phœnix* neuer knew a nobler death.
DOL. Nay, now you court the courtier: and destroy
What you would build. This art, sir, i' your words,
Calls your whole faith in question. MAM. By my soule——
DOL. Nay, oathes are made o' the same aire, sir. MAM. Nature
Neuer bestow'd vpon mortalitie,

IV. i. 49 want] Want *Q originally* guilt] gilt *corr. F2* 53 drug,] *Drug*, Q: drug *Ff* 55 chin!] chinne. *Q* 58 nose.] Nose; *Q* 62 not how! it] not, how; It *Q* 63 e'en] ee'n *Q*, *Ff* 64 After 'laugh.' *Aside and exit.* G 66 beautie!] beauty. *Q* 70 court] court, *Q originally* courtier:] Courtier, *Q* 71 art, . . . words, *Ff*: Art . . . words *Q originally*: Art, . . . words, *corr. Q*

A more vnblam'd, a more harmonious feature:
Shee play'd the step-dame in all faces, else.
Sweet madame, le' me be particular——
DOL. Particular, sir? I pray you, know your distance.
MAM. In no ill sense, sweet lady, but to aske
How your faire graces passe the houres? I see
Yo'are lodg'd, here, i'the house of a rare man,
An excellent Artist: but, what's that to you?
DOL. Yes, sir. I studie here the *mathematiques*,
And distillation. MAM. O, I crie your pardon.
H'is a diuine instructer! can extract
The soules of all things, by his art; call all
The vertues, and the miracles of the Sunne,
Into a temperate fornace: teach dull nature
What her owne forces are. A man, the Emp'rour
Has courted, aboue KELLEY: sent his medalls,
And chaines, t'inuite him. DOL. I, and for his physick, sir——
MAM. Aboue the art of ÆSCVLAPIVS,
That drew the enuy of the Thunderer!
I know all this, and more. DOL. Troth, I am taken, sir,
Whole, with these studies, that contemplate nature:
MAM. It is a noble humour. But, this forme
Was not intended to so darke a vse!
Had you beene crooked, foule, of some course mould,
A cloyster had done well: but, such a feature
That might stand vp the glorie of a kingdome,
To liue recluse! is a mere *solœcisme*,
Though in a nunnery. It must not be.
I muse, my lord your brother will permit it!
You should spend halfe my land first, were I hee.
Do's not this diamant better, on my finger,
Then i' the quarrie? DOL. Yes. MAM. Why, you are like it.

IV. i. 80 houres] howers *Q* 84 your] you *F2* 86 art;] art, *Q* 93 Thunderer!] *Thunderer.* Q 96 humour] Humor *Q*: humor *F2* 97 intended] entended *Q* vse!] vse. *Q* 101 recluse!] recluse? *Q* *solœcisme*] *solæcisme* Q, Ff 103 it!] it: *Q* 106 Then] Than *F2*

You were created, lady, for the light!
Heare, you shall weare it; take it, the first pledge
Of what I speake: to binde you, to beleeue me.
D o l. In chaines of adamant? M a m. Yes, the strongest
bands.
And take a secret, too. Here, by your side,
Doth stand, this houre, the happiest man, in *Europe*.
D o l. You are contented, sir? M a m. Nay, in true
being:
The enuy of Princes, and the feare of States.
D o l. Say you so, sir E p i c v r e! M a m. Yes, & thou
shalt proue it,
Daughter of honor. I haue cast mine eye
Vpon thy forme, and I will reare this beautie,
Aboue all stiles. D o l. You meane no treason, sir!
M a m. No, I will take away that iealousie.
I am the lord of the *Philosophers stone*,
And thou the lady. D o l. How sir! ha' you that?
M a m. I am the master of the *maistrie*.
This day, the good old wretch, here, o' the house
Has made it for vs. Now, hee's at *proiection*.
Thinke therefore, thy first wish, now; let me heare it:
And it shall raine into thy lap, no shower,
But flouds of gold, whole cataracts, a deluge,
To get a nation on thee! D o l. You are pleas'd, sir,
To worke on the ambition of our sexe.
M a m. I'am pleas'd, the glorie of her sexe should know,
This nooke, here, of the *Friers*, is no climate
For her, to liue obscurely in, to learne
Physick, and surgery, for the Constables wife
Of some odde Hundred in *Essex*; but come forth,
And tast the aire of palaces; eate, drinke
The toyles of *Emp'ricks*, and their boasted practice;
Tincture of pearle, and corrall, gold, and amber;

IV. i. 107 the light!] light. *Q* 112 houre] hower *Q* in] of *Q* 115 Dol.] Dol, *Q* Epicvre!] *Epicure?* Q 118 sir!] Sir? *Q* 121 sir!] Sir, *Q* 135 palaces;] *Palaces,* Q 136 *Emp'ricks*] *Empricks* Q

Be seene at feasts, and triumphs ; haue it ask'd,
What miracle shee is ? set all the eyes
Of court a-fire, like a burning glasse,
And worke 'hem into cinders ; when the iewells
Of twentie states adorne thee ; and the light
Strikes out the starres ; that, when thy name is mention'd,
Queenes may looke pale : and, we but shewing our loue,
NERO's POPPÆA may be lost in storie !
Thus, will we haue it. DOL. I could well consent, sir.
But, in a monarchy, how will this be ?
The Prince will soone take notice ; and both seize
You, and your *stone :* it being a wealth vnfit
For any priuate subiect. MAM. If he knew it.
DOL. Your selfe doe boast it, sir. MAM. To thee, my life.
DOL. O, but beware, sir ! You may come to end
The remnant of your daies, in a loth'd prison,
By speaking of it. MAM. 'Tis no idle feare !
Wee'll therefore goe with all, my girle, and liue
In a free state ; where we will eate our mullets,
Sous'd in high-countrey wines, sup phesants egges,
And haue our cockles, boild in siluer shells,
Our shrimps to swim againe, as when they liu'd,
In a rare butter, made of dolphins milke,
Whose creame do's looke like opalls : and, with these
Delicate meats, set our selues high for pleasure,
And take vs downe againe, and then renew
Our youth, and strength, with drinking the *elixir,*
And so enioy a perpetuitie
Of life, and lust. And, thou shalt ha' thy wardrobe,
Richer then *Natures,* still, to change thy selfe,
And vary oftener, for thy pride, then shee :
Or *Art,* her wise, and almost-equall seruant.

IV. i. 144 we] we, *Q* 145 POPPÆA *F2* : POPPæA *F1* storie !] story. *Q* 148 notice ;] notice, *Q* 149 *stone :*] *Stone,* Q 152 sir !] Sir. *Q* 154 feare !] feare. *Q* 155 with all] withall *F2* 156 state ;] *State,* Q 163 againe,] againe ; *Q* 164 *elixir,*] *Elixir :* Q 167–8 then] than *F2* 169 -equall] -æquall *Q* After 169 *Re-enter Face.* G

FAC. Sir, you are too loud. I heare you, euery word,
Into the laboratory. Some fitter place.
The garden, or great chamber aboue. How like you her?
MAM. Excellent! *Lungs.* There's for thee. FAC. But, doe you heare?
Good sir, beware, no mention of the *Rabbines.*
MAM. We thinke not on 'hem. FAC. O, it is well, sir. SVBTLE!

Act IIII. *Scene* II.

FACE, SVBTLE, KASTRIL, DAME PLIANT.

DOst thou not laugh? SVB. Yes. Are they gone? FAC. All's cleare.
SVB. The widdow is come. FAC. And your quarrelling disciple?
SVB. I. FAC. I must to my Captaine-ship againe, then.
SVB. Stay, bring 'hem in, first. FAC. So I meant. What is shee?
A *Bony-bell?* SVB. I know not. FAC. Wee'll draw lots,
You'll stand to that? SVB. What else? FAC. O, for a suite,
To fall now, like a cortine: flap. SVB. To th' dore, man.
FAC. You'll ha' the first kisse, 'cause I am not readie.
SVB. Yes, and perhaps hit you through both the nostrils.
FAC. Who would you speak with? KAS. Wher's the Captaine? FAC. Gone, sir,
About some businesse. KAS. Gone? FAC. Hee'll returne straight.
But master Doctor, his Lieutenant, is here.

IV. i. 171 laboratory.] *Laboratory*: Q: labaratory. *Ff* place.] place, *Q* 175 After "hem.' *Exeunt Mam. and Dol.* G SVBTLE!] *Subtle*— Q
IV. ii. *Enter Subtle.* G, continuing the scene 1 cleare.] cleare *F1 originally* 5 *-bell?*] *-Bell??* Q 7 cortine] Curtine *Q*: Curtain *F3* 8 *Exit.* add G 10–11 FAC. . . . KAS. . . .] *Face.* [*within.*] . . . *Kas.* [*within.*] G (for all speeches) After 12 *Enter Kastril, followed by Dame Pliant.* G

SVB. Come neere, my worshipfull Boy, my *terræ Fili*,
That is, my Boy of land; make thy approches:
Welcome, I know thy lusts, and thy desires,
And I will serue, and satisfie 'hem. Beginne,
Charge me from thence, or thence, or in this line;
Here is my center: Ground thy quarrell. KAS. You lie.
SVB. How, child of wrath, and anger! the loud lie?
For what, my sodaine Boy? KAS. Nay, that looke you too,
I am afore-hand. SVB. O, this's no true *Grammar*,
And as ill *Logick!* You must render causes, child,
Your first, and second *Intentions*, know your *canons*,
And your *diuisions*, *moodes*, *degrees*, and *differences*,
Your *prædicaments*, *substance*, and *accident*,
Series externe, and *interne*, with their *causes*
Efficient, *materiall*, *formall*, *finall*,
And ha' your *elements* perfect—— KAS. What is this
The angrie tongue he talkes in? SVB. That false precept,
Of being afore-hand, has deceiu'd a number;
And made 'hem enter quarrells, often-times,
Before they were aware: and, afterward,
Against their wills. KAS. How must I doe then, sir?
SVB. I crie this lady mercy. Shee should, first,
Haue beene saluted. I doe call you lady,
Because you are to be one, ere't be long,
He kisses her. My soft, and buxome widdow. KAS. Is shee, i-faith?
SVB. Yes, or my art is an egregious lyar.
KAS. How know you? SVB. By inspection, on her fore-head,
He kisses her againe. And subtiltie of her lip, which must be tasted
Often, to make a iudgement. 'Slight, shee melts
Like a *Myrobalane!* Here is, yet, a line
In *riuo frontis*, tells me, he is no knight.
PLI. What is he then, sir? SVB. Let me see your hand.

IV. ii. 15 lusts] lust *F2* 20 sodaine] sudden *F3* (*so usually*) too,] too; *Q*: to, *F3* 22 *Logick!*] *Logick.* Q 28 perfect——] perfect. *Q* this *Q*: this! *Ff* 29 After 'in?' *Aside.* G precept] præcept *Q* 37, 40 *Stage directions not in Q* 38 SVB.] SUR. *F2*

O, your *linea Fortunæ* makes it plaine;
And *stella*, here, in *monte Veneris:*
But, most of all, *iunctura annularis.*
He is a souldier, or a man of art, lady:
But shall haue some great honour, shortly. PLI. Brother,
Hee's a rare man, beleeue me! KAS. Hold your peace.
Here comes the tother rare man. 'Saue you Captaine.
FAC. Good master KASTRIL. Is this your sister?
KAS. I, sir.
Please you to kusse her, and be proud to know her?
FAC. I shall be proud to know you, ladie. PLI. Brother,
He calls me ladie, too. KAS. I, peace. I heard it.
FAC. The *Count* is come. SVB. Where is he? FAC. At the dore.
SVB. Why, you must entertaine him. FAC. What'll you doe
With these the while? SVB. Why, haue 'hem vp, and shew 'hem
Some fustian booke, or the darke glasse. FAC. 'Fore god,
Shee is a delicate dab-chick! I must haue her.
SVB. Must you? I, if your fortune will, you must.
Come sir, the Captaine will come to vs presently.
I'll ha' you to my chamber of *demonstrations*,
Where I'll shew you both the *Grammar*, and *Logick*,
And *Rhetorick* of quarrelling; my whole method,
Drawne out in tables: and my instrument,
That hath the seuerall scale vpon't, shall make you
Able to quarrell, at a strawes breadth, by *Moone*-light.
And, lady, I'll haue you looke in a glasse,
Some halfe an houre, but to cleare your eye-sight,
Against you see your fortune: which is greater,
Then I may iudge vpon the sodaine, trust me.

IV. ii. 50 me!] me. *Q* After 'me!' *Re-enter Face, in his uniform.* G 55 *Takes her aside.* add G 59 god] God *Q* 60 *Exit.* add G 61 Must] Must, *Q* 65 quarrelling;] Quarrelling, *Q* 66 tables:] Tables, *Q* 67 scale] Scales *F3* 70 houre] hower *Q* 71 fortune:] Fortune, *Q* 72 Then] Than *F2* After 72 *Exit, followed by Kast. and Dame P.* G

Act IIII. *Scene* III.

FACE, SVBTLE, SVRLY.

WHere are you, Doctor? SVB. I'll come to you presently.
FAC. I will ha' this same widdow, now I ha' seene her,
On any composition. SVB. What doe you say?
FAC. Ha' you dispos'd of them? SVB. I ha' sent 'hem vp.
FAC. SVBTLE, in troth, I needs must haue this widdow.
SVB. Is that the matter? FAC. Nay, but heare me.
SVB. Goe to,
If you rebell once, DOL shall know it all.
Therefore be quiet, and obey your chance.
FAC. Nay, thou art so violent now—— Doe but conceiue:
Thou art old, and canst not serue—— SVB. Who, cannot I?
'Slight, I will serue her with thee, for a—— FAC. Nay,
But vnderstand: I'll gi' you composition.
SVB. I will not treat with thee: what, sell my fortune?
'Tis better then my birth-right. Doe not murmure.
Winne her, and carrie her. If you grumble, DOL
Knowes it directly. FAC. Well sir, I am silent.
Will you goe helpe, to fetch in *Don*, in state?
SVB. I follow you, sir: we must keepe FACE in awe,
Or he will ouer-looke vs like a tyranne.
Surly like a Spaniard. Braine of a taylor! Who comes here? *Don* ION!
SVR. *Sennores, beso las manos, à vuestras mercedes.*
SVB. Would you had stoup'd a little, and kist our *anos.*

IV. iii. *Re-enter Face.* G, continuing the scene 1 SVB.] *Sub.* [*within.*] G 3 After 'composition.' *Re-enter Subtle.* G SVB.] SVB.. *Q* 4 ha' sent] h'sent *F2* 9 now——] now. *Q* 11 'Slight] 'Sblood *Q* 12 gi'] giue *Q* 14 then] than *F2* 17 *Exit.* add G 18 sir:] Sir, *Q* 19 tyranne] Tyrant *F3* After 19 *Re-enter Face, introducing Surly disguised as a Spaniard.* G 20, 42 *Stage directions not in Q* 20 ION] *John* F3 21 *beso las* Q, F2: *besolas* F1

FAC. Peace SVBTLE. SVB. Stab me; I shall neuer
hold, man.
He lookes in that deepe ruffe, like a head in a platter,
Seru'd in by a short cloake vpon two tressils!
FAC. Or, what doe you say to a collar of brawne, cut
downe
Beneath the souse, and wriggled with a knife?
SVB. 'Slud, he do's looke too fat to be a *Spaniard.*
FAC. Perhaps some *Fleming,* or some *Hollander* got him
In D'ALVA's time: *Count* EGMONTS bastard. SVB.
Don,
Your sciruy, yellow, *Madrid* face is welcome.
SVR. *Gratia.* SVB. He speakes, out of a fortification.
'Pray god, he ha' no squibs in those deepe sets.
SVR. *Por dios, Sennores, muy linda casa!*
SVB. What sayes he? FAC. Praises the house, I thinke,
I know no more but's action. SVB. Yes, the *Casa,*
My precious DIEGO, will proue faire inough,
To cossen you in. Doe you marke? you shall
Be cossened, DIEGO. FAC. Cossened, doe you see?
My worthy *Donzel,* cossened. SVR. *Entiendo.*
SVB. Doe you intend it? So doe we, deare *Don.*
Haue you brought pistolets? or portagues? *He feeles his pockets.*
My solemne *Don?* Dost thou feele any? FAC. Full.
SVB. You shall be emptied, *Don;* pumped, and drawne,
Drie, as they say. FAC. Milked, in troth, sweet *Don.*
SVB. See all the monsters; the great lyon of all, *Don.*
SVR. *Con licencia, se puedè ver à esta Sennorà?*
SVB. What talkes he now? FAC. O'the *Sennora.*
SVB. O, *Don,*
That is the lyonesse, which you shall see
Also, my *Don.* FAC. 'Slid, SVBTLE, how shall we doe?
SVB. For what? FAC. Why, DOL's emploi'd, you
know. SVB. That's true!

IV. iii. 25 tressils!] tressils. *Q, F2* 31 *Madrid*] *Madril* Q 33 god] God *Q* 36 *Casa,*] *Casa!* F2 46 SVB.] SWB. *F2* 47 *Sennorà*] *Sennora* F2 51 true!] true. *Q*

'Fore heau'n I know not: He must stay, that's all.

FAC. Stay? That he must not by no meanes. SVB. No, why?

FAC. Vnlesse you'll marre all. 'Slight, hee'll suspect it.
And then he will not pay, not halfe so well.
This is a trauell'd punque-master, and do's know
All the delayes: a notable hot raskall,
And lookes, already, rampant. SVB. 'Sdeath, and MAMMON
Must not be troubled. FAC. MAMMON, in no case!

SVB. What shall we doe then? FAC. Thinke: you must be sodaine.

SVR. *Entiendo, que la Sennora es tan hermosa, que codìcio tan*
à verla, como la bien auenturánça de mi vida.

FAC. *Mi vida?* 'Slid, SVBTLE, he puts me in minde o'the widow.
What dost thou say to draw her to it? ha?
And tell her, it is her fortune. All our venter
Now lies vpon't. It is but one man more,
Which on's chance to haue her: and, beside,
There is no maiden-head, to be fear'd, or lost.
What dost thou thinke on't, SVBTLE? SVB. Who, I? Why——

FAC. The credit of our house too is engag'd.

SVB. You made me an offer for my share e're while.
What wilt thou gi' me, i-faith? FAC. O, by that light,
Ile not buy now. You know your doome to me.
E'en take your lot, obey your chance, sir; winne her,
And weare her, out for me. SVB. 'Slight. I'll not worke her then.

FAC. It is the common cause, therefore bethinke you.
DOL else must know it, as you said. SVB. I care not.

SVR. *Sennores, por que se tarda tanta?*

IV. iii. 54 hee'll] he will *G* 59 MAMMON] MAMMOM *F2* 62 *à* om. G *verla* G: *ver la* Q, Ff *auenturánça*] *auenturánza* F2 64 to it *G*: to't *Q, Ff* 65 venter] venture *F3* 75 her, out] her out, *F3* 78 *porque* G: *por que* Q, Ff *tarda tanta*] *tàrda tánta* Q: *tarda tanto* G

SVB. Faith, I am not fit, I am old. FAC. That's now no reason, sir.
SVR. *Puede ser, de hazer burla de mi amor.*
FAC. You heare the *Don*, too? By this ayre, I call,
And loose the hinges. DOL. SVB. A plague of hell——
FAC. Will you then doe? SVB. Yo'are a terrible rogue,
Ile thinke of this: will you, sir, call the widow?
FAC. Yes, and Ile take her too, with all her faults,
Now I doe thinke on't better. SVB. With all my heart, sir,
Am I discharg'd o'the lot? FAC. As you please. SVB. Hands.
FAC. Remember now, that, vpon any change,
You neuer claime her. SVB. Much good ioy, and health to'you, sir.
Marry a whore? *Fate*, let me wed a witch first.
SVR. *Por estas honrada's barbas*—— SVB. He sweares by his beard.
Dispatch, and call the brother too. SVR. *Tiengo dùda, Sennores,*
Que on me hágan alguna traycion.
SVB. How, issue on? Yes, *præsto Sennor*. Please you
Enthratha the *chambratha*, worthy *Don*;
Where if it please the *Fates*, in your *bathada*,
You shall be sok'd, and strok'd, and tub'd, and rub'd:
And scrub'd, and fub'd, deare *Don*, before you goe.
You shall, in faith, my sciruie babioun *Don*:
Be curried, claw'd, and flaw'd, and taw'd, indeed.
I will the heartilier goe about it now,
And make the widdow a punke, so much the sooner,
To be reueng'd on this impetuous FACE:
The quickly doing of it is the grace.

IV. iii. 81 call, *Q*: call. *Ff* 82 hinges. *Q*: hinges, *Ff* 84 widow] Widodw *F2* 86 sir,] Sir. *Q* 87 *They take hands.* add G 88 that, *Q*: that *Ff* 89 to'you *Q*: to you *Ff* 90 witch] Witch, *Q* 92 After 'too.' *Exit Face.* G *Tiengo*] *Tengo* G 99 babioun] Babion *Q*: Baboon *F3* After 104 *Exeunt Sub. and Surly.* G

Act IIII. *Scene* IIII.

FACE, KASTRIL, DA. PLIANT, SVBTLE, SVRLY.

COme ladie : I knew, the Doctor would not leaue,
Till he had found the very nick of her fortune.
KAS. To be a *Countesse*, say you ? ⟨FAC.⟩ A *Spanish Countesse*, sir.
PLI. Why ? is that better then an *English Countesse ?*
FAC. Better ? 'Slight, make you that a question, ladie ?
KAS. Nay, shee is a foole, Captaine, you must pardon her.
FAC. Aske from your courtier, to your innes of court-man,
To your mere millaner : they will tell you all,
Your *Spanish* iennet is the best horse. Your *Spanish*
Stoupe is the best garbe. Your *Spanish* beard
Is the best cut. Your *Spanish* ruffes are the best
Weare. Your *Spanish Pauin* the best daunce.
Your *Spanish* titillation in a gloue
The best perfume. And, for your *Spanish* pike,
And *Spanish* blade, let your poore Captaine speake.
Here comes the Doctor. SVB. My most honor'd ladie,
(For so I am now to stile you, hauing found
By this my *scheme*, you are to vnder-goe
An honorable fortune, very shortly.)
What will you say now, if some—— FAC. I ha' told her all, sir.
And her right worshipfull brother, here, that shee shall be
A *Countesse :* doe not delay 'hem, sir. A *Spanish Countesse*.
SVB. Still, my scarse worshipfull Captaine, you can keepe

IV. iv. SCENE II. | *Another Room in the same.* | *Enter Face, Kastril, and Dame Pliant.* G 3 FAC. *Q* : *om. Ff* 4 then] than *F2* (*so* 44) 8 millaner : they] Millaner ; They *Q* 16 After 'Doctor.' *Enter Subtle with a paper.* G honor'd] honour'd *F2* 17–19 (For . . . shortly.)] For . . . shortly. *Q* 19 honorable] honourable *Q, F2* 20 ha'] had *F2*

No secret. Well, since he has told you, madame,
Doe you forgiue him, and I doe. KAS. Shee shall doe that, sir.
I'le looke to't, 'tis my charge. SVB. Well then. Nought rests
But that shee fit her loue, now, to her fortune.
PLI. Truely, I shall neuer brooke a *Spaniard*. SVB. No?
PLI. Neuer, sin' *eighty-eight* could I abide 'hem,
And that was some three yeere afore I was borne, in truth.
SVB. Come, you must loue him, or be miserable:
Choose, which you will. FAC. By this good rush, perswade her,
Shee will crie straw-berries else, within this twelue-month.
SVB. Nay, shads, and mackrell, which is worse. FAC. Indeed, sir?
KAS. Gods lid, you shall loue him, or Ile kick you. PLI. Why?
Ile doe as you will ha' me, brother. KAS. Doe,
Or by this hand, I'll maull you. FAC. Nay, good sir,
Be not so fierce. SVB. No, my enraged child,
Shee will be rul'd. What, when shee comes to tast
The pleasures of a Countesse! to be courted——
FAC. And kist, and ruffled! SVB. I, behind the hangings.
FAC. And then come forth in pomp! SVB. And know her state!
FAC. Of keeping all th'idolaters o'the chamber
Barer to her, then at their prayers! SVB. Is seru'd
Vpon the knee! FAC. And has her pages, huishers,
Foot-men, and coaches—— SVB. Her sixe mares——
FAC. Nay, eight!
SVB. To hurry her through *London*, to th'*Exchange*,
Bet'lem, the *China*-houses—— FAC. Yes, and haue

IV. iv. 30 borne,] borne *Q* 37 sir,] Sir. *Q* 39 What,] What *Q* 40 Countesse!] Countesse, *Q* 41 ruffled!] ruffled—— *Q* 42 pomp!] pompe—— *Q* SVB.] SUR. *F2* (*so* 44) state!] State—— *Q* 44 prayers!] prayers—— *Q* 45 knee!] knee—— *Q* huishers] ushers *F2* 46 eight!] eight—— *Q* 48 -houses] -house *F2*

The citizens gape at her, and praise her tyres!
And my-lords goose-turd bands, that rides with her!
KAS. Most braue! By this hand, you are not my suster,
If you refuse. PLI. I will not refuse, brother.
SVR. *Que es esto, Sennores, que non se venga?*
Esta tardanza me mata! FAC. It is the *Count* come!
The Doctor knew he would be here, by his art.
SVB. *En gallanta Madama, Don! gallantissima!*
SVR. *Por tódos los dioses, la mas acabada*
Hermosura, que he visto en mi vìda!
FAC. Is't not a gallant language, that they speake?
KAS. An admirable language! Is't not *French?*
FAC. No, *Spanish*, sir. KAS. It goes like law-*French*,
And that, they say, is the court-liest language. FAC. List, sir.
SVR. *El Sol ha perdido su lumbre, con el*
Resplandor, que tràe esta dama. Valgame dios!
FAC. He'admires your sister. KAS. Must not shee make curtsie?
SVB. 'Ods will, shee must goe to him, man; and kisse him!
It is the *Spanish* fashion, for the women
To make first court. FAC. 'Tis true he tells you, sir:
His art knowes all. SVR. *Per que no se acùde?*
KAS. He speakes to her, I thinke? FAC. That he do's sir.
SVR. *Por el amor de dios, que es esto, que se tàrda?*
KAS. Nay, see: shee will not vnderstand him! Gull.
Noddy. PLI. What say you brother? KAS. Asse, my suster,
Goe kusse him, as the cunning man would ha' you,
I'll thrust a pinne i' your buttocks else. FAC. O, no sir.
SVR. *Sennora mia, mi persona muy indigna esta*
A llegar à tànta Hermosura.

IV. iv. 49 tyres!] Tires, *Q* 50 her!] her. *Q* After 52 *Enter Surly*. G 53 SVR.] SUB. *F2* *esto*] *èsto* Q 54 come!] come. *Q* 58 *Hermosura*] *Hermosùra* Q 63 *lumbre*] *lúmbre* Q 64 *Resplandor*] *esplandor* G *Valgame* G: *Valga me* Q, Ff 66 him!] him: *Q* 72 him!] him. *Q* 74 you,] you. *Q* 77 *A llegar* Schelling: *Alle gar* Q, Ff: *Allegar* G *Hermosura*] *Hermofura* F2

FAC. Do's he not vse her brauely? KAS. Brauely, i-faith!
FAC. Nay, he will vse her better. KAS. Doe you thinke so?
SVR. *Sennora, si sera seruida, entremos.*
KAS. Where do's he carry her? FAC. Into the garden, sir;
Take you no thought: I must interpret for her.
SVB. Giue DOL the word. Come, my fierce child, aduance,
Wee'll to our quarrelling lesson againe. KAS. Agreed.
I loue a *Spanish* Boy, with all my heart.
SVB. Nay, and by this meanes, sir, you shall be brother
To a great *Count*. KAS. I, I knew that, at first.
This match will aduance the house of the KASTRILS.
SVB. 'Pray god, your sister proue but pliant. KAS. Why,
Her name is so: by her other husband. SVB. How!
KAS. The widdow PLIANT. Knew you not that? SVB. No faith, sir.
Yet, by erection of her *figure*, I gest it.
Come, let's goe practice. KAS. Yes, but doe you thinke, Doctor,
I e'er shall quarrell well? SVB. I warrant you.

Act IIII. *Scene* V.

DOL, MAMMON, FACE, SVBTLE.

FOr, *after* ALEXANDERS *death*—— MAM. Good lady—— *In her fit of talking.*
DOL. *That* PERDICCAS, *and* ANTIGONVS *were slaine,*

IV. iv. 80 *entremos* Schelling: *entremus* Q, Ff *Exit with dame Pliant.* add G 81 sir;] Sir, *Q* 82 thought:] thought, *Q* 83 After word.' *Aside to Face, who goes out.* G child, aduance] Child. Aduance *Q* 89 god] God *Q, F2* 90 so:] so, *Q* 93 Doctor,] Doctor. *Q* 94 *Exeunt.* add G IV. v. SCENE III. | *Another Room in the same.* | *Enter Dol in her fit of raving, followed by Mammon.* G SVBTLE.] SVBTLE: *F1* *The stage directions at* ll. 1, 25, 33, 55, 62, 66, 77 *are not in Q* 1–23 *Dol's speeches in roman in Q*

The two that stood, Selevc', *and* Ptolomee——
Mam. Madame. Dol. *Made vp the two legs, and the fourth Beast.*
That was Gog-north, and Egypt-south: which after
Was call'd Gog Iron-leg, and South Iron-leg—— Mam. Lady——
Dol. *And then Gog-horned. So was Egypt, too.*
Then Egypt clay-leg, and Gog clay-leg—— Mam. Sweet madame.
Dol. *And last Gog-dust, and Egypt-dust, which fall*
In the last linke of the fourth chaine. And these
Be starres in story, which none see, or looke at——
Mam. What shall I doe? Dol. *For, as he sayes, except*
We call the Rabbines, and the heathen Greekes——
Mam. Deare lady. Dol. *To come from Salem, and from Athens,*
And teach the people of great Britaine—— Fac. What's the matter, sir?
Dol. *To speake the tongue of* Eber, *and* Iavan—— Mam. O,
Sh'is in her fit. Dol. *We shall know nothing*—— Fac. Death, sir,
We are vn-done. Dol. *Where, then, a learned Linguist*
Shall see the antient vs'd communion
Of vowells, and consonants—— Fac. My master will heare!
Dol. *A wisedome, which* Pythagoras *held most high*——
Mam. Sweet honorable lady. Dol. *To comprise*
All sounds of voyces, in few markes of letters——
Fac. Nay, you must neuer hope to lay her now.

They speake together.

Dol. And so we may arriue by *Talmud* skill,

Fac. How did you put her in-to't? Mam. Alas I talk'd

IV. v. 7–9 *Egypt*] *Ægypt* Q 9 *-dust* :] *-Dust,* Q 15 After '*Britaine*' *Enter Face hastily in his servant's dress.* G 17 Sh'is] Sh's *F2* *originally* (*corrected*) 22 honorable] honourable *F2* 25–33 *F2* *prints in roman in one column, with Dol's speech first. Corrected to italic in l. p. copy. The stage direction* 'They speake together' *loses all point by being placed in the margin and appearing to refer to Face and Mammon's speeches*

And profane *greeke*, to raise the building vp
Of HELENS house, against the *Ismaelite*,
King of *Thogarma*, and his *Habergions*
Brimstony, blew, and fiery; and the force
Of King ABADDON, and the Beast of *Cittim:*
Which *Rabbi* DAVID KIMCHI, ONKELOS,
And ABEN-EZRA doe interpret *Rome.*

Of a fift *Monarchy* I would erect,
With the *Philosophers stone* (by chance) and shee
Fals on the other foure, straight. FAC. Out of BROVGHTON!
I told you so. 'Slid stop her mouth. MAM. Is't best?
FAC. She'll neuer leaue else. If the old man heare her,
We are but *fæces*, ashes. SVB. What's to doe there?
FAC. O, we are lost. Now she heares him, she is quiet.

MAM. Where shall I hide me? SVB. How! What sight is here! *Vpon Subtles entry they disperse.*
Close deeds of darknesse, and that shunne the light!
Bring him againe. Who is he? What, my sonne!
O, I haue liu'd too long. MAM. Nay good, deare father,
There was no'vnchast purpose. SVB. Not? and flee me,
When I come in? MAM. That was my error. SVB. Error?
Guilt, guilt, my sonne. Giue it the right name. No maruaile,
If I found check in our *great worke* within,
When such affaires as these were managing!
MAM. Why, haue you so? SVB. It has stood still this halfe houre:
And all the rest of our *lesse workes* gone back.
Where is the instrument of wickednesse,
My lewd false drudge? MAM. Nay, good sir, blame not him.
Beleeue me, 'twas against his will, or knowledge.
I saw her by chance. SVB. Will you commit more sinne,
T'excuse a varlet? MAM. By my hope, 'tis true, sir.

IV. v. 25, 29 MAM. *Q, F2*: MAN. *F1* 26 fift] fifth *F2* 27 With] Which *Q* *stone* om. F2 originally (corrected), F3 28 foure,] foure *Q* 29 Brimstony] Brimstoni *F2 originally* (*corrected*) 30 ABADDON *F2*: ABADDON *F1* 31 *fæces* F2: *fœces* Q, F1 31 SVB.] *Sub.* [*within.*] G 36 O,] O *F2 originally* (*corrected*) 41 managing!] managing. *Q* 42 stood still] gone back *Q* 43 gone back] stand still *Q*

Svb. Nay, then I wonder lesse, if you, for whom
The blessing was prepar'd, would so tempt heauen:
And loose your fortunes. Mam. Why, sir? Svb. This'll retard
The *worke*, a month at least. Mam. Why, if it doe,
What remedie? but thinke it not, good father:
Our purposes were honest. Svb. As they were,
So the reward will proue. How now! Aye me.
A great crack and noise within.
God, and all Saints be good to vs. What's that?
Fac. O sir, we are defeated! all the *workes*
Are flowne *in fumo:* euery glasse is burst.
Fornace, and all rent downe! as if a bolt
Of thunder had beene driuen through the house.
Retorts, Receiuers, Pellicanes, Bolt-heads,
All strooke in shiuers! Helpe, good sir! Alas,
Subtle falls downe as in a swoune.
Coldnesse, and death inuades him. Nay, sir Mammon,
Doe the faire offices of a man! You stand,
As you were readier to depart, then he.
One knocks.
Who's there? My lord her brother is come. Mam. Ha, *Lungs?*
Fac. His coach is at the dore. Auoid his sight,
For hee's as furious, as his sister is mad.
Mam. Alas! Fac. My braine is quite vn-done with the fume, sir,
I ne'er must hope to be mine owne man againe.
Mam. Is all lost, *Lungs?* Will nothing be preseru'd,
Of all our cost? Fac. Faith, very little, sir.
A peck of coales, or so, which is cold comfort, sir.
Mam. O my voluptuous mind! I am iustly punish'd.
Fac. And so am I, sir. Mam. Cast from all my hopes——
Fac. Nay, certainties, sir. Mam. By mine owne base affections.

iv. v. 51 loose] lose *F2* This'll retard] This will hinder *Q* After 56 *Re-enter Face.* G 57 defeated!] defeated: *Q* 58 *fumo:* euery] *fumo.* Euery *Q* 59 downe!] downe: *Q* 62 strooke] struck *F2* shiuers!] shiuers. *Q* sir!] Sir. *Q* 64 man!] man. *Q* 65 then] than *F2* 68 sister is] sister's *G* 74 voluptuous] voluptuouos *F1*

SVB. O, the curst fruits of vice, and lust! MAM. Good father, *Subtle seemes come to himselfe.*
It was my sinne. Forgiue it. SVB. Hangs my roofe
Ouer vs still, and will not fall, ô iustice,
Vpon vs, for this wicked man! FAC. Nay, looke, sir,
You grieue him, now, with staying in his sight:
Good sir, the nobleman will come too, and take you,
And that may breed a *tragœdie*. MAM. I'll goe.
FAC. I, and repent at home, sir. It may be,
For some good penance, you may ha' it, yet,
A hundred pound to the boxe at *Bet'lem*—— MAM. Yes.
FAC. For the restoring such as ha' their wits. MAM. I'll do't.
FAC. Ile send one to you to receiue it. MAM. Doe.
Is no *proiection* left? FAC. All flowne, or stinks, sir.
MAM. Will nought be sau'd, that's good for med'cine, thinkst thou?
FAC. I cannot tell, sir. There will be, perhaps,
Something, about the scraping of the shardes,
Will cure the itch: though not your itch of mind, sir.
It shall be sau'd for you, and sent home. Good sir,
This way: for feare the lord should meet you. SVB. FACE.
FAC. I. SVB. Is he gone? FAC. Yes, and as heauily
As all the gold he hop'd for, were in his bloud.
Let vs be light, though. SVB. I, as balls, and bound
And hit our heads against the roofe for ioy:
There's so much of our care now cast away.
FAC. Now to our *Don*. SVB. Yes, your yong widdow, by this time
Is made a *Countesse*, FACE: Sh'has beene in trauaile
Of a yong heire for you. FAC. Good, sir. SVB. Off with your case,

IV. v. 77 and] aod *F2* 82 nobleman] noble man *F1* 83 *tragœdie*] *Tragedy* Q 85 ha' it] ha't *F2* 86 *Bet'lem*——] *Betlem*. Q 87 as ha'] as——have *G* 95 way:] way, *Q* After 'you.' *Exit Mammon.* G SVB.] *Sub.* [*raising his head.*] G 97 in his] in 's *G* 98 SVB.] *Sub.* [*leaping up.*] G 99 ioy:] ioy. *Q* 103 yong] young *F2*

And greet her kindly, as a bride-groome should,
After these common hazards. FAC. Very well, sir.
Will you goe fetch *Don* DIEGO off, the while?
SVB. And fetch him ouer too, if you'll be pleas'd, sir:
Would DOL were in her place, to pick his pockets now.
FAC. Why, you can doe it as well, if you would set to't.
I pray you proue your vertue. SVB. For your sake, sir.

Act IIII. *Scene* VI.

SVRLY, DA. PLIANT, SVBTLE, FACE.

LAdy, you see into what hands, you are falne;
Mongst what a nest of villaines! and how neere
Your honor was t'haue catch'd a certaine clap
(Through your credulitie) had I but beene
So punctually forward, as place, time,
And other circumstance would ha' made a man:
For yo'are a handsome woman: would yo' were wise, too.
I am a gentleman, come here disguis'd,
Onely to find the knaueries of this *Citadell*,
And where I might haue wrong'd your honor, and haue not,
I claime some interest in your loue. You are,
They say, a widdow, rich: and I am a batcheler,
Worth nought: Your fortunes may make me a man,
As mine ha' preseru'd you a woman. Thinke vpon it,
And whether, I haue deseru'd you, or no. PLI. I will, sir.
SVR. And for these houshold-rogues, let me alone,
To treat with them. SVB. How doth my noble DIEGO?
And my deare madame, *Countesse?* Hath the *Count*
Beene courteous, lady? liberall? and open?
Donzell, me thinkes you looke melancholike,

IV. V. 106 DIEGO off,] *Deigo* off *Q* 108 were] were, *Q* 110 *Exeunt.* add G IV. VI. SCENE IV. | *Another Room in the same.* | *Enter Surly and Dame Pliant.* G 3 catch'd] catc'd *F2* 6 circumstance] circumstances *F2* 13 nought:] naught. *Q* 16 SVR.] SVB. *F1* 17 After 'them.' *Enter Subtle.* G

After your *coitum*, and scuruy! True-ly,
I doe not like the dulnesse of your eye:
It hath a heauy cast, 'tis *vpsee Dutch*,
And say's you are a lumpish whore-master.
Be lighter, I will make your pockets so. *He falls to picking of them.*
SVR. Will you, *Don* bawd, and pick-purse? How now? Reele you?
Stand vp sir, you shall find since I am so heauy,
I'll gi' you equall weight. SVB. Helpe, murder! SVR. No, sir.
There's no such thing intended. A good cart,
And a cleane whip shall ease you of that feare.
I am the *Spanish Don*, that should be cossened,
Doe you see? cossened? Where's your Captayne FACE?
That parcell-broker, and whole-bawd, all raskall.
FAC. How, SVRLY! SVR. O, make your approach, good Captaine.
I'haue found, from whence your copper rings, and spoones
Come, now, wherewith you cheate abroad in tauernes.
'Twas here, you learn'd t'anoint your boot with brimstone,
Then rub mens gold on't, for a kind of touch,
And say 'twas naught, when you had chang'd the colour,
That you might ha't for nothing? And this Doctor,
Your sooty, smoakie-bearded compeere, he
Will close you so much gold, in a bolts-head,
And, on a turne, conuay (i'the stead) another
With *sublim'd Mercurie*, that shall burst i'the heate,
And flye out all *in fumo?* Then weepes MAMMON:
Then swounes his worship. Or, he is the FAVSTVS,
That casteth figures, and can coniure, cures
Plague, piles, and poxe, by the *Ephemerides*,
And holds intelligence with all the bawdes,
And midwiues of three shires? while you send in——

IV. vi. 26 SVR.] *Sur.* [*Throws open his cloak.*] G After '-purse?' *strikes him down.* G 28 equall] æquall *Q* murder!] Murder. *Q* After 33 *Enter Face in his uniform.* G 37 anoint] annoint *Q* 45 *fumo ?*] *fumo.* Q 46 After 'worship.' *Face slips out.* G 50 shires ?] Shires. *Q*

Captaine, (what is he gone?) dam'sells with child,
Wiues, that are barren, or, the waiting-maide
With the greene-sicknesse? Nay, sir, you must tarrie
Though he be scap't; and answere, by the eares, sir.

Act IIII. *Scene* VII.

FACE, KASTRIL, SVRLEY, SVBTLE,
DRVGGER, ANANIAS, DA.
PLIANT, DOL.

WHy, now's the time, if euer you will quarrell
Well (as they say) and be a true-borne child.
The Doctor, and your sister both are abus'd.
KAS. Where is he? which is he? he is a slaue
What ere he is, and the sonne of a whore. Are you
The man, sir, I would know? SVR. I should be loth, sir,
To confesse so much. KAS. Then you lie, i'your throate.
SVR. How?
FAC. A very errant rogue, sir, and a cheater,
Employd here, by another coniurer,
That dos not loue the Doctor, and would crosse him
If he knew how—— SVR. Sir, you are abus'd. KAS. You lie:
And 'tis no matter. FAC. Well said, sir. He is
The impudent'st raskall—— SVR. You are indeed. Will you heare me, sir?
FAC. By no meanes: Bid him be gone. KAS. Be gone, sir, quickly.
SVR. This's strange! Lady, doe you informe your brother.
FAC. There is not such a foyst, in all the towne,
The Doctor had him, presently: and findes, yet,
The *Spanish Count* will come, here. Beare vp, SVBTLE.

IV. vi. 53 -sicknesse?] -sicknesse. *Q* After '-sicknesse?' *seizes Subtle as he is retiring*. G IV. vii. *Re-enter Face with Kastril*. G, continuing the scene 11 lie:] lie, *Q* 14 meanes:] meanes. *Q*

SVB. Yes, sir, he must appeare, within this houre.
FAC. And yet this rogue, would come, in a disguise,
By the temptation of another spirit,
To trouble our art, though he could not hurt it. KAS. I,
I know——Away, you talke like a foolish mauther.
SVR. Sir, all is truth, she saies. FAC. Doe not beleeue him, sir:
He is the lying'st Swabber! Come your wayes, sir.
SVR. You are valiant, out of companie. KAS. Yes, how then, sir?
FAC. Nay, here's an honest fellow too, that knowes him,
And all his tricks. (Make good what I say, ABEL,
This cheater would ha' cossen'd thee o'the widdow.)
He owes this honest DRVGGER, here, seuen pound,
He has had on him, in two-penny'orths of *tabacco*.
DRV. Yes sir. And h'has damn'd himselfe, three termes, to pay mee.
FAC. And what do's he owe for *lotium?* DRV. Thirtie shillings, sir:
And for sixe *syringes*. SVR. HYDRA of villanie!
FAC. Nay, sir, you must quarrell him out o'the house. KAS. I will.
Sir, if you get not out o' dores, you lie:
And you are a pimpe. SVR. Why, this is madnesse, sir,
Not valure in you: I must laugh at this.
KAS. It is my humour: you are a Pimpe, and a Trig,
And an AMADIS *de Gaule*, or a *Don* QVIXOTE.
DRV. Or a Knight o'the *curious cox-combe*. Doe you see?
ANA. Peace to the houshold. KAS. Ile keepe peace, for no man.
ANA. Casting of dollers is concluded lawfull.

IV. vii. 19 houre] hower *Q* 23 After 'Away,' *To his sister*. G 26 valiant,] valiant *Q* After 26 *Enter Drugger with a piece of damask*. G 28 (Make] Make *Q* ABEL,] *Abel*, Q: ABEL,) *Ff* 29 widdow.)] Widdow. *Q*: widdow. *Ff* 32 h'has] he hath *Q* himselfe,] himselfe *Q* 36 lie:] lie *Q* 38 valure] valor *F3* 39 humour] humor, *Q* After 41 *Enter Ananias*. G

KAS. Is he the Constable? SVB. Peace, ANANIAS.
FAC. No, sir.
KAS. Then you are an *Otter*, and a *Shad*, a *Whit*,
A very *Tim*. SVR. You'll heare me, sir? KAS. I will not.
ANA. What is the motiue? SVB. Zeale, in the yong gentleman,
Against his *Spanish* slops—— ANA. They are profane,
Leud, superstitious, and idolatrous breeches.
SVR. New raskals! KAS. Will you be gone, sir?
ANA. Auoid *Sathan*,
Thou art not of the light. That ruffe of pride,
About thy neck, betrayes thee: 'and is the same
With that, which the vncleane birds, in *seuenty-seuen*,
Were seene to pranke it with, on diuers coasts.
Thou look'st like *Antichrist*, in that leud hat.
SVR. I must giue way. KAS. Be gone, sir. SVR. But Ile take
A course with you—— (ANA. Depart, proud *Spanish* fiend)
SVR. Captain, & Doctor—— ANA. Child of perdition.
KAS. Hence, sir.
Did I not quarrell brauely? FAC. Yes, indeed, sir.
KAS. Nay, and I giue my mind to't, I shall do't.
FAC. O, you must follow, sir, and threaten him tame.
Hee'll turne againe else. KAS. I'll re-turne him, then.
FAC. DRVGGER, this rogue preuented vs, for thee:
We had determin'd, that thou shouldst ha' come,
In a *Spanish* sute, and ha' carried her so; and he,
A brokerly slaue, goes, puts it on himselfe.
Hast' brought the damaske? DRV. Yes sir. FAC. Thou must borrow,

IV. vii. 47 motiue?] Motiue. *Q*: motiue! *Ff* 57 (ANA. . . . fiend) *corr. F1*: (ANA. . . . fiend. *F1 originally*: ANA. . . . *Fiend.* Q: ANA. . . . fiend. *F2* 58 Doctor——] Doctor. *Q* *Exit Surly.* add G 60 and] an' *F2* do't.] do't, *Q* After 62 *Exit.* | *Subtle takes Ananias aside.* G 64 We had *F2*: We'had *Q, F1*: *query*, We, had 65 he,] he *Q, Ff* 67 Hast' *F2*: Hast *Q, F1*

A *Spanish* suite. Hast thou no credit with the players?
DRV. Yes, sir, did you neuer see me play the foole?
FAC. I know not, NAB: thou shalt, if I can helpe it.
HIERONYMO's old cloake, ruffe, and hat will serue,
Ile tell thee more, when thou bringst 'hem. ANA. Sir, I know
The *Spaniard* hates the *Brethren*, and hath spies
Vpon their actions: and that this was one
I make no scruple. But the holy *Synode*
Haue beene in prayer, and meditation, for it.
And 'tis reueal'd no lesse, to them, then me,
That casting of money is most lawfull. SVB. True.
But here, I cannot doe it; if the house
Should chance to be suspected, all would out,
And we be lock'd vp, in the tower, for euer,
To make gold there (for th' state) neuer come out:
And, then, are you defeated. ANA. I will tell
This to the *Elders*, and the weaker *Brethren*,
That the whole companie of the *Separation*
May ioyne in humble prayer againe. (SVB. And fasting.)
ANA. Yea, for some fitter place. The peace of mind
Rest with these walls. SVB. Thanks, courteous ANANIAS.
FAC. What did he come for? SVB. About casting dollers,
Presently, out of hand. And so, I told him,
A *Spanish* minister came here to spie,
Against the faithfull—— FAC. I conceiue. Come SVBTLE,
Thou art so downe vpon the least disaster!
How wouldst tho'ha' done, if I had not helpt thee out?
SVB. I thanke thee FACE, for the angrie Boy, i-faith.
FAC. Who would ha' lookt, it should ha' beene that raskall?
SVRLY? He had dy'd his beard, and all. Well, sir,
Here's damaske come, to make you a suit. SVB. Where's DRVGGER?

Subtle hath whisperd with him this while.

IV. vii. 70 NAB: thou] *Nab.* Thou *Q* 72 *Stage direction not in Q* *Exit Drugger.* add G 77 then] than *F2* 80 out,] out. *Q* 82 there] there: *Q* out:] out. *Q* 88 After 'walls.' *Exit.* G 98 SVB.] SVB, *Q*

FAC. He is gone to borrow me a *Spanish* habite,
Ile be the *Count*, now. SVB. But where's the widdow?
FAC. Within, with my lords sister: Madame DOL
Is entertayning her. SVB. By your fauour, FACE,
Now shee is honest, I will stand againe.
FAC. You will not offer it? SVB. Why? FAC. Stand to your word,
Or——here comes DOL. She knowes—— SVB. Yo'are tyrannous still.
FAC. Strict for my right. How now, DOL? Hast' told her,
The *Spanish Count* will come? DOL. Yes, but another is come,
You little look'd for! FAC. Who's that? DOL. Your master:
The master of the house. SVB. How, DOL! FAC. Shee lies.
This is some trick. Come, leave your quiblins, DOROTHEE.
DOL. Looke out, and see. SVB. Art thou in earnest? DOL. 'Slight,
Fortie o'the neighbours are about him, talking.
FAC. 'Tis he, by this good day. DOL. 'Twill proue ill day,
For some on vs. FAC. We are vndone, and taken.
DOL. Lost, I'am afraid. SVB. You said he would not come,
While there dyed one a weeke, within the liberties.
FAC. No: 'twas within the walls. SVB. Was't so? Cry'you mercy:
I thought the liberties. What shall we doe now, FACE?
FAC. Be silent: not a word, if he call, or knock.
I'll into mine old shape againe, and meet him,
Of IEREMIE, the butler. I' the meane time,

IV. vii. 104 SVB. *Q*: SVR. *Ff* After 105 *Enter Dol hastily.* G 106 Hast' told] Hast thou told *G* 108 for!] for. *Q* 109 DOL!] *Dol?* Q 111 After 'see.' *Face goes to the window.* G 'Slight,] 'Slight. *F2* 115 I'am *F1, F3*: I am *Q*: I'm *F2* 119 silent:] silent, *Q*

Doe you two pack vp all the goods, and purchase,
That we can carry i' the two trunkes. I'll keepe him
Off for to day, if I cannot longer : and then
At night, Ile ship you both away to *Ratcliffe*,
Where wee'll meet to morrow, and there wee'll share.
Let MAMMON's brasse, and pewter keepe the cellar :
Wee'll haue another time for that. But, DOL,
'Pray thee, goe heate a little water, quickly,
SVBTLE must shaue me. All my Captaines beard
Must off, to make me appeare smooth IEREMIE.
You'll do't? SVB. Yes, Ile shaue you, as well as I can.
FAC. And not cut my throte, but trim me? SVB. You shall see, sir.

Act V. *Scene* I.

LOVE-WIT, NEIGHBOVRS.

HAs there beene such resort, say you? NEI. 1. Daily, sir.
NEI. 2. And nightly, too. NEI. 3. I, some as braue as lords.
NEI. 4. Ladies, and gentlewomen. NEI. 5. Citizens wiues.
NEI. 1. And knights. NEI. 6. In coches. NEI. 2. Yes, & oyster-women.
NEI. 1. Beside other gallants. NEI. 3. Sailors wiues. NEI. 4. *Tabacco*-men.
NEI. 5. Another *Pimlico!* LOV. What should my knaue aduance,
To draw this companie? He hung out no banners
Of a strange Calfe, with fiue legs, to be seene?
Or a huge Lobster, with sixe clawes? NEI. 6. No, sir.
NEI. 3. We had gone in then, sir. LOV. He has no guift

IV. vii. 126 there] then *Q* 129 'Pray thee] 'Pr'y thee *F2* 133 *Exeunt.* add G V. i. ACT V. SCENE I. | *Before Lovewit's door.* | *Enter Lovewit, with several of the neighbours.* G 6 *Pimlico!*] *Pimlico.* Q 9 Lobster] Lobstar *Q*

Of teaching i' the nose, that ere I knew of!
You saw no Bills set vp, that promis'd cure
Of agues, or the tooth-ach? Nei. 2. No such thing, sir.
Lov. Nor heard a drum strooke, for Babiouns, or Puppets?
Nei. 5. Neither, sir. Lov. What deuice should he bring forth now!
I loue a teeming wit, as I loue my nourishment.
'Pray god he ha' not kept such open house,
That he hath sold my hangings, and my bedding:
I left him nothing else. If he haue eate 'hem,
A plague o'the moath, say I. Sure he has got
Some bawdy pictures, to call all this ging;
The Frier, and the Nun; or the new *Motion*
Of the Knights courser, couering the Parsons mare;
The Boy of sixe yeere old, with the great thing:
Or 't may be, he has the Fleas that runne at tilt,
Vpon a table, or some Dog to daunce?
When saw you him? Nei. 1. Who sir, Ieremie?
Nei. 2. Ieremie butler?
We saw him not this mon'th. Lov. How! Nei. 4. Not these 5. weeks, sir.
Nei. ⟨1.⟩ These six weeks, at the least. Lov. Yo' amaze me, neighbours!
Nei. 5. Sure, if your worship know not where he is,
Hee's slipt away. Nei. 6. Pray god, he be not made away!
He knocks.
Lov. Ha? It's no time to question, then. Nei. 6. About
Some three weekes since, I heard a dolefull cry,
As I sate vp, a mending my wiues stockings.
Lov. This's strange! that none will answere! Didst thou heare

v. i. 14 Babiouns] Babouns *Q*: Baboons *F3* or] ot *F2* 17 god] God *Q* (*so* 31) 28 mon'th] mont'h *Q*, *F1*: month *F2* 29, 1 *Ed. conj.*: 6. *F2*. *The* '1' *has dropped out after the* '1' *of* 'Nei.' 31 away !] away. *Q* 32 *Stage direction not in Q* 34 wiues] wifes *F2*

A cry, saist thou? NEI. 6. Yes, sir, like vnto a man
That had beene strangled an houre, and could not speake.
  NEI. 2. I heard it too, iust this day three weekes, at two a clock
Next morning. LOV. These be miracles, or you make 'hem so!
A man an houre strangled, and could not speake,
And both you heard him cry? NEI. 3. Yes, downeward, sir.
  LOV. Thou art a wise fellow: Giue me thy hand, I pray thee.
What trade art thou on? NEI. 3. A smith, and't please your worship.
  LOV. A smith? Then, lend me thy helpe, to get this dore open.
  NEI. 3. That I will presently, sir, but fetch my tooles——
  NEI. 1. Sir, best to knock againe, afore you breake it.

Act V. *Scene* II.

LOVE-WIT, FACE, NEIGHBOVRS.

I Will. FAC. What meane you, sir? NEI. 1. 2. 4. O, here's IEREMIE!
  FAC. Good sir, come from the dore. LOV. Why! what's the matter?
  FAC. Yet farder, you are too neere, yet. LOV. I'the name of wonder!
What meanes the fellow? FAC. The house, sir, has beene visited.
  LOV. What? with the plague? stand thou then farder. FAC. No, sir,
I had it not. LOV. Who had it then? I left

v. i. 37, 40 houre] hower *Q* 42 hand, *Q*: hand *Ff* 43 thou] thou, *Q* and't] an't *F2* 45 *Exit.* add G 46 Sir, best] Sir. Best *Q* v. ii. *Enter Face, in his butler's livery.* G, continuing the scene 2 sir, come] Sir. Come *Q* Why!] Why? *Q* 3, 5 farder] farther *F3* (*so* 15) 3 wonder!] wonder, *Q*

None else, but thee, i'the house! Fac. Yes, sir. My fellow,
The cat, that kept the buttry, had it on her
A weeke, before I spied it: but I got her
Conuay'd away, i'the night. And so I shut
The house vp for a month—— Lov. How! Fac. Purposing then, sir,
T'haue burnt rose-vinegar, triackle, and tarre,
And, ha' made it sweet, that you should ne'er ha' knowne it:
Because I knew the newes would but afflict you, sir.
Lov. Breath lesse, and farder off. Why, this is stranger!
The neighbours tell me all, here, that the dores
Haue still been open—— Fac. How, sir! Lov. Gallants, men, and women,
And of all sorts, tag-rag, beene seene to flock here
In threaues, these ten weekes, as to a second *Hogs-den*,
In dayes of *Pimlico*, and *Eye-bright!* Fac. Sir,
Their wisedomes will not say so! Lov. To day, they speake
Of coaches, and gallants; one in a *French*-hood,
Went in, they tell me: and another was seene
In a veluet gowne, at the windore! diuerse more
Passe in and out! Fac. They did passe through the dores then,
Or walls, I assure their eye-sights, and their spectacles;
For here, sir, are the keyes: and here haue beene,
In this my pocket, now, aboue twentie dayes!
And for before, I kept the fort alone, there.
But, that 'tis yet not deepe i'the after-noone,
I should beleeue my neighbours had seene double
Through the black-pot, and made these apparitions!
For, on my faith, to your worship, for these three weekes,
And vpwards, the dore has not beene open'd. Lov. Strange!

v. ii. 7 Fac.] Face. Fac. *F2* 11 month——] month - - *Q* sir,] Sir. *Q* 17 open——] open. *Q* 20 -*bright!*] *bright*. Sir,] Sir. *Q* 24 windore!] windore. *Q*: window! *F3* 25 out!] out. *Q* 27 keyes:] keyes; *Q* 28 dayes!] dayes. *Q* 32 apparitions!] apparitions: *Q*

NEI. 1. Good faith, I thinke I saw a coach! NEI. 2. And I too,
I'ld ha' beene sworne! LOV. Doe you but thinke it now?
And but one coach? NEI. 4. We cannot tell, sir: IEREMIE
Is a very honest fellow. FAC. Did you see me at all?
NEI. 1. No. That we are sure on. NEI. 2. I'll be sworne o' that.
LOV. Fine rogues, to haue your testimonies built on!
NEI. 3. Is IEREMIE come? NEI. 1. O, yes, you may leaue your tooles,
We were deceiu'd, he sayes. NEI. 2. He'has had the keyes:
And the dore has beene shut these three weekes. NEI. 3. Like enough.
LOV. Peace, and get hence, you changelings. FAC. SVRLY come!
And MAMMON made acquainted? They'll tell all.
(How shall I beate them off? What shall I doe?)
Nothing's more wretched, then a guiltie conscience.

Act V. *Scene* III.

SVRLY, MAMMON, LOVE-WIT, FACE, NEIGHBOVRS, KASTRIL, ANANIAS, TRIBVLATION, DAPPER, SVBTLE.

NO, sir, he was a great physitian. This,
It was no bawdy-house: but a meere *Chancell*.
You knew the lord, and his sister. MAM. Nay, good SVRLY——

v. ii. 36 I'ld] I'lld] *Q*, *F1*: I'll *F2* 37 sir:] Sir. *Q* After 40 *Re-enter third Neighbour, with his tools.* G 41 NEI. 1.] MEI. 1. *Q originally* 42 deceiu'd,] deceiu'd *Q originally* He'has] He has *Q*, *F2* keyes:] keyes, *Q originally* 44 After 'changelings.' *Enter Surly and Mammon.* G 47 then] than *F2* v. iii. *G continues the scene.* ANANIAS.] ANA. *Q* *The stage directions at ll.* 9, 33, 44, 63 *are not in Q*

S v r. The happy word, *be rich*—— M a m. Play not the tyranne——

S v r. Should be to day pronounc'd, to all your friends.
And where be your andirons now? and your brasse pots?
That should ha' beene golden flaggons, and great wedges?

M a m. Let me but breath. What! They ha' shut their dores,
Me thinks! S v r. I, now, 'tis holy-day with them. M a m. Rogues,
Coseners, impostors, bawds. F a c. What meane you, sir?

Mammon and Surly knock.

M a m. To enter if we can. F a c. Another mans house?
Here is the owner, sir. Turne you to him,
And speake your businesse. M a m. Are you, sir, the owner?

L o v. Yes, sir. M a m. And are those knaues, within, your cheaters?

L o v. What knaues? what cheaters? M a m. S v b t l e, and his *Lungs*.

F a c. The gentleman is distracted, sir! No lungs,
Nor lights ha' beene seene here these three weekes, sir,
Within these dores, vpon my word! S v r. Your word,
Groome arrogant? F a c. Yes, sir, I am the house-keeper,
And know the keyes ha' not beene out o' my hands.

S v r. This's a new F a c e? F a c. You doe mistake the house, sir!
What signe was't at? S v r. You raskall! This is one
O' the confederacie. Come, let's get officers,
And force the dore. L o v. 'Pray you stay, gentlemen.

S v r. No, sir, wee'll come with warrant. M a m. I, and then,
We shall ha' your dores open. L o v. What meanes this?

F a c. I cannot tell, sir! N e i. i. These are two o'the gallants,
That we doe thinke we saw. F a c. Two o' the fooles?

v. iii. 8 breath] breathe *F2* 16 sir!] Sir. *Q* 18 word!] word. *Q* 21 Face?] *Face!* Q 23 officers, *F1*: Officers! *Q originally*: Officers, *corr. Q, F2* 26 After 'open.' *Exeunt Mam. and Surly.* G

You talke as idly as they. Good faith, sir,
I thinke the *Moone* has cras'd 'hem all! (O me,
The angrie Boy come too? Hee'll make a noyse,
And nere away till he haue betray'd vs all.)
KAS. What rogues, bawds, slaues, you'll open the dore anone. *Kastrill knocks.*
Punque, cocatrice, my suster. By this light
I'll fetch the marshall to you. You are a whore,
To keepe your castle—— FAC. Who would you speake with, sir?
KAS. The bawdy Doctor, and the cosening Captaine,
And PVS my suster. LOV. This is something, sure!
FAC. Vpon my trust, the dores were neuer open, sir.
KAS. I haue heard all their tricks, told me twice ouer,
By the fat knight, and the leane gentleman.
LOV. Here comes another. FAC. ANANIAS too?
And his *Pastor?* TRI. The dores are shut against vs.
ANA. Come forth, you seed of sulphure, sonnes of fire, *They beat too, at the dore.*
Your stench, it is broke forth: abomination
Is in the house. KAS. I, my suster's there. ANA. The place,
It is become a cage of vncleane birds.
KAS. Yes, I will fetch the scauenger, and the constable.
TRI. You shall doe well. ANA. Wee'll ioyne, to weede them out.
KAS. You will not come then? punque, deuice, my suster!
ANA. Call her not sister. Shee is a harlot, verily.
KAS. I'll raise the street. LOV. Good gentlemen, a word.
ANA. *Sathan*, auoid, and hinder not our zeale.
LOV. The world's turn'd *Bet'lem*. FAC. These are all broke loose,

v. iii. 30 *Enter Kastril.* G 33 you'll] you'il *Q* anone. *Q*: anone, *F1*: anon, *F2* 36 castle——] Castle. *Q* 42 After 'another.' *Enter Ananias and Trib-ulation.* G 44 sulphure] Vipers *Q* fire] *Belial* Q 45 stench, it] wickednesse *Q* abomination] Abhomination *Q* 46 I, my] My *Q* 48 Yes] I *Q* 51 Shee is] she's *F2* 53 *Sathan*] *Satan* F2 After 53 *Exeunt Ana. Trib. and Kast.* G

Out of S. KATHER'NES, where they vse to keepe,
The better sort of mad-folkes. NEI. 1. All these persons
We saw goe in, and out, here. NEI. 2. Yes, indeed, sir.
NEI. 3. These were the parties. FAC. Peace, you drunkards. Sir,
I wonder at it! Please you, to giue me leaue
To touch the dore, I'll trie, an' the lock be chang'd.
LOV. It mazes me! FAC. Good faith, sir, I beleeue,
There's no such thing. 'Tis all *deceptio visus*.

Dapper cryes out within.

Would I could get him away. DAP. Master Captayne, master Doctor.
LOV. Who's that? FAC. (Our clark within, that I forgot!) I know not, sir,
DAP. For gods sake, when wil her *Grace* be at leisure? FAC. Ha!
Illusions, some spirit o'the aire: (his gag is melted,
And now he sets out the throte.) DAP. I am almost stiffled——
(FAC. Would you were altogether.) LOV. 'Tis i'the house.
Ha! List. FAC. Beleeue it, sir, i'the aire! LOV. Peace, you——
DAP. Mine aunts *Grace* do's not vse me well. SVB. You foole,
Peace, you'll marre all. FAC. Or you will else, you rogue.
LOV. O, is it so? Then you conuerse with spirits!
Come sir. No more o' your tricks, good IEREMIE,
The truth, the shortest way. FAC. Dismisse this rabble, sir.
What shall I doe? I am catch'd. LOV. Good neighbours,
I thanke you all. You may depart. Come sir,
You know that I am an indulgent master:

v. iii. 55 KATHER'NES] *Katherines* Q keepe,] keep *F2* 60 an'] and *Q* 61 FAC.] *Face.* [*Goes to the door.*] G 63 After 'away.' *Aside.* G 64 forgot!)] forgot) *Q* 65 gods] Gods *Q* 67 stiffled] stifled *Q*, *F3* 69 aire!] ayre. *Q* 71 FAC.] *Face.* [*speaks through the key-hole, while Lovewit advances to the door unobserved.*] G 72 spirits!] spirits. *Q* 75 After 'catch'd.' *Aside.* G 76 After 'depart.' *Exeunt Neighbours.* G

And therefore, conceale nothing. What's your med'cine,
To draw so many seuerall sorts of wild-fowle?
FAC. Sir, you were wont to affect mirth, and wit:
(But here's no place to talke on't i' the street.)
Giue me but leaue, to make the best of my fortune,
And onely pardon me th'abuse of your house:
It's all I begge. I'll helpe you to a widdow,
In recompence, that you shall gi' me thankes for,
Will make you seuen yeeres yonger, and a rich one.
'Tis but your putting on a *Spanish* cloake,
I haue her within. You need not feare the house,
It was not visited. LOV. But by me, who came
Sooner then you expected. FAC. It is true, sir.
'Pray you forgiue me. LOV. Well: let's see your widdow.

Act V. *Scene* IIII.

SVBTLE, DAPPER, FACE, DOL.

HOw! ha' you eaten your gag? DAP. Yes faith, it crumbled
Away i' my mouth. SVB. You ha' spoil'd all then. DAP. No,
I hope my aunt of *Faery* will forgiue me.
SVB. Your aunt's a gracious lady: but in troth
You were to blame. DAP. The fume did ouer-come me,
And I did do't to stay my stomack. 'Pray you
So satisfie her *Grace*. Here comes the Captaine.
FAC. How now! Is his mouth downe? SVB. I! he has spoken!
FAC. (A poxe, I heard him, and you too.) Hee's vndone, then.
(I haue beene faine to say, the house is haunted

v. iii. 81 (But . . . street.)] But . . . street. *Q* 90 then] than *F2* 91 *Exeunt.* add G v. iv. SCENE II. | *A Room in the same.* | *Enter Subtle, leading in Dapper, with his eyes bound as before.* G 4 lady:] Lady, *Q* troth] truth, *Q* 7 After '*Grace.*' *Enter Face in his uniform.* G 8 I!] I, *Q* 10–15 (I . . . it.)] I . . . it. *Q*

With spirits, to keepe churle back. SVB. And hast thou done it ?
FAC. Sure, for this night. SVB. Why, then triumph, and sing
Of FACE so famous, the precious king
Of present wits. FAC. Did you not heare the coyle,
About the dore ? SVB. Yes, and I dwindled with it.)
FAC. Shew him his aunt, and let him be dispatch'd :
I'll send her to you. SVB. Well sir, your aunt her *Grace*,
Will giue you audience presently, on my sute,
And the Captaines word, that you did not eate your gag,
In any contempt of her *Highnesse*. DAP. Not I, in troth, sir.

Dol like the Queene of Faery.

SVB. Here shee is come. Downe o' your knees, and wriggle :
Shee has a stately presence. Good. Yet neerer,
And bid, God saue you. DAP. Madame. SVB. And your aunt.
DAP. And my most gracious aunt, god saue your *Grace*.
DOL. Nephew, we thought to haue beene angrie with you :
But that sweet face of yours, hath turn'd the tide,
And made it flow with ioy, that eb'd of loue.
Arise, and touch our veluet gowne. SVB. The skirts,
And kisse 'hem. So. DOL. Let me now stroke that head,
Much, nephew, shalt thou win ; much shalt thou spend ;
Much shalt thou giue away : much shalt thou lend.
SVB. (I, much, indeed.) Why doe you not thanke her *Grace ?*
DAP. I cannot speake, for ioy. SVB. See, the kind wretch !
Your *Graces* kins-man right. DOL. Giue me the *Bird*.
Here is your *Fly* in a purse, about your neck, cosen,

v. iv. 13 famous,] famous *some copies of Q* 17 After ' you.' *Exit Face*. G 20 After '*Highnesse.*' *Unbinds his eyes*. G After 20 *Enter Dol like the Queen of Fairy*. G 21 *Stage direction not in Q* 22 After ' presence.' *Dapper kneels, and shuffles towards her*. G 23 you] *her* Q 24 god] God *Q* 25 angrie] angry, *Q* 31 *away* :] *away*, Q 32 (I . . . indeed.)] I . . . indeede. *Q*

Weare it, and feed it, about this day seu'night,
On your right wrist—— Svb. Open a veine, with a pinne,
And let it suck but once a weeke: till then,
You must not looke on't. Dol. No. And, kins-man,
Beare your selfe worthy of the bloud you come on.
Svb. Her grace would ha' you eate no more *Wool-sack* pies,
Nor *Dagger* frume'ty. Dol. Nor breake his fast,
In *heauen*, and *hell*. Svb. Shee's with you euery where!
Nor play with Costar-mongers, at *mum-chance*, *tray-trip*,
God make you rich, (when as your aunt has done it:) but keepe
The gallant'st company, and the best games—— Dap. Yes, sir.
Svb. *Gleeke* and *primero*: and what you get, be true to vs.
Dap. By this hand, I will. Svb. You may bring's a thousand pound,
Before to morrow night, (if but three thousand,
Be stirring) an' you will. Dap. I sweare, I will then.
Svb. Your *Fly* will learne you all games. Fac. Ha' you done there?
Svb. Your grace will command him no more duties? Dol. No:
But come, and see me often. I may chance
To leaue him three or foure hundred chests of treasure,
And some twelue thousand acres of *Faerie* land:
If he game well, and comely, with good gamesters.
Svb. There's a kind aunt! kisse her departing part.
But you must sell your fortie marke a yeare, now:
Dap. I, sir, I meane. Svb. Or, gi't away: pox on't.
Dap. I'le gi't mine aunt. Ile goe and fetch the writings.

v. iv. 37 wrist——] wrist. *Q* 38 weeke: till] weeke. Till *Q* 42 frume'ty] Frumenty *Q* 43 where!] where. *Q* 44 *-trip,* Q: *-trip.* Ff 46 games——] Games. *Q* 49 thousand,] thousand *Q* 50 an'] if *Q* 51 Fac.] *Fac.* [*within.*] G 55 twelue] fiue *Q* 58 your *Q, F2*: you *F1* now:] now. *Q* 59 away: pox] away. A poxe *Q* 60 Dap. *F2*: Fac. *Q, F1* *Exit.* add G

SVB. 'Tis well, away. FAC. Where's SVBTLE?
SVB. Here. What newes?
FAC. DRVGGER is at the doore, goe take his suite,
And bid him fetch a Parson, presently:
Say, he shall marrie the widdow. Thou shalt spend
A hundred pound by the seruice! Now, queene DOL,
Ha' you pack'd vp all? DOL. Yes. FAC. And how doe you like
The lady PLYANT? DOL. A good dull innocent.
SVB. Here's your HIERONIMO's cloake, and hat.
FAC. Giue mee 'hem.
SVB. And the ruffe too? FAC. Yes, I'll come to you presently.
SVB. Now, he is gone about his proiect, DOL,
I told you of, for the widow. DOL. 'Tis direct
Against our articles. SVB. Well, wee'll fit him, wench.
Hast thou gull'd her of her iewels, or her bracelets?
DOL. No, but I will do't. SVB. Soone at night, my DOLLY,
When we are shipt, and all our goods aboord,
East-ward for *Ratcliffe*; we will turne our course
To *Brainford*, westward, if thou saist the word:
And take our leaues of this ore-weaning raskall,
This peremtorie FACE. DOL. Content, I'am weary of him.
SVB. Tho'hast cause, when the slaue will runne a wiuing, DOL,
Against the instrument, that was drawne betweene vs.
DOL. I'll plucke his bird as bare as I can. SVB. Yes, tell her,
She must by any meanes, addresse some present
To th' cunning man; make him amends, for wronging
His art with her suspition; send a ring;

v. iv. 61 After 'away.' *Re-enter Face*. G   65 seruice!] seruice. *Q* After 'seruice!' *Exit Subtle*. G   66 FAC. *om. F2*   After 67 *Re-enter Subtle*. G   *Exit*. add G   79 Content,] Content. *Q*   80 Tho'hast] Thou'hast *Q, F2*   84 man;] man, *Q*   amends,] amends *Q*   85 suspition; . . . ring;] suspition, . . . Ring, *Q*

Or chaine of pearle ; shee will be tortur'd else
Extremely in her sleepe, say : and ha' strange things
Come to her. Wilt thou ? D o l. Yes. S v b. My fine flitter-mouse,
My bird o'the night ; wee'll tickle it at the *pigeons*,
When we haue all, and may vn-lock the trunkes,
And say, this's mine, and thine, and thine, and mine—— *They kisse.*
F a c. What now, a billing ? S v b. Yes, a little exalted
In the good passage of our stock-affaires.
F a c. D r v g g e r has brought his Parson, take him in, S v b t l e,
And send N a b back againe, to wash his face.
S v b. I will : and shaue himselfe ? F a c. If you can get him.
D o l. You are hot vpon it, F a c e, what ere it is !
F a c. A trick, that D o l shall spend ten pound a month by.
Is he gone ? S v b. The Chaplaine waits you i'the hall, sir.
F a c. I'll goe bestow him. D o l. Hee'll now marry her, instantly.
S v b. He cannot, yet, he is not readie. Deare D o l,
Cosen her of all thou canst. To deceiue him
Is no deceipt, but iustice, that would breake
Such an inextricable tye as ours was.
D o l. Let me alone to fit him. F a c. Come, my venturers,
You ha' pack'd vp all ? Where be the trunkes ? Bring forth.
S v b. Here. F a c. Let's see 'hem. Where's the money ? S v b. Here,
In this. F a c. M a m m o n s ten pound : eight score before.
The *Brethrens* money, this. D r v g g e r s, and D a p p e r s.

v. iv. 86 pearle ;] Pearle, *Q* 87 say :] say, *Q* 88 her. Wilt] her, wilt *Q* 91 *Stage direction not in Q* After 91 *Re-enter Face.* G 94 Parson,] Parson ; *F2* 95 Nab] him *Q* 96 After 'himselfe?' *Exit.* G 97 is !] is. *Q* After 98 *Re-enter Subtle.* G 100 After 'him.' *Exit.* G 103 iustice,] Iustice ; *Q* 105 After 'him.' *Re-enter Face.* G venturers,] Venturers. *Q*: ventures, *F3* 107 Let's] Let us *W*

What paper's that? Dol. The iewell of the waiting maides,
That stole it from her lady, to know certaine——
Fac. If shee should haue precedence of her mistris?
Dol. Yes.
Fac. What boxe is that? Svb. The fish-wiues rings, I thinke:
And th'ale-wiues single money. Is't not Dol?
Dol. Yes: and the whistle, that the saylors wife
Brought you, to know, and her husband were with Ward.
Fac. Wee'll wet it to morrow: and our siluer-beakers,
And tauerne cups. Where be the *French* petti-coats,
And girdles, and hangers? Svb. Here, i'the trunke,
And the bolts of lawne. Fac. Is Drvggers damaske, there?
And the *tabacco*? Svb. Yes. Fac. Giue me the keyes.
Dol. Why you the keyes! Svb. No matter, Dol: because
We shall not open 'hem, before he comes.
Fac. 'Tis true, you shall not open them, indeed:
Nor haue 'hem forth. Doe you see? Not forth, Dol.
Dol. No!
Fac. No, my smock-rampant. The right is, my master
Knowes all, has pardon'd me, and he will keepe 'hem.
Doctor, 'tis true (you looke) for all your figures:
I sent for him, indeed. Wherefore, good partners,
Both hee, and shee, be satisfied: for, here
Determines the *indenture tripartite*,
Twixt Svbtle, Dol, and Face. All I can doe
Is to helpe you ouer the wall, o' the back-side;
Or lend you a sheet, to saue your veluet gowne, Dol.
Here will be officers, presently; bethinke you,
Of some course sodainely to scape the dock:
Some knock. For thether you'll come else. Harke you, thunder.

v. iv. 112 mistris] mistresse *Q* 116 and] an' *F2* 121 *tabacco*] *Tobacco* Q 122 Dol:] *Dol*, Q 127 'hem. *Q*: 'hem, *F1*: 'hem; *F2* 128 figures:] Figures. *Q* 130 satisfied: for,] satisfied. For *Q* 137 *St.-dir. not in Q*

SVB. You are a precious fiend! OFF. Open the dore.
FAC. DOL, I am sorry for thee i-faith. But hearst thou?
It shall goe hard, but I will place thee some-where:
Thou shalt ha' my letter to mistris AMO. DOL. Hang you——
FAC. Or madame *Cæsarean.* DOL. Poxe vpon you, rogue,
Would I had but time to beat thee. FAC. SVBTLE,
Let's know where you set vp next; I'll send you
A customer, now and then, for old acquaintance:
What new course ha' you? SVB. Rogue, I'll hang my selfe:
That I may walke a greater diuell, then thou,
And haunt thee i'the flock-bed, and the buttery.

Act V. *Scene* V.

LOVE-WIT, OFFICERS, MAMMON, SVRLY, FACE, KASTRIL, ANANIAS, TRIBVLATION, DRVGGER, DA. PLIANT.

WHat doe you meane, my masters? MAM. Open your dore,
Cheaters, bawds, coniurers. OFF. Or wee'll breake it open.
LOV. What warrant haue you? OFF. Warrant inough, sir, doubt not:
If you'll not open it. LOV. Is there an officer, there?
OFF. Yes, two, or three for fayling. LOV. Haue but patience,
And I will open it straight. FAC. Sir, ha' you done?

v. iv. 138 SVB.] SYB. *Fi* OFF.] *Offi.* [*without.*] G 142 *Cæsarean*] *Imperiall.* Q 143 Would] I would *T. Keightley conj.* 148 *Exeunt.* add G v. v. SCENE III. | *An outer Room in the same.* | *Enter Lovewit in the Spanish dress, with the Parson.* [*Loud knocking at the door.*] G *The stage directions at ll.* 37, 58, 90, 115, 125, *are not in Q* 1 MAM.] *Mam.* [*without.*] G 2, 3, 5 OFF.] *Offi.* [*without.*] G 3 not:] not, *Q* 6 After 'straight.' *Enter Face as Butler.* G

Is it a marriage? perfect? LOV. Yes, my braine.

FAC. Off with your ruffe, and cloake then, be your selfe, sir.

SVR. Downe with the dore. KAS. 'Slight, ding it open.

LOV. Hold.

Hold gentlemen, what meanes this violence?

MAM. Where is this Colliar? SVR. And my Captaine FACE?

MAM. These day-Owles. SVR. That are birding in mens purses.

MAM. Madame *Suppository*. KAS. *Doxey*, my suster.

ANA. Locusts

Of the foule pit. TRI. Profane as BEL, and the *Dragon*.

ANA. Worse then the Grasse-hoppers, or the Lice of *Egypt*.

LOV. Good gentlemen, heare me. Are you officers,

And cannot stay this violence? OFF. Keepe the peace.

LOV. Gentlemen, what is the matter? Whom doe you seeke?

MAM. The *Chymicall* cousoner. SVR. And the Captaine *Pandar*.

KAS. The *Nun* my suster. MAM. Madame *Rabbi*.

ANA. Scorpions,

And Caterpillers. LOV. Fewer at once, I pray you.

OFF. One after another, gentlemen, I charge you,

By vertue of my staffe—— ANA. They are the vessells

Of pride, lust, and the cart. LOV. Good zeale, lie still,

A little while. TRI. Peace, Deacon ANANIAS.

LOV. The house is mine here, and the dores are open:

If there be any such persons, as you seeke for,

Vse your authoritie, search on o' gods name.

I am but newly come to towne, and finding

v. v. 7 braine. *Ff*: Braine? *Q originally*: Braine. *corr. Q* 8 then], then; *F2* 9 SVR.] *Sur.* [*without.*] G KAS.] *Kas.* [*without.*] G LOV.] *Love.* [*opening the door.*] G After 10 *Mammon, Surly, Kastril, Ananias, Tribulation, and Officers rush in.* G 13 suster] Suster *Q*: sister *Ff* 15 then] than *F2* *Egypt*] *Ægypt* Q 22 OFF.] 2 *Offi.* G 24 pride, lust, and the cart] shame, and of dishonour *Q* 28 gods] Gods *Q*

This tumult 'bout my dore (to tell you true)
It somewhat maz'd me ; till my man, here, (fearing
My more displeasure) told me ⟨he⟩ had done
Somewhat an insolent part, let out my house
(Belike, presuming on my knowne auersion
From any aire o'the towne, while there was sicknesse)
To a Doctor, and a Captaine : who, what they are,
Or where they be, he knowes not. MAM. Are they gone? *They enter.*
LOV. You may goe in, and search, sir. Here, I find
The emptie walls, worse then I left 'hem, smok'd,
A few crack'd pots, and glasses, and a fornace,
The seeling fill'd with *poesies* of the candle :
And MADAME, with a *Dildo*, writ o' the walls.
Onely, one gentlewoman, I met here,
That is within, that said shee was a widdow——
KAS. I, that's my suster. I'll goe thumpe her. Where
is shee?
LOV. And should ha' marryed a *Spanish Count*, but he,
When he came to't, neglected her so grosly,
That I, a widdower, am gone through with her.
SVR. How! Haue I lost her then? LOV. Were you
the *Don*, sir?
Good faith, now, shee do's blame yo'extremely, and sayes
You swore, and told her, you had tane the paines,
To dye your beard, and vmbre o'er your face,
Borrowed a sute, and ruffe, all for her loue ;
And then did nothing. What an ouer-sight,
And want of putting forward, sir, was this!
Well fare an old Hargubuzier, yet,
Could prime his poulder, and giue fire, and hit,
All in a twinckling. MAM. The whole nest are fled! *Mammon comes forth.*
LOV. What sort of birds were they? MAM. A kind of
Choughes,

v. v. 32 he *F2* 36 Captaine :] Captaine, *Q* 38 After 'sir.' *Mammon, Ana. and Trib. go in.* G 39 then] than *F2* 43 Onely,] Onely *Q* 45 *Goes in.* add G 46 but he] buthe *Q originally* 56 Hargubuzier] Harquebuzier *F2* 57 poulder] Powder *F3* 59 Choughes] Coughes *F2*

Or theeuish Dawes, sir, that haue pickt my purse
Of eight-score, and ten pounds, within these fiue weekes,
Beside my first materialls ; and my goods,
That lye i'the cellar : which I am glad they ha' left,
I may haue home yet. LOV. Thinke you so, sir ? MAM. I.
LOV. By order of law, sir, but not otherwise.
MAM. Not mine owne stuffe ? LOV. Sir, I can take no knowledge,
That they are yours, but by publique meanes.
If you can bring certificate, that you were gull'd of 'hem,
Or any formall writ, out of a court,
That you did cosen your selfe : I will not hold them.
MAM. I'll rather loose 'hem. LOV. That you shall not, sir,
By me, in troth. Vpon these termes they'are yours.
What should they ha' beene, sir, turn'd into gold all ? MAM. No.
I cannot tell. It may be they should. What then ?
LOV. What a great losse in hope haue you sustain'd ?
MAM. Not I, the common-wealth has. FAC. I, he would ha' built
The citie new ; and made a ditch about it
Of siluer, should haue runne with creame from *Hogsden* :
That, euery sunday in *More*-fields, the younkers,
And tits, and tom-boyes should haue fed on, *gratis*.
MAM. I will goe mount a turnep-cart, and preach
The end o'the world, within these two months. SVRLY,
What ! in a dreame ? SVR. Must I needs cheat my selfe,
With that same foolish vice of honestie !
Come let vs goe, and harken out the rogues.
That FACE I'll marke for mine, if ere I meet him.
FAC. If I can heare of him, sir, I'll bring you word
Vnto your lodging : for in troth, they were strangers
To me, I thought 'hem honest, as my selfe, sir.

v. v. 63 ha'] haue *Q* left, *Q*: left. *Ff* 66 knowledge,] knowledge. *F2* 70 selfe :] selfe ; *Q* 71 loose] lose *F2* (*so* 90) 72 they'are] they, are *Q* *originally* 80 on,] on *Q* 82 world,] world *Q* After 89 *Exeunt Mam. and Sur.* | *Re-enter Ananias and Tribulation.* G

TRI. 'Tis well, the *Saints* shall not loose all yet. Goe, *They come forth.*
And get some carts—— LOV. For what, my zealous friends?

ANA. To beare away the portion of the righteous,
Out of this den of theeues. LOV. What is that portion?

ANA. The goods, sometimes the Orphanes, that the *Brethren*
Bought with their siluer pence. LOV. What, those i'the cellar,
The knight sir MAMMON claimes? ANA. I doe defie
The wicked MAMMON, so doe all the *Brethren*,
Thou prophane man. I aske thee, with what conscience
Thou canst aduance that Idol, against vs,
That haue the seale? Were not the shillings numbred,
That made the pounds? Were not the pounds told out,
Vpon the second day of the fourth weeke,
In the eight month, vpon the table dormant,
The yeere, of the last patience of the *Saints*,
Sixe hundred and ten? LOV. Mine earnest vehement botcher,
And *Deacon* also, I cannot dispute with you,
But, if you get you not away the sooner,
I shall confute you with a cudgell. ANA. Sir.

TRI. Be patient ANANIAS. ANA. I am strong,
And will stand vp, well girt, against an host,
That threaten GAD in exile. LOV. I shall send you
To *Amsterdam*, to your cellar. ANA. I will pray there,
Against thy house: may dogs defile thy walls,
And waspes, and hornets breed beneath thy roofe,
This seat of false-hood, and this caue of cos'nage.

LOV. Another too? DRV. Not I sir, I am no *Brother*. *Drugger enters, and he beats him away.*

LOV. Away you HARRY NICHOLAS, doe you talke?

v. v. 94 *Brethren*] *Brethren*, F1 99 Idol] *Nemrod* Q 103 eight] eigth *F2* 105 ten? *F2*: tenne. *Q*: ten. *F1* 108 you] you, *Q* 112 *Amsterdam*] *Amstredam* Q After 115 *Exeunt Ana. and Trib. Enter Drugger* G 117 *Stage directions in F1 at l.* 118

**To the Parson.*

FAC. No, this was ABEL DRVGGER. *Good sir, goe,
And satisfie him; tell him, all is done:
He stay'd too long a washing of his face.
The Doctor, he shall heare of him at *Westchester;*
And of the Captayne, tell him at *Yarmouth:* or
Some good port-towne else, lying for a winde.
If you get off the angrie Child, now, sir——

To his sister.

KAS. Come on, you yew, you haue match'd most sweetly, ha' you not?
Did not I say, I would neuer ha' you tupt
But by a dub'd Boy, to make you a lady-*Tom?*
'Slight, you are a mammet! O, I could touse you, now.
Death, mun' you marry with a poxe? LOV. You lie, Boy;
As sound as you: and I am afore-hand with you. KAS. Anone?
LOV. Come, will you quarrell? I will feize you, sirrah.
Why doe you not buckle to your tooles? KAS. Gods light!
This is a fine old Boy, as ere I saw!
LOV. What, doe you change your copy, now? Proceed,
Here stands my doue: stoupe at her, if you dare.
KAS. 'Slight I must loue him! I cannot choose, i-faith!
And I should be hang'd for't. Suster, I protest,
I honor thee, for this match. LOV. O, doe you so, sir?
KAS. Yes, and thou canst take *tabacco*, and drinke, old Boy,
I'll giue her fiue hundred pound more, to her marriage,
Then her owne state. LOV. Fill a pipe-full, IEREMIE.
FAC. Yes, but goe in, and take it, sir. LOV. We will.
I will be rul'd by thee in any thing, IEREMIE.
KAS. 'Slight, thou art not hide-bound! thou art a *Iouy'* Boy!
Come let's in, I pray thee, and take our whiffes.

V. V. 118 *The asterisk in F1 is placed at the beginning of the line.* 122 *Yarmouth :*] *Yarmouth,* Q 123 *Exit Parson.* G 124 get] can get *Q* After 124 *Enter Kastril dragging in his sister.* G 130 -hand with] -handwith *Q* 138 honor] honour *Q* 139 *tabacco*] *Tobacco* Q and] an' *F2* 141 Then] Than *F2* 144 *Iouy'*] *Iouy* Q 145 I *not in Q* pray thee] pr'y thee *F2*

LOV. Whiffe in with your sister, brother Boy. That master
That had receiu'd such happinesse by a seruant,
In such a widdow, and with so much wealth,
Were very vngratefull, if he would not be
A little indulgent to that seruants wit,
And helpe his fortune, though with some small straine
Of his owne candor. Therefore, gentlemen,
And kind Spectators, if I haue out-stript
An old mans grauitie, or strict canon, thinke
What a yong wife, and a good braine may doe:
Stretch ages truth sometimes, and crack it too.
Speake for thy selfe, knaue. FAC. So I will, sir. Gentlemen,
My part a little fell in this last *Scene*,
Yet 'twas *decorum*. And though I am cleane
Got off, from SVBTLE, SVRLY, MAMMON, DOL,
Hot ANANIAS, DAPPER, DRVGGER, all
With whom I traded; yet I put my selfe
On you, that are my countrey: and this pelfe,
Which I haue got, if you doe quit me, rests
To feast you often, and inuite new ghests.

THE END.

v. v. 146 After 'Boy.' *Exeunt Kas. and Dame P.* G 152 After 'candor.' [*advancing.*] G 157 After 'sir.' [*advancing to the front of the stage.*] G 165 ghests] Guests *F3* *Exeunt.* add G

This Comoedie was first acted, in the yeere 1610.

By the Kings Maiesties

SERVANTS.

The principall Comœdians were,

RIC. BVRBADGE.	IOH. HEMINGS.
IOH. LOWIN.	WILL. OSTLER.
HEN. CONDEL.	IOH. VNDERWOOD.
ALEX. COOKE.	NIC. TOOLY.
ROB. ARMIN.	WILL. EGLESTON.

With the allowance of the Master of REVELLS.

This page was added in F1. In F2 the statements about the date, the company, and the Master of the Revels were omitted, and the list of ' The principall Comœdians ' *was transferred to the back of the half-title, where it followed* ' *THE SCENE* LONDON '.

CATILINE

THE TEXT

The first edition of the tragedy of *Catiline* was not entered on the Stationers' Register. It was published by Walter Burre in 1611 with the title *Catiline his Conspiracy.* The printer is unknown. The collation, A to N in fours with three leaves of O, is in detail: A 1 recto, title-page; A 1 verso, blank; A 2, dedication to Lord Pembroke; A 3 recto, 'To the Reader in ordinary' and 'To the Reader extraordinary'; A 3 verso, a complimentary poem by Francis Beaumont and part of a similar poem by John Fletcher; A 4 recto, Fletcher's poem concluded, and a poem by Nathan Field; A 4 verso, 'The names of the Actors'; B to O 3 verso, the text of the play. The running title is '*CATJLINE*'.

Five copies of the Quarto have been collated for the text of the present edition:

The British Museum copy, with shelf-mark 644.b.55 (marked A in the following list);

The Bodleian copy, with shelf-mark Malone 188 (6) (marked B);

The copy in the Cambridge University Library, with shelf-mark Syn. 7–61–12, inscribed at the bottom of the last page in a seventeenth-century hand 'for the mutch honorid my very good Lord the Earle of Bristow; these presentes' (marked C);

The copy in the Dyce Library (marked D);

Mr. T. J. Wise's copy (marked E).

In addition, Mr. C. K. Edmonds, who has collated the Devonshire and Bridgewater copies of the Quarto in the Huntington Library, has supplied variants in the inner forme of D. Jonson's proof-corrections may well have extended to other sheets of the Quarto, but the variants we have been able to trace are as follows:

Sig. A 4r	Field's poem, l. 10	eare *B, C, D, E*	Yeare *A*
Sig. B 1r	I. 20	voice *A, B, D*	voice ! *C, E*
Sig. B 3r	160	with debts *A, B, D*	with their debts *C, E*
	167	be *A, B, D*	be, *C, E*
Sig. B 4v	268	They had *A, B, D, E*	They'had *C*

Sig. C 3r	411	you ! *D, E*	you. *A, B, C*
Sig. C 4v	531–2	Can nothing great... Remaine so long ? *D, E*	CAn nothing great... Remaine so long ? *A, B, C*
Sig. D 1v	II. 2	hether *Devonshire*	hither *the rest*
Sig. D 3v	145	yonr *Devonshire*	your *the rest*
	163	to *Devonshire*	too *the rest*
	165	dos *Devonshire*	do's *the rest*
Sig. D 4r	170	so, imperious *Devonshire*	so imperious *the rest*
Sig. H 1r	III. 658	him lost, *A*	him, lost : *B, C, D, E*
Sig. I 1v	IV. 61	Stayer *C*	STAYER *A, B, D, E*
	64–5	Which may be happy, and auspicious still | To *Rome*, and hers. *C*	*Which may be happy, and auspicious still* | *To* Rome, *and hers.* A, B, D, E
	65	conscript *C*	Conscript *A, B, D, E*
	67	state *C*	State *A, B, D, E*
	68	night ; *C*	night, *A, B, D, E*
	77	seem'd ; *C*	seem'd, *A, B, D, E*
	81	effects ; Then *C*	effects, then *A, B, D, E*
	83	one ; *C*	one : *A, B, D, E*
	84	sithence *C*	yet since *A, B, D, E*
	86	loose *C*	loose, *A, B, D, E*
	89	greater, . . . all, *C*	greater ; . . . all : *A, B, D, E*
Sig. I 2r	105	wife *C*	Wife *A, B, D, E*
	120	Nature *C*	Nature, *A, B, D, E*
	127	licentiousnesse ; *C*	licentiousnesse : *A, B, D, E*
Sig. I 3v	201	state's *C*	State's *A, B, D, E*
	205	rust, *C*	rust ; *A, B, D, E*
	207	liu'st, *C*	liu'st : *A, B, D, E*
	209	Fathers *C*	Fathers, *A, B, D, E*
	214	iawes . . . *Hetruria*, C	iawes, . . . *Hetruria ;* A, B, D, E
	216	walles, *C*	walles : *A, B, D, E*
	217	publique *C*	Publique *A, B, D, E*
	218	If *C*	If, *A, B, D, E*
	222	meale *C*	meale, *A, B, D, E*
	229	leaue : . . . liu'st, *C*	leaue ; . . . liu'st : *A, B, D, E*
	231	state *C*	State *A, B, D, E*
	235	night, can . . . darknesse *C*	Night can, . . . darknesse, *A, B, D, E*
	236	house *C*	House *A, B, D, E*

Sig. I 4^r	237	Can . . . walles *C*	Can, . . . walles, *A*, *B*, *D*, *E*
	238	conspiracy, if *C*	conspiracy : If *A*, *B*, *D*, *E*
	241	told *C*	told, *A*, *B*, *D*, *E*
	257	And *C*	Where *A*, *B*, *D*, *E*
	261	thee; *C*	thee, *A*, *B*, *D*, *E*
	263	buisinesse *C*	businesse *A*, *B*, *D*, *E*
	267	met ? *C*	met. *A*, *B*, *D*, *E*
	269	thee ; *C*	thee : *A*, *B*, *D*, *E*
Sig. L 1^r	596	I' ha' *D*, *E*	I ha' *A*, *B*, *C*
Sig. O 2^r	v. 602	by, a sword *D*, *E*	by' a sword *A*, *B*, *C*

The twenty-seven corrections in the inner forme of I show Jonson's characteristic vigilance. The four corrections in the outer forme of B show a second reading of the proof on B 4 verso where Jonson's final correction was a metrical apostrophe in the words 'They'had' in Act I, line 268. The type-correction of the large initial capital for the opening lines of the first chorus on C 4 verso is a signal instance of Jonson's exactness ; the other choruses start with a similar capital. The catchword 'FVL.' on signature D 4 recto is without the stop in the Dyce and Wise copies ; probably this is only a failure to print it.

The Folio text of 1616 was printed from a revised copy of the Quarto. There are few changes of reading, as if Jonson found little to correct in what he believed to be his best tragedy.[1] There are retouchings of single words, as in the demand of the blood-thirsty Cethegus, 'Swell mee my bowle yet fuller' for 'Crowne me my bowle' (I. 499), where Jonson dropped Virgil's 'Vina coronant'.[2] The most striking alteration is in Act III, line 729—'To betray headie husbands' for the more violent expression of the Quarto, 'To strangle head-strong Husbands'. But Jonson completely recast the punctuation in order to bring it into line with the system he adopted in the Folio ; his minute and incessant changes are recorded in the critical apparatus except where

[1] So he tells Lord Pembroke in the dedication, line 11.

[2] We are reminded of the lyric in *Poetaster*, III. i. 8, 'Swell me a bowle with lustie wine'.

there is an obvious loss of a stop in the Quarto. He inserted freely the note of exclamation, the dash, and the bracket for parentheses; and he employed far more sparingly the inverted commas used at the beginning of a 'sentence' or aphorism.[1] The metrical apostrophe once more gave trouble to the printer.[2] We have inserted it on the authority of the Quarto in the following passages where it has disappeared in the Folio:

> BESTIA,' AVTRONIVS (I. 156)
> —thou' art (III. 214)[3]
> we' intend (III. 555)
> to' you (V. 43)
> to' vs (V. 397)
> the' immortall gods (V. 693).

The printer's difficulties are shown by his absurd substitution of a comma in the Quarto text of Act v, line 602, 'by, a sword', which was promptly corrected, and by his omission of a comma where the two stops coincided in 'No' in troth' (II. 75) and 'practise on me' or finde' (II. 248). In such passages as 'And that hath plac'd thee, CICERO, at the helme' (III. 62) and 'These things for mine owne glorie, and false greatnesse' (IV. 78), Jonson's manuscript probably had 'CICERO', at' and 'glorie', and', but, as Jonson himself passed the text for the press, we have left the responsibility with him. In such minutiae he here fell far below his rigid standard of correctness. It is something of a shock to find that we have had to make nearly fifty corrections, most of them, of course, extremely trivial.[4] There are hardly any serious blunders; the only noteworthy one is 'engines' for 'enginers' (III. 760), which was corrected by Gifford. It is as if Jonson, secure of the text as a whole

[1] See the introduction to the text of *Sejanus* in vol. iii, pp. 335–6.
[2] Ibid., pp. 338–42.
[3] 'thou'rt' in *Q*; 'thou'art' in *F2*.
[4] The curious may track them out in the critical apparatus at I. 291, 297, 459, 527; II. 57, 75, 178, 248, 273, 285; III. 114, 148, 207, 216, 219, 342, 408, 413, 684, 759, 760, 862, 874; IV. 62, 325, 382, 504, 596, 727, 730, 732, 764, 806, 824, 833; V. 148, 214, 220, 327, 402, 413, 427, 451, 496, 498, 521, 571, 577, 578.

and feeling that it needed little revision, read his proofs too rapidly.

A second Quarto was published in 1635, two years before Jonson's death. It was printed by Nicholas Okes for John Spenser, who had acquired the copyright from Mistress Burre in 1630. Probably Jonson knew nothing about it. The collation is: A 1, blank; A 2 recto, the title-page; A 3 recto, 'To the Reader'; A 3 verso, Beaumont's poem, and part of Fletcher's; A 4 recto, Fletcher's poem continued, and Field's poem; A 4 verso, 'The names of the Actors'; B to M in fours, the text of the play. For this edition the first Quarto served as copy, not, as would certainly have been the case if Jonson had been consulted, the revised text of the Folio.

The 1635 Quarto is a grossly careless reprint, and we have not judged it necessary to encumber the critical apparatus with the misreadings, numbering well over a hundred, with which Okes corrupted the text. He omitted two lines;[1] he printed a line of Petreius's speech[2]—

The rest are a mixt kind, all sorts of furies—

in the unmetrical form, 'The rest are but a mixt kinde, of all sorts of furies'; and he wrecked the passage where Cicero asks Lentulus in the Senate if he recognized the seal on his intercepted letter—

LEN. Yes, it is mine. CIC. Whose image is that, on it?
LEN. My grand-fathers. CIC. What, that renowm'd
good man,—[3]

by omitting 'Whose image is that, on it?' and substituting 'What, that renowm'd good man?' which he printed at the end of both lines. When Catiline tells the conspirators of Marius' standard which he worshipped in a shrine built

Of purpose to it. Pledge then all your hands,
To follow it, with vowes of death, and ruine,
Strooke silently, and home.—[4]

Okes printed nonsense by leaving out the words 'Pledge

[1] III. 627, V. 581. [2] V. 44. [3] V. 170–1. [4] III. 569–71.

then all your hands, To follow it'. He constantly drops single words, usually monosyllables, to the detriment of the metre: thus, 'A small praise, and that wrung out by force'[1] should be 'A most small praise'. Misreadings which he foisted into the text include 'salvation' for 'salutation' (I. 201), 'feele thirst' for 'fell thirst' (ibid., 492), 'unconstant' for 'constant' (II. 159), 'fall' for 'all' (III. 460), 'covenant' for 'conuent' (IV. 295), 'prodigallity' for 'prodigally' (ibid., 668). His worst blunder, because this was a deliberate tampering with the text, is at the point where Catiline sends Vargunteius to hold Cethegus back from an ill-advised attempt to fire Cicero's house at night.[2] The first Quarto reads:

CAT. Follow him, *Vargunteius*, . . .
. . . Intreat, and coniure him.
In all our names. LEN. By all our vowes, and friendships.

These words end the page on signature H recto. H verso begins with a scene heading,

SEMPRONIA, AVRELIA, FVLVIA, to them.

The formula 'To them' is a frequent stage direction in the Folio; it marks the entrance of a new character or characters, and saves repeating the names of those already on the stage. But this being the only time Jonson used it in the Quarto, Okes did not know what to make of it. Finding it in roman lower-case, like the body of the text, he decided that it was wrongly taken over from the speech on the previous page; so he printed

LEN. By all our vowes and friendships to them.—

ignoring the troublesome detail that the pronoun 'them' had nothing to refer to grammatically in the context.

The Folio of 1640 was printed from its predecessor of 1616. From time to time it revises the punctuation, though it frequently omits the metrical apostrophe. There are some careless misprints: for example, '*Circes*' for '*Circei*' (I.

[1] III. 6. [2] III. 674 foll.

390); 'bend Upon occasion' for 'bend Vnto occasion' (III. 196); 'the old porter TITAN' for 'old potter' as a description of Prometheus (ibid., 542); and 'How dost thou heare this?' for 'beare this' (IV. 362). It makes one attempt at an emendation—

> I could desire, grave *Fathers*, to be found

for

> I could desire, *Fathers*, to be found—

treating 'desire' as a dissyllable through not understanding Jonson's pronunciation.[1]

In one respect the text of *Catiline* is unique. Two quarto editions were published at the Restoration. It was produced at the Theatre Royal on 18 December 1668, and Pepys, who saw it on the second day, described it as 'the least diverting' play he had ever seen. Hart played Catiline, Mohun Cethegus, Burt Cicero, Mrs. Corey Sempronia, and Nell Gwyn spoke a prologue 'Merrily' 'in an Amazonian habit'. It was published next year, 'Printed for *A. C.*', i.e. Andrew Crooke, 'and are to be sold by *William Cademan* at the *Pope's Head* in the Lower walk of the *New-Exchange.* 1669'. It was published in February, 'Price 1*s*', according to the entry in the *Term Catalogues.* Crooke had, with John Legatt, acquired the copyright of *Bartholomew Fair* and *The Staple of News* from Allot in 1637; he probably acquired the copyright of *The Devil is an Ass* in 1640.[2] The collation, A to M in fours, is in detail: A 1 blank; A 2 recto, title-page; A 2 verso, blank; A 3 recto, Nell Gwyn's prologue; A 3 verso, 'THE EPILOGVE, By the same'; A 4 recto, 'The Persons of the Play'; A 4 verso, 'The Principal Tragœdians'; B to M, the text of the Play. On M 4 verso, after 'The End' is appended the list, taken from the 1616 Folio, of 'The principal Tragœdians, when first Acted in the year 1611'. The interesting fact about this Quarto is that it aims at being a reprint of the 1616 Folio; it modernizes the spelling, but it often retains

[1] IV. 209.
[2] See S. G. Dunn in *The Times Literary Supplement*, 28 July 1921.

Jonson's peculiar punctuation, which was obsolete in 1669. There are some bad misprints. In I. 297–8 'Dare they looke day In the dull face?' is not improved by printing 'In the full face'. But there is one interesting attempt at an emendation: the alexandrine in Act V, line 427,

With money to corrupt the poore artificers

is normalized to blank verse by omitting 'poore'. At two points in the play an omission has been stamped in after the text had been printed off: the letter *s* in ''gin's to move' (III. 761) and the words 'and he', which had dropped out at the end of Act IV, line 792.

The 1669 Quarto was reprinted in 1674 (1) with an identical title-page, (2) with the imprint:

Printed for *William Crook*, at the green *Drag-gon* without *Temple-bar*. 1674.

The *Term Catalogues* announce it as published in July. The actor list of the 1668 revival was omitted. The collation is A^2, $B–L^4$. All that this Quarto does is to add a new crop of misprints; one effort to correct a faulty reading may be quoted. In Act III, l. 454, 'And lay it to thy brest, how much the gods', the 1669 Quarto printed 'host' for 'how'; the printer of 1674, seeing that 'host' was nonsense, thought he had restored sense by printing 'haste'.

The Folio text of 1616 was reprinted by Dr. Lynn Harold Harris in *Yale Studies in English*, no. LIII, in 1916; the proof-reading is careless, especially in the matter of dropped words; the critical apparatus is inaccurate; and the existence of the third Quarto is unknown to the editor.

CATILINE
his
CONSPIRACY.

VVritten
by
BEN: IONSON.

——*His non Plebecula gaudet.*
Verum Equitis quoq;, iam migrauit ab aure voluptas,
Omnis, ad incertos oculos, & gaudia vana.

LONDON,
Printed for *Walter Burre.*
1611.

The title-page of the first Quarto, 1611.

CATILINE
HIS
CONSPIRACY.

A Tragœdie.

Acted in the yeere 1611. By the
Kings MAIESTIES
Seruants.

The Author B. I.

HORAT.

———*His non plebecula gaudet:*
Verum equitis quoq;, iam migrauit ab aure voluptas
Omnis, ad incertos oculos, & gaudia vana.

LONDON,
Printed by WILLIAM STANSBY.

M. DC. XVI.

The title-page of the 1616 Folio.

CATILINE
HIS
CONSPIRACY.

VVRITTEN
BY
BEN: IONSON.

And now Acted by his MAIESTIES Servants with great Applause.

——*His non Plebecula gaudet.*
Verum Equitis quoq; jam migravit ab aure voluptas
Omnis, ad incertos oculos, & gaudia vana.

LONDON:
Printed by N. OKES, for *I. S.*
1635.

The title-page of the second Quarto, 1635.

CATILINE
HIS
CONSPIRACY.

A Tragedy.

First Acted in the yeare 1611. By the
Kings MAIESTIES
SERVANTS.

With the allowance of the Master
of REVELLS.

The Author *B. J.*

HORAT.

——*His non plebecula gaudet:*
Verùm equitis quoque jam migravit ab aure voluptas
Omnis, ad incertos oculos, & gaudia vana.

LONDON,
Printed by RICHARD BISHOP.

M. DC. XL.

Eee 3

The title-page of the second Folio, 1640.

CATILINE
HIS
CONSPIRACY.
A
Tragœdie.

As it is now Acted by His
MAJESTIE'S Servants;
at the Theatre *ROYAL*.

The Author *B. J.*

HORAT.
-------*His non plebecula gaudet:*
Verum equitis quoq;, jam migravit ab aure voluptas
Omnis, ad incertos oculos, & gaudia vana.

LONDON,
Printed for *A. C.* and are to be ſold by *William Cademan* at the *Pope's Head* in the Lower walk of the *New-Exchange*. 1669.

The title-page of the third Quarto, 1669.

CATILINE
HIS
CONSPIRACY.
A
Tragœdie.

As it is now Acted by His
MAJESTIE'S Servants;
at the Threatre *ROYAL.*

The Author *B. J.*

HORAT.
——*His non plebecula gaudet:*
Verum equitis quoq; jam migravit ab aure voluptas
Omnis, ad incertos oculos, & gaudia vana.

LONDON,

Printed for *A. C.* and are to be ſold by *William*
Cademan at the *Pope's Head* in the Lower
walk of the *New-Exchange.* 1674

The title-page of the fourth Quarto, 1674.

TO THE GREAT EXAMPLE OF HONOR, AND VERTVE,

THE MOST NOBLE

William,

EARLE OF PEMBROKE,

LORD CHAMBERLAINE, &c.

MY LORD,

In so thick, and darke an ignorance, as now almost couers the age, I craue leaue to stand neare your light: and, by that, to bee read. Posteritie may pay your benefit the honor, & thanks: when it shall know, that you dare, in these Iig-giuen times, to countenance a legitimate Poeme. I must call it so, against all noise of opinion: from whose crude, and ayrie reports, I appeale, to that great and singular faculty of iudgement in your Lordship, able to vindicate truth from error. It is the first (of this race) that euer I dedicated to any person, and had I not thought it the best, it should haue beene taught a lesse ambition. Now, it approcheth your censure cheerefully, and with the same assurance, that innocency would appeare before a magistrate.

Your Lo. most faithfull
honorer,
BEN. IONSON.

DEDICATION. HONOR] HONOUR *F2* PEMBROKE] *PENBROOKE* Q LORD CHAMBERLAINE *not in Q* 4 *honor*] honour *F2* 6 *Poeme*] Poëme *Q* 10 *error*] errour *F2* 17 honorer,] *Honorer.* Q

TO THE READER IN ORDINAIRIE.

The Muses forbid, that I should restrayne your medling, whom I see alreadie busie with the Title, and tricking ouer the leaues: It is your owne. I departed with my right, when I let it first abroad. And, now, so secure an Interpreter I am of my chance, that neither praise, nor dispraise from you can affect mee. Though you commend the two first Actes, with the people, because they are the worst; and dislike the Oration of Cicero, *in regard you read some pieces of it, at Schoole, and vnderstand them not yet; I shall finde the way to forgiue you. Be anything you will be, at your owne charge. Would I had deseru'd but halfe so well of it in translation, as that ought to deserue of you in iudgment, if you haue any. I know you will pretend (whosoeuer you are) to haue that, and more. But all pretences are not iust claymes. The commendation of good things may fall within a many, their approbation but in a few; for the most commend out of affection, selfe tickling, an easinesse, or imitation: but men iudge only out of knowledge. That is the trying faculty. And, to those works that will beare a Iudge, nothing is more dangerous then a foolish prayse. You will say I shall not haue yours, therfore; but rather the contrary, all vexation of Censure. If I were not aboue such molestations now, I had great cause to think vnworthily of my studies, or they had so of mee. But I leaue you to your exercise. Beginne.*

To the Reader extraordinary.

You I would vnderstand to be the better Man, though Places in Court go otherwise: to you I submit my selfe, and worke. Farewell.

BEN: IONSON.

TO THE READER *om. Ff*

The Persons of the Play.

SYLLA'S GHOST.

CATILINE.	CICERO.
LENTVLVS.	ANTONIVS.
CETHEGVS.	CATO.
CVRIVS.	CATVLVS.
AVTRONIVS.	CRASSVS.
VARGVNTEIVS.	CAESAR.
LONGINVS.	QV. CICERO.
LECCA.	SYLLANVS.
FVLVIVS.	FLACCVS.
BESTIA.	POMTINIVS.
GABINIVS.	SANGA.
STATILIVS.	SENATORS.
CEPARIVS.	ALLOBROGES.
CORNELIVS.	PETREIVS.
VOLTVRTIVS.	SOVLDIERS.
AVRELIA.	PORTER.
FVLVIA.	LICTORS.
SEMPRONIA.	SERVANTS.
GALLA.	PAGES.

CHORVS.

THE SCENE

ROME.

THE PERSONS OF THE PLAY] *The names of the Actors* Q CATILINE] L. Sergius Catiline *G* LENTVLVS] Publius Lentulus *G* CETHEGVS] Caius Cethegus *G* CVRIVS] Quintus Curius *G* LONGINVS] Lucius Cassius Longinus *G* LECCA] Porcius Lecca *G* BESTIA] Lucius Bestia *G* GABINIVS] Gabinius Cimber *G* CORNELIVS] Caius Cornelius *G* AVRELIA] Aurelia Orestilla *G* ANTONIVS] Caius Antonius *G* SANGA] Quintus Fabius Sanga *G* *THE SCENE* ROME *not in Q*: The SCENE partly at Rome, and partly in Fesulæ. *G* *After* The Scene *F2 inserts the names of* The principall Tragœdians *given in F1 at the end of the Play.*

CATILINE.

Act I.

SYLLA'S *Ghost.*

DO'st thou not feele me, *Rome?* not yet? Is night
So heauy on thee, and my weight so light?
Can SYLLA's Ghost arise within thy walls,
Lesse threatning, then an earth-quake, the quick falls
Of thee, and thine? shake not the frighted heads
Of thy steepe towers? or shrinke to their first beds?
Or, as their ruine the large *Tyber* fills,
Make that swell vp, and drowne thy seuen proud hills?
What sleepe is this doth seize thee, so like death,
And is not it? Wake, feele her, in my breath:
Behold, I come, sent from the *Stygian* sound,
As a dire vapor, that had cleft the ground,
T'ingender with the night, and blast the day;
Or like a pestilence, that should display
Infection through the world: which, thus, I doe. *Discouers Catiline in his study.*
PLVTO be at thy councells; and into
Thy darker bosome enter SYLLA's spirit:
All, that was mine, and bad, thy brest inherit.
Alas, how weake is that, for CATILINE!
Did I but say (vaine voice!) all that was mine?
All, that the GRACCHI, CINNA, MARIVS would;
What now, had I a body againe, I could,
Comming from hell; what Fiends would wish should be;
And HANNIBAL could not haue wish'd to see:
Thinke thou, and practice. Let the long-hid seeds

Act I] ACT I. SCENE I. | *A Room in Catiline's House.* | *The Ghost of Sylla rises.* G I. 10 breath:] breath. *Q* 15 *Stage direction not in Q*: *The curtain draws, and Catiline is discovered in his study.* G 20 voice! *corr. Q, Ff*: voice *Q originally*

Of treason, in thee, now shoot forth in deeds,
Ranker then horror ; and thy former facts
Not fall in mention, but to vrge new acts :
Conscience of them prouoke thee on to more.
Be still thy incests, murders, rapes before
Thy sense ; thy forcing first a *Vestall* nunne ;
Thy parricide, late, on thine owne onely sonne,
After his mother ; to make emptie way
For thy last wicked nuptialls ; worse, then they,
That blaze that act of thy incestuous life,
Which got thee, at once, a daughter, and a wife.
I leaue the slaughters, that thou didst for me,
Of *Senators ;* for which, I hid for thee
Thy murder of thy brother, (being so brib'd)
And writ him in the list of my proscrib'd
After thy fact, to saue thy little shame :
Thy incest, with thy sister, I not name.
These are too light. *Fate* will haue thee pursue
Deedes, after which, no mischiefe can be new ;
The ruine of thy countrey : thou wert built
For such a worke, and borne for no lesse guilt.
What though defeated once th'hast beene, and knowne,
Tempt it againe : That is thy act, or none.
What all the seuerall ills, that visite earth,
(Brought forth by night, with a sinister birth)
Plagues, famine, fire could not reach vnto,
The sword, nor surfets ; let thy furie doe :
Make all past, present, future ill thine owne ;
And conquer all example, in thy one.
Nor let thy thought find any vacant time
To hate an old, but still a fresher crime
Drowne the remembrance : let not mischiefe cease,
But, while it is in punishing, encrease.
Conscience, and care die in thee ; and be free

I. 27 then] than *F2* (*et passim*) 32 thine] thy *F2* onely *Ff*: naturall *Q* 33 mother ;] Mother, *Q* 35 blaze *Ff* : fame *Q* 37 slaughters,] *The comma faint or lost in F1* 46 guilt.] guilt : *Q* 51 fire] fire, *F2*

Not heau'n it selfe from thy impietie :
Let night grow blacker with thy plots ; and day,
At shewing but thy head forth, start away
From this halfe-spheare : and leaue *Romes* blinded walls
T'embrace lusts, hatreds, slaughters, funeralls,
And not recouer sight, till their owne flames
Doe light them to their ruines. All the names
Of thy confederates, too, be no lesse great
In hell, then here : that, when we would repeat
Our strengths in muster, we may name you all,
And *Furies*, vpon you, for *Furies*, call.
Whilst, what you doe, may strike them into feares,
Or make them grieue, and wish your mischiefe theirs.

CATILINE.

IT is decree'd. Nor shall thy Fate, ô *Rome*,
Resist my vow. Though hills were set on hills,
And seas met seas, to guard thee ; I would through :
I, plough vp rocks, steepe as the *Alpes*, in dust ;
And laue the *Tyrrhene* waters, into clouds ;
But I would reach thy head, thy head, proud citie.
The ills, that I haue done, cannot be safe
But by attempting greater ; and I feele
A spirit, within me, chides my sluggish hands,
And sayes, they haue beene innocent too long.
Was I a man, bred great, as *Rome* her selfe ?
One, form'd for all her honors, all her glories ?
Equall to all her titles ? that could stand
Close vp, with ATLAS ; and sustaine her name
As strong, as he doth heau'n ? And, was I,
Of all her brood, mark'd out for the repulse
By her no voice, when I stood *Candidate*,
To be commander in the *Pontick* warre ?
I will, hereafter, call her step-dame, euer.
If shee can loose her nature, I can loose
My pietie ; and in her stony entrailes

I. 71 may] doth *Q* After 72] *Sinks.* G 92 loose] lose *F2*

Dig me a seate: where, I will liue, againe,
The labour of her wombe, and be a burden,
Weightier then all the prodigies, and monsters,
That shee hath teem'd with, since shee first knew MARS.

CATILINE, AVRELIA.

WHo's there? AVR. 'Tis I. CAT. AVRELIA?
AVR. Yes. CAT. Appeare,
And breake, like day, my beautie, to this circle:
Vpbraid thy *Phœbus*, that he is so long
In mounting to that point, which should giue thee
Thy proper splendor. Wherefore frownes my sweet?
He kisseth them. Haue I too long beene absent from these lips,
This cheeke, these eyes? What is my trespasse? speake.
AVR. It seemes, you know, that can accuse your selfe.
CAT. I will redeeme it. AVR. Still, you say so. When?
CAT. When ORESTILLA, by her bearing well
These my retirements, and stolne times for thought,
Shall giue their effects leaue to call her Queene
Of all the world, in place of humbled *Rome*.
AVR. You court me, now. CAT. As I would alwayes, Loue,
By this *ambrosiack* kisse, and this of *nectar*,
Wouldst thou but heare as gladly, as I speake.
Could my AVRELIA thinke, I meant her lesse;
When, wooing her, I first remou'd a wife,
And then a sonne, to make my bed, and house
Spatious, and fit t'embrace her? These were deeds
Not t'haue begun with, but to end with more,
And greater: " He that, building, stayes at one
" Floore, or the second, hath erected none.
'Twas how to raise thee, I was meditating;
To make some act of mine answere thy loue:
That loue, that, when my state was now quite sunke,
Came with thy wealth, and weigh'd it vp againe,
And made my'emergent-fortune once more looke

I. Before 98 CATILINE, AVRELIA.] *Enter Aurelia Orestilla.* G, continuing the scene 98 CAT.] AVR. *Q* 102 splendor] splendour *Q* 103 *Stage direction not in Q* 125 emergent-] emergent *Q, F2*

Aboue the maine; which, now, shall hit the starres,
And stick my ORESTILLA, there, amongst 'hem,
If any tempest can but make the billow,
And any billow can but lift her greatnesse.
But, I must pray my loue, shee will put on
Like habites with my selfe. I haue to doe
With many men, and many natures. Some,
That must be blowne, and sooth'd; as LENTVLVS,
Whom I haue heau'd, with magnifying his bloud,
And a vaine dreame, out of the SYBILL's bookes,
That a third man, of that great family,
Whereof he is descended, the CORNELII,
Should be a king in *Rome*: which I haue hir'd
The flatt'ring AVGVRES to interpret him,
CINNA, and SYLLA dead. Then, bold CETHEGVS,
Whose valour I haue turn'd into his poyson,
And prais'd so into daring, as he would
Goe on vpon the gods, kisse lightning, wrest
The engine from the CYCLOP's, and giue fire
At face of a full cloud, and stand his ire:
When I would bid him moue. Others there are,
Whom enuy to the state drawes, and puts on,
For contumelies receiu'd, (and such are sure ones)
As CVRIVS, and the fore-nam'd LENTVLVS,
Both which haue beene degraded, in the *Senate*,
And must haue their disgraces, still, new rub'd,
To make 'hem smart, and labour of reuenge.
Others, whom meere ambition fires, and dole
Of *prouinces* abroad, which they haue fain'd
To their crude hopes, and I as amply promis'd:
These, LECCA, VARGVNTEIVS, BESTIA', AVTRONIVS.
Some, whom their wants oppresse, as th'idle Captaynes
Of SYLLA's troops: and diuers *Roman* Knights
(The profuse wasters of their patrimonies)

I. 127 'hem] 'em *F3* (*et passim*) 145 ire:] ire, *Q* 156 BESTIA'] *Bestia'* Q: BESTIA *Ff*

So threatned with their debts as they will, now,
Runne any desperate fortune, for a change.
These, for a time, we must relieue, AVRELIA,
And make our house the safe-guard : like, for those,
That feare the law, or stand within her gripe,
For any act past, or to come. Such will
From their owne crimes, be factious, as from ours.
Some more there be, slight ayrelings, will be wonne,
With dogs, and horses ; or, perhaps, a whore ;
Which must be had : and, if they venter liues,
For vs, AVRELIA, we must hazard honors
A little. Get thee store, and change of women,
As I haue boyes ; and giue 'hem time, and place,
And all conniuence : be thy selfe, too, courtly ;
And entertayne, and feast, sit vp, and reuell ;
Call all the great, the faire, and spirited *Dames*
Of *Rome* about thee ; and beginne a fashion
Of freedome, and community. Some will thanke thee,
Though the sowre *Senate* frowne, whose heads must ake
In feare, and feeling too. We must not spare
Or cost, or modestie. It can but shew
Like one of IVNO's, or of IOVE's disguises,
In either thee, or mee : and will as soone,
When things succeed, be throwne by, or let fall,
As is a vaile put off, a visor chang'd,
Or the *scene* shifted, in our *theaters*—— *A noyse without.*
Who's that? It is the voyce of LENTVLVS.
AVR. Or of CETHEGVS. CAT. In, my faire AVRELIA,
And thinke vpon these arts. They must not see,
How farre you are trusted with these priuacies ;
Though, on their shoulders, necks, and heads you rise.

I. 160 their debts *corr. Q, Ff*: debts *Q originally* 163 the] their *Q* safe-guard : like *Ff*: saue-gard. Like *Q* 167 be, *corr. Q, Ff*: be *Q originally* 169 venter] venture *F3* 176 thee ;] thee, *Q* 181 disguises,] disguises *Q* 183 fall,] fall ; *Q* 185 *theaters*——] *Theaters.* Q *Stage direction not in Q* 188 arts.] artes: *Q* 190 on *Ff*: by *Q* *Exit Aurelia.* add G Before 191 LENTVLVS . . . CATILINE.] *Enter Lentulus, in discourse with Cethegus.* G, continuing the scene

LENTVLVS, CETHEGVS,
CATILINE.

IT is, me thinks, a morning, full of fate!
It riseth slowly, as her sollen carre
Had all the weights of sleepe, and death hung at it!
Shee is not rosy-finger'd, but swolne black!
Her face is like a water, turn'd to bloud,
And her sick head is bound about with clouds,
As if shee threatned night, ere noone of day!
It does not looke, as it would haue a haile,
Or health, wish'd in it, as on other mornes.
CET. Why, all the fitter, LENTVLVS: our comming
Is not for salutation, we haue business.
CAT. Said nobly, braue CETHEGVS. Where's AVTRONIVS?
CET. Is he not come? CAT. Not here. CET. Nor VARGVNTEIVS?
CAT. Neither. CET. A fire in their beds, and bosomes,
That so will serue their sloth, rather then vertue.
They are no *Romanes*, and at such high need
As now. LEN. Both they, LONGINVS, LECCA, CVRIVS,
FVLVIVS, GABINIVS, gaue me word, last night,
By LVCIVS BESTIA, they would all be here,
And early. CET. Yes? As you, had I not call'd you.
Come, we all sleepe, and are meere dormice; flies,
A little lesse then dead: more dulnesse hangs
On vs, then on the morne. W'are spirit-bound,
In ribs of ice; our whole bloud are one stone;
And honor cannot thaw vs; nor our wants:
Though they burne, hot as feuers, to our states.
CAT. I muse they would be tardy, at an houre
Of so great purpose. CET. If the gods had call'd
Them, to a purpose, they would iust haue come

I. 191 fate!] *Fate.* Q 193 it!] it. *Q* 194 black!] blacke. *Q*
197 day!] day. *Q* 198–9 haile . . . health] *Hayle* . . . *Health* Q
215 honor] Honour *Q* wants:] wants, *Q*

With the same tortoyse speed ! that are thus slow
To such an action, which the gods will enuy :
As asking no lesse meanes, then all their powers
Conioyn'd, t'effect. I would haue seene *Rome* burn't,
By this time ; and her ashes in an vrne :
The kingdome of the *Senate*, rent a-sunder ;
And the degenerate, talking gowne runne frighted,
Out of the aire of *Italie*. CAT. Spirit of men !
Thou, heart of our great enterprise ! how much
I loue these voices in thee ! CET. O, the dayes
Of SYLLA's sway, when the free sword tooke leaue
To act all that it would ! CAT. And was familiar
With entrailes, as our *Augures !* CET. Sonnes kild fathers,
Brothers their brothers. CAT. And had price, and praise.
All hate had licence giuen it : all rage raines.
CET. Slaughter bestrid the streets, and stretch'd himselfe
To seeme more huge ; whilst to his stayned thighes
The gore he drew flow'd vp : and carryed downe
Whole heaps of limmes, and bodies, through his arch.
No age was spar'd, no sexe. CAT. Nay, no degree.
CET. Not infants, in the porch of life were free.
The sick, the old, that could but hope a day
Longer, by natures bountie, not let stay.
Virgins, and widdowes, matrons, pregnant wiues,
All dyed. CAT. 'Twas crime inough, that they had liues.
To strike but onely those, that could doe hurt,
Was dull, and poore. Some fell to make the number,
As some the prey. CET. The rugged CHARON fainted,
And ask'd a nauy, rather then a boate,
To ferry ouer the sad world that came :
The mawes, and dens of beasts could not receiue
The bodies, that those soules were frighted from ;
And e'en the graues were fild with men, yet liuing,
Whose flight, and feare had mix'd them, with the dead
CAT. And this shall be againe, and more, and more,

I. 220 speed !] speed, *Q* 226 gowne] Gowne, *Q* 253 flight] fligh *F2*

Now LENTVLVS, the third CORNELIVS,
Is to stand vp in *Rome*. LEN. Nay, vrge not that
Is so vncertaine. CAT. How! LEN. I meane, not clear'd.
And, therefore, not to be reflected on.
CAT. The SYBILL's leaues vncertayne? or the comments
Of our graue, deepe, diuining men not cleare?
LEN. All prophecies, you know, suffer the torture.
CAT. But this, already, hath confess'd, without.
And so beene weigh'd, examin'd, and compar'd,
As 't were malicious ignorance in him,
Would faint in the beliefe. LEN. Doe you beleeue it?
CAT. Doe I loue LENTVLVS? or pray to see it?
LEN. The *Augures* all are constant, I am meant.
CAT. They'had lost their science else. LEN. They count from CINNA.
CAT. And SYLLA next, and so make you the third;
All that can say the sunne is ris'n, must thinke it.
LEN. Men marke me more, of late, as I come forth!
CAT. Why, what can they doe lesse? CINNA, and SYLLA
Are set, and gone: and we must turne our eyes
On him that is, and shines. Noble CETHEGVS,
But view him with me, here! He lookes, already,
As if he shooke a scepter, o're the *Senate*,
And the aw'd purple dropt their rods, and axes!
The statues melt againe; and houshold gods
In grones confesse the trauaile of the citie;
The very walls sweat bloud before the change;
And stones start out to ruine, ere it comes.
CET. But he, and we, and all are idle still.
LEN. I am your creature, SERGIVS: And what ere
The great CORNELIAN name shall winne to be,

I. 259 leaues] leafes *F2* 268 They'had *corr. Q, Ff*: They had *Q originally* 271 forth!] forth. *Q* 275 here!] here: *Q* 277 axes!] axes. *Q* 279 trauaile] travailes *F2*

It is not *Augury*, nor the SYBILS bookes,
But CATILINE that makes it. CAT. I am shaddow
To honor'd LENTVLVS, and CETHEGVS here,
Who are the heires of MARS. CET. By MARS himselfe,
CATILINE is more my parent: for whose vertue
Earth cannot make a shaddow great inough,
Though enuy should come too. O, there they are.
Now we shall talke more, though we yet doe nothing.

AVTRONIVS, VARGVNTEIVS, LONGINVS,
CVRIVS, LECCA, BESTIA, FVLVIVS,
To them. GABINIVS, &c.

HAile LVCIVS CATILINE. VAR. Haile noble
SERGIVS.
LON. Haile PVBLIVS LENTVLꝰ. CVR. Haile the
third CORNELIꝰ.
LEC. CAIVS CETHEGVS haile. CET. Haile sloth,
and words,
In steed of men, and spirits. CAT. Nay, deare CAIVS——
CET. Are your eyes yet vnseel'd? Dare they looke day
In the dull face? CAT. Hee's zealous, for the'affaire,
And blames your tardy comming, gentlemen.
CET. Vnlesse, we had sold our selues to sleepe, and ease,
And would be our slaues slaues—— CAT. Pray you for-
beare.
CET. The north is not so starke, and cold. CAT.
CETHEGVS——
BES. We shall redeeme all; if your fire will let vs.
CAT. You are too full of lightning, noble CAIVS.
Boy, see all doores be shut, that none approch vs,
On this part of the house. Goe you, and bid

I. 291 After 'too.' *Noise within.* G they are] they'are *Q, Ff* Before 293 AVTRONIVS . . . &c.] *Enter Autronius, Vargunteius, Longinus, Curius, Lecca, Bestia, Fulvius, Gabinius, &c. and Servants.* G, continuing the scene *To them* not in Q 294 PVBLIVS] *Publius* Q: PVB: *F1*: PUB. *F2* 296 CAIVS——] *Caius*; Q 297 CET.] GET. *F1* vnseel'd *Q*: vnsee'ld *F1*: unsee'ld *F2* 301 slaues——] slaues. *Q* 302 CETHEGVS——] *Cethegus.* Q 306 After 'house.' *Exit Servant.* G

The Priest, he kill the slaue I mark'd last night;
And bring me of his bloud, when I shall call him:
Till then, wait all without. VAR. How is't, AVTRONIVS!
AVT. LONGINVS? LON. CVRIVS? CVR. LECCA? VAR. Feele you nothing?
LON. A strange, vn-wonted horror doth inuade me,
I know not what it is! LEC. The day goes back,
Or else my senses! CVR. As at ATREVS feast!
FVL. Darknesse growes more, and more! LEN. The *vestall* flame,
A darknesse comes ouer the place.
I thinke, be out. GAB. What grone was that? CET. Our phant'sies.
A grone of many people is heard vnder ground.
Strike fire, out of our selues, and force a day.
AVR. Againe it sounds! BES. As all the citie gaue it! *Another.*
CET. We feare what our selues faine. VAR. What light is this?
A fiery light appeares.
CVR. Looke forth. LEN. It still growes greater! LEC. From whence comes it?
LON. A bloudy arme it is, that holds a pine
Lighted, aboue the *Capitoll!* and, now,
It waues vnto vs! CAT. Braue, and omenous!
Our enterprise is seal'd. CET. In spight of darkeness,
That would discountenance it. Looke no more;
We loose time, and our selues. To what we came for,
Speake LVCIVS, we attend you. CAT. Noblest *Romanes*,
If you were lesse, or that your faith, and vertue
Did not hold good that title, with your bloud,
I should not, now, vnprofitably spend
My selfe in words, or catch at empty hopes,
By ayrie wayes, for solide certainties.
But since in many, and the greatest dangers,
I still haue known you no lesse true, then valiant,
And that I tast, in you, the same affections,

I. 309 After 'without.' *Exeunt Servants.* G 313, 316, 318, 319 *Stage directions not in Q* 321 *Capitoll !*] *Capitoll :* Q 322 omenous] ominous *F2* 325 loose] lose *F2* 327 or] or, *Q*

To will, or nill, to thinke things good, or bad,
Alike with me: (which argues your firme friendship)
I dare the boldlier, with you, set on foot,
Or leade, vnto this great, and goodliest action.
What I haue thought of it afore, you all
Haue heard apart. I then express'd my zeale
Vnto the glorie; now, the neede enflames me:
When I fore-thinke the hard conditions,
Our states must vnder-goe, except, in time,
We doe redeeme our selues to libertie,
And break the yron yoke, forg'd for our necks.
For, what lesse can we call it? when we see
The common-wealth engross'd so by a few,
The giants of the state, that doe, by turnes,
Enioy her, and defile her! All the earth,
Her Kings, and *Tetrarchs*, are their tributaries;
People, and nations, pay them hourely stipends:
The riches of the world flowes to their coffers,
And not, to *Romes*. While (but those few) the rest,
How euer great we are, honest, and valiant,
Are hearded with the vulgar; and so kept,
As we were onely bred, to consume corne;
Or weare out wooll; to drinke the cities water;
Vngrac'd, without authoritie, or marke;
Trembling beneath their rods: to whom, (if all
Were well in *Rome*) we should come forth bright axes.
All places, honors, offices are theirs!
Or where they will conferre 'hem! They leaue vs
The dangers, the repulses, iudgements, wants:
Which how long will you beare, most valiant spirits?
Were we not better to fall, once, with vertue,
Then draw a wretched, and dishonor'd breath,
To loose with shame, when these mens pride will laugh?
I call the faith of gods, and men to question,

I. 340 apart.] apart; *Q*: a part. *F2* 349 defile her!] defile her. *Q* 356 corne;] corne, *Q* 357 out] our *F2* wooll;] wooll, *Q* 359 rods:] rods, *Q* 361 theirs!] theirs; *Q* 362 'hem!] 'hem: *Q* 367 loose] lose *Q* 368 question,] question; *Q*

The power is in our hands ; our bodies able ;
Our mindes as strong ; o'th' contrary, in them,
All things growne aged, with their wealth, and yeeres :
There wants, but onely to beginne the businesse,
The issue is certaine. CET. LON. On, let vs goe on.
CVR. BES. Goe on, braue SERGIVS. CAT. It doth strike my soule,
(And, who can scape the stroke, that hath a soule,
Or, but the smallest aire of man within him ?)
To see them swell with treasure ; which they powre
Out i' their riots, eating, drinking, building,
I, i' the sea ! planing of hills with valleyes ;
And raysing vallies aboue hills ! whilst we
Haue not, to giue our bodies necessaries.
They ha' their change of houses, mannors, lordships ;
We scarce a fire, or poore houshold *Lar !*
They buy rare *Atticke* statues, *Tyrian* hangings,
Ephesian pictures, and *Corinthian* plate,
Attalicke garments, and now, new-found gemmes,
Since POMPEY went for *Asia*, which they purchase
At price of *prouinces !* The riuer *Phasis*
Cannot affoord 'hem fowle ; nor *Lucrine* lake
Oysters enow : *Circei*, too, is search'd
To please the witty gluttony of a meale !
Their ancient habitations they neglect,
And set vp new ; then, if the eccho like not
In such a roome, they pluck downe those, build newer,
Alter them too : and, by all frantick wayes,
Vexe their wild wealth, as they molest the people,
From whom they force it ! yet, they cannot tame,
Or ouer-come their riches ! Not, by making
Bathes, orchards, fish-pooles ! letting in of seas

I. 371 yeeres :] yeares. *Q* 380 hills ! *F1* : Hilles, *Q* : hils ; *F2* 383 poore] a poore *F2* *Lar !*] *Lar.* Q 386 and now, new-found] and, now new-found, *Q* 387 *Asia*,] *Asia ;* Q 388 *prouinces !*] *Prouinces.* Q 389 affoord] affourd *Q* 390 *Circei*] *Circes* F2 391 meale !] meale. *Q* 394 those,] those ; *Q* 395 too :] too ; *Q* 397 it !] it. *Q* 398 riches !] riches. *Q* 399 -pooles !] -pooles, *Q*

Here ! and, then there, forcing 'hem out againe,
With mountaynous heaps, for which the earth hath lost
Most of her ribs, as entrailes ! being now
Wounded no lesse for marble, then for gold.
We, all this while, like calme, benum'd Spectators,
Sit, till our seates doe cracke ; and doe not heare
The thundring ruines : whilst, at home, our wants,
Abroad, our debts doe vrge vs ; our states daily
Bending to bad, our hopes to worse : and, what
Is left, but to be crush'd ? Wake, wake braue friends,
And meet the libertie you oft haue wish'd for.
Behold, renowne, riches, and glory court you.
Fortune holds out these to you, as rewards.
Me thinkes (though I were dumbe) th'affaire it selfe,
The opportunity, your needs, and dangers,
With the braue spoile the warre brings, should inuite you.
Vse me your generall, or souldier : neither,
My minde, nor body shall be wanting to you.
And, being *Consul*, I not doubt t'effect,
All that you wish, if trust not flatter me,
And you'd not rather still be slaues, then free.

CET. Free, free. LON. 'Tis freedom. CVR. Freedom we all stand for.

CAT. Why, these are noble voyces ! Nothing wants then,
But that we take a solemne sacrament,
To strengthen our designe. CET. And so to act it.
Differring hurts, where powers are so prepar'd.

AVT. Yet, ere we enter into open act,
(With fauour) 'twere no losse, if 't might be enquir'd,
What the condition of these armes would be ?

VAR. I, and the meanes, to carry vs through ? CAT. How, friends !

I. 400 Here ! *F1*: Here ; *Q*: Here, *F2* 401 heaps,] heapes ; *Q* 402 entrailes !] entrayles, *Q* 406 ruines :] ruines, *Q* 407 vs ;] vs, *Q* 411 you. *corr. Q, Ff*: you ! *Q originally* 413 selfe, *F2*: selfe *Q, F1* 419 wish,] wish : *Q* 420 you'd not] you had *Q* 422 voyces !] voices. *Q* 425 so] most *Q* 429 through?] through. *Q*

Thinke you, that I would bid you, graspe the winde?
Or call you to th'embracing of a cloud?
Put your knowne valures on so deare a businesse,
And haue no other second then the danger,
Nor other gyrlond then the losse? Become
Your owne assurances. And, for the meanes,
Consider, first, the starke securitie
The common wealth is in now; the whole *Senate*
Sleepy, and dreaming no such violent blow;
Their forces all abroad; of which the greatest,
That might annoy vs most, is fardest off,
In *Asia*, vnder POMPEY: those, neare hand,
Commanded, by our friends; one army'in *Spaine*,
By CNEVS PISO; th'other in *Mauritania*,
By NVCERINVS; both which I haue firme,
And fast vnto our plot. My selfe, then, standing
Now to be *Consul;* with my hop'd Colleague
CAIVS ANTONIVS; one, no lesse engag'd
By'his wants then we: and, whom I'haue power to melt,
And cast in any mould. Beside, some others
That will not yet be nam'd, (both sure, and great ones)
Who, when the time comes, shall declare themselues,
Strong, for our party: so, that no resistance
In nature can be thought. For our reward, then,
First, all our debts are paid; dangers of law,
Actions, decrees, iudgements against vs quitted;
The rich men, as in SYLLA's times, proscrib'd,
And publication made of all their goods;
That house is yours; that land is his; those waters,
Orchards, and walkes a third's; he has that honor,
And he that office: Such a *prouince* falls
To VARGVNTEIVS: this to' AVTRONIVS: that
To bold CETHEGVS: *Rome* to LENTVLVS.
You share the world, her magistracies, priest-hoods,

I. 434 gyrlond] Garland *F3* 437 in] in, *Q* 447 ANTONIVS;] *Antonius*, Q 448 By'his] By's *F3* 459 he has] He' has *Q*: he' has *Ff* 460 office:] Office. *Q* 462 LENTVLVS] *Lentulus:* Q

Wealth, and felicitie amongst you, friends;
And CATILINE your seruant. Would you, CVRIVS,
Reuenge the contumely stuck vpon you,
In being remoued from the *Senate?* Now,
Now, is your time. Would PVBLIVS LENTVLVS
Strike, for the like disgrace? Now, is his time.
Would stout LONGINVS walke the streets of *Rome,*
Facing the *Prætor?* Now, has he a time
To spurne, and tread the *fasces,* into dirt,
Made of the vsurers, and the *Lictors* braines.
Is there a beautie, here in *Rome,* you loue?
An enemie you would kill? What head's not yours?
Whose wife, which boy, whose daughter, of what race,
That th'husband, or glad parents shall not bring you,
And boasting of the office? only, spare
Your selues, and you haue all the earth beside,
A field, to exercise your longings in.
I see you rais'd, and reade your forward mindes
High, in your faces. Bring the wine, and bloud
You haue prepar'd there. LON. How! CAT. I'haue kill'd a slaue,
And of his bloud caus'd to be mixt with wine.
Fill euery man his bowle. There cannot be
A fitter drinke, to make this *sanction* in.
Here, I beginne the sacrament to all.
O, for a clap of thunder, now, as loud,
As to be heard through-out the vniuerse,
To tell the world the fact, and to applaud it.
Be firme, my hand; not shed a drop: but powre
Fiercenesse into me, with it, and fell thirst
Of more, and more, till *Rome* be left as bloud-lesse,
As euer her feares made her, or the sword.
And, when I leaue to wish this to thee, step-dame,
Or stop, to effect it, with my powers fainting;
So may my bloud be drawne, and so drunke vp

I. 482 in] i' *Q* 483 After 'there.' *Enter Servants with a bowl.* G
491 powre] poure *Q* 492 it,] it; *Q* 493 more, till] more: Till *Q*

As is this slaues. LON. And so be mine. LEN. And mine. *They drinke.*
AVT. And mine. VAR. And mine. CET. Swell mee my bowle yet fuller.
Here, I doe drinke this, as I would doe CATO's,
Or the new fellow CICERO's: with that vow
Which CATILINE hath giuen. CVR. So doe I.
LEC. And I. BES. And I. FVL. And I. GAB. And all of vs.
CAT. Why, now's the businesse safe, and each man strengthned.
Sirrah, what aile you? PAG. Nothing. BES. Somewhat modest. *He spies one of his boyes not answere—*
CAT. Slaue, I will strike your soule out, with my foot,
Let me but find you againe with such a face:
You whelp—— BES. Nay, LVCIVS. CAT. Are you coying it,
When I command you to be free, and generall
To all? BES. You'll be obseru'd. CAT. Arise, and shew
But any least auersion i' your looke
To him that bourds you next, and your throat opens.
Noble confederates, thus farre is perfect.
Only your suffrages I will expect,
At the assembly for the choosing *Consuls*,
And all the voyces you can make by friends
To my election. Then, let me worke out
Your fortunes, and mine owne. Meane while, all rest
Seal'd vp, and silent, as when rigid frosts
Haue bound vp brookes, and riuers, forc'd wild beasts
Vnto their caues, and birds into the woods,
Clownes to their houses, and the countrey sleeps:
That, when the sodaine thaw comes, we may breake
Vpon 'hem like a deluge, bearing downe
Halfe *Rome* before vs, and inuade the rest
With cryes, and noise able to wake the vrnes

I. 498, 505 *Stage directions not in Q* 499 Swell] Crowne *Q*
508 whelp——] Whelpe. *Q*

Of those are dead, and make their ashes feare.
The horrors, that doe strike the world, should come
Loud, and vnlook'd for : till they strike, be dumbe.
CET. Oraculous SERGIVS! LEN. God-like CATILINE!

CHORVS.

CAn nothing great, and at the height
Remaine so long? but it's owne weight
Will ruine it? Or, is't blinde chance,
That still desires new states t'aduance,
And quit the old? Else, why must *Rome*,
Be by it selfe, now, ouer-come?
Hath shee not foes inow of those,
Whom shee hath made such, and enclose
Her round about? Or, are they none,
Except shee first become her owne?
O wretchednesse of greatest states,
To be obnoxious to these fates:
That cannot keepe, what they doe gaine;
And what they raise so ill sustaine!
Rome, now, is Mistris of the whole
World, sea, and land, to either pole;
And euen that fortune will destroy
The power that made it: shee doth ioy
So much in plentie, wealth, and ease,
As, now, th'excesse is her disease.
Shee builds in gold; and, to the starres;
As, if shee threatned heau'n with warres:
And seekes for hell, in quarries deepe,
Giuing the fiends, that there doe keepe,
A hope of day. Her women weare
The spoiles of nations, in an eare,

I. 527 feare. *Q*: feare, *F1*: feare; *F2* 528–9 "Thee . . ." Loud *Q* 530 SERGIVS! . . . CATILINE!] *Sergius*. . . . *Catiline*. Q *Exeunt.* add G 531–2 CAn nothing great . . . Remaine . . . *corr. Q, Ff*: Can nothing great . . . Remaine . . . *Q originally* 536 selfe, *F2*: selfe; *Q, F1* 544 raise] raise, *F2* sustaine!] sustaine. *Q* 548 it: shee] it. Shee *Q*

Chang'd for the treasure of a shell;
And, in their loose attires, doe swell
More light then sailes, when all windes play:
Yet, are the men more loose then they!
More kemb'd, and bath'd, and rub'd, and trim'd,
More sleek'd, more soft, and slacker limm'd;
As prostitute: so much, that kinde
May seeke it selfe there, and not finde.
They eate on beds of silke, and gold;
At yuorie tables; or, wood sold
Dearer then it: and, leauing plate,
Doe drinke in stone of higher rate.
They hunt all grounds; and draw all seas;
Foule euery brooke, and bush; to please
Their wanton tasts: and, in request
Haue new, and rare things; not the best!
  Hence comes that wild, and vast expence,
That hath enforc'd *Romes* vertue, thence,
Which simple pouerty first made:
And, now, ambition doth inuade
Her state, with eating auarice,
Riot, and euery other vice.
Decrees are bought, and lawes are sold,
Honors, and offices for gold;
The peoples voyces: and the free
Tongues, in the *Senate*, bribed bee.
Such ruine of her manners *Rome*
Doth suffer now, as shee's become
(Without the gods it soone gaine-say)
Both her owne spoiler, and owne prey.
  So, *Asia*, 'art thou cru'lly euen
With vs, for all the blowes thee giuen;
When we, whose vertue conquer'd thee,
Thus, by thy vices, ruin'd bee.

I. 557 shell;] shell! *F2* 560 they!] they, *Q* 562 sleek'd] *sleek* F3 571 tasts] *Taste* F3 572 best!] best. *Q* 581 voyces:] voyces, *F2*

Act II.

FVLVIA, GALLA, SERVANT.

THose roomes doe smell extremely. Bring my glasse,
And table hither. GALLA. GAL. Madame. FVL. Looke
Within, i' my blew cabinet, for the pearle
I'had sent me last, and bring it. GAL. That from CLODIVS?
FVL. From CAIVS CAESAR. You'are for CLODIVS, still.
Or CVRIVS. Sirrha, if QVINTVS CVRIVS come,
I am not in fit moode; I keepe my chamber:
Giue warning so, without. GAL. Is this it? madame.
FVL. Yes, helpe to hang it in mine eare. GAL. Beleeue me,
It is a rich one, madame. FVL. I hope so:
It should not be worne there else. Make an end,
And binde my haire vp. GAL. As 'twas yesterday?
FVL. No, nor the t'other day. When knew you me
Appeare, two dayes together, in one dressing?
GAL. Will you ha't i'the globe, or spire? FVL. How thou wilt;
Any way, so thou wilt doe it, good impertinence.
Thy company, if I slept not very well
A nights, would make me, an errant foole, with questions.
GAL. Alas, madame—— FVL. Nay, gentle halfe o'the dialogue, cease.
GAL. I doe it, indeed, but for your exercise,
As your physitian bids me. FVL. How! Do's he bid you
To anger me for exercise? GAL. Not to anger you,
But stirre your bloud a little: There's difference

Act II.] ACT II. SCENE I. | *A Room in Fulvia's House.* | *Enter Fulvia, Galla, and Servant.* G 1 extremely.] extremely; *Q* 2 hither.] hither, *corr. Q*: hether, *Q originally* 6 After 'CVRIVS.' *Exit Galla.* G 8 After 'without.' *Exit Servant.* | *Re-enter Galla.* G 19 Alas, madame——] Alas Madam. *Q*

Betweene luke-warme, and boyling, madame. FVL. IOVE!
Shee meanes to cooke me, I thinke? Pray you, ha' done.
GAL. I meane to dresse you, madame. FVL. O, my IVNO,
Be friend to me! Offring at wit, too? Why, GALLA!
Where hast thou been? GAL. Why? madam! FVL. What hast thou done
With thy poore innocent selfe? GAL. Wherefore? sweet madame!
FVL. Thus to come forth, so sodainely, a wit-worme?
GAL. It pleases you to flout one. I did dreame
Of lady SEMPRONIA—— FVL. O, the wonder is out.
That did infect thee? Well, and how? GAL. Me thought,
Shee did discourse the best—— FVL. That euer thou heard'st?
GAL. Yes. FVL. I' thy sleepe? Of what was her discourse?
GAL. O'the *republike*, madame, and the state,
And how shee was in debt, and where shee meant
To raise fresh summes: Shee's a great states-woman!
FVL. Thou dream'st all this? GAL. No, but you know she is, madam,
And both a mistris of the *latine* tongue,
And of the *greeke*. FVL. I, but I neuer dreamt it, GALLA,
As thou hast done, and therefore you must pardon me.
GAL. Indeed, you mock me, madame. FVL. Indeed, no.
Forth, with your learned lady. Shee has a wit, too?
GAL. A very masculine one. FVL. A shee-*Critick*, GALLA?
And can compose, in verse, and make quick iests,
Modest, or otherwise? GAL. Yes, madame. FVL. Shee can sing, too?
And play on instruments? GAL. Of all kindes, they say.

II. 29 Wherefore?] Wherefore, *Q* 30 sodainely] suddenly *F2* 32 SEMPRONIA——] *Sempronia. Q* 34 best——] best. *Q* 38 -woman!] -woman. *Q* 39 dream'st] dreampt'st *Q* 41 dreamt] dreampt *Q* 44 Forth,] Forth *Q* lady.] Ladie: *Q*

FVL. And doth dance rarely? GAL. Excellent! So well,
As a bald *Senator* made a iest, and said,
'Twas better, then an honest woman need.
FVL. Tut, shee may beare that. Few wise womens honesties
Will doe their courtship hurt. GAL. Shee's liberall too, madame.
FVL. What! of her money, or her honor, pray thee?
GAL. Of both, you know not which shee doth spare least.
FVL. A comely commendation. GAL. Troth, 'tis pitty,
Shee is in yeeres. FVL. Why, GALLA? ⟨GAL.⟩ For it is.
FVL. O, is that all? I thought thou'hadst had a reason.
GAL. Why, so I haue. Shee has beene a fine lady.
And, yet, shee dresses her selfe (except you, madame)
One o'the best in *Rome:* and paints, and hides
Her decayes very well. FVL. They say, it is
Rather a visor, then a face shee weares.
GAL. They wrong her verily, madame, shee do's sleeke
With crums of bread, and milke, and lies a nights
In as neat gloues——But shee is faine of late
To seeke, more then shee's sought to (the fame is)
And so spends that way. FVL. Thou know'st all! But, GALLA,
What say you to CATILINES lady, ORESTILLA?
There is the gallant! GAL. Shee do's well. Shee has
Very good sutes, and very rich: but, then,
Shee cannot put 'hem on. Shee knowes not how
To weare a garment. You shall haue her all
Iewels, and gold sometimes, so that her selfe
Appeares the least part of her selfe. No', in troth,
As I liue, madame, you put 'hem all downe

II. 49 Excellent!] Excellent. *Q* So *Q*: So, *Ff* 54 honor, pray thee] honour, pr'y thee *F2* 57 GAL. *Q2*, *F2*: GAI. *Q*: *om. F1* 66 gloues——] gloues. *Q* 68 all!] all. *Q* 70 gallant!] Gallant. *Q* 72 not] not, *Q* 75 No',] No' *Q*, *Ff*

With your meere strength of iudgement! and doe draw, too,
The world of *Rome* to follow you! you attire
Your selfe so diuersly! and with that spirit!
Still to the noblest humors! They could make
Loue to your dresse, although your face were away, they say.
FVL. And body too, and ha' the better match on't?
Say they not so too, GALLA? Now! What newes
Trauailes your count'nance with? SER. If 't please you, madame,
The lady SEMPRONIA is lighted at the gate;
GAL. CASTOR, my dreame, my dreame. SER. And comes to see you.
GAL. For VENVS sake, good madame see her. FVL. Peace,
The foole is wild, I thinke. GAL. And heare her talke,
Sweet madame, of state-matters, and the *Senate.*

SEMPRONIA, FVLVIA, GALLA.

FVLVIA, good wench, how dost thou? FVL. Well, SEMPRONIA.
Whither are you thus early addrest? SEM. To see
AVRELIA ORESTILLA. Shee sent for me.
I came to call thee, with me, wilt thou goe?
FVL. I cannot now, in troth, I haue some letters
To write, and send away. SEM. Alas, I pitty thee.
I ha' beene writing all this night (and am
So very weary) vnto all the *tribes,*
And *centuries,* for their voyces, to helpe CATILINE,
In his election. We shall make him *Consul,*
I hope, amongst vs. CRASSVS, I, and CAESAR
Will carry it for him. FVL. Do's he stand for't?

II. 77 iudgement!] iudgement; *Q* 78 follow you!] follow you: *Q*: follow! *F2* 79 diuersly! . . . spirit!] diuersly, . . . spirit, *Q* 80 humors!] humors. *Q* 83 After 'GALLA?' *Re-enter Servant.* G 87 After 'her.' *Exit Servant.* G Before 90 SEMPRONIA . . . GALLA.] *Enter Sempronia.* G, continuing the scene 93 me,] mee; *Q, F2*

SEM. H'is the chiefe *Candidate.* FVL. Who stands beside?
(Giue me some wine, and poulder for my teeth.
SEM. Here's a good pearle in troth! FVL. A pretty one.
SEM. A very orient one!) There are competitors,
CAIVS ANTONIVS, PVBLIVS GALBA, LVCIVS
CASSIVS LONGINVS, QVINTVS CORNIFICIVS,
CAIVS LICINIVS, and that talker, CICERO.
But CATILINE, and ANTONIVS will be chosen.
For foure o' the other, LICINIVS, LONGINVS,
GALBA, and CORNIFICIVS will giue way.
And CICERO they will not choose. FVL. No? why?
SEM. It will be cross'd, by the nobilitie.
GAL. (How shee do's vnderstand the common businesse!)
SEM. Nor, were it fit. He is but a new fellow,
An in-mate, here, in *Rome* (as CATILINE calls him)
And the *Patricians* should doe very ill,
To let the *Consul*-ship be so defil'd
As 't would be, if he obtain'd it! A meere vpstart,
That has no pedigree, no house, no coate,
No ensignes of a family? FVL. He'has vertue.
SEM. Hang vertue, where there is no bloud: 'tis vice,
And, in him, sawcinesse. Why should he presume
To be more learned, or more eloquent,
Then the nobilitie? or boast any qualitie
Worthy a noble man, himselfe not noble?
FVL. 'Twas vertue onely, at first, made all men noble.
SEM. I yeeld you, it might, at first, in *Romes* poore age;
When both her Kings, and *Consuls* held the plough,
Or garden'd well: But, now, we ha' no need,
To digge, or loose our sweat for't. We haue wealth,
Fortune and ease, and then their stock, to spend on,

II. 103 (Giue] Giue *Q* 104 troth!] troth. *Q* 105 one!)] one. *Q* 110 o'] of *Q* 111 way.] way, *Q* 114 (How . . . businesse!)] How . . . busines! *Q* 119 it!] it? *Q* 121 He'has] He has *F2* 131 loose] lose *F2*

Of name, for vertue ; which will beare vs out
'Gainst all new commers : and can neuer faile vs,
While the succession stayes. And, we must glorifie,
A mushrome ? one of yesterday ? a fine speaker ?
'Cause he has suck'd at *Athens ?* and aduance him,
To our owne losse ? No, FVLVIA. There are they
Can speake *greeke* too, if need were. CAESAR, and I,
Haue sate vpon him ; so hath CRASSVS, too :
And others. We haue all decreed his rest,
For rising farder. GAL. Excellent rare lady !
FVL. SEMPRONIA, you are beholden to my woman, here.
Shee do's admire you. SEM. O good GALLA, how dost thou ?
GAL. The better, for your learned ladiship.
SEM. Is this grey poulder, a good dentifrice ?
FVL. You see I vse it. SEM. I haue one is whiter.
FVL. It may be so. SEM. Yet this smells well. GAL. And clenses
Very well, madame, and resists the crudities.
SEM. FVLVIA, I pray thee, who comes to thee, now ?
Which of our great *Patricians ?* FVL. Faith, I keepe
No catalogue of 'hem. Sometimes I haue one,
Sometimes another, as the toy takes their blouds.
SEM. Thou hast them all. Faith, when was QVINTVS CVRIVS,
Thy speciall seruant, here ? FVL. My speciall seruant ?
SEM. Yes, thy idolater, I call him. FVL. He may be yours,
If you doe like him. SEM. How ! FVL. He comes, not, here,
I haue forbid him, hence. SEM. VENVS forbid !
FVL. Why ? SEM. Your so constant louer. FVL. So much the rather.

II. 133 vertue ;] Vertue, *Q* 139 CAESAR,] *Cæsar Q* 140 too :] too ; *Q* 145 your *corr. Q* : yonr *Q originally* 148 so.] so, *F2* 157 here,] here ; *F2*

I would haue change. So would you too, I am sure.
And now, you may haue him. SEM. Hee's fresh yet,
FVLVIA:
Beware, how you doe tempt me. FVL. Faith, for me,
He'is somewhat too fresh, indeed. The salt is gone,
That gaue him season. His good gifts are done.
He do's not yeeld the crop that he was wont.
And, for the act, I can haue secret fellowes,
With backs worth ten of him, and shall please me
(Now that the land is fled) a myriade better.
SEM. And those one may command. FVL. 'Tis true: these Lordings,
Your noble *Faunes*, they are so imperious, saucy,
Rude, and as boistrous as *Centaures*, leaping
A lady, at first sight. SEM. And must be borne
Both with, and out, they thinke. FVL. Tut, Ile obserue
None of 'hem all: nor humour 'hem a iot
Longer, then they come laden in the hand,
And say, here's t'one, for th'tother. SEM. Do's CAESAR giue well?
FVL. They shall all giue, and pay well, that come here,
If they will haue it: and that, iewells, pearle,
Plate, or round summes, to buy these. I'am not taken
With a cob-swan, or a high-mounting bull,
As foolish LEDA, and EVROPA were,
But the bright gold, with DANAE. For such price,
I would endure, a rough, harsh IVPITER,
Or ten such thundring gamsters: and refraine
To laugh at 'hem, till they are gone, with my much suffring.
SEM. Th'art a most happy wench, that thus canst make
Vse of thy youth, and freshnesse, in the season:
And hast it, to make vse of. FVL. (Which is the happinesse.)

II. 163 too *corr. Q, Ff*: to *Q originally* 165 do's *corr. Q, Ff*: dos *Q originally* 169 true:] true, *Q* Lordings] Lordlings *F2* 170 so imperious *corr. Q, Ff*: so, imperious *Q originally* 171 *Centaures*,] *Centaures*; *Q* 174 humour] humor *Q* 178 that, iewells] that, jewels *F2*: that iewels *Q*: that iewells *F1* 184 gamsters:] Gamsters; *Q* 188 it,] it *Q*

SEM. I am, now, faine to giue to them, and keepe
Musique, and a continuall table, to inuite 'hem;
FVL. (Yes, and they study your kitchin, more then you)
SEM. Eate myselfe out with vsury, and my lord, too,
And all my officers, and friends beside,
To procure moneyes, for the needfull charge
I must be at, to haue 'hem: and, yet, scarce
Can I atchieue 'hem, so. FVL. Why, that's because
You affect yong faces onely, and smooth chinnes,
SEMPRONIA. If you'ld loue beards, and bristles,
(One with another, as others doe) or wrinkles——
Who's that? Looke GALLA. GAL. 'Tis the party, madame.
FVL. What party? Has he no name? GAL. 'Tis QVINTVS CVRIVS.
FVL. Did I not bid 'hem, say, I kept my chamber?
GAL. Why, so they doe. SEM. Ile leaue you, FVLVIA.
FVL. Nay, good SEMPRONIA, stay. SEM. In faith, I will not.
FVL. By IVNO, I would not see him. SEM. Ile not hinder you.
GAL. You know, he will not be kept out, madame. SEM. No,
Nor shall not, carefull GALLA, by my meanes.
FVL. As I doe liue, SEMPRONIA—— SEM. What needs this?
FVL. Goe, say, I am a-sleepe, and ill at ease.
SEM. By CASTOR, no, I'le tell him, you are awake;
And very well. Stay GALLA; Farewell FVLVIA:
I know my manners. Why doe you labour, thus,
With action, against purpose? QVINTVS CVRIVS,
Shee is, yfaith, here, and in disposition.
FVL. Spight, with your courtesie! How shall I be tortur'd!

II. 189–90 *G divides at* 'music | And' 191 (Yes . . . you)] Yes . . . you: *Q* 197 yong] young *F2* 198 you'ld *F2*: youl'd *Q, F1* 200 *Knocking within.* add G 208 SEMPRONIA——] *Sempronia.* Q 210 no,] no; *Q* 214 *Exit.* add G 215 courtesie!] courtesie. *Q*

CVRIVS, FVLVIA, GALLA.

WHere are you, faire one, that conceale your selfe,
And keepe your beautie, within locks, and barres, here,
Like a fooles treasure? FVL. True, shee was a foole,
When, first, shee shew'd it to a thiefe. CVR. How, pretty solennesse!
So harsh, and short? FVL. The fooles artillery, sir.
CVR. Then, take my gowne off, for th'encounter. FVL. Stay sir.
I am not in the moode. CVR. I'le put you into't.
FVL. Best put your selfe, i'your case againe, and keepe
Your furious appetite warme, against you haue place for't.
CVR. What! doe you coy it? FVL. No sir. I'am not proud.
CVR. I would you were. You thinke, this state becomes you?
By HERCVLES, it do's not. Looke i'your glasse, now,
And see, how sciruely that countenance shewes;
You would be loth to owne it. FVL. I shall not change it.
CVR. Faith, but you must; and slack this bended brow;
And shoot lesse scorne: there is a fortune comming
Towards you, Daintie, that will take thee, thus,
And set thee aloft, to tread vpon the head
Of her owne statue, here, in *Rome*. FVL. I wonder,
Who let this promiser in! Did you, good diligence?
Giue him his bribe, againe. Or if you had none,
Pray you demand him, why he is so ventrous,
To presse, thus, to my chamber, being forbidden,
Both, by my selfe, and seruants? CVR. How! This's handsome!
And somewhat a new straine! FVL. 'Tis not strain'd, sir.
'Tis very naturall. CVR. I haue knowne it otherwise,

II. Before 216 CVRIVS . . . GALLA] *Enter Curius.* G, continuing the scene 216 selfe,] selfe; *Q* 219 solennesse] sullennesse *F2* 221 th'encounter] the'encounter *Q*

Betweene the parties, though. F v L. For your fore-knowledge,
Thanke that, which made it. It will not be so,
Hereafter, I assure you. C v R. No, my mistris?
F v L. No, though you bring the same materialls. C v R. Heare me,
You ouer-act when you should vnder-doe.
A little call your selfe againe, and thinke.
If you doe this to practise on me', or finde
At what forc'd distance you can hold your seruant;
That'it be an artificiall trick, to enflame,
And fire me more, fearing my loue may need it,
As, heretofore, you ha' done: why, proceede.
F v L. As I ha' done heretofore? C v R. Yes, when you'ld faine
Your husbands iealousie, your seruants watches,
Speake softly, and runne often to the dore,
Or to the windore, forme strange feares that were not;
As if the pleasure were lesse acceptable,
That were secure. F v L. You are an impudent fellow.
C v R. And, when you might better haue done it, at the gate,
To take me in at the casement. F v L. I take you in?
C v R. Yes, you my lady. And, then, being a-bed with you,
To haue your well taught wayter, here, come running,
And cry, her lord, and hide me without cause,
Crush'd in a chest, or thrust vp in a chimney.
When he, tame crow, was winking at his farme;
Or, had he beene here, and present, would haue kept
Both eyes, and beake seal'd vp, for sixe *sesterces*.
F v L. You haue a slanderous, beastly, vnwash'd tongue,
I' your rude mouth, and sauouring your selfe,
Vn-manner'd lord. C v R. How now! F v L. It is your title, sir.

II. 244 mistris] Mistresse *Q* (*so* 351) 245 No,] No *Q* 246 ouer-act . . . vnder-doe] ouer act . . . vnderdoe *Q* 248 me',] me' *Q*, *Ff* 252 done :] done ; *Q* 256 windore] Window *F3* 267 seal'd] seel'd *W*

Who (since you ha' lost your owne good name, and know not
What to loose more) care not, whose honor you wound,
Or fame, you poyson with it. You should goe,
And vent your selfe, i' the region, where you liue,
Among the suburbe-brothels, bawdes, and brokers,
Whither your broken fortunes haue design'd you.
CVR. Nay, then I must stop your fury, I see; and pluck
He offers to force her, and shee drawes her knife.
The tragick visor off. Come, lady CYPRIS,
Know your owne vertues, quickly. Ile not be
Put to the wooing of you thus, a-fresh,
At euery turne, for all the VENVS in you.
Yeeld, and be pliant; or by POLLVX—— How now?
Will LAIS turne a LVCRECE? FVL. No, but by CASTOR,
Hold off your rauishers hands, I pierce your heart, else.
Ile not be put to kill my selfe, as shee did,
For you, sweet TARQVINE. What? doe you fall off?
Nay, it becomes you graciously! Put not vp.
You'll sooner draw your weapon on me, I thinke it,
Then on the *Senate,* who haue cast you forth
Disgracefully, to be the common tale
Of the whole citie; base, infamous man!
For, were you other, you would there imploy
Your desperate dagger. CVR. FVLVIA, you doe know
The strengths you haue vpon me; doe not vse
Your power too like a tyran: I can beare,
Almost vntill you breake me. FVL. I doe know, sir,
So do's the *Senate,* too, know, you can beare.
CVR. By all the gods, that *Senate* will smart deepe
For your vpbraidings. I should be right sorry
To haue the meanes so to be veng'd on you,
(At least, the will) as I shall shortly on them.
But, goe you on still; fare you well, deare lady:

II. 272 loose] lose *F2* 273 fame,] fame' *Q, F1*: fame *F2* 278 *Stage direction not in Q* 285 did, *F3*: did *Q, Ff* 291 man !] Man : *Q* 295 tyran] Tyrant *F3* 298 that] the *F2*

You could not still be faire'vnlesse you were proud.
You will repent these moodes, and ere 't be long, too.
I shall ha' you come about, againe. F V L. Doe you thinke so?
C V R. Yes, and I know so. F V L. By what augurie?
C V R. By the faire entrailes of the matrons chests,
Gold, pearle, and iewells, here in *Rome*, which F V L V I A
Will then (but late) say that shee might haue shar'd:
And, grieuing, misse. F V L. Tut, all your promis'd mountaynes,
And seas, I am so stalely acquainted with——
C V R. But, when you see the vniuersall floud
Runne by your coffers; that my lords, the *Senators*,
Are sold for slaues, their wiues for bond-women,
Their houses, and fine gardens giuen away,
And all their goods, vnder the speare, at out-cry,
And you haue none of this; but are still F V L V I A,
Or perhaps lesse, while you are thinking of it:
You will aduise then, Coynesse, with your cushion,
And looke o' your fingers; say, how you were wish'd;
And so, he left you. F V L. Call him againe, G A L L A:
This is not vsuall! something hangs on this
That I must winne out of him. C V R. How now, melt you?
F V L. Come, you will laugh, now, at my easinesse!
But, 'tis no miracle: Doues, they say, will bill,
After their pecking, and their murmuring. C V R. Yes,
And then 'tis kindly. I would haue my loue
Angrie, sometimes, to sweeten off the rest
Of her behauiour. F V L. You doe see, I studie
How I may please you, then. But you thinke, C V R I V S,
'Tis couetise hath wrought me: if you loue me,
Change that vnkinde conceipt. C V R. By my lou'd soule,
I loue thee, like to it; and 'tis my studie,
More then mine owne reuenge, to make thee happy.

II. 316 out-cry] out cry *F1* 321 After 'you.' *Exit.* G After 'GALLA' *Exit Galla.* G 322 vsuall!] vsuall, *Q* 323 After 'him.' *Re-enter Curius.* G 324 easinesse!] easinesse? *Q* 331 me:] me; *Q*

F v l. And 'tis that iust reuenge doth make me happy
To heare you prosequute : and which, indeed,
Hath wonne me, to you, more, then all the hope
Of what can else be promis'd. I loue valour
Better, then any lady loues her face,
Or dressing : then my selfe do's. Let me grow
Still, where I doe embrace. But, what good meanes
Ha' you t'effect it ? Shall I know your proiect ?
C v r. Thou shalt, if thou'lt be gracious. F v l. As I can be.
C v r. And wilt thou kisse me, then ? F v l. As close as shells
Of cockles meet. C v r. And print 'hem deepe ? F v l. Quite through
Our subtle lips. C v r. And often ? F v l. I will sow 'hem,
Faster, then you can reape. What is your plot ?
C v r. Why, now my F v l v i a lookes, like her bright name !
And is her selfe ! F v l. Nay, answere me, your plot :
I pray thee tell me, Q v i n t v s. C v r. I, these sounds
She kisses and flatters him along still. Become a mistris. Here is harmonie !
When you are harsh, I see, the way to bend you
Is not with violence, but seruice. Cruell,
A lady is a fire : gentle, a light.
F v l. Will you not tell me, what I aske you ? C v r. All,
That I can thinke, sweet loue, or my brest holds,
Ile poure into thee. F v l. What is your designe, then ?
C v r. Ile tell thee ; C a t i l i n e shall now be *Consull :*
But, you will heare more, shortly. F v l. Nay, deare loue——
C v r. Ile speake it, in thine armes, let vs goe in.
Rome will be sack'd, her wealth will be our prize ;
By publique ruine, priuate spirits must rise.

II. 336 prosequute] prosecute *F2* 341 But,] But *Q* 348 name !] name, *Q* 349 selfe !] selfe. *Q* 350 pray thee] pr'ythee *F2* 351 harmonie !] harmony. *Q* *Stage direction not in Q* 359 loue——] Loue. *Q* 360 armes,] armes ; *Q* 362 *Exeunt.* add G

CHORVS.

GReat father MARS, and greater IOVE,
By whose high auspice, *Rome* hath stood
So long; and, first, was built in blood
Of your great nephew, that then stroue
Not with his brother, but your rites:
Be present to her now, as then,
And let not proud, and factious men
Against your wills oppose their mights.
Our *Consuls*, now, are to be made;
O, put it in the publique voice
To make a free, and worthy choice:
Excluding such as would inuade
The common wealth. Let whom we name
Haue wisedome, fore-sight, fortitude,
Be more with faith, then face endu'd,
And studie conscience, aboue fame.
Such, as not seeke to get the start
In state, by power, parts, or bribes,
Ambition's bawdes: but moue the *tribes*
By vertue, modestie, desart.
Such, as to iustice will adhere,
What euer great one it offend:
And from the'embraced truth not bend
For enuy, hatred, gifts, or feare.
That, by their deeds, will make it knowne,
Whose dignitie they doe sustaine;
And life, state, glorie, all they gaine,
Count the republiques, not their owne.
Such the old BRVTI, DECII were,
The CIPI, CVRTII, who did giue
Themselues for *Rome*: and would not liue,
As men, good, only for a yeere.
Such were the great CAMILLI, too;
The FABII, SCIPIO's; that still thought

II. 381 bawdes:] baudes; *Q* 383 adhere] adhære *Q*

No worke, at price inough, was bought,
That for their countrey they could doe.
And, to her honor, so did knit;
As all their acts were vnderstood
The sinewes of the publique good:
And they themselues, one soule, with it.
These men were truely magistrates;
These neither practis'd force, nor formes:
Nor did they leaue the helme, in stormes!
And such they are make happy states.

Act III.

CICERO, CATO, CATVLVS, ANTONIVS, CRASSVS, CÆSAR, CHORVS, LICTORS.

GReat honors are great burdens: but, on whom
They'are cast with enuie, he doth beare two loades.
His cares must still be double to his ioyes,
In any dignitie; where, if he erre,
He findes no pardon: and, for doing well
A most small praise, and that wrung out by force.
I speake this, *Romanes*, knowing what the weight
Of the high charge, you'haue trusted to me, is.
Not, that thereby I would with art decline
The good, or greatnesse of your benefit;
For, I ascribe it to your singular grace,
And vow, to owe it to no title else,
Except the gods, that CICERO' is your *Consul*.
I haue no vrnes; no dustie moniments;
No broken images of ancestors,
Wanting an eare, or nose; no forged tables

II. 405 stormes!] stormes: *Q* Act III] ACT III. SCENE I. | *The Field of Mars.* | *Enter Cicero, Cato, Catulus, Antonius, Crassus, Cæsar, Chorus, Lictors, and People.* G 1 honors] honours *F2* 4 erre, *F2*: erre *Q*, *F1* 6 out] out, *Q* 14 moniments] monuments *F2*

Of long descents ; to boast false honors from :
Or be my vnder-takers to your trust.
But a new man (as I am stil'd in *Rome*)
Whom you haue dignified ; and more, in whom
Yo'haue cut a way, and left it ope for vertue
Hereafter, to that place : which our great men
Held shut vp, with all ramparts, for themselues.
Nor haue but few of them, in time beene made
Your *Consuls*, so ; new men, before me, none :
At my first suite ; in my iust yeere ; preferd
To all competitors ; and some the noblest——
CRA. Now the vaine swels. CAES. Vp glorie. CIC. And to haue
Your loud consents, from your owne vtter'd voices ;
Not silent bookes : nor from the meaner *tribes*,
But first, and last, the vniuersall concourse !
This is my ioy, my gladnesse. But my care,
My industrie, and vigilance now must worke,
That still your counsells of me be approu'd ;
Both, by your selues, and those, to whom you haue,
With grudge, prefer'd me : two things I must labour,
That neither they vpbraid, nor you repent you.
For euery lapse of mine will, now, be call'd
Your error, if I make such. But, my hope is,
So to beare through, and out, the *Consul*-ship,
As spight shall ne're wound you, though it may me.
And, for my selfe, I haue prepar'd this strength,
To doe so well ; as, if there happen ill
Vnto me, it shall make the gods to blush :
And be their crime, not mine, that I am enui'd.
CAES. O confidence ! more new, then is the man !
CIC. I know well, in what termes I doe receiue
The common wealth, how vexed, how perplex'd :

III. 17 descents ;] descents, *Q* 22 place :] place, *Q* 23 ramparts] rampires *Q* 25 *Consuls*,] *Consuls* Q 27 noblest——] noblest. *Q* 31 concourse !] concourse. *Q* 34 counsells] counsell *Q* 39 error,] error ; *Q* 44 blush :] blush, *Q* 45 enui'd.] enui'd ; *Q*

In which, there's not that mischiefe, or ill fate,
That good men feare not, wicked men expect not.
I know, beside, some turbulent practises
Alreadie on foot, and rumors of moe dangers——
CRA. Or you will make them, if there be none. CIC. Last,
I know, 'twas this, which made the enuie, and pride
Of the great *Romane* bloud bate, and giue way
To my election. CAT. MARCVS TVLLIVS, true;
Our need made thee our *Consul*, and thy vertue.
CAES. CATO, you will vn-doe him, with your praise.
CATO. CAESAR will hurt himselfe, with his owne enuie.
CHOR. The voice of CATO is the voice of *Rome*.
CATO. The voice of *Rome* is the consent of heauen!
And that hath plac'd thee, CICERO, at the helme,
Where thou must render, now, thy selfe a man,
And master of thy art. Each petty hand
Can steere a ship becalm'd; but he that will
Gouerne, and carry her to her ends, must know
His tides, his currents; how to shift his sailes;
What shee will beare in foule, what in faire weathers;
Where her springs are, her leakes; and how to stop 'hem;
What sands, what shelues, what rocks doe threaten her;
The forces, and the natures of all winds,
Gusts, stormes, and tempests; when her keele ploughs hell,
And deck knocks heauen: then, to manage her,
Becomes the name, and office of a pilot.
CIC. Which I'le performe, with all the diligence,
And fortitude I haue; not for my yeere,
But for my life; except my life be lesse,
And that my yeere conclude it: if it must,
Your will, lou'd gods. This heart shall yet employ
A day, an houre is left me, so, for *Rome*,
As it shall spring a life, out of my death,
To shine, for euer glorious in my facts.

III. 52 moe] more *F3* dangers——] dangers. *Q* 61 heauen!] Heauen; *Q* 82 facts.] facts: *Q*

The vicious count their yeeres, vertuous their acts.
CHOR. Most noble *Consul!* Let vs wait him home.
CAES. Most popular *Consul* he is growne, me thinks!
CRA. How the rout cling to him! CAES. And CATO leads 'hem!
CRA. You, his colleague, ANTONIVS, are not look't on.
ANT. Not I, nor doe I care. CAES. He enioyes rest,
And ease, the while. Let th'others spirit toile,
And wake it out, that was inspir'd for turmoile.
CATV. If all reports be true, yet, CAIVS CAESAR,
The time hath need of such a watch, and spirit.
CAES. Reports? Doe you beleeue 'hem CATVLVS,
Why, he do's make, and breed 'hem for the people;
T'endeare his seruice to 'hem. Doe you not tast
An art, that is so common? Popular men,
They must create strange monsters, and then quell 'hem;
To make their artes seeme something. Would you haue
Such an HERCVLEAN actor in the scene,
And not his HYDRA? They must sweat no lesse
To fit their properties, then t'expresse their parts.
CRA. Treasons, and guiltie men are made in states
Too oft, to dignifie the magistrates.
CATV. Those states be wretched, that are forc'd to buy
Their rulers fame, with their owne infamy.
CRA. We therefore, should prouide that ours doe not.
CAES. That will ANTONIVS make his care. ANT. I shall.
CAES. And watch the watcher. CATV. Here comes CATILINE.
How do's he brooke his late repulse? CAES. I know not.
But hardly sure. CAT⟨V⟩. LONGINVS, too, did stand?

III. 83 *Gnomic pointing in Q*: "The After 84 *Exeunt Cato, Cicero, Lictors, and People.* G 85 thinks!] thinkes. *Q* 89 while.] while: *Q* 102–5 *Gnomic pointing in Q*: "CRA. . . . "Too . . . "CATV. . . . "Their . . . 105 fame,] fame *F2* 106 therefore, should] therefore should, *F2*: *query,* We, therefore, should 110, 114 CATV.] CATU. *F2*

CAES. At first: but he gaue way vnto his friend.

CATV. Who's that come? LENTVLVS? CAES. Yes. He is againe
Taken into the *Senate*. ANT. And made *Prætor*.

CAT⟨V⟩. I know't. He had my suffrage, next the *Consuls*.

CAES. True, you were there, Prince of the *Senate*, then.

CATILINE, ANTONIVS, CATVLVS, CÆSAR, CRASSVS, LONGINVS, LENTVLVS.

HAile noblest *Romanes*. The most worthy *Consul*,
I gratulate your honor. ANT. I could wish
It had beene happier, by your fellowship,
Most noble SERGIVS, had it pleas'd the people.

CATI. It did not please the gods; who'instruct the people:
And their vnquestion'd pleasures must be seru'd.
They know what's fitter for vs, then our selues;
And 'twere impietie, to thinke against them.

CATV. You beare it rightly, LVCIVS; and, it glads me,
To find your thoughts so euen. CATI. I shall still
Studie to make them such to *Rome*, and heauen.
(I would with-draw with you, a little, IVLIVS.

CAES. Ile come home to you: CRASSVS would not ha' you
To speake to him, 'fore QVINTVS CATVLVS.

CATI. I apprehend you.) No, when they shall iudge
Honors conuenient for me, I shall haue 'hem,
With a full hand: I know it. In meane time,
They are no lesse part of the common-wealth,
That doe obey, then those, that doe command.

III. 112 that] that's *F2* 114 *Consuls.*] *Consuls;* Q, Ff Before 116 CATILINE . . . LENTVLVS] *Enter Catiline, Longinus, and Lentulus*, G. continuing the scene 127, 130 (I . . . you.)] I . . . you. *Q* 131 Honors] Honours *F2*

CATV. O, let me kisse your fore-head, LVCIVS.
How are you wrong'd! CATI. By whom? CATV. Publike report.
That giues you out, to stomack your repulse;
And brooke it deadly. CATI. Sir, shee brookes not me.
Beleeue me rather, and your selfe, now, of me:
It is a kinde of slander, to trust rumour.
CATV. I know it. And I could be angrie with it.
CATI. So may not I. Where it concernes himselfe,
Who's angrie at a slander, makes it true.
CATV. Most noble SERGIVS! This your temper melts me.
CRA. Will you doe office to the *Consul*, QVINTVS?
CAES. Which CATO, and the rout haue done the other?
CATV. I wait, when he will goe. Be still your selfe.
He wants no state, or honors, that hath vertue.
CATI. Did I appeare so tame, as this man thinkes me?
Look'd I so poore? so dead? So like that nothing,
Which he calls vertuous? O my breast, breake quickly;
And shew my friends my in-parts, lest they thinke
I haue betraid 'hem. (LON. Where's GABINIVS? LEN. Gone.
LON. And VARGVNTEIVS? LEN. Slipt away; all shrunke:
Now that he mist the *Consul*-ship.) CATI. I am
The scorne of bond-men; who are next to beasts.
What can I worse pronounce my selfe, that's fitter?
The owle of *Rome*, whom boyes, and girles will hout!
That were I set vp, for that woodden god,
That keeps our gardens, could not fright the crowes,
Or the least bird from muiting on my head.
(LON. 'Tis strange how he should misse it. LEN. Is't not stranger,

III. 138 Sir,] Sir: *Q* 146 Which] That *Q* 148 honors] honours *F2* vertue. *F2*: vertue, *Q, F1* *Exeunt Catulus, Antonius, Cæsar, Crassus, Lictors, &c.* G 153–5 (LON. . . . -ship.)] LON. . . . -ship. *Q* 158 hout!] hout; *Q* 161 muiting] muting *Q* 162–5 (LON. . . . true.)] LON. . . . true. *Q*

The vpstart CICERO should carrie it so,
By all consents, from men so much his masters?
LON. 'Tis true.) CATI. To what a shaddow, am I melted!
(LON. ANTONIVS wan it but by some few voices.)
CATI. Strooke through, like aire, and feele it not. My wounds
Close faster, then they're made. (LEN. The whole designe,
And enterprise is lost by't. All hands quit it,
Vpon his faile.) CATI. I grow mad at my patience.
It is a visor that hath poison'd me.
Would it had burnt me vp, and I died inward:
My heart first turn'd to ashes. (LON. Here's CETHEGVS yet.)

CATILINE, CETHEGVS, LENTVLVS, LONGINVS, CATO.

REpulse vpon repulse? An in-mate, *Consul?*
That I could reach the axell, where the pinnes are,
Which bolt this frame; that I might pull 'hem out,
And pluck all into *chaos,* with my selfe.
CET. What, are we wishing now? CATI. Yes, my CETHEGVS.
Who would not fall with all the world about him?
CET. Not I, that would stand on it, when it falls;
And force new nature out, to make another.
These wishings tast of woman, not of *Romane.*
Let vs seeke other armes. CATI. What should we doe?
CET. Doe, and not wish; something, that wishes take not:
So sodaine, as the gods should not preuent,
Nor scarce haue time, to feare. CATI. O noble CAIVS!

III. 166 (LON. . . . voices.)] LON. . . . voyces. *Q* 168–70 (LEN. . . . faile.)] LEN. . . . fayle. *Q* 173 (LON. . . . yet.)] LON. . . . yet. *Q* Before 174 CATILINE . . . CATO] *Enter Cethegus.* G, continuing the scene 185 sodaine] sudden *F2*

CET. It likes me better, that you are not *Consul.*
I would not goe through open dores, but breake 'hem;
Swim to my ends, through bloud; or build a bridge
Of carcasses; make on, vpon the heads
Of men, strooke downe, like piles; to reach the liues
Of those remaine, and stand: Then is't a prey,
When danger stops, and ruine makes the way.

CATI. How thou dost vtter me, braue soule, that may not,
At all times, shew such as I am; but bend
Vnto occasion? LENTVLVS, this man,
If all our fire were out, would fetch downe new,
Out of the hand of IOVE; and riuet him
To *Caucasus*, should he but frowne: and let
His owne gaunt Eagle flie at him, to tire.

LEN. Peace, here comes CATO. CATI. Let him come, and heare.
I will no more dissemble. Quit vs all;
I, and my lou'd CETHEGVS here, alone
Will vndertake this giants warre, and carrie it.

LEN. What needs this, LVCIVS? LON. SERGIVS, be more warie.

CATI. Now, MARCVS CATO, our new *Consuls* spie,
What is your sowre austeritie sent t'explore?

CATO. Nothing in thee, licentious CATILINE:
Halters, and racks cannot expresse from thee
More, then thy deeds. 'Tis onely iudgement waits thee.

CATI. Whose? CATO's? shall he iudge me? CATO. No, the gods;
Who, euer, follow those, they goe not with:
And *Senate;* who, with fire, must purge sicke *Rome*
Of noisome citizens, whereof thou'art one.
Be gone, or else let me. 'Tis bane to draw
The same aire with thee. CET. Strike him. LEN. Hold, good CAIVS.

III. 191 strooke] strucke *F2*   196 Vnto] Upon *F2*   Before 205 *Re-enter Cato.* G   207 explore? *F2*: explore. *Q, F1*   212 *Gnomic pointing in Q*: "Who . . .   214 thou'art *F2*: thou'rt *Q*: thou art *F1*   216 CAIVS. *F2*: *Caius;* Q: CAIVS; *F1*

CET. Fear'st thou not, CATO? CATO. Rash CETHEGVS, no.
'Twere wrong with *Rome*, when CATILINE and thou
Doe threat, if CATO fear'd. CATI. The fire you speake of,
If any flame of it approch my fortunes,
Ile quench it, not with water, but with ruine.
CATO. You heare this, *Romanes*. CATI. Beare it to the *Consul*.
CET. I would haue sent away his soule, before him.
You are too heauie, LENTVLVS, and remisse;
It is for you we labour, and the kingdome
Promis'd you by the SYBILL'S. CATI. Which his *Prætor*-ship,
And some small flatterie of the *Senate* more,
Will make him to forget. LEN. You wrong me, LVCIVS.
LON. He will not need these spurres. CET. The action needs 'hem.
These things, when they proceed not, they goe backward.
LEN. Let vs consult then. CET. Let vs, first, take armes.
They that denie vs iust things, now, will giue
All that we aske; if once they see our swords.
CAT. Our obiects must be sought with wounds, not words.

CICERO, FVLVIA.

IS there a heauen? and gods? and can it be
They should so slowly heare, so slowly see!
Hath IOVE no thunder? or is IOVE become
Stupide as thou art? ô neere-wretched *Rome*,
When both thy *Senate*, and thy gods doe sleepe,
And neither thine, nor their owne states doe keepe!
What will awake thee, heauen? what can excite

III. 217, 231 CET.] CET, *Q* 219 of, *F2*: of *Q, F1* 220 flame] flames *F2* 222 *Exit.* add G 230 *Gnomic pointing in Q*: " These . . . 234 *Exeunt.* add G Before 235 CICERO, FULVIA] SCENE II. | *Cicero's House.* | *Enter Cicero and Fulvia.* G

Thine anger, if this practice be too light?
His former drifts partake of former times,
But this last plot was onely CATILINES.
O, that it were his last. But he, before
Hath safely done so much, hee'll still dare more.
Ambition, like a torrent, ne're lookes back;
And is a swelling, and the last affection
A high minde can put off: being both a rebell
Vnto the soule, and reason, and enforceth
All lawes, all conscience, treades vpon religion,
And offereth violence to natures selfe.
But, here, is that transcends it! A black purpose
To confound nature: and to ruine that,
Which neuer age, nor mankinde can repaire!
Sit downe, good lady; CICERO is lost
In this your fable: for, to thinke it true
Tempteth my reason. It so farre exceedes
All insolent fictions of the tragick *scene!*
The common-wealth, yet panting, vnder-neath
The stripes, and wounds of a late ciuill warre,
Gasping for life, and scarce restor'd to hope;
To seeke t'oppresse her, with new crueltie,
And vtterly extinguish her long name,
With so prodigious, and vnheard-of fiercenesse!
What sinke of monsters, wretches of lost minds,
Mad after change, and desp'rate in their states,
Wearied, and gall'd with their necessities,
(For all this I allow them) durst haue thought it?
Would not the barbarous deeds haue beene beleeu'd,
Of MARIVS, and SYLLA, by our children,
Without this fact had rise forth greater, for them?
All, that they did, was pietie, to this!
They, yet, but murdred kinsfolke, brothers, parents,
Rauish'd the virgins, and, perhaps, some matrons;
They left the citie standing, and the temples:

III. 253 it!] it. *Q* 255 repaire!] repaire. *Q* 259 *scene!*] *Scene. Q* 272 Without] Without, *Q* 273 this!] this. *Q*

The gods, and maiestie of *Rome* were safe yet!
These purpose to fire it, to dispoile them,
(Beyond the other euils) and lay wast
The farre-triumphed world: for, vnto whom
Rome is too little, what can be inough?
FVL. 'Tis true, my lord, I had the same discourse.
CIC. And, then, to take a horride sacrament
In humane bloud, for execution
Of this their dire designe; which might be call'd
The height of wickednesse: but that, that was higher,
For which they did it! FVL. I assure your lordship,
The extreme horror of it almost turn'd me
To aire, when first I heard it; I was all
A vapor, when 'twas told me: and I long'd
To vent it any where. 'Twas such a secret,
I thought, it would haue burnt me vp. CIC. Good FVLVIA,
Feare not your act; and lesse repent you of it.
FVL. I doe not, my good lord. I know to whom
I haue vtter'd it. CIC. You haue discharg'd it, safely.
Should *Rome*, for whom you haue done the happy seruice,
Turne most ingrate; yet were your vertue paid
In conscience of the fact: so much good deedes
Reward themselues. FVL. My lord, I did it not
To any other aime, but for it selfe.
To no ambition. CIC. You haue learn'd the difference
Of doing office to the publike weale,
And priuate friendship: and haue shewne it, lady.
Be still your selfe. I haue sent for QVINTVS CVRIVS,
And (for your vertuous sake) if I can winne him,
Yet, to the common-wealth; he shall be safe too.
FVL. Ile vnder-take, my lord, he shall be won.
CIC. Pray you, ioyne with me, then: and helpe to worke him.

III. 277 yet!] yet. *Q* 287 it!] it. *Q* 288 horror] horrour *F2* 290 me:] me; *Q* 291 where.] where; *Q* 303 friendship:] friendship, *Q* 307 shall] will *Q*

CICERO, LICTOR, FVLVIA,
CVRIVS.

HOw now? Is he come? LIC. He'is here, my lord.
CIC. Go presently,
Pray my colleague ANTONIVS, I may speake with him,
About some present businesse of the state;
And (as you goe) call on my brother QVINTVS,
And pray him, with the *Tribunes* to come to me.
Bid CVRIVS enter. FVLVIA, you will aide me?
FVL. It is my dutie. CIC. O, my noble lord!
I haue to chide you, yfaith. Giue me your hand.
Nay, be not troubled; 't shall be gently, CVRIVS.
You looke vpon this lady? What! doe you ghesse
My businesse, yet? Come, if you frowne, I thunder:
Therefore, put on your better lookes, and thoughts.
There's nought but faire, and good intended to you;
And I would make those your complexion.
Would you, of whom the *Senate* had that hope,
As, on my knowledge, it was in their purpose,
Next sitting, to restore you: as they ha' done
The stupide, and vngratefull LENTVLVS
(Excuse me, that I name you thus, together,
For, yet, you are not such) would you, I say,
A person both of bloud and honor, stock't
In a long race of vertuous ancestors,
Embarke your selfe for such a hellish action,
With parricides, and traytors; men turn'd *furies*,
Out of the wast, and ruine of their fortunes!
(For 'tis despaire, that is the mother of madnesse)
Such as want (that, which all conspirators,
But they, haue first) meere colour for their mischiefe?
O, I must blush with you. Come, you shall not labour
To extenuate your guilt, but quit it cleane;

III. Before 309 CICERO . . . CVRIVS] *Enter a Lictor.* G, continuing the scene 314 After 'enter.' *Exit Lictor.* G 315 After 'dutie.' *Enter Curius.* G 326 LENTVLVS] *Lentulus;* Q 332 traytors;] Traitors, *Q* 333 fortunes!] fortunes; *Q* 338 To extenuate] To'extenuate *F2*

Bad men excuse their faults, good men will leaue 'hem.
He acts the third crime, that defends the first.
Here is a lady, that hath got the start,
In pietie, of vs all; and, for whose vertue,
I could almost turne louer, againe: but that
TERENTIA would be iealous. What an honor
Hath shee atchieued to her selfe! What voices,
Titles, and loud applauses will pursue her,
Through euery street! What windores will be fill'd,
To shoot eyes at her! What enuy, and griefe in matrons,
They are not shee! when this her act shall seeme
Worthier a chariot, then if POMPEY came,
With *Asia* chain'd! All this is, while shee liues.
But dead, her very name will be a statue!
Not wrought for time, but rooted in the minds
Of all posteritie: when brasse, and marble,
I, and the *Capitol* it selfe is dust!
FVL. Your honor thinks too highly of me. CIC. No:
I cannot thinke inough. And I would haue
Him emulate you. 'Tis no shame, to follow
The better precedent. Shee shewes you, CVRIVS,
What claime your countrey layes to you; and what dutie
You owe to it: be not afraid, to breake
With murderers, and traytors, for the sauing
A life, so neere, and necessary to you,
As is your countries. Thinke but on her right.
No child can be too naturall to his parent.
Shee is our common mother, and doth challenge
The prime part of vs; doe not stop, but giue it:
He, that is void of feare, may soone be iust.
And no religion binds men to be traitors.
FVL. My lord, he vnderstands it; and will follow
Your sauing counsell: but his shame, yet, stayes him.

III. 339–40 *Gnomic pointing in Q*: "Bad ... "He ... 342 pietie,] piety, *Q*: pietie *F1*: piety *F2* 352 a *om. F2* statue!] Statue, *Q* 354 posteritie:] posterity; *Q* 355 dust!] dust. *Q* 365 *Gnomic pointing in Q*: "No ... 368–9 *Gnomic pointing in Q*: "He ... "And ... 371 counsell: but] counsell. But *Q*

I know, that he is comming. CVR. Doe you know it?
FVL. Yes, let me speake with you. CVR. O you are—— FVL. What am I?
CVR. Speake not so loud. FVL. I am, what you should be,
Come, doe you thinke, I'ld walke in any plot,
Where madame SEMPRONIA should take place of me,
And FVLVIA come i'the *rere*, or o'the *by?*
That I would be her second, in a businesse,
Though it might vantage me all the sunne sees?
It was a silly phant'sie of yours. Apply
Your selfe to me, and the *Consul*, and be wise;
Follow the fortune I ha' put you into:
You may be something this way, and with safetie.
CIC. Nay, I must tolerate no whisperings, lady.
FVL. Sir, you may heare. I tell him, in the way,
Wherein he was, how hazardous his course was.
CIC. How hazardous? how certayne to all ruine.
Did he, or doe, yet, any of them imagine
The gods would sleepe, to such a *Stygian* practice,
Against that common-wealth, which they haue founded
With so much labour, and like care haue kept,
Now neere seuen hundred yeeres? It is a madnesse,
Wherewith heauen blinds 'hem, when it would confound 'hem,
That they should thinke it. Come, my CVRIVS,
I see your nature's right; you shall no more
Be mention'd with them: I will call you mine,
And trouble this good shame, no farder. Stand
Firme for your countrey; and become a man
Honor'd, and lou'd. It were a noble life,
To be found dead, embracing her. Know you,
What thankes, what titles, what rewards the *Senate*
Will heape vpon you, certaine, for your seruice?
Let not a desperate action more engage you,

III. 373 After 'you.' *Takes him aside,* G are——] -are. *Q* After 374 *Lowering her voice.* G 377 o'] on *Q* 380 silly] seely *Q* 398 your] you *F2*

Then safetie should : and wicked friendship force
What honestie, and vertue cannot worke.

FVL. He tells you right, sweet friend : 'Tis sauing counsaile.

CVR. Most noble *Consul*, I am yours, and hers ;
I mean my countries : you, haue form'd me new.
Inspiring me, with what I should be, truely.
And I intreat, my faith may not seeme cheaper
For springing out of penitence. CIC. Good CVRIVS,
It shall be dearer rather, and because
I'ld make it such, heare, how I trust you more.
Keepe still your former face : and mixe againe
With these lost spirits. Runne all their mazes with 'hem :
For such are treasons. Find their windings out,
And subtle turnings, watch their snaky wayes,
Through brakes, and hedges, into woods of darkenesse,
Where they are faine to creepe vpon their brests
In paths ne're trod by men, but wolues, and panthers.
Learne, beside CATILINE, LENTVLVS, and those,
Whose names I haue ; what new ones they draw in ;
Who else are likely ; what those great ones are,
They doe not name ; what wayes they meane to take ;
And whither their hopes point : to warre, or ruine,
By some surprize. Explore all their intents,
And what you finde may profit the republique,
Acquaint me with it, either, by your selfe,
Or this your vertuous friend, on whom I lay
The care of vrging you. I'le see, that *Rome*
Shall proue a thankefull, and a bounteous mother :
Be secret as the night. CVR. And constant, sir.

CIC. I doe not doubt it. Though the time cut off
All vowes. The dignitie of truth is lost,
With much protesting. Who is there ! This way,

III. 404 should :] should ; *Q* 408 you,] you' *Q*, *Ff* 413 I'ld] Il'd *Q*, *Ff* 414 face :] face ; *Q* 415 'hem :] 'hem ; *Q* 422 haue ;] haue, *Q* 425 point : . . . warre,] point ; . . . warre : *Q* 430 you.] you ; *Q* 434 *Gnomic pointing in Q* : " The . . . 435 After 'there!' *Enter a Servant.* G

Lest you be seene, and met. And when you come,
Be this your token, to this fellow. Light 'hem. *He whispers with him.*
O *Rome*, in what a sicknesse art thou fall'n!
How dangerous, and deadly! when thy head
Is drown'd in sleepe, and all thy body feu'ry!
No noise, no pulling, no vexation wakes thee,
Thy *lethargie* is such: or if, by chance,
Thou heau'st thy eye-lids vp, thou dost forget
Sooner, then thou wert told, thy proper danger.
I did vn-reuerendly, to blame the gods,
Who wake for thee, though thou snore to thy selfe.
Is it not strange, thou should'st be so diseas'd,
And so secure? But more, that the first symptomes
Of such a maladie, should not rise out
From any worthy member, but a base
And common strumpet, worthlesse to be nam'd
A haire, or part of thee? Thinke, thinke, hereafter,
What thy needes were, when thou must vse such meanes:
And lay it to thy brest, how much the gods
Vpbraid thy foule neglect of them; by making
So vile a thing, the author of thy safetie.
They could haue wrought by nobler wayes: haue strooke
Thy foes with forked lightning; or ramm'd thunder;
Throwne hills vpon 'hem, in the act; haue sent
Death, like a dampe, to all their families;
Or caus'd their consciences to burst 'hem. But,
When they will shew thee what thou art, and make
A scornefull difference 'twixt their power, and thee,
They helpe thee by such aides, as geese, and harlots.
How now? What answer? Is he come? LIC. Your brother,
Will streight be here; and your colleague ANTONIVS
Said, coldly, he would follow me. CIC. I, that
Troubles me somewhat, and is worth my feare.

III. 437 *Stage direction not in Q*: *Exit Servant with Curius and Fulvia.* add G 457 strooke] strucke *F2* After 464 *Re-enter Lictor.* G 467 After 'me.' *Exit.* G 468 feare.] feare; *Q*

He is a man, 'gainst whom I must prouide,
That (as hee'll doe no good) he doe no harme.
He, though he be not of the plot, will like it,
And wish it should proceed : for, vnto men,
Prest with their wants, all change is euer welcome.
I must with offices, and patience win him ;
Make him, by art, that which he is not borne,
A friend vnto the publique ; and bestow
The *prouince* on him ; which is by the *Senate*
Decreed to me : that benefit will bind him.
'Tis well, if some men will doe well, for price :
So few are vertuous, when the reward's away.
Nor must I be vnmindfull of my priuate ;
For which I haue call'd my brother, and the *tribunes,*
My kins-folke, and my clients to be neere me :
He that stands vp 'gainst traytors, and their ends,
Shall need a double guard, of law, and friends :
Especially, in such an enuious state,
That sooner will accuse the magistrate,
Then the delinquent ; and will rather grieue
The treason is not acted, then beleeue.

CÆSAR, CATILINE.

THe night growes on ; and you are for your meeting :
Ile therefore end in few. Be resolute,
And put your enterprise in act : the more
Actions of depth, and danger are consider'd,
The lesse assuredly they are perform'd.
And thence it hapneth, that the brauest plots
(Not executed straight) haue beene discouer'd.
Say, you are constant, or another, a third,

III. 470 harme.] harme ; *Q* 472 proceed :] proceede ; *Q* 479 price :] price ; *Q* 480 *Gnomic pointing in Q* : " So . . . away.] away : *Q* 483 me :] me ; *Q* 484–9 *Gnomic pointing in Q* : " He . . . " Shall . . . " Especially . . " That . . . " Then . . . " The . . . 489 *Exit.* add G Before 490 ' CÆSAR, CATILINE '] SCENE III. | *A Room in Catiline's House.* | *Enter Cæsar and Catiline.* G 493–4 *Gnomic pointing in Q, which should have begun with* The *in l.* 492 : " Actions . . . " The . . .

Or more ; there may be yet one wretched spirit,
With whom the feare of punishment shall worke
'Boue all the thoughts of honor, and reuenge.
You are not, now, to thinke what's best to doe,
As in beginnings ; but, what must be done,
Being thus entred : and slip no aduantage
That may secure you. Let 'hem call it mischiefe ;
When it is past, and prosper'd, 'twill be vertue.
Th'are petty crimes are punish'd, great rewarded.
Nor must you thinke of perill ; since, attempts,
Begunne with danger, still doe end with glory :
And, when need spurres, despaire will be call'd wisdome.
Lesse ought the care of men, or fame to fright you ;
For they, that win, doe seldome receiue shame
Of victorie : how ere it be atchiu'd ;
And vengeance, least. For who, besieg'd with wants,
Would stop at death, or any thing beyond it ?
Come, there was neuer any great thing, yet,
Aspired, but by violence, or fraud :
And he that sticks (for folly of a conscience)
To reach it—— CAT. Is a good religious foole.
CAES. A superstitious slaue, and will die beast.
Good night. You know what CRASSVS thinkes, and I,
By this : Prepare you wings, as large as sayles,
To cut through ayre, and leaue no print behind you.
A serpent, ere he comes to be a dragon,
Do's eate a bat : and so must you a *Consul*,
That watches. What you doe, doe quickly SERGIVS.
You shall not stir for me. CAT. Excuse me, lights there.
CAES. By no meanes. CAT. Stay then. All good thoughts to CAESAR.
And like to CRASSVS. CAES. Mind but your friends counsells.

III. 505–6 *Gnomic pointing in Q*: "When . . . "Th'are . . . 507–9 *Gnomic pointing in Q*: " Attempts . . . " Begunne . . . " And . . . 507 attempts,] attempts; *F2* 511–12 *Gnomic pointing in Q*: " For . . . " Of . . . 519 superstitious] superstitiou s *F1* 524 you] y ou *F1* 528 *Exit.* add G

CATILINE, AVRELIA, LECCA.

OR, I will beare no mind. How now, AVRELIA?
Are your confederates come? the ladies? AVR. Yes.
CAT. And is SEMPRONIA there? AVR. She is.
CAT. That's well.
Shee ha's a sulphurous spirit, and will take
Light at a sparke. Breake with them, gentle loue,
About the drawing as many of their husbands,
Into the plot, as can: if not, to rid 'hem.
That'll be the easier practice, vnto some,
Who haue beene tir'd with 'hem long. Sollicite
Their aydes, for money: and their seruants helpe,
In firing of the citie, at the time
Shall be design'd. Promise 'hem states, and empires,
And men, for louers, made of better clay,
Then euer the old potter TITAN knew.
Who's that? O, PORCIVS LECCA! are they met?
LEC. They are all, here. CAT. Loue, you haue your instructions:
Ile trust you with the stuffe you haue to worke on.
You'll forme it? PORCIVS, fetch the siluer eagle
I ga' you in charge. And pray 'hem, they will enter.

CATILINE, CETHEGVS, CVRIVS, LENTVLVS, VARGVNTEIVS, LONGINVS, GABINIVS, CEPARIVS, AVTRONIVS, &c.

O, Friends, your faces glad me. This will be
Our last, I hope, of consultation.
CET. So, it had need. CVR. We loose occasion, daily.
CAT. I, and our meanes: whereof one wounds me most,

III. Before 'CATILINE . . . LECCA' *Enter Aurelia.* G, continuing the scene 538 money:] money; *Q* 542 potter] porter *F2* Before 543 *Enter Lecca.* G 546 After 'it?' *Exit Aurelia.* G 547 *Exit Lecca.* add G Before 548 CATILINE . . . &c.] *Enter Cethegus, Curius, Lentulus, Vargunteius, Longinus, Gabinius, Ceparius, Autronius, &c.* G, continuing the scene 550 CET.] CAT. *Q* loose] lose *F2*

That was the fairest. PISO is dead, in *Spaine.*
CET. As we are, here. LON. And, as it is thought, by enuy
Of POMPEY's followers. LEN. He too's comming backe,
Now, out of *Asia.* CAT. Therefore, what we'intend,
We must be swift in. Take your seates, and heare.
I haue, already, sent SEPTIMIVS
Into the *Picene* territorie; and IVLIVS,
To raise force, for vs, in *Apulia:*
MANLIVS at *Fesulæ*, is (by this time) vp,
With the old needie troops, that follow'd SYLLA:
And all doe but expect, when we will giue
The blow at home. Behold this siluer eagle,
'Twas MARIVS standard, in the *Cimbrian* warre,
Fatall to *Rome;* and, as our augures tell me,
Shall still be so: for which one ominous cause,
I'haue kept it safe, and done it sacred rites,
As to a god-head, in a chappell built
Of purpose to it. Pledge then all your hands,
To follow it, with vowes of death, and ruine,
Strooke silently, and home. So waters speake
When they runne deepest. Now's the time, this yeere,
The twenti'th, from the firing of the *Capitol*,
As fatall too, to *Rome*, by all predictions:
And, in which, honor'd LENTVLVS must rise
A king, if he pursue it. CVR. If he doe not,
He is not worthy the great destinie.
LEN. It is too great for me, but what the gods,
And their great loues decree me, I must not
Seeme carelesse of. CAT. No, nor we enuious.
We haue enough beside, all *Gallia*, *Belgia*,
Greece, *Spaine*, and *Africke.* CVR. I, and *Asia*, too,
Now POMPEY is returning. CAT. Noblest *Romanes*,

III. 555 we'intend *Q*: we intend, *Ff* 561 SYLLA:] *Sylla;* Q 563 After 'home.' *Re-enter P. Lecca with the eagle.* G 564 'Twas] Was *Q* 566 ominous] omenous *Q* 568 god-head,] Godhead; *Q* 574 predictions:] predictions; *Q* 575 honor'd] honour'd *F2*

Me thinkes our lookes, are not so quicke and high,
As they were wont. CVR. No? whose is not? CAT. We haue
No anger in our eyes, no storme, no lightning:
Our hate is spent, and fum'd away in vapor,
Before our hands be'at worke. I can accuse
Not any one, but all of slacknesse. CET. Yes,
And be your selfe such, while you doe it. CAT. Ha?
'Tis sharply answer'd, CAIVS. CET. Truly, truly.
LEN. Come, let vs each one know his part to doe,
And then be accus'd. Leaue these vntimely quarrells.
CVR. I would there were more *Romes* then one, to ruine.
CET. More *Romes?* More worlds. CVR. Nay then, more gods, and natures,
If they tooke part. LEN. When shall the time be, first?
CAT. I thinke the *Saturnalls*. CET. 'Twill be too long.
CAT. They are not now farre off, 'tis not a month.
CET. A weeke, a day, an houre is too farre off,
Now, were the fittest time. CAT. We ha' not laid
All things so safe, and readie. CET. While we'are laying,
We shall all lye; and grow to earth. Would I
Were nothing in it, if not now. These things
They should be done, e're thought. CAT. Nay, now your reason
Forsakes you, CAIVS. Thinke, but what commodity
That time will minister; the cities custome
Of being, then, in mirth, and feast—— LEN. Loos'd whole
In pleasure and securitie—— AVT. Each house
Resolu'd in freedome—— CVR. Euery slaue a master——
LON. And they too no meane aides—— CVR. Made from their hope
Of libertie—— LEN. Or hate vnto their lords.
VAR. 'Tis sure, there cannot be a time found out

III. 591 CAIVS.] *Caius*, *Q* 607 feast——] feast. *Q* 608 securitie——] securitie. *Q* 609 freedome—— . . . master——] freedome. . . . master. *Q* 610 aides——] aides. *Q* 611 libertie——] liberty. *Q*

More apt, and naturall. LEN. Nay, good CETHEGVS,
Why doe your passions, now, disturbe our hopes?
CET. Why doe your hopes delude your certainties?
CAT. You must lend him his way. Thinke, for the order,
And processe of it. LON. Yes. LEN. I like not fire:
'Twill too much wast my citie. CAT. Were it embers,
There will be wealth enough, rak't out of them,
To spring a new. It must be fire, or nothing.
LON. What else should fright, or terrifie 'hem? VAR. True.
In that confusion, must be the chiefe slaughter.
CVR. Then we shall kill 'hem brauest. CEP. And in heaps.
AVT. Strew sacrifices. CVR. Make the earth an altar.
LON. And *Rome* the fire. LEC. 'Twill be a noble night.
VAR. And worth all SYLLA's dayes. CVR. When husbands, wiues,
Grandsires, and nephewes, seruants, and their lords,
Virgins, and priests, the infant, and the nurse
Goe all to hell, together, in a fleet.
CAT. I would haue you, LONGINVS, and STATILIVS,
To take the charge o' the firing, which must be,
At a signe giuen with a trumpet, done
In twelue chiefe places of the citie, at once.
The flaxe, and sulphure, are alreadie laid
In, at CETHEGVS house. So are the weapons.
GABINIVS, you, with other force, shall stop
The pipes, and conduits: and kill those that come
For water. CVR. What shall I doe? CAT. All will haue
Employment, feare not: Ply the execution.
CVR. For that, trust me, and CETHEGVS. CAT. I will be
At hand, with the armie, to meet those that scape.

III. 615 your certainties] our certainties *F2* 620 a new. *F1*: a new: *Q*: anew *F2* 625 LON.] LON, *Q* 633 places] places, *F2*

And LENTVLVS, begirt you POMPEY's house,
To seize his sonnes aliue: for they are they
Must make our peace with him. All else cut off,
As TARQVINE did the poppy heads; or mowers
A field of thistles; or else, vp, as ploughes
Doe barren lands; and strike together flints,
And clods; th'vngratefull *Senate*, and the people:
Till no rage, gone before, or comming after,
May weigh with yours, though horror leapt her selfe
Into the scale; but, in your violent acts,
The fall of torrents, and the noyse of tempests,
The boyling of *Charybdis*, the seas wildnesse,
The eating force of flames, and wings of winds,
Be all out-wrought, by your transcendent furies.
It had beene done, e're this, had I beene *Consul;*
We'had had no stop, no let. LEN. How find you ANTONIVS?
CAT. The'other ha's wonne him, lost: that CICERO
Was borne to be my opposition,
And stands in all our wayes. CVR. Remoue him first.
CET. May that, yet, be done sooner? CAT. Would it were done.
CVR. VAR. I'll do't. CET. It is my prouince; none vsurpe it.
LEN. What are your meanes? CET. Enquire not. He shall die.
Shall, was too slowly said. He'is dying. That
Is, yet, too slow. He'is dead. CAT. Braue, only *Romane*,
Whose soule might be the worlds soule, were that dying;
Refuse not, yet, the aides of these your friends.
LEN. Here's VARGVNTEIVS holds good quarter with him.
CAT. And vnder the pretext of clientele,
And visitation, with the morning haile,
Will be admitted. CET. What is that to me?

III. 651 scale;] scale: *Q* 658 him, lost *corr. Q, Ff*: him lost *Q originally* 667 friends.] friends: *Q* 670 haile] *Hayle* Q

VAR. Yes, we may kill him in his bed, and safely.

CET. Safe is your way, then; take it. Mine's mine owne.

CAT. Follow him, VARGVNTEIVS, and perswade,
The morning is the fittest time. LON. The night
Will turne all into tumult. LEN. And perhaps
Misse of him too. CAT. Intreat, and coniure him,
In all our names—— LEN. By all our vowes, and friendships.

SEMPRONIA, AVRELIA, FULVIA. *To them.*

WHat! is our counsell broke vp first? AVR. You say,
Women are greatest talkers. SEM. We ha' done;
And are now fit for action. LON. Which is passion.
There's your best actiuitie, lady. SEM. How
Knowes your wise fatnesse that? LON. Your mothers daughter
Did teach me, madame. CAT. Come SEMPRONIA, leaue him:
He is a giber. And our present businesse
Is of more serious consequence. AVRELIA
Tells me, you'haue done most masculinely within,
And plaid the orator. SEM. But we must hasten
To our designe as well, and execute:
Not hang still, in the feuer of an accident.

CAT. You say well, lady. SEM. I doe like our plot
Exceeding well, 'tis sure; and we shall leaue
Little to fortune, in it. CAT. Your banquet stayes.
AVRELIA, take her in. Where's FVLVIA?

SEM. O, the two louers are coupling. CVR. In good faith,
Shee's very ill, with sitting vp. SEM. You'ld haue her
Laugh, and lye downe? FVL. No, faith, SEMPRONIA,

III. 673 *Exit.* add G 677 him,] him. *Q* 678 names——] names. *Q* *Exit Vargunteius.* add G Before 679 SEMPRONIA . . . FULVIA] *Enter Sempronia, Aurelia, and Fulvia.* G, continuing the scene. FULVIA, to them. *Q* 680 After 'talkers.' *Whispers with Catiline while Fulvia takes Curius aside.* G 684 CAT.] CET. *Q, Ff* 688 plaid] play *F2* 696 You'ld] Youl'd *Q, Ff* 697 downe ?] downe. *Q*

I am not well: I'le take my leaue, it drawes
Toward the morning. CVRIVS shall stay with you.
Madame, I pray you, pardon me, my health
I must respect. AVR. Fare-well, good FVLVIA.
CVR. Make hast, and bid him get his guards about him.
For VARGVNTEIVS, and CORNELIVS
Haue vndertane it, should CETHEGVS misse:
Their reason, that they thinke his open rashnesse
Will suffer easier discouerie,
Then their attempt, so vayled vnder friendship.
Ile bring you to your coach. Tell him, beside,
Of CAESARS comming forth, here. CAT. My sweet madame,
Will you be gone? FVL. I am, my lord, in truth,
In some indisposition. CAT. I doe wish
You had all your health, sweet lady: LENTVLVS,
You'll doe her seruice. LEN. To her coach, and dutie.

Curius whispers this to Fuluia.

CATILINE.

WHat ministers men must, for practice, vse!
The rash, th' ambitious, needy, desperate,
Foolish, and wretched, eu'n the dregs of mankind,
To whores, and women! still, it must be so.
Each haue their proper place; and, in their roomes,
They are the best. Groomes fittest kindle fires,
Slaues carry burdens, butchers are for slaughters,
Apothecaries, butlers, cookes for poysons;
As these for me: dull, stupide LENTVLVS,
My stale, with whom I stalke; the rash CETHEGVS,
My executioner; and fat LONGINVS,
STATILIVS, CVRIVS, CEPARIVS, CIMBER,
My labourers, pioners, and incendiaries;
With these domesticke traytors, bosome theeues,
Whom custome hath call'd wiues; the readiest helps,

III. 698 well:] well; Q 702 *Stage direction not in Q* 707 attempt,] attempt; Q 713 *Exeunt all but Catiline.* G, continuing the scene 725 CIMBER,] *Cimber.* Q 726 labourers] laborers Q

To betray headie husbands; rob the easie:
And lend the moneys, on returnes of lust.
Shall CATILINE not doe, now, with these aides,
So sought, so sorted, something shall be call'd
Their labour, but his profit? and make CAESAR
Repent his ventring counsells, to a spirit,
So much his lord in mischiefe? when all these,
Shall, like the brethren sprung of dragons teeth,
Ruine each other; and he fall amongst 'hem:
With CRASSVS, POMPEY, or who else appeares,
But like, or neere a great one. May my braine
Resolue to water, and my bloud turne phlegme,
My hands drop off, vnworthy of my sword,
And that b⟨e⟩'inspired, of it selfe, to rip
My brest, for my lost entraills; when I leaue
A soule, that will not serue: and who will, are
The same with slaues, such clay I dare not feare.
The cruelty, I meane to act, I wish
Should be call'd mine, and tarry in my name;
Whil'st, after-ages doe toile out themselues,
In thinking for the like, but doe it lesse:
And, were the power of all the fiends let loose,
With fate to boot, it should be, still, example.
When, what the *Gaule*, or *Moore* could not effect,
Nor emulous *Carthage*, with their length of spight,
Shall be the worke of one, and that my night.

CICERO, FVLVIA, QVINTVS.

I Thanke your vigilance. Where's my brother, QVINTVS?
Call all my seruants vp. Tell noble CVRIVS,
And say it to your selfe, you are my sauers;

III. 729 betray headie] strangle head-strong *Q* 733 labour] labor *Q* 741 hands] hands, *Q* 744 serue: and] serue. And *Q* 748 Whil'st,] Whil'st *Q* themselues,] themselues *Q* 753 emulous] æmulous *Q* 754 *Exit.* add G Before 755 CICERO . . . QVINTVS] SCENE IV. | *A Room in Cicero's House.* | *Enter Cicero, Fulvia, and Attendant.* G 756 After 'vp.' *Exit Attendant.* G

But that's too little for you, you are *Romes*:
What could I, then, hope lesse? O brother! now,
The engine⟨r⟩s I told you of, are working;
The machine 'gin's to moue. Where are your weapons?
Arme all my house-hold presently. And charge
The porter, he let no man in, till day.
QVI. Not clients, and your friends? CIC. They weare those names,
That come to murther me. Yet send for CATO,
And QVINTVS CATVLVS; those I dare trust:
And FLACCVS, and POMTINIVS, the *Prætors*,
By the backe way. QVI. Take care, good brother MARCVS,
Your feares be not form'd greater, then they should;
And make your friends grieue, while your enemies laugh.
CIC. 'Tis brothers counsell, and worth thankes. But doe
As I intreat you. I prouide, not feare.
Was CAESAR there, say you? FVL. CVRIVS sayes, he met him,
Comming from thence. CIC. O, so. And, had you a counsell
Of ladies too? Who was your speaker, madame?
FVL. Shee that would be, had there beene fortie more;
SEMPRONIA, who had both her *greeke*, and *figures*;
And, euer and anone, would ask vs, if
The witty *Consul* could haue mended that?
Or Orator CICERO could haue said it better?
CIC. Shee's my gentle enemy. Would CETHEGVS
Had no more danger in him. But, my guards
Are you, great powers; and th'vnbated strengths
Of a firme conscience, which shall arme each step
Tane for the state: and teach me slacke no pace
For feare of malice. How now, brother? QVI. CATO,

III. 759 I,] I *Q, Ff* After 'lesse?' *Enter Quintus Cicero.* G 760 enginers *G conj.*: engines that *W conj.* 765 murther] murder *F2* 772 After 'you.' *Exit Quintus.* G 785 state:] State; *Q* 786 After 'malice.' *Re-enter Quintus.* G

And QVINTVS CATVLVS were comming to you,
And CRASSVS with 'hem. I haue let 'hem in,
By th' garden. CIC. What would CRASSVS haue?
QVI. I heare
Some whispering 'bout the gate; and making doubt,
Whether it be not yet too early, or no?
But I doe thinke, they are your friends, and clients,
Are fearefull to disturbe you. CIC. You will change
To'another thought, anone. Ha' you giu'n the porter
The charge, I will'd you? QVI. Yes. CIC. With-draw, and hearken.

VARGVNTEIVS, CORNELIVS, PORTER,
CICERO, CATO, CATVLVS,
CRASSVS.

THe dore's not open, yet. COR. You'were best to knocke.
VAR. Let them stand close, then: And, when we are in,
Rush after vs. COR. But where's CETHEGVS? VAR. He
Has left it, since he might not do't his way.
POR. Who's there? VAR. A friend, or more. POR. I may not let
Any man in, till day. VAR. No? why? COR. Thy reason?
POR. I am commanded so. VAR. By whom? COR. I hope
We are not discouer'd. VAR. Yes, by reuelation.
Pray thee, good slaue, who has commanded thee?
POR. He that may best, the *Consul*. VAR. We are his friends.
POR. All's one. COR. Best giue your name. VAR. Do'st thou heare, fellow?

III. 795 CIC. *om. F2* *Exeunt.* add G Before 796 VARGVNTEIVS . . . CRASSVS.] SCENE V. | *The Street before Cicero's House.* | *Enter Vargunteius and Cornelius with armed men.* G 799 *Knocks.* add G 800 POR.] *Por.* [*within.*] G: so for his other speeches. 804 Pray thee] Pr'y thee *F2*

I haue some instant businesse with the *Consul*.
Cicero speakes to them from aboue.
My name is VARGVNTEIVS. CIC. True, he knowes it;
And for what friendly office you are sent.
CORNELIVS, too, is there? VAR. We are betraid.
CIC. And desperate CETHEGVS, is he not?
VAR. Speake you, he knowes my voyce. CIC. What say you to't?
COR. You are deceiu'd, sir. CIC. No, 'tis you are so;
Poore, misse-led men. Your states are yet worth pitty,
If you would heare, and change your sauage minds.
Leaue to be mad; forsake your purposes
Of treason, rapine, murder, fire, and horror:
The common-wealth hath eyes, that wake as sharpely
Ouer her life, as yours doe for her ruine.
Be not deceiu'd, to thinke her lenitie
Will be perpetuall; or, if men be wanting,
The gods will be, to such a calling cause.
Consider your attempts, and while there's time,
Repent you of 'hem. It doth make me tremble
There should those spirits yet breath, that when they cannot
Liue honestly, would rather perish basely.
CATO. You talke too much to 'hem, MARCVS, they'are lost.
Goe forth, and apprehend 'hem. CATV. If you proue
This practice, what should let the common-wealth
To take due vengeance? VAR. Let vs shift, away.
The darkenesse hath conceal'd vs, yet. Wee'll say
Some haue abus'd our names. COR. Deny it all.
CATO. QVINTVS, what guards ha' you? Call the *Tribunes* aide,
And raise the citie. *Consul*, you are too mild,
The foulenesse of some facts takes thence all mercy:
It thunders, and lightens violently on the sodaine.
Report it to the *Senate*. Heare: The gods
Grow angrie with your patience. 'Tis their care,

III. 808 *Stage direction not in Q*: *appears at the window above, with Cato, Catulus, and Crassus.* G 814 misse-led] misled *Q* 827 they'are] they are *F2* 831 yet.] yet: *Q* 832 *Exeunt below.* add G 835 *Gnomic pointing in Q*: "The . . . 836 *Stage direction not in Q*

And must be yours, that guiltie men escape not.
As crimes doe grow, iustice should rouse it selfe.

CHORVS.

WHat is it, heauens, you prepare
  With so much swiftnesse, and so sodaine rising?
There are no sonnes of earth, that dare,
  Againe, rebellion? or the gods surprising?
The world doth shake, and nature feares,
  Yet is the tumult, and the horror greater
Within our minds, then in our eares:
  So much *Romes* faults (now growne her fate) doe threat her.
The priests, and people runne about,
  Each order, age, and sexe amaz'd at other;
And, at the ports, all thronging out,
  As if their safety were to quit their mother:
Yet finde they the same dangers there,
  From which they make such hast to be preserued;
For guiltie states doe euer beare
  The plagues about them, which they haue deserued.
And, till those plagues doe get aboue
  The mountayne of our faults, and there doe sit;
Wee see 'hem not. Thus, still we loue
  The'euill we doe, vntill we suffer it.
But, most, ambition, that neere vice
  To vertue, hath the fate of *Rome* prouoked;
And made, that now *Rome's* selfe⟨'s⟩ no price,
  To free her from the death, wherewith shee's yoked.
That restlesse ill, that still doth build
  Vpon successe; and ends not in aspiring:
But there begins. And ne're is fill'd,
  While ought remaines that seemes but worth desiring.

III. 837–9 *Gnomic pointing in Q*: "Tis . . ." And . . . "As . . . 839 *Exeunt above*. G 843 rebellion?] rebellion: *Q* 848 priests] Priest *F2* 857 mountayne] mountaines *F2* 859 The'euill] The evill *F2* 862 selfe's *G conj*.

Wherein the thought, vnlike the eye,
To which things farre, seeme smaller then they are,
Deemes all contentment plac'd on high:
And thinkes there's nothing great, but what is farre.
O, that in time, *Rome* did not cast
Her errors vp, this fortune to preuent;
T'haue seene her crimes, ere they were past:
And felt her faults, before her punishment.

Act IIII.

Diuers Senators passe by, quaking, and trembling.

ALLOBROGES.

CAn these men feare? who are not onely ours,
But the worlds masters? Then I see, the gods
Vpbraid our suffrings, or would humble them;
By sending these affrights, while we are here:
That we might laugh at their ridiculous feare,
Whose names, we trembled at, beyond the *Alpes*.
Of all that passe, I doe not see a face
Worthy a man; that dares looke vp, and stand
One thunder out: but downe-ward all, like beasts,
Running away from euery flash is made.
The falling world could not deserue such basenesse.
Are we emploid here, by our miseries,
Like superstitious fooles (or rather slaues)
To plaine our griefs, wrongs, and oppressions,
To a meere clothed *Senate*, whom our folly
Hath made, and still intends to keepe our tyrannes?
It is our base petitionarie breath
That blowes 'hem to this greatnesse; which this pricke
Would soone let out, if we were bold, and wretched.
When they haue taken all we haue, our goods,

III. 874 crimes, ere] crimes 'ere *Q, Ff*: *Jonson may have written* crimes, e're   IV. Act IV] ACT IV. SCENE I. | *A Street at the foot of the Capitol.* | [*The storm continued.*] *Enter the Allobrogian Ambassadors. Divers Senators* . . . G   *Divers* . . . *trembling.* not in Q   1 Can] 1 *Am.* Can *G*   8 man;] man, *Q*   9 out:] out; *Q*   18 *Points to his sword.* add G   20 haue,] haue; *Q*

Crop, lands, and houses, they will leaue vs this:
A weapon, and an arme will still be found,
Though naked left, and lower then the ground.

CATO, CATVLVS, CICERO, ALLOBROGES.

DOe; vrge thine anger, still: good heauen, and iust.
Tell guiltie men, what powers are aboue them.
In such a confidence of wickednesse,
'Twas time, they should know something fit to feare.
CATV. I neuer saw a morne more full of horror.
CATO. To CATILINE, and his: But, to iust men,
Though heauen should speake, with all his wrath at once,
That, with his breath, the hinges of the world
Did cracke, we should stand vpright, and vnfear'd.
CIC. Why, so we doe, good CATO. Who be these?
CATV. Ambassadors, from the ALLOBROGES,
I take 'hem, by their habits. ALL. I, these men
Seeme of another race; let's sue to these,
There's hope of iustice, with their fortitude.
CIC. Friends of the *Senate*, and of *Rome*, to day
We pray you to forbeare vs: on the morrow
What sute you haue, let vs, by FABIVS SANGA,
(Whose patronage your state doth vse) but know it,
And, on the *Consul's* word, you shall receiue
Dispatch, or else an answere, worth your patience.
ALL. We could not hope for more, most worthy *Consul.*
This magistrate hath strooke an awe into me,
And, by his sweetnesse, wonne a more reguard
Vnto his place, then all the boystrous moodes
That ignorant greatnesse practiseth, to fill
The large, vnfit authoritie it weares.
How easie is a noble spirit discern'd
From harsh, and sulphurous matter, that flies out

IV. Before 24 ALLOBROGES *not in Q*: *Enter Cato, Catulus, and Cicero.* G, continuing the scene 32 cracke,] cracke; *Q* 35 ALL.] 1 *Am.* G 36 these,] these *Q* 44 ALL.] 2 *Am.* G After 44 *Exeunt Cato, Catulus, and Cicero.* G 46 reguard] regard *F2*

In contumelies, makes a noyse, and stinkes!
May we find good, and great men: that know how
To stoupe to wants, and meete necessities,
And will not turne from any equall suites.
Such men, they doe not succour more the cause,
They vnder-take, with fauour, and successe;
Then, by it, their owne iudgements they doe raise,
In turning iust mens needs, into their praise.

THE SENATE.

PRAE. Roome for the *Consuls.* Fathers, take your places.
Here, in the house of IVPITER, the STAYER,
By edict from the *Consul,* MARCVS TVLLIVS,
You'are met, a frequent *Senate.* Heare him speake.
CIC. *What may be happy, and auspicious still*
To Rome, and hers. Honor'd, and conscript Fathers,
If I were silent, and that all the dangers
Threatning the state, and you, were yet so hid
In night, or darkenesse thicker in their brests,
That are the blacke contriuers; so, that no
Beame of the light could pierce 'hem: yet the voyce
Of heau'n, this morning, hath spoke loud inough,
T'instruct you with a feeling of the horror;
And wake you from a sleepe, as starke, as death.
I haue, of late, spoke often in this *Senate,*
Touching this argument, but still haue wanted
Either your eares, or faith: so'incredible
Their plots haue seem'd, or I so vaine, to make

IV. 52 stinkes!] stinkes. *Q* 53 men:] men, *Q* 54 stoupe] stoope *F2* 56–9 *Gnomic pointing in Q*: "Such . . . "They . . . "Then . . . "In . . . 57 fauour] fauor *Q* 59 *Exeunt.* add G Before 60 THE SENATE.] SCENE II. | *The Temple of Jupiter Stator.* | *Enter Cicero, Antonius, Cato, Catulus, Cæsar, Crassus, and many other Senators, Prætor, Officers, &c.* G 61 STAYER *corr. Q, Ff*: Stayer *Q originally* 62 TVLLIVS,] *Tullius,* Q: TVLLIVS. *F1*: TULLIUS. *F2* 64–5 *The formula in roman type in Q originally, but corrected to italic.* 64 *What*] *Which* Q 65 Honor'd,] Honor'd *Q* conscript *Q originally, Ff*: Conscript *corr. Q* 67 state *Q originally, F1*: State *corr. Q, F2* 68 night, *corr. Q, Ff*: night; *Q originally* 73 starke] dead *Q* 77 seem'd, *corr. Q, Ff*: seem'd; *Q originally*

These things for mine owne glorie, and false greatnesse,
As hath beene giuen out. But be it so.
When they breake forth, and shall declare themselues,
By their too foule effects, then, then, the enuy
Of my iust cares will find another name.
For me, I am but one: and this poore life,
So lately aim'd at, not an houre yet since,
They cannot with more eagernesse pursue,
Then I with gladnesse would lay downe, and loose,
To buy *Romes* peace, if that would purchase it.
But when I see, they'ld make it but the step
To more, and greater; vnto yours, *Romes*, all:
I would with those preserue it, or then fall.
CAES. I, I, let you alone, cunning artificer!
See, how his gorget 'peeres aboue his gowne;
To tell the people, in what danger he was.
It was absurdly done of VARGVNTEIVS,
To name himselfe, before he was got in.
CRA. It matters not, so they denie it all:
And can but carry the lye constantly.
Will CATILINE be here? CAES. I'haue sent for him.
CRA. And ha' you bid him to be confident?
CAES. To that his owne necessitie will prompt him.
CRA. Seeme to beleeue nothing at all, that CICERO
Relates vs. CAES. It will mad him. CRA. O, and helpe
The other partie. Who is that? his brother?
What new intelligence ha's he brought him now?
Quintus Cicero brings in the Tribunes, and guards.
CAES. Some cautions from his wife, how to behaue him.
CIC. Place some of them without, and some bring in.
Thanke their kind loues. It is a comfort yet,
That all depart not from their countries cause.
CAES. How now, what meanes this muster? *Consul*, ANTONIVS?

IV. 79 so.] so: *Q* 81 effects, then *corr. Q, Ff*: effects; Then *Q originally* 83 one: *corr. Q, Ff*: one; *Q originally* 84 yet since *corr. Q, Ff*: sithence *Q originally* 86 loose, *corr. Q, F1*: lose, *F2*: loose *Q originally* 89 greater; . . . all: *corr. Q, Ff*: greater, . . . all, *Q originally* 92 'peeres] peeres *Q* 95 *Aside to Crassus.* add G 104 *Stage direction not in Q* 105 wife *Q originally, Ff*: Wife *corr. Q*

ANT. I doe not know, aske my colleague, hee'll tell you.
There is some reason in state, that I must yeeld to;
And I haue promis'd him: Indeed he has bought it,
With giuing me the *Prouince.* CIC. I professe,
It grieues me, *Fathers,* that I am compell'd
To draw these armes, and aides for your defence;
And, more, against a citizen of *Rome,*
Borne here amongst you, a *Patrician,*
A man, I must confesse, of no meane house,
Nor no small vertue, if he had employ'd
Those excellent gifts of fortune, and of nature,
Vnto the good, not ruine of the state.
But, being bred in's fathers needy fortunes,
Brought vp in's sisters prostitution,
Confirm'd in ciuill slaughter, entring first
The common-wealth, with murder of the gentrie;
Since, both by studie, and custome, conuersant
With all licentiousnesse: what could be hop'd
In such a field of riot, but a course
Extreme pernicious? Though, I must protest,
I found his mischiefs, sooner, with mine eyes,
Then with my thought; and with these hands of mine,
Before they touch'd, at my suspicion.
CAES. What are his mischiefs, *Consul?* you declame
Against his manners, and corrupt your owne:
No wise man should, for hate of guiltie men,
Loose his owne innocence. CIC. The noble CAESAR
Speakes god-like truth. But, when he heares, I can
Conuince him, by his manners, of his mischiefs,
He might be silent: and not cast away
His sentences in vaine, where they scarce looke
Toward his subiect. CATO. Here he comes himselfe.
If he be worthy any good mans voyce,

Catiline sits downe, and Cato rises, from him.

IV. 120 nature, *F1*: Nature, *corr. Q, F2*: Nature *Q originally* 127 licentiousnesse: *corr. Q, Ff*: licentiousnesse; *Q originally* 135–6 *Gnomic pointing in Q*: " No . . . " Loose 140 looke] looke. *Q* 141 CATO.] CAT. *Q* 142 worthy] wo thy *Q* *Stage direction not in Q* rises,] *rises* F2

That good man sit downe by him : CATO will not.
  CATV. If CATO leaue him, I'le not keepe aside.
  CATI. What face is this, the *Senate* here puts on,
Against me, *Fathers !* Giue my modestie
Leaue, to demand the cause of so much strangenesse.
  CAES. It is reported here, you are the head
To a strange faction, LVCIVS. CIC. I, and will
Be prou'd against him. CATI. Let it be. Why, *Consul,*
If in the common-wealth, there be two bodies,
One leane, weake, rotten, and that hath a head ;
The other strong, and healthfull, but hath none :
If I doe giue it one, doe I offend ?
Restore your selues, vnto your temper, *Fathers ;*
And, without perturbation, heare me speake.
Remember who I am, and of what place,
What petty fellow this is, that opposes ;
One, that hath exercis'd his eloquence,
Still to the bane of the nobilitie :
A boasting, insolent tongue-man. CATO. Peace, leud traytor,
Or wash thy mouth. He is an honest man
And loues his countrey, would thou didst so, too.
  CATI. CATO, you are too zealous for him. CATO. No ;
Thou art too impudent. CATV. CATILINE, be silent.
  CATI. Nay then, I easily feare, my iust defence
Will come too late, to so much preiudice.
  (CAES. Will he sit downe ?) CATI. Yet, let the world forsake me,
My innocence must not. CATO. Thou innocent ?
So are the *Furies.* CIC. Yes, and *Ate,* too.
Do'st thou not blush, pernicious CATILINE ?
Or, hath the palenesse of thy guilt drunke vp
Thy bloud, and drawne thy veines, as drie of that,

IV. 143 him :] him. *Q* 144 *Rises.* add G 148 reported] re- por ted *F1* 150 CATI.] CAT. *Q* 156 speake.] speake : *Q* 163 countrey,] Countrey ; *Q* 164 No ;] No, *Q* 168 (CAES. . . . downe ?)] CAES. . . . downe ? *Q*

As is thy heart of truth, thy brest of vertue?
Whither at length wilt thou abuse our patience?
Still shall thy furie mocke vs? To what licence
Dares thy vnbridled boldnessé runne it selfe?
Doe all the nightly guards, kept on the palace,
The cities watches, with the peoples feares,
The concourse of all good men, this so strong
And fortified seate here of the *Senate*,
The present lookes vpon thee, strike thee nothing?
Do'st thou not feele thy counsells all laid open?
And see thy wild conspiracie bound in
With each mans knowledge? which of all this order
Canst thou thinke ignorant (if they'll but vtter
Their conscience to the right) of what thou didst
Last night, what on the former, where thou wert,
Whom thou didst call together, what your plots were?
O age, and manners! This the *Consul* sees,
The *Senate* vnderstands, yet this man liues!
Liues? I, and comes here into counsell with vs;
Partakes the publique cares: and with his eye
Markes, and points out each man of vs to slaughter.
And we, good men, doe satisfie the state,
If we can shunne but this mans sword, and madnesse.
There was that vertue, once, in *Rome*, when good men
Would, with more sharpe coërcion, haue restrain'd
A wicked citizen, then the deadliest foe.
We haue that law still, CATILINE, for thee;
An act as graue, as sharpe: The state's not wanting,
Nor the authoritie of this *Senate*; we,
We, that are *Consuls*, onely faile our selues.
This twentie dayes, the edge of that decree
We haue let dull, and rust; kept it shut vp,
As in a sheath, which drawne should take thy head.
Yet still thou liu'st: and liu'st not to lay by

IV. 201 state's *Q originally, F1*: State's *corr. Q, F2* 205 rust; *corr. Q, Ff*: rust, *Q originally* 207 liu'st: *corr. Q, Ff*: liu'st, *Q originally*

Thy wicked confidence, but to confirme it.
I could desire, *Fathers*, to be found
Still mercifull, to seeme, in these maine perills
Grasping the state, a man remisse, and slacke;
But then, I should condemne my selfe of sloth,
And trecherie. Their campe's in *Italie*,
Pitch'd in the iawes, here, of *Hetruria;*
Their numbers daily increasing, and their generall
Within our walls: nay, in our counsell! plotting
Hourely some fatall mischiefe to the publique.
If, CATILINE, I should command thee, now,
Here, to be taken, kill'd; I make iust doubt,
Whether all good men would not thinke it done
Rather too late, then any man too cruell.
CATO. Except he were of the same meale, and batch.
CIC. But that, which ought to haue been done long since,
I will, and (for good reason) yet forbeare.
Then will I take thee, when no man is found
So lost, so wicked, nay, so like thy selfe,
But shall professe, 'tis done of need, and right.
While there is one, that dares defend thee, liue;
Thou shalt haue leaue; but so, as now thou liu'st:
Watch'd at a hand, besieged, and opprest
From working least commotion to the state.
I haue those eyes, and eares, shall still keepe guard,
And spiall on thee, as they haue euer done,
And thou not feele it. What, then, canst thou hope?
If neither night can, with her darknesse, hide,
Thy wicked meetings; nor a priuate house

IV. 209 *Fathers,* F1: Fathers, *corr. Q*: Fathers *Q originally*: grave *Fathers* F2 (cf. V. 490) 210 perills] perils, *Q* 214 iawes, *corr. Q, F1*: jawes, *F2*: iawes *Q originally* *Hetruria;* corr. Q, Ff: *Hetruria,* Q originally 216 walls: *Ff*: walles: *corr. Q*: walles, *Q originally* nay, . . . Counsell!] nay . . . Councell, *Q* 217 Hourely] Howerly *Q* publique] Publique *corr. Q* 218 If, *corr. Q, Ff*: If *Q originally* 222 meale, *corr. Q, Ff*: meale *Q originally* 229 leaue; . . . liu'st: *corr. Q, F1*: leave; . . . liv'st: *F2*: leaue: . . . liu'st, *Q originally* 231 state *Q originally, F1*: State *corr. Q, F2* 235 night can, . . . darknesse, *Ff*: Night can, . . . darknesse, *corr. Q*: night, can . . . darknesse *Q originally* 236 house] House *corr. Q*

Can, in her walls, contayne the guiltie whispers
Of thy conspiracie : if all breake out,
All be discouered, change thy mind at last,
And loose thy thoughts of ruine, flame, and slaughter.
Remember, how I told, here, to the *Senate*,
That such a day, thy Lictor, CAIVS MANLIVS,
Would be in armes. Was I deceiued, CATILINE?
Or in the fact, or in the time? the houre?
I told too, in this *Senate*, that thy purpose
Was, on the fifth (the kalends of *Nouember*)
T'haue slaughter'd this whole order : which my caution
Made many leaue the citie. Canst thou here
Denie, but this thy blacke designe was hindred,
That very day, by me? thy selfe clos'd in
Within my strengths, so that thou could'st not moue
Against a publique reed? when thou wert heard
To say, vpon the parting of the rest,
Thou would'st content thee, with the murder of vs,
That did remaine. Had'st thou not hope, beside,
By a surprize, by night, to take *Præneste?*
Where when thou cam'st, did'st thou not find the place
Made good against thee, with my aides, my watches?
My garrisons fortified it. Thou do'st nothing, SERGIVS,
Thou canst endeauour nothing, nay not thinke,
But I both see, and heare it; and am with thee,
By, and before, about, and in thee, too.
Call but to mind thy last nights businesse. Come,
Ile vse no circumstance : at LECCA's house,
The shop, and mint of your conspiracie,
Among your sword-men, where so many associates
Both of thy mischiefe, and thy madnesse, met.

IV. 237 Can, . . . walles, *corr. Q, F1*: Can, . . . walls, *F2*: Can . . . walles *Q originally* 238 conspiracie: if *Ff*: conspiracy: If *corr. Q*: conspiracy, if *Q originally* 239 discouered] discover'd *F2* 240 loose] lose *F2* 241 told, *corr. Q, Ff*: told *Q originally* 243 CATILINE?] *Catiline*, Q 244 houre] hower *Q* 246 fifth (the . . . *Nouember*)] fifth, the . . . Nouember, *Q* 250 me?] mee, *Q* 257 Where *corr. Q, Ff*: And *Q originally* 261 thee, *corr. Q, Ff*: thee; *Q originally* 263 businesse] buisinesse *Q originally* 267 met. *corr. Q, Ff*: met? *Q originally*

Dar'st thou denie this ? wherefore art thou silent ?
Speake, and this shall conuince thee : Here they are,
I see 'hem, in this *Senate*, that were with thee.
O, you immortall gods ! in what clime are we ?
What region doe we liue in ? in what ayre ?
What common-wealth, or state is this we haue ?
Here, here, amongst vs, our owne number, *Fathers*,
In this most holy counsell of the world,
They are, that seeke the spoyle of me, of you,
Of ours, of all ; what I can name 's too narrow :
Follow the sunne, and find not their ambition.
These I behold, being *Consul ;* nay, I aske
Their counsells of the state, as from good *Patriots :*
Whom it were fit the axe should hew in pieces,
I not so much as wound, yet, with my voyce.
Thou wast, last night, with LECCA, CATILINE,
Your shares, of *Italie*, you there diuided ;
Appointed who, and whither, each should goe ;
What men should stay behind, in *Rome*, were chosen ;
Your offices set downe ; the parts mark'd out,
And places of the citie, for the fire ;
Thy selfe (thou'affirmd'st) wast readie to depart,
Onely, a little let there was, that stay'd thee,
That I yet liu'd. Vpon the word, stept forth
Three of thy crew, to rid thee of that care ;
Two vnder-tooke this morning, before day,
To kill me in my bed. All this I knew,
Your conuent scarce dismiss'd, arm'd all my seruants,
Call'd both my brother, and friends, shut out your clients,
You sent to visite me ; whose names I told
To some there, of good place, before they came.
CATO. Yes, I, and QVINTVS CATVLVS can affirme it.
CAES. He's lost, and gone. His spirits haue forsooke
him.
CIC. If this be so, why, CATILINE, do'st thou stay ?

IV. 269 thee : *corr. Q, Ff* : thee ; *Q originally* 286 behind,] behind *F2* 291 liu'd.] liu'd : *Q* 300 *Aside.* add G

Goe, where thou mean'st. The ports are open; forth.
The campe abroad wants thee, their chiefe, too long.
Lead with thee all thy troupes out. Purge the citie.
Draw drie that noysome, and pernicious sinke,
Which left, behind thee, would infect the world.
Thou wilt free me of all my feares, at once,
To see a wall betweene vs. Do'st thou stop
To doe that now, commanded; which before,
Of thine owne choice, thou'rt prone to? Goe. The *Consul*
Bids thee, an enemie, to depart the citie.
Whither, thou'lt aske? to exile? I not bid
Thee that. But aske my counsell, I perswade it.
What is there, here, in *Rome*, that can delight thee?
Where not a soule, without thine owne foule knot,
But feares, and hates thee. What domesticke note
Of priuate filthinesse, but is burnt in
Into thy life? What close, and secret shame,
But is growne one, with thy knowne infamy?
What lust was euer absent from thine eyes?
What leud fact from thy hands? what wickednesse
From thy whole body? where's that youth drawne in
Within thy nets, or catch'd vp with thy baits,
Before whose rage, thou hast not borne a sword,
And to whose lusts thou hast not held a torch?
Thy latter nuptialls I let passe in silence;
Where sinnes incredible, on sinnes, were heap't:
Which I not name, lest, in a ciuill state,
So monstrous facts should either appeare to be,
Or not to be reueng'd. Thy fortunes, too,
I glance not at, which hang but till next *Ides*.
I come to that, which is more knowne, more publike;
The life, and safetie of vs all, by thee
Threatned, and sought. Stood'st thou not in the field,
When LEPIDVS, and TVLLVS were our *Consuls*,
Vpon the day of choice, arm'd, and with forces,

IV. 302 mean'st.] mean'st: *Q* 325 held *F2*: 'held *Q*, *F1*

To take their liues, and our chiefe citizens?
When, not thy feare, nor conscience chang'd thy mind,
But the meere fortune of the common-wealth
With-stood thy actiue malice? Speake but right.
How often hast thou made attempt on me?
How many of thy assaults haue I declin'd
With shifting but my body (as wee'ld say)
Wrested thy dagger from thy hand, how oft?
How often hath it falne, or slip't by chance?
Yet, can thy side not want it: which, how vow'd,
Or with what rites, 'tis sacred of thee, I know not,
That still thou mak'st it a necessitie,
To fixe it in the body of a *Consul*.
But let me loose this way, and speake to thee,
Not as one mou'd with hatred, which I ought,
But pitty, of which none is owing thee.
CAT. No more then vnto TANTALVS, or TITYVS.
CIC. Thou cam'st, e're-while, into this *Senate*. Who
Of such a frequency, so many friends,
And kindred thou hast here, saluted thee?
Were not the seates made bare, vpon thy entrance?
Riss' not the consular men? and left their places,
So soone as thou sat'st downe? and fled thy side,
Like to a plague, or ruine? knowing, how oft
They had beene, by thee, mark'd out for the shambles?
How dost thou beare this? Surely, if my slaues
At home fear'd me, with halfe th'affright, and horror,
That, here, thy fellow-citizens doe thee,
I should soone quit my house, and thinke it need too.
Yet thou dar'st tarry here? Goe forth, at last;
Condemne thy selfe to flight, and solitude.
Discharge the common-wealth, of her deepe feare.
Goe; into banishment, if thou wait'st the word.
Why do'st thou looke? They all consent vnto it.
Do'st thou expect th'authoritie of their voyces,

IV. 337 citizens ?] Citizens ; *Q* 343 body] bodie, *Q* 350 loose] lose *F2* 360 ruine ?] ruine ; *Q* 362 beare] heare *F2*

Whose silent wills condemne thee? While they sit,
They approue it; while they suffer it, they decree it;
And while they'are silent to it, they proclaime it.
Proue thou there honest, Ile endure the enuie.
But there's no thought, thou should'st be euer he,
Whom either shame should call from filthinesse,
Terror from danger, or discourse from furie.
Goe; I intreat thee: yet, why doe I so?
When I alreadie know, they'are sent afore,
That tarry for thee'in armes, and doe expect thee
On the AVRELIAN way. I know the day
Set downe, 'twixt thee, and MANLIVS; vnto whom
The siluer eagle too is sent, before:
Which I doe hope shall proue, to thee as banefull,
As thou conceiu'st it to the common-wealth.
But, may this wise, and sacred *Senate* say,
What mean'st thou MARCVS TVLLIVS? If thou know'st
That CATILINE be look'd for, to be chiefe
Of an intestine warre; that he'is the author
Of such a wickednesse; the caller out
Of men of marke in mischiefe, to an action
Of so much horror; Prince of such a treason;
Why do'st thou send him forth? why let him scape?
This is, to giue him libertie, and power:
Rather, thou should'st lay hold vpon him, send him
To deseru'd death, and a iust punishment.
To these so holy voices, thus I answere.
If I did thinke it timely, *Conscript Fathers*,
To punish him with death, I would not giue
The Fencer vse of one short houre, to breath;
But when there are in this graue order, some,
Who, with soft censures, still doe nource his hopes;
Some, that with not beleeuing, haue confirm'd
His designes more, and whose authoritie

IV. 380 they'are] they're *F2* 382 On the *Q*: On th' *Ff* 395 is,] is *Q* 401 houre] hower *Q* 403 nource] nourse *F2*

The weaker, as the worst men, too, haue follow'd :
I would now send him, where they all should see
Cleere, as the light, his heart shine ; where no man
Could be so wickedly, or fondly stupide,
But should cry out, he saw, touch'd, felt, and grasp't it.
Then, when he hath runne out himselfe ; led forth
His desp'rate partie with him ; blowne together
Aides of all kindes, both shipwrack'd mindes and fortunes :
Not onely the growne euill, that now is sprung,
And sprouted forth, would be pluck'd vp, and weeded ;
But the stocke, roote, and seed of all the mischiefes,
Choking the common-wealth. Where, should we take,
Of such a swarme of traytors, onely him,
Our cares, and feares might seeme a while relieu'd,
But the maine perill would bide still enclos'd
Deepe, in the veines, and bowells of the state.
As humane bodies, labouring with feuers,
While they are tost with heate, if they doe take
Cold water, seeme for that short space much eas'd,
But afterward, are ten times more afflicted.
Wherefore, I say, let all this wicked crew
Depart, diuide themselues from good men, gather
Their forces to one head ; as I said oft,
Let 'hem be seuer'd from vs with a wall ;
Let 'hem leaue off attempts, vpon the *Consul*,
In his owne house ; to circle in the *Prætor* ;
To girt the court with weapons ; to prepare
Fire, and balls, swords, torches, sulphure, brands :
In short, let it be writ in each mans fore-head
What thoughts he beares the publike. I here promise,
Fathers Conscript, to you, and to my selfe,
That diligence in vs *Consuls*, for my honor'd
Colleague, abroad, and for my selfe, at home ;
So great authoritie in you ; so much
Vertue, in these, the gentlemen of *Rome* ;

IV. 410 out,] out *Q* 411 himselfe ;] himselfe, *Q* 422 labouring] laboring *Q* 437 honor'd] honour'd *Q*

Whom I could scarce restraine to day, in zeale,
From seeking out the parricide, to slaughter;
So much consent in all good men, and minds,
As, on the going out of this one CATILINE,
All shall be cleere, made plaine, oppress'd, reueng'd.
And, with this *omen*, goe, pernicious plague,
Out of the citie, to the wish'd destruction
Of thee, and those, that, to the ruine of her,
Haue tane that bloudie, and black sacrament.
Thou IVPITER, whom we doe call the STAYER,
Both of this citie, and this empire, wilt
(With the same auspice thou didst raise it first)
Driue from thy altars, and all other temples,
And buildings of this citie; from our walls;
Liues, states, and fortunes of our citizens;
This fiend, this furie, with his complices.
And all the'offence of good men (these knowne traytors
Vnto their countrey, theeues of *Italie*,
Ioyn'd in so damn'd a league of mischiefe) thou
Wilt with perpetuall plagues, aliue, and dead,
Punish for *Rome*, and saue her innocent head.
  CATI. If an oration, or high language, *Fathers*,
Could make me guiltie, here is one, hath done it:
H'has stroue to emulate this mornings thunder,
With his prodigious rhetoricke. But I hope,
This *Senate* is more graue, then to giue credit
Rashly to all he vomits, 'gainst a man
Of your owne order, a *Patrician*;
And one, whose ancestors haue more deseru'd
Of *Rome*, then this mans eloquence could vtter,
Turn'd the best way: as still, it is the worst.
  CATO. His eloquence hath more deseru'd to day,
Speaking thy ill, then all thy ancestors
Did, in their good: and, that the state will find,
Which he hath sau'd. CATI. How, he? were I that enemie,

IV. 450 STAYER,] STAYER *Q*   464 emulate] æmulate *Q*   471 way:] way, *Q*

That he would make me: I'ld not wish the state
More wretched, then to need his preseruation.
What doe you make him, CATO, such a HERCVLES?
An ATLAS? A poore petty in-mate! CATO. Traytor.
CATI. He saue the state? A burgesse sonne of *Arpinum.*
The gods would rather twentie *Romes* should perish,
Then haue that contumely stucke vpon 'hem,
That he should share with them, in the preseruing
A shed, or signe-post. CATO. Peace, thou prodigie.
CATI. They would be forc'd themselues, againe, and lost
In the first, rude, and indigested heape;
Ere such a wretched name, as CICERO,
Should sound with theirs. CATV. Away, thou impudent head.
CATI. Doe you all backe him? are you silent too?
Well, I will leaue you, *Fathers;* I will goe.
But—— my fine daintie speaker—— CIC. What now, *Furie?* *He turnes sodainly on Cicero.*
Wilt thou assault me here? (CHO. Helpe, aide the *Consul.*)
CATI. See, *Fathers,* laugh you not? who threatned him?
In vaine thou do'st conceiue, ambitious orator,
Hope of so braue a death, as by this hand.
(CATO. Out, of the court, with the pernicious traytor.)
CATI. There is no title, that this flattering *Senate,*
Nor honor, the base multitude can giue thee,
Shall make thee worthy CATILINES anger. (CATO. Stop,
Stop that portentous mouth.) CATI. Or, when it shall,
Ile looke thee dead. CATO. Will none restraine the monster?

IV. 476 I'ld *F2*: Il'd *Q, F1* 480 burgesse] *Burgesse'* Q 485 forc'd] runne *Q* 491 *Stage direction not in Q* 492 (CHO. . . . *Consul.*)] CHO. . . . Consul. *Q* 496 (CATO. . . . traytor.)] CATO. . . traytor. *Q* 498 honor] honour *Q* 499–500 (CATO. . . . mouth.)] CATO. . . . mouth. *Q*

CATV. Parricide. QVI. Butcher, traytor, leaue the *Senate.*
CATI. I'am gone, to banishment, to please you, *Fathers.*
Thrust head-long forth! CATO. Still, do'st thou murmure, monster?
CATI. Since, I am thus put out, and made a—— CIC. What?
CATV. Not guiltier then thou art. CATI. I will not burne
Without my funerall pile. CATO. What saies the fiend?
CATI. I will haue matter, timber. CATO. Sing out scrich-owle.
CATI. It shall be in—— CATV. Speake thy imperfect thoughts.
CATI. The common fire, rather then mine owne.
For fall I will with all, ere fall alone.
CRA. H'is lost, there is no hope of him. CAES. Vnlesse
He presently take armes; and giue a blow,
Before the *Consuls* forces can be leui'd.
CIC. What is your pleasure, *Fathers*, shall be done?
CATV. See, that the common-wealth receiue no losse.
CATO. Commit the care thereof vnto the *Consuls.*
CRA. 'Tis time. CAES. And need. CIC. Thankes to this frequent *Senate.*
But what decree they, vnto CVRIVS,
And FVLVIA? CATV. What the *Consul* shall thinke meete.
CIC. They must receiue reward, though't be not knowne;
Lest when a state needs ministers, they ha' none.
CATO. Yet, MARCVS TVLLIVS, doe not I beleeue,
But CRASSVS, and this CAESAR here ring hollow.
CIC. And would appeare so, if that we durst proue 'hem.
CATO. Why dare we not? What honest act is that,
The *Roman Senate* should not dare, and doe?

IV. 504 forth!] forth? *Q, Ff* 511 *Rushes out of the Senate.* add G 518 After 'need.' *Goes aside with Crassus.* G

CIC. Not an vnprofitable, dangerous act,
To stirre too many serpents vp at once.
CAESAR, and CRASSVS, if they be ill men,
Are mightie ones; and, we must so prouide,
That, while we take one head, from this foule *Hydra*,
There spring not twentie more. CATO. I 'proue your counsell.
CIC. They shall be watch'd, and look'd too. Till they doe
Declare themselues, I will not put 'hem out
By any question. There they stand. Ile make
My selfe no enemies, nor the state no traytors.

CATILINE, LENTVLVS, CETHEGVS, CVRIVS, GABINIVS, LONGINVS, STATILIVS.

FAlse to our selues? All our designes discouer'd
To this state-cat? CET. I, had I had my way,
He'had mew'd in flames, at home, not i' the *Senate*:
I'had sing'd his furres, by this time. CAT. Well, there's, now,
No time of calling backe, or standing still.
Friends, be your selues; keepe the same *Roman* hearts,
And readie minds, you'had yester-night. Prepare
To execute, what we resolu'd. And let not
Labour, or danger, or discouerie fright you.
Ile to the armie: you (the while) mature
Things, here, at home. Draw to you any aides,
That you thinke fit, of men of all conditions,
Or any fortunes, that may helpe a warre.
Ile bleede a life, or winne an empire for you.
Within these few dayes, looke to see my ensignes,
Here, at the walls: Be you but firme within.

IV. 537 *Exeunt.* add G Before 538 CATILINE . . . STATILIVS.] SCENE III. | *Catiline's House.* | *Enter Catiline, Lentulus, Cethegus, Curius, Gabinius, Longinus, and Statilius.* G 544 you'had] you had *F2* 546 Labour] Labor *Q* 550 Or] Of *F2*

Meane time, to draw an enuy on the *Consul*,
And giue a lesse suspicion of our course,
Let it be giuen out, here in the citie,
That I am gone, an innocent man, to exile,
Into *Massilia*, willing to giue way
To fortune, and the times; being vnable
To stand so great a faction, without troubling
The common-wealth: whose peace I rather seeke,
Then all the glory of contention,
Or the support of mine owne innocence.
Farewell the noble LENTVLVS, LONGINVS,
CVRIVS, the rest; and thou, my better Genius,
The braue CETHEGVS: when we meete againe,
Wee'll sacrifice to libertie. CET. And reuenge.
That we may praise our hands once. LEN. O, you *Fates*,
Giue *Fortune* now her eyes, to see with whom
Shee goes along, that shee may ne're forsake him.
CVR. He needs not her, nor them. Goe but on, SERGIVS.
A valiant man is his owne fate, and fortune.
LON. The fate, and fortune of vs all goe with him.
GAB. STA. And euer guard him. CAT. I am all your creature.
LEN. Now friends, 'tis left with vs. I haue alreadie
Dealt, by VMBRENVS, with the ALLOBROGES,
Here resiant in *Rome*; whose state, I heare,
Is discontent with the great vsuries,
They are oppress'd with: and haue made complaints
Diuers, vnto the *Senate*, but all vaine.
These men, I'haue thought (both for their owne oppressions,
As also that, by nature, they'are a people
Warlike, and fierce, still watching after change,
And now, in present hatred with our state)
The fittest, and the easiest to be drawne

IV. 572 *Gnomic pointing in Q*: "A . . . 574 *Exit.* add G 580 all] all, *F2* 581 I'haue] I have *F2* thought (both] thought, both *Q* 582 they'are] they are *F2* 583 Warlike] Warlick *F2* 584 state)] State, *Q*

To our societie, and to aide the warre.
The rather, for their seate; being next bordrers
On *Italie;* and that they'abound with horse:
Of which one want our campe doth onely labour.
And I haue found 'hem comming. They will meete
Soone, at SEMPRONIA's house, where I would pray you
All to be present, to confirme 'hem more.
The sight of such spirits hurt not, nor the store.
GAB. I will not faile. STA. Nor I. CVR. Nor I.
CET. Would I
Had somewhat by my selfe, apart, to doe.
I ha' no Genius to these many counsells.
Let me kill all the *Senate*, for my share,
Ile doe it at next sitting. LEN. Worthy CAIVS,
Your presence will adde much. CET. I shall marre more.

CICERO, SANGA, ALLOBROGES.

THe state's beholden to you, FABIVS SANGA,
For this great care: And those ALLOBROGES
Are more then wretched, if they lend a listning
To such perswasion. SAN. They, most worthy *Consul*,
As men employ'd here, from a grieued state,
Groning beneath a multitude of wrongs,
And being told, there was small hope of ease
To be expected, to their euills, from hence,
Were willing, at the first to giue an eare
To any thing, that sounded libertie:
But since, on better thoughts, and my vrg'd reasons,
They'are come about, and wonne, to the true side.
The fortune of the common-wealth hath conquer'd.
CIC. What is that same VMBRENVS, was the agent?
SAN. One that hath had negotiation
In *Gallia* oft, and knowne vnto their state.

IV. 589 labour] labor *Q* 591 Soone,] Soone *Q* 596 I ha' *corr. Q*: I'ha' *Q originally, Ff* 599 *Exeunt.* add G Before 600 CICERO . . . ALLOBROGES.] SCENE IV. | *The House of Brutus.* | *Enter Cicero and Sanga.* G (*For* ' Brutus ' *read* ' Cicero ') 600 to] unto *F2*

CIC. Are th'Ambassadors come with you? SAN. Yes.
CIC. Well, bring 'hem in, if they be firme, and honest,
Neuer had men the meanes so to deserue
Of *Rome*, as they. A happy, wish'd occasion,
And thrust into my hands, for the discouery,
And manifest conuiction of these traytors.
The Allobroges enter.
Be thank'd, ô IVPITER. My worthy lords,
Confederates of the *Senate*, you are welcome.
I vnderstand by QVINTVS FABIVS SANGA,
Your carefull patron here, you haue beene lately
Sollicited against the common-wealth,
By one VMBRENVS (take a seate, I pray you)
From PVBLIVS LENTVLVS, to be associates
In their intended warre. I could aduise,
That men, whose fortunes are yet flourishing,
And are *Romes* friends, would not, without a cause,
Become her enemies; and mixe themselues
And their estates, with the lost hopes of CATILINE,
Or LENTVLVS, whose meere despaire doth arme 'hem:
That were to hazard certainties, for aire,
And vnder-goe all danger, for a voice.
Beleeue me, friends, loud tumults are not laid
With halfe the easinesse, that they are rais'd.
All may beginne a warre, but few can end it.
The *Senate* haue decreed, that my colleague
Shall leade their armie, against CATILINE,
And haue declar'd both him, and MANLIVS traytors.
METELLVS CELER hath alreadie giuen
Part of their troops defeate. Honors are promis'd
To all, will quit 'hem; and rewards propos'd
Euen to slaues, that can detect their courses.
Here, in the citie, I haue by the *Prætors*,
And *Tribunes*, plac'd my guards, and watches so,
That not a foote can treade, a breath can whisper,

IV. 616 th'Ambassadors] the'Ambassadors *Q* 619 After 'they.' *Exit Sanga.* G 622 *Stage direction not in Q, omitted in F2: Re-enter Sanga with the Allobrogian Ambassadors.* G 637–9 *Gnomic pointing in Q*: " Loud . . . " With . . . "All . . .

But I haue knowledge. And be sure, the *Senate*,
And people of *Rome*, of their accustom'd greatnesse,
Will sharply, and seuerely vindicate,
Not onely any fact, but any practice,
Or purpose, 'gainst the state. Therefore, my lords,
Consult of your owne wayes, and thinke which hand
Is best to take. You, now, are present suters
For some redresse of wrongs; Ile vnder-take
Not onely that shall be assur'd you: but
What grace, or priuiledge else, *Senate*, or people,
Can cast vpon you, worthy such a seruice,
As you haue now the way, and meanes, to doe 'hem,
If but your wills consent, with my designes.

ALL. We couet nothing more, most worthy *Consul*.
And how so e're we haue beene tempted lately,
To a defection, that not makes vs guiltie:
We are not yet so wretched in our fortunes,
Nor in our wills so lost, as to abandon
A friendship, prodigally, of that price,
As is the *Senate*, and the people of *Romes*,
For hopes, that doe precipitate themselues.

CIC. You then are wise, and honest. Doe but this, then:
(When shall you speake with LENTVLVS, and the rest?

ALL. We are to meete anone, at BRVTVS house.

CIC. Who? DECIVS BRVTVS? He is not in *Rome*.

SAN. O, but his wife SEMPRONIA. CIC. You instruct me,
Shee is a chiefe.) Well, faile not you to meete 'hem,
And to expresse the best affection
You can put on, to all that they intend.
Like it, applaud it, giue the common-wealth,
And *Senate* lost to 'hem. Promise any aides
By armes, or counsell. What they can desire,
I would haue you preuent. Onely, say this,
You'haue had dispatch, in priuate, by the *Consul*,

IV. 658 you :] you, *Q* 659 grace,] grace *Q* 661 'hem,] 'hem; *Q* 663 ALL.] 1 *Am*. G. *So* 673, 702, 706 670 precipitate] præcipitate *Q* 672, 676 (When . . . chiefe.)] When . . . Chiefe. *Q*

Of your affaires, and for the many feares
The state's now in, you are will'd by him, this euening,
To depart *Rome:* which you, by all sought meanes,
Will doe, of reason to decline suspicion.
Now, for the more authoritie of the businesse
They'haue trusted to you, and to giue it credit
With your owne state, at home, you would desire
Their letters to your *Senate*, and your people,
Which shewne, you durst engage both life, and honor,
The rest should euery way answere their hopes.
Those had, pretend sodaine departure, you,
And, as you giue me notice, at what port
You will goe out, Ile ha' you intercepted,
And all the letters taken with you: So
As you shall be redeem'd in all opinions,
And they conuicted of their manifest treason.
Ill deedes are well turn'd backe, vpon their authors:
And 'gainst an iniurer, the reuenge is iust.
This must be done, now. ALL. Chearefully, and firmely.
We'are they, would rather hast to vndertake it,
Then stay, to say so. CIC. With that confidence, goe:
Make your selues happy, while you make *Rome* so.
By SANGA, let me haue notice from you. ALL. Yes.

SEMPRONIA, LENTVLVS, CETHEGVS, GABINIVS, STATILIVS, LONGINVS, VOLTVRTIVS, ALLOBROGES.

WHen come these creatures, the Ambassadors?
I would faine see 'hem. Are they any schollers?
LEN. I think not, madame. SEM. Ha' they no *greeke?*
LEN. No surely.
SEM. Fie, what doe I here, wayting on 'hem then?
If they be nothing but meere states-men. LEN. Yes,

IV. 692 honor] honour *F2* 694 sodaine] sudden *F2* departure,] departure *Q* 700–1 *Gnomic pointing in Q*: "Ill . . . "And . . . 706 *Exeunt.* add G Before 707 SEMPRONIA . . . ALLOBROGES.] SCENE V. | *A Room in Brutus'* (*Sempronia's*) *House.* | *Enter Sempronia, and Lentulus.* G

Your ladiship shall obserue their grauitie,
And their reseruednesse, their many cautions,
Fitting their persons. SEM. I doe wonder much,
That states, and common-wealths employ not women,
To be Ambassadors, sometimes! we should
Doe as good publike seruice, and could make
As honorable spies (for so THVCIDIDES
Calls all Ambassadors.) Are they come, CETHEGVS?
CET. Doe you aske me? Am I your scout, or baud?
LEN. O, CAIVS, it is no such businesse. CET. No?
What do's a woman at it then? SEM. Good sir,
There are of vs can be as exquisite traytors,
As ere a male-conspirator of you all.
CET. I, at smock treason, matron, I beleeue you;
And if I were your husband; but when I
Trust to your cobweb-bosomes any other,
Let me there die a flie, and feast you, spider.
LEN. You are too sowre, and harsh CETHEGVS. CET. You
Are kind, and courtly. I'ld be torne in pieces,
With wild HIPPOLYTVS, nay proue the death,
Euery limbe ouer, e're I'ld trust a woman,
With wind, could I retaine it. SEM. Sir. They'll be trusted
With as good secrets, yet, as you haue any:
And carry 'hem too, as close, and as conceal'd,
As you shall for your heart. CET. Ile not contend with you
Either in tongue, or carriage, good CALIPSO:
LON. Th'ambassadors are come. CET. Thanks to thee MERCVRY,
That so hast rescu'd me. LEN. How now, VOLTVRTIVS?
VOL. They doe desire some speech with you, in priuate.

IV. 719 After 'Ambassadors' *Enter Cethegus.* G 724 ere] e're *F2* 727 cobweb- *Q*: cob-web- *Ff* other, *F2*: other *Q, F1* 728 flie,] Flie; *Q* 730 I'ld]: Il'd *Q F1* 732 I'ld *Q*: Il'd *F1* Before 738 *Enter Lentulus.* G 739 After 'me.' *Enter Volturtius, Statilius, and Gabinius, with the Allobrogian Ambassadors.* G

LEN. O! 'tis about the prophecie, belike,
And promise of the SIBYLLS. GAB. It may be.
SEM. Shun they, to treat with me, too? GAB. No, good lady,
You may partake: I haue told 'hem, who you are.
SEM. I should be loth to be left out, and here too.
CET. Can these, or such, be any aides, to vs?
Looke they, as they were built to shake the world,
Or be a moment, to our enterprise?
A thousand, such as they are, could not make
One atome of our soules. They should be men
Worth heauens feare, that looking vp, but thus,
Would make IOVE stand vpon his guard, and draw
Himselfe within his thonder; which, amaz'd,
He should discharge in vaine, and they vn-hurt.
Or, if they were, like CAPANEVS, at *Thebes*,
They should hang dead, vpon the highest spires,
And aske the second bolt, to be throwne downe.
Why, LENTVLVS, talke you so long? This time
Had beene enough, t'haue scatter'd all the starres,
T'haue quench'd the sunne, and moone, and made the world
Despaire of day, or any light, but ours.
LEN. How doe you like this spirit? In such men,
Mankind doth liue. They are such soules, as these,
That moue the world. SEM. I, though he beare me hard,
I, yet, must doe him right. He is a spirit
Of the right MARTIAN breed. ALL. He is a MARS!
Would we had time to liue here, and admire him.
LEN. Well, I doe see you would preuent the *Consul*.
And I commend your care: It was but reason,
To aske our letters, and we had prepar'd them.
Goe in, and we will take an oath, and seale 'hem.
You shall haue letters, too, to CATILINE,
To visite him i'the way, and to confirme

IV. 742 SIBYLLS.] *Sibylls;* Q After 'SIBYLLS.' *He takes them apart.* G 748 moment,] moment *Q* 753 thonder] thunder *F2* 757 bolt] charge *Q* 764 SEM. *F2*: SEN. *Q, F1* 766 ALL.] 1 *Am.* G MARS!] *Mars.* Q

The association. This our friend, VOLTVRTIVS,
Shall goe along with you. Tell our great generall,
That we are readie here; that LVCIVS BESTIA
The *Tribune*, is prouided of a speech,
To lay the enuie of the warre on CICERO;
That all but long for his approach, and person:
And then, you are made free-men, as our selues.

CICERO, FLACCVS, POMTINIVS, SANGA.

I Cannot feare the warre but to succeed well,
Both for the honor of the cause, and worth
Of him that doth command. For my colleague,
Being so ill affected with the gout,
Will not be able to be there in person;
And then PETREIVS, his lieutenant, must
Of need take charge o'the armie: who is much
The better souldier, hauing beene a *Tribune*,
Prefect, *Lieutenant*, *Prætor* in the warre,
These thirtie yeeres, so conuersant i'the armie,
As he knowes all the souldiers, by their names.
FLA. They'll fight then, brauely, with him. POM. I, and he
Will lead 'hem on, as brauely. CIC. They'haue a foe
Will aske their braueries, whose necessities
Will arme him like a furie. But, how euer,
I'le trust it to the manage, and the fortune
Of good PETREIVS, who's a worthy patriot:
METELLVS CELER, with three legions, too,
Will stop their course, for *Gallia*. How now, FABIVS?
SAN. The traine hath taken. You must instantly
Dispose your guards vpon the *Miluian* bridge:
For, by that way, they meane to come. CIC. Then, thither
POMTINIVS, and FLACCVS, I must pray you

IV. 778 on] upon *F2* 780 *Exeunt.* add G Before 781 CICERO . . . SANGA.] SCENE VI. | *A Room in Cicero's House.* | *Enter Cicero, Flaccus, and Pomtinius.* G 782 honor] honour *F2* 797 patriot:] Patriot. *Q* 799 After '*Gallia.*' *Enter Fabius Sanga.* G

To lead that force you haue; and seize them all:
Let not a person scape. Th'ambassadors
Will yeeld themselues. If there be any tumult,
Ile send you aide. I, in meane time will call
LENTVLVS to me, GABINIVS, and CETHEGVS,
STATILIVS, CEPARIVS, and all these,
By seuerall messengers: who no doubt will come,
Without sense, or suspicion. Prodigall men
Feele not their owne stocke wasting. When I haue 'hem,
Ile place those guards, vpon 'hem, that they start not.
SAN. But what'll you doe with SEMPRONIA? CIC. A states anger
Should not take knowledge eyther of fooles, or women.
I do not know whether my ioy or care
Ought to be greater; that I haue discouer'd
So foule a treason: or must vndergoe
The enuie of so many great mens fate.
But, happen what there can, I will be iust,
My fortune may forsake me, not my vertue:
That shall goe with me, and before me, still,
And glad me, doing well, though I heare ill.

PRAETORS, ALLOBROGES, VOLTVRTIVS.

FLA. Stand, who goes there? ALL. We are th' ALLOBROGES,
And friends of *Rome*. POM. If you be so, then yeeld
Your selues vnto the *Prætors*, who in name
Of the whole *Senate*, and the people of *Rome*,
Yet, till you cleare your selues, charge you of practise
Against the State. VOL. Die friends, and be not taken.

IV. 806 tumult, *F2*: tumult *Q, F1* 807 After 'aide.' *Exeunt Flaccus and Pomtinius.* G 811–12 *Gnomic pointing in Q*: "Prodigall . . . "Feele . . . 814–15 *Gnomic pointing in Q*: "A . . . "Should . . . 814 A states anger] "A State *Q* 823 *Exeunt.* add G Before 824 PRAETORS . . . VOLTVRTIVS.] SCENE VII. | *The Milvian Bridge.* | *Enter Flaccus and Pomtinius, with Guards, on one side, and Volturtius with the Allobrogian Ambassadors on the other.* G 824, 830 ALL.] 1 *Am.* G 824 ALLOBROGES,] *Allobroges*, Q: ALLOBROGES *Ff*

FLA. What voyce is that? Downe with 'hem all.
ALL. We yeeld.
POM. What's he stands out? Kill him there. VOL.
Hold, hold, hold.
I yeeld vpon conditions. FLA. We giue none
To traytors, strike him downe. VOL. My name's VOLTVRTIVS,
I know POMTINIVS. POM. But he knowes not you,
While you stand out vpon these trayterous termes.
VOL. I'le yeeld vpon the safety of my life.
POM. If it be forfeyted, we cannot saue it.
VOL. Promise to doe your best. I'am not so guilty,
As many others, I can name; and will:
If you will grant me fauour. POM. All we can
Is to deliuer you to the *Consul.* Take him,
And thanke the gods, that thus haue saued *Rome.*

CHORVS.

NOw, do our eares, before our eyes,
Like men in mists,
Discouer, who'ld the state surprise,
And who resists?
And, as these clouds doe yeeld to light,
Now, do we see,
Our thoughts of things, how they did fight,
Which seem'd t'agree?
Of what strange pieces are we made,
Who nothing know;
But, as new ayres our eares inuade,
Still censure so?
That now doe hope, and now doe feare,
And now enuy;
And then doe hate, and then loue deare,
But know not, why:

IV. 833 traytors,] traytors; *F2* VOLTVRTIVS,] *Volturtius*: Q: VOLTVRTIVS *F1*: VOLTURTIUS, *F2* 838 I'am] I am *F2* 841 *Consul*] Consul *Q, Ff* 842 *Exeunt.* add G

Or, if we doe, it is so late,
  As our best mood,
Though true, is then thought out of date,
  And emptie of good.
How haue we chang'd, and come about
  In euery doome,
Since wicked CATILINE went out,
  And quitted *Rome?*
One while, we thought him innocent;
  And, then, w⟨e⟩'accus'd
The *Consul*, for his malice spent;
  And power abus'd.
Since, that we heare, he is in armes,
  We thinke not so:
Yet charge the *Consul*, with our harmes,
  That let him goe.
So, in our censure of the state,
  We still doe wander;
And make the carefull magistrate
  The marke of slander.
What age is this, where honest men,
  Plac'd at the helme,
A sea of some foule mouth, or pen,
  Shall ouer-whelme?
And call their diligence, deceipt;
  Their vertue, vice;
Their watchfulnesse, but lying in wait;
  And bloud, the price.
O, let vs plucke this euill seede
  Out of our spirits;
And giue, to euery noble deede,
  The name it merits.
Lest we seeme falne (if this endures)
  Into those times,
To loue disease: and brooke the cures
  Worse, then the crimes.

Act v.

PETREIVS. *The Armie.*

IT is my fortune, and my glorie, Souldiers,
This day, to lead you on; the worthy *Consul*
Kept from the honor of it, by disease:
And I am proud, to haue so braue a cause
To exercise your armes in. We not, now,
Fight for how long, how broad, how great, and large
Th'extent, and bounds o'th' people of *Rome* shall be;
But to retaine what our great ancestors,
With all their labours, counsells, arts, and actions,
For vs, were purchasing so many yeeres.
The quarrell is not, now, of fame, of tribute,
Or of wrongs, done vnto confederates,
For which, the armie of the people of *Rome*
Was wont to moue: but for your owne republique,
For the rais'd temples of th'immortall gods,
For all your fortunes, altars, and your fires,
For the deare soules of your lou'd wiues, and children,
Your parents tombes, your rites, lawes, libertie,
And, briefly, for the safety of the world:
Against such men, as onely by their crimes
Are knowne; thrust out by riot, want, or rashnesse.
One sort, SYLLA's old troops, left here in *Fesulæ*,
Who sodainely made rich, in those dire times,
Are since, by their vn-bounded, vast expence,
Growne needy, and poore: and haue but left t'expect,
From CATILINE, new bills, and new proscriptions.
These men (they say) are valiant; yet, I thinke 'hem
Not worth your pause: For either their old vertue
Is, in their sloth, and pleasures lost; or, if
It tarry with 'hem, so ill match to yours,
As they are short in number, or in cause.

v. Act V] PETREIVS. THE ARMY. *Q*: ACT V. SCENE I. | *Etruria. The Country near Fesulæ.* | *Enter Petreius, marching, at the head of his army.* G 11 of tribute] or tribute *F2* 25 poore:] poore, *Q*

The second sort are of those (city-beasts,
Rather then citizens) who whilst they reach
After our fortunes, haue let flie their owne;
These, whelm'd in wine, swell'd vp with meates, and weakned
With hourely whoredomes, neuer left the side
Of CATILINE, in *Rome;* nor, here, are loos'd
From his embraces: such, as (trust me) neuer
In riding, or in vsing well their armes,
Watching, or other militarie labour,
Did exercise their youth; but learn'd to loue,
Drinke, dance, and sing, make feasts, and be fine gamsters:
And these will wish more hurt to'you, then they bring you.
The rest are a mixt kind, all sorts of furies,
Adulterers, dicers, fencers, out-lawes, theeues,
The murderers of their parents, all the sinke,
And plague of *Italie,* met in one torrent,
To take, to day, from vs the punishment,
Due to their mischiefes, for so many yeeres.
And who, in such a cause, and 'gainst such fiends,
Would not now wish himselfe all arme, and weapon?
To cut such poysons from the earth, and let
Their bloud out, to be drawne away in cloudes,
And pour'd, on some inhabitable place,
Where the hot sunne, and slime breeds nought but monsters?
Chiefly, when this sure ioy shall crowne our side,
That the least man, that falls vpon our partie
This day (as some must giue their happy names
To fate, and that eternall memorie
Of the best death, writ with it, for their countrey)
Shall walke at pleasure, in the tents of rest;
And see farre off, beneath him, all their host
Tormented after life: and CATILINE, there,
Walking a wretched, and lesse ghost, then he.

v. 42 gamsters:] gamsters. *Q* 43 to'you *Q*: to you *Ff* 50 and *om. F3*

Ile vrge no more : Moue forward, with your eagles,
And trust the *Senates*, and *Romes* cause to heauen.
ARM. To thee, great father MARS, and greater IOVE.

CÆSAR, CRASSVS.

I Euer look'd for this of LENTVLVS,
When CATILINE was gone. CRA. I gaue 'hem lost,
Many dayes since. CAES. But, wherefore did you beare
Their letter to the *Consul*, that they sent you,
To warne you from the citie ? CRA. Did I know
Whether he made it ? It might come from him,
For ought I could assure me : if they meant,
I should be safe, among so many, they might
Haue come, as well as writ. CAES. There is no losse
In being secure. I haue, of late, too, ply'd him
Thicke, with intelligences, but they'haue beene
Of things he knew before. CRA. A little serues
To keepe a man vpright, on these state-bridges,
Although the passage were more dangerous.
Let vs now take the standing part. CAES. We must,
And be as zealous for't, as CATO. Yet
I would faine helpe these wretched men. CRA. You cannot.
Who would saue them, that haue betraid themselues ?

CICERO, QVINTVS, CATO.

I Will not be wrought to it, brother QVINTVS.
There's no mans priuate enmitie shall make
Me violate the dignitie of another.
If there were proofe 'gainst CAESAR, or who euer,
To speake him guiltie, I would so declare him.
But QVINTVS CATVLVS, and PISO both,
Shall know, the *Consul* will not, for their grudge,

v. 67 *Exeunt.* G Before 68 CÆSAR, CRASSVS.] SCENE II. | *Rome. A Street near the Temple of Concord.* | *Enter Cæsar and Crassus.* G 85 *Exeunt.* add G Before 86 CICERO . . . CATO] SCENE III. | *Cicero's House.* | *Enter Cicero, Q. Cicero, and Cato.* G

Haue any man accus'd, or named falsly.
 QVI. Not falsly: but if any circumstance,
By the ALLOBROGES, or from VOLTVRTIVS,
Would carry it. CIC. That shall not be sought by me.
If it reueale it selfe, I would not spare
You, brother, if it pointed at you, trust me.
 CATO. Good MARCVS TVLLIVS (which is more, then great)
Thou had'st thy education, with the gods.
 CIC. Send LENTVLVS forth, and bring away the rest.
This office, I am sorry, sir, to doe you.

THE SENATE.

WHat may be happy still, and fortunate,
To Rome, and to this Senate: Please you, *Fathers*,
To breake these letters, and to view them round.
If that be not found in them, which I feare,
I, yet, intreate, at such a time, as this,
My diligence be not contemn'd. Ha' you brought
The weapons hither, from CETHEGVS house?
 PRAE. They are without. CIC. Be readie, with VOLTVRTIVS,
To bring him, when the *Senate* calls; and see
None of the rest, conferre together. *Fathers*,
What doe you reade? Is it yet worth your care,
If not your feare, what you find practis'd there?
 CAES. It hath a face of horror! CRA. I'am amaz'd!
 CATO. Looke there. SYL. Gods! Can such men draw common aire?
 CIC. Although the greatnesse of the mischiefe, *Fathers*,
Hath often made my faith small, in this *Senate*,
Yet, since my casting CATILINE out (for now

v. 94 falsly :] falsly, *Q* 102 *Exeunt.* add G Before 103 THE SENATE.] SCENE IV. | *The Temple of Concord.* | *Enter Lictors, Cicero* (*with letters*), *Cato, Q. Cicero, Cæsar, Crassus, Syllanus, and other Senators.* G 108 After 'contemn'd.' *Gives the letters to the Senate.* | *Enter* (*the Prætors*) *Flaccus and Pomtinius.* G 112 After 'together.' *Exeunt Prætors.* G 115 horror! . . . amaz'd!] horror. . . . amaz'd. *Q*

I doe not feare the enuy of the word,
Vnlesse the deed be rather to be fear'd,
That he went hence aliue; when those I meant
Should follow him, did not) I haue spent both dayes,
And nights, in watching, what their fury'and rage
Was bent on, that so staid, against my thought:
And that I might but take 'hem in that light,
Where, when you met their treason, with your eyes,
Your minds, at length, would thinke for your owne safetie.
And, now, 'tis done. There are their hands, and seales.
Their persons, too, are safe, thankes to the gods.
Bring in VOLTVRTIVS, and the'ALLOBROGES.
These be the men, were trusted with their letters.
VOL. *Fathers*, beleeue me, I knew nothing: I
Was trauailing for *Gallia*, and am sorry——
CIC. Quake not, VOLTVRTIVS, speake the truth, and hope
Well of this *Senate*, on the *Consuls* word.
VOL. Then, I knew all. But truely'I was drawne in
But t'other day. CAES. Say, what thou know'st, and feare not.
Thou hast the *Senates* faith, and *Consuls* word,
To fortifie thee. VOL. I was sent with letters——
He answeres with feare and interruptions.
And had a message too——from LENTVLVS——
To CATILINE——that he should vse all aides——
Seruants, or others——and come with his armie,
Assoone, vnto the citie as he could——
For they were readie, and but staid for him——
To intercept those, that should flee the fire——
These men (the ALLOBROGES) did heare it too.
ALL. Yes, *Fathers*, and they tooke an oath, to vs,
Besides their letters, that we should be free;
And vrg'd vs, for some present aide of horse.
CIC. Nay, here be other testimonies, *Fathers*,
The weapons and armes are brought forth.

v. After 131 *Re-enter Prætors, with Volturtius and the Allobrogian Ambassadors.* G   137 truely'I] *The apostrophe clear in Q, faint or missing in F1*: *om. F2*   140, 151 *Stage directions not in Q*   148 ALL.] 1 *Amb.* G   vs,] vs. *Q, F1*: us. *F2*

CETHEGVS armourie. CRA. What, not all these?
CIC. Here's not the hundred part. Call in the Fencer,
That we may know the armes to all these weapons.
Come, my braue sword-player, to what active vse,
Was all this steele prouided? CET. Had you ask'd
In SYLLA's dayes, it had beene to cut throats;
But, now, it was to looke on, only: I lou'd
To see good blades, and feele their edge, and points.
To put a helme vpon a blocke, and cleaue it,
And, now and then, to stab an armour through.
CIC. Know you that paper? That will stab you through.
Is it your hand? Hold, saue the pieces. Traytor,
Hath thy guilt wak'd thy furie? CET. I did write,
I know not what; nor care not: That foole LENTVLVS
Did dictate, and I t'other foole, did signe it.
CIC. Bring in STATILIVS: Do's he know his hand too?
And LENTVLVS. Reach him that letter. STA. I
Confesse it all. CIC. Know you that seale yet, PVBLIVS?
LEN. Yes, it is mine. CIC. Whose image is that, on it?
LEN. My grand-fathers. CIC. What, that renowm'd good man,
That did so only'embrace his countrey', and lou'd
His fellow citizens! Was not his picture,
Though mute, of power to call thee from a fact,
So foule—— LEN. As what, impetuous CICERO?
CIC. As thou art, for I doe not know what's fouler.
Looke vpon these. Doe not these faces argue
Thy guilt, and impudence? LEN. What are these to me?
I know 'hem not. ALL. No PVBLIVS? we were with you,

v. After 154 *Enter Cethegus, guarded.* G 163 After 'hand?' *Cethegus tears the letters.* G 168 After 'LENTVLVS.' *Enter Statilius and P. Lentulus, guarded.* G 171 renowm'd] renown'd *F3* 177 After 'these.' *Points to the Allobrogian Ambassadors.* G 179 ALL.] *Amb.* G: *so* 181, 188, 196

At BRVTVS house. VOL. Last night. LEN. What did you there?
Who sent for you? ALL. Your selfe did. We had letters
From you, CETHEGVS, this STATILIVS here,
GABINIVS CIMBER, all, but from LONGINVS,
Who would not write, because he was to come
Shortly, in person, after vs (he said)
To take the charge o' the horse, which we should leuy.
CIC. And he is fled, to CATILINE, I heare.
LEN. Spies? spies? ALL. You told vs too, o' the SIBYLLS bookes,
And how you were to be a king, this yeere,
The twentieth, from the burning of the *Capitoll*.
That three CORNELII were to raigne, in *Rome*,
Of which you were the last: and prais'd CETHEGVS,
And the great spirits, were with you, in the action.
CET. These are your honorable Ambassadors,
My soueraigne lord. CAT. Peace, that too bold CETHEGVS.
ALL. Besides GABINIVS, your agent, nam'd
AVTRONIVS, SERVIVS SVLLA, VARGVNTEIVS,
And diuers others. VOL. I had letters from you,
To CATILINE, and a message, which I'haue told
Vnto the *Senate*, truely, word for word:
For which, I hope, they will be gracious to me.
I was drawne in, by that same wicked CIMBER,
And thought no hurt at all. CIC. VOLTVRTIVS, peace.
Where is thy visor, or thy voyce, now, LENTVLVS?
Art thou confounded? Wherefore speak'st thou not?
Is all so cleere, so plaine, so manifest,
That both thy eloquence, and impudence,
And thy ill nature, too, haue left thee, at once?
Take him aside. There's yet one more, GABINIVS,
The enginer of all. Shew him that paper,

v. 194 honorable] honourable *F2* 197 SVLLA] SYLLA *F2* 209 more,] more. *Q* 210 enginer] Engineer *F3* After 'all.' *Gabinius Cimber is brought in.* G

If he doe know it? GAB. I know nothing. CIC. No?
GAB. No. Neither will I know. CAT. Impudent head!
Sticke it into his throate; were I the *Consul*,
I'ld make thee eate the mischiefe, thou hast vented.
GAB. Is there a law for't, CATO? CAT. Do'st thou aske
After a law, that would'st haue broke all lawes,
Of nature, manhood, conscience, and religion?
GAB. Yes, I may aske for't. CAT. No, pernicious CIMBER.
Th'inquiring after good, do's not belong
Vnto a wicked person. GAB. I, but CATO
Do's nothing, but by law. CRA. Take him aside.
There's proofe enough, though he confesse not. GAB. Stay,
I will confesse. All's true, your spies haue told you.
Make much of 'hem. CET. Yes, and reward 'hem well,
For feare you get no more such. See, they doe not
Die in a ditch, and stinke, now you ha' done with 'hem;
Or beg, o' the bridges, here in *Rome*, whose arches
Their actiue industrie hath sau'd. CIC. See, *Fathers*,
What mindes, and spirits these are, that, being conuicted
Of such a treason, and by such a cloud
Of witnesses, dare yet retayne their boldnesse?
What would their rage haue done, if they had conquer'd?
I thought, when I had thrust out CATILINE,
Neither the state, nor I, should need t'haue fear'd
LENTVLVS sleepe here, or LONGINVS fat,
Or this CETHEGVS rashnesse; it was he,
I onely watch'd, while he was in our walls,
As one, that had the braine, the hand, the heart.
But now, we find the contrary! Where was there
A people grieu'd, or a state discontent,

v. 212 Neither . . . know] Nor I will not know *Q* Neither *corr. F1, F2*: Neyther *F1 originally* head!] head? *Q* 214 I'ld] Il'd *Q, Ff* 219–20 *Gnomic pointing in Q*: " Th'inquiring . . . " Vnto . . . 220 I, *Q*: I *Ff* 239 But] Bnt *Q* contrary!] contrary. *Q*

Able to make, or helpe a warre 'gainst *Rome*,
But these, th'ALLOBROGES, and those they found?
Whom had not the iust gods beene pleas'd to make
More friends vnto our safety, then their owne,
As it then seem'd, neglecting these mens offers,
Where had we beene? or where the common-wealth?
When their great Chiefe had beene call'd home? this man,
Their absolute king (whose noble grand-father,
Arm'd in pursuit of the seditious GRACCHVS,
Tooke a braue wound, for deare defence of that,
Which he would spoile) had gather'd all his aides
Of ruffians, slaues, and other slaughter-men?
Giuen vs vp for murder, to CETHEGVS?
The'other ranke of citizens, to GABINIVS?
The citie, to be fir'd by CASSIVS?
And *Italie*, nay the world, to be laid wast
By cursed CATILINE, and his complices?
Lay but the thought of it, before you, *Fathers*,
Thinke but with me you saw this glorious citie,
The light of all the earth, tower of all nations,
Sodainely falling in one flame. Imagine,
You view'd your countrey buried with the heapes
Of slaughter'd citizens, that had no graue;
This LENTVLVS here, raigning, (as he dreamp't)
And those his purple *Senate*; CATILINE come
With his fierce armie; and the cryes of matrons,
The flight of children, and the rape of virgins,
Shriekes of the liuing, with the dying grones
On euery side t'inuade your sense; vntill
The bloud of *Rome*, were mixed with her ashes!
This was the spectacle these fiends intended
To please their malice. CET. I, and it would
Haue beene a braue one, *Consul*. But your part
Had not then beene so long, as now it is:

v. 247 home?] home; *Q* 252 ruffians] Ruffins *Q* -men?] -men; *Q* 253 CETHEGVS?] *Cethegus;* Q 254 GABINIVS?] *Gabinius;* Q 255 CASSIVS?] *Cassius;* Q 257 complices?] complices. *Q* 270 ashes!] ashes. *Q*

I should haue quite defeated your oration;
And slit that fine rhetoricall pipe of yours,
I' the first *Scene*. CAT. Insolent monster! CIC. *Fathers*,
Is it your pleasures, they shall be committed
Vnto some safe, but a free custodie,
Vntill the *Senate* can determine farder?
SEN. It pleaseth well. CIC. Then, MARCVS CRASSVS,
Take you charge of GABINIVS: send him home
Vnto your house. You CAESAR, of STATILIVS.
CETHEGVS shall be sent to CORNIFICIVS;
And LENTVLVS, to PVBLIVS LENTVLVS SPINTHER,
Who now is *Ædile*. CAT. It were best, the *Prætors*
Carryed 'hem to their houses, and deliuered 'hem.
CIC. Let it be so. Take 'hem from hence. CAES. But, first,
Let LENTVLVS put off his *Prætor*-ship.
LEN. I doe resigne it here vnto the *Senate*.
CAES. So, now, there's no offence done to religion.
CAT. CAESAR, 'twas piously, and timely vrg'd.
CIC. What doe you decree to th'ALLOBROGES?
That were the lights to this discouery?
CRA. A free grant, from the state, of all their suites.
CAES. And a reward, out of the publike treasure.
CAT. I, and the title of honest men, to crowne 'hem.
CIC. What to VOLTVRTIVS? CAES. Life, and fauour 's well.
VOL. I aske no more. CAT. Yes, yes, some money, thou need'st it.
'Twill keepe thee honest: want made thee a knaue.
SYL. Let FLACCVS, and POMTINIVS, the *Prætors*,
Haue publike thankes, and QVINTVS FABIVS SANGA,
For their good seruice. CRA. They deserue it all.
CAT. But what doe we decree vnto the *Consul*,
Whose vertue, counsell, watchfulnesse, and wisedome,
Hath free'd the common-wealth, and without tumult,

v. 276 rhetoricall] rhethoricall *F2* 286 *Ædile*] Ædile *Q, Ff*
After 290 *Exeunt Prætors and Guards, with Lentulus, Cethegus, Statilius, and Gabinius.* G 298 fauour 's] fauor's *Q*

Slaughter, or bloud, or scarce raysing a force,
Rescu'd vs all out of the iawes of fate?
CRA. We owe our liues vnto him, and our fortunes.
CAES. Our wiues, our children, parents, and our gods.
SYL. We all are saued, by his fortitude.
CATO. The common-wealth owes him a *ciuicke* gyrland.
He is the onely father of his countrey.
CAES. Let there be publike prayer, to all the gods,
Made in that name, for him. CRA. And in these words.
For that he hath, by his vigilance, preseru'd
Rome *from the flame, the* Senate *from the sword,*
And all her citizens from massacre.
CIC. How are my labours more than paid, graue *Fathers,*
In these great titles, and decreed honors!
Such, as to me, first, of the ciuill robe,
Of any man, since *Rome* was *Rome,* haue hap'ned;
And from this frequent *Senate:* which more glads me,
That I now see, yo'haue sense of your owne safety.
If those good dayes come no lesse gratefull to vs,
Wherein we are preseru'd from some great danger,
Then those, wherein we'are borne, and brought to light,
Because the gladnesse of our safetie is certaine,
But the condition of our birth not so;
And that we are sau'd with pleasure, but are borne
Without the sense of ioy: why should not, then,
This day, to vs, and all posteritie
Of ours, be had in equall fame, and honor,
With that, when ROMVLVS first rear'd these walls,
When so much more is saued, then he built?
CAES. It ought. CRA. Let it be added to our *Fasti.*
CIC. What tumult's that? FLA. Here's one TARQVINIVS taken,
Going to CATILINE; and sayes he was sent
By MARCVS CRASSVS: whom he names, to be

v. 312 gyrland] garland *F2* 324 yo'haue] you' haue *Q* 327 we'are *F2*: w' are *Q, F1* brought] brought, *Q, Ff* 333 honor] honour *F2* 336 *Noise without.* add G 337 After 'that?' *Re-enter Flaccus.* G

Guiltie of the conspiracy. Cic. Some lying varlet.
Take him away, to prison. Cra. Bring him in,
And let me see him. Cic. He is not worth it, Crassvs.
Keepe him vp close, and hungrie, till he tell,
By whose pernicious counsell, he durst slander
So great, and good a citizen. (Cra. By yours
I feare, 'twill proue.) Syl. Some o' the traytors, sure,
To giue their action the more credit, bid him
Name you, or any man. Cic. I know my selfe,
By all the tracts, and courses of this businesse,
Crassvs is noble, iust, and loues his countrey.
Fla. Here is a libell too, accusing Caesar,
From Lvcivs Vectivs, and confirm'd by Cvrivs.
Cic. Away with all, throw it out o' the court.
Caes. A tricke on me, too? Cic. It is some mens malice.
I said to Cvrivs, I did not beleeue him.
Caes. Was not that Cvrivs your spie, that had
Reward decreed vnto him, the last *Senate*,
With Fvlvia, vpon your priuate motion?
Cic. Yes. Caes. But, he has not that reward, yet?
Cic. No.
Let not this trouble you, Caesar, none beleeues it.
Caes. It shall not, if that he haue no reward.
But if he haue, sure I shall thinke my selfe
Very vntimely, and vnsafely honest,
Where such, as he is, may haue pay t'accuse me.
Cic. You shall haue no wrong done you, noble Caesar,
But all contentment. Caes. *Consul*, I am silent.

The Armie.

Catiline.

I Neuer yet knew, Souldiers, that, in fight,
Words added vertue vnto valiant men;
Or, that a generalls oration made

v. 345–6 (Cra. . . . proue.)] Cra. . . . proue. *Q* 353 throw it] throw'it *Q* 359 But,] But *Q* 366 *Exeunt.* add G Before 367 Catiline. The Armie. *Q*: Scene v. | *The Country near Fesulæ.* | *Enter Catiline with his Army.* G

An armie fall, or stand : but how much prowesse
Habituall, or naturall each mans brest
Was owner of, so much in act it shew'd.
Whom neither glory'or danger can excite,
'Tis vaine t'attempt with speech : for the minds feare
Keepes all braue sounds from entring at that eare.
I, yet, would warne you some few things, my friends,
And giue you reason of my present counsailes.
You know, no lesse then I, what state, what point
Our affaires stand in ; and you all haue heard,
What a calamitous misery the sloth,
And sleepinesse of LENTVLVS, hath pluck'd
Both on himselfe, and vs : how, whilst our aides
There, in the citie look'd for, are defeated,
Our entrance into *Gallia*, too, is stopt.
Two armies wait vs : one from *Rome*, the other
From the *Gaule-Prouinces*. And, where we are,
(Although I most desire it) the great want
Of corne, and victuall, forbids longer stay.
So that, of need, we must remoue, but whither
The sword must both direct, and cut the passage.
I onely, therefore, wish you, when you strike,
To haue your valours, and your soules, about you ;
And thinke, you carrie in your labouring hands
The things you seeke, glorie, and libertie,
Your countrie, which you want now, with the *Fates*,
That are to be instructed, by our swords.
If we can giue the blow, all will be safe to'vs.
We shall not want prouision, nor supplies.
The colonies, and free townes will lye open.
Where, if we yeeld to feare, expect no place,
Nor friend, to shelter those, whom their owne fortune,
And ill-vs'd armes haue left without protection.
You might haue liu'd in seruitude, or exile,

v. 373–5 *Gnomic pointing in Q*: "Whom . . . "Tis . . . "Keepes . . . 388 victuall] victuals *F2* 393 labouring] laboring *Q* 397 to'vs *Q*: to vs *F1*: to us *F2* 402 ill-vs'd] ill vs'd *Q*, *F1*: ill us'd *F2*

Or safe at *Rome*, depending on the great ones ;
But that you thought those things vnfit for men.
And, in that thought, you then were valiant.
For no man euer yet chang'd peace for warre,
But he, that meant to conquer. Hold that purpose.
There's more necessitie, you should be such,
In fighting for your selues, then they for others.
Hee's base, that trusts his feet, whose hands are arm'd.
Me thinkes, I see *Death*, and the *Furies*, waiting
What we will doe ; and all the heau'n at leisure
For the great spectacle. Draw, then, your swords :
And, if our destinie enuie our vertue
The honor of the day, yet let vs care
To sell our selues, at such a price, as may
Vn-doe the world, to buy vs ; and make *Fate*,
While shee tempts ours, feare her owne estate.

THE SENATE.

SEN. What meanes this hastie calling of the *Senate?*
SEN. We shall know straight. Wait, till the *Consul* speakes.
POM. *Fathers Conscript*, bethinke you of your safeties,
And what to doe, with these conspirators ;
Some of their clients, their free'd men, and slaues
'Ginne to make head : there is one of LENTVLVS bawds
Runnes vp and downe the shops, through euery street,
With money to corrupt the poore artificers,
And needie tradesmen, to their aide. CETHEGVS
Hath sent, too, to his seruants ; who are many,
Chosen, and exercis'd in bold attemptings,
That forth-with they should arme themselues, and proue
His rescue : All will be in instant vproare,
If you preuent it not, with present counsailes.

v. 411 *Gnomic pointing in Q*: " Hee's . . . 413 heau'n] Heauen' *Q*: heauen' *F1*: heaven' *F2* 418 world,] world *Q* 419 *Exeunt, marching.* add G Before 420 THE SENATE] SCENE VI. | *The Temple of Jupiter Stator.* | *Enter Lictors, Prætors,* (*Pomptinius and Flaccus,*) *Cicero, Syllanus, Cæsar, Cato, Crassus, and other Senators.* G 427 money] Money, *F3* corrupt *F2*: corrupt, *Q, F1*

We haue done what we can, to meet the furie,
And will doe more. Be you good to your selues.
CIC. What is your pleasure, *Fathers*, shall be done?
SYLLANVS, you are *Consul* next design'd.
Your sentence, of these men. SYL. 'Tis short, and this.
Since they haue sought to blot the name of *Rome*,
Out of the world; and raze this glorious empire
With her owne hands, and armes, turn'd on her selfe:
I thinke it fit they die. And, could my breath
Now, execute 'hem, they should not enioy
An article of time, or eye of light,
Longer, to poyson this our common ayre.
SEN. I thinke so too. SEN. And I. SEN. And I.
SEN. And I.
CIC. Your sentence, CAIVS CAESAR. CAES. *Conscript Fathers*,
In great affaires, and doubtfull, it behooues
Men, that are ask'd their sentence, to be free
From either hate, or loue, anger, or pittie:
For, where the least of these doe hinder, there
The mind not easily discernes the truth.
I speake this to you, in the name of *Rome*,
For whom you stand; and to the present cause:
That this foule fact of LENTVLVS, and the rest,
Weigh not more with you, then your dignitie;
And you be more indulgent to your passion,
Then to your honor. If there could be found
A paine, or punishment, equall to their crimes,
I would deuise, and helpe: but, if the greatnesse
Of what they ha' done, exceed all mans inuention,
I thinke it fit, to stay, where our lawes doe.
Poore pettie states may alter, vpon humour,
Where, if they'offend with anger, few doe know it,
Because they are obscure; their fame, and fortune
Is equall, and the same. But they, that are

v. 451 doe hinder] doehinder *F1* 463 humour] humor *Q*
466 same.] same: *Q*

Head of the world, and liue in that seene height,
All mankind knowes their actions. So wee see,
The greater fortune hath the lesser licence.
They must nor fauour, hate, and least be angrie:
For what with others is call'd anger, there,
Is crueltie, and pride. I know SYLLANVS,
Who spoke before me, a iust, valiant man,
A louer of the state, and one that would not,
In such a businesse, vse or grace, or hatred;
I know, too, well, his manners, and modestie:
Nor doe I thinke his sentence cruell (for
'Gainst such delinquents, what can be too bloudie?)
But that it is abhorring from our state;
Since to a citizen of *Rome*, offending,
Our lawes giue exile, and not death. Why then
Decrees he that? 'Twere vaine to thinke, for feare;
When, by the diligence of so worthy a *Consul*,
All is made safe, and certaine. Is't for punishment?
Why, death's the end of euills, and a rest,
Rather then torment: It dissolues all griefes.
And beyond that, is neither care, nor ioy.
You heare, my sentence would not haue 'hem die.
How then? set free, and increase CATILINES armie?
So will they, being but banish'd. No, graue *Fathers*,
I iudge 'hem, first, to haue their states confiscate,
Then, that their persons remaine prisoners
I'the free townes, farre off from *Rome*, and seuer'd:
Where they might neither haue relation,
Hereafter, to the *Senate*, or the people.
Or, if they had, those townes, then, to be mulcted,
As enemies to the state, that had their guard.

SEN. 'Tis good, and honorable, CAESAR hath vtterd.

CIC. *Fathers*, I see your faces, and your eyes
All bent on me, to note of these two censures,

v. 470 fauour] fauor *Q* 476 well,] well *Q* and] and his *Q* 486 griefes.] griefes; *F2* 493 seuer'd] seuerd' *Q* 496 then,] then *Q, Ff* 498 honorable] honourable *Q* CAESAR] CAESAR, *Ff*: *Cæsar*, *Q*

Which I incline to. Either of them are graue,
And answering the dignitie of the speakers,
The greatnesse of th'affaire, and both seuere.
One vrgeth death : and he may well remember
This state hath punish'd wicked citizens so.
The other bonds : and those perpetuall, which
He thinkes found out for the more singular plague.
Decree, which you shall please. You haue a *Consul*,
Not readier to obey, then to defend,
What euer you shall act, for the republique ;
And meet with willing shoulders any burden,
Or any fortune, with an euen face,
Though it were death : which to a valiant man
Can neuer happen foule, nor to a *Consul*
Be immature, or to a wise man wretched.
SYL. *Fathers*, I spake, but as I thought : the needes
O'th' common-wealth requir'd. CAT. Excuse it not.
CIC. CATO, speake you your sentence. CAT. This it is.
You here dispute, on kinds of punishment,
And stand consulting, what you should decree
'Gainst those, of whom, you rather should beware.
This mischiefe is not like those common facts,
Which, when they are done, the lawes may prosequute.
But this, if you prouide not, ere it happen,
When it is happen'd, will not wait your iudgement.
Good CAIVS CAESAR, here, hath very well,
And subtilly discours'd of life, and death,
As if he thought those things, a prettie fable,
That are deliuer'd vs of hell, and furies,
Or of the diuers way, that ill men goe
From good, to filthy, darke, and vgly places.
And therefore, he would haue these liue ; and long too ;
But farre from *Rome*, and in the small free townes,
Lest, here, they might haue rescue : As if men,

v. 501 incline] encline *Q* 521 beware. *Q* : beware, *F1* : beware ; *F2* 531 vgly] ougly *Q*

Fit for such acts, were only in the citie,
And not throughout all *Italie ?* or, that boldnesse
Could not doe more, where it found least resistance ?
'Tis a vaine counsaile, if he thinke them dangerous.
Which, if he doe not, but that he alone,
In so great feare of all men, stand vn-frighted,
He giues me cause, and you, more to feare him.
I am plaine, *Fathers*. Here you looke about,
One at another, doubting what to doe ;
With faces, as you trusted to the gods,
That still haue sau'd you ; and they can do't : But,
They are not wishings, or base womanish prayers,
Can draw their aides ; but vigilance, counsell, action :
Which they will be ashamed to forsake.
'Tis sloth they hate, and cowardise. Here, you haue
The traytors in your houses, yet, you stand,
Fearing what to doe with 'hem ; Let 'hem loose,
And send 'hem hence with armes, too ; that your mercie
May turne your miserie, as soone as 't can.
O, but, they, are great men, and haue offended,
But, through ambition. We would spare their honor :
I, if themselues had spar'd it, or their fame,
Or modestie, or either god, or man :
Then I would spare 'hem. But, as things now stand,
Fathers, to spare these men, were to commit
A greater wickednesse, then you would reuenge.
If there had beene but time, and place, for you,
To haue repair'd this fault, you should haue made it ;
It should haue beene your punishment, to'haue felt
Your tardie error : but necessitie,
Now, bids me say, let 'hem not liue an houre,
If you meane *Rome* should liue a day. I haue done.
SEN. CATO hath spoken like an oracle.
CRA. Let it be so decreed. SEN. We are all fearefull.

v. 549 Here,] Here *Q, F2* 555 But,] But *Q* 561 place,] place *Q* 565 houre] hower *Q* 567 oracle.] Oracle, *Q* 568 are all] all were *Q*

SYL. And had beene base, had not his vertue rais'd vs.
SEN. Goe forth, most worthy *Consul*, wee'll assist you.
CAES. I am not yet chang'd in my sentence, *Fathers*.
CAT. No matter. What be those? SER. Letters, for CAESAR.
CAT. From whom? let 'hem be read, in open *Senate;*
Fathers, they come from the conspirators.
I craue to haue 'hem read, for the republique.
CAES. CATO, reade you it. 'Tis a loue-letter,
From your deare sister, to me: though you hate me,
Doe not discouer it. CAT. Hold thee, drunkard. *Consul*,
Goe forth, and confidently. CAES. You'll repent
This rashnesse, CICERO. PRAE. CAESAR shall repent it.
CIC. Hold friends. PRAE. Hee's scarce a friend vnto the publike.
CIC. No violence. CAESAR, be safe. Leade on:
Where are the publike executioners?
Bid 'hem wait on vs. On, to SPINTHERS house.
Bring LENTVLVS forth. Here, you, the sad reuengers
Of capitall crimes, against the publike, take
This man vnto your iustice: strangle him.
LEN. Thou do'st well, *Consul*. 'Twas a cast at dice,
In FORTVNES hand, not long since, that thy selfe
Should'st haue heard these, or other words as fatall.
CIC. Leade on, to QVINTVS CORNIFICIVS house.
Bring forth CETHEGVS. Take him to the due
Death, that he hath deseru'd: and let it be
Said, He was once. CET. A beast, or, what is worse,
A slaue, CETHEGVS. Let that be the name
For all that's base, hereafter: That would let
This worme pronounce on him; and not haue trampled

v. 571 I am] I'am *Q, Ff* 572 After 'those?' *Enter a Messenger with letters.* G SER.] SEN. *F2* 577 me,] me. *Q, Ff* 578 After 'it.' *Aside to Cato.* G drunkard] dronkard *Q* *Consul,* F2: Consul. *Q*: *Consul.* F1 580 *The Prætors attempt to seize him.* add G 582 on :] on. *F2* After 'on:' *They rise.* G 585 After 'forth.' *He is brought out* G 590 *Exit Lentulus guarded.* add G 592 After 'CETHEGVS.' *He is brought out.* G

His body into——Ha! Art thou not mou'd?
CIC. Iustice is neuer angrie: Take him hence.
CET. O, the whore FORTVNE! and her bawds the *Fates!*
That put these tricks on men, which knew the way
To death by'a sword. Strangle me, I may sleepe:
I shall grow angrie with the gods, else. CIC. Leade
To CAIVS CAESAR, for STATILIVS.
Bring him, and rude GABINIVS, out. Here, take 'hem
To your cold hands, and let 'hem feele death from you.
GAB. I thanke you, you doe me a pleasure. STA. And me too.
CAT. So, MARCVS TVLLIVS, thou maist now stand vp,
And call it happy *Rome*, thou being *Consul.*
Great parent of thy countrie, goe, and let
The old men of the citie, ere they die,
Kisse thee; the matrons dwell about thy necke;
The youths, and maides, lay vp, 'gainst they are old,
What kind of man thou wert, to tell their nephewes,
When, such a yeere, they reade, within our *Fasti*,
Thy *Consul*-ship. Who's this? PETREIVS? CIC. Welcome,
Welcome, renowned souldier. What's the newes?
This face can bring no ill with't, vnto *Rome*.
How do's the worthy *Consul*, my colleague?
PET. As well as victorie can make him, sir.
He greets the *Fathers*, and to me hath trusted
The sad relation of the ciuill strife;
For, in such warre, the conquest still is black.
CIC. Shall we with-draw into the house of *Concord?*
CAT. No, happy *Consul*, here; let all eares take

v. 599 *Gnomic pointing in Q*: " Iustice . . . 602 by'a] by, a *Q originally* 603 After 'else.' *Exit, guarded.* G 604 CAESAR] *Cæsars Q* 605 After 'out.' *They are brought out.* G 606 you.] you: *Q* 607 *Exeunt Gabinius and Statilius guarded.* G 613 maides, . . . old,] Maids . . . old *Q* 616 After '*Consul*-ship.' *Enter Petreius.* G 622 strife;] strife, *Q* 625 *Consul*, here] *Consul*. Here *F2*

The benefit of this tale. If he had voyce,
To spread vnto the poles, and strike it through
The center, to the *Antipodes ;* It would aske it.
PET. The streights, and needs of CATILINE being such,
As he must fight, with one of the two armies,
That then had neere enclos'd him ; It pleas'd *Fate*,
To make vs th'obiect of his desperate choise,
Wherein the danger almost paiz'd the honor :
And as he riss', the day grew black with him ;
And *Fate* descended neerer to the earth,
As if shee meant, to hide the name of things,
Vnder her wings, and make the world her quarrie.
At this we rous'd, lest one small minutes stay
Had left it to be'enquir'd, what *Rome* was.
And (as we ought) arm'd in the confidence
Of our great cause, in forme of battaile, stood.
Whilst CATILINE came on, not with the face
Of any man, but of a publique ruine :
His count'nance was a ciuill warre it selfe.
And all his host had standing in their lookes,
The palenesse of the death, that was to come.
Yet cryed they out like vultures, and vrg'd on,
As if they would precipitate our fates.
Nor staid we longer for 'hem ; But himselfe
Strooke the first stroke : And, with it, fled a life.
Which cut, it seem'd, a narrow necke of land,
Had broke betweene two mightie seas ; and either
Flow'd into other ; for so did the slaughter :
And whirl'd about, as when two violent tides
Meet, and not yeeld. The *Furies* stood, on hills,
Circling the place, and trembled to see men
Doe more, then they : whilst pietie left the field,
Grieu'd for that side, that, in so bad a cause,
They knew not, what a crime their valour was.

v. 630 fight,] *the comma faint or missing in F1* 633 paiz'd the honor] poiz'd the honour *F2* 636 meant,] meant *Q* 648 precipitate] præcipitate *Q* 655 hills,] hilles *Q*

The sunne stood still, and was, behind the cloud
The battaile made, seene sweating, to driue vp
His frighted horse, whom still the noyse droue backward.
And now had fierce ENYO, like a flame,
Consum'd all it could reach, and then it selfe;
Had not the fortune of the common-wealth
Come PALLAS-like, to euery *Roman* thought.
Which CATILINE seeing, and that now his troops
Couer'd that earth, they'had fought on, with their trunkes,
Ambitious of great fame, to crowne his ill,
Collected all his furie, and ran in
(Arm'd with a glorie, high as his despaire)
Into our battaile, like a *Lybian* lyon,
Vpon his hunters, scornefull of our weapons,
Carelesse of wounds, plucking downe liues about him,
Till he had circled in himselfe with death:
Then he fell too, t'embrace it where it lay.
And as, in that rebellion 'gainst the gods,
MINERVA holding forth MEDVSA's head,
One of the gyant brethren felt himselfe
Grow marble at the killing sight, and now,
Almost made stone, began t'inquire, what flint,
What rocke it was, that crept through all his limmes,
And, ere he could thinke more, was that he fear'd;
So CATILINE, at the sight of *Rome* in vs,
Became his tombe: yet did his looke retayne
Some of his fiercenesse, and his hands still mou'd,
As if he labour'd, yet, to graspe the state,
With those rebellious parts. CAT. A braue bad death.
Had this beene honest now, and for his countrey,
As 'twas against it, who had ere fallen greater?
CIC. Honor'd PETREIVS, *Rome*, not I, must thanke you.
How modestly has he spoken of himselfe!
CAT. He did the more. CIC. Thanks to the'immortall gods,

v. 687 labour'd] labor'd *Q* 693 the'immortall *Q*: the immortall *Ff*

Romans, I now am paid for all my labours,
My watchings, and my dangers. Here conclude
Your praises, triumphs, honors, and rewards,
Decreed to me : only the memorie
Of this glad day, if I may know it liue
Within your thoughts, shall much affect my conscience,
Which I must alwayes studie before fame.
Though both be good, the latter yet is worst,
And euer is ill got, without the first.

THE END.

v. 701–2 *Gnomic pointing in Q*: " Though . . . " And . . . 702
Exeunt. add G

This Tragoedie was first
Acted, in the yeere
1611.

By the KINGS *Maiesties*

SERVANTS.

The principall Tragœdians were,

RIC. BVRBADGE.	IOH. HEMINGS.
ALEX. COOKE.	HEN. CONDEL.
IOH. LOWIN.	IOH. VNDERWOOD.
WIL. OSTLER.	NIC. TOOLY.
RIC. ROBINSON.	WIL. EGLESTONE.

With the allowance of the Master of REVELLS.

This page was added in F1. In F2 the statements about the date, the company, and the Master of the Revels were omitted, and the list of 'The principall Tragœdians' *was transferred to the back of the dedication, where it followed* 'The Persons of the Play'.

ADDITIONAL NOTES AND CORRECTIONS TO VOLUME IV

The Editor apologizes for the following misprints, most of which have been noted by Mr. George W. Whiting:

p. 7, l. 13. *For* too *read* two.
l. 18. *E* (*the Huntington quarto*) *reads* humour.
p. 10, l. 5. *Omit E from the first column.*
p. 12, column 1, l. 5. *For* Ladie *read* Lady.
p. 13, column 2, l. 39. *For* Roome *read* Roome. *with a period.*
p. 15, column 1, l. 20. *For* choyse, *read* choyse *without a comma.*
column 1, l. 23. *For* Beauty *read* Beauty. *with a period.*
p. 16, l. 37. V. x. 110–12: *prefix* Sig. L 3 recto.
p. 115, l. 238 of the text. *For* my *read* thy.
p. 191, column 1, l. 11. *For* you'd *read* you'ld.
p. 192, column 1, l. 13. *For* doe; *read* doe:
p. 203, l. 2 of the text. *For* splendour *read* splendor.
p. 254, l. 267 of the text. *For* me *read* mee.
p. 294, Scene ii, l. 7. *For* the surfet *read* and surfet.
p. 342, l. 29. *For* in *read* is.
p. 355, l. 16 of the text. *For* authors *read* pale authors.
p. 371, l. 499 of the text. *For* long. *read* long,
p. 415, l. 666 of the text. *For* choice *read* choise.
p. 439, l. 73 of the text. *For* now *read* now,
p. 480, note on Act IV, l. 114. For *detestandâ* read *detestandâ fraude.*

CYNTHIA'S REVELS

Outer forme of C

p. 6, l. 23. Sig. C 1 recto. In I. iii. 38 transpose the readings of *B*, *D* to the first column.

p. 7, ll. 31, 32. The one reading of C 3 verso should have been given as a correction of the inner forme and printed on page 8 after line 10.

pp. 6–8. There are four states in the outer forme of C: (1) *B*, which has two readings (I. iii. 25, 27) altered in all the other copies; (2) *D*, which, after correcting these two readings, retains most of the other original readings; (3) *E*, which retains the original reading at I. iv. 73, 120, while correcting all the others; (4) *A*, *C*, which are correct throughout.

Inner forme of D

p. 8, ll. 11, 12. Transpose the readings of *D* and *A*, *B*, *C*. Probably the printer originally set 'mouth. Hee's', was directed to alter the period to a comma, but failed to remove the capital 'H'.

Outer forme of F

pp. 8–12. There are three states of the text: (1) the Dyce copy (*C*), as is shown by two readings 'Houres' for 'Houers' (III. iv. 45) and

'*Cart:*' for 'Court:' (III. v. 75); (2) the Huntington copy (*E*), which prints the colon after 'himselfe' at III. iv. 19; (3) the British Museum, Bodleian, and Wise copies (*A*, *B*, *D*). The *C* readings should be transposed to the first column.

Inner forme of F

pp. 12–16. Here again *C* represents one state and *A*, *B*, *D*, *E* another state. The correction of the signature E 2 (*C*) to F 2 (*A*, *B*, *D*, *E*) tells in favour of *A*, *B*, *D*, *E* being the second state, and, if so, the *C* readings should be transposed to the first column.

But, alike in the outer and the inner forme of F, these readjustments involve serious difficulty. They reveal a number of bad miscorrections. To begin with there is a liberal sprinkling of wrong fount in the punctuation. The roman stops are wrongly corrected to italic in 'Presence:' (III. ii. 31), 'Sparke?' (l. 45), 'Fanne:' (III. iv. 70), 'place:' (l. 81), 'eares?' (III. iii. 9), 'me?' (l. 18), 'hearing:' (l. 22), 'stir'd:' (l. 24), 'friends?' (III. iv. 2), 'So?' (III. v. 40). Popular spellings are substituted for those which Jonson is likely to have used in 'deuided' for 'diuided' (III. iv. 47), 'howers' for 'houres' where the metre condemns the dissyllable (l. 92), '*coulored*' for '*coloured*' (III. v. 77), 'pursew' and 'pursewd' for 'pursue' and 'pursude' (III. iv. 106, v. 103). The re-spelling is intelligible, but what of the punctuation? As the printer originally used a wrong-fount capital 'T' seven times on F 2 recto, it is clear that his stock of this letter failed when he was setting up the inner forme: he had it in use for another book. He corrected this defect, or Jonson made him correct it. But was he in a similar difficulty over his roman stops, taking them out of the text and not replacing them? He made other blunders when he had to correct a crowded line: in Act III, scene ii, lines 63–5—

my heart, he hates such barren shifts, yet to doe thee a pleasure—

he corrected the comma after 'shifts' to a semicolon and altered 'heart' to 'hart', taking out the *e* to justify the spacing; in Act III, scene 5, line 4—

Tis wel enterd sir. Stay, you come on too fast; your Pace is too—

he corrected to 'Tis wel enter'd Sir' and removed the comma after 'Stay' to save space afterwards; in line 10—

hath sufficiently whited your face: then (stifling a sigh or two and—

he at first corrected 'face' to 'Face' and took the 'and' over to the next line; finding 'Face' had lost its stop he inserted a pointless italic question-mark 'Face?then' without adjusting the spacing; in lines 24–5 '*sweete Honor*, or by what other title you please to remember her, *me thinkes you are Melancholy.*' he was directed to make a parenthesis of the words 'or by . . . her', so he put in the second bracket at the end and left out the first; in line 45 he altered 'pretie' to 'prerty', probably because he was directed to correct it to 'pretty'—an error of foul case, as *t* and *r* are often confused:

compare '*teturne*' and '*returne*' in this very play (v. vii. 7). A few other errors may be attributed to derangement of the type: for example, 'insuspect' in Act III, scene ii, line 54. Of course, *A*, *B*, *D*, *E* make a number of true corrections: it is sufficient to note 'talke' for 'take' (III. iii. 28) and the Jonsonian 'then' for 'than' (III. v. 110). The printer could not plead that he was printing from bad or disordered copy: Jonson wrote a clear and beautiful hand, and we may be sure that he prepared his manuscript with special care.

Inner forme of G

p. 16. Probably *A*, *E* give the first state, and the imperfect reading '*He*)' for '*Hedon*)' in IV. ii. 10 is only an accidental disturbance of the type.

Outer forme of L

There are only three variants, but they are more difficult to account for than any others in the play. *B*, *C*, *D* must have the first state of the stage direction in Act V, scene x, ll. 110–12; they were rearranged in *A*, *E* to correspond with the setting of the earlier stage direction at line 94. But *C* has 'Your wes' for 'Your Arrowes' in line 88, and 'Dotard' instead of 'dotard' in line 96. When 'Dotard' was capitalized, the type was deranged, and four letters dropped out of 'Arrowes': this is the second state. The third state was to reset the stage direction in lines 110–12 in two lines and to restore 'Arrowes': this is found in *E*. Finally in *A* the initial of 'Dotard' was changed back to lower-case. A puzzling solution for a complicated problem.

POETASTER

p. 195, ll. 3, 4. The printer was Richard Bishop, who printed the whole of the first volume of the 1640 Folio and put his device on the title-page of *Poetaster*. The imprint '*LONDON*, Printed by ROBERT YOUNG' is merely an acknowledgement of the copyright which he had acquired in 1630. (Dr. W. W. Greg.) Bishop's imprint appears in all the other plays printed in this volume and also on the general title-page. It was necessary to put his device on the title-page of *Poetaster*; in the other plays he puts only an ornament.

SEJANUS

p. 330. Dr. W. W. Greg (privately) and Professor H. de Vocht in his edition of the Quarto (Louvain, 1935) have pointed out that the title-page with the imprint 'by *G. Ellde*' is not a cancel, but a first state of the page. The printer took out the final *e* of his name and did not adjust the spacing; he left an ugly gap between the 'by' and the '*G.*'. Possibly he meant to take out the second *l* as well, for he usually spelt his name 'Eld', but he omitted to do this.

ADDITIONAL NOTE TO VOLUME V

p. 148. To the three large-paper copies of the 1616 Folio which contain the reset quire Y y, two other copies may be added—the copy formerly at Britwell, now in America, and the Hoe-Huntington copy at Passadena, described by Mr. George W. Whiting in *Modern Language Notes*, vol. xlviii, 1933, pages 537–8.

REPRINTED LITHOGRAPHICALLY IN GREAT BRITAIN
AT THE UNIVERSITY PRESS, OXFORD
BY VIVIAN RIDLER
PRINTER TO THE UNIVERSITY